FREDERICK COUNTY MILITIA
in the
WAR OF 1812

A Record of Approximately 3,000 of Those
Men of Frederick County, Maryland
Who Were Called to Serve in the
Defense of Maryland and
Washington, D.C.

INCLUDING

A

CHRONOLOGY OF EVENTS AND
GENEALOGICAL DATA ON
THE FAMILIES

Sallie A. Mallick and F. Edward Wright

HERITAGE BOOKS
2008

HERITAGE BOOKS
AN IMPRINT OF HERITAGE BOOKS, INC.

Books, CDs, and more—Worldwide

For our listing of thousands of titles see our website
at
www.HeritageBooks.com

Published 2008 by
HERITAGE BOOKS, INC.
Publishing Division
100 Railroad Ave. #104
Westminster, Maryland 21157

Copyright © 1992 Sallie A. Mallick and F. Edward Wright

All rights reserved. No part of this book may be reproduced or transmitted in any form or by any means, electronic or mechanical, including photocopying, recording or by any information storage and retrieval system without written permission from the author, except for the inclusion of brief quotations in a review.

International Standard Book Numbers
Paperbound: 978-1-58549-212-1
Clothbound: 978-0-7884-7271-8

CONTENTS

Preface	v
Militia Organization	1
Initial Units Activated in 1812	4
Militia Units Activated in 1812	6
Regular Army Enlistees Who were Natives of Frederick County	8
Specially Formed 1st, 2nd and 3rd Regiments	8
Activation of Frederick County Units in 1814	10
Battle of Bladensburg	11
Desertions	15
British Prisoners	15
Defense of Baltimore	16
Later Years	21
Appendix A:	
Sources	27
Abbreviations	29
The Veterans	30
Appendix B: Adjutant General Papers	317
Appendix C: The Commission Books	327
Appendix D: Muster Rolls of Active Units	330
Index	367

Bounty land warrant issued to John A. Porter of Frederick County for 120 acres, based on his service under Captain John Brengle. Typical of most veterans and their widows, the warrant was sold, probably to a land speculator.

PREFACE

As with our previous studies of Maryland Militia in the War of 1812 in other counties, we began with the muster and pay rolls and based on the names found in these lists we sought to find the many applications for bounty land warrants and pensions. We have examined these files to learn about the veterans, their families and their roles in the War of 1812 - individually and collectively.

A large number of Frederick County militiamen were called to serve during the war. Perhaps as many as 800 faced the British at Bladensburg and still more served in the defense of Baltimore where the British invaders were turned back. A number of Frederick County companies were activated on several separate occasions to serve at Annapolis when the state officials sensed the possibility of an attack on that city. The county provided infantry companies, an artillery company and at least three cavalry units during the war.

Many others were recruited by the regular army. The army enlistment registers reveal natives of Frederick County who enlisted, i.e., men born in Frederick County, Maryland; they do not indicate where the men were living at the time of enlistment. Judging by the place of enlistment, one concludes that many had migrated south by the time of the war. Of those still in Frederick County we counted at least thirty-one militiamen of Frederick County who enlisted in the army while serving on active militia duty. We must assume that there were other Frederick Countians whose enlistments went undetected.

Of the militia rolls there were a few companies for which we were unable to find the muster rolls despite the clear evidence that they had been active. We suspect that the rolls of Captain Riggs' company has been mis-shelved; those of Captain Farquhar were probably lost sometime after the war and may never be recovered. The roll of Captain Turbutt's company is shown by Williams, in *History of Frederick County Maryland*, and is probably based on a privately held copy. We have not been able to find an original. Pension applications and bounty land claims for a few veterans indicate that the Frederick County companies of Ely Brashear, Robert Fulton and Jacob Creager were also active; these rolls are also missing. We have no accurate method to determine how many of the bounty land applications or pension applications went undetected by our search, although we were able to form one estimate on the basis of a copy of the complete muster roll of Captain Brengle's company submitted by Ormond Butler in 1862. In it he showed those men or their widows who had received bounty land warrants. Slightly less than one-third of the bounty land claims had been missed by us. The variation in spellings of the names of these veterans was the major factor in our omissions. The spelling of the veterans' names in Butler's list varied with the spelling of the names as shown in the

FREDERICK COUNTY MILITIA IN THE WAR OF 1812

original muster rolls and with the spelling shown in the abstracted service records and the benefit files (bounty land and pension). It thus follows that if the abstract of the bounty land or pension application is not shown as a source in Appendix A of this work and if the veteran or his widow or minor children were alive in 1850, 1855, 1871 or 1878, there is a significant likelihood that files exist, perhaps placed under an incorrect spelling of the veteran's name and/or a mispelling of the veteran's captain or colonel.

Applications submitted under the bounty land laws of 1850 and 1855 revealed the following:

(1) If submitted by the veteran himself: his age, residence at the time of application, captain's name, and some indication of dates of service, perhaps some recollection on his involvement in the war.

(2) If submitted by the widow: her age, her residence; date and place of marriage; name of minister (or justice of the peace); whether either had married previously with names of earlier wives or husbands; date and place of husband's death; name of her deceased husband's captain and when and where he served (if recalled); affidavits attesting to her marriage and other facts.

(3) If submitted for minor children (father deceased, mother deceased or remarried): ages or dates of birth of minor children, name of father's captain.

Pension applications submitted under the laws of 1871 and 1878 revealed the following:

(1) If submitted by the veteran himself: his age, residence at the time of application; name of wife; captain's name; dates of service.

(2) If submitted by the widow: the same information required in Bounty Land claims - plus a description of her husband at the time of his enrolling in the militia - age, occupation, color of eyes, complexion and height; places of her husband's residence since discharge.

Published lists. The appendix found in William M. Marine, *The British Invasion of Maryland 1812-1815*, reprinted by Genealogical Publishing Co., 1977, contains a listing by Louis Dielman of militiamen and some regular army men who served from Maryland. It is incomplete since Dielman was unable to obtain the muster and pay rolls from the War Department. [His listing probably represents less than half of the men who actually served.]

We are especially grateful to the following persons who furnished information on some of the veterans: Mrs. Virginia Stenley, Mrs. Virginia S. Poling; Frank D. Bittle, Ms. Bonnie Miller, Leonard J. Six, Mrs. Donna Younkin Logan, Jay Lipps and Mrs. Carol L. Porter.

THE VETERANS

Most of the data taken from newspaper articles, *Bridge in Time*, and *Names in Stone*, were compiled by Mary Fitzhugh Hitselberger, adding greatly to the value of this work.

The reader is cautioned that the sources which we have consulted for data on the personal lives of the veterans represent only a few of the many sources available. You are encouraged to investigate others.

F. Edward Wright
Westminster, Maryland
1992

MILITIA ORGANIZATION

Prior to the War of 1812 the Maryland Militia was organized in three divisions which were subdivided into twelve brigades. The Seventh Brigade consisted of regiments of Lower Frederick and Upper Montgomery counties, 3rd, 13th, 28th, 29th and 44th regiments of which the 13th and 29th were from Frederick County. The Ninth Brigade covered Upper Frederick County, consisting of the 16th, 20th, 28th and 47th regiments. [The 16th Regiment consisted of the 1st Battalion for the city of Frederick and the 2nd Battalion called the Country Battalion.] Each county was laid out in regiments; unfortunately few of the records of the boundaries of these regiments have been found. Likewise companies were assigned to captains whose companies drew from local regions within the regimental boundaries. From time to time questions regarding the regimental boundaries arose. On 18 April 1808, Lt. Colonel Joseph S. Smith, Taneytown, sent an inquiry to Annapolis,

> "In the year seventeen Hundred and Ninety four or five the bounds of the different regiments composing the Ninth Brigade was deposited in the Council Chambers, I will take it as a particular favor if you will send me the bounds of the 47 Regiment as we are in confusion for the want of them...."[1]

In April of 1812 the 28th Regiment planned to meet in order to revise its boundaries.[2]

In examining the actual readiness of the organization it becomes apparent that only a fraction of the companies were formed during the period from 1794 to 1811. Still fewer were adequately equipped. General Mountjoy Bayly, commanding the 9th Brigade, reported in August 1794 that one troop of horse had been organized with no officers selected and an artillery company was not yet formed.[3] In 1797 the Frederick Artillery Company requested that the Governor furnish two field pieces with the promise that "... you may depend upon their being taken particular care of, and the Companys being Uniformed and Organized in as small a space of time as possible."[4]

There were a significant number of Frederick Countians who were not supportive of the newly enacted militia laws of 1793. In his letter to the Governor Gen. Bayly said " ...I cannot flatter your Excellency that the quota you have called for from this county will be made up from Volunteers tho there is not doubt but they will be completed by draft within the time directed - As there appears to be a diversity of sentiment prevailing here among the people respecting the conduct of the insurgents Westward ..."[5] The "insurgents westward" to whom General Bayly referred, were, of course, the "Whiskey Boys" who had rebelled against the newly established Federal tax on whiskey.

Attendance at company drills was compulsory for those who had been enrolled. Fines of fifty cents were assessed in 1797 on those who failed to attend.[6]

There is some indication that the pacifist view of the local Quakers was also felt, as in the letter of 11 July 1795 of Lieutenant Colonel Philemon Griffith who resigned his commission. In explaining his reasons for leaving the militia he said that, "My neighbours chiefly are Quakers who will not adhere to any law that Nature only has compeld..."[7]

In 1803 the Maryland Militia was still not fully organized, including the 7th and 9th Brigades of Frederick and Montgomery Counties. During that year a letter was received by the Governor and Council from John McPherson of Frederick County whose patience had run out. In his letter he said "...It has been totally impracticable for me to comply with the Governors order respecting a return of the Regt. I have had the Command of. The deranged state of the Militia with respect to officers & the difficulty of getting characters of the smallest semblance of decency, to agree to be recommended for appointments, has determined me to make a tender of my resignation ... "[8]

In 1807 Gen. Robert Cumming, Liberty Town, reported to Governor Wright,

> "I am sorry to inform your Excellency of the total disorganization of three of the Regiments, impairing part of my Brigade. The event has been inevitable in my part, for, I continued to issue orders for Battalion & Regimental meetings, till within Eighteen Months past; but, was only obeyd by Colonel Barrick of the 29th who, much to his Honor persisted in his duty ..., I believe Colonel Barracks Regt. can be drafted in (probably) two weeks."[9]

MILITIA ORGANIZATION

Despite the poor state of the militia General Cumming sensed a strong anti-British feeling. In his letter to the Governor he added, "It will doubtless, be matter of high gratification to your Excellency to learn that, a Spirit of resentment (in these parts) is universally exhibited against the late insult offered to our National dignity, to a degree that, at present includes all party considerations; in ...[?], the pulse of our country appears to beat in union."[10]

The entire militia organization was political in nature. The company officers were elected by the members of the company subject to approval by the Governor and Council. Naturally political squabbling and name calling found their way into militia affairs. The Adjutant General Papers, held by the Maryland State Archives, contain several personal attacks, such as the following:

(1) In 1795 Lt. Colonel Jamison described John Wachtel and John Gaver as "ignorant and least qualified as officers."

(2) Henry Kuhn and David Shriver described Joshua Stevenson as "totally unsuited by habit of intoxication."

(3) Lt. Colonel John Wampler requested the revocation of the commission of Captain John Williams of the 20th Regiment. "Whereas John Williams at present holds the command as the Captain of a company in the Regt. No. 20 of the militia of this state in Frederick County. He has for some time past been very cumbersome to his under offices and privates composing his company. To my own knowledge on the subject at whatever place or time, have seen Captain Williams tumbling about in a despert state of intoxication, almost destitute of his reason, And this is the absolute knowledge & report of his company and neighbours, who appear very anctious to have him removed from holding a military commission amongst them. ..."

(4) Major John S. Hall who had moved to Frederick Town, "a considerable distance from the whole of the men composing the said Battalion... That the said Major John S. Hall is much given to intoxication, in deed he is never sober scarcely if he can procure liquor enough to make him drunk, and besides he is by no means proper character to be trusted with any monies that may come into his hands, in virtue of his officers, having lately cleared out by the insolvent law, after having been confined for a length of time in the common jail of Frederick County...."

FREDERICK COUNTY MILITIA IN THE WAR OF 1812

Despite the unpreparedness of the militia, there were some units ready to be called at a moment's notice. John Adlum notified the Governor and Council in 1804 of his unit's availability as Select Militia.

"To Gov. and Council. 1804, June 17. From John Adlum, Henry Steiner, Ezra Mantz, ..."The petition of the undersigned showeth to your honorable body that they have been directed by the company who formerly addressed a memorial to our honors upon the subject of organising a select company of militia in this place, to request that you will decide upon the contents of the said petition. The company are particularly anxious to obtain the arms, the commissions are not so much an object except only as they may be necessary to authorise the executive to give them the use of the arms. Your petitioners and the company are desirous of a speedy decision..."[11]

In 1811 the Maryland Legislature November session, passed two acts (chapters 182 and 213, Nov. sess. 1811) for regulating and governing the militia of the State. Among the many specifications of the acts, they required all white male citizens between the ages of eighteen and forty-five to perform military duty. The acts exempted certain persons such as civil officers of Federal and State governments, professors, doctors, ferrymen, pilots, and sailors in the coasting trade. Persons with religious scruples against war were also exempted with the proviso that they pay dues of three dollars annually. Details were given on the conduct of militia drills, meetings, etc. The new acts established cavalry districts of which Washington and Frederick Counties constituted the 1st Cavalry District. Washington County was designated the 1st Regiment and Frederick County the 2nd Regiment. Revision of militia boundaries was to be considered prior to 1 May 1812.

INITIAL UNITS ACTIVATED IN 1812

Because of the almost constant threat of the British fleet in the Chesapeake the Maryland militia units were frequently called into service from the spring of 1812 through the fall of 1814. Those militia units of Maryland west of the Chesapeake Bay were called up to defend Annapolis, Baltimore and the Capitol. There were few who would be able to avoid service. In the 9 May 1812 issue of *Frederick-Town Herald* were published Regimental orders to the 16th Regiment

INITIAL UNITS ACTIVATED IN 1812

Maryland Militia to enroll in their respective districts all able bodied, free white male citizens, from 18 to 45 years of age - ordered by "John Ritchie, Lieut. Colonel, Fredericktown."[12] The other regiments of Frederick County issued similar notices.

In their *History of Frederick County Maryland*, T. J. C. Williams and Folger McKinsey state,

> "On the 28th of May 1812, the Sixteenth Regiment was ordered to assemble in Frederick at the usual parade ground for settling the plan to furnish two captains, one lieutenant, one ensign, seventy-five infantrymen and forty artillerymen to the United States being the number apportioned to this regiment. At this time the Fifth Regiment of United States Infantry under command of Colonel William D. Beall, was stationed in Frederick at the Barracks. In August the Hagerstown Volunteers under Captain Thomas Quantrill arrived in Frederick escorted by Captain Henry Steiner's Company of Artillery and Captain Stephen Steiner's Company of Infantry. The whole body was commanded by Major Ezra Mantz and Adjutant John Rigney. These troops pitched their tents in the Barracks lot. A few days later they left for Annapolis to which place 850 troops had been called to protect the city from a descent of the British by water."[13]

During the following summer the company of Captain Thomas Contee Worthington was one of the first to be called out.[14] Worthington's company, comprised of about 70 men, left for Annapolis on 17 August 1812. The *Frederick Gazette* gave news of the departure,

> "On Thursday Captain Worthington's company of drafted militia from the town and neighbourhood marched for Annapolis. These men, we understand are to supply the place of a part of the 5th Regiment, United States Infantry, which have been ordered to the northward. Captain Worthington was escorted out of town by the uniform companies commanded by Captain Henry Steiner and Captain Stephen Steiner."[15]

Worthington's company was stationed at Fort Severn under the command of Lieutenant Colonel Jacob Small. Members of Worthington's company served at intervals between 17 August and 31 December 1812.

FREDERICK COUNTY MILITIA IN THE WAR OF 1812

MILITIA UNITS ACTIVATED IN 1813

On 16 April 1813 the British fleet threatened the City of Baltimore and while it lay off the city, preparations for the city's defense progressed. On the 26th of April an attack on Annapolis was rumored.

In response to the threat on Baltimore Captain George Flautt's company of Frederick County riflemen was called up on 29 April 1813 and placed in the service of the United States a few days later. Many of the men came from the Emmittsburg area. They served under the command of Lieut. Colonel William C. Miller of Cecil County at Baltimore. Several veterans said they stood guard at Ft. McHenry for about 3 weeks. They were discharged on 29 June 1813. Captain Flautt later (1850) said he was discharged at Fort McHenry around 20 July 1813.

Captain Henry Steiner's artillery company was called into service and formed in Fredericktown on 1 May 1813. Seven days later they left for Baltimore where they were placed in the "service of the United States," under the command of Lt. Colonel Miller. This unit served from 28 April through 29 June 1813. They returned home, having received praise for their conduct.[16]

Captain Samuel Ogle's company, from the Fredericktown and Emmittsburgh area was called up on 1 May 1813 and marched to Baltimore County. Benjamin Gump said the company was stationed at the "Old Orchard." They were probably discharged at Spring Gardens in Baltimore County around 5 July 1813. However, some veterans said the place of discharge was Federal Hill; others recalled they had been dismissed at the Patapsco Encampment near the city of Baltimore. Private George Reed recalled that his company was not in any engagement; their regiment was at Fort McHenry for one week.

The company of Captain Samuel Dawson served 1 May - 5 July 1813 in Baltimore City. [In examining the records no specific details of their deployment have surfaced.]

During the period, 23 through 29 May, a company of militia was drafted from the Woodsboro area [about 83 members] and formed under Captain Philip Smith. They were ordered into service by Brigadier General H. Barrick in response to concern that the British were probably preparing to attack Annapolis. When Captain Smith's company reached Annapolis he and his men were placed under the command of Colonel Gassaway Watkins who was in charge of the Annapolis Harbor. The company was discharged verbally around 8 September 1813 at the State House. During the period the company was active, there were 31 desertions; several returned before the company was discharged. On 5 June 1813 rewards were offered for

> "Christian Geary, living near Christian Harman's, south mountain, draughted in Captain Willhide's rifle company, 29th regiment Md. militia, aged about 23 yrs, 5 ft 6-7 inches, had on long blue coat, linen pantaloons and white hat; and Thomas Gasaway, aged 28 yrs, 5 ft 8-9 inch, living about 4-5 miles from New Market near Reel's mill on Bush creek; and Nathan Vanpherson living in New Market, aged about 23 yrs, 5 ft 7-8 inch, had on blue chambray cotton coat, black-corded pantaloons and took with him one blue cloth coat. The two latter persons are from the extra battalion, 7th brigade, Md. militia - Philip Smith, Capt Commandt., 3rd company Md. Militia, stationed at Fort Severn, Annapolis Harbor."[17]

Captain Jacob Getzendanner's rifle company, called variously as the First Company, Washingtonian Rifle Greens, or Washingtonian Green Volunteers, were called out with a notice appearing in the *Frederick-Town Herald* on 31 July 1813.[18] They left for Annapolis around 9 August 1813 with a total of about 44 men. On Sept. 17, 1813, Captain Getzendanner's company of Washington Rifle Greens, returned to Frederick from Annapolis. They announced their arrival by firing a volley.[19]

On Monday evening, the 16th of August, 1813, it was reported that "a company of the mountain boys of this county, commanded by Captain Marker, reached town on their march to Annapolis, for which place they proceeded next morning. This company is composed of a fine, hardy, healthy set of men, accustomed to labour and fatigue. They were all armed with their own rifles, in the use of which they are very expert...."[20] This company, called "Mountain Rangers," was under the command of Captain Daniel Marker (28th Regiment) and was from the Middletown area.

The *Frederick-Town Herald* announced on 18 September 1813 that the British fleet having nearly all left the Chesapeake Bay, the militia stationed at Annapolis had been discharged. It stated that "Captain

FREDERICK COUNTY MILITIA IN THE WAR OF 1812

Marker's Rifle company from this county, reached here on their return on Thursday evening last and Capt Getzendanner's Washington Rifle Greens on last evening." Marker's company passed through Frederick escorted by Captain Henry Steiner's company of artillery and Captain Stephen Steiner's company of infantry.

REGULAR ARMY ENLISTEES WHO WERE NATIVES OF FREDERICK COUNTY

Many men of Frederick County enlisted in the regular army. Williams says, "On May 13, 1813, Ensign W. G. Shade marched off with 37 recruits, all recruited in Frederick County, who had enlisted in the regular army."[21] In addition many were recruited directly from the militia. There were 31 annotations in the militia muster rolls reading, "enlisted," indicating that these Frederick Countians were recruited into the regular army while serving on active duty with the militia. The service of many of these men is revealed in the army enlistment records. Many served on the Western frontiers and in New York state as part of the Canadian expedition.[22]

SPECIALLY FORMED 1ST, 2ND AND 3RD REGIMENTS

The regiments of Frederick, Washington and Allegany Counties seem to have merged into at least three newly and temporarily designated regiments during the course of the war as they were ordered into the "service of the United States." These temporary regiments were numbered one, two and three, notwithstanding the earlier designation of other first, second and third regiments in the militia of the state.[23] Similarly the integrity of the companies was not always maintained. Men from several companies were sometimes melded into a newly formed company and marched off under a captain with whom they had never drilled. Some officers were given higher ranks when placed in the service of the United States and others given lesser ranks -in order to conform to the existing organizations.

In 1813 a specially formed first regiment, "in the service of the United States" at Baltimore was placed under the command of Lieut. Colonel William C. Miller of Cecil County. Captain George Flautt's company of Frederick County served in this regiment, along with Steiner's Artillery company. The following year a specially formed first regiment was

SPECIALLY FORMED 1ST, 2ND AND 3RD REGIMENTS

commanded by Colonel John Ragan [from the regular 24th Militia Regiment] probably established circa 21 July 1814, a month before their participation in the Battle of Bladensburg, and continued until 10 January 1815 when they were discharged. During the battle Colonel Ragan was captured and during the brief period of his captivity Lt. Colonel Stephen Steiner temporarily replaced him. The field and staff were made up primarily of officers from Frederick and Washington Counties The quartermaster was from Baltimore. Second in command was Lieutenant Colonel Stephen Steiner [from the 16th Regiment] who was promoted from Major to Lt. Col on the day following the Battle of Bladensburg, 25 August 1814. The companies, formed in this special 1st Regiment, were from Frederick, Washington, Allegany and Baltimore (a few men) Counties.

Serving in the first Regiment in the service of the U.S. were the companies of John Brengle, 25 August - 19 September 1814; Samuel Dawson 21 July 1814 - 10 January 1815; James F. Huston, Lewis Weaver and Joseph Green, serving as captain in that order, 23 July 1814 - 10 January 1815; George Shryock (from Hagerstown), 23 July 1814 - 10 January 1815; Henry Lowrye, 24 August - 10 January 1815; George W. Magee, 22 July - 10 January 1815; Joseph Wood, 3 August 1814 - 28 October 1814; William P. Farquhar (formed ca. 26 July 1814, discharged ?). The companies of Shryock and Lowrye were from Washington County; the others were from Frederick County. There were two men from Frederick County who served under Shryock's company. Dawson's company was comprised of men from Frederick County and Washington County with a few men from Baltimore County. Eventually Lowrye's company picked up some men from Allegany and Baltimore Counties.

A Second Regiment was formed in 1813 under Lieutenant Colonel Richard Key Heath. The Fields and Staff served from 1 May until 29 June 1813. It included the Frederick County companies of Samuel Dawson and Samuel Ogle, serving from 1 May until 5 July 1813. Also in the regiment were two companies from Washington County under Captain John Miller and Captain David Stephens, serving for the same period.

Another Second Regiment appeared in 1814, frequently called Hood's Regiment; it was created with the following General Orders:

"Annapolis August 1814

FREDERICK COUNTY MILITIA IN THE WAR OF 1812

> The companies from the 2d Brigade [Washington County] will form one Battalion, those from the 7th [Lower Frederick County and Upper Montgomery County] will form another Battalion, Captain Alexander's and Captain Gitzendanner's companies for the present will be attached to the first Battalion and those of Captains Burgess and Belmear to the 2d. Lt. Colonel Hood will take command of the whole.... Lev. Winder."[24]

A Detachment under Captain Jacob Alexander from the 32nd Regiment was attached to Lt. Colonel Hood's Regiment. They served from 22 July to 19 September, participating in the Battle of Bladensburg on 24 August. Hood's Regiment marched first to Annapolis then to Bladensburg, arriving just 15 minutes before the battle.[25]

The specially formed 3rd Regiment was commanded by Lt. Colonel Henry Stembel. The staff served circa 27 August - 27 October 1814. All the officers on the staff were from Frederick County except for the 1st major, John Reynolds, of Washington County. The muster roll for the staff of this regiment is also shown in Appendix C. Serving in the 3rd Regiment were the companies of Captains John Galt, 31 August - 29 October 1814; George W. Ent, 24 August - 30 September 1814; Nicholas Turbutt, 2 September - 27 October 1814; John Fonsten (2nd Batt.), 2 September - 27 October 1814; Mathew Murray, 25 August - 27 October 1814; Captain Daniel Marker, 25 August - 27 October 1814; and Captain Daniel Shawen, 5 September - 27 October 1814.

ACTIVATION OF FREDERICK COUNTY UNITS IN 1814

One of the first companies to be placed into service during 1814 was that of Captain Jacob Alexander. Colonel Henry Stembel, commander of the 28th Regiment, and later the "3rd Regiment in the service of the United States," received the following orders from General Winder.

> "To Colonel Henry Stembel, Middletown, Frederick County. Annapolis July 9th 1814.
> Sir, Sometime since we received yours, making a tender of the service of Captain Alexander and forty one of his company. It is but recently we have had occasion to call into service any part of the militia; and being desirous as much as possible to avoid calling them a great distance from home untill the

ACTIVATION OF UNITS IN 1814

harvest was gathered in. [Ordered] ... that he march immediately to this place to perform a tour of duty ..."[26]

Less than 40 men of Captain Alexander's company were actually put into service, according to the *Frederick-Town Herald* of July 23, 1814. One-third refused to march, abetted by remarks made by General Swearingen who, if the *Herald*'s report was accurate, clearly discouraged the men to volunteer.

In July 1814, Captain Jacob Alexander's Company of volunteers left Middletown Valley for Annapolis. They arrived on Friday, the 22nd at 12 noon.[27] Their service continued until 19 September, participating in the Battle of Bladensburg on 24 August, where one of their company, James Bryant, died on the field of battle and David Stotelmyer was wounded. This company continued on to Baltimore and participated in its defense. They departed Baltimore around 20 September, arriving home in about three days.

Approximately one week after Captain Alexander received his orders to march to Annapolis the Seventh Brigade was ordered to furnish additional men.[28]

The company of Captain Jacob Getzendanner (16th Regiment) arrived in Annapolis around 26 July 1814. Many of the same men had marched with Captain Getzendanner on the previous deployment to Annapolis in the summer of 1813. (According to the *Frederick-Town Herald* of July 23, 1814, fifteen to twenty men refused to go.) The company was discharged at Annapolis on 21 August 1814 and allowed 5 days for the march home, a distance of 75 miles.

BATTLE OF BLADENSBURG

Participating in the Battle of Bladensburg were an estimated 500 to 800 men from Frederick County.[29] This figure is based on the known companies of Frederick County for which muster rolls or pay rolls are available and the evidence of the presence of other companies from the bounty land and pension applications of the veterans. Among those from Frederick County were companies of Dawson, Magee, Farquhar and Weaver, who marched under Lieutenant Colonel Ragan from Baltimore on 20 August to join General Winder at Bladensburg.

FREDERICK COUNTY MILITIA IN THE WAR OF 1812

The following companies of Frederick County are known to have been present at the Battle of Bladensburg:

(1) Captain Jacob Alexander's company [from Middletown Valley] served 22 July - 19 September 1814. Stationed at Annapolis under Colonel Hood, they arrived at Bladensburg about 15 minutes before the enemy appeared. A member of this company, James Bryant, was killed on the field of battle 24 August. David Stotelmyer was wounded.

(2) Captain Denton Darby's company, 3 August - 8 November 1814, was placed in the service of the United States; one veteran said they were discharged at Gun Powder Hill, Washington D. C. around 1 December 1814. Captain Darby stated that he was placed under Lieutenant Colonel Cramer and at some point he was placed under Major Kizer of the U. S. Army. In Washington, following the Bladensburg disaster, he was attached to the "City Brigade." During the period the company was active, two men drowned, one on 16 August. Aquila Teller was wounded in action. Andrew Wilson died on 5 September. Henry Zimmerman was taken prisoner on 24 August. Jesse Brandenburgh said that he was enrolled at the Frederick Barricks. Privates Philip Harding and Walter White said they were drafted at New Market.

(3) The Company of Captain Samuel Dawson was called into service a second time from 21 July (many didn't join until the 26th) 1814 until 10 January 1815 when the company was discharged at Annapolis. They participated in the Battle of Bladensburg and the defense of Baltimore. They were discharged at Spring Gardens (according to Private George B. Walker).

(4) Captain Basil Dorsey's company was called up on 30 July 1814. Dorsey's company was discharged at Baltimore around 27 September 1814, having served in Annapolis, Bladensburg and Baltimore. Many of the men were from the New Market area. [Throughout the muster roll of Dorsey's company are annotations of discharge by General Foreman, indicating that this company was under the command of the 1st Brigade while at Baltimore.]

(5) Captain Samuel Duvall's company left Frederick County around 3 August 1814, participated in the Battle of Bladensburg and were discharged in Georgetown, D.C. around 8 November 1814. Many of the members were drafted from the Woodsboro area. The muster rolls

cover the period 3 August - 3 October 1814; however several members said they were discharged in November and others said in December. According to Christian Fout, private in Duvall's company (in his pension application in 1871) the company went from Frederick through Georgetown to Bladensburgh, then towards the bay to meet the enemy, the enemy going around, they fell back to Washington and then on the next day went to Bladensburgh, and then had an engagement, then went on to Montgomery County Courthouse, then ordered to Baltimore and made one day march, then ordered to Washington City and then discharged. Sergeant Simpson Hamond said he joined the company at Fredericktown in July of 1814, marched from Fredericktown Barracks to Bladensburg, from thence to the Old Fields, then back to Washington City and next morning met the British at Bladensburg; gave battle and had to retreat; went to the city from thence, continued on to Montgomery Court House and from there marched back to Bladensburgh, thence to Washington City and encamped on Windmill Hill between the President's house and the Potomac River.

(6) Captain William P. Farquhar's company, whose muster rolls were lost when Colonel Ragan decided to set aside the regimental muster taken by Lt. Colonel Stephen Steiner. (Steiner took charge of the regiment when Ragan was captured by the British). This company marched from Taneytown around 26 July 1814 to Camp Fairfield near Baltimore City, then went on to serve at Bladensburg; they returned to Baltimore to be stationed on Chincapin Hill and were discharged at Camp Diehl around 1 October 1814. According to Jacob Heck (served as private in Captain Galt's company) Captain Farquhar's company had been dissolved (around the end of September) by the time the latter muster was taken. When the company was dissolved some of the men were transferred to other companies (according to sergeant Jacob Baumgardner).

(7) The company of Captain George Washington Magee was from the New Windsor area; they served 22 July 1814 - 10 January 1815. Most of the company went on to Baltimore from Bladensburg. Charles Bond who served under Captain Magee during this period, said he was drafted at Westminster into the company of Captain David Dutterow and sent to a company commanded by Captain Magee; marched off in the middle of the wheat harvest, first to Camp Fairfield near Baltimore, next to Bladensburg, when the company was dispersed after one fire at the enemy. After their participation in the defense of Baltimore (in the entrenchments at Chincapin Hill) they were sent to Annapolis.

FREDERICK COUNTY MILITIA IN THE WAR OF 1812

(8) The company of Captain Lewis Weaver (Emmittsburg area) served from 23 July until 10 January 1815. They served at Bladensburg, Annapolis and Baltimore. According to one veteran, Captain Lewis Weaver commanded the company at the battle of Bladensburg and after that he took the company to Baltimore. They arrived at camp on 4 September outside Baltimore. At some point he was cashiered and succeeded by Captain James F. Huston who in turn was succeeded by Captain Joseph Green [from Emmittsburg] who remained in command until the company was discharged on 10 January 1815 at Annapolis. William Gillen stated that Weaver was court martialed for improper conduct the day after the bombardment of Fort McHenry. In attempting to prove the service of an acquaintance, Christian Correll, as a member of Weaver's company [whose name neither the 3d auditor nor these compilers were able to find in the rolls], two veterans of Captain Galt's company made the following remarks.

In 1878 Felix B. Taney remembered that Captain Weaver was from Emmittsburg. Taney visited the company while they were at Baltimore in Camp. "It was Wednesday, August 31, 1814, that we were mustered into service and on Sunday following which would be Sept. 21, 1814, Captain Weaver's company arrived and I with half a dozen others went over to their camp which was about a mile ..." They were discharged on the following Tuesday. "When they had started we went out and wished them good luck and wished it was ourselves." Samuel Barton, age 79, in 1878, resident of Emmittsburg, remembered Captain Ward's company, Captain Creager's company, Captain Fulton's company and Captain Weaver's company.

(9) At least three cavalry companies of the First Cavalry District, 2nd Regiment (Frederick County), were called up as the British approached Washington, D.C. The muster rolls reveal that the cavalry companies of Reid, Hall and Zacharias of the 2nd Regiment, 1st Cavalry District, were called up during this period. They were in the command of Major John Cook, under Lieut. Colonel Henry Kemp. The troop of horse under 1st Lieutenant Upton Reid served in Washington, D. C. from 26 August to 3 September 1814. The troops of horse of Captain Nicholas Hall and Captain Daniel Zacharias, both served from 7 August until 10 September 1814. Hall's unit formed at Frederick and according to several of his men, engaged in the Battle of Indian Head. Zacharias's troop formed at Westminster and was discharged at Port Tobacco, Charles County.

BATTLE OF BLADENSBURG

There were also Frederick County men who served in companies which originated in other areas; for example there were six men of Frederick County who served in Henry Lowrye's company of Washington County.[30] Serving under Lowrye was 2nd Lieutenant Hugh Thomson of Taneytown who was wounded at Bladensburg. Four Frederick County men served at Bladensburg under Captain Shryock of Hagerstown.[31]

The defeat at Bladensburg on the 24th of August is well known. Many veterans referred to the flight of the American defenders as the "Bladensburg Races." Most regrouped at Montgomery County Court House (now Rockville). From there many of the companies marched to Baltimore and to a much prouder outcome.

DESERTIONS

There were a large number of desertions recorded on the muster rolls. Appearing in the Frederick newspaper, Engine of Liberty, dated 5 October 1814, were the names of twenty-one men who deserted from the companies of Captain Samuel Duvall and Captain Denton Darby while camped at Bladensburg and later at Montgomery Court House and in Washington, D.C.[32] A reward of five dollars was offered for each man. Their descriptions are contained in their individual entries in this book. In the units from Frederick County in 1812 there were only a few who deserted (only a few companies were called into service); in 1813 there were over 50 desertions; in 1814 there were over 200 Frederick Countians who deserted.[33] Many men left their units after the British had departed the Chesapeake, no doubt feeling that the need at home was much greater. In later years some of the men would argue that the notation of desertion in their record was unfounded.

BRITISH PRISONERS

Some British prisoners and British deserters were marched up from Washington following the Battle of Bladensburg. Thirty-four men of Captain Markey's company (16th Regiment), under the command of 1st Lieutenant William Kolb, were engaged in guarding the British prisoners at the Barracks at Frederick.[34] This unit served from 13 Oct, or earlier, until 15 November 1814.

FREDERICK COUNTY MILITIA IN THE WAR OF 1812

DEFENSE OF BALTIMORE

Following their participation in the Battle of Bladensburg the companies of Captains Alexander, Weaver, Dawson, Dorsey and Magee went on to participate in the defense of Baltimore. [Weaver's company arrived at Camp Hampstead on 4 September.] In addition to these companies the following companies of Frederick County were activated for the defense of Baltimore:

(1) Captain Matthew Murray's company was called "The Middletown Blues." The men were drafted at Middletown, around 25 August 1814 and had marched as far as Montgomery County when the Battle of Bladensburg took place. From there they marched to Baltimore where they participated in the defense of the city. They were discharged at Camp Hampstead around 31 October 1814.

(2) Captain George W. Ent's company (called the Fredericktown Blues Company) was drafted at Fredericktown, Maryland, around 23 August 1814; stationed at Hampstead Hill; discharged at Baltimore, last of October 1814 to 11 November 1814.

(3) Captain John Brengle's company left Fredericktown, according to one veteran, around 23 August 1814 and marched to Clarksburgh on the way to the City of Washington, but at Clarksburg the orders were countermanded to return to Frederick. They were then ordered to march to Baltimore where they were placed in the service of the United States in the First Regiment on 25 August. Private Reuben Grove of this company stated he was one of fifty men, detailed on special service to advance to a certain point, to fire one shot to draw the British, and then retire. The company was discharged at Baltimore on 19 September 1814.[35] The company served at the entrenchments during the battle of North Point.[36]

(4) The rifle company of Captain William Durbin, Jr., (20th Regiment) made its rendezvous at New Windsor on 24 August 1814 and marched to Baltimore. They were discharged at Camp Diehl, Baltimore, on 27 October. One of the members of the company, Peter Burns, said in 1871 that he saw General Ross fall from his horse when he was killed.

(5) Captain Nicholas Turbutt[37] from the Fredericktown area served from 1 September until 27 October 1814 when they were discharged at Camp Hampstead, Baltimore. Jacob Crumbaker, who served as 1st

DEFENSE OF BALTIMORE

lieutenant of the company, later gave his account of the preparations and the battle from his vantage point. He said,

> "We marched from Frederick Town the 2nd Day of September and arrived at Camp Hampstead below [sic] Baltimore on Sunday the 4th Sept. and we could not get tents until the Sunday following and During that time we had to live in a rope walk; and the Second Night we lay there, their [there] were alarm guns fired when we formed our company all under arms without a single cartrige and expecting an attack by the Enemy but in about an hour we found out that it was a false alarm and went to Rest; and on the Eleventh there was alarm guns fired again and in a short time the Enemy came in sight with about Twenty sail.

> "When we struck our tents and marched about half a mile and their [there] we lay on our arms that day and night and about 6 o'clock the next day the Enemy began bombarding on our fort and continued without intervils untill about 10 o'clock on the 13th when they weighed anker and stood out on.

> "On the night between the 12th and 13th the roaring of cannons and the bursting of boms was like one continuel peal of thunder in the night. 3 of their vessels run up on the Patapsico side of the fort without being heard & when they got above the fort they gave three cheers thinking they would throw their bombs in Baltimore not knowing their [there] was a little battery above the fort but when they came even with that they let loose our Bull Dogs on their ships and soon made them cry for mercy and in a little time 2 of their ships were cut to peices and the third made a narrow escape for when she came down again even with the fort they let loose on her and raked her fore & aft so that terminated with the loss on our side of four men & one woman and on the side of the Enemy with the loss of two of their vessels and about two hundred men.

> "During the time of their bombarding it is supposed by the best judges that they throwed between twelve and fifteen hundred bombs.

> "On the night of the twelvth we lay about forty yards in the

rear of the entrenchments on our arms all night without any sleep. Our men were permitted to let down some times but were roused very often as our piquots fired four or five times during the night.

"That night about eight thousand of the enemy's land forces lay within a mile and a half of us. We could see them at their fires and could hear the hogs squeal as they killed them in their camp. But about three o'clock in the morning when they found they could not silence our fort they threw some rockets down the bay as a signal for the land forces to retreat which they did in great haste and left some of their straglers behind wich were taken prisoners by our men next day and on the next day our baggage waggons returned about 3 o'clock when we had orders to march to our camp and pitch our tents. But before we were quite done pitching them we had orders to strike them again and march off to the Federal Hill that the enemy were landing there and so we lay another night exposed to the Dew of Heaven.

"Next morning we came back to our camp again, pitched our tents and went to rest for awhile...."[38]

(6) The volunteer company of Captain Henry Steiner served from 25 August to 27 September 1814. They were discharged at Baltimore October 1814. Stationed on Louderslagers Hill, they fought at the Battle of North Point. (One member said that Captain Steiner was reported as sick.)

(7) Captain John Galt's company left Emmittsburg around 26 August 1814, marched to Taneytown and then to Baltimore. Most of the men were from the Emmittsburg/Taneytown area. They arrived at Camp Hampstead on 31 August and were placed as reserves in the entrenchments. Henry Green recalled the company being stationed at the Chincapin Hill entrenchments. "It rained a great deal. Mud and water were almost knee deep." Some men said they were discharged as late as 3 November 1814. The muster roll reads, 31 August - 27 October 1814.

Nicholas Snider, the 1st lieutenant of the company, was from Taneytown. A family history of the Thomson family credits him with the following account. According to him just before the Battle of North

DEFENSE OF BALTIMORE

Point the company was on picket duty many more hours than usual, and the members were almost starved. They dared not leave their post, and no one seemed to think of them. Then a large black man came along with a dirty horse bucket full of hot coffee. Lieutenant Snider bought a cup full and afterwards said it was the most delicious beverage he had ever tasted. At any other time the very sight of the bucket would have made him sick. They were relieved just as the first cannon was fired. Otherwise they would have been in the thickest of the fight. They were ordered to Federal Hill, near Baltimore, for a few hours rest and then again put on duty. They stood up in water to their armpits in the trenches where Saratoga Street, Baltimore, now is. The firing was heard very plainly at Taneytown where Lieutenant Snider's wife was living. Her brother, Hugh Thomson, observed, "Many a poor fellow will bite the dust tonight." The soldier's wife reflected on her husband's being in harms way - and fainted.[39]

In one of his men's application for bounty land Snider said, "After the Genl. Order of discharge was received at Camp Hampstead, Balto. Octr. 30th 1814 of 'Stansbury & Foremans Brigades' to which Captn Galts compy was attached, such was the enxiety of the troops to return to their homes that very few remained to receive their pay or certificates of discharge. Lieut. Jacob Row & myself remained with the Paymaster until the rolls were prepared, money recd., and pd to thos entitled a few days after our return to Taney Town & Emmitsburg, Fredk. County, averaging 50 miles from place of discharge to their several homes. Those facts account for so few certificates of discharge from Public Service being given by the Officer in Command."

According to Lieutenant Snider, Galt's company was designated 1st company of the 2nd Battalion commanded by Major George M. Eichelberger of the 3rd Regiment under Lieutenant Colonel Stemble.

(8) Captain Daniel Marker's Mountain Rangers from Middletown were activated a second time on 25 August 1814, this time for Baltimore. The company was discharged at Camp Hampstead, on 27 October 1814.

(9) The volunteer rifle company of Captain William Knox of the 1st Battalion of Major Beall Randall served during the period 26 August - c. 30 October 1814. The company was organized of men from the Taneytown area including some men from Emmittsburg. According to one of the members, this unit was encamped at the Rope Walk on Federal Hill. One member said he witnessed the destruction of the

three barges that passed the Fort. During the Battle of North Point the regiment marched down on the bayside to prevent the soldiers engaged in battle from being flanked. According to Joshua Green, the company was positioned in a corn field in sight of the British Army with orders to fire on the British if the Americans were driven back. After the battle the command was employed in guarding Baltimore.

(10) Captain Daniel Shawen's company was comprised of men from the Fredericktown and Middletown area; they served 5 September - 27 October 1814.

(11) The company of Captain Barton Hackney, from the Fredericktown and Middletown area, participated in the Battle of North Point, in the entrenchments. Their service covered the approximate period of 1 September - 29 October 1814.

(12) Captain Joseph Wood's company served from 3 August until 28 October 1814. They were at the entrenchments during the Battle of North Point. Many of the men were from the Woodsboro area; the company was discharged at Camp Diehl.

(13) The company of Captain Upton Norris (later succeeded by Captain John Fonsten) served from 2 September through 31 October 1814. The men were enrolled at Uniontown, Sulphur Spring, New Windsor and Westminster and marched from Westminster to Baltimore where they were engaged in the defense of the city. They lay in the rope walks two days awaiting tents and straw, before being mustered into the regiment.[40] According to Lewis Green, the day of the battle was a hot one. Then it blew up cold the following morning. The company remained on the ground for some time. Green stated, "Norris [Captain Norris] being a weakley man was taking with the colick and went into town to the Doctor whereupon Captain Norris and the Colonel had some words and Captain Norris went home. At this point Fonsten took charge of the company. According to George Fringer, "... we were attached to Colonel Stemple's regiment - so we remained untill the night that we expected the British to attack our fortifications. The intrenchments were filled with soldiers except Captain Norrises company. They were stationed back of the intrenchment, perhaps one hundred yards; it was a very dark night. The Colonel came riding amongst us. He inquired what troops were these. Then someone answered Captain Norris's Company. The Colonel asked where the Captain was. Someone answered, 'he is sick.' The Colonel said, 'sick,

hell, a pretty time to be sick, [just] when the British will be on [us] directly.' Then the Colonel asked where the Lieutenant was. He asked what was to hinder these troops from being cut to pieces by the British. He ordered us to be moved back under the hill. Then is the time and place that Lieutenant Fonsten took command of us...."[41]

Bazil Hahn of Norris's company said that during the battle of Baltimore and the bombardment of Ft. McHenry, he was doing guard duty over the magazine at Spring Garden.

(14) The company of Captain Henry Riggs, 27 August - 2 October 1814, 1st Regiment probably formed at New Market; they were discharged at Baltimore. Riggs' widow said he was a Captain in the first Regiment commanded by Colonel Stephen Steiner or Colonel Ragan. One of his lieutenants was William Sellman. The muster rolls can not be located.

(15) Reference was made by Joshua Turner to there being a company of Captain Ely Brashears at the Battle of Baltimore. See entry for Joshua Turner in Appendix A: The Veterans. No muster roll has been found for a company commanded by Brashears.

(16) Reference was made to the company of Captain Robert Fulton by privates, Richard Davis, John B. Stimmel, and Henry Shryock. Shryock who was in Captain Wood's company said the Fulton's company was camped next to Wood's company and consisted of men from the Creagerstown area. No muster rolls have been found.

(17) Reference is made to the company of Captain Jacob Creager of Creagerstown by John Frederick Saylor. He said the company formed at Annapolis and participated in the Battle of Bladensburg and the defense of Baltimore. Reference is also made to this company by Daniel Shaffer, and Solomon Smith whose widow said the company was in the 32nd Regiment under Colonel Hood. No muster rolls have been found.

LATER YEARS

By 1858 veterans of the War in Frederick County had formed an association called "United Brethren [or Brothers] of the War of 1812." Their activities included an annual celebration of the defense of Baltimore, escort duties at the funerals of their comrades in arms, and attendance at other public functions.

FREDERICK COUNTY MILITIA IN THE WAR OF 1812

NOTES AND REFERENCES

1. Adjutant General Papers, Maryland State Archives.
2. *Frederick-Town Herald*, dated Apr. 18, 1812, announced the meeting of company officers of the 28th Regiment, Md. Militia, at Jonathan Levy's tavern, in Middletown, "to revise and fix the bounds of the several districts - by order of the Colonel, John Shafer, Jun. Adjutant of the 28th Regt."
3. Adjutant General Papers. Brig. Gen. M. Bayley to the Governor, dated 23 Aug. 1794.
4. Adjutant General Papers. From Henry Myers and others, Frederick Town, May 2nd, 1797 - to Gov. and Council.
5. Adjutant General Papers. Letter from Brig. Gen. M. Bayley to Governor dated 23 Aug. 1794.
6. A list of absentees of Captain Fleming's company is found in the Adjutant General Papers.

    "At the meeting of my company of maletia on the 28th of November 1795, at Roll call the following persons were absent to wit (each fined 50 cents) John Miller, George Shoup, John Wardeck, George Hinklie, Adam Densmore, Lewis Fout, Thomas McCarlin, Jacob Fout, Baltzer Smith, Jacob Schlyock, Peter Frans, Godig(?) Grammer, Anthony Woodward, John Marloy, Jonathen Ballet, Peter Hoff, Benjamin Ireland, John Gaston, Jacob Staley of Joseph, Elias Bruner, John Staley, Joseph Staley Jr., Thomas Weirs. Arthur Fleming, Capt."

7. Adjutant General Papers. Those excused from militia duty because of religious scruples were required to pay a penalty.
8. Adjutant General Papers. Letter from John McPherson, Frederick County, Apr. 6th, 1803.
9. Adjutant General Papers.
10. *Ibid.*
11. *Ibid.*
12. *Frederick-Town Herald*, May 9, 1812.
13. T. J. C. Williams and Folger McKinsey, *History of Frederick County Maryland* (hereafter cited as Williams), Baltimore, Md., 1979, p. 166. We have been unable to locate the musters rolls for the staff or the companies.
14. A notice appeared in the *Frederick-Town Herald*, Aug. 15, 1812: "Volunteers and draughts of the 16th Regiment, Md. Militia, and those who have become substitutes, will repair to the barracks, in Fredericktown - Thomas Contee Worthington, Capt."
15. *Frederick Gazette*, Aug. 22, 1812.

NOTES AND REFERENCES

16. Williams on p. 166 states, "On July 3, 1813, a general discharge of troops called to the defense of Baltimore took place and Captain Henry Steiner's company of Frederick Artillery was particularly extolled and the other Western Maryland troops received praise for their conduct."
17. *Frederick-Town Herald*, June 5, 1813.
18. The announcement in the *Frederick-Town Herald*, July 31, 1813, read, "First Company, Washingtonian Green Volunteers, to meet at John Getzendanner's lower meadow spring in Full Uniform, with arms and twenty rounds of blank cartridges - John A. Dean, 1st Lieut."
19. Williams, p. 167.
20. *Frederick-Town Herald*, Aug. 21, 1813.
21. Williams, p. 166.
22. A large number of these men have been identified in the registers of enlistment, Microfilm Group M233 at the National Archives. This information is included with the soldier in Appendix A of this work.
23. Earlier a designation of First Regiment was assigned to Charles County, Second Regiment to Anne Arundel County and Third Regiment to Montgomery County.
24. Letterbook, Adjutant General, Maryland State Archives.
25. Marine, *British Invasion of Maryland, 1812-1815*, Baltimore, Md., 1913, reprinted, 1977, p. 86 (quoting General Winder's account).
26. Adjutant General Letterbook.
27. *Maryland Republican* (Annapolis), dated 23 July 1814.
28. The order read, "To Genl. Barrick, Annapolis July 17th 1814
 Sirs,
 I have just received information that the enemy have received a considerable reinforcement of Ships and some land forces, that they were as high up the bay on yesterday as Patuxent; it therefore becomes necessary to call on you to afford some . . . from your Brigade. You will cause five hundred men to be detached from your Brigade, organized with a due proportion of officers and marched with all expedition to this place - it will probably facilitate their movement to send them by companies. You will cause them to be furnished with waggons at the rate of one waggon to a hundred men, . . . I trust as the militia of your Brigade have hitherto had little duty to do, they will enable you to comply with this order promptly. An order issued yesterday from the Adj. Genl. Office which will be forwarded by this conveyance to furnish your quota of 6000 men ordered by the President of the United States this order is entirely distinct from the one of yesterday, you will detach this 500 with utmost expedition and proceed as speedily as possible to furnish your quota agreeably to their order of yesterday. Lev. Winder." Adjutant General Papers.

FREDERICK COUNTY MILITIA IN THE WAR OF 1812

*29. Williams, *History of Frederick County*, pp. 167, erroneously states, "the Frederick troops . . . arrived too late for the affair at Bladensburg." An examination of the muster rolls held by the National Archives, shows he was quite in error. We estimate that there were about 700 men from Frederick County on the battlefield. The issue dated August 27, 1814 of the *Frederick-Town Herald* stated,

"Since our last [issue] several hundred more of the militia of this county have been marched for Annapolis and Bladensburg. the whole number now in service from this county amounts to not less than 1500, and in all probability a further call will be made in the course of new week...."

30. The men of Frederick County serving in the company of Lowrye were Michael Umberger, 4th corporal; Rufus Bett (Belt?), 5th corporal; and privates, George Booses, Otho Hughes and John Harding. They made their rendezvous with the company at New Market.

31. These men were James Curry, Phillip Flenner, George Sergent and James Sergent.

32. Deserted from Camp at Bladensburg were the following men: Daniel Misinger, Philip Bidinger, Benjamin Butler, John Redenour, William Hinton, Amos Harbaugh, Henry Lear, James Jemeson, Hezekiah Metcalf, William Swan, Elijah Chaney, James Fillery, Thomas Goodlin, William Johnson, Samuel Lishure, John Lishure, Joshua Lishure, Bennoni Belt. William Fields and Jacob Litt were reported as deserting from Montgomery Court House. Peter Cartnail was listed as having deserted in Washington, D. C. The physical description of these men as given in the newspaper advertisement are shown here in the individual entries of the veterans, found in Appendix A.

33. En route to Baltimore from New Windsor was the company of Captain Upton Norris. According to one of its members, private, Bazil Hahn, their company arrested about 60 deserters who had run from the Battle of Bladensburg. Pension applications for Bazil Hahn, SO 518, SC 23343, WO 41606, WC 32440.

34. Marine's *British Invasion of Maryland, 1812-1815*. According to Marine the prisoners numbered around 80 privates and two officers.

35. A slightly different account of this company was given by J. Thomas Scharf, in the *History of Western Maryland, p. 193*. According to Scharf, the company of John Brengle was "raised in four hours by marching through the streets of Frederick, Aug. 25, 1814. This was the day after the battle of Bladensburg, when the news of that battle was received. Rev. David F. Schaeffer rode by the side of Captain Brengle through Fredericktown, encouraging men to volunteer..."

36. *(Frederick) Examiner*, 15 Apr. 1863.

NOTES AND REFERENCES

37. In the *History of Frederick County*, Williams incorrectly spelled his name as "Turnbull."
38. From a typewritten copy lent to the Monument by John Crumbaker, 416 E. North Ave., Baltimore, Maryland. The original letter was in the possession of his father, Mr. M. W. Crumbaker, New Concord, Ohio, 26 Jul. 1942. Crumbaker also described the following event.

"Some time afterwards [following the Battle of Baltimore] we got a quarter of beef that was bad and we went to Brigade Major Haslet for advice and he told us to summon a Board of seven officers out of the regiment to inspect the same which was done, but that being contrary to the rules of the Militia but the rules were that the quarter-master of the regiment was to choose one man and the contractor to choose another which being the two gentlemen appointed were Dr. Bantz and Capt. Murray and they pronounced the meat good which the seven officers condemned. Our men would not be imposed on by those two gentlemen but would soon fast one day than to eat unholsum food. So they left the meat laying at the quartermasters until the next morning when they buried it in the following manner: Two men dug a hole and four of them put straw bands round their hats as pall bearers and took meat on two poles while the company marched after and the drum beating a dead march before and after they buried the meat they gave three cheers and returned to their quarters.

"The two gentlemen who passed the meat to be good lost the confidence of our company, officers and men in a great measure.

"Another time we got meat that was not good and there was two gentelmen appointed agin to inspect it but they being men of better judgement (or no partiality) they condemned the meat and we got good meat in place of it."

39. A hand written narrative entitled, "An Account of William Thomson, the first of the name in America and his children." It was acquired by Virginia Stenley, Taneytown, at an antique show in recent years.
40. Bounty land claim of Lewis Green, 55-160-44745; Pension, SO1638, SC23351.
41. Bounty land claims and pension applications of George Fringer. Bounty land claims, 50-40-89642, 55-120-64579; Pension, SO21158. Still another veteran, Charles W. Michael, stated in this bounty land claim that Captain Norris was accused of deserting his company and punished.

DISCHARGE PAPER OF PRIVATE ABRAHAM HAHN OF CARROLL COUNTY (then Frederick County). This scrap of paper is representative of the many discharge papers found in the Bounty Land application files of the National Archives. It reads,
Camp Hampstead Octr. 31st 1814.
I hereby Certify that Abraham Hahn a private in Capt. John Fonstens Company of M. Militia in service of the United States was Honourably discharged by order of Major General Scott after performing a Tour of duty. /s/ John Fonsten Capt.

APPENDIX A

VETERANS OF THE MILITIA AND REGULAR ARMY

The military service of the following veterans is based on muster and pay rolls held by the National Archives, in the case of the militia; and the enlistment registers held by the National Archives, in the case of regular army members. Regular army units are designated by numerical regiments preceded by "U.S.," for example, "36th U.S. Inf." Other units are Maryland Militia units. The phrase, Crawford's "company," indicates volunteers of a militia company which was organized somewhere near Westminster, but never approved by the State. The period of service of the militia units is based on muster and pay rolls held by the National Archives. These rolls sometimes cover only a portion of the actual period served. Service in the regular army was taken from the Regular Army Register on microfilm at the National Archives. Information on the dates of militia commissions was based primarily on the Adjutant General Commission Book held by the Maryland State Archives. Other sources of information are shown following "Sources." Acquaintances, abbreviated as "acq." and "witnessses" refer to names found in the affidavits of bounty land and pension applications.

Sources

FMml-*Fredrick County Marriage Licenses* by Magaret Myers. 1778-1810 and 1811-1840. (Family Line Publications)

Rcds. of Ref. Ch., Frederick - *Records of the Evangelical Reformed Church in Frederick, Maryland, 1746-1800*, originally tanslated by William J. Hinke. (Family Line Publications)

Names in Stone - *Names in Stone: 75,000 Cemetery Inscriptions From Frederick County, Maryland*, compiled by Jacob Mehrling Holdcraft (Genealogical Publishing Co., Inc., 1985)

Bridge in Time - *Bridge in Time: the Complete 1850 Census of Frederick County, Maryland*, compiled by Mary Fitzhugh Hitselberger and John Philip Dern (Monocacy Book Company, 1978).

Md. German Church Records. *Maryland German Church Records*, compiled by Pastor Frederick S. Weiser. On going series published by Historical Society of Carroll County, Westminster, MD.

Moravian Families of Graceham, Md. - *Moravian Families of Graceham, Maryland: The Families Belonging to the Moravian Community and Congregation at Graceham in Maryland and Some of Their Neighbors. 1754-1871.* Translated by Henry James Young (Family Line Publications, 1988).

West. Md. Genealogy - *Western Maryland Genealogy*, subscription magazine published by Catoctin Press, Donna Valley Russell, ed.

Hist. of Fred. Co. - *History of Frederick County, Maryland*, by T. J. C. Williams and Folger McKinsey, (Regional Publishing Co., 1979).

Williams' Frederick Directory, City Guide and Business Mirror, 1859-60 (Reprinted by Family Line Publications, repr. 1985).

Englebrecht Diary - In three volumes. Given here is the volume number followed by page number. Available at the Frederick County Historical Society, Inc., Frederick, Maryland.

Marr. and Deaths of Fred. & Montg., 1831-1840 - *Abstracts of Marriages and Deaths And Other Articles of Interest in the Newspapers of Frederick and Montgomery Counties, Maryland* From 1831-1840, by L. Tilden Moore (Heritage Books, Inc., 1991).

Monocacy and Catoctin, by Calvin Schildknecht (Volume 1 published by White Mane, Shippensburg; Volume 2 published by Family Line Publications).

Hist. of West. Md. - *History of Western Maryland*, by J. Thomas Scharf, a history of Frederick, Montgomery, Carroll, Washington, Allegeny, and Garrett Counties. 2 vols. (1882), Repr. Baltimore Regional Pub. Co. 1968.

Abstracts of Carroll County Newspapers, 1831-1846 by Marlene S. Bates and Martha Reamy (Family Line Publications, 1988).

The Register of General Society of the War of 1812 (pub. by the Society, 1972).

Divorces and Names Changed in Maryland by Act of Legislature 1634-1867, Pipe Creek Publications, Inc., 1991.

NEWSPAPER SOURCES:

(Frederick) *Examiner, Maryland Union, Fredericktown Herald, Maryland Herald and Hagers-Town Weekly Advertiser, Wyandot Pioneer, U.,* (Sandusky Ohio).

ABBREVIATIONS

acq. - acquaintance(s), acquainted
appt'd - appointed
b. - born
Balt. - Baltimore
bapt. - baptized
bro. - brother
bur. - buried
c. - about

capt. - captain
Cath. - Catholic
cem. - cemetery
ch. - church
corpl. - corporal
d. - died
dau(s) - daughter(s)
dec'd. - deceased

THE VETERANS

m. - married
m(1) - married first to
m(2) - married second to
marr. - marriage
mbr. - member
Meth. - Methodist
MM - Maryland Militia
mos. - months
obit. - obituary
Presby. - Presbyterian
prev. - previously
poss. - possibly
prob. - probably

pvt. - private
Ref. - Reformed (church)
regt. - regiment
rep. - representative
res. - resident, residing at/in. A placename in parentheses following a date indicates known residence on that date only.
resp. - respectively
rev - Reverend
sergt. - sergeant
twp - township
w/o - wife of
yrs - years

TERMS

Enlistment - used in this work to indicate entering into regular army.

Enrollment - used in this work to indicate entering into active militia service.

Brackets [ ] are used to indicate that information inside brackets may possibly pertain to subject veteran.

FREDERICK COUNTY MILITIA IN THE WAR OF 1812

ADAMS, John C. Pvt. in Capt. Flautt's rifle company, 29 Apr-11 May 1813; "dec'd. 11 May 1813."

ADAMS, William. Pvt. under Capt. William Durbin, Jr. Aug 24 - Oct 27, 1814.

ADKINS, Benjamin. Never joined company under Capt. Turbutt, on 1 Sep 1814.

ADLUM, Joseph. 2nd Sergt. under Capt. Brengle, 25 Aug - 19 Sep 1814. [Joseph Adlum m. Mrs. Mary Crum 1 Apr 1819.]
Source: Frederick-town Herald, 3 Apr 1819.

AERHART, Valentine. Pvt. under Capt. Fonsten, 2 Sep - 27 Oct 1814.

AGNEW, Henry. Pvt. under Capt. Nicholas Turbutt, 1 Sep - 27 Oct 1814.

AGNEW [Egnew], Samuel. 2nd Sergt. under Capt. Samuel Ogle, 1 May - 5 Jul 1813.

ALBAUGH Family. [Died last night (13 Jan 1832) in the 76th year of his age, born Jun 30, 1756, Mr. Christian Ahlbach ... father of Messrs. David, Absolom, Solomon, and Daniel Albaugh of this town. ... buried on the German Reformed Grave yard... - *Engelbrecht Diary*: 1:67.]

ALBAUGH, Absalom. Pvt. under Capt. George W. Ent, 24 Aug - 30 Sep 1814; b. c.1793; m. c.21 Jan 1819 Rebecca Rice (b. c.1801); d. 15 Jul 1856, in his 64th year; res. Fredericktown, 1850. Rebecca d. 12 Jul 1853, aged 52 yrs and 4 days. [See "Albaugh Family above.]
Sources: Bridge in Time; (Frederick) Examiner, 27 Jul 1853, 17 Jul 1856; FCmL

ALBAUGH [Albach], Adam. Pvt. under Capt. William Knox, 26 Aug - 27 Oct 1814. [Adam Albach m. Maria Kreis 20 Nov 1787 - Luth. Ch. of Fredericktown.]

ALBAUGH, Isaac. Appt'd 15 Jun 1813 cornet in Capt. Enoch Taylor's Troop of Horse, 2nd Regt., 1st Regt. Dist.

ALBAUGH, Jacob. Capt. in 20th Regt., MM; resigned 22 Jan 1814.

ALBAUGH, Samuel. Capt., 28th Regt.; d. prior to 6 Apr 1814 [See Adjutant General (MD) Papers.]

ALBAUGH, Solomon. Pvt. under Capt. Getzendanner, 26 Jul - 21 Aug 1814; b. c.1796-1798; m. c.3 Sep 1818 Elizabeth Kantner (b. 1799, d. 1843); he d. 1853. 1850 census of Fredericktown: Solomon Albaugh, carpenter; Morris age 25, shoemaker; Louesa 23; George 22, carpenter; Adeline 17; Annie M. 13; Amanda 11; Frances 9; Emma J. 8. Solomon and wife bur. Frederick Ref. Cem. (abandoned). George Kantner appt'd guardian fol. minor children of Solomon Albaugh (ages on 19 Jan 1856): Amanda E., 17; Sally Francis, 15; Emma Jane 13. Earlier George Kantner was guardian of Mary Ann Albaugh, presumably older dau of Solomon Albaugh. Acq. (1853): John J. Woodward, Maurice Albaugh. [See "Albaugh Family" above.]
Sources: Bounty land claim, 55-120-87968; Names in Stone; Bridge in Time. FCmL

ALBAUGH, William H. Pvt. under Capt. Turbutt, 2 Sep - 27 Oct 1814; b. 8 July 1795; m(1) c.9 Sep 1824, Susanna (Hickson) Snider (b. 1797, d. 13 Apr 1862, age 65 yrs, 7 months, 25 days, widow of John N. Snider). They were married by Rev. Helfenstein. William H. Albaugh m(2) 10 Oct 1863 Susan Snyder (widow of George Holida, b. c.1819) in Fredericktown, MD by Rev. Daniel Zacharias. They res. Fredericktown 1850 where he was carpenter and coach painter. Geo. Holida d. Berkley Co. VA, 9 Jun 1860. William H. Albaugh res. Fred. Co., MD, 1850, 1851 and 1871; mbr. of Frederick delegation of "United Brothers of the War of 1812" in 1859; d. Fredericktown 28 Aug 1872 from a fall from a pear tree in his garden. He and first wife bur. Fredericktown Ref. Ch. His widow res. Berkley Co., WV in 1878; she d. 12 Nov 1887 Kearneysville, Berkley Co. WV. Acq. (1878): Samuel Carmack, age 85, res. at 63 W. Patrick St., Frederick City, and John H. Keller, age 50, res. 2nd St., Frederick, acq. with Susan Albaugh 12 and 15 yrs, resp.

Sources: Pensions, SO25306, SC21180, WO19293, WC11881; Bounty land claims, 50-40-29949, 55-120-20841; **Bridge in Time; FCml;** Names in Stone; Williams' **Frederick Directory,** City Guide, and Business Mirror, 1859-60; (Frederick) Examiner, 14 Sep 1859, 23 Apr 1862; Md. Union, 5 Sep 1872; **Engelbrecht Diary:** 1:295.

ALBERT, William. 3rd corpl. under Capt. Getzendanner, 9 Aug - 17 Sep 1813; 4th corpl. under Capt. Getzendanner, 26 Jul - 21 Aug 1814.

ALBERT, William. Pvt. under Capt. Daniel Shawen, 5 Sep - 27 Oct 1814.

ALCOT, Joel. Pvt. under Samuel Ogle, 1 May 1813 - 5 Jul 1813.

ALDWORTH, John. Pvt. under Capt. James F. Huston 23 Jul - 20 Sep 1814 and under Capt. Joseph Green; joined 20 Sep 1814; deserted 10 Nov 1814.

ALER, Jacob. Pvt. under Capt. Barton Hackney, 1 Sep - 27 Oct 1814.

ALEXANDER, George. Pvt. under Capt. Matthew Murray, 25 Aug - 27 Oct 1814; b. c.1770. res. Petersville Dist. in 1850 with Hellen, 35, Tilghman, 32, laborer; Sarah, 25, Maria, 22 and Matilda C., 1.

Sources: Bounty land claim, 50-40-97269; **Bridge in Time.**

ALEXANDER, Henry. Pvt. under Capt. Samuel Dawson, 1 May - 5 Jul 1813 and 21 Jul - 13 Oct 1814.

ALEXANDER, Henry. Pvt. under Capt. Matthew Murray; joined 25 Aug 1814; deserted 23 Oct 1814.

ALEXANDER, Jacob. Jr. From Middletown. Capt. of company, 28th Regt.; served 22 Jul - 19 Sep 1814; resigned commission 2 Jan 1816. [Adj. General - Military Papers]

ALEXANDER, Jacob. Pvt. under Capt. Samuel Dawson, 1 May - 5 Jul 1813, and Capt. Jacob Alexander, 22 Jul - 19 Sep 1814.

ALEXANDER, Muhail [Michael?] G. Pvt. under Capt. Samuel Duvall, 3 Aug - 3 Oct 1814.

ALEXANDER, Robertson. 1st sergt. under Capt. Brengle, 25 Aug - 19 Sep 1814.

ALEXANDER, Valentine. Pvt. under Capt. Jacob Alexander, 22 Jul - 19 Sep 1814. After discharge res. VA, 4 yrs; b. c.1790; m(1) Rebecca (Rebeckey) Burgan 23 Mar 1820 by Rev. Kurtz; m(2) at Boonsborough, MD, 7 Aug 1824,

FREDERICK COUNTY MILITIA IN THE WAR OF 1812

Elizabeth Cross (b. c.1802); d. 15 Feb 1871 Cresap Town, MD. Elizabeth, res. Frostburg, MD 1879. Acq.: 1879 - Jonas Whitacre, 66, James Whitacre, 29, James S. McKinzie, 33 and James L. Hays, 45 all res. Frostburg, acq. with Elizabeth 25 yrs.

Sources: Bounty land claims, 50-40-47477, 55-120- 30566; Pension, WO36746, WC28628; Md. Herald and Hagers-Town Weekly Advertiser, 28 Mar 1820.

ALGUIRE. See Allgoyer [Allgeyer].

ALLEN, Alexander. Pvt. under Capt. Daniel Marker, 25 Aug - 27 Oct 1814.

ALLEN, Henry. 1st corpl. under Capt. Daniel Marker, 25 Aug - 27 Oct 1814.

ALLGOYER [Allgeyer, Alguire, Aulquire], Henry. Pvt. under Capt. Joseph Wood; joined 27 Aug 1814; enlisted regular army 11 Oct 1814 Balt. by Lt. Barret for 5 yrs, 5 ft, 4 inches, brown eyes, brown hair, brown complexion, age 32, tailor, b. Holland. In 38th U.S. Inf. Transferred to 4th U.S. Inf. by 31 Aug 1815. Mustered at Fort Moultrie 31 Dec 1815. Absent sick at Mobile 31 Mar 1819, d. Mobile 1 May 1819.

ALLISANDER, Jacob. Pvt. under Capt. Daniel Shawen's company, 5 Sep - 27 Oct 1814.

ALLISON, John P. Pvt. under Capt. Darby, 3 Aug - 8 Nov 1814 (absent 30 days); said he served as pvt. in Capt. Dade's company about 1 week and balance of time in Darby's company; substitute for Thomas Alnut who was drafted for 3 mos. at Bladensburg c.24 Jun 1814; b. c.1792. res. Clarke Co., VA 1850, 1855. Bachelor in 1872, res. Harpers Ferry, WV. Acq. 1850: John F. Cunningham and Thomas Watkins, both res. Sandy Hook, MD.

Sources: Pension, SO27798, SC21081; Bounty land claims, 50-40-99116, 55-120-40119.

ALLNUTT, Jesse. Pvt. under Capt. Denton Darby, 1 Sep - 8 Nov 1814.

ALSOP, Joseph. Pvt. under Capt. Samuel Dawson; joined 1 May 1813; deserted 5 Jun; returned 25 Jun; discharged 5 Jul 1813.

ALSOP, Joseph. Pvt. under Capt. Barton Hackney; joined 1 Sep 1814; deserted 23 Oct 1814.

AMBROSE, Matthias. Pvt. in U.S. Artillery under Capt. Thomas Biddle/Col. W. Scott; enlisted 15 or 21 Sep 1814 by Lt. Lamar for 5 yrs. At enlistment: 5 ft, 8 inches; dark eyes, light hair, fair complexion; age 27; occupation currier; b. Fred. Co., MD; mustered Fort Moultrie 17 Jul 1815; absent, in pursuit of deserters 31 Oct 1815. Reported deserted at Fort Moultrie 30 Jun 1816.

AMBROSE, Peter. Pvt. in company of artillery of Capt. Henry Steiner, 28 Apr - 29 Jun 1813 and 25 Aug - 27 Sep 1814. Poss. son of John Ambrose, early settler of Catoctin Dist., Fred. Co. or son of Christopher Ambrose who d. 1795 and whose rep. were: Mary w/o Robert Mossman, Peter Ambrose, age 18; Catherine Ambrose, age 15; Catherine Miller w/o David Miller; and the widow - all of Fayette Co. PA, on 10 Aug 1810.

Sources: Williams, Hist. of Fred. Co., Md., p. 869; West. Md. Genealogy, v. 4:2 (descents).

AMICH [Amick], George. Pvt. under Capt. G. W. Magee, 14 Oct 1814 - 10 Jan 1815. Captured at Battle of Bladensburg.

THE VETERANS

Source: Marine, **British Invasion of Md., 1812-1815.**

ANDERS [Andrews], Henry. Pvt. (named Andrews on the rolls) in Capt. Fonsten's company, 2 Sep - 27 Oct 1814; b. c.1794; m. Elizabeth Vaughn Fred. Co. 25 May 1817. He res. Woodsboro, Fred. Co., MD 1871. Acq.: 1871 - Samuel Carmack, res. Patrick St., Frederick and Benjamin Smith, Woodsboro.
Source: Pension, SO6870, rejected (insufficient service).

ANDERS, John. Pvt. under Capt. Samuel Dawson, 21 Jul - 13 Oct 1814.

ANDERSON, Alexander. Pvt. under Capt. Samuel Duvall, 3-13 Aug 1814.

ANDERSON, George. Pvt. under Capt. Basil Dorsey, 30 Jul - 27 Sep 1814; m. 28 Dec 1814, Elizabeth Saltkild (b. c.1798) New Market, MD, by Justice of Peace [later Elizabeth stated they were married by Rev. James Higgins]; 1st marr. for both. Widow said he served as substitute for James Walker under Capt. Darby. After discharge he res. Fred. Co.; since 1830 in Meigs Creek, OH; d. Meigs Creek, Bristol Twp, Morgan Co., OH, 12 Aug 1838. Widow res. Morgan Co., OH (1855), Meigs Creek, OH (1878, 1879). In 1814 he was 5 ft, 11 inches, black hair, fair complexion, blue eyes, miller. Acq.: H. Margratt and Thomas Stevens (1855), res. Bristol Township, Morgan Co., OH; Thomas K. Mcgrath age 70 and Daniel Lawrance age 78 - both res. Meigs Creek (1878) acq. 45 yrs; Ephraim Roberts, 60 (1879), P. Roberts, 30 (1879).

[Family Record reveals marr. of George and Elizabeth Anderson and Lewis Dodge and Lusindia Anderson m. 18 Nov 1841; James Anderson and Margarett Ann Kirkpatrick m. 7 Jun 1855; John Weeks and Sharloty Anderson m. 19 Apr 1838; Bernard T. Wear and Louisa Anderson m. 6 Sep 1838; John Anderson and Mary Frazier m. 30 Sep 1840.]
Sources: Bounty land claim, 55-160-114510; Pension, WO30087, WC29384. Discharge paper in pension file.

ANDERSON, J. M. Mbr. of the Frederick delegation of "United Brothers of the War of 1812" in 1859. "He was on the excursion of the Old Soldiers to Baltimore, and upon the arrival of the train at the Washington Junction, he stepped out upon the platform of the car; while there, the sudden starting of the train threw him down on the track, in such a manner, that four of the cars passed over him without inflicting the slightest injury. His escape was miraculous." [FCml issued to Jonathan M. Anderson and Ann Easter on 26 Nov 1810. He d. c.27 Apr 1864, age 80 yrs, one of the Old Defenders.]
Source: **(Frederick) Examiner**, 14 Sep 1859, 27 Apr 1864; FCml.

ANDREW, Bernard. Pvt. from Balt., under Capt. Joseph Green, 14 Oct 1814 - 10 Jan 1815, substitute for William Gillen. "Deserted."

ANDREW, Herbert. Pvt. under Capt. Samuel Ogle, 1 May 1813 - 5 Jul 1813.

ANDREWS, Adam. Pvt. under Capt. Samuel Ogle; joined 1 May 1813; deserted 8 Jun 1813.

FREDERICK COUNTY MILITIA IN THE WAR OF 1812

ANDREWS, Henry. Res. 8 miles from Westminster. Pvt. under Capt. Fonsten, 2 Sep - 27 Oct 1814.

ANDREWS, Jacob. Commissioned lieut. under Capt. Upton Noris 24 Jan 1814.
Source: Adjutant (MD) General Papers.

ANGEL [Angle], David. Corpl. in the U.S. Rifles; b. Fred. Co. MD, enlisted in regular army 25/26 Oct 1813 at Hanover, PA, by Lt. McKenney, to serve until 26 Oct 1818. At enlistment, 5 ft, 8 inches, grey eyes, sandy hair, light complexion, age 23, hatter. Province Island Barracks, 1813. Mustered at Sacketts Harbor, reported absent sick "at Buffalo or Williamsville."

ANGEL [Angle], George. Pvt. under Capt. William Knox, 26 Aug - 27 Oct 1814; b. c.1792; res. Carroll Co., MD, 1850 and 1855.

ANGLE, Isaac. Mbr. of Crawford's "company." [FCml issued to Isaac Angel and Catharine Devilbiss 12 Dec 1814.]

ANGLE, John. Mbr. of Crawford's "company."

ANKRUM [Ankrom], George. Pvt. from Fredericktown, under Capt. James F. Huston 23 Jul - 20 Sep 1814, then Capt. Joseph Green, until 10 Jan 1815.

ANNON, Robert L. Appt'd 24 Oct 1796, 2nd lieut. Capt. William Emmitt's company of Light Dragoons, attached to 9th Brigade.

ANTHONY, Henry. Pvt. under Capt. Dawson, 21 Jul - 13 Oct 1814.

APPLEBEE, Hezekiah. Pvt. under Capt. Brengle, 25 Aug - 19 Sep 1814.

APPLEBEE, Hezekiah. Pvt. under Capt. Nicholas Turbutt, 2 Sep - 27 Oct 1814.

APPLEBER [Appler], William. Pvt. under Capt. Denton Darby, 3 Aug - 8 Nov 1814 (absent 6 days).

ARAWALD, Antony. Mbr. of Crawford's "company."

ARBAGH, Jacob. Stated he was drafted Fred. Co., MD, c.1 Aug 1814; went to Washington City, then down Potomac River to Mulberry Bottom [St. Mary's Co.?] c.1 Nov 1814; taken sick before company was discharged and taken to Port Tobacco where he was discharged; substitute of John Stonecypher in Zacharias's company of Light Horsemen - b. c.1795; m. Elizabeth Arbaugh, Fred. Co., MD, 15 Sep 1821; res. Brook Co., VA 1852 & 1853; Jefferson Co., OH, 1855; Steubenville, Jefferson Co., OH, 1871. Acq.: Rezin Harris (1851), pvt., Turbutt's company. John Stonecypher (1854) said he volunteered in Zacharias's company, then employed Jacob Arbough as substitute. John Woolverton (1852) former res. Carroll Co. MD, now res. Jefferson Co, OH. James M. Elliott, Steubenville, OH (1871) and Rassellas Castner, res. Steubenville, OH. Daniel Hensell, Jefferson Co, OH, acq. with Jacob Arbaugh when Hensell's Regt. was serving in Balt.
Sources: Bounty land claims, 50-40-102167, 55-120-89568; Pension, SO6565, rejected.

ARCHIBALD. See Archbold.

ARCHBOLD, James or James K. Pvt., 12th U.S. Inf.; Fort Covington, 28 Feb

1815, discharged there 30 Mar 1815; b. Fred. Co., MD [possibly VA]. Enlisted regular army 7 May 1814 by Lt. Harrison or Lt. Robinson; in recruiting rolls at Staunton, VA, 8 Aug 1814. At enlistment: 5 ft, 6 inches, blue eyes, black hair, dark complexion, age 21, farmer.
Source: Bounty land claim, 12-160-5282.

ARMSTRONG, James. Pvt. under Capt. Philip Smith, 23 May - 8 Sep 1813 and Capt. Basil Dorsey 30 Jul - 27 Sep 1814.

ARMSTRONG, James. Pvt. under Capt. Joseph Wood, 27 Aug - 28 Oct 1814.

ARMSTRONG, Oliver. Res. 1 mile of Taneytown; 3rd corpl. under Capt. John Galt; joined 31 Aug 1814; deserted 15 Sep 1814.

ARMSTRONG, Richard. Pvt. under Capt. Turbutt; joined 8 Sep 1814, deserted 12 Oct 1814.

ARMSTRONG, William. Pvt. under Capt. William Knox, 26 Aug - 27 Oct 1814.

ARNOLD, John. Pvt., Capt. Flautt's rifle company; joined 29 Apr 1813 ; deserted 15 May 1813.

ARNOLD, John. Pvt. under Capt. Daniel Marker, 25 Aug - 27 Oct 1814. 1850 census: John Arnold, 56, farmer; Sarah, 50; Sarah, 21; Ezra, 19; Joshua, 17; Mahlon, 15; Martin, 13; Thomas, 11. Tomb-stone inscriptions for Burkitsville, Pleasant View Brethren Ch.: John Arnold, Sr., 5 Aug 1860, age 65; wife Sarah, 2 Aug 1878, age 80; dau Matilda, 16 Feb 1855, age 28 yrs, 8 mos., 9 days.
Sources: **Bridge in Time, Names in Stone.**

ARNOLD, Samuel. Pvt., 17th U.S. Inf.; b. Westminster, MD. Enlisted regular army 17 Oct 1813 at Cadiz, OH, by Lt. Milligan for duration of war. At enlistment: 5 ft, 6 inches, blue eyes, red hair and red complexion, age 35, farmer. At Erie, PA 28 Feb 1814 or 1815; Lt. W. Featherstone's company near Chillicothe, OH, 31 May 1815. Discharged Chillicothe 9 Jun 1815.
Source: Bounty land claim, 12-160-6536.

ARTHUR, Daniel. Appt'd 16 Jun 1813 Lieut. in company of Capt. Thomas Hammond, 29th Regt.

ARTHUR, John. Pvt. under Capt. William Durbin, 24 Aug - 27 Oct 1814, absent without leave 25 Oct.; b. c.1795, prob. son of Daniel Arthur who in 1800, bound son John to Frederick Arthur, blacksmith and sicklesmith, until 2 Aug 1803. John Arthur (of Middle Creek Factory) m. Susan Zimmerman (b. c.1803) of Liberty Twp, Adams Co., PA. 20 Jan 1825, by Rev. Boerstler. John and Susan Arthur res. Creagerstown E.D., 1850; with them were Celestia E. 16, Sarah C.13, Nerva F. 10, Maranda, 6. John Arthur d. 23 May 1873, age 78 yrs, 6 mos., 15 days. Family bur. Thurmont United Brethren Cem. Wife Susan d. 18 May 1873, age 74 yrs, 3 mos., 5 days. Acq. (1871): John H. Bowers, George A. Miller, Westminster; and Isaac E. Pearson.
Sources: Pension SO3246; **West. Md. Genealogy, vol. 5; Adams Centinal; Bridge in Time; Names in Stone.**

ARTZ, Abraham. His widow stated he enlisted at Fredericktown, MD and fol-

FREDERICK COUNTY MILITIA IN THE WAR OF 1812

discharge he res. Fredericktown, MD until 1826; moved to Montgomery Co., OH; m. Miss Mattie [Martha] L. Miller (b. c.1828) at Dayton, OH, 17 Mar 1864, by Rev. David Winters, German Ref. Ch., Dayton; previously m. Catherine Rudy who d. 14 Oct 1862/bur. Woodland Cem., Dayton. At enlistment: farmer, b. PA, 5 ft 6 inch, black hair, black eyes, dark complexion. He d. Dayton, OH, 25 Feb 1877; bur. 27 Feb 1877 Woodland Cem. His widow res. Dayton OH, 1889; res. 217 S. Perry St, Dayton, OH with Caroline C. Miller and Marianna Lydenberg, 49, acq. 35 and 49 yrs resp. Acq.: 1900 - Catherine A. Marat, age 62, res. 18 New St., Dayton and Marianna Lydenberg, age 50, res. 217 S. Perry, Dayton; acq. 30 and 50 yrs, resp.

Source: Pension, WO44889.

ATIR [Eader?], Lazurus. Pvt. under Capt. Denton Darby 3 Aug - 8 Nov 1814. See Lazarus Eader.

ATIR [Eader?], Solomon. Pvt. under Capt. Denton Darby 3 Aug - 8 Nov 8 1814, absent 6 days.

ATKINS, Charles. Pvt. under Capt. Jacob Getzendanner 9 Aug - 17 Sep 1813.

ATKINS, Charles of William. Pvt. under Capt. Thomas Contee Worthington, 17 Aug - 31 Dec 1812. Charles son of William and Kaby Adkins b. 4 Mar 1786; bapt. Luth. Ch. of Frederick.

Source: Md. German Ch. Rcds., v.4, p.29.

ATKINS, James. Pvt. under Capt. Thomas Worthington, 17 Aug - 31 Dec 1812. b. c.1795; m. Mary Brown (b. c.1796) Fredericktown, MD, 16 Jul 1818 by Rev. Martin, Meth. pastor. James Atkins d. Almshouse Fredericktown, Aug 1831. 1850 census: Mary Atkins, 50, pauper - in household of William Beall, 30. Witnesses: Conrad Young, James Atkins; acq.: Charles Burkett, Maria R. Watts.

Sources: Bounty land claim, 55-80-5072; **Bridge in Time.**

ATKINS, James. b. Fred. Co., MD. Enlisted regular army 25 Jun 1814 at Fredericktown, MD, by Ens. Philip Fisher; 36th U.S. Inf. under Col. H. Carbury. At enlistment, 5 ft, 8 inches, 40 yrs old.

ATKINS, Samuel. b. Fred. Co., MD. Enlisted regular army 15/16 Mar 1814, Charlestown, VA, by Lt. McDonald for duration of war. At enlistment, dark eyes, dark hair and fair or sallow complexion, age 20 or 22, shoemaker. Pvt. 12th U.S. Inf. under Col. Cole. Fort Washington 31 Dec 1814 and 28 Feb 1815; lost 4 days because of desertion, later reported as invalid, unfit for service. At Fort Meigs and 17th U.S. Inf. in New York in 1813. "Absent sick, sent to Lower Sandusky."

ATLESPURIER, Sebastian. Res. 3 miles of Taneytown; pvt. under Capt. John Galt, 31 Aug - 27 Oct 1814.

ATTIC, George. Pvt. under Capt. Fonsten, 2 Sep - 27 Oct 1814.

ATLOO [Altoo, Atho], Samuel. b. Fred. Co., MD. Enlisted 1 Feb 1815 by Lt. Jones for 5 yrs. At enlistment, 5 ft 5-6 inches tall, black eyes, black hair, dark complexion, age 25, wagoner or laborer. Pvt., 38th U.S. Inf. Mustered by Capt.

THE VETERANS

Thomas Sangster's Det., Fort Covington 30 Apr 1815; discharged Annapolis, MD, 24 Jul 1815 as supernumerary.

ATWOOD, William. m(1) Priscilla Hilleary (b. c.1795) Sep 1817 at Fredericktown, by Father Maroney, Cath. Priest. [Date of marr. given by widow; however FCml issued 19 Feb 1818.]; d. Loudoun Co, VA, 22 Sep 1852. Widow res. Newburg, WV 1878.

According to widow he served under Capt Denton Darby; said he was drafted at Bunker Hill 10 Jun 1814 for 6 mos. and at enlistment was about 23 yrs of age, carpenter, b. near Poolesville, Montgomery Co, 6 ft, dark eyes and hair, fair complexion; fol. discharge he res. Montgomery Co., MD until 1816; Fred. Co., MD until 1847; then Loudoun Co., VA. In 1866 she came to Newburg, Preston Co, WV. Acq. (1878): F. M. Ford, 45, res. Kingwood, Preston Co, WV and C.W. Fawcett, 34, res. Kingwood, Preston Co; acq. with Priscilla Atwood 10 yrs.

Source: Pension, WO24349 (rejected, name not on rolls).

AUBERT, Jacob. Pvt. in Capt. Jacob Getzendanner's rifle company, 9 Aug - 17 Sep 1813; b. 9 Apr 1792, d. 4 Dec 1882 at the residence of his son, A.E. Aubert on 2nd St., Fredericktown; m. Hannah Grove (b. 22 Jul 1798, d. 25 Dec 1857), c.1827 [FCml issued 25 Apr 1827]. 1850 census, Fred. E.D.: Jacob Aubert 53, laborer, Hannah Aubert 53 and Louesa 16. [Amanda Louisa Creager d. near Rocky Spring of "childbed fever," 1 Nov 1865, at age 27 yrs, 5 days, m., bur.

Doubs Graveyard, b. near Rocky Spring, dau of Jacob Aubert of same place.] Jacob Aubert among 1812 veterans present in 1876 ceremony in Frederick. Jacob and Hannah Aubert bur. Rocky Springs (or Doubs) Cem. Acq. (1871): George Shoacre and Frederick Kline, res. Fred. Co.; (1875): James Bartgis, res. East South St., Frederick City and Reuben Grove res. West South St., Frederick City.

Sources: Pension, WO7262, WC22607; Bounty land claims, 50-40-78490, 55-120-48512; Names in Stone; Bridge in Time; FCml; Scharf's Hist. of West. Md.; (Frederick) Examiner, 30 Dec 1857, 6 Dec 1882.

AUD, Asa. Orderly sergt. in company of Capt. Nicholas Turbutt, 2 Sep - 27 Oct 1814; b. c.1790, near Buckeystown, MD; m. c.1817 Catharine Hickman (b. c.1803), near Poolesville, MD, Montgomery Co. by Rev. Clingan, Bapt. minister, 1st marr. for both. In 1814 he was a farmer, c.5 ft, 9 inches; dark brown hair and eyes, dark complexion. Widow, Catharine Aud said they m. 15 Sep 1829.* Asa Aud d. 1 Apr 1860 near Edwards Ferry, Montgomery Co. After discharge he res. Fred. Co. 5 yrs, then Culpepper Co., Va. 4 yrs and then Montgomery Co., MD, for rest of his life. He d. 1 Apr 1860. She res. Montgomery Co. 1865 and 1878 (Poolesville); d. 29 Nov 1887. Acq. (1882): R. W. Williams and John O. Merchant, Poolesville, Montgomery Co, MD.

* Copy of marr. license [Frederick County] of Asa Aud and Catharine Hickman issued 13 Sep 1817 was presented by Wm. E. Aud to the Na-

FREDERICK COUNTY MILITIA IN THE WAR OF 1812

tional Archives through Walter Robertson to prove that marr. did not occur on 15 Sep 1829 "as indicated in the official pension file."

Sources: Bounty land claims 50-40-17659, Duplicate/ 55-120-69358; Pension, WO38036, WC32414; FCmL

BABB, Charles. Pvt., 2nd U.S. Inf. under Capt. Bracham/ Col. T. H. Cushing; b. Fred. Co., MD, c.1775; enlisted regular army 23 Dec 1807 at Staunton, VA by Capt. Bracham for 5 yrs. At enlistment: 5 ft, 11 inches tall, blue eyes, light hair, fair complexion, age 32, farmer. Tried at C.C. Springs 13 Sep 1809, being drunk, given 50 lashes, remitted. Tried 17 Jul 1810 for insolence - acquitted. At Natchez 2 Nov - 7 Dec 1810. Tried at Fort Stoddart 17 Aug 1811 for disobedience of orders, given 35 lashes - remitted. Discharged 22 Dec 1812. Re-enlisted 29 Dec 1812 at Mt. Vernon for 5 yrs; appt'd corpl. 15 Jan 1813; d. at New Orleans 16 Apr 1815.

BACHMAN, Fredrick. Pvt. under Capt. Zacharias, 7 Aug -10 Sep 1814, 2nd Regt., 1st Cav. Dist.

BACON, Stephen. Pvt. under Capt. George W. Ent, 24 Aug - 30 Sep 1814.

BADER, Gabriel. Pvt. under Capt. Galt, 31 Aug 1814.

BAER - See Bear.

BAER [Bear], David. Pvt. under Capt. John Brengle, 25 Aug - 19 Sep 1814.

BAER, Jacob. Appt'd surgeon, 6th Regt., MM; served in 3rd Regt., MM, c.27 Aug - 27 Oct 1814, (according to him); served in "same corps" as Michael S. Baer, M.D. and John Nelson, who attested to his service; b. 22 May 1783; m. 12 Jan 1813, Miss Elizabeth W. Dorsey (d. 28 May 1865), dau of Caleb Dorsey, of Elk Ridge, Anne Arundel Co.; d. at his residence, West Patrick St., 10 Apr 1866, after a lingering illness; bur. Mt. Olivet, Frederick. [In the Adjutant General file - Military Papers, 7 Feb 1814: letter to Governor from George Baer, recommending nephew, Dr. Jacob Baer to replace Dr. John Fisher, dec'd., as surgeon in Col. John Ritchie's Regt.]

Sources: Bounty land claim, 55-120-60206; Frederick-town Herald, 5 Jun 1824; (Frederick) Examiner, 16 Jan 1813, 31 May 1865, 18 Apr 1866.

BAER, Michael S. Surgeon's Mate under Col. Stemble, 1 Sep 1814 to ?; b. c.1799; m. Matilda C. Ridgely dau of Judge Richard Ridgely, at home of her father, in Recess, Elk Ridge, Anne Arundel Co., 27 May 1824, by Alfred H. Dashiell, minister of the Epis. Ch. Dr. Michael S. Baer d. Balt. City 8 Jun 1854. His widow d. Balt. City 22 Aug 1874 in her 74th year. Acq.: Lucretia C. Wellmore and William H. Stewart, res. Balt. City.

Sources: Bounty land claim, 55-120-24990; (Frederick) Examiner, 5 Jun 1824, 14 Jun 1854, 2 Sep 1874.

BAER, Michael of John. Pvt. under Capt. Henry Steiner, 28 Apr 1813 - 29 Jun 1813 and 25 Aug - 27 Sep 1814; m. morning of 16 Jan 1817, Miss Charlotte Kiefer, dau of Christian Kiefer; both from Fred. Co., by Rev. Helfenstein. He d. 11 or 12 Apr 1823, leaving a wife and several small children; bur. German Reformed grave yard. His widow, Charlotte Baer, m. 15 Jan 1832, James Fin-

THE VETERANS

ney. Ezra Baer, son of Michael Baer of John d. 25 Dec 1835 in his 19th year. 1850 census of Buckeys Town Dist.: James Finney, 60, farmer, b. PA; Charlotte, 52, b. MD; Christian K. Finney, 16; Mary F., 10; Anne E. Candler, 30; Mariah L., 10; Osker H., 8; Augusta B., 6; Sarah C., 5; Adelade S., 2; Mary Reamous, 17, b. Germany. Miss Ann E. Baer m. Daniel H. Candler of Montgomery Co., MD, 4 Dec 1838. [Michael Baer son of Johannes Baer and Anna Maria, b. 8 Dec 1791, bapt. 24 Apr 1792 - Rcds. of Evan. Ref. Ch.]
Sources: **(Frederick) Examiner**, 18 Jan 1817; Rds. of Evan. Ref. Ch.; **Engelbrecht Diary**: 1:213, 2:325; **Bridge in Time**.

BAER, William (of Henry). Pvt. under Capt. Henry Steiner, 28 Apr - 29 Jun 1813, and according to him he also served under Capt. John D. Miller. Muster rolls of Capt. George W. Ent show a pvt. William Baer serving, 24 Aug - 30 Sep 1814. b. 1787 in Fredericktown; d. of cancer 7 Jun 1866 in Frederick; m. 1 Sep 1812 (evening) Miss Harriet Mantz (b. c.1790) by Rev. Jonathan Helfenstein at Frederick. In 1851 and 1855 he res. Carroll Co. Harriet res. Frederick City; d. 25 Aug 1871 at her residence on East Patrick St. in her 83rd year. Both bur. Mt. Olivet Cem., Frederick. Acq. (1871): J. Stapleton Bonsall and Joseph M. Ebberts, Frederick. Professor Baer lived in Baltimore and near Sykesville.
Sources: Bounty land claim, 50-40-77703, 55-120-4629; **Frederick-town Herald**; Scharf, **Hist. of West, Md.**; (Frederick) **Examiner**, 13 Jun 1866, 30 Aug 1871.

BAIL, Abraham. Ensign of Crawford's "company; lived c.5 miles sw of Westminster, c.2 miles east of New Windsor. Juryman in 1840.
Sources: **Carrolltonian, 25 Jan 1839, 10 Apr 1840.**

BAIL, Ludwick. Mbr. of Crawford's "company," d. 28 Sep 1853, aged 69 yrs; bur. Presby. Cem., New Windsor. FCml issued to Ludwick Bail and Sarah Haines 15 Mar 1823. The *Carrolltonian*, 28 Mar 1835, announced death of Eliza Baile on Sunday - "last dau of Ludwick Baile, Esq., of Westminster Dist."
Sources: FCml; Names in Stone; **Carrolltonian**, 28 Mar 1835.

BAIL, William. Mbr. of Crawford's "company." FCml issued to William Bail and Elizabeth Kline on 17 Dec 1804.
Sources: FCml; **Political Examiner**, 3 May 1836.

BAILY, William. Pvt. under Capt. Barton Hackney, 1 Sep - 27 Oct 1814.

BAKER, Basil. Appt'd 23 Mar 1814 ensign under Capt. Joseph Wood, 29th Regt., MM.

BAKER, Henry. Pvt. under Capt. John Galt, 31 Aug - 27 Oct 1814; res. 10 miles from Taneytown.

BAKER, Henry. Trumpeter under Capt. Hall, 7 Aug - 10 Sep 1814, 2nd Regt., 1st Cav. Dist.

BAKER, Jacob. Pvt. under Capt. John Galt 10 Sep - 27 Oct 1814; res. 10 miles from Hampstead.

BAKER, Jacob. Pvt. under Capt. Matthew Murray, 25 Aug - 27 Oct 1814; entry in rolls: "Sick present"; m. 5 Sep 1824 Hannah Youtzey (b. 3 Apr 1798) in Fred. Co., MD by Rev. Snae. Jacob

FREDERICK COUNTY MILITIA IN THE WAR OF 1812

Baker d. Fred. Co. 6 Jul 1833. Widow res. Fred. Co. 1850 (Middletown Dist.), 1852 and 1855; d. 1 Sep 1867; bur. at Middletown Luth. Cem. Acq.: 1852 - Mahlon Rhoderick and John Lorentz, res. Fred. Co. 1855 - Christian Remsburg, George W. Remsburg.
Sources: Bounty land claim, 55-120-31684; Names in Stone; Bridge in Time.

BAKER, Philip. Pvt., 5th U.S. Inf. under Lt. J. B. Taylor/ Col. J. Bowyer; b. Fred. Co., MD, c.1783; enlisted 3 Mar 1814, Harrisburg, PA, by Lt. Rea for 5 yrs: 5 ft, 6 inches, brown eyes, black hair, dark complexion, 31, laborer. On 31 Dec 1814 and 16 Feb 1815 he was mustered by Capt. J. R. Carbaley's company. At "New Jail Barracks" 28 Feb 1815. "Absent, taken by the Sheriff" 25 Feb 1815.

BALDERSTON [Balderson], John. Pvt. under Capt. John Brengle, 25 Aug - 19 Sep 1814; elected Bagman of Washington Hose Company of Ward # 2 in 1837; b. Lancashire, England; occupation weaver; d. 19 Oct 1852, (age 60 yrs according to newspaper, age 65 on tombstone); wife Margaret d. 23 or 25 Apr 1860, age 57. Both bur. Mt. Olivet, Frederick. 1850 census of Fredericktown: John Balderson, 60, weaver, b. England; Margaret Balderson, 45, b. MD; Drucilla Balderson, 18; William Burger, 12, b. Germany.
Sources: Political Examiner, Feb 1, 1837; (Frederick) Examiner, Oct 1852, 2 May 1860; Names in Stone; Bridge in Time.

BALDWIN, George. Pvt. under Capt. Fonsten, 2 Sep - 27 Oct 1814; res. 6 miles from Westminster.

BALDWIN, Isaac. Pvt. under Capt. Galt, 31 Aug - 27 Oct 1814; res. 3 miles from Taneytown.

BALDWIN, Nicholas. Pvt. under Capt. Huston; joined 23 Jul 1814; deserted 2 Aug 1814.

BALDWIN, Peter. Pvt. under Capt. Fonsten, 2 Aug - 27 Oct 1814; res. 4 miles from Westminster.

BALL, John D. Pvt. under Capt. Denton Darby, 3 Aug - 8 Nov 1814. Absent 4 days.

BALL, Samuel B. Pvt. under Capt. Barton Hackney, 1 Sep - 27 Oct 1814 (substitute for William Cassil of Frederick-town according to Ball); b. c.1790; res. Miami Township, Logan Co., OH, 1850 and Darke Co., OH, 1855.
Source: Bounty land claim, 55-120-39819.

BALTZELL, Charles. Appt'd major 17 Sep 1811, 29th Regt., MM.

BALTZELL, John of Nicholas. 2nd Sergt. under Capt. Jacob Getzendanner, 9 Aug - 17 Sep 1813; b. c.1792; d. 6 Dec 1881; m. 12 Oct 1824, Charlotte Miller (b. c.1805) in Frederick City by Rev. Helphenstine, first marr. for both. Newspaper announced the marr. of John Baltzell of Kentucky and Miss Charlotte dau of Dr. Samuel Miller of this city. They res. Frankfort KY 1852, 1855, 1871. She res. Main St. Frankfort KY in 1882. Acq. in 1882: Pat. McDonald, Main St., Frankfort, KY and L. L. Cox, Frankfort, KY; and William Strobridge of Frankfort, 77, acq. with John Baltzell for 33 yrs previous to Baltzell's death.

THE VETERANS

Sources: Bounty land claim, 50-40-84189, 55-120-27696; Williams, **Hist. of Fred. Co.**

BALTZELL, John. Pvt. under Capt. Nicholas Turbutt, 2 Sep - 27 Oct 1814; occupation hatter.

BALTZELL, John. Surgeon's Mate, 16th Regt., appt'd Sep 3 1799, promoted to Surgeon 14 Feb 1815; b. 11 Feb 1775. 1850 census, Fredericktown: John Baltzell, 75, physician $9,000; Ruth, 50; Eliza A., 25; John R., 22, lawyer; Alice, 13; Fanny, 11. - all b. MD. He d. 6 or 7 Sep 1854 of paralysis. Wife Ruth was dau of Charles Ridgely of Balt. Co.; she d. 25 Jul 1867 at age 67 at Leonardtown, MD at the residence of her son-in-law, Robert Ford. Both, John and Ruth bur. at Mt. Olivet Cem., Frederick. Also bur. at Mt. Olivet were: Albert, 21 Feb 1834 - 2 Jul 1854; son Frederick, 24 Sep 1830 - 18 Jun 1831; son Philip Thomas, 21 Dec 1828 - 16 Jun 1829; dau Cornelia, 9 Nov 1825 - 14 Aug 1826.

Sources: Adjutant (MD) General Papers; **Bridge in Time; Names in Stone**; **(Frederick) Examiner**, 31 Jul 1867.

BAND, Elijah. Mbr. of Crawford's "company."

BANKARD, Jacob. In his pension application Jacob Banker, on 1 Nov 1871, age 78, res. Clay Co., IL, said he enrolled at Fredericktown during War of 1812; m. Mary Vanhorn, Butler Co., OH, 5 May 1818. Acq.: Michael Kerney, Joseph Beard. No record of service.

Source: Pension, SO2520.

BANKARD, John. Pvt. under Capt. Jacob Getzendanner, 9 Aug - 17 Sep 1813; b. c.1791, Liberty, MD. At enlistment: 22 yrs old, labourer, 5 ft, 10 inches, black hair, dark eyes, dark complexion. Fol. discharge res. at or near Fredericktown, MD, c.6 mos.; moved to Butler Co.; res. there until at least 1878; d. 1 Jul 1881. Acq. (1878): Jacob Banker, 60 yrs and W. P. Poast, 45, res. Poast Town, acq. 50 and 35 yrs, resp.

Sources: Pension, SO31468, SC22180 (admitted 18 May 1878); Bounty land claim, 55-160-28142.

BANKER, John. Pvt. under Capt. George W. Magee; joined 22 Jul 1814; deserted 1 Oct 1814; b. c.1791; res. Carroll Co., MD, 1851. Source: Bounty land claim, 50-rejected-2664.

BANKERT, Mathias. Pvt. under Capt. Fonsten, 2 Sep - 27 Oct 1814; b. c.1785; res. Westmoreland Co., PA, in 1855.

Source: Bounty land claim, 55-rejected-196083 for reason: "Not on rolls of Cap. Andw. Baggs." On his application for bounty land he said he served as pvt. under Capt. Beggs.

BANKERT [Bankerd], Samuel. Appt'd lieut. 26 Jun 1812 in Capt. Simmons' company, 13th Regt.

Source: Adjutant (MD) General Papers.

BANKHART, Peter. Appt'd 28 Feb 1812 as capt. of company in 20th Regt., MM.

Source: Adjutant (MD) General Papers.

BANTZ, Henry. Corpl. under Capt. John Brengle, 25 Aug - 19 Sep 1814. [Died near St. Genevieve, MO, 27 Jun 1854, formerly of Frederick, aged about 58 yrs. *(Frederick) Examiner* - 7 Jun 1854]

BANTZ, John. Pvt. under Capt. John Brengle, 25 Aug - 19 Sep 1814.

BARING, Jesse. Mbr. of Crawford's "company."

BARKDOLL, Christian. Pvt. under Capt. John Galt; joined 31 Aug 1814; deserted 13 Sep 1814; b. c.1787; res. Carroll Co., MD, in 1850 and 1855. He recalled that he was in service for 15 days and sent home from the camp at Oldtown, near Balt., because of sickness (rheumatism) from which he did not recover until sometime following spring; has been a cripple ever since.
Source: Bounty land claim, 55-rejected-177303.

BARKMAN [Barrickman], Daniel. 4th sergt. under Capt. Jacob Alexander, Jul 22 - Sep 19 1814; d. near Dayton, OH, 23 May 1861; m. 5 Sep 1811 Catherine Stotelmyer (b. 1791) by Rev. George Craver, at Middletown, MD. [FCml issued to Daniel Barrickman and Catharine Stottlemier 2 Nov 1812.] Widow res. Montgomery Co., OH, 1855 and 1871 (Mad River Twp). Acq. (1871): Daniel Barkman and Henry Atwood, res. 1st St., Dayton, OH. [From the *Independent American Volunteer* (Fredericktown), 21 Sep 1808 - Daniel Barckmon age around 19, well looking lad, absconded as an apprentice to blacksmithing; reward offered by Benedict Joy, Carroll Manor.]
Sources: Pension, WO2408, WC798 (admitted 10 Oct 1871); Bounty land claim, 50-40-5270, 55-120-34404.

BARNERD, Hezekiah. Pvt. under Capt. Philip Smith, 23 May - 8 Sep 1813.

BARNES, Henry. Widow stated her husband was drafted at Cooksville 1 Aug 1814. Later she said he was drafted at New Market, MD. He d. Fred. Co., Sep 1842; m. 14 Feb 1820 Mary Cain (b. between 1790 and 1801?) in Anne Arundel Co. by Rev. Hood, Meth. Ch. Acq. (1855): John Barnes, Anne Lavina Barnes.
Source: Bounty land claim, 55-120-7134.

BARNES, Samuel. Pvt. from Fred. Co. under Capt. Henry Steiner, 25 Aug - 27 Sep 1814; b. 20 Feb 1788 in Kent Co., MD; m. 21 Mar 1833, Miss Ellen Ridgely Locke, dau of Nathaniel Locke of Balt. City. Samuel Barnes res. Balt. City 1852 and 1855. *(Frederick) Examiner* noted that Samuel Barnes, founded *The Political Examiner* in Frederick and was connected with the editorial management of the *Baltimore Clipper*. Engelbrecht in his diary noted that Major Sheppard C. Leakin, bro.-in-law of Samuel Barnes had been elected Sheriff of Baltimore City and County. "Major" Samuel Barnes d. at his residence near the Relay House 15 Dec 1858. [The *Examiner* published a lengthy obit. in which was stated that he served as major in War of 1812. In another item, the *Examiner* noted that Samuel Barnes was major of the 9th Brigade of MM in 1823.]
Sources: Bounty land claim, 55-120-2664; (Frederick) Examiner, 27 Jul 1853, 22 Dec 1858, 8 May 1878; Engelbrecht Diary: 1:103; Marr. and Deaths of Fred. & Montg., 1831-1840.

BARNETT, David. Ensign under Capt. Joseph Green, 14 Oct 1814 - 10 Jan 1815.

BARNHART, Solomon. Pvt. under Capt. Samuel Duvall, 3 Aug - 3 Oct 1814; drafted at Woodbury [Woodsboro], MD; b. c.1794; res. Montgomery Co., IN, 1850 (Darlington), and Montgomery Co., IN,

THE VETERANS

1855. Acq. (1865): George W. Cook and John B. Lowman, Montgomery Co., IN.
Source: Bounty land claim, 55-120-16332.

BARNHOUSE, Richard. Pvt. under Capt. Samuel Duvall, 3 Aug - 3 Oct 1814. Fred. Co.; m. c.17 Jan 1816 (date of FCml) Margaret Jane White. On 16 Aug 1855 James A. May, res. Washington, D.C., applied for bounty land for his wards, Jonas P. Barnhouse and Sarah Jane Barnhouse, (wife of James A. May). They were minor children of Richard Barnhouse and Margaret Jane Barnhouse. Margaret Jane m. Joseph Barnhouse bro. of her former husband, c.19 Nov 1849. On 30 Sep 1859 Joshua Stocks and William Stocks, res. Loudoun Co., VA, gave the birth dates of the children of Richard Barnhouse: Jonas P. Barnhouse, b. 29 Mar 1836; Sarah Jane May, 29 Mar 1836; John Barnhouse b. 14 Sep 1819, Randolph Barnhouse b. 12 Feb 1827; Sidney Barnhouse b. 17 Feb 1831. Acq.(1855): Mary W. Marlow and Martha L. Smith, res. Loudoun Co., VA.

On 12 Apr 1862 James Wilcott and Harrison Harper state that they were informed by Sarah Jane May that her bro. Jonas P. Barnhouse was engaged in rebel services against U.S. and had been so engaged for about 12 mos. He belonged to Capt. Mead's Cav. Company, Leesburg, VA.
Source: Bounty land claim, 55-160-101099

BARNOVER, David. Res. New Windsor; pvt. under Capt. Samuel Ogle 1 May - 5 Jul 1813 and ensign under Capt. George W. Magee, 22 Jul - 10 Jan 1815. Appt'd ensign on 12 Jul 1814 under Capt. John Matthias, 20th Regt., MM.

BARNOVER, George. Pvt., 14th U.S. Inf.; b. Fred. Co., MD, c.1774; enlisted in regular army 12 May 1812 by Lt. Gist. At enlistment: hazel eyes, dark hair and dark complexion, age 38. Mustered under Capt. F. Montgomery, Lewiston, 31 Jul 1813; reported absent sick at Williamsville; wounded at Brownstown and discharged at Chillicothe 22 Dec 1814.

BARNS. See Barnes and Burns.

BAROLL, Lewis. Pvt. under Capt. Samuel Ogle, 1 May - 5 Jul 1813.

BARR, John. Pvt. under Capt. Samuel Dawson, 14 Oct 1814 - 10 Jan 1815.

BARRET, William. Pvt. under Capt. Basil Dorsey, 30 Jul - 27 Sep 1814.

BARRICK, Cornelius. Pvt. under Capt. Joseph Wood, 27 Aug - 28 Oct 1814; he said he was a substitute for William Cramer; joined at Woodsboro, MD, 26 Aug 1814; carpenter; b. c.1792; res. Fred. Co., MD, 1850 and 1855. 1850 census of Creagerstown E.D. shows him with members of the family: Edward, 24; Sophia, 20; Abert, 18; Joshua, 16; Robert, 16; Simon, 14; Isaiah, 12; Mary J. 10.
Sources: Bounty land claim, 55-120-48511; **Bridge in Time.**

BARRICK, Ezra. 2nd Sergt. under Capt. Joseph Wood, 27 Aug - 28 Oct 1814; b. c.1794; d. at Carlinville, IL, 12 Apr 1864; m. 26 Aug 1826, Sarah S. Small (b. c.1809), near Louisville, Jefferson Co., KY, by Rev. John Blackburn, each for first time. In 1814 he was 18 yrs old; 5 ft, 9 inches; had fair com-

FREDERICK COUNTY MILITIA IN THE WAR OF 1812

plexion, dark hair, hazel eyes; carpenter or farmer. Following discharge he res. MD, KY and IL. He and Sarah res. Macoupin Co. IL, 1850 and 1855. Widow res. Macoupin Co., IL, 1878 and 1879. In 1879 fol. children of Ezra and Sarah Barrick were living: Richard H. b. 21 Jun 1829 at Oldham Co., KY; Ann Eliza (now Otwill) b. 13 Jul 1836, Oldham Co., KY; Charles d. b. 19 Nov 1839, at Carlinville, IL.; Ellen (now Brown) b. 20 Oct 1844 at Carlinville, IL.; and George Lewis b. 3 Jan 1846 at Carlinville, IL.

Acq.: 1878 - George R. Hughes, age 50; William Farrell, age 43 - acq. 25 yrs. 1879 - Catharine Blackburn, 67; Rhoda Fishback, 65 - knew Ezra Barrick and Sarah S. Small previous to their marr.; knew that Ezra and Sarah moved to Macoupin Co., IL, in Oct 1836. 1879 - Thomas C. Davis.

Sources: Pension, WO34336, WC22168 (admitted 20 Mar 1879, last paid 4 Dec 1885, dropped 14 Aug 1886, because of death); Bounty land claim, 50-40-7288, 55-120-16334.

BARRICK, Frederick. Appt'd Capt. of company, 29th Regt., MM, 12 May 1811; appt'd Lt. Col. 12 Feb 1818.

BARRICK, George of Peter. Appt'd Lieut. 12 May 1812 Capt. Frederick Barrick's company, 29th Regt., MM. Served as 1st Lieut. under Capt. Joseph Wood, 3 Aug - 28 Oct 1814; b. 8 Mar 1779; d. near Woodsboro 19 Feb 1863; bur. Walkersville, Glade Ref. Cem.

Source: (Frederick) Examiner, 4 Mar 1863.

BARRICK, Henry. Appt'd Brig. General, MM, 28 Dec 1812; d. 8 May 1834, at Ridgeville, age 77 yrs, "soldier of the Revolution."

Source: Frederick Herald, 17 May 1834.

BARRICK, John. Pvt. under Capt. Creager, Washington Co.; joined 1 Aug 1814; leg broken, on furlough 21 days. d. Woodsboro 13 Oct 1844; m. 29 Jan 1818 Esther Kurtz (b. c.1783) in Fredericktown by Rev. J. Helfenstein. In 1850 Esther res. with John W. Barrick [her son? in the Woodsboro Dist.]. In the household were John W. Barrick, 32, farmer; Elizabeth Barrick, 22; Eugenia, 2; Ester, 12 and Ester, 67; also George W. Horner age 15, laborer. Acq.: George Barrick b. c.1795; John Holbrunner b. c.1793, stated John Barrick was wounded at Annapolis en route to Bladensburg and taken home.

Sources: Bounty land claim, 50-40-83499, The Times and Democratic Advocate, Apr 26, 1838.

BARRICK, Lewis. Appt'd 2nd Lieut. 23 Apr 1808 in Capt. James Clemson's artillery company.

BARRICK, Samuel. Pvt. under Capt. Henry Steiner, 28 Apr - 29 Jun 1813, and Capt. Reid's troop of horse, 1st Cav. Dist., 26 Aug - 3 Sep 1814; b. c.1790. Appearing in Tippacanoe Co., IN, 1855, was Nancy Lucretia Maxwell (b. 29 May 1835), only minor child of Samuel Barrick. She appeared with her husband, Thomas Maxwell and two witnesses, Henry and Josephine Squire. Henry Squire was a son-in-law of Samuel Barrick; he stated that family bible contained dates of birth of Samuel Barrick, birth and death of his two wives, and births of 10 children and 2 grandchildren.

THE VETERANS

[Samuel Barrick of New Philadelphia, OH, m. 13 Sep 1832 Miss Hetty Crum of Fred. Co. by Rev. Wachter.]
Sources: Bounty land claim, 55-120-22568; Frederick-town Herald, 15 Sep 1832.

BARRICK, William. Enlisted 23 Apr 1814 by Lt. Fletcher; he was 5 ft, 8 1/2 inches, had grey eyes, dark hair and light complexion, age 25, occupation cooper, b. Fred. Co. Served in the 38th U.S. Inf. Mustered 1 Jun 1814, at Balt.; discharged at Balt. on 6 Apr 1815.

BARRICKMAN [Barickman, Barrukman, Birckman, Berkman], Christian. Pvt. under Capt. Samuel Duvall, 3 Aug - 3 Oct 1814, as substitute for his bro. Henry Barickman who was drafted near New Market in Frederick Co, MD; b. c.1799; d. 26 Feb 1865, Columbia Township; m. 15 Aug 1839 Elizabeth Hapler by Rev. J. W. Steel, Meth. minister in Butler Co., OH; res. Jennings Co., IN, 1855. Widow res. Zenas, Jennings Co., IN, 1878; stated her husband was German and not well acquainted with English language, generally spelled his name Birckman, but pronounced it Barickman, and was called Berkman. Acq. (1878): Enock Barickman, 31, son of Christian and Elizabeth Barrickman; and John Himelick, 30, res. Columbia Township.
Sources: Pension, WO23623, WC21112; Bounty land claim, 55-160-23505.

BARROLL - See Baroll.

BART, Cornelius. Appt'd 24 Jan 1814, ensign under Capt. Norris, 20th Regt., MM.

BARTEL, Christian. Pvt. under Capt. John Brengle, 25 Aug - 19 Sep 1814.

BARTGIS, Benjamin F. Appt'd 26 Jun 1812, lieut. under Capt. Gilbert Kemp, 16th Regt.

BARTGIS, Mathias E. 2nd Lieut. under Capt. Samuel Dawson, 1 May - 5 Jul 1813, and 1st Lieut. under Capt. John Brengle, 25 Aug - 19 Sep 1814. Appt'd capt. of company, 24 Jul 1813; b. 29 Dec 1790; d. of jaundice in Frederick 5 Aug 1849, age 58 yrs, 7 mos., 7 days (had been ill for 21 days); m. 23 Apr 1811 Margret Dartzabaugh (b. 24 Jan 1788) by Rev. David F. Shaffer, Luth. minister. Margret d. 23 Sep 1849 at the residence of her son-in-law, Dennis Scholl in Fredericktown.

Acq.: George Dartzabaugh, Ormond F. Butler, Perry Rice and Winchester Clingan - all res. Fredericktown. Printer; edited and published newspaper in Frederick for many yrs; proprietor of an inn for 33 yrs; elected sheriff of Fred. Co. 1833.

Matthias E. Bartgis was the son of Matthias Bartgis, who brought the first press or printing-office to Frederick Co. (from Philadelphia).
Sources: Bounty land claim, 55-120-6663; Scharf, Hist. of West. Md., Williams, Hist. of Fred. Co.; (Frederick) Examiner, 15 Aug 1849.

BARTHALOW, Elias. Pvt. under Capt. Samuel Duvall, 3 Aug-3 Oct 1814. He stated he was a pvt. in the company of Capt. Woodward and transferred to Capt. S. Duvall; he was 5 ft, 10 inches tall, had light complexion, blue eyes and light hair; b. c.1792; d. 16 Apr 1854 in Balt; bur. Whatcoat Cem.; m. 18 Oct 1818, Hester Ann Hooper (b. c.1802, d. 22 Oct 1878), each for the first time, by

FREDERICK COUNTY MILITIA IN THE WAR OF 1812

Rev. Jonathan Forrester. [FCml issued to Elias Barthelow and Esther Hooper 19 Oct 1818]. Fol. discharge he res. Smith Lane 8-9 yrs, 62 Poppleton St, 10 yrs, and Pennsylvania Ave. near Fremont for 28 yrs, all in Balt. City. In 1878 she res. 62 Poppleton, Balt. City. Acq.: 1855 - Andrew J. Bartholow and Thomas Jenkins; 1878 - Miss Urilla Hooper age 46, and Mrs. Ann B. Glascow, age 63 - both res. 56 Fayette St., Balt., acq. 40 and 60 yrs resp. - and William McCly, age 66 undertaker; Adoram Phelps, age 63; and Lydia H. McKey, age 55, all of Balt. City. On 9 Jan 1880 Andrew J. Bartholow, res. 59 N. Poppleton St., Balt., certified that Hester Ann Bartholow d. 22 Oct 1878, of apoplexy.

Sources: Bounty land claim, 50-40-46679, 55-120-3327; Pension, WO12820, WC7665.

BARTHALOW, John. Mbr. of Crawford's "company."

BARTHALOW, Joshua. Mbr. of Crawford's "company."

BARTHOLOW, Michael. Mbr. of Crawford's "company."

BARTLE, Christian - See Bartel.

BARTLET, Joseph. Pvt. under Capt. William Knox, Aug 26-Oct 27 1814; b. c.1794; res. Preston Co., VA, 1850, and Frenchtown, Monroe Co., MI, in 1855.

Source: Bounty land claim, 55-120-46428.

BARTON, Samuel. Pvt. under Capt. John Galt, 31 Aug - 27 Oct 1814; b. 25 Nov 1791; m. 2 Nov 1820 Amy McWilliams at Graceham, Fred. Co.; res. Taneytown, 1812-1814; Fred. Co., 1850, 1851, 1855 and 1871 (Emmittsburg).

1850 census, 5th E.D. (in addition to Samuel Barton):, wife Amy, 58; Sarah E. Barton, 20; and Mary Carter, 70; Samuel owned a thirty-acre farm; d. 3 Jan 1878. According to Williams, "He was a Baptist for many yrs, but a short time before his death allied himself with Luth. Ch. He lived to be nearly 93 yrs old." Samuel's wife, Amy, d. on 25 Jan 1857 at age 67. Their dau Sarah Elizabeth d. 16 Jun 1852 at the age of 27 yrs, 4 mos., 12 days.

Sources: Bounty land claims, 50-40-47457, 55-120-62809; Pension, SO13531, SC8629; Williams, **Hist. of Fred. Co.; Bridge in Time; Names in Stone.**

BARTZELL, John. Appt'd Lieut. 15 Jul 1814 under Capt. Matthias E. Bartgis.

BASFORD, Thomas. Pvt. under Capt. Denton Darby, 3 Aug-8 Nov 1814.

BATLES, John. From Fred. Co. Musician in the Washington Co. company commanded by Capt. William Curtis, 14 Oct 1814 - 10 Jan 1815.

BAUGHER - See Bougher.

BAUGHMAN, Adam. Pvt. under Capt. Barton Hackney, 17 Sep - 27 Oct 1814.

BAUMGARTEN [Baungantous, Jr.?], Jacob. Appt'd lieut. under Capt. Galt 23 Jun 1808, 47th Regt., MM.

BAUSTON, Philip. Pvt. under Capt. Joseph Wood, 27 Aug - 28 Oct 1814.

BAYER, Abraham. Pvt. under Capt. Samuel Ogle, 1 May - 5 Jul 1813.

BEACHTLE, George. Pvt. under Capt. Barton Hackney; joined 25 Sep 1814; deserted 23 Oct 1814.

THE VETERANS

[George Bechtell, laborer, bound his son George Bechtell, age 3 yrs on 12 Jan 1794, to David Mullendore, wheelwright, on 23 May 1794. He also bound his sons Samuel and Jacob.]
Source: West. Md. Genealogy, 4:3.

BEAL, David. Pvt. under Capt. John Fonsten, joined 2 Sep 1814; discharged by certificate 26 Sep 1814.

BEALL, Benjamin. Pvt. under Capt. Nicholas Hall, 7 Aug - 10 Sep 1814, 2nd Regt., 1st Cav. Dist.; volunteered at Hyattstown, MD; b. 1786; res. Fred. Co., 1855.
Source: Bounty land claim, 55-120-2614.

BEALL, Ninian. Pvt. under Capt. Nicholas Turbutt, 2 Sep - 27 Oct 1814; served as substitute for Stephen Ramsparke; b. c.1793; res. Lee Co., IA, 1855. Acq. (1855): Zepheniah Beall.
Source: Bounty land claim, 55-rejected-180288.

BEALL [Bealle], Thomas. Pvt. under Capt. Samuel Dawson, 1 May - 5 Jul 1813 and under Capt. Barton Hackney, 1 Sep - 27 Oct 1814. On one occasion he substituted for Isaac Rumm. He was b. 1790; d. 4 Jun 1851, New Market, MD; m. 6 Aug 1801 Catharine Hotter (b. c.1780). 1850 census showed Thomas Beall res. New Market Dist., age 60, chair maker; with Daniel Beall, age 47 and Catherine Beall, age 70. Both he and Catherine were listed as "pensioners." Acq. (1851): Peter Ott.
Source: Bounty land claim, 50-80-49712.

BEALL, Thomas N. Pvt. under Capt. Huston; joined 23 Jul 1814; deserted 27 Oct 1814.

BEAM [Beams], Jacob. Pvt. under Capt. William Durbin, Jr. 24 Aug - 29 Oct 1814; b. 1793; m. 1814, Elizabeth Englar, in Westminster Dist., MD; res. Balt., MD, 1851 and 1855 Carroll Co., MD, in 1871 (Hoods Mill). She d. Balt. 25 Dec 1853. Acq. (1871): Jacob Reese, George E. Wampler.
Sources: Pension, SO28140, SC19924; Bounty land claims, 50-40-39719, 55-120-59941; Democrat and Carroll County Republican, dated 1 Jan 1854.

BEAM, William. Newspaper item states he was veteran of the War of 1812; b. c.1777; d. at Montevue, MD, 6 Mar 1874, age 82 yrs, merchant; long-time Justice of the Peace; coroner; bur. Mechanicstown. 1850 census of Creagerstown E.D.: William Beams, 53, merchant; Anna Beams, 47; Mary E. Willhide, 6; Isabella Briscoe, 16. Anna Beam b. 8 Nov 1807, d. 23 May 1865; bur. Thurmont Unite Brethren Cem.
Sources: Names in Stone; Bridge in Time.

BEAR - See also Baer.

BEAR, George. Pvt. under Capt. Daniel Marker, 25 Aug - 27 Oct 1814; b. Jan 1789; m. 17 May 1817 Fred. Co. Mary Fink; res. Fred. Co. 1850, 1851, 1852, 1855, and 1871. 1850 census, Middletown: George Bear 61, carpenter; Mary Bear 60; Elizabeth Turner 22. Tombstone inscription: Elder George Bear, 16 Apr 1872, age 83 yrs, 2 mos., 25 days at the residence of C.F. Adolphus Fox, Frederick; wife Mary, d. 14 or 17 Oct 1863, age 74 yrs, 1 month, 28 days; bur. Burkittsville, Pleasant View Brethren Ch. She d. at the residence of G. C. Rhoderick in Middletown. Acq. (1871): Mahlon Rhoderick, near

FREDERICK COUNTY MILITIA IN THE WAR OF 1812

Frederick, MD, and Frederick Harmon, Market St., Frederick.
Sources: Pension, SO7273, SC4230; Bounty land claims, 50-40-70243, 55-120-28503; **Names in Stone; Bridge in Time; Md. Union, 18 Apr 1871;** (Frederick) Examiner, 28 Oct 1863, 17 Apr 1872.

BEAR, Michael. Pvt. under Capt. Denton Darby, 3 Aug - 8 Nov 1814, absent 6 days. [FCml issued to Michael Bear and Catharine Walker on 5 Feb 1802.]

BEARD, Daniel. Pvt. in 4th U.S. Rifles under Capt. M.G. Magee; b. Fred. Co., MD, c.1789; enlisted in regular army 10 Dec 1814 by Lt. Getz for duration of war. At enlistment: 5 ft, 10 1/2 inches, grey eyes, light hair, red complexion, age 25, laborer. Discharged at Carlisle Barracks 25 Mar 1815.

BEARD, Jacob. Pvt. under Capt. Nicholas Turbutt, 2 Sep - 27 Oct 1814.

BEARD, Jacob. Appt'd ensign 17 Sep 1811, under Capt. Philip Smith, 16th Regt.
Source: Adjutant (MD) General Papers.

BEARD, John. Pvt. in company of Capt. Jacob Alexander, 22 Jul - 19 Sep, 1814; volunteered Middletown, MD, 1814 as substitute for Peter Fressong; d. 21 Sep 1831; m. Amelia --- (d. 24 Sep 1830); James Elder Beard youngest child b. 25 Jan 1830, res. Athens Co., OH 1851. Acq. (1851): William Holter, Abraham Beard. [On 31 Dec 1802 John Beard, an orphan, age 16 yrs, 6 mos., bound to Benjamin Routzan, hatter, until age 21. In 1806 Benjamin Routzong, (7 miles from Middletown), offered reward for John Beard, apprentice to hatting business, about 13 yrs of age, brown hair.]

Sources: Bounty land claims, 50-40-70243, 55-120-28503; Pension, SO7273, SC4230; **West. Md. Genealogy, vol 5; Frederick Hornet, 11 Mar 1806.**

BEARD, John. Pvt. under Capt. James F. Huston 23 Jul - 20 Sep 1814 and then under Joseph Green; deserted 8 Dec 1814.

BEARD, John. Pvt. under Capt. Galt, 31 Aug - 27 Oct 1814; lived within one mile of Taneytown.

BEARD, Richard. Pvt. under Capt. Dawson; joined 14 Oct 1814; deserted Dec 1814.

BEARSHANK, William. Pvt. under Capt. Ent, 24 Aug - 30 Sep 1814.

BEATTY, Ebenezer. Pvt. in 36th U.S. Inf. under Col. Henry Carbury; b. Fred. Co./Charles Co.?; enlisted Georgetown, D.C. for 5 yrs by Capt. H. C.Neal 22 or 28 May 1814. At enlistment: 5 ft, 6 1/2 inches, blue eyes, dark hair, fair complexion, age 29 or 32, farmer; serving at Fort Covington 1815. Discharged at Fort Crawford 22 or 24 May 1819.

BEATTY, Lewis A. Appt'd 2nd lieut. in Capt. Thomas Gist's troop of horse on 31 May 1813 and 1st lieut. in Gist's company on 28 Jul 1813.

BEAUMONT, Bazil. Pvt. under Capt. Joseph Wood, 27 Aug - 28 Oct 1814.

BEAVER [Bever], John. Pvt. under Capt. Fonsten, 2 Sep - 28 Oct 1814 as a substitute for Andrew Powder; b. 8 Nov 1796; m. 1819, Mary Robertson (b. 2 Apr 1802), near Westminster, Carroll Co., MD, by Rev. Burges Nelson - each for first time. In 1814 he was 5 ft 8-9 inches tall; had brown hair and eyes,

THE VETERANS

farmer, res. 2 miles from Westminster. After discharge he always res. Carroll Co., near Westminster; started tombstone business; son Andrew J. Beaver was a stone-cutter in 1850. The company was the predecessor to Joseph L. Mathias, Inc. which provides cem. monuments today. He d. 15 Dec 1877, at his residence in Carroll Co; widow res. Carroll Co. (P.O. Westminster) in 1878. She d. 21 Nov 1887 Carroll Co. Both John and Mary bur. Westminster Cem. Children mentioned in his will.] Acq.: 1871 - Ira E. Crouse and Thomas B. Gist, res. Westminster. 1878 - William Lockard of John, 65 and William Lockard, 78 - both of Carroll Co. Letter dated 5 Jan 1888, Westminster, MD, from John Beaver, grandson of Mary Beaver in file.

Sources: Pension, SO1384 (rejected, insufficient time in service), WO13195, WC11924; Bounty land claims, 50-40-40921, 55-120-1766; Harold Jesse Robertson, **The Robertson Family of Carroll County, Maryland.** p. 189.

BECHTELL. See Beachtle.

BECKENBAUGH, John. Pvt. under Capt. Matthew Murray, 25 Aug - 27 Oct 1814; b. c.1789; res. Fred. Co. 1851 and 1855. 1850 census: John Beckenbaugh, age 62, farmer, $4000; Mary Beckenbaugh, 50; Peter, age 25; Sarah A., 23; Henry, 21; Catharine, 18; Susan, 15; Ann R., 12; John T., 10; Elizabeth, 8; Cornelia Alexander, 35. Bur. Middletown Ref. Ch.: John Beckenbaugh, d. 18 May 1861, age c.76 and Mary Beckenbaugh, d. 26 Nov 1872, age c.72.

Sources: Bounty land claim, 50-120-28513; **Bridge in Time; Names in Stone.**

BECKETT, Benjamin. 3rd sergt. under Capt. Nicholas Turbutt 2 Sep - 27 Oct 1814.

BECKLEY, Henry. Pvt. under Capt. Daniel Shawen, 5 Sep - 27 Oct 1814; m. 14 Mar 1819 Ann [also called Nancy] Bailey by Bishop Newcomer (poss. Meth. minister), Washington Co., MD. Henry Beckley d. Balt. City, 23 Mar 1828. Widow res. Balt. City, 1859. Acq. (1859): Margaret Adams, stated Henry and Ann Beckley raised family of children.

Source: Bounty land claim, 55-160-87705.

BECKWORTH [Beckwith], Lenox. 1st sergt. under Capt. Jacob Alexander, Jul 22 - Sep 19 1814. "Sick on furlough." FCml issued to Lenox Beckwith and Rebecca Ridgely 24 Nov 1812. Rebecca Beckwith age 54 b. in MD, d. Feb 1850 of unknown causes; she had been ill for 7 days. [Benjamin Beckwith, Allegany Co., MD, bound his son, Lenox Beckwith, aged 12 yrs, to Jacob Alexander, Jr., of Fred. Co., hatter, for 9 mos., on 22 Mar 1803.]

Sources: FCml; **West. Md. Genealogy; Bridge in Time.**

BEEKLESS, Philip. b. Fred. Co., MD, c.1772; enlisted on 17 May 1813 at Balt. by John Fendall for 5 yrs; he was 5 ft, 7 inches, had dark eyes, dark hair and dark complexion, age 41, farmer. Served in 5th U.S. Inf. under Lt. W. C.Bird. At Balt. (Capt. Jas. Dorman's Co. Book) 1814.

BELL, George. b. c.1777 Fred. Co., MD; enlisted 28 Apr 1814 Washington, D.C. by Lt. Hobbs for duration of war. He was 5 ft, 5 1/2 inches, had blue eyes,

FREDERICK COUNTY MILITIA IN THE WAR OF 1812

black hair and fair complexion, age 37, shoemaker. Served in 36th U.S. Inf. under Col. Henry Carbery at Balt. in Thomas Carbery's company. Discharged Balt. 31 Mar 1815.

BELL, Thomas. Pvt. under Capt. Matthew Murray, 25 Aug - 27 Oct 1814.

BELL, Thomas N. Res. Upper Fred. Co. Pvt. under James F. Huston, 23 Jul - 20 Sep 1814; then under Capt. Joseph Green until he deserted on 27 Oct.

BELT, Bennoni. Pvt. under Capt. Denton Darby; joined 3 Aug 1814; deserted 18 Aug 1814 when described as 25 yrs of age, 5 ft, 10-11 inches tall, light complexion, black hair, labourer.
Source: Engine of Liberty, 5 Oct 1814.

BELT, Lloyd. Pvt. under Capt. Henry Steiner, Aug 25 - Sep 27 1814. [FCml issued to Lloyd Belt and Elizabeth Causlet Metcalfe Thomas 16 Dec 1790.]

BENGLBRECK - See Englebrecht.

BENITT, Lloyd. Mbr. of Crawford's "company."

BENN, John. b. in Fred. Co., MD, c.1792. Enlisted Front Royal 21 Oct 1814 by Lt. Lewis for 5 yrs. At enlistment: 5 ft, 10 inches, blue eyes, dark hair, fair complexion, age 22, blacksmith. Fifer in 20th U.S. Inf. under Capt. M.M. Payne. Ordered to Norfolk 31 Mar 1815. At Craney Island 1 Jul 1815. At Fort Moultrie 30 Apr 1816, Pensacola 31 Aug 1818, Fort Mifflin 5 Mar 1819, Capt. John McIntosh's Company at Trader's Hill 30 Apr 1819. Discharged 12 Oct 1819.

BENNETT, David. Pvt. under Capt. Samuel Ogle, 1 May - 5 Jul 1813, and under Capt. Ent, 24 Aug - 30 Sep 1814.

BENNETT, James. b. Uniontown, MD; enlisted 13 Aug 1814, Uniontown, MD, by Capt. Scott for 5 yrs; 5 ft, 7 1/4 inches, grey eyes, black hair and fair complexion, age 20 or 28, shoemaker. Pvt., 4th U.S. Rifles. 30 Apr 1815 reported as unfit for duty. Mustered by Lt. L. Hickman's Company, U.S. Rifles, Detroit on 31 Aug 1815. With Capt. E. Shipp's Company, Prairie du Chien 30 Jun 1819, discharged at Fort Crawford 13 Aug 1819.

BENNETT, John B. Pvt. under Capt. Samuel Dawson, 1 May - 5 Jul 1813 and joined again on 21 Jul 1814; deserted 6 Aug 1814.

BENNETT, Robert. Mbr. of Crawford's "company." FCml issued to Robert Bennet and Elizabeth Laurence 20 Jan 1808. In 1838 and 1841 Robert Bennett res. near Sams Creek; d. 26 Mar 1856 aged 78; Elizabeth Bennett d. 4 Jan 1846, aged 78. Both bur. Bethel M.E. Churchyard.
Sources: FCml; Names in Stone; Carrolltonian, 12 Jan 1838, 24 Dec 1841.

BENTLEY, George. Pvt. under Capt. William Knox, 26 Aug - 27 Oct 1814.

BENTZ. See also Bantz.

BENTZ, John, Jr. Pvt. under Capt. George W. Ent, 24 Aug - 30 Sep 1814.

BEONER [Booner], John. Res. Upper Frederick; 1st Sergt. under Capt. James F. Huston, 23 Jul - 13 Oct 1814.

BERNARD, Hezekiah. Enlisted 20 Dec 1814 for duration of war. He was 5 ft, 8 inches, had grey eyes, brown hair and dark complexion, age 21, a farmer, b. Fred. Co., MD. Served in 38th U.S. Inf.; discharged Balt. on 6 Apr 1815.

BERRY, John. Pvt. under Capt. Denton Darby, 1 Sep - 8 Nov 1814; m. Miss Mary Getzendanner dau of Capt. Jacob Getzendanner of Frederick Co 8 Apr 1823 by Rev. D. F. Schaeffer. [James Berry bound his son John Berry to Thomas Pack, shoemaker, "to age 21 or 8 yrs from 25 Jul next," on 11 Apr 1804.]
Sources: **Fredericktown Herald**, 12 Apr 1823; **West. Md. Genealogy**, 6:1, p. 24

BERRY, Samuel. Pvt. under Capt. Barton Hackney; joined 1 Sep 1814; deserted 14 Sep 1814.

BERTIN, Benjamin. Pvt. under Capt. Samuel Dawson; joined 14 Oct 1814; deserted 24 Oct 1814.

BETT, Rufus. From New Market. 5th Corpl. under Capt. Lowrye, 27 Aug - 28 Oct 1814. He made a rendezvous at New Market with the company, from Washington Co.

BEVANS [Bivins], Alexander. Pvt. under John Brengle, 25 Aug - 19 Sep 1814.

BICKETT, James. Pvt. under Capt. James F. Huston, 23 Jul - 13 Oct 1814.

BIDDLE [Bittle], Thomas. Lieut. under Capt. Daniel Marker 16 Aug 1813 - 18 Sep 1813; b. 22 Feb 1783, son of George Michael Bittle and Ann Marie Elizabeth (Beale) Bittle; m. Mary Baer, c.11 Mar 1811 [date of marr. license]; dau of Philip Baer. Philip Baer and his 2 bros., Moses and Jacob migrated from Westphalia to the Middletown Valley where they settled near the Bittle family. Thomas and Mary Bittle had three daus: Lydia who m. Hezekiah Floyd (8 children), Mary who m. Isaac Poffenberger (9 children) and Elizabeth who m. Benjamin Routzahn (13 children). Thomas and Mary spent their latter yrs with Mary (Bittle) Poffenberger. Their two sons were David Frederick Bittle and Daniel Howard Bittle. David F. graduated from the Gettysburg Seminary, m. the sister of its president and became a Luth. minister in VA; had five sons and two daus. In 1842 he became the first pres., Roanoke College, Salem VA. Daniel Howard Bittle became the first pres. of North Carolina College; m. Susan Bigelow (no children).
Sources: Frank D. Bittle, Palm Beach Gardens, FL; Schildknecht, **Monocacy and Catoctin**, vol. 1.

BIDINGER, Philip. Deserted 14 Aug 1814 from camp at Bladensburg and described as 29-30 yrs old, 5 ft, 8-9 inches tall, light complexion, light hair, grey eyes, laborer.
Source: **Engine of Liberty**, 5 Oct 1814.

BIERSHING [Biershenk], Henry. Fifer under Capt. Thomas C. Worthington, 17 Aug - 31 Dec 1812; d. Hagerstown, 13 Apr 1843; m. Rachael Steele (b. c.1800, d. c.1889), first marr. for both, in Hagerstown, MD, 27 Sep 1817, by Rev. Irvin, Epis. minister. Fol. discharge he res. Hagerstown and nowhere else. Acq. - 1854: Jacob Haller and George Fagler. 1878: David C. Hammond, age 65; James J. Hurley, age 66; Henry K. Tice, age 67; Rebecca Williamson, 71 - all res. Hagerstown. Witnesses in 1855

FREDERICK COUNTY MILITIA IN THE WAR OF 1812

were David Steele and F. J. Posey, res. Hagerstown.
Sources: Pension, WO21800, WC17213; Bounty land claims, 50-80-43413, 55-80-33584.

BIGGLE, Jacob. Pvt. under Capt. Fonsten, 2 Sep - 27 Oct 1814, res. 8 miles from Westminster.

BIGHAM, Robert. Appt'd 24 Oct 1796 cornet in Capt. William Emmitt's troop of horse.

BILLINGSLEY, Walter R. Pvt. under Capt. Basil Dorsey, 30 Jul - 27 Sep 1814; b. c.1797; res. Kosciusko Co., IN, in 1855.
Source: Bounty land claim, 55-160-20933.

BIRELY, Lewis. Ensign under Capt. Shawen, 5 Sep - 27 Oct 1814.

BIRELY, Valentine. Sergt. under Capt. Andrew E. Warner's company, 39th Regt. (Balt.), 19 Aug - 27 Oct 1814; m. evening of 27 Jun 1820 Charlotte Mantz, by Rev. David Martin. She was dau of Francis Mantz of Frederick-town. She d. morning of 19 Aug 1821. Valentine Birely was a tanner; later m. Evalina Severs (b. 18 Oct 1807), dau of Henry Severs of Fred Co. VA. Valentine Birely d. Frederick from cancer in his neck, 21 Jun 1860, in his 69th year; bur. Mt. Olivet. His widow d. 31 Aug 1887 in Balt.
Source: (**Frederick**) **Examiner**, 1 Jul 1820, 25 Aug 1821, 27 Jun 1860; Frederick-town Herald, 1 Jul 1820, 25 Aug 1821; **Engelbrecht Diary**, v. 1:85.

BITTLE - See also Biddle.

BITTLE, Henry. Pvt. under Capt. John Fonsten, 2 Sep - 27 Oct 1814, as a substitute for Henry Beachtel; b. c.1783; res. Adams Co., PA, in 1855. Acq.: 1855

- Adam Bowers, age 65; Jacob Stone, age 66 - both res Carroll Co., MD, and pvts. under Capt. John Fonsten.
Source: Bounty land claim, 55-160-39408.

BIVENS, Alexander. Pvt. under Lieut. William Kolb in a det. assigned to guard the British prisoners at the Frederick Barracks, 13 Oct - 15 Nov 1814. [The muster roll lists Alexander Bivens and the payroll lists Benjamin Bivens vice Alexander Bivens.]

BIVENS, Henry. Pvt., joined 2 Sep 1814 Capt. Fonsten's militia company; enlisted regular army 2 Oct 1814.

BIVINS - See Bivens and Bevins

BLACK, Henry. Pvt. under Capt. George W. Magee, 22 Jul - 13 Oct 1814.

BLACK, Henry. Pvt. under Capt. John Galt, 1 Sep - 27 Oct 1814; b. c.1785-1792; m. 1819 Rebecca Reck; res. Carroll Co., MD 1851, 1855 and 1871; res. Littlestown, PA, 1874. Acq.: Josiah Adlesperger and John Boose, res. Carroll Co. 1871.
Sources: Pension, SO3673; Bounty land claim, 55-120-57546 [in file separate from pension].

BLACK, Henry. Served at Balt. in 14th U.S. Inf.; b. c.1786, Fred. Co., MD; enlisted in regular army 24 Jan 1814 by Lt. Gale for 5 yrs; at enlistment: 6 ft, 10 inches, age 28.

BLACK, Isaac. Pvt. under Capt. Magee; joined 22 Jul 1814; reported as missing 24 Aug 1814.

BLACK, Jacob. Pvt. under Capt. John Gault, 31 Aug - 29 Oct 1814; b. c.1790; d. c.1875; m. Oct 1826, Sarah Ocker, Fred. Co., MD; res. Wyandot Co., OH, in 1852 and 1856, in Seneca (P.O.: Mc-

Cutchinsville), Wyandot Co., OH 1874. Sarah d. prior to 28 May 1874. Acq. (1874): J. R. Philips and George Heckman(?).
Sources: Pension, SO29782, SC21458; Bounty land claims, 50-40-60961, 55-120-87014.

BLACK, John. Pvt. in 27th U.S. Inf. under Col. Hugh Brady; b. Fred. Co., MD, c.1789; enlisted in regular army 21 Mar 1814 at Chambersburg by Lt. J. Culbertson, the enlistment to last until 18 Mar 1819. At enlistment: 5 ft, 8 inches, grey eyes, dark hair, dark complexion, age 25, laborer. At Pittsburg 30 Apr 1814. Deserted 30 Oct 1814.

BLACK, Philip. Pvt. under Capt. George W. Magee, 22 Jul - 12 Oct 1814.

BLACK, Sam. From New Windsor. Servant under Capt. George W. Magee, 14 Oct - 8 Dec 1814.

BLACKFORD, Thomas Thornburg. Pvt. in Capt. Henry Steiner's Artillery Company, 25 Aug - 27 Sep 1814; b. c.1798 at Pine Grove Furnace, PA; d. Lynchburg, VA, 1863; m. 24 Oct 1820, Caroline Steinberger (b. c.1801, d. c.1888), in Shenandoah Co., VA, by Rev. Lanston, both for first time. In 1814 he was c.20, medical student, 6 ft, gray eyes, brown hair. After discharge he res. Fredericktown; Lurray, Page Co., Va; and Lynchburg, VA. In 1878 she res. 390 Eutau Place, Balt., MD, c/o W. H. Blackford. Letter dated 27 Sep 1878 from William H. Blackford (her son., manager of South-Eastern Department, of --- Insurance Co., No. 8 South St., Balt.). Caroline Blackford res. Richmond, VA, at No. 1014 E. Broad St., Richmond, VA, in 1878. Acq. (1878): Thomas H. Harris, age 47, res. 305 Madison Ave., Balt. and Alexander T. Leftwich, age 33, res. 158 N. Howard St., Balt. City, both acq. 25 yrs; William Otway Owen, age 57 and Thomas L. Walker, age 59, res. of Lynchburg, VA, the latter two being the physicians attending Thomas Blackford at the time of his death; and Henry R. Crane, age 33.
Sources: Pension, WO17035, WC10134, Bounty land claim, 55-160-3230.

BLANCHFORD, James. Pvt. in Capt. Flautt's rifle company, 29 Apr - 29 Jun 1813.

BLAXFORD, Oswald. Pvt. under Capt. George W. Ent, 24 Aug - 30 Sep 1814.

BLAZE, William. Enlisted at "Fincastle" 29 Dec 1814 by Lt. Houston for 5 yrs. At enlistment: 5 ft, 10 inches, gray eyes, dark hair and dark complexion, age 31, farmer, b. Fred. Co., MD. Pvt. in 12th U.S. Inf. under Lt. R. Houston. Mustered 16 Feb 1815 by Capt. Page's Company and at Carlisle Barracks, PA on 30 Apr 1815. Discharged Camp Jefferson 1 Mar 19 in consequence of a stiff ankle joint.

BLESSING, Abraham. Appt'd lieut. 2 Sep 1811 in Capt. Hackney's company, 20th Reg., MM; served as lieut. in Capt. Flautt's rifle company, 29 Apr - 29 Jun 1813; m. 3 Feb 1829, Miss Mary M. Ent, only dau of Capt. George W. Ent, by Rev. Schaeffer. A newspaper announcement referred to Abraham Blessing as a merchant, of Trap-town. Bur. at Petersville, St. Mark's Epis. Ch. was Abraham Blessing, 15 May 1779 -

FREDERICK COUNTY MILITIA IN THE WAR OF 1812

24 Jun 1844. 1850 census of Buckeys Town Dist.: Mary Blessing, 40; William H. Blessing, 22; Francis T. Blessing, 20; George W. Blessing, 18; Elizabeth E. Blessing, 15; Mary J. Blessing, 16; Penelope R. Blessing, 13; Anna M. Blessing, 5. Englebrecht refers to him as Abraham Blessing, Junr.

Sources: **Fredericktown Herald**, 7 Feb 1829; **Bridge in Time**; **Names in Stone**; **Englebrecht Diary**, v.2, 428.

BLESSING, Jacob. Pvt. in Capt. Flautt's rifle company, 29 Apr - 29 Jun 1813.

BLEWBOUGH, John. Res. New Windsor. Pvt. under Capt. George W. Magee; 22 Jul - 10 Jan 1815 - "in confinement at Fort McHenry."

BLIZZARD, Beal. Res. New Windsor. Pvt. under Capt. George W. Magee, 22 Jul - 13 Oct 1814. Deserted 6 Dec 1814??.

BLOIS, Mordicai. Pvt., 14th U.S. Inf.; b. Fred. Co., MD, c.1792. Enlisted 4 May 1812 at Washington by Ens. Clarke for 5 yrs. At enlistment: 5 ft, 7 3/4 inches, light eyes, light hair and light complexion, age 20, farmer. Prisoner of war, exchanged 15 Apr 1814. Present at Boston 2 May 1814. Promoted to corpl. 1 Feb 1815. Joined company at Williamsville 4 Jan 1815. At Greenbush 1 Mar and 30 Apr 1815. Mustered by Capt. Alex. Cummings' Company, 4th U.S. Inf. at Annapolis 31 Aug 1815, deserted from Fort Severn (Annapolis) 17 Jul 1815.

BLOOM, Peter. Pvt. under Capt. Fonsten, 2 Sep - 27 Oct 1814; m. Catherine Hiteshew (b. c.1786), 15 Aug 1806, by Rev. Grubb; d. Fred. Co. 28 Mar 1834. Widow res. Fred. Co. 1850 and Carroll Co. in 1855. Acq: 1850 - Adam Bloom and Sophia Yingling, res. Carroll Co., MD. 1855 - Sophia L. Yingling, Hannah Hiteshew.

Source: Bounty land claim, 55-120-67487.

BLUFFORD, Henry. Pvt. under Capt. George W. Magee, 22 Jul - 13 Oct 1814. Absent (sick) 24 Aug 1814.

BOCHMAN, Andrew. Pvt. under Capt. Matthew Murray, 25 Aug - 27 Oct 1814.

BODEN, Samuel. Never joined company of Capt. Matthew Murray which served 25 Aug-27 Oct 1814.

BOERSTLER, Charles G. Son of Dr. Christian Boerstler, of Funkstown; d. while stationed at New Orleans, LA, 21 Nov 1817. Commanded First Division of Maryland troops under Col. Winder at battle of Queenstown in projected invasion of Canada, 1812.

Source: Scharf, **Hist. of West. Md.**

BOHAM, Peter. Pvt., Capt. Flautt's rifle company, 29 Apr - 29 Jun 1813.

BOHAN, Jacob. 4th corpl. in company of Mathew Murray, 25 Aug - 27 Oct 1814; b. c.1793; m. Elizabeth Mercer, Washington Co., OH, 5 Feb 1854. Res. Monroe Co., OH. 1850, 1855 and 1871 (Liberty Township).

Sources: Pension, SO3675, SC2183 (Dropped 2 Jan 1880 - failure to claim pension, last paid $8.00 for period up to 4 Sep 1875); Bounty land claims, 50-40-6619, 55-120-70609.

BOHER, Henry. Pvt. under Capt. Samuel Ogle; joined 1 May 1813; deserted 25 May 1813.

THE VETERANS

BOLDING, Benjamin. See Bowlin.

BOLY, Daniel. Pvt., 2nd U.S. Inf., under Col. T. H. Cushing; b. in Fred. Co., MD, c.1777; enlisted in regular army 14 Mar 1808, Staunton, VA, by Lt. Sevier for 5 yrs. At enlistment: 5 ft, 9 3/4 inches, blue eyes, light hair, fair complexion, age 31, occupation saddler. Tried by court martial in Capt. Laurence's company 6 Aug 1810 for drunkenness, received 7 days at hard labor. Sick in hospital at Washington, 5 Dec 1810 - "Dead."

BOND Alexander. Pvt. under Capt. Daniel Marker 16 Aug - 18 Sep 1813. [Note: Christian Stover was appt'd as guardian of Alexander Bond on 26 Apr 1810. - *West. Md. Genealogy.*]

BOND, Benjamin. Pvt. under Capt. John Fonsten, 2 Sep - 28 Oct 1814; b. c.1791; res. Carroll Co. 1851 and 1855 (P.O. Office: Sams Creek); d. 12 Sep 1863 at age 72; bur. Union-town, Pipe Creek Cem.

Sources: Bounty land claim, 55-120-46050; **Bridge in Time.**

BOND, Charles. Pvt. under Capt. George W. Magee, 22 Jul 1814 - 10 Jan 1815. He and two others in the company were supposed not old enough, but within a few days their ages were ascertained and "one of them had to go" [was released from service?]. b. c.1796; m. Emeline Vaughan, at Fredericktown, 7 Aug 1831, by Rev. Joshua Jones, Meth. minister who lived about 7 miles se. of Liberty. Charles Bond res. Guernsey Co., OH, in 1851, Morristown, Belmont Co., OH, 1852, Guernsey Co., OH, 1855, 1871; d. Londonderry, Guernsey Co., OH, 3 Nov 1875. Widow res. Londonderry, OH, 1878; d. 23 Sep 1894. Acq. (1878): Anthony Arnold and Alfred C.Clay, res. Guernsey Co., OH.

Sources: Pensions, SO19602, SC19704, WO19911, WC12004 (Veteran's pension admitted 20 Nov 1872, Widow's pension admitted 16 Sep 1878; dropped 29 Sep 1894); Bounty land claims, 50-40-46911 (canceled), 50-80-44032, 55-80-8639.

BOND, Elijah. Mbr. of Crawford's "company."

BOND, John. Pvt. under Capt. Fonsten, 2 Sep - 27 Oct 1814; res. 10 miles from Westminster.

BOND, Joshua. Mbr. of Crawford's "company." [FCml issued to Joshua Bond and Abigail Murry on 2 May 1812.]

BOND, Peter. Mbr. of Crawford's "company." FCml issued to Peter Bond and Juliana Lindsey 9 Jan 1822. 1850 census, 8th E.D.: Peter Bond, 58, owns 35-acre farm; Juliann, 54; Caroline F. 18; Sarah E. 16; Mary J. 14 and Jacob Stitely 16.

Sources: **FCml; Bridge in Time.**

BONER, Joseph. Pvt. under Capt. John Gault, 31 Aug - 20 Oct 1814; said he was substitute for George Gaden (who had been drafted at Emmittsburg, MD); b. c.1794; m. Jane Conner, Germantown, OH, 4 Mar 1826; res. Wabash Co., IN, 1855; Troy, Miami Co., OH 1871.

Sources: Pension, SO11712, SC16869 (admitted 14 May 1872); Bounty land claims, 50-40-53590, 55-120-71706.

BOONE, Robert. Pvt. under Capt. Henry Steiner, 25 Aug - 27 Sep, 1814; b. c.1790; res. Fred. Co. 1850, 1851, 1855;

FREDERICK COUNTY MILITIA IN THE WAR OF 1812

d. 30 Dec 1861, age 71; wife Catherine F. d. 17 Jan 1872; both bur. Frederick, St. John's Cath. Cem. 1850 census, Fredericktown: Robert Boone, no occupation, $2750, Catherine Boone 59, Jerningham Boone 26, physician, and many others. Robert Boone owned 5 slaves. Treasurer of the "United Brothers of the War of 1812" in 1859. Catherine Boone d. at the residence of her son, Dr. Jerningham Boone, near Buckeystown, in her 85th year; bur. in Cath. grave-yard. Acq. (1855): Louis H. Dill, Samuel Haller, res. Fred. Co. Robert Boone was appt'd Judge of the Orphans' Court in 1837; elected Director of Mutual Fire Insurance Co. of Frederick in 1848.

Sources: Bounty land claim, 55-120-48513; **Bridge in Time; (Frederick) Examiner**, 14 Sep 1859, 14 Jan 1872; **Engelbrecht Diary**: 1:266, 463.

BOONER - See Beoner.

BOOSES [Booser], George. Pvt. from New Market under Capt. Lowrye, 27 Aug - 28 Oct 1814. Lowrye's company was from Washington County. Booser made his rendezvous with it at New Market; discharged at Camp Deal.

BOOTMAN Jacob. Pvt. under Capt. Daniel Marker 16 Aug - 18 Sep 1813.

BOOVEY, Jacob. Pvt. from Hagerstown, under Capt. Samuel Dawson, 14 Oct 1814 - 10 Jan 1815.

BOPST [Bobst, Pobst], Daniel. Pvt. under Capt. Turbutt, 2 Sep -27 Oct 1814; b. c.1796; d. 15 Feb 1840, age 44, at Shookstown, Fred. Co., MD; m. 10 Sep 1818 in Fred. Co., Mary Shook (8 Jun 1798 - 11 Aug 1861) by Rev. David F. Schaeffer, Luth. pastor. 1850 census of Frederick E.D.: Mary Bopst, 52; Ann M. Bopst, 25; Joshua D. Bopst, 21; Marietta Bopst, 15; Ruanna Bopst, 13; John H. Bopst 11; David McDade, 5. Daniel and Mary bur. Shook family cem., Shookstown. Acq.: 1851 - George Staley and William Bopst; 1852 - Peter Ott.

Sources: Bounty land claim, 55-120-60207; **Bridge in Time; Names in Stone.**

BOPST [Bobst, Pobst] John. Pvt. under Lieut. William Kolb 13 Oct - 15 Nov 1814, detachment assigned to guard the British prisoners at Frederick Barracks; m. 4 Jun 1818, Lydia Shook (b. 19 Nov 1800), each for the first time, in Fredericktown, by Rev. Helfenstine, German Reformed Congregation; d. Shookstown, MD 21 Sep 1829. Their children: Samuel A., eldest, b. 5 Jan 1819, Fred. Co., MD; Othaniel A.; Elizabeth and Sophia. Acq. - 1855: Z. James Gittinger, Ormond F. Butler; 1875: Samuel Bopst res. Morenci, Lenowee Co., MI, aged 60 yrs; Ada K. McKenzie, age 24 - P.O. address: Morenci, MI, acq. for 20 and 55 yrs. Letter dated 1895 in pension file from Elizabeth Ramsburg, dau of Lydia Bopst.

Sources: Pension, WO36636, WC26533; Bounty land claim, 55-160-2537.

BORDER, David. Pvt. under Capt. Samuel Ogle, 1 May - 5 Jul 1813. Mathias Ickes age 75 in 1851, res. Bedford Co., also a former res. Fred. Co., MD, said that he returned from military duty in Balt. with David Border and stayed all night at his (Border's) house on their return. David Border b. c.1785; m. 1833 Shellsburg, PA, Ellen Smith

THE VETERANS

(dec'd. as of 23 Sep 1871); he res. Bedford Co., PA 1851, Napier Twp, Bedford Co. 1855, Cumberland, MD 1871; reported to be old and feeble in letter of 25 Sep 1871 from Jacob Brown; d. Cumberland, MD 16 Jun 1872. Acq. in 1871: Percival Rowland and Theo A. Ogle.

Sources: Bounty land claims, 50-40-51871, 55-120-46575; Md. Union, 4 Jul 1872.

BOREING [Boring], Peter. Pvt. under Capt. Samuel Ogle, 1 May - 5 Jul 1813, and 1st Corpl. under Capt. George W. Magee, 22 Jul - 13 Oct 1814.

BORING, Zachariah. Pvt. under Capt. Samuel Ogle, 1 May - 5 Jul, 1813.

BORING, Zacharias. Pvt. under Capt. Fonsten; joined 2 Sep 1814; deserted 30 Sep 1814.

BOROUGHS - See Buroughs.

BOSTAIN, Philip. Newspaper obit. announced death of Philip Bostain on 14 Sep 1881 with his family connection in Van's Valley, Delaware Co., OH, "Old Defender in the last war with Great Britain" and a native of Fred. Co., age 99 yrs and 9 days.

Source: (Frederick) Examiner, 26 Oct 1881.

BOSTON George. Pvt. under Capt. Samuel Duvall, 3 Aug - 3 Oct 1814.

BOTELER, Edward L. 3rd sergt. under Capt. Daniel Marker; joined 25 Aug 1814; furloughed 1 Oct 1814; b. c.1796, m. 4 Sep 1833, Boonsboro, MD, Prudence Chaney; res. Washington Co., MD in 1851, 1855 and 1871 (Brownsville, Washington Co).

Sources: Pension, SO25184, SC19344; Bounty land claims, 50-40-31820, 55-120-16148.

BOTELER, Edward Sims. "A soldier of the war of 1812, died at the residence of his son, Jeff. O. Boteler, Esq., in this city, on Thursday last, at the age of 75 yrs, 8 months and 1 day. His remains were interred in Mount Olivet Cemetery, on Saturday afternoon, and were attended to their final resting place, by the association of the "United Brethren of the war of 1812," the "United Guards," Capt. J. T. Sinn, "Independent Riflemen," Act. Capt. U. Hobbs, accompanied by Hubbard's Cornet Band and a large concourse of mourning relatives and friends. Mr. Boteler served his country for four yrs in the Second War of Independence, and was taken prisoner by the British at Detroit upon Hull's surrender; he was carried thence into Canada, where he remained sometime in captivity. ..."

Source: (Frederick) Examiner, 1 Dec 1858.

BOTELER, Lingen. Appt'd 16 Mar 1812 1st lieut in Christian Cost's company of light dragoons.

BOUGHER, Jacob. Pvt. under John Brengle, 25 Aug - 19 Sep 1814.

BOWER, Christian. Appt'd major, 20th Regt. under Col. John Wampler on 18 Apr 1808.

BOWERS, Adam. Pvt. under Capt. Fonsten, 2 Sep - 27 Oct 1814; res. 6 miles from Westminster.

BOWERS, Jacob. Enlisted 25 May 1812 at Westminster, MD, by Lt. Gist; b. Fred. Co., MD, c.1773. At enlistment: 5 ft, 8 1/2 inches tall, dark eyes, black hair, dark complexion, age 36; 14th U.S.

FREDERICK COUNTY MILITIA IN THE WAR OF 1812

Inf. under Capt. Samuel Lane. Killed in action on Niagara River 28 Nov 1812.

BOWERSOCK [Bowersoch], Daniel. Res. 3 miles of Taneytown. Pvt. under Capt. John Galt, 31 Aug-27 Oct 1814.

BOWHAN [Bowhorn], George. Pvt. under Capt. John Fonsten, 2 Sep - 29 Oct 1814; b. c.1793; res. 16 miles from Westminster, 1814; Fred. Co., MD, 1851 and 1855.
Source: Bounty land claim, 55-120-737.

BOWHORN [Bowhan], William. Pvt. under Capt. John Fonsten, 2 Sep - 27 Oct 1814; res. 16 miles from Westminster.

BOWLES, David. Paymaster, 28th Regt.

BOWLIN [Bolding], Benjamin. Pvt. under Capt. William Durbin, Jr., 24 Aug - 27 Oct 1814.

BOWMAN, George, Pvt. under Capt. William Knox, 26 Aug - 27 Oct 1814; b. c.1777; res. Washington Co., MD, in 1851 and 1855.
Source: Bounty land claim, 55-120-69752

BOWMASTER, John. Pvt. under Capt. John Galt, 20 Oct - 27 Oct 1814; res. 5 miles of Taneytown.

BOYD, David. Pvt. in artillery company of Capt. Henry Steiner, 28 Apr - 29 Jun 1813 and 25 Aug - 27 Sep 1814; weaver & blue dyer; b. Fredericktown, 20 Aug 1790; m. 30 May 1811 Miss Mary Mixell (b. 18 Sep 1794) by Rev. David Martin, both of Fredericktown. 1850 census, Frederick E.D.: David Boyd 59, prosperous farmer, 301 acres, 3 slaves; $42,511; Mary 56; Hamilton 17; Caline 14; David 11, Frances E. Ball 33 and several Ball children. David Boyd d. 24 Dec 1862 at his res., E. 2nd St, Frederick; mbr. of Masonic Lodge; mbr. of "United Brothers of the War of 1812" in 1859; his widow Mary d. 19 Feb 1871. Both bur. Mt. Olivet, Frederick. Engelbrecht, in his diary, on 30 Mar 1826, noted that Mrs. Meixsell, mother-in-law of David Boyd moved from Fredericktown to the "Clear Spring," near Hagerstown, MD. In his diary, Engelbrecht noted that John H. Boyd, son of David Boyd d. 1 Jan 1842 in his 18th year; bur. Meth. Grave yard, "I presume." Marriages: 3 Jan 1839, Auberry Jones to Miss Mary Boyd, 2nd dau of David Boyd; 18 Nov 1842, Owen D. Ball of Baltimore to Miss Frances Elizabeth Boyd, eldest dau of David Boyd.
Sources: Bounty land claim, 55-120-65181; Hornet, dated 5 Jun 1811; Names in Stone; Bridge in Time; (Frederick) Examiner, 31 Dec 1862, 22 Feb 1871, 12 Apr 1871; Engelbrecht Diary: 1:386; 2:327, 427. There are many more items re the David Boyd family in the Engelbrecht Diary.

BOYD, William. Corpl. under Capt. Samuel Duvall, 3 Aug - 3 Oct 1814; b. c.1781, m. 2 Feb 1806, Edna Brashear (b. c.1789), in City of Washington by --- McCormick. He d. 13 Apr 1853 Ralls Co., MO. They raised a large family of children, some of whom continued to res. Ralls Co., MO. William Boyd res. Ralls Co., MO, in 1850 and 1855. Widow res. Ralls Co. in 1872; Pike, MO, P.O. address: Madisonville, MO. Acq. - 1855: Singleton W. Boyd and Robert A. Carriel, res. Ralls Co, MO; 1872: Richard M. Brashear and John Liter; Liter had known Edna Boyd since 1828

THE VETERANS

and Richard Brashear had known her since he was a small boy (now over 60).
Sources: Pension, WO9510, WC5411; Bounty land claim, 50-80-5560, 55-80-41677.

BOYER. See also Byer.

BOYER John. Pvt. under Capt. Thomas Contee Worthington; joined 17 Aug 1812; deserted 12 Oct 1812.

BOYER, Jonathan [Johnathan]. Pvt. under Capt. Matthew Murray; joined 25 Aug 1814; on furlough from 21 Oct 1814; b. c.1773; res. Miami Co., OH, 1855.
Source: Bounty land claim, 55-120-34161.

BOYER, Jonathan. Pvt. under Capt. Daniel Shawen; joined 5 Sep 1814; deserted 1 Oct 1814.

BOYLE, Charles. Pvt. under Capt. Samuel Dawson; joined 21 Jul 1814; deserted 23 Aug 1814.

BOYLE, Peter. Pvt., 1st Cav. Dist., 26 Aug - 3 Sep 1814. [FCml issued to Peter Boyle and Elizabeth Livers on 24 Nov 1809. 1850 census: Elizabeth Boyle, age 76, res. 5th E.D. with Joseph Worthan 26; Elizabeth Worthan 23; Joseph Worthan 3 mos.]
Sources: Bridge in Time; FCml.

BRACK, Frederick. Pvt. under Capt. William Knox; joined 26 Aug 1814; deserted 26 Sep 1814.

BRADSHAW, Solomon. Pvt. under Capt. Dawson, 1 May - 5 Jul 1813.

BRAIN, John. Pvt. under Capt. Getzendanner, 26 Jul - 21 Aug 1814.

BRAMWELL [Bromwell], William. Pvt. under Capt. William Knox, 26 Aug - 27 Oct 1814.

BRANNARD, George. Pvt., 39th U.S. Inf. under Col. J. Williams; b. Fred. Co., MD, c.1789; enlisted 28 Oct 1814 at Knoxville, TN by C. Reynolds for 5 yrs. At enlistment: 6 ft, 1 inch, blue eyes, black hair, fair complexion, age 25, farmer; mustered under Lt. W. A. Covington 30 Apr 1815, re-enlisted; d. 17 Feb 1815.

BRANDENBURGH, Jesse. Pvt. under Capt. Denton Darby, 3 Aug - 8 Nov 1814, as substitute for his bro. Jacob Brandenburgh; b. c.1795; m. Matilda Turner near Flushing, OH, May 1818; res. Flushing Township, OH 1850, Belmont Co., OH 1855, Harrison Co., OH 1871. Witnesses (1855): Joseph Cook and Allen T. Brandenburgh, res. Flushing Township, and 1871 witnesses were Thomas Lindsay of Flushing, OH and Allen C. Turner of Cadiz, OH. Letters of inquiry from: Edwin F. Severn, Helethorpe, MD, Nov 1937; Frank E. Brandenburg, N. Arlington, NJ, 29 Sep 1934; grandson, Howard Wilson Brandenburg, Boston, MA, 27 Oct 1918; grandson, O. D. Brandenburg, Madison, WI, 1 Apr 1918.

[*Rcds. of Evan. Ref. Ch. of Fred., Md., 1746-1800* shows baptism of Jesse of Jacob Brandenberger and Elisabeth b. 8 Jul 1795.]
Sources: Bounty land claim, 50-40-38038, 55-120-50535; Pension, SO6908, SC7613; **Rcds. of Evan. Ref. Ch. in Fred., Md., 1746-1800.**

BRANNARD. See Branard.

BRASHEARS, Eli - Appt'd capt. of a militia company 16 Sep 1797. Statement by Joshua Turner suggests that Eli Brashears may have commanded a

FREDERICK COUNTY MILITIA IN THE WAR OF 1812

company at the defense of Balt. No muster roll has been found.

BRAWNER, Emanuel. Mbr. of Crawford's "company."

BRAWNER, William. Mbr. of the Crawford's "company."

BREADSHAW, Solomon. Pvt. under Capt. Dawson, 1 May - 5 Jul 1813.

BREADY, David. Pvt. under Capt. Turbutt, 2 Sep - 27 Oct 1814; d. 19 Nov 1869, at his residence in Sandy Spring, Montgomery Co., MD, in the 74th year of his age.
Sources: Md. Union, 2 Dec 1869; (Frederick) Examiner, 1 Dec 1869.

BREADY, John. Pvt. under Capt. Jacob Getzendanner, 9 Aug - 17 Sep 1813 and 26 Jul - 21 Aug 1814.
[According to *Hist. of Fred. Co.* by Williams, George A. Bready was father of large family, namely: George, John, David, Calvin, Edward, Eugene, Richard, Luther, Mary, Elizabeth, Ormond, E. Tobias and Curtis.]
Source: Williams, Hist. of Fred. Co., p. 854.

BRENGLE [Brengel, Branckel, Brenckel, Prengel], John. Corpl. [promoted from pvt. on 16 May 1813] under Capt. Henry Steiner 28 Apr - 29 Jun 1813 (he said he also enrolled under Capt. Getzendanner c.Aug 1814); m. Fred. Co., 17 Mar 1818, by Rev. Helphenstine, German Ref. minister, Lucy Todd (b. c.1800); d. Bedford, PA, 21 Jun 1851. Widow res. Fred. Co., 1852 and 1855.

Witnesses (1855): Benjamin Todd, Juliann Pickett, Roderick Dorsey of Fred. Co. and Henry Bussard of Carroll Co.
Source: Bounty land claim, 55-12-47737.

BRENGLE [Brenckel], John [Johannes]. Appt'd Lieut. under Capt. Michael Hausar 2 Aug 1799; served as capt. of company, 25 Aug - 19 Sep 1814 (1st Regt.); b. 15 or 18 Feb 1772; d. 24 or 25 Aug 1835, son of Lawrence [Lorenz] and Eva Brengle; m. 29 Mar 1803 Elizabeth Ziehler (8 Dec 1774 - 19 Mar 1809), dau of Henry Ziehler; children of John Brengle: Lawrence John b. 4 Dec 1805, Elizabeth b. 24 May 1807, Eva Margaret b. 19 Mar 1809, Anna Maria b. 25 Nov 1810, Daniel b. 10 Nov 1812. [Marriage information taken from article in *Md. Hist. Mag.* Newspaper article and Names in Stone show Mrs. Elizabeth Brengle, relict of Capt. John Brengle d. 18 Oct 1850 in her 76th year; both John and Elizabeth (2nd wife named Elizabeth?) bur. at Mt. Olivet.]
Sources: Md. Hist. Mag. 7:91-94; Rcds. of Evan. Ref. Ch. in Fred., Md., 1746-1800; Names in Stone; (Frederick) Examiner, 25 Aug 1835, 23 Oct 1850.

BRENGLE, John Nicholas. Appt'd 2nd lieut. in Capt. Hauer's company in First Cav. Dist., 16 Jun 1812; b. 4 Oct 1776 son of Lawrence [Lorenz] Brengle; m Maria [Mary] Mantz dau of Major Peter and Catharine (Hauer) Mantz; d. 9 Dec 1843; bur. Mt. Olivet, Frederick with dau Margaret (d. 5 Dec 1830 at age 32).
Sources: Md. Historical Magazine, 7:91-94; Adjutant (MD) General Papers; Names in Stone.

THE VETERANS

BRENGLE, Lawrence (of Christian).* Pvt. under Capt. John Brengle, 25 Aug - 19 Sep 1814; b. c.1797; m. 18 Dec 1819 Mary Menchey (b. 2 Jul 1799) Fred. Co., Luth. Ch. by Rev. David F. Schaeffer, their pastor. When enrolled: dark complexion, dark eyes, dark hair. He d. on night of 11 Jan 1836 Fred. Co. She res. Fred. Co., MD in 1855 and 1878; d. 24 Nov 1884 (note from her son-in-law, Dennis Ramsburgh confirming her death). Acq.: Ezra Ely, age 78 (1878) and George Marquest(?), age 85, both res. Fredericktown.
Sources: **Bounty land claim #3223; Political Examiner,** 13 Jan 1836.

* There were two men named Lawrence Brengle. In addition to above there was Lawrence Brengle, sheriff and county surveyor, who d. at Washington 6 Jun 1820, in his 57th year. (*Frederick-town Herald*, 8 Jun 1820. His widow, Catherine, dau of Andrew Shriver, near Westminster, d. 9 Oct 1832. (Fredericktown Herald, 20 Oct 1832)

BRIANT, Samuel. Pvt. under Capt. Henry Steiner, 25 Aug - 27 Sep 1814.

BRICKER, David. Res. New Windsor; pvt. under Capt. George W. Magee, 22 Jul 1814 - 10 Jan 1815.

BRICKER, George. Pvt. under Capt. William Durbin, Jr.; joined 24 Aug 1814; absent without leave on 25 Oct 1814; b. c.1788; res. Columbia Co, OH, 1850 and 1855.

BRICKER, Henry. Res. New Windsor in 1814; pvt. under Capt. George Magee, 22 Jul 1814 - 10 Jan 1815.

BRIGGS, Asa. Pvt. under Capt. Samuel Dawson, 1 May - 5 Jul 1813.

BRIGHTWELL, Thomas. Pvt. under Capt. Fonsten, 2 Sep - 27 Oct 1814; res. 16 miles from Westminster.

BRILY, Coloson. Pvt. under Capt. Samuel Duvall, 3 Aug - 3 Oct 1814. FCml of Collison Briley and Sarah Nicholas issued 2 Mar 1814.
Source: FCmL

BRILY, Joseph. b. in MD; enlisted in regular army 1 Jun 1814 in KY.

BRISH, David. Res. Upper Frederick Co.; pvt. under Capt. James F. Huston/Joseph Green; joined 23 Jul 1814; deserted 12 Dec 1814; m. Miss Ann Linton 22 Dec 1818 by Rev. Armstrong. Prob. the same David Brish in 1850 census, age 60, insane. *(Frederick) Examiner* stated he wandered about the streets with infirm mind but harmless disposition. Names in *Stone*: David Brish, d. 2 Nov 1848 [prob. mistakened for 1858], age 68; and wife Ann d. 10 Jan 1863, age 68 yrs, 2 mos., 6 days; bur. Fred. Ref. Cem. There is another David Brish, formerly of Frederick, who d. Washington Co. Almshouse 29 Nov 1873.
Sources: FCml; **Bridge in Time; Names in Stone; Frederick-Town Herald,** 2 Jan 1819; (Frederick) Examiner, 24 Nov 1858, 10 Dec 1873.

BRITTEN [Britton], John. Res. Fredericktown; pvt., 23 Jul 1814 - 10 Jan 1815, under Capt. James F. Huston/Capt. Joseph Green.

BROMWELL - See Bramwell.

BROONER. See Brunner.

BROOKE, Richard. Appt'd Brigade Inspector of 9th Brigade 6 Jan 1812.

BROOKE, Richard. Res. Fredericktown; pvt., under Capt. James F. Hus-

FREDERICK COUNTY MILITIA IN THE WAR OF 1812

ton/Capt. Joseph Green; joined 23 Jul 1814; deserted 27 Oct 1814.

BROOKOVER, William. 4th corpl. under Capt. Daniel Marker, 25 Aug - 27 Oct 1814; b. c.1790, m. twice; both wives dead as of 31 Mar 1871; res. Licking Co., OH 1853, and Gratiot, Muskingum Co., OH, 1871. Acq. (1871): Howard Chappel res. Gratiot, and Robert M. Smart, res. Zenesville, Muskingum Co., OH.

BROONER, John. Pvt. under Capt. Samuel Ogle, 1 May - 5 Jul 1813.

BROWN, Benjamin. Pvt. under Capt. Darby 3 Aug - 8 Nov 1814; enrolled at New Market; m. 28 Dec 1815, in Fred. Co., Sarah Williams; res. Belmont Co., OH, 1851; Flushing Co., OH 1855, and Cassville, Harrison Co., OH, 1871.

Sources: Bounty land claim, 50-40-82917, 55-120-36229; Pension, SO12480, SC8421.

BROWN, Christian. b. Fred. Co., MD, c.1787; enlisted regular army 7 Feb 1814 at Hagerstown by Lt. Fletcher for duration of war; pvt., 38th U.S. Inf. At enlistment; 5 ft, 8 inches, blue eyes, brown or sandy hair, fair complexion, age 27, farmer. Mustered in Capt. H. H. Hook's Company 1 Jun 1814, mustered near Fort Covington 31 Dec 1814, discharged 24 Nov 1814 on surgeon's certificate at Balt., ruptured.

BROWN, Emanuel, Junr. Mbr. of Crawford's "company."

BROWN, Francis. Pvt. under Capt. Thomas Contee Worthington, 17 Aug - 31 Dec 1812.

BROWN, Frederick. From New Market; corpl. under Capt. Denton Darby, 3 Aug - 8 Nov 1814, "sick." [FCml issued to Frederick Brown and Catharine Engle, 23 Jul 1796 and to Frederick Brown and Jane Ervin, 4 Mar 1816. 1850 census, New Market Dist.: Frederick Brown, 58, owns 112-acre farm; Jane Brown, 58; Deborah Brown, 85; Mary Brown, 20.]

BROWN, John. Pvt. under Capt. William Knox, 26 Aug - 27 Oct 1814.

BROWN, John. Pvt. under Capt. Fonsten, 2 Sep - 27 Oct 1814; m. 12 Jul 1821 in Uniontown, Richland Co., OH, Rebecca Anderson; d. 20 Feb 1859, Delonaga, Wapello Co., IA; res. Canton, Fulton Co., IL, 1850; Flushing Co., OH, 1855; Chariton, Lucas Co., IA, 1871. She d. c.1893.

Sources: Bounty land claims, 50-40-19699, 55-120-77595; Pension, WO24399, WC26680

BROWN, John. b. in Fred. Co., MD; enlisted in regular army 1796-1800 at Greenville, transferred to Capt. Clinch's company. Mustered at Washington 9 Aug 1813; fifer, 5th U.S. Inf. under Capt. Sparks. At enlistment: 5 ft, 4 inches, gray eyes, red hair, fair complexion, age 37, farmer.

BROWN, Robert. Pvt. under Capt. Fonsten, 2 Sep - 27 Oct 1814; res. 15 miles from Westminster.

BROWN, Thomas. b. Fred. Co., MD; Enlisted 11 Jun 1814 (1813?) by Capt. Sangster for the duration of war. At enlistment: 5 ft, 4 inches, grey eyes, brown hair, light complexion, age 36, laborer, pvt., 12th U.S. Inf.; mustered at Staunton, VA on 8 Aug 1814, detained at Winchester, VA, as witness. Discharged at Fort Covington 30 Mar 1815.

BROWN, William. 2nd lieut. under Capt. William Durbin, Jr., 24 Aug - 27 Oct 1814.

BROWN, William. b. Fred. Co. MD; Enlisted 19 Feb 1814 at Georgetown, D.C.; served under Col. Henry Carberry in 36th U.S. Inf. At enlistment: 5 ft, 10 inches, age 23, mustered in Georgetown Mar 1814.

BROWNING, Archibald. 2nd sergt. under Capt. Nicholas Hall, 2nd Regt., 1st Cav. Dist., 7 Aug - 10 Sep 1814. [FCml issued to Archibald Browning, Jr., and Rebecca Lewis on 7 Nov 1812.]

BROWNING [Brawning], David. Pvt. under Capt. Hall, 7 Aug - 10 Sep 1814; m. 10 Feb 1801 in Anne Arundel Co., MD, Achsah Warfield (b. c.1784), by Archabald Brawning, Meth. minister; d. Ross Co., OH, 31 Jan 1839. Widow res. Ross Co., OH 1853 and 1855. Acq.(1855): Hugh Cochran, Allen Cochran, res. Ross Co., OH.

Source: Bounty land claim, 55-120-24531.

BROWNING, Jonathan. Pvt. under Capt. Denton Darby, 3 Aug - 8 Nov 1814; b. c.1790; m. 24 Apr 1813 at New Market, Maria Falconer (recorded variously as Falkner or Fortner; possibly Farquhar), by Rev. Pitts, Meth. pastor; d. near Liberty, Fred. Co. 11 Sep 1850 [this date given by widow; she later gave date of death as 11 Nov 1850]. Widow res. Liberty, Fred. Co, 1871; d. near Liberty 25 Jul 1879, age 84. Acq.: Henry Baker of Liberty (1871).

Sources: Pension, WO1119, WC637; Bounty land claims, 50-40-33543, 55-120-63012; **(Frederick) Examiner.**

BRUNER, John. b. Fred. Co., MD, c.1792; enlisted 20 Apr 1814 at Fredericktown by Lt. J. Neal for the duration of war. At enlistment: 5 ft, 10 inches tall, dark eyes, dark hair, dark complexion, age 22, occupation whitesmith. Pvt. in 36th U.S. Inf.; mustered 28 Feb 1815 at Fort Covington, discharged near Fort Covington 30 Mar 1815.

BRUNNER [Brooner], John (of Jacob). 3rd sergt. under Capt. John Brengle, 25 Aug - 19 Sep 1814. John Brunner m(1) 14 Dec 1816 by Rev. J. Helfenstein, Maria Stickle, by whom he had fol. children: Valentine S., Mary who m. Lewis Markell, Lewis A. and Edward J. John Brunner m(2) a Miss Doll by whom he had Caroline who m. William S. Buntz and Ellen C. who m. Martin N. Rohrback, of Frederick.

Sources: Williams, Hist. of Fred. Co., Md.; West. Md. Genealogy, 4:4; The Frederick-town Herald, Dec 1816

BRUNNER, John, Jr. Appt'd Capt. of a company, 28th Regt. 22 Apr 1814.

BRYAN, William. Pvt. under Capt. Barton Hackney, 1 Sep - 27 Oct 1814.

BRYANT, James. Pvt. under Capt. Jacob Alexander. 22 Jul 1814; d. on field of battle 24 Aug 1814. [FCml issued to James Bryan and Amey Hall 29 Aug 1793.]

BUCKEY, George. Appt'd lieut. in Capt. Jacob Freshour's company, 9 Jun 1809.

BUCKEY, George. Pvt. under Capt. George W. Ent, 24 Aug - 30 Sep 1814.

FREDERICK COUNTY MILITIA IN THE WAR OF 1812

BUCKEY, John. Pvt. under Capt. Henry Steiner, Apr 28-Jun 29 1813 and Aug 25 - Sep 27 1814; b. c.1792; m. 8 May 1810, Miss Susan Hauser dau of Michael Hauser in Frederick, MD, by Rev. Wagner; d. Frederick Town 10 Jan 1829, "in his 48th year" after a long and severe illness, a hatter. Bur. Luth. graveyard, "though he belonged to Ger. Ref." Susan Buckey res. Harpers Ferry 1853, VA and Jefferson Co. VA ', 1855. Witnesses in 1855 were Benjamin Wentzel and Jacob Crowl, res. Jefferson Co., VA. Letter dated 17 Jan 1940 from Grace A. Wentzell states her great grandfather was John Buckey, proper spelling Bouquet; lived all his life in Fred. Co., MD, at Buckeystown, named after the family. Henry Buckey bro. of John Buckey, d. 2 Mar 1829 in the Alms House, age 43 yrs. Miss Catherine Buckey 3rd dau. of John Buckey m. Ambrose Ingrman 25 Jun 1839. Miss Matilda Buckey, youngest dau of John Buckey, m. Dennis Smook 26 Aug 1841.

[Note: On 9 Jan 1799 John Bucky bound his son John Bucky to Henry Steiner, hatter, for 3 yrs, and 8 mos., until age 21. If this is the veteran, John Buckey then the above estimated date of birth is incorrect.]

Sources: Bounty land claims, 50-40-86087, 55-120-3420; **Fredericktown Herald**, 17 Jan 1829; **West. Md. Genealogy**, 5:33; **Engelbrecht's Diary**, 1:343, 526, 534, 2:346, 377.

BUCKEY, Michael. Appt'd 16 Jun 1812 as cornet in Capt. Daniel Hauer's troop of horse.

BUCKINGHAM, Basil. Mbr. of Crawford's "company."

BUCKINGHAM, Ephraim. Mbr. of Crawford's "company."

BUFFINGTON, John. Pvt. under Capt. Samuel Duvall, 3 Aug - 3 Oct 1814.

BURCH, Henry. Pvt. under Capt. Samuel Duvall, 3 Aug - 3 Oct 1814.

BURCKHEAD, Daniel of Christopher. Appt'd ensign under Capt. Kemp 18 Sep 1812; "moved away" [after the war].

BURESS, Nicholas. Pvt. under Capt. Denton Darby, 3 Aug - 8 Nov 1814. Absent 12 days.

BURESS, Proverb. Pvt. under Capt. Denton Darby, 3 Aug - 8 Nov 1814. Absent 12 days.

BURGEE, Miel. Cornet under Capt. Nicholas Hall in the 2nd Regt., 1st Cav. Dist., 7 Aug - 10 Sep 1814.

BURGEE, Thomas, Jr. Appt'd 16 Nov 1812 cornet in Capt. John Cook's troop of horse, 2nd Regt., 1st Cav. Dist. Appt'd 1st lieut. in same company on 22 Dec 1812. Served as lieut. under Capt. Hall, 7 Aug - 10 Sep 1814, 1st Regt'l Dist, 2nd Regt.; m. Ann Waters (b. c.1789) in Fred. Co. by Parson Rennels, Epis. minister. FCml issued to Thomas Burgee and Anne Waters 14 May 1805. They had "large family of children." Thomas Burgee d. Fred. Co. 15 Mar 1852; his widow res. Fred. Co. 1853. 1850 census, New Market Dist.: Thomas Burgee, 70, farmer, pensioner; Ann Burgee, 60; Thomas, 36; Mary, 30. Acq. - 1853: Adam Hagan and Ephraim Davis, res. Fred. Co., Md.

Sources: Bounty land claim, 50-40-84976; FCml; **Bridge in Time**.

64

BURGESS, Henry. Pvt. under George W. Ent, 24 Aug - 30 Sep 1814.

BURGOON, Jacob. Pvt. under Capt. Fonsten, 2 Sep - 28 Oct 1814; b. 28 Aug 1788; m. Catharine Dehoof, at Taneytown, MD, Jun or Jul 1810; res. Perry Co., OH, 1850 and 1855 and Somerset, Perry Co., OH, 1871; d. Somerset, OH, 9 Dec 1874. Discharge paper in file, "Camp Hampstead October 31st 1814. I do hereby Certify that Jacob Burgoon, a pvt. in Capt. John Fonsten's Company 2d Bat. 3rd Regt., 2nd Divn., 11th Brigade M. Militia in the service of the United States was Honourably discharged by order of Major General Scott after Serving his Regular Tour of duty. /s/ John Fonsten, Capt."
Sources: Pension, SO13558 (rejected 13 Apr 1872 by reason of insufficient service); Bounty land claim, 55-160-19361 [copy of canceled warrant is in file]. Register of the General Society of the War of 1812, publ. by the Society in 1972, gives descendancy to Norman Aaron Burgoon (elected to Society in 1964) from William Burgoon bro. of veteran Jacob Burgoon. According to this source, William Burgoon, bro. of the veteran, b. Fred. Co., 12 May 1792; d. Silver Run, MD, 21 Apr 1862; m. Sarah Eckert (d. 20 Nov 1879).

BURK, Daniel. Res. upper Frederick County during war; pvt. under Capt. James F. Huston/Capt. Joseph Green; joined 23 Jul 1814; deserted on 16 Dec 1814.

BURK, Isaac. Pvt. under Capt. Samuel Duvall, 3 Aug - 3 Oct 1814.

FCml issued to Isaac Burke and Elizabeth Clay 31 Oct 1818. In 1850 Isaac Burk, New Market Dist. owned 28-acre farm, age 56, farmer; in same household was Elizabeth Burk age 62 and Milton Burk age 20, laborer.
Source: Bridge in Time.

BURK, Michael. Corpl. under Capt. Flautt, 29 Apr - 29 Jun 1813.

BURK, Michael. Pvt. under Capt. William Knox, 26 Aug - 27 Oct 1814; m. 13 Nov 1810 Elizabeth Fuss (b. c.1790) at Emmittsburg, in Ref. Ch., Emmittsburg; d. 29 (or 27) 1828. Acq.: Henry Appenzellar; Joseph Ovelman, res. Franklin Co., PA; Patrick Burk and James Rodgers, res. Carroll Co., MD who served with Michael Burk. Widow res. Franklin Co., PA, in 1855.
Source: Bounty land claim, 55-160-38169.

BURK, Patrick. 4th sergt. under Capt. William Knox, 26 Aug - 27 Oct 27 1814; b. c.1790; res. Carroll County, 1850, 1855; appt'd Commissioner of Taneytown Dist., 1838 and candidate for Road Supervisor in 1853.
Sources: **Carrolltonian**, dated 4/5/1838; Bounty land claim, 55-120-1910.

BURKARD [Burkhard], Jacob. Pvt. under Capt. Philip Smith, 23 May - 8 Sep 1813.

BURKE, John. Pvt. under Capt. Farquhar. According to his widow her husband served in the company of Capt. Farquhar and continued on the rolls of Capt. Galt, Capt Curtis or Capt. Farquhar; d. 5 Dec 1839 near Taneytown; bur. Cath. Cem., Taneytown; m. 10 Jun 1821 Mary (called Polly) Gribbel (b. c.1798), at Conewago Ch. in Adams Co., PA, by Father Leckhue, Cath. priest. John Burke previously m. Catharine Storm who d. 7 Sep 1819.

John Burke d. 5 Dec 1839 near Taneytown, Carroll Co. MD; bur. Cath. graveyard at Taneytown. Mary Burke res. Westminster, MD in 1878; d. Westminster 24 Jan 1881. Acq.: 1878 - John B. Boyle, age 66, and George T. Wering, age 45, res. Carroll Co., acq. with Mary Burke for 55 and 30 yrs, resp. 1880 - John B. Boyle, age 69, res. Westminster, MD.; Dr. Samuel Swope, age 73, res. Taneytown.

Letter from Mary Burke dated 7 Jun 1880, Westminster, MD, stating "that the house in which I lived and occupied on upper room, was, on or about the 18th day of December 1878, consumed by fire ... my life was only saved by the timely arrival and exertion of my near neighbors."

Letter dated 27 Oct 1883, Wheeling. WV, from Thomas C.Burke, stating that "I and my brother William A. Burke, are the only living heirs of Mrs. Mary Burke."

Letter from Postmaster, P.O. Westminster, MD., A. J. Huber, saying Mrs. Mary Burke is "very old and feeble. Her circumstances approach destitution. She is compelled to accept charity."

Source: Pension, 17884. "Third Auditor's office - There are no rolls of Capt. Farquhar's company of MM War of 1812 on file in this office..."

BURKET, Jacob. Res. Mechanickstown; served as pvt. under Capt. George W. Magee, 14 Oct 1814 - 10 Jan 1815.

BURKHARD, Jacob. See Burkard.

BURKHART, Daniel. Pvt. under Capt. Henry Steiner, 28 Apr - 29 Jun 1813 and 25 Aug - 27 Sep 1814.

BURKHART, Daniel. Ensign, under Capt. Nicholas Turbutt, 8 Sep - 27 Oct 1814.

BURKHART, John. Pvt. in Capt. Flautt's rifle company, 29 Apr - 29 Jun 1813.

BURNS, Andrew. b. Fred. Co., MD, ca.1781; enlisted Westminster, MD, 14 May 1813 by Ens. Philip Fisher for 1 year. At enlistment: 5 ft, 11 inches, age 32; served in 36th U.S. Inf. under Col. Carbury. On 31 Dec 1813 and 30 Apr 1814 he was mustered under Capt. James Hook.

BURNS, George. Pvt. under Capt. William Durbin, Jr., 24 Aug - 27 Oct 1814.

BURNS, Jacob. Pvt. under Capt. Shawen, 5 Sep - 27 Oct 1814.

BURNS, James. Res. upper Fred. Co.; pvt. under James F. Huston; joined company 23 Jul 1814; on 12 Aug 1814 he enlisted in the regular army at Annapolis in 38th U.S. Inf.; at time of enlist. had blue eyes, dark brown hair, light complexion, b. County Whitlow, Ireland; enlisted by Ensign Raticker for duration of war; discharged at Fort McHenry 28 Mar 1815.

BURNS, John. Pvt. under Capt. William Durbin, 24-27 Oct 1814; b. 11 Jun 1785; m. Jul 1819 near Millerstown, Adams Co., PA, Mary Fisher (b. c.1802) by Amos McQuiley, Justice of the Peace. First marr. for both. John Burns d. Franklin Co., PA, 5 Aug 1845, bur. churchyard near Scotland, PA, age 60 yrs, 2 mos., 25 days. Their children

THE VETERANS

(living in 1878): Ann Rebeca Fuller b 25 Dec 1826, George Frederic b 13 Nov 1828, Jarvis Francis b 12 Dec 1836, Mary J. F. Walter b 28 Mar 1841. Widow said her husband "sometimes insisted his name was Barns." In 1878 her dau, Ann Rebecca, stated she was a widow now living with her mother; the children older than she were John Jeremiah (b 14 Jul 1821, d 21 Jan 1845) and David (b 9 Jul 1824, d 16 Jun 1849). Witnesses at marr. of John Burns and Mary Fisher were Mrs. Jane Agnew, Mrs. Carson, Joseph Shepperd, John Shafer and wife, and Authur Bennett and Margaret his wife. When called into service John Burns was medium size, had rather dark complexion, dark brown eyes, black hair. After discharge res. Adams Co. for 22 1/2 yrs and Franklin Co. about 3 1/2 yrs until his death. She res. Leitersburg St., Waynesboro, 1878. Acq. (1878): Catherine E. Weagly, age 68, Main St. ,Waynesboro; and Sanford Shroder of Fountain Dale, Adams Co - acq. for 23 yrs and 25 yrs resp.

Source: Pension, WO35997 rejected.

BURNS, Peter. Pvt. under Capt. William Durbin, Jr.; joined 24 Aug 1814; absent without leave on 25 Oct 1814; b. c.1783, m. Nov 1816 Polly Horns in Fred. Co. In 1855 Peter Burns applied for a bounty warrant at the courthouse in Ashland Co., Oh; in 1871, res. Richland Co., OH.

Sources: Pension, SO19656, SC18494; Bounty land claim, 50-40-6885, 55-120-33885.

BUROUGHS [Burroughs, Boroughs], Isaac. Pvt. under Capt. Dawson; joined 21 Jul 1814; discharged 27 Oct 1814; sick in Balt. on 12 Oct.

BURRISS (Burris, Burrows), Nicholas R. Pvt. under Capt. Darby, 3 Aug - 8 Nov 1814. "Absent 12 days." He stated he was drafted near Rockville 15 Jul 1814; b. c.1796; m. Sarah Howser Feb 1820, Montgomery Co., MD; res. Montgomery Co., MD, 1850, 1855, 1871 (Tennellytown), and 1872 (Georgetown, D.C.); d. c.1883. Acq.: John Wesly Robisson (signed Robson) and John F. Ward.

Sources: Bounty land claim, 50-40-71733, 55-120-11705; Pension, SO773, SC779.

BUSSARD, Daniel. From New Market area; pvt. under Capt. Philip Smith; joined 23 May 1813; deserted 19 Jun 1813.

[Possible connections: (1) A FCml was issued to Daniel Bussard and Eleanor Aldridge 21 Jan 1817. (2) Daniel Bussard d. Georgetown, D. C.13 May 1830, in his 59th year, mbr. of Board of Aldermen.]

Sources: Williams, Hist. of Fred. Co. (see section on Bussard Family, p. 861); Marr. & Deaths of All. & Wash. Cos.

BUTLER, Benjamin. Deserted from Capt. Duvall's company at camp at Bladensburg 16 Aug 1814, described as 19-20 yrs old, 5 ft, 9-10 inches tall, darkish complexion, blue eyes, black hair, laborer, substitute from Creager's Town. His name is not on the muster rolls.

Source: Engine of Liberty, dated 5 Oct 1814.

BUTLER, Elias. b. Fred. Co. MD, c.1795; enlisted 20 Jun at Hagerstown by Lt. Cochran for duration of war;

served in 38th U.S. Inf. At enlistment: 5 ft, 6 inches, dark eyes, light hair, light complexion, age 19, laborer.

BUTLER, James. Pvt. under Capt. George W. Magee, 22 Jul 1813 until discharged by surgeon 1 Sep 1813.

BUTLER, Ormon F. Appt'd ensign 19 Sep 1809 in Capt. David Markey's company, 16th Regt., MM. 3rd Lieut. under Capt. Samuel Ogle, from 1 May until transferred to Capt. Mathews 15 Jun 1813, and served as ensign under Capt. John Brengle, in the 1st Regt., 25 Aug - 19 Sep 1814; b. 4 May 1787; elected to the Friendship Fire Co., Ward 5 as Engineman in 1837; m(1) c. 16 Dec 1813, Elizabeth Bortle (d. 21 Mar 1852, age 60 yrs, 3 mos., 2 days); m(2) c.Mar 1853, Mariah Barbara Showbaker, widow of Christian Brengle, Senr. FCml issued to Barbara Showbaker and Christian Brengle, Senr. 29 Dec 1835. Ormond F. Butler was mbr. of Frederick delegation of the "United Brothers of the War of 1812" in 1859. He d. Fredericktown 8 Apr 1863, age 75 yrs, 11 mos., 4 days. She d. 25 Sep 1871, age 80 yrs, 17 days. 1850 census of Fredericktown: Barbara Brengle, 58; Elizabeth Scott, 41. Their children: Ann Elizabeth Butler eldest dau, m. 28 May 1833, George Bready; Richard; Charles; Ormond; George; Robert; Sarah m. Henry Baker; Amelia m. George French; Harriet m. John Neir; Christina Mocabee. Died on 23 Oct 1838, John Bartel at the house of his bro.-in-law, Ormond F. Butler, at the Inclined Planes.

[Note: There was more than one Ormond F. Butler. Mrs. Mary A. Butler d. 14 Dec 1869, relict of Ormond F. Butler. She was b. 29 Sep 1811. (Frederick) Examiner, 22 Dec 1869]

Sources: Bounty land claim, 55-120-13300; FCml; Bridge in Time; (Frederick) Examiner, 1 Mar 1837, 30 Mar 1853, 14 Sep 1859, 15 Apr 1863, 16 Aug 1865, 9 Oct 1871; Engelbrecht Diary; Names in Stone.

BUTLER, Richard. Served under Capt. Thomas Contee Worthington, 17 Aug - 31 Dec 1812. Reduced from 1st corpl. to pvt. on 22 Sep 1812.

[Possible connections: (1) FCml issued to Richard Butler and Amelia Fischer on 20 May 1786. (2) Records of Luth. Ch. of Frederick include baptisms of children of Richard and Anna Maria Butler: Anna Margareth b. 3 Mar 1787; Richardt William b. 22 Jan 1792; Catharina Barbara b. 30 Dec 1790; John Tobias b. 25 Apr 1793; Maria Anna b. 6 Jul 1794.]

Sources: FCml; Md. German Ch. Rcds., v.4.

BUTLER, Richard W. b. Fred. Co. MD, c.1792; enlisted 18 Mar 1813 for 18 mos.; corpl. in 14th U.S. Inf. At enlistment: 5 ft, 9-10 inches, grey eyes, light hair, light complexion, age 21, clerk; discharged at Plattsburgh 10 May 1814, re-enlisted in Rifle Co., discharged Plattsburgh 24 Aug 1815.

BUTLER, Thomas. Pvt. under Capt. Samuel Duvall, 3 Aug - 3 Oct 1814. [Possible connection: Thomas Butler and Jane Gittings m. at her father's house 29 Dec 1795. *Rcds. of Evan. Ref. Ch. in Fred., Md., 1746-1800.*]

BUTLER, Tobias H. Pvt. under Capt. John Brengle, 25 Aug - 19 Sep 1814; b. c.1794; m(1) Elizabeth [called Betzy]

THE VETERANS

Waller (d. 1821) at Jefferson co, KY, in 1818; m(2) Sallie Reed; m(3) Sallie Goss; m(4) Elizabeth Russell (b. c.1806), 3 Nov 1856, Fishersville, Jefferson Co., KY, by Elijah Sutton in presence of Stephen H. Read and John Russell. The first two wives d. KY, the third in Indiana. This was the first and only marr. for Elizabeth Russell Butler; she had no children. At time of enrollment he was 5 ft, 8 inches; had dark eyes and dark hair; was a tanner and currier. Fol. discharge he res. c.3 yrs in MD, then c.5 yrs in KY, and since then in IN. Morgan Co., IN, 1873, 1879 and 1880 (P.O. Address: Paragon). d. 8 May 1885 in Alaska, IN. Widow res. Alaska, Morgan Co., IN, 1885; Morgan Co., IN, 1886. Acq.: 1879 - Charles H. Dow, age 51, and Mortimer D. Costin, age 39, res. Ray Township, Morgan Co., IN. 1885 - Thomas J. Pottorff, aged 52, res. Alaska, IN; and Thomas Dunagan, age 60, res. Gosport, Owen co., IN. 1886 - Elender Whitaker and James K. Whittaker, acq. with Sallie (Goss) Butler, 3rd wife of Tobias H. Butler; Richard Butler and Catherine Phillips, res. Louisville, KY, who knew first two wives.

Sources: Pensions, SO29282, SC25408, WO43898, WC34471; Bounty land claim, 55-160-114490.

BUZARD [Bussard, Bussard], Peter. Pvt. under Capt. Samuel Duvall, 3 Aug - 3 Oct 1814; b. 6 May 1792; d. 27 Nov 1864; m. Miss Sarah Reidenour 11 Apr 1822 by Rev. J. R. Reiley. She d. 23 Jul 1872, age 72 yrs, 3 mos, 27 days. 1850 census of Catoctin Dist: Peter Bussard, 59, farmer; Sarah 50. Both are buried at Thurmont United Brethren/Blue Ridge Cemeteries.

Sources: Williams, Hist. of Fred. Co.; Marr. & Deaths of All. & Washington Cos, Md.; Md. Union, 1 Aug 1872.; Names in Stone.

BUZZARD, David. Pvt. under Capt. Mathew Murray, 25 Aug - 27 Oct 1814; b. c.1790-1793; m. 26 Dec 1816 Mary Shank (b. c.1796) by Rev. Jacob Bowles [Powles] in Middletown, MD, each for first time. Bro.-in-law, Peter Shank, served with him. When enrolled: stone and brick mason; b. Fred. Co., MD, 5 ft, 8 inches, black hair, black eyes, dark complexion; res. Frederick Co, MD, until 1823 when he moved to Montgomery Co., OH, then moved to Carroll Co., IN, 1844, where he remained; 1879 P.O. Address: Delphi. David Buzzard d. 21 Jul 1860 in Delphia, IN; widow d. Aug 1885, Buck Creek, IN. Acq.: 1879 - Soloman Bossard, aged 53, near Delphia, IN; and Abram B. Martin, age 44; Conley M. Knight; Peter Shank, M.D., aged 87 yrs (bro. of Mary Buzzard) of Montgomery Co, OH, b. Frederick Co, M.D, 8 Mar 1793, in same company as David Buzzard; other acq. James P. Dugan and John Burr.

Sources: Pension, WO35662, WC25354; Bounty land claims, 50-40-74069, canceled, 55-160-10615 (certificate for 40 acres in file).

BUZZARD [Buzerd], Samuel. Pvt. under Capt. Daniel Shawen, 5 Sep - 27 Oct 1814.

Sources: Pension, WO4000, WC3459; Bounty land claim, 50-40-57612, 55-120-88746.

BYER, David. On muster roll of Capt. William Durbin, Jr., 24 Aug - 27 Oct 1814; never joined his company.

FREDERICK COUNTY MILITIA IN THE WAR OF 1812

BYER [Boyer], George. He served under Capt. Thomas Contee Worthington; joined 17 Aug 1812; promoted to 4th corpl. on 22 Sep 1812; d. 13 Dec 1814.

BYERLY, Lewis. Appt'd ensign 15 Jul 1814 under Capt. Otho Woltz, 16th Regt., MM.

BYERS, Michael. Pvt. under Capt. Fonsten, 2 Sep - 27 Oct 1814; res. within 3 miles of Westminster. According to Williams, Michael Byers m. Elizabeth Dutrow; FCml issued on 26 May 1820 to Michael Byers and Margt. Duttero.

According to Williams, the name Byers, formerly Boyer, has German origin. Gabriel Boyer, came to America from Germany in early manhood and settled near Westminster, MD. "Michael Byers, was a cooper and farmer; spent his whole life near Westminster. He was a soldier in the War of 1812 ... the sword he carried is in the possession of his dau, Mrs. Joseph Byers."

Sources: Williams, **Hist. of Fred. Co.**, p. 860; FCml.

BYRODD [Byroad], Peter. Pvt. under Capt. Joseph Wood, 27 Aug 1814 until he deserted on 29 Sep 1814.

CABLE, Henry. Pvt., 38th U.S. Inf., under Capt. James H. Hook. At enlist.: 5 ft 4 or 6 inches, grey or blue eyes, dark hair, dark or ruddy complexion, bricklayer, b. in Frederick or Anne Arundel County, MD. Enlisted 1814 at Alexandria [VA] by Capt. Hook for duration of the war. Discharged at Fort Covington 31 Mar 1815 for disability contracted in the service.

CAFFMAN, Henry. See Kauffman.

CAIL, Joseph. Mbr. of the Crawford's "company."

CAIN, Benjamin. Pvt. under Capt. Fonsten; joined 2 Sep 1814; deserted 13 Sep 1814; b. 1789; m. Oct 1810 Mary Dalauter (b. c.1793) in Hagerstown, MD, by Ref. minister; res. Montgomery Co., OH, 1851 and 1855; d. there 6 Mar 1868; widow res. Montgomery Co, OH, (P.O. Address: German-town) 1871. Acq.(1871): Lewis Zehring and William E. Miller, both res. Germantown; Jacob De Lawter (b. 20 Aug 1795) and Sarah his wife (b. 21 Jun 1797); John Stump, age 65, shinglemaker, b. MD.

Source: **Bridge in Time.**

CAIN, Jacob. Pvt. under Capt. Ogle; joined 1 May 1813; enlisted 6 Jun 1813 in 38th U.S. Inf., by Lieut. Duncan for 1 year; served under Capt. Mittenberger; transferred to Capt. Haslett's Company.

CAIN, Thomas. Pvt. under Capt. Philip Smith, 23 May - 8 Sep 1813.

CAIN, Thomas. Pvt. under Capt. Samuel Duvall, 3 Aug - 3 Oct 1814; m. Leticia Hix (b. c.1790), by Rev. Snyder, Meth. minister; d. c.1835 at Liberty, MD; she res. Libertytown, Fred. Co., MD, 1850. 1850 census of Fred. Co.: Leticia Cain, age 70, pauper, living with Solomon Cain, age 34, laborer; Elizabeth Cain, 48; Mary J. Cain, 15; Levinia Cain, 13; Sarah A. Cain, 11; John T. Cain, 9; Joseph E. Cain, 1; and Elizabeth Kessler, age 44. Acq.: 1850 - John Glisan and Abraham Furry; said Thomas and Laticia Cain had 5 or 6 children and Laticia has since lived with said children.

THE VETERANS

Sources: Bounty land claim, 50-rejected-51804; Bridge in Time.

CALF, Martin. Pvt. under Capt. William Knox; joined 26 Aug 1814; deserted 10 Sep 1814.

CALHOON, Robert L. Pvt. under Capt. Samuel Dawson, 1 May - 5 Jul 1813.

CALL, Mathew. Pvt. in Capt. Flautt's rifle company, 29 Apr - 29 Jun 1813.

CALL, Mathew or Mathias. Res. New Windsor; pvt. under Capt. George W. Magee, 22 Jul 1814 - 10 Jan 1815.

CAMPBELL, Benjamin. Pvt. under Capt. Zacharias, 7 Aug -10 Sep 1814, 2nd Regt., 1st Cav. Dist.

CAMPBELL, George. Pvt. under Capt. Darby, 3 Aug - 8 Nov 1814. Absent 17 days.

CAMPBELL, John. Pvt. under Capt. Philip Smith, 23 May - 8 Sep 1813. [John Campbell, Jr., d. Monday 24 Sep 1827 at his residence near Libertytown, in his 60th year. *Frederick-town Herald*.]

CAMPBELL, William. Pvt. under Capt. Zacharias, 7 Aug -10 Sep 1814, 2nd Regt., 1st Cav. Dist.

CANADAY, John. Mbr. of Crawford's "company."

CANNON, Jacob. Pvt. under Capt. Getzendanner; joined 26 Jul - 21 Aug 1814; b. c.1793; res. Fred. Co. in 1850 and 1855. [A marr. license was issued in Fred. Co. to Jacob Cannon and Elizabeth Mattern 19 Jul 1831. 1850 census of Frederick E.D.: Jacob Cannon, 54, laborer; Elizabeth, 50; Julian M., 17; Christian, 20; Daniel, 16; Elizabeth, 9.]

Sources: Bounty land claim, 55-80-6087 (a certificate for 40 acres is in the file); Bridge in Time.

CARBIN (Carlin?), Nicholas. Pvt. under Capt. Samuel Ogle, 1 May - 5 Jul 1813.

CAREY, Cyrus. 4th sgt. under George W. Ent, 24 Aug - 30 Sep 1814.

CARLEN, Bennet. Pvt. under Lieut. William Kolb, guarding British prisoners, 13 Oct - 15 Nov 1814; substitute for Thomas Young; b. c.1798; res. Fred. Co., VA, in 1855.

Source: Bounty land claim, 55-160-2426.

CARLEN, James. Pvt. under Lieut. Kolb, guarding British prisoners at Frederick Barracks, 13 Oct - 15 Nov 1814.

CARLIN, Cornelius. Pvt. under Capt. Samuel Dawson, 1 May - 5 Jul 1813 and pvt. under Capt. Getzendanner, 9 Aug - 17 Sep 1813.

CARLIN, Nicholas. Pvt. under Capt. Ogle, 1 May - 5 Jul 1813.

CARLTON [Carleton], Thomas. Lieut. under Capt. Thomas Contee Worthington, 17 Aug - 31 Dec 1812; appt'd 20 Sep 1813 as capt. of a company, 16th Regt., MM; m. Mary Pickel (b. c.1784), in Fredericktown, 1811, by Rev. Wagner, of Ref. Ch.; d. 23 Nov 1835 at Fredericktown, aged 54 yrs; eldest son, Edward A., d. 20 Dec 1834; second dau, Ann Rebecca, m. Lewis A. Brengle 22 May 1834; dau Eliza m. Rev. Charles Martin of Martinsburg, VA 11 May 1837. Thomas Carlton served as sheriff of Fred. Co., c.1824-1827 and mayor of Fredericktown, 1829-1835. Mary Carlton res. alone in Frederick-town in

1850; Acq.: 1851 - Perry Rice and Lewis A. Brengle, res. Fred. Co. 1855 - Jacob Reese, Jacob Sinn, res. Fred. Co. Edward Carlton, father of Thomas Carlton d. 24 Jul 1821 in his 93yrd year; he was Roman Cath. Marriages of the children of Thomas Carlton: 22 May 1834, Ann Rebecca Carlton 2nd dau of to Lewis A. Brengle of Peter; 11 May 1837, Eliza Jenett Carlton (d. New York City 10 Apr 1846), eldest dau to Rev. Charles Martin of Germantown, PA; 25 Jun 1840, William (Register of Frederick, d. 22 Dec 1840) to Miss Mary P. Neill, dau of John W. Neill of Phila (cousins). Edward A. Carlton, eldest son of Thomas Carlton, d. 20 Dec 1834 in his 28th year.

Sources: Bounty land claim, 55-80-4713; **The Times and Democratic Advocate**, dated 25 May 1837; **Frederick Herald** dated 27 Dec 1834; **Bridge in Time**; **Engelbrecht Diary**: 2:78, 113, 140, 183, 250, 371, 385, 401, 445.

CARMACK, Samuel. 4th sergt. under Capt. Samuel Duvall, 3 Aug - 3 Sep 1814; served later as Quartermaster sergt. to Col. Cramer; b. 29 Aug 1792; m. 28 May 1818 Caroline Smith (b. 22 Mar 1800) in Fredericktown, MD, by Jonathan Helfenstein; fol. discharge res. Fredericktown except for a short period in Allegany and Washington Counties; res. Fredericktown, MD, in 1852, 1855 and 1871; he d. 4 Aug 1879. Became capt. of Everhart Grays, later col.; mbr. of Meth. Ch.; mbr. of Independent Hose Company; Chief Marshal of the Frederick Delegation of the "United Brothers of the War of 1812" in 1859. Widow res. Court St. Fredericktown, 1879; she d. 28 Feb 1881. Both bur. Mt. Olivet, Frederick with daus, Salome, 27 Feb 1819 - 19 Mar 1878, Isabelle, 26 Feb 1827 - 3 Jan 1895. Acq.: 1879 - William H. McCaffrey, age 35 and Horatio Waters, age 45; John B. Stimmel, age 88, res. Mt. Pleasant, Fred. Co.; George Metzger, age 77, res. Fred. Co., and John Fauble, age 84, res. Fredericktown. Inquiry dated 7 May 1913 from George S. Miles of 1330 N. Mount St., Balt., MD.

Sources: Pensions, SO6932, SC4420, WO37782, WC27668; Bounty land claims, 50-40-93653, 55-120-13770; **Names in Stone**; **Fredericktown Herald**, 30 May 1818.

CARMACK, William. Corpl. under Capt. Joseph Wood, 27 Aug - 13 Oct 1814; b. c.1792; m. Lydia Ott at his father's house Dec 1815 [FCml issued 19 Dec 1815]; res. Carroll Co., MD, 1853 and 1871 (Double Pipe Creek). Bur. Detour, Meth. Protestant Cem. are fol. members of family: Wm. Carmack d. at his residence 1 mile southwest of Keysville, Carroll Co. on 7 Aug 1876, age 84 yrs, 5 mos., 29 days; Lydia (Ott), d. 15 Feb 1876, age 81 yrs, 6 mos., ? days; son Francis, 1823-1903; dau Sarah Jane, 1826-1906. William Carmack was the father-in-law of William J. Black, one of the Judges of the Orphans' Court.

Sources: Pension, SO13016, SC7967; Bounty land claims, 50-40-87974, 55-120-84618; **Names in Stone**; **FCml**; (Frederick) **Examiner**, 16 Aug 1876.

CARMICKLE, James. Pvt., 1st U.S. Inf., under Capt. S. Owens. At enlistment in regular army: 5 ft, 7 3/4 inches, hazel eyes, dark hair, fair complexion, age 19, laborer; b. Fred. Co., MD; enlisted Winchester 2 Aug 1809 by Capt. Owens for 5 yrs. Tried by General Court

THE VETERANS

Martial at Belle Fontaine 6 Jan 1812 for intoxication, given 25 lashes, whiskey stopped 2 weeks, police duty for 2 weeks, stripes remitted; d. Fort Clark 30 Jan 1814.

CARNE, Adam. Pvt. under Capt. Jacob Alexander, 22 Jul - 19 Sep 1814.

CARNES [Carns], Jacob. Pvt. under Capts. Huston/Green; joined 23 Jul 1814; discharged 6 Dec by the regtl. surgeon.

CARNES, John. Servant to Quartermaster, John Markall, 20 Jul 1814 - 10 Jan 1815.

CARNES, Thomas. Pvt. under Capt. Samuel Dawson; joined 21 Jul 1814; d. 30 Dec 1814.

CARNEY, Patrick. Pvt. under Capt. Samuel Dawson; joined 21 Jul 1814; deserted 26 Oct 1814.

CARNEY, William. Pvt. under Capt. Hall, 7 Aug - 10 Sep 1814, 2nd Regt., 1st Cav. Dist.

CARPENTER, Emanuel. Pvt. under Capt. George W. Ent, 24 Aug - 1 Sep 1814.

CARPENTER, John. Pvt., 14th U.S. Inf. At enlist.: 5 ft 4 or 7 inches; grey or dark eyes, dark hair and dark complexion; age 16 or 17; farmer; b. Frederick or Washington Co.; enlisted 26 May 1812 at Cumberland, MD, by Lt. Nelson. In Boston 2 May 1814. Prisoner of war exchange 15 Apr 1814. Greenbush on 1 Mar and 30 Apr, 1815. Capt. Alex. Cummings' Company, 4th U.S. Inf., Annapolis 31 Aug 1815. Deserted from Fort Severn 16 Jul 1815.

CARPENTER, Solomon. Pvt. under Capt. Samuel Duvall, 3 Aug - 3 Oct 1814.

CARR, Thomas. Pvt. under Capt. Philip Smith, 23 May - 8 Sep 1813, [according to our transcription of the muster roll]. However note in bounty land files states he served "from 23rd to 31st May 1813"; b. c.1781. Res. Chillicothe in Ros(?) Co., OH, in 1851.
Source: Bounty land claim.

CARTER, Joseph. Pvt. under Capt. Thomas Contee Worthington; joined 17 Aug 1812; deserted 5 Sep 1812. [FCml issued to Joseph Carter and Catherine Fisher 16 May 1805.]

CARTER, William. Pvt. under Capt. Samuel Ogle, 1 May - 5 Jul 1813.

CARTNAIL, Jacob. Pvt. under Capt. Barton Hackney, 1 Sep - 27 Oct 1814. [FCml issued Jacob Cartnail and Eleanor Brookover 2 Mar 1807.]

CARTY, James. Pvt. under Capt. Jacob Alexander, 22 Jul - 19 Sep 1814.

CARTY, John. Pvt. under Capt. Jacob Alexander, 22 Jul- 19 Sep 1814. [FCml issued to John Carty and Margaret Holtz 21 May 1816.]

CARVEL, William. Pvt. under Capt. Magee; joined 22 Jul 1814; deserted 29 Jul 1814.

CARY, Cyrus. 2nd corpl. under Capt. Worthington, 17 Aug - 31 Dec 1812. Promoted to 4th sergt. on 22 Sep. [Cyrus Cary, formerly of Fredericktown, m. Miss Mary Arbuckle of Lewisburg, Greenbriar Co., VA, 22 Jul 1824; he d. Lewisburg, 1 Apr 1832 in his 38th year.]
Sources: **Engelbrecht Diary**: 1:286, 2:6.

FREDERICK COUNTY MILITIA IN THE WAR OF 1812

CARY, Joseph. Pvt. under Capt. Denton Darby, 3 Aug - 8 Nov 1814.

CASEY, Jason. Pvt. under Capt. Dawson; joined 21 Jul 1814; deserted 8 Dec 1814.

CASNER [Cassner], Jacob. Pvt. under Capt. Samuel Ogle, 1 May - 5 Jul 1813 and 3rd corpl. under Capt. William Durbin, Jr., 24 Aug - 27 Oct 1814. [FCml issued to Jacob Casner and Eleanor Swales 18 Dec 1815.]

CASNER, John. From New Windsor; pvt. under Capt. Magee, 22 Jul 1814 - 10 Jan 1815.

CASNER [Cassner], John. From New Windsor; pvt. under Capt. Samuel Dawson, 21 Jul - 13 Oct 1814.

CASS. See Coss.

CASTLE, Eli. Pvt. under Capt. Daniel Marker, 25 Aug - 27 Oct 1814, as substitute for John McNeil [McNeal]; b. c.1793; res. Brownsville, MD, 1855; d. 12 Nov 1869 near Brownsville, Washington Co., age 76 yrs, 11 mos., 7 days. Acq. (1855): George Bear, in same company, and Joseph Ramsburg who served in company of Capt. Shawen, in same regt., rcs. Frcd. Co. [FCml: Ely Castle and Nancy Brown, 8 May 1819]

Sources: Bounty land claim, 55-120-15293; (Frederick) Examiner, 24 Nov 1869; Md. Union, 25 Nov 1869.

CASTLE, Elisha. Pvt. under Capt. Samuel Dawson, 21 Jul 1814 - 10 Jan 1815.

CASTLE, George V. Pvt. under Capt. James Neal in a company of regular troops, 36th U.S. Inf. His widow said he enlisted at Fred. Co., MD, c.14 Sep 1813; discharged at Balt. around 14 Sep 1814; participated in Battle of Bladensburg; m. Catharine Horine (b. c.1786) 4 Dec 1805 [the date given by widow] in Fredericktown by Rev. Craver. [A marr. license was issued to George Castle and Catharine Horine on 22 Nov 1806.] George V. Castle d. 7 Jul 1850 in Butler Co., OH. Widow res. Cass Co., IN, 1854, 1855, 1871 (Logansport, Hamon Twp). On 1 Apr 1855 Catharine Castle mailed a warrant for 160 acres of bounty land to Noah Castle, authorizing him to locate the land. It never reached the destination [confirmed by Noah Castle, age 42 in 1855, res. Cass Co.]. Witnesses: 1855 - Sarah A. Castle and Catherine Cafry. Acq.: 1855 - Noah Castle, age 42, res. Cass Co.; Sarah A. Castle and Catherine Cafry. 1871 - Joseph McCoy and Thomas P. Castle, acq. for 20 and 45 yrs, resp.

Sources: Pension --; Bounty land claim, 50-160-26971.

CASTLE, John H. P. 2nd sergt. under Capt. Daniel Shawen, 5 Sep - 27 Oct 1814; b. 1786; res. Bond Co., IL 1850 and Jamestown, Clinton Co., IL, 1855.

Source: Bounty land claim, 55-120-40133.

CASY, Daniel. Pvt. under Capt. Daniel Shawen, 5 Sep - 27 Oct 1814.

CAUGH, Balser. Mbr. of Crawford's "company."

CAUGH, David. Mbr. of Crawford's "company."

CAUGH, Jacob. Mbr. of Crawford's "company."

THE VETERANS

CAYWOOD [Cawood], Thomas. Pvt. under George W. Ent, 24 Aug - 30 Sep 1814; as substitute for Samuel Fleming; b. 16 Apr 1793; m. 29 Sep 1822 Fredericktown Hannah Huffer (b. 12 Feb 1803), by Rev. McCally, first marr. for both; he d. 1 Oct 1871 in Farmington, IL, of cancer under his right arm, affecting his lungs (according to John Gregory, M.D.). When enrolled: a shoe-maker; auburn hair, blue eyes, light complexion; res. Peoria Co., IL, 1851 and 1855; res. Peoria Co. (P.O. address: Farmington, Fulton Co.), IL, 1871; res. Farmington, IL, 1878 and Bradford, IL in 1886. Thomas and Hannah Caywood had res. MD and OH, previously. Acq. Catharine Watson, aged 52, 21 Jan 1879, quoted fol. from family bible: their children: William Caywood b. 5 Jul 1823; Mahjala Caywood b. 18 Dec 1824; Catherin Caywood b. 17 Apr 1826; Joseph Caywood b. 25 Feb 1828; Elizabeth Caywood b. 6 Dec 1829; Thomas Caywood b. 1 Jul 1831; John Caywood b. 13 Jun 1833; Samuel Caywood b. 28 Dec 1837; Martin Caywood b. 5 Nov 1841; William Caywood d. 1 Oct 1823. Acq.: 1871 - John McClallen and David R. Gregory, res. Peoria, IL. 1878 - Catharine Watson, age 52 and Abraham Marant, age 79, both res. Farmington, IL. 1887 - Samuel Caywood, age 50, gunsmith, son of Hannah Caywood, states his mother d. Bradford, IL, 6 Feb 1886; he paid expenses of her last illness, funeral, erected tomb-stone. Telegram from E. D. Christman, dated 6 Feb 1886, to Samuel Caywood, Bradford, IL, stated, "Mother died this morning at three thirty, inform Christr. [Christy?] and Frank Christman." Letter in file from Miss Alta Chrisman, 3051 Starr St., Lincoln, NE, dated 30 Jul 1923, regarding service in War of 1812 of Thomas Caywood of MD and George P. Chrisman of Berkeley Co, VA. She said that Thomas Caywood res. Dayton and Sandusky, OH, then Farmington, IL.
Sources: Pensions, SO11073, SC11034, WO25187, WC19066; Bounty land claims, 50-40-54358, 55-120-44940.

CEARLY [Searly], Joseph. Pvt. and corpl. under Capt. Daniel Marker, 16 Aug - 18 Sep 1813.

CEASE, John. Pvt., 12th U.S. Inf. At enlistment: 5 ft, 5 1/2 inches; grey eyes; black hair and dark complexion; age 20, laborer; b. Fred. Co., MD; enlisted 19 20 May 1812 at Middletown by Lt. Morgan to serve until 19 May 1817. Mustered by Capt. Andrew L. Madison's Company, Burlington, 28 Feb 1814. Prisoner of war from Halifax; d. 1 Dec 1814 Buffalo of an accident.

CECIL, Henry B. Served in the 19th U.S. Inf., under Col. Jno. Miller. At enlistment: 5 ft, 11 inches; black eyes, dark hair, fair complexion; age 31; blacksmith; b. Fred. Co., MD; enlisted 2 or 4 Apr 1814 at Detroit by Lt. Atchison for 5 yrs or duration of war; mustered at Chillicothe, OH, 30 Apr 1814; discharged from Capt. James Herron's Company, 17th U.S. Inf. at Chillicothe, OH, 9 Jun 1815 as sergt.

CHAMBERLAIN, Walter. Pvt. under Capt. Fonsten, 2 Sep - 27 Oct 1814. Sick absent on 3 Oct 1814.

FREDERICK COUNTY MILITIA IN THE WAR OF 1812

CHAMPER, John. 1st corpl., later as pvt., under Capt. Joseph Wood; joined 27 Aug 1814; deserted 23 Oct 1814.

CHANEY, Charles J. Pvt. under Capt. Samuel Dawson, 1 May - 5 Jul 1813.

CHANEY, Elijah. Pvt. under Denton Darby; joined 3 Aug 1814; deserted 22 Aug 1814; b. c.1787; m(1) c.7 May 1813 Mary Flemming; m(2) c.20 Nov 1833 Aurella Aldrige, "on Mr. Dorsey's farm," Fred. Co., by Rev. James Higgins. At enlist.: 5 ft, 2 inches; light hair, hazel eyes, light complexion; fol. discharge he res. Fred. Co. near New Market; res. Fred. Co., MD, in 1850. [FCml was issued to Elijah Chaney and Mary Fleming on 7 May 1813 and to Elijah Cheney and Corrilla Aldridge 8 Feb 1825.] In 1869 Elijah Chaney of Mt. Airy, MD, assigned power of attorney to William Van Marter & Co., because of "want of education and blindness." He d. 10 Mar 1871 at Plane No. 4, MD. In 1878 Aurella Chaney res. Frederick Co, MD, No. 4, Balt. and Ohio Railroad.

Sources: Pension, WO25324 (rejected 9 Apr 1878 because of desertion); Bounty land claim, 55-rejected-156754 (separate from pension file); FCml.

CHANEY, John. Appt'd 16 Mar 1812, 2nd Lieut under Capt. Edward G. Williams.

CHARLES, Negro. Servant to the lieut. colonel, 1st Regt., 14 Oct 1814 - 10 Jan 1815; discharged at Annapolis.

CHEW, William. Pvt. under Capt. Dawson, 1 May - 5 Jul 1813.

CHEW, William. Pvt. under Capt. Samuel Duvall, 3 Aug - 3 Oct 1814.

CHEW, William. Pvt. under Capt. Fonsten; joined 2 Sep 1814; deserted 6 Sep 1814.

CHRIST [Crist], Jacob. Corpl. under Capt. Samuel Duvall, 3 Aug - 3 Oct 1814; b. 22 Sep 1789; gun stock maker of Graceham, m. 14 Mar 1809, Christina Leinbach (b. 24 Feb 1787, d. 23 May 1842), dau of Christian and Anna Rosina Leinbach. Their children: John Rudolph b. 11 Oct 1809; Anna Sophia b. 27 Jan 1812; William Henry b. 24 Nov 1813; Israel b. 29 Dec 1815; Anna Juliana b. 16 Jan 1818, m. George Hosler; Maria Elizabeth b. 2 Aug 1820; Charlotte Emilia b. 12 Oct 1822; Rebecca Louisa b. 18 Apr 1825; Henrietta Angelica b. 27 Aug 1827. Bur. Uniontown, Ch. of God Cem. are fol. members of family: Jacob Christ, 22 Sep 1789 - 30 Nov 1872; wife Elizabeth d. 16 May 1867 age 68 yrs, 10 mos., 12 days; son Jesse B., 16 Apr 1836 - 16 Feb 1858.

Sources: **Moravian Families of Graceham, Md.; Names in Stone; Carroll County, Md. 1860 Census Index.**

CHURCHHILL, Israel. Pvt., 35th U.S. Inf., under Col. Joseph Goodwyn. At enlist.: 5 ft, 5 1/2 inches or 5 ft, 7 inches; grey eyes, dark hair, dark complexion; age 22 or 23, farmer; b. Fred. Co. Enlisted 14 Feb 1812 at Craney Island by Lt. Williams for duration of war. Discharged Norfolk 15 Mar 1815.

CLABAUGH, Jacob. Pvt. under Capt. William Knox, 26 Aug 1814; deserted 15 Sep 1814. [Bur. Taneytown Ref. Ch. is Jacob Clabaugh, age 48 - **no dates given.**]

FREDERICK COUNTY MILITIA IN THE WAR OF 1812

CLABAUGH [Claybaugh], Thomas. Pvt. under Capt. Fonsten, 2 Sep - 27 Oct 1814; res. 9 miles from Westminster. 1850 census of 5th E.D.: Thomas Clabaugh, Sr., 64; Mary Clabaugh, 63; John Clabaugh, 37, harness maker.
Source: **Bridge in Time**.

CLANTZ [Clants], Charles. Pvt. under Capt. Philip Smith, 29 May - 8 Sep 1813; also pvt. in Capt. Creagar's company in Hood's Regt.; b. c.1786; m. Mary Ann Catharine Andes 21 Mar 1825 in Frederick Co, MD; res. Perry Township, Tuscavras Co., OH 1850, alive in 1872. Witnesses: Buzaleel (?) Steel and Andrew Steel.
Sources: Pension, SO27543, SC19062; Bounty land claims, 50-80-15600, 55-80-13978.

CLAPSADDLE, Michael. Sergt. under Capt. Zacharias, 7 Aug - 10 Sep 1814, in 2nd Regt., 1st Cav. Dist.; b. c.1771; res. Carroll Co., MD, 1852 and 1855. Acq.(1855): Basil Hayden and Jacob Grove who served in same company.
Source: Bounty land claim, 55-120-6912.

CLAPSADDLE, Paul. Pvt., 14th U.S. Inf., under Capt. Samuel Lane and Col. C.Boerstler. At enlistment: 5 ft, 11 inches; grey eyes, light hair, fair complexion; age 21, blacksmith; b. Woodsboro, MD; enlisted 6 Jun 1812 at Westminster/Winchester by Lt. Gist until 6 Jun 1817. Fort Severn on 30 Jun 1815. Deserted from Fort Severn 15 Jul 1815.

CLARK, John. Pvt. under Capt. Samuel Dawson; joined 10 Sep 1814; deserted 29 Oct 1814.

CLARK, Jonah [Josiah?]. Pvt. under Capt. Samuel Dawson, 21 Jul 1814 - 10 Jan 1815.

CLARK, Levi. Pvt. under Capt. Denton Darby, 3 Aug - 8 Nov 1814. Absent 6 days.

CLARK, Richard. Corpl. under Capt. Philip Smith, 23 May - 8 Sep 1813; Commissioned ensign in Denton Darby's company, 13th Regt., MM 10 Dec 1813; promoted to lieut. 10 Sep 1814; served under Capt. Denton Darby, 3 Aug - 8 Nov 1814. According to him he served under Capt. Darby and Eli Brashers; m. 30 Dec 1813, Fred. Co. Martha Basford (b. c.1788) by James Day, Meth. minister; d. Center Township, Guernsey Co., OH, 22 Apr 1850. They had fol. children: Martha Ann b. 7 Apr 1815, m. --- Cunningham; Margaret b. 18 Feb 1821; John Henry b. 16 Aug 1822; Arthur[?] Younzey b. 19 Dec 1823; Rhoday b. 19 Dec 1825; Richard, Jr. b. 13 Oct 1827; Mary b. 19 Mar 1830; Ann Maria b. 9 Jan 1832 (dec'd. as of 29 Sep 1852). Martha Clark res. Washington, Guernsey Co., OH, 1850.

CLARK, Richard. Pvt., 5th U.S. Inf., under Capt. Dale and Col. D. Bissell. At enlistment: 5 ft, 4 1/2 inches; dark eyes, black hair, fair complexion; farmer; b. Fred. Co. Mustered at New Orleans on 4 May 1809. Tried for desertion, acquitted 24 Jun 1809. Court martial in Capt. Bankhead's company 23 Oct 1810 for loading musket without orders, sentenced to receive 25 lashes, pardoned. Appears to have again enlisted on 6 or 13 Apr 1812 at Frederick by Capt. Johnson for 5 yrs at age 21. Mustered in

FREDERICK COUNTY MILITIA IN THE WAR OF 1812

Capt. Dorman's company at Ft George, NC, 31 Aug 1813. Buffalo [NY] on 28 Feb and 30 Apr 1815. Fort Crawford 28 Feb 1817. Re-enlisted.

CLARK, Thomas S. Corpl., 22nd U.S. Inf., under Col. Hugh Brady. At enlistment: 5 ft, 8 inches; blue eyes, sandy hair, fair complexion; age 25; laborer; b. Franklin Co., PA, or Fred. Co., MD. Enlisted 23 Mar 1814, Chambersburg by Lt. J. Culbertson, until 23 Mar 1819. Mustered at Pittsburg 30 Apr 1814. Wounded at Williamsville. Sacketts Harbor 30 Dec 1814. Left sick at Williamsville since 26 Oct 1814. Discharged from Hospital 8 Nov 1814. Deserted.

CLARKE, Hugh. Pvt. under Capt. Thomas Contee Worthington, 17 Aug - 31 Dec 1812.

CLARY [Clairy], Adin. Enlisted regular army 21 May 1814 by Lt. Jaquet for 5 yrs. At enlistment: 5 ft, 11 inches, black eyes, black hair, dark complexion, age 38, laborer, b. Fred. Co., MD. Pvt. in 4th U.S. Rifles under Capt. J. Kean; mustered 28 Feb 1815 Conjoiquita Creek, as absent sick at General Hospital; d. hospital 30 Apr 1815.

CLARY, Daniel. Pvt. under Capt. Fonsten; joined 2 Sep 1814; deserted 20 Sep 1814.

CLARY, Nathaniel. Pvt. under Capt. Basil Dorsey, during period, 30 Jul - 27 Sep 1814; b. c.1786; res. Noble Co., IN, 1851.

Source: Bounty land claim, 50-40-81382.

CLARY, Samuel. Pvt. under Capt. Fonsten, 2 Sep - 27 Oct 1814; "sick absent," on 16 Sep.

CLARY [Cleary], Zachariah. Pvt., 19th U.S. Inf., under Col. George Paull. At enlistment: 5 ft, 11 inches or 5 ft, 11 3/4 inches; dark or grey eyes, dark hair, dark complexion; age 34; tailor; b. Fred. Co. Enlisted 29 Sep 1814 at Franklinton by Lt. Granger for 5 yrs. In Capt. George Kissling's company on 16 Feb 1815. Deserted near Springfield, OH, 16 Sep 1815.

CLAY, Henry. Mbr. of Crawford's "company."

CLEMSON, James. Appt'd capt. of artillery company, attached to 7th Brigade.

CLINE, ---. Pvt. under Jacob Getzendanner, 26 Jul - 21 Aug 1814.

CLINE [Klein], Casper. Pvt. under George W. Ent, 24 Aug - 30 Sep 1814; b. Hanover, PA, 1795, son of Alexander; d. 18 Apr 1871, age 76, of pneumonia; mbr. Meth. Ch.; m(1) Catherine Evans dau of Robert Evans; she d. 8 Aug 1854, age 56. He m(2) Corilla Evans sister to first wife; she was b. 12 Apr 1801, d. 24 Nov 1882 at age 81, of congestion of the heart. Casper and both wives bur. Mt. Olivet Cem. Fredericktown 1850 census: Casper Cline, 55, tanner, b. PA, Catherine Cline, 50, b. MD; Nicholas Cline, 15, b. MD; Currilla Evans, 40; Harriet Crum, 32; Edward L. Crum, 7; Caspar Crum, 7; Isaac Crum, 5.

Sources: **Names in Stone; Bridge in Time; (Frederick) Examiner,** 19 Apr 1871, 29 Oct 1881, 29 Nov 1882; **Md. Union,** 20 Apr 1871; Williams, **Hist. of Fred. Co.**

CLINE, Charles. Appt'd lieut.; d. before 27 Jan 1816.

THE VETERANS

CLINE, Frederick. Pvt. under Capt. Barton Hackney; joined 1 Sep 1814; deserted 14 Sep 1814. Frederick Kline, veteran of the War of 1812, d. 28 Jul 1876 near Rocky Springs School House, age c.86 yrs. Article in the Examiner relates an incident on the anniversary of Washington's birthday, in the hoisting of the flag, which "delved upon the two older soldiers of the late Second War of Independence, Mr. Frederick Cline of this vicinity, and his veteran bro., now living in Ohio. ..." [The 1850 census of Fred. Co. shows a Frederick Kline and a Frederick Cline.]
Sources: **Bridge in Time;** (Frederick) **Examiner,** 27 Feb 1861, 2 Aug 1876.

CLINE [Kline], Philip. He said he served as musician in Capt. Marker's company, enrolling at Myerville c.18 Jul 1812; discharged c.30 Sep 1812, Frederick; b. 1787 in Germany and d. age 85 (according to *Williams*); m. 16 May 1808, Elizabeth Ambrose (23 Nov 1791 - 1 May 1856) at Middletown. Philip Cline d. 13 Mar 1874, bur. Ellerton St. John's Luth. Ch. His P.O. address, 1873: Elerton, Fred. Co. Acq.: 1873 - Ernst A. C. Fox.
Sources: Pension, SO29293 (Rejected 16 Oct 1873); Williams, **Hist. of Fred. Co.,** p. 1142; **Names in Stone; Bridge in Time.**

CLINEFERBURCK, Cornelius. Pvt. under Capt. Samuel Ogle, 1 May - 5 Jul 1813.

CLINGAN, William. Pvt. under Capt. William Knox, 26 Aug - 27 Oct 1814. [FCml issued to William Clingan and Elizabeth McGuffin 16 Mar 1815.]

CLINK, Andrew. Enlisted in regular army 3 Oct 1814 by Lt. Kline for 5 yrs. Pvt. in 22nd U.S. Inf. under Capt. Jack Carmack. At enlistment: 5 ft, 7 inches, brown eyes, sandy hair, dark complexion, age 39, weaver, b. Fred. Co., MD. Mustered Fort Fayette 31 Dec 1814 and Plattsburgh, NY, 28 Feb 1815, absent, deserted 12 Nov 1814.

CLOPPER, Andrew M. 4th sergt. under Capt. Barton Hackney, 1 Sep - 27 Oct 1814; from Balt. to home - 58 miles; b. c.1792; res. Hamilton Co., OH, 1852.
Source: Bounty land claim, 50-40-73903

CLOPPER, Nicholas. Pvt. under Lieut. William Kolb, guarding British prisoners at Frederick Barracks, 25 Oct - 15 Nov 1814.

COAKER, Walter. Res. New Windsor; pvt. under Capt. George W. Magee, 22 Jul 1814 - 10 Jan 1815.

COBLENTS [Coblentz], Jacob. Pvt. under Capt. William Knox; joined 26 Aug 1814; discharged by doctor 8 Sep 1814. [A FCml issued to Dr. Jacob Coblentz and Malinda Staley on 22 Nov 1819.]

[A chancery case in 1824 states that John Ecard, by his last will devised to Magdalena Buffington, his sister, part Maryland Tract, in fee. Magdalena d. intestate and left fol. persons her heirs: Henry Ecard, John Coblentz and Elizabeth his wife, Peter Coblentz and Catharine Coblentz, the children of Jacob Coblentz, Barbara Renner, wife of Solomon Renner, Catharine Elizabeth M'Crea, Ann Mary M'Crea, Margaret Jane M'Crea and James Wil-

FREDERICK COUNTY MILITIA IN THE WAR OF 1812

liam Thomson M'Crea. John Coblentz and his wife, Jacob Coblentz, Peter Coblentz and Catharine Coblentz res. OH at that time.]

COCHRAN, James. 5th sergt. under Capt. Samuel Duvall, 3 Aug - 3 Oct 1814.

COCHRAN, James. From Upper Fred. Co.; pvt. under Capt. James F. Huston/Capt. Joseph Green; joined 23 Jul 1814; enlisted 3 Nov 1814. [FCml issued to James Cochran and Rachel Bradfield 23 Mar 1815.]

COCHRAN, John. Pvt. under Capt. Knox, 26 Aug - 30 Oct 1814. [FCml issued to John Cochran and Rachel Starling 26 Mar 1801.]

COCKEY, John C. Cornet in the company of Capt. Zacharias, 7 Aug - 10 Sep 1814, 2nd Regt., 1st Cav. Dist.

COFFMAN [Caufman], Christian. Enlisted in regular army 16 Jun 1813 by Capt. J. Rothrock for 1 year. At enlistment: 5 ft, 10 inches, dark eyes, dark hair, dark complexion, butcher, b. Fredericktown, MD. Pvt. in 38th U.S. Inf. Sent to Hospital sick Oct 1813. Appears to have re-enlisted 20 Feb 1814 at Craney Island by Capt. Rothrock for duration of war, at age 22. Promoted to corpl. Discharged at Craney Island 15 Mar 1815.

COLBERT, Joseph. Pvt. from Washington Co. under Capt. Daniel Shawen; joined 5 Sep 1814; deserted 13 Oct 1814.

COLE, Enser. From New Windsor; pvt. under George W. Magee; joined 22 Jul 1814; deserted 6 Dec 1814.

COLE, Humphrey. Pvt. under Capt. Thomas Contee Worthington, 17 Aug - 31 Dec 1812.

COLE [Coale], William. Pvt. under Capt. Samuel Dawson, 14 Oct 1814 - 10 Jan 1815.

COLEGATE, George. Appt'd surgeon 23 Apr 1813, 20th Regt., MM.

COLELASURE, Abraham. Pvt. under Capt. Brengle; joined 25 Aug 1814; deserted. [On 27 Jul 1797 Abraham Colgazier, age 12 on 18 Feb 1798, with consent of mother Mary Colgazier, was bound to Frederick Rool of Fredericktown, weaver, til age 21.]
Source: West. Md. Genealogy.

COLLENS, Mathew. Pvt. from Washington Co., under Capt. Daniel Shawen, 5 Sep - 27 Oct 1814.

COLLIFLOWER, George. Pvt. under Capt. Joseph Wood, 27 Aug - 28 Oct 1814.

COLLIFLOWER, Michael. Pvt. under Capt. Joseph Wood, 27 Aug - 28 Oct 1814; b. 1790; m. c.1820 Mary Bowers at Frederick Co., MD; res. New Castle, Henry Co., IN 1871. Acq.: Benjamin Parrish and Priscilla Bumpers, both res. Henry Co., IN.
Source: Pension, SO11789 (rejected for want of proof of loyalty during civil war); FCml.

COLLIFLOWER, Samuel. Pvt. under Capt. Joseph Wood, 27 Aug - 28 Oct 1814; b. c.1792; m(1) Hannah Reichart 11 Dec 1822; m(2) Susannah Hay, 26 Nov 1843 in Woodsfield, Monroe Co., OH; res. Guernsey Co., OH, 1850 and Beaver Twp, Noble Co., OH, 1872; d. 26

Apr 1872; widow d. 27 Sep 1894. Acq.: Philip Finley and Nathan House.
Sources: Pension, SO21990, SC13792, WO35239, WC23930; Bounty land claim: 50-40-25223, 55-120-44529.

COLLINGER, Phillip. Pvt. under Capt. Daniel Shawen, 5 Sep - 27 Oct 1814.

COLLINS, Daniel. Orderly sergt. under Capt. Hall, 7 Aug - 10 Sep 1814; b. c.1781; res. Montgomery Co., MD, 1850, 1855.
Source: Bounty land claim, 55-120-29896.

COLLINS, Elijah. Pvt. under Capt. Samuel Dawson, 1 May - 5 Jul 1813.

COLLINS, James. Pvt., 12th U.S. Infantry, under Capt. Thomas Post and Col. Cole. At enlistment: 5 feet, 6 inches; grey eyes, black hair; age 18; tanner; b. Frederick Co.; enlisted 4 Feb 1814 at Washington Co., MD by Capt. Post for 5 yrs or duration of the war. Buffalo [NY] on 16 Feb, 28 Feb and 30 Apr, 1815. Discharged at Buffalo on 20 Jun 1815, procured a substitute.

COLWELL, Charles. Pvt. under Capt. Daniel Shawen; joined 5 Sep 1814; discharged 11 Oct 1814.

COLWELL, David. Pvt. under Capt. Galt, 31 Aug - 27 Oct 1814. Sick absent 15 Oct.

CONDON, Edward. Pvt. under Capt. Joseph Wood, 27 Aug - 28 Oct 1814.

CONDON, Thomas. Pvt. from Mechanickstown under Capt. Philip Smith, 23 May - 8 Sep 1813; "transferred" 23 Sep 1814 to Capt. George W. Magee and reduced from corpl. to pvt.

CONNER, Aquila. Pvt. under Capt. Jacob Alexander, 22 Jul - 19 Sep 1814; b. c.1782 - 1786; m. Martha White (b. c.1795) 19 Oct 1814 by Rev. James Day, M.E. Ch., at her father's house near New Market; res. Jeromeville, Ashland Co., OH, 1850, Wootten, Wayne Co., OH, 1855. Acq.: 1871 - Emanuel Schuckers, Pittsburg Ave, Wooster; and Amanda M. Miller, Liberty St., Wooster.
Sources: Pension, WO731 (rejected 4 May 1872 - lack of evidence); Bounty land claim: 55-120-22526.

CONNER, James Pvt. under Capt. Jacob Alexander, 22 Jul - 19 Sep 1814. [On 29 May 1795 James Conner, free mulatto, son of Peggy Conner, age 2 yrs on Apr 1795, bound to Michael Hardman, blacksmith, until age 21.]
Source: West. Md. Genealogy.

CONNER, Thomas. Pvt. from Fredericktown under Capt. Huston/ Capt. Green, 23 Jul 1814; furloughed from 4 Oct 1814; 1850 census.

CONNER, Thomas. Pvt. under Capt. Daniel Marker, 25 Aug - 27 Oct 1814.

CONNER, Thomas. [prob. one of the above], veteran of the War of 1812 (b. c.1798) m. Catherine --- (b. c.1792.); she d. 26 Dec 1861, age 63 yrs, 11 mos, 4 days; bur. M.E. cem.
Source: (Frederick) Examiner, 1 Jan 1862.

CONNER, William. Pvt. under George W. Ent, 24 Aug - 30 Sep 1814.

CONRAD, Crisher. See Coonrod Crisher.

CONRAD [Conradt], Joseph. Pvt. from Fredericktown under Capt. James

FREDERICK COUNTY MILITIA IN THE WAR OF 1812

F. Huston/Capt. Joseph Green; joined 23 Jul 1814; deserted 21 Dec 1814; returned 2 Jan 1815; discharged 10 Jan 1815; d. 8 Feb 1861 in his 72nd year; bur. Luth cem. [Elizabeth wife of Joseph Conrad, d. 14 Aug 1851, age 52 yrs, 3 mos., 14 days; bur. Mt. Olivet.]
Source: (Frederick) Examiner, 13 Feb 1861.

COOK, Benjamin. Pvt. under Capt. Nicholas Turbutt, 1 Sep - 27 Oct 1814.

COOK, John. Pvt. under Capt. Samuel Dawson, 26 Jul - 13 Oct 1814.

COOK, John. Appt'd 13 Feb 1812 as capt. of a troop of horse; promoted 18 Sep 1812, Major of 2nd Regt., 1st Cav. Dist.; promoted to lieut. col. in place of Henry Kemp 21 Dec 1814.

COOK, John. Appt'd 3 Oct 1807 as capt. of a company, 13th Regt., MM.

COOK, Thomas. Pvt. under Capt. Fonsten, 2 Sep - 27 Oct 1814.

COOKERLY, William. Appt'd 23 Apr 1808 as 2nd lieut. of a company of light dragoons under Capt. Elie Phillips. The *Frederick-Town Herald* announced the death of Major William Cookerly, aged about 45 yrs on Wednesday, 20 Aug 1823. He left a wife and six children.
Sources: Frederick-Town Herald, 30 Aug 1823; Englebrecht Diary, v.1, 233.

COOLEY, James. Pvt. under Capt. Barton Hackney; joined 1 Sep 1814; sick in hospital 15 Sep 1814.

COOLEY, Joseph. Pvt. from Upper Frederick Co., under James F. Huston and Green; joined 23 Jul 1814; missing from 24 Aug 1814.

COOMES, John. Mbr. of Crawford's "company."

COOMES, William. 1st sergt. under Capt. George W. Magee, 23 Jul - 13 Oct 1814. [FCml issued to William Coomes and Elizabeth Green 6 May 1814.]

COOPER, John. Pvt. from Mechanickstown under Capt. George W. Magee, 23 Jul - 25 Nov 1814; discharged on 25 Nov as over age; b. c.1769 Fr. Co.; res. 5th E.D., Fr. Co.
Source: Bridge in Time.

COOSHING, Joseph. Mbr. of Crawford's "company.".

COOSIX [or Coosin], Joseph. Pvt. from Baltimore Town under Capt. George W. Magee, 22 Jul 1814 - 10 Jan 1815.

COPENHAVER, Jacob. Appt'd 1st lieut. 13 Jul 1814 under Capt. John Matthias, 20th Regt., MM.; served as 1st lieut. under Capt. Funsten, 2 Sep - 27 Oct 1814.

COPENHAVER, John. Pvt. under Capt. Nicholas Turbutt, 1 Sep - 27 Oct 1814. [FCml issued to John Copenhaver and Barbara Miller 19 Jun 1790.]

COPENHAVER, William. Pvt. from New Windsor under Capt. George W. Magee; joined 22 Jul 1814; deserted 6 Dec 1814.

COPLAND, Samuel. Pvt. under Capt. Daniel Marker, 25 Aug - 27 Oct 1814. [Bur. at Buckeystown, Cath. St. Joseph's Carrollton Manor Cath. Ch.: Samuel B. Copelin, d. 31 Oct 1822, age 29, wife Elizabeth 28 Dec 1839, age 44 yrs, 14 days.]
Source: Names in Stone.

COPPERSMITH, Jacob. Pvt. under Capt. Zacharias, 7 Aug - 10 Sep 1814, 2nd Regt., 1st Cav. Dist.; m. 15 Apr 1797

THE VETERANS

Elizabeth Mason in Fred. Co., by Rev. Darnel Shrader, Luth. preacher; d. 18 Dec 1846, Carroll Co. Widow res. Carroll Co. 1855. Family Bible lost in a fire c.1825. Bur. at McKinstrys Mill, Sams Creek Meth. Prot. Ch.: Jacob Coppersmith, 15 Dec 1845, age 66; wife Elizabeth, 28 Jan 1860, age 77. Acq.(1855): George Lippy, John Froock, res. Carroll Co.
Sources: Bounty land claim, 55-160-23816; Names in Stone.

CORBIN, Nicholas. Pvt. under Capt. Zacharias, 7 Aug - 10 Sep 1814, 2nd Reg., 1st Cav. Dist. [6 Jun 1805 - Nicholas Corbin son of Edward Corbin was bound to John Watson, house painter and glazier, until age of 21.]
Source: West. Md. Genealogy, 6:2.

CORCORAN, John. 1st sergt. under Capt. Joseph Wood, 27 Aug - 28 Oct 1814.

CORD, Stephen. Pvt., 5th U.S. Inf., under Col. D. Bissell. At enlistment: 5 feet, 8 inches; blue eyes, light hair, fair complexion; age 27; shoemaker; b. Fred. Co.; enlisted 29 Jan 1812 at Hagerstown by Lt. Miller for 5 yrs. Mustered by Capt. Green's company, 3rd U.S. Inf., Detroit, 31 Oct 1815. Discharged at Michelmackinac 26 Jan 1817.

CORNEL [Cornell], Richard. Pvt. under Capt. John Galt, 31 Aug - 27 Oct 1814; b. c.1776; res. 5 miles of Taneytown 1814; res. Guernsey Co., OH, 1850, 1855. Acq.: 1855 - Robert Kirkwood and Abraham Armstrong.
Source: Bounty land claim: 55-120-79769.

CORNELL, Smith. Appt'd 22 May 1812 as capt. of a company in 47th Regt., MM.

CORNELL, Thomas. Pvt. under Capt. Knox, 26 Aug - 27 Oct 1814.

CORRELL, Christian. He said he served under Capt. Isaac Dern and Capt. Farquhar; drafted in Capt. Isaac Dern's company and then went with Capt. Farquhar into Col. Ragan's regt. around 1 Jun 1814 and after the Battle of Bladensburg he transferred to Capt. Weaver's company and then to an Allegany County company. [No roll of Capt. Lewis Weaver's company in the pension office. b. c.1795; m(1) 11 Jun 1818 Elizabeth Gillilan [Gilleland, Gillan] at her father's house; she d. at Bridgeport 25 Dec 1856; later m(2) Mary E. Smith (b. c.1827) near Bridgeport in Carroll Co., 9 Mar 1865 by R. S. Grear, Presby. minister. At enlistment: 18 yrs old; dark brown hair, light blue eyes, fair complexion; 6 ft, 1 inch; d. at Bridgeport 6 Nov 1875; widow res. Bridgeport, Frederick Co., 1878. Acq.: Felix B. Taney, age 81, res. Emmitsburg; remembered that Christian Correll served under Capt. Lewis Weaver. Taney visited the company while they were at Baltimore in Camp. Christian lived halfway between Emmitsburg and Taneytown. Also appeared was Samuel Barton, age 79, res. Emmitsburg. In 1812 and 1814 he res. Taneytown; pvt. under Capt. John Galt; remembers Capt. Ward's company, Capt. Creager's company, Capt. Fulton's company and Capt. Weaver's company.

FREDERICK COUNTY MILITIA IN THE WAR OF 1812

Source: Pension, SO13588. Suspended for want of proof of service. WO24140. Rejected 5/23/79.

COSNEL [Gosnell?], Richard. Pvt. under Capt. Galt, 31 Aug 1814.

COSS, Peter. Pvt. from Washington Co., under Capt. Samuel Dawson, 14 Oct 1814 - 10 Jan 1815; b. c.1792; m. Susanna Tritt (b. c.1790) at Maryland Tract 14 Apr 1811 by Rev. Bond. [FCml issued to Peter Coss and Susanna Tritt 12 Apr 1811.] He res. Columbiana Co., OH, 1850, 1855; d. 15 Apr 1866 Columbiana Co.; widow res. Columbiana Co., OH (P.O. Dungannon) 1874. Acq.: 1874 - Hiram Gaver, acq. 18 yrs prior to death of Peter Coss, and B. C. Iden - both res. Columbiana Co.

Sources: Pension, WO11016, WC6380; Bounty land claim: 50-80-5533, 55-80-1689.

COSSELL, William. Pvt. under Capt. Henry Steiner, 25 Aug - 27 Sep 1814.

COST, Christian. Appt'd 13 Feb 1812 as capt. of a troop of horse, 2nd Regt., 1st Cav. Dist.

COUGH, Jacob. Mbr. of Crawford's "company." [FCml issued to Jacob Cough and Mary Senseny 5 May 1807.]

COVER, Jacob. 4th corpl. under Capt. Galt 31 Sep - 27 Oct 1814; b. 20 Jan 1785; m. Margaret Stimmel (b. 7 Jun 1797), in Frederick Co., 19 Nov 1816, by Rev. W. Runkles; d. at his farm near Mechanicstown, MD, 9 May 1842; widow was res. Frederick Co., 1850, 1855. Acq.: 1850 - Abraham Tooney and William Cover; 1855 - Nicholas Snyder and George Harman. Living with widow in 1850 (Creagerstown Dist.): Sophia, 21; Cyrus, 20; Eveline, 12; Adeline, 12; Jacob H., 8; she d. 30 Oct 1867. Both Jacob and Margaret bur. Thurmont, Apples Ref. Ch.

Sources: Bounty land claim, 55-128-3800; Names in Stone.

COVER, Joseph. Pvt. under Capt. Galt, 20 Sep - 29 Oct 1814; m. Susannah Koch (b. 2 May 1795, Fred. Co.), in Graceham, Frederick Co., 7 Apr 1816 by Rev. Blick [Plech], dau of George and Maria (Duckness) Koch; d. at Upper Sanduskey 16 Dec 1849; widow res. Sewico (?) Co., OH 1851 and Wyandott Co., OH, 1855. Their children: Anna Rebecca b. 11 Jan 1817; Susanna b. 29 Feb 1820; Joseph Hanson b. 28 Feb 1822; George Alfred b. 1 Jan 1824; Wesley Alexander b. 4 Mar 1826, d. 30 Aug 1827; Levi b. 18 Aug 1828; Erastus b. 12 Jul 1831. Acq.: 1851 - David Cover, bro. of Joseph Cover.

Sources: Bounty land claim: 55-128-3800; Moravian Families of Graceham, Md.

COX, Jacob. Never joined service during the period his company was active, 24 Aug - 27 Oct 1814, commanded by Capt. William Durbin, Jr.

COX, William. Pvt. from Upper Frederick Co. under Capt. James F. Huston and Capt. Joseph Green; joined 23 Jul 1814; deserted 8 Dec 1814.

CR..., Nathan. Pvt. under Capt. Samuel Dawson, 1 May - 5 Jul 1813.

CRABSTER, Peter. See Crapster.

CRAGER [Krieger, Creeger], Samuel. Musician under Capt. Samuel Duvall, 3 Aug - 3 Oct 1814. Samuel Krieger, shoemaker, of Graceham, son of Lawrence and Anna Maria (Harbaugh) Krieger; b. in Frederick Co., 22 Mar

1791; m. 7 Dec 1815, Elizabeth Favorite (b. in Frederick Co. 1793); she d. 16 Apr 1827 of an ardent gall fever. Their children: Eliza b. 15 Sep 1818, d. of convulsions 16 Jan 1817; George Washington b. 23 Jan 1818, m. Rebecca Late; Jeremiah Augustus b. 27 Mar 1821; d. of convulsions 8 Apr 1821; Mary Ann b. 13 Aug 1822, m. George Washington Late; she d 12 Dec 1898; Sarah Anna b. 23 Dec 1823; Elizabeth b. 26 Oct 1826. Source: **Moravian Families of Graceham, Md.** which contains additional information on the family.

CRAMER, Jacob. Appt'd lieut. colonel, 29th Regt., MM, 12 Feb 1818; called into service at Woodsboro, Frederick Co., around 1 Aug 1814; discharged at Washington City around 10 Nov 1814; commanded a regiment at Washington called "Cramer's Regiment." He m. Magdalena Stimmel (b. c.1774), in Frederick Co., 7 Apr 1795, by Rev. Runkles, German Ref. Ch. Witnesses to marriage were Peter Stimmel and Peter Kramer. His youngest dau, Mary M., m. David Coblentz of Middletown on 24 Mar 1836. Jacob Cramer d. on his farm in Frederick Co. on 28 Jul 1849 in Creagerstown Dist. Acq.: 1850 - John W. Porter, minister of Meth. Ch. who bur. Jacob Cramer on 29 Jul 1849, and Eve Catharine Cramer. The *(Frederick) Examiner*, dated 26 March 1856, announced the death "near Utica Church, on the 22d ult., [of] Margaret Cramer, relict of the late Colonel Cramer, aged 81 yrs, 6 mos. and 2 days..."

Sources: **Rcds. of Ref. Ch. of Fred. Md., 1746-1800; Political Examiner**, 13 Apr 1836, 23 Jul 1849; **(Frederick) Examiner**, 26 March 1856.

CRAMLET (Cranslet), Andrew. Pvt. under Capt. Fonsten; joined 2 Sep 1814; deserted 14 Sep 1814.

CRANDLE, James. Pvt. under Capt. Samuel Dawson; joined 14 Oct 1814; deserted 8 Dec 1814.

CRAP, Boler. From Baltimore. Pvt. under Capt. Daniel Marker, servant to one of the commissioned officers; 25 Aug - 27 Oct 1814.

CRAPSTER, John. Resigned his militia commission circa 13 March 1809, "being now over age." [Adjutant General - Military Papers]

CRATON, James. Pvt. under Capt. John Galt, 6 Sep - 27 Oct 1814; res. 8 miles of Hampstead.

CRAVER, Clements. Pvt. under Thomas Contee Worthington; joined 17 Aug 1812; deserted 3 Sep 1812 and as pvt. under Capt. Samuel Dawson, 1 May - 5 Jul 1813.

CRAVER, Henry. Pvt. under Capt. William Durbin, Jr., 24 Aug - 27 Oct 1814. Absent without leave on 25 Oct.

CRAWELL, Michael. Mbr. of Crawford's "company."

CRAWFORD, Evan L. A letter, dated 4 Dec 1811, from Major Sabritt Sollers stated that Evan L. Crawford was elected Capt. of a company in his battalion, along with Henry Willis as Lieut. and Abraham Beail, as Ensign. Earlier L/Col. Wampler, commanding the 20th Regiment, recommended that Evan Crawford not be given any office of

THE VETERANS

trust. Not surprisingly, Crawford never held a commission despite his being elected by the company. [Adjutant General - Military Papers]

CRAWFORD, James. According to his widow he served under Capt. Smith; was present at the Battle of Bladensburg and saw the Capitol burning; b. c.1790; m(1) Scena --- who d. Cumberland, OH, c.8 Feb 1855; m(2) Rebecca Furguson (b. c.1819 at Norwich, OH) 29 Nov 1859 at Cumberland, Guernesy Co., OH, by Rev. Thomas Thomas. At the enlistment: 22 yrs old; 6 ft, 2 inches; black eyes, black hair; d. at Rix Mills, OH, 1 Apr 1884; moved from MD to OH 1838 and always res. at Cumberland except for last two yrs at Rix Mills, Muskingum Co., OH. Rebecca res. Cumberland from 1856. Acq.: 1886 - William J. Crow, 78, and William G. Johnson, 45, both res. Cumberland, OH, both acq. 30 yrs with Rebecca Crawford. A letter from J. Purkey, dated 8 Nov 1886, Cumberland, OH, stated he had talked with two daus of James Crawford; the oldest dau said that her father started from Rockville. MD. In letter from George W. Crawford, Zanesville, OH, 227 North 7 St., dated 2/25/1889 he said that his mother, Rebeca Crawford, had d.
Source: Pension, WO44106.

CRAWFORD, Robert. Pvt. under Capt. Zacharias, 2nd Regt., 1st Cav. Dist., 7 Aug - 10 Sep 1814; b. c.1775; m. 4 Sep 1800 Eve Haubert in Hanover, PA, by Rev. Daniel Shrader, Luth. minister; res. Carroll Co. 1851; d. near Union Mills, Carroll Co., 18 Aug 1852;

widow d. c.1 Oct 1856. Acq. (1852): Isaac Biehl, Isaac Bankert; (1857): John G. Fritchey, minister who preached at funeral service for Eve Crawford 3 Oct 1856.
Source: Bounty land claim, 55-rejected-212859. In file is letter from George Crawford son of Robert and Eve Crawford.

CRAWFORD, Samuel. Pvt. in company of Capt. Fonsten, 2 Sep - 27 Oct 1814; res. 7 miles form Westminster.

CRAWFORD, William. Pvt. in the company of Capt. Fonsten, 2 Sep - 27 Oct 1814; res. 8 miles from Westminster.

CRAWMER, Daniel. Pvt. under Capt. Fonsten, 2 Sep - 27 Oct 1814; b. c.1780; res. Muskingam Co., OH, 1855; Witnesses: 1855 - George Crawmer and Basil Crawmer, res. Muskingum, OH.
Source: Bounty land claim: 55-160-51223.

CRAWMER, Helpher. Pvt. under Capt. Funston, 2 Sep - 27 Oct 1814; b. c.1790; m. Margaret Gosnell (b. c.1794) in Fredericktown 28 Oct 1815 by Rev. Shaeffer - first time for both. At enlistment: 5 feet, 10 inches; dark complexion, blue eyes, dark hair. After discharge res. Fred. Co.; res. Carroll Co. 1855; d. near New Windsor 17 Apr 1869; widow res. near New Windsor 1878. Acq.: 1878 - Samuel Hoffman, age 67, New Windsor; and William T. Smith, age 45, near New Windsor.
Sources: Pension, WO22613 (rejected 27 Jul 1879); Bounty land claim: 55-160-41135.

CRAYTON, Hugh. Pvt., 12th U.S. Inf. At enlistment: 5 ft, 8 inches; light eyes, light hair, light complexion; age 25; plasterer; b. Fred. Co., MD; enlisted 18

Aug 1812 at Charlestown by Lieut. Callis until 18 Aug 1817. Absent sick at Lewistown since 25 Sep 1813. Near Buffalo on 28 Feb and 30 Apr 1815. Discharged 18 Aug 1817.

CREAGER. See Crager, Krieger.

CREAGER, Jacob. Appt'd 12 May 1812 as capt. of a company in 29th Regt., MM. No muster rolls found for this company.

CREAGER, John of Lawrence. Appt'd 1 Jan 1813 as cornet in troop of horse of Capt. Baker Johnson, 2nd Reg., 1st Cav. Dist.

CREAGER, William. Pvt. under Capt. Joseph Wood, 27 Aug - 18 Sep 1814; on furlough on 18 Sep 1814.

CREAK, George. Pvt. in Capt. Flautt's rifle company, 29 Apr until 30 May 1813; dec'd. 30 May 1813.

CREGLOW, George. Pvt. under Lieut. William Kolb of Capt. Markey's company, guarding British prisoners at the Frederick Barracks, 13 Oct - 15 Nov 1814.

CRETIN [Craton], James. Pvt. under Capt. Galt, 6 Sep - 27 Oct 1814; b. c.1788; m. Mary A. Livers, at Mt. St. Mary's Ch., Fred. Co., 27 Jun 1830 by Father Brute(?), a priest - both for the first time. At enlistment: grey eyes, dark curly hair; spare man; laborer; res. Frederick Co., 1855. They continued to res. on farm near Emmitsburg at Mothers Station; he d. 17 Feb 1857, age 69; bur. St. Anthony, old Mt. St. Mary's Cath. Cem.; she was still living on the farm in 1878. Witness: 1850 - John T. Cretin. Acq.: 1878 - Mary C. Dielman, age 43, near Emmitsburg, and A. F. Orndorff, age 50, acq. 40 and 10 yrs, resp.; and Lewis M. Motter of Emmitsburg. In 1916 Mary A. Cretin's dau, Mrs. John J. Mahoney res. Sharon Hill, Delaware Co., PA. In 1916 reference was made to other children of Mary A. Cretin. It was stated in a letter that the father of Mary A. Cretin also served in the War of 1812.

Sources: Pension, 33933; Bounty land claim: 50-40-94999, 55-120-63037; **Names in Stone.**

CREW, William. Pvt. under Capt. Thomas Contee Worthington; joined 16 Oct 1812 as a substitute for William B. Thompson; b. c.1780; m. Elizabeth Wilson (b. c.1785), in Baltimore City, Apr 1813, by "a circuit preacher" res. Baltimore City 1850, 1851; d. Balt. 9 Sep 1852; widow res. Baltimore City 1855.

Source: Bounty land claim: 55-120-23549.

CRILLY, Michael. Pvt. from Upper Frederick Co. under Capt. James F. Huston and Capt. Joseph Green; joined 23 Jul 1814; deserted 8 Dec 1814.

CRISE, George. In the pension file of Crise is copy from company books of Capt. John Galt, "in the service of the U.S. in 1814 3 Regt. Inf., 11 Brigade. Camp Hampstead Baltimore Sep 29 1814. I John Hynson jr. do hereby acknowledge that I by the consent of my father have this day become a substitute for Geo. Crise now in the service of the U.S. under command of Jno. Galt. signed ..." His widow said that he served until 5 Oct 1814 when he furnished a substitute. The company served from 31 Aug until 27 Oct 1814.

George Crise m. 7 Jun 1809 Barbara Little in Adams Co., PA [another entry

FREDERICK COUNTY MILITIA IN THE WAR OF 1812

says they m. 10 Aug 1810 in Frederick Co.]. George Crise d. at home 30 Sep 1824; widow res. Taneytown, MD, in 1871. Acq.: 1871 - Theodore Derr, D. Scott Boyle.
Source: Pension, WO303.

CRISHER, Coonrod. From New Windsor. Pvt. under Capt. George W. Magee, 22 Jul 1814 - 10 Jan 1815. He was "sick his last muster" and "furloughed 15 days." The army enlistment register shows Conrad Crisher was enlisted at Westminster, MD, on 4 May 1813 by Ens. Philip Fisher. At enlistment: he 5 feet, 6 inches, 21 yrs of age. He served in 36th U.S. Inf. under Col. Carbury; mustered at Westminster on 9 May 1813.

CRIST, John. Appt'd 20 Sep 1813 as 2nd lieut. under Capt. John Crist, 16th Regt., MM.

CROMBACKER. See Crumbaker.

CRONISE [Crouse, Cronice], Henry. Pvt. under Capt. George W. Ent, 24 Aug - 30 Sep 1814.

CROSBERY, James B. Pvt. under Capt. George W. Magee; joined 22 Jul 1814; deserted 20 Aug 1814.

CROSS, Thomas. Pvt. under Capt. Samuel Dawson; joined 26 Jul 1814; "sick in Balt., deserted 8 Dec 1814."

CROUS, William. Res. within 2 miles of Westminster; pvt. under Capt. Fonsten, 2 Sep - 27 Oct 1814.

CROUSE, Christian. Pvt. under Capt. William Knox; joined 26 Aug 1814; deserted 11 Sep 1814. He stated he was absent on furlough for a few days and before the expiration of his furlough his company was discharged. He appears on the muster rolls as Christopher Crouse; b. c.1778. Res. Bedford Co., PA, 1852; Napier Township, Bedford Co., PA, in 1855. Acq.: 1852 - Jacob Hiteshew of Bedford Co., PA, and Gideon Hiteshew of Carroll Co. attest that he served in the same company and that Christian Crouse and Christopher Crouse are the one and same.
Source: Bounty land claim, 55-120-46577.

CROUSE [Krouse], John. Pvt. under Samuel Ogle, 1 May - 5 Jul 1813, as substitute for William Houck; b. ca.1796; m. Jun 1818 Salley Eckert at her father's residence; res. Carroll Co. 1851, 1855 and 1871 (Westminster). Acq.: 1871 - Isaac E. Pearson, William S. Brown, res. Carroll Co.
Sources: Pension, SO1417, SC649; Bounty land claims, 50-40-19158, 55-160-7986 (certificate for 40 acres in the file).

CROUSE, Joseph. Pvt. under Capt. Samuel Ogle, 1 May - 5 Jul 1813. [FCm] issued to Joseph Crouse and Elizabeth Heitchew 8 Nov 1813. Bur. at Taneytown Ref. Ch. are Joseph Crouse, d. 1 May 1850, age 52 yrs, 11 mos., and wife Elizabeth, 26 Oct 1850, age 52 yrs, 2 mos. - *Names in Stone*.]

CROUSE, Lewis. Pvt. under Capt. Galt, 5 Sep - 27 Oct 1814.

CROUSE [Crous, Krouse], William. Pvt. in Capt. Fonston's company, 2 Sep - 27 Oct 1814; res. 2 miles from Westminster; b. 1793; m. 15 Feb 1818 Margaret Shaffer (b. c.1798) at Westminster, by Rev. Jacob Geiger, each for first time. At enrollment: 21 yrs old; blacksmith; 5 ft, 9 inches; dark hair and eyes and fair complexion; weighed about 160 pounds. He res. Carroll Co. 1851, 1855, 1871 and 1878; d. 16 Mar 1882 in Westminster; widow res. Westminster 1882; d. 30 Nov 1884, Westminster. Acq.: 1871 - George M. Parke and Thomas B. Gist. 1882 - Charles P. Cassell, age 26, Main St., Westminster; Jeremiah Yingling, 62, Main St., Westminster; George A. Miller, age 35, Westminster; James A. Diffenbaugh, age 28, Westminster; William Baker.

Sources: Pensions, SO7769, SC22940; WO42170, WC32701; Bounty land claim, 50-40-42684, 55-120-67367.

CROUT, John. Pvt. under Capt. Samuel Ogle, 1 May - 5 Jul 1813; m. 9 May 1811 Miss Rachel Fetterling of Fr. Co., by Rev. Green.

Source: (Frederick) Hornet, 22 May 1811.

CROWL, David. Lived within 2 miles of Westminster; pvt. under Capt. Fonsten, 2 Sep - 27 Oct 1814.

CRUM, Abraham. Pvt. under George W. Ent, 24 Aug - 30 Sep 1814; "drafted at Fredericktown"; b. c.1795; res. Washington Co., MD, 1850 and 1855. [In records of Ref. Ch. of Frederick appears baptism of Abraham Crum son of William and Elisabetha Crum, b. 31 May 1796. Also note FCml issued to Abraham Crum and Susanna Ringer on 6 Mar 1797.]

Sources: Bounty land claim, 55-120-15294; Rcds. of Evan. Ref. Ch. in Fred., Md., 1746-1800; FCml.

CRUMAGE, Frederick. Pvt. under Capt. George W. Magee, 23 Jul - 13 Oct 1814.

CRUMBAKER [Crumbecker], David F. Pvt. under Capt. Huston /Capt. Green; joined 23 Jul 1814; deserted 14 Dec 1814; from Upper Fred. Co.; b. c.1795; m. 20 Aug 1849 Mary Fisher at Chester Twp, Meigs Co., OH; res. Chester Twp, 1871. Acq.: 1871 - John P.[?] Will and Jerim Howell.

Sources: Pension, SO11815; Bounty land claim, 55-120-34158 (separate from the pension file).

CRUMBAKER [Crombacker], Jacob. Appt'd 28 Apr 1813 as 1st lieut. under Capt. Nicholas Turbutt, 16th Regt., MM; served as 1st lieut. under Capt. Nicholas Turbutt, 1 Sep 27 - Oct 1814. In a letter, now on display in the museum at the Fort McHenry National Monument and Historic Shrine, he gives details on his company's involvement and a description of some of the preparations of Balt.'s defense. [See pp. 17-18.]

Jacob Crumbaker b. 21 [or 23] Jun 1776 in Fred. Co. MD, son of John Crumbacher who was one of the sons of Hans Crumbacher who moved to Fred. Co. c.1765. Jacob moved with his parents to Loudoun Co. VA c.1786; m. Rosanna Smitley, in Loudon Co., VA, 1798, by Rev. Craver (she was from Loudon Co.); moved to his native Fred. Co. and owned land in Middletown Valley. He sold his land in Maryland and acquired land in Salt Creek Township, Muskingum Co., OH c.1818-19; res. Muskingum Co., OH, 1851; d. 5 Jun 1853, Salt Creek Township, Muskingum Co., OH. In 1855 James Officer, son-in-law of Jacob Crumbaker declared fol. excerpted [edited here] from papers of the dec'd. Jacob Crumbaker: Jacob

FREDERICK COUNTY MILITIA IN THE WAR OF 1812

Crumbaker b. 21 Jun 1776; m. Rossanna Smitley by Rev. Craner, minister of the Gospel. His children: Sarah Crumbaker b. 13 Nov 1799; Elisabeth Crumbaker b. 23 Aug 1801; Zikiah[?] Crumbaker b. 15 Nov 1803; Joshua Randolph Crumbaker b. 21 Apr 1808; Elias Smitley Crumbaker b. 5 Jan 1811; Grofton Porter[?] Crumbaker b. 21 Jun 1814; Joseph Monroe Crumbaker b. 13 Sep 1817; Oliver Hazzard Perry Crumbaker b. 24 Apr 1821. Jacob's bro., John Crumbacker, served in War of 1812, from VA. Acq.: 1855 - George Smitley and Eve Smitley, aged 72 yrs and 64 yrs, resp., res. Salt Creek Township, and bro. and sister of Rosanna Crumbaker.

Sources: Bounty land claim, 55-120-61074; Virginia S. Poling, 233 Oak Valley Drive, Hagerstown, MD, 21740, who published **The Hans Crumpacker Family**, dealing with the Crumpackers who moved from Chester Co. PA, to Fred. Co., MD.

CRUMBECKER - See Crumbaker.

CRUMRINE [Krumrine], Henry. Pvt. under Capt. Samuel Ogle, 1 May - 5 Jul 1813; m. 26 Feb 1818 Judith Sterner (b. c.1798) at Hanover, PA, by Rev. Jacob Weistling of the German Ref. Ch.; res. Carroll Co., MD, 1855 and 1878 near Silver Run; d. 28 Mar 1845 Carroll Co.; bur. 30 Mar 1845; widow d. c.1886. Acq.: 1855 - Daniel Yeiser and Jacob Leister.

Sources: Pension, WO16765; Bounty land claim, 55-160-27234.

CRUMRINE, John. Pvt. under Capt. Fonsten, 2 Sep - 27 Oct 1814; res. 9 miles from Westminster.

CRUMRINE, Peter. Pvt. under Capt. Fonsten, 2 Sep - 27 Oct 1814; res. 12 miles from Westminster.

CRUTCHER, Vincent. Pvt. under George W. Ent, 24 Aug - 30 Sep 1814; discharged 27 Oct 1814; m. 18 Jul 1809 Barbara Smith (b. c.1789), in Fred. Co., MD, by Rev. Myers; d. 13 Aug 1846, at Lancaster, Fairfield Co., OH; widow res. Pickaway Co., OH, 1851; Fairfield Co., OH, 1855; Lancaster, Fairfield Co., OH, 1871. Acq.: 1853 - Benjamin Connel, age 62, and William H. Shutt, age 36, res. Fairfield Co., OH, acq. 2 yrs prior to the death of Vincent Crutcher. 1871 - Isaac W. Julian, John Stonebunn. 1873 - Ann R. Leonard and Samuel Ewing, Lancaster, Fairfield Co., OH, acq. since 1841.

Sources: Pension, WO3320, WC5046; Bounty land claims, 50-40-96682, 55-120-43093.

CULLER, Henry. Lieut. under Capt. Daniel Shawen, 5 Sep - 27 Oct 1814; b. 10 Nov 1786; m. c.6 Apr 1809, Anna Fister; res. Fred. Co. 1850 and 1855; res. Jefferson Dist.; farming and milling, mbr. of the state legislature; d. 1 Feb 1861 of inflamation of the stomach; bur. Jefferson Union Cem. with wife Anna (17 Aug 1789 - 16 Dec 1856).

Sources: Bounty land claim, 55-120-14721; **Bridge in Time; Names in Stone; (Frederick) Examiner**, 13 Feb 1961.

CULLISON [Culison], Joseph. He never joined the service while his company (Capt. Durbin) was active, 24 Aug - 27 Oct 1814.

CUNNINGHAM, James. Pvt. in Capt. Flautt's rifle company, 29 Apr - 29 Jun 1813.

THE VETERANS

CURENCE, Elijah. Corpl. under Capt. Flautt, 29 Apr - 29 Jun 1813.

CURFMAN, Adam. Claims to have served under Capt. Barton Hackney although his name is not in the rolls; b. Balt. Co. 1791; m. Feb 1831 Elizabeth Claybaugh at Franklin Co., OH. He stated at time of enrollment he was age 21, farmer, 5 ft, 6 inches; had light hair and blue eyes, and fair complexion. Res. Fulton Co., IL, 1874 (P.O. address: Lewistown). Acq.: 1872 - Andrew Warfield and Joseph McGee, both res. Cass, IL. 1874 - Gilbert McElroy and E. T. Campbell. 1878 - James C.Watson, age 88 and John Ellis, age 52, acq. for 40 and 25 yrs, resp. - both res. Smithfield, IL.
Source: Pension, SO28441.

CURFMAN [Kirfman], Christopher [called Christ; in the muster roll as Christian]. Pvt. under Capt. Basil Dorsey, 30 Jul - 27 Sep 1814. He said that his father, Adam Curfman, was in the same company. [There is no Adam Curfman listed in the existing rolls of Capt. Dorsey for the War of 1812; perhaps Christopher Curfman was referring to a period prior to the War.]
Christopher Curfman b. c.1790; m. 9 Aug 1822 Rebecca Carman in Stubenville, Jefferson Co., OH, by Justice of the Peace. Christ Kurfman res. Wirt Co., WV, 1856 and Three Forks of Reedy, Roane Co., WV 1871; d. 7 Apr 1882, Mt. Hoge, WV. Widow res. Mt. Hoge, Wurt Co., WV 1882; d. prior to 11 Jun 1883. Acq.: 1871 - Jonathan Kelly and William Patterson - witnesses at the wedding. 1871 - John W. Cain, John E. Goodwin, res. Reedy Twp, Wirt Co.

1882 - J. W. Cain, age 62; Louisa A. Cain, age 56 - first acq. in 1841.
Sources: Pensions, SO1124, SC15373; WO42140, WC32622; Bounty land claim, 55-160-65570.

CURRY, James. Pvt. under Capt. Philip Smith, joined 23 May 1813; deserted 15 Aug; returned 26 Aug; discharged 8 Sep 1813.

CURRY, James. Pvt. under Capt. George Shryock, joined 14 Oct 1814; discharged on 10 Jan 1815 at Annapolis.

CURRY, John. Pvt. under Capt. Samuel Duvall, 3 Aug - 3 Oct 1814.

CURSMAN [Kursman], Christian. Pvt. under Capt. Getzendanner, 9 Aug - 17 Sep 1813 and pvt. under Capt. Getzendanner, joined 26 Jul 1814; discharged 21 Aug 1814.

CUSTARD, Jacob. 2nd corpl. under Capt. Matthew Murray, 25 Aug - 27 Oct 1814.

CUSTARD, John. Pvt. under Capt. Daniel Marker, 25 Aug - 27 Oct 1814.

CUTSHALL, Samuel. He said served under Capt. Samuel Dawson and discharged by reason of furnishing a substitute whose name was Joseph Lowery; b. c.1790; m. 1 Jan 1812 Mary Darner in Fred. Co., MD.
Source: Pension, SO25387. Rejected - no proof of service. [Corpl. Joseph Lowery served in Capt. Samuel Dawson's company from 21 Jul 1814 to 10 Jan 1815.]

DADDS, Robert. Mbr. of Crawford's "company."

DAGEN, John. Mbr. of Crawford's "company."

DAGETT, Joab. Hospital Steward(?) on staff of 1st Regt., 23 Dec 1814 - 10 Jan 1815.

DAHOOF, Andrew. From Upper Fred. Co. Pvt. under Capt. James F. Huston, 23 Jul - 13 Oct 1814.

DAHOOF, Christian. Pvt. under Capt. Fonsten; joined 2 Sep 1814; deserted 20 Sep 1814.

DAILEY, Archibald. Pvt. under Capt. Samuel Ogle, 1 May 1813 - 5 Jul 1813.

DAILY, John. Pvt. under Capt. Daniel Marker, 25 Aug - 27 Oct 1814.

DAMOOT, John. Pvt.; served as a substitute under Capt. William Knox, 26 Aug - 27 Oct 1814. [In Henry Young's Moravian Families of Graceham, Maryland, there is a Johann Demuth who m. Catharine ---; issue: Sophia Theresia b. 23 Aug 1797 at 11:45.]

DANIEL. Negro. Servant to Major Cole of the 1st Regt., 14 Oct 1814 - 10 Jan 1815.

DARBY, Denton. Appt'd capt. 20 Aug 1813, 13th Regt., MM; served as Capt. of a company, 3 Aug - 8 Nov 1814; stated he was a capt. of militia company in the Bladensburg detachment, commanded by Lieut. Colonel Creamer; he volunteered at New Market, Fred. Co., 1 Aug 1814, discharged at the City of Washington about last of Oct 1814. He was first organized and consolidated under Major Kizer, of the U.S. Army, and after reaching the City of Washington he was attached to the City Brigade. He was b. c.1787; res. Logan Co., KY, 1852 and 1855.

Source: Bounty land claim, 55-120-74947.

DARBY, Perry. Pvt. under Capt. Basil Dorsey, 30 Jul - 27 Sep 1814; b. c.1795; m(1) c.2 Dec 1849 Elizabeth Michael (d. Vermillion, OH); m(2) 18 Jul 1850 Miss Zemiah B. Akers, Milan, Erie Co., OH, by Rev. Newton Barrett; res. Erie Co., OH, 1852, 1856; d. 3 Jul 1873, at Brownhelm, Lorain Co., OH; widow res. Vermillion, Erie Co., OH, 1879; d. 27 Nov 1893, Vermillion, OH. Acq. (1879): Joseph B. Clarke, aged 62 and Peter G. Akers, aged 60, both res. Oberlin, OH, acq. of Zemiah Darby 25 and 50 yrs resp.

Sources: Bounty land claim, 55-160-37875; Pension, WO37370, WC27282.

DARNELL, Benedick. Pvt. under Capt. Philip Smith; joined 23 May 1813; deserted 20 Jul 1813.

DATROFF, Andrew. Res. Fredericktown; pvt. under Capt. Joseph Green, 14 Oct 1814 - 10 Jan 1815.

DAUS, Francis. 5th corpl. under Capt. Barton Hackney, 1 Sep - 27 Oct 1814.

DAVIDSON, Jesse. Pvt. under Capt. William Knox, 26 Aug - 27 Oct 1814; b. c.1782; res. Fred. Co. 1855.

Source: Bounty land claim, 55-120-30649.

DAVIDSON [Davison], Samuel. Pvt. under Capt. Basil Dorsey, 30 Jul - 27 Sep 1814. Also served under Capt. Townsend Dade [Montgomery Co, MD]; he remained in Dade's company until after the battle of Bladensburg. From this place he went home for clothes and was there informed that his Capt. and company had gone to Balt.; then enrolled in company of "Bazil Dowsey." He was b. 4 Nov 1788; m. 8 Mar 1814 Catherine Ryan, Fred. Co.;

THE VETERANS

res. Knox Co., OH, 1850, 1855 and 1871 (Bladensburg); d. c.1880. Acq.: 1871 - John W. Boggs, Daniel Nicholls, res. Bladensburg, Knox Co., OH. Letter in file from Ella May Davidson, P.O. Box 314, Hood River, OR, dated 10 Nov 1931, seeking information on Samuel Davidson who served in War of 1812 from Fred. Co., and m. Catherine Rine [sic].
Sources: Bounty land claim, 50-40-24316; Pension, SO2620, SC5082.

DAVIS Alban. Pvt. under Capt. William Durbin, Jr.; joined 24 Aug 1814; deserted 5 Sep 1814.

DAVIS, Alexander. Pvt. under Capt. Samuel Ogle, 1 May 1813 - 5 Jul 1813.

DAVIS, Elijah. Pvt. under Capt. Daniel Marker, 25 Aug - 27 Oct 1814.

DAVIS, Eli. Pvt., 38th U.S. Inf., under Capt. John Rothrock. At enlistment: 5 ft, 11 inches; light eyes, brown hair, dark complexion; age 23; farmer; b. Fred. Co., MD; enlisted 11 Jul 1813 or 19 Feb 1814 at Craney Island by Capt. Rothrock, for duration of war. Discharged at Craney Island 15 March 1815.

DAVIS, George E. Pvt. under Capt. Nicholas Hall, 7 Aug - 10 Sep 1814, in the 2nd Regt., 1st Cav. Dist.; b. 3 Feb 1775, Lancaster Co., PA; moved to Montgomery Co., MD, where he engaged in mercantile business at Hyattstown; m. 12 Aug 1803 Elizabeth Hyatt (b. c.1785, Montgomery Co., MD) dau of Eli Hyatt by Rev. Dade. They bought a farm in New Market Dist.; had four sons and four daus. Second son, Eli, b. 5 Nov 1809, New Market Dist.; m. 18 Aug 1831 at Clarksburg, Montgomery Co., Rachel, only child of William Morsell. William Morsell was Quaker and native of Fred. Co., MD. George E. Davis, farmer, d. 6 May 1850, age 78, after 3-day illness of palsy, near New Market. The 1850 census of 5th E.D. shows Elizabeth Davis, age 69, res. in home of Henry Nurser, age 45, shoemaker, and Ann Nurser, 41, and their two children. Elizabeth d. 13 May 1855. Acq.(1851): Ezra Greentree, William Lowe.
Sources: Bounty land claim, 55-120-51046; Bridge in Time; Williams, Hist. of Fred. Co., p. 839.

DAVIS, Isaac. Pvt. under Capt. Hall, 7 Aug - 10 Sep 1814, 2nd Regt., 1st Cav. Dist.; m. 1816 Mary Ann Sides (b. c.1786) in Anne Arundel Co., MD, by Rev. James Day, Meth. minister. [FCml issued to Isaac Davis and Mary Ann Sides 11 March 1816.] Isaac Davis d. 19 Jun 1819, Anne Arundel Co. Acq. - 1855: Ann Shipley and Charlotta Pecor, res. Balt. City.
Source: Bounty land claim, 55-160-27237.

DAVIS, James. Pvt. under Capt. Nicholas Turbutt, 2 Sep - 27 Oct 1814; b. PA. 1850 census of Creagerstown Dist.: James Davis, 60, and Elizabeth Davis, 56, res. with Henry and Susan Willhide.
Source: **Bridge in Time.**

DAVIS, John. From Balt.; pvt. under Capt. Samuel Dawson, 21 Jul 1814 - 10 Jan 1815; sick in Balt. 1850 census of New Market Dist.: John Davis, 70, labourer, pensioner, and Permilla Davis, 74, pensioner.
Source: **Bridge in Time.**

FREDERICK COUNTY MILITIA IN THE WAR OF 1812

DAVIS, John. Pvt. under Capt. John Fonsten; joined 2 Sep 1814; deserted 30 Sep 1814.

DAVIS, Jonathan. Pvt. under Samuel Dawson, 21 Jul 1814 - 10 Jan 1815.

DAVIS, Joseph. Pvt. under Capt. Denton Darby; joined 3 Aug 1814; drowned 16 Aug 1814.

DAVIS, Joshua. Res. 3 miles of Taneytown, 1814; pvt. under Capt. Galt, 31 Aug - 27 Oct 1814; 1850 census, Fred. E.D.: Joshua Davis, 55, Jane Davis, 46 and John Davis, 8; Heneretta T. Butler, 13, and James F. Frederick, 1.

DAVIS, Joshua. 1st Sergt. under Capt. Nicholas Turbutt, 2 Sep - 27 Oct 1814.

DAVIS, Joshua. Ordered to serve as pvt. under Capt. Thomas Contee Worthington 17 Aug - 31 Dec 1812. Never joined.

DAVIS, Levi. Res. Fredericktown; 4th corpl. under Capt. Huston and 1st corpl. under Capt. Joseph Green, 23 Jul 1814 - 10 Jan 1815.

DAVIS, Nathan. Pvt. under Capt. Samuel Dawson; joined 21 Jul; absent without leave 19 - 28 Aug; deserted 8 Dec 1814.

DAVIS, Paris. Pvt. under Capt. Samuel Dawson, 21 Jul - deserted 23 Aug 1814.

DAVIS, Richard. Pvt. under Capt. Riggs and Capt. Fulton; m. c.19 Jun 1812 Elizabeth Penn (b. c.1795) near Ridgeville, MD, by Rev. James L. Higgins; d. near New Market Sep 1820, bur. New Market. She m(2) James Thompson, who d. 30 Nov 1845, Muskingum Co., OH. She res. Muskingum Co., OH, 1858. Acq.: (1858): James J. King and Jesse L. Manly, res. Muskingum Co., OH; Jesse Wright, present at marriage and funeral; Sarah Salmon, res. Fred. Co., MD. Acq. (1869): Sarah Ann Davis, dau of Richard Davis and administrator of the estate of Elizabeth Thompson of Hopewell, OH; John B. Stimmell, res. Mt. Pleasant, MD, and served under Capt. Robert Fulton with pvt. Richard Davis. He stated that all the men of this company were residents of the neighborhood. Acq.: Henry Shryock, res. Creagerstown, MD, who res. Creagerstown during the War of 1812, and served under Capt. Joseph Wood; he said that the company of Capt. Fulton was "camped very near us and I use to see the members very often and personally acq. with the members of this company [Fulton's] as they were men from this neighborhood in which I lived."

Source: Bounty land claim, 55-160-111071.

DAVIS, Richard. Mbr. of Crawford's "company."

DAVIS, Richard. Pvt. under Capt. Joseph Wood, 27 Aug - absent 27 Oct 1814.

DAVIS, Thomas. Pvt. under Capt. Joseph Wood, 27 Aug - 13 Oct 1814; deserted 21 Sep 1814. [Note: On 5 Dec 1797 Thomas Davis, age 15 yrs, 3 Aug 1797, with the consent of his mother, was bound to Balser Conrod, house carpenter, joiner and cabinet maker.]

Source: West. Md. Genealogy.

DAVIS, Walter. Pvt. under Capt. Daniel Marker, 25 Aug - 27 Oct 1814.

THE VETERANS

DAVIS, William. Pvt., 2nd U.S. Inf., under Capt. W. R. Boote. At enlistment: 6 ft, 1 inches; blue eyes, red hair, light complexion; age 29; blacksmith; b. Fred. Co., MD. Name in Company book 1805-1810. Deserted 25 Aug 1809. Ft. Stoddert - Swore in presence of Sgt. Cochran, that if the Americans made an attack on Mobile, he would fight against them till he spilt the last drop of his blood. Discharged Columbian Springs, 8 Nov 1809.

DAVISON, Samuel. Pvt. under Capt. Basil Dorsey, 30 July - 27 Sep 1814.

DAVISON, William. Pvt. under Capt. Basil Dorsey, 30 Jul - 27 Sep 1814.

DAWES [Davis], James. Pvt., 36th U.S. Inf. At enlistment: 6 ft 1/2 or 1 1/2 inches; age 24; b. Middletown, Fred. Co., MD; enlisted 23 Nov 1814 at Norfolk by Capt. Nelson. Absent sick at Norfolk, discharged 13 March 1815.

DAWSON, Nicholas. Pvt. under Capt. Barton Hackney; joined 1 Sep 1814; deserted 14 Sep 1814.

DAWSON, Samuel. Blacksmith from Funkstown [according to Daniel Matzenbaugh]. Capt. of a company; served 21 Jul 1814 - 10 Jan 1815.

DAYHOOF, Christian. Pvt. under Capt. John Fonsten; joined 2 Sep 1814; deserted 20 Sep 1814.

DAYS, Henry. Pvt. under Capt. George W. Ent, 24 Aug - 30 Sep 1814.

DEAN, James. 1st corpl. under Capt. Jacob Getzendanner 9 Aug - 17 Sep 1813 and 26 Jul - 21 Aug 1814; m. 26 Apr 1819 Elizabeth Pennybaker (b. c.1791), in Fredericktown, by Rev. Davison, Presby. Ch.; d. Fred. Co., 17 Jan 1833. Acq.: 1850 - George Lease, Peter Dean, res. Fred. Co.; 1855 - Ormond W. Hammond, Robert Dean, res. Fred. Co.

Source: Bounty land claim, 55-120-2412.

DEAN, John A. Appt'd 18 Sep 1812 as 1st lieut. under Capt. Jacob Getzendanner; served as 1st lieut. under Capt. Jacob Getzendanner, 9 Aug - 17 Sep 1813 and 26 Jul 21 Aug 1814.

DEAN, Joshua. Pvt. under Capt. John Brengle, 25 Aug - 19 Sep 1814.

DEAN, Robert. 2nd corpl. under Capt. Jacob Getzendanner, 9 Aug - 17 Sep 1813 and 26 Jul - 21 Aug 1814.

DEAN, Thomas. Pvt. under Capt. Henry Steiner, 28 Apr - 29 Jun 1813 and 25 Aug - 27 Sep 1814; b. c.1795; m. 6 Dec 1818 Catharine Weaver, at Fredericktown; res. Balt. City in 1852, 1855, 1871; d. c.May 1888. Acq. (1871): Hezekiah Vanorsdel, Howard St., Balt.; John Tudor, 354 W. Fayette, Balt.

Sources: Bounty land claims, 50-40-79441, 55-120-37813; Pension, SO3756, SC3166.

DEAVER, Benjamin. Appt'd ensign 22 May 1812, under Capt. Barton Hackney, 28 Regt., MM.

DEGRANGE, John. Drummer under Capt. Nicholas Turbutt, 2 Sep - 27 Oct 1814; b. 2 Aug 1796; m. Elizabeth Archbold (b. 28 Dec 1799), Fredericktown, 30 Nov 1820. The 1850 census of the Buckeystown Dist. shows, John Degrange, 52, farmer, $6255; Elizabeth Degrange, 50; George W., 22; Catharine M., 19; Ann R., 17; David J. 19; Nathaniel C., 11; Daniel W. F., 9. He also res. Fred. Co., MD, 1851, 1855,

1871 (Frederick City). John d. 17 March 1879 at residence of Eli Wasskey; his wife Elizabeth d. 17 Nov 1869. Both are bur. at Mt. Olivet with other members of the family. Acq.: William H. Albaugh, F. Haneman.

Sources: Bounty land claims, 50-40-55885, 55-120-23962; Pension, SO16996, SC11085; **Names in Stone; Bridge in Time**; (Frederick) Examiner, 24 Nov 1869, 19 Mar 1879.

DEHAVEN, William. Pvt. under Capt. Matthew Murray, 25 Aug - 27 Oct 1814.

DEHOOF, John. Pvt. under Capt. George W. Magee; enrolled 22 Jul 1814; deserted 1 Oct 1814.

DELAPLAIN [Delaplane], Daniel. Pvt. under Capt. Upton Reed, 1st Cav. Dist., 26 Aug - 3 Sep 1814; b. c.1770; res. Highland Co., OH, 1850 [age 80 yrs]. He stated he volunteered at "Tonatown," [Taneytown] Frederick Co., MD in Jun 1814.

Source: Bounty land claim, 50-rejected-84480.

DELASHMITT, Bazil. Pvt. under Capt. Samuel Dawson, 21 Jul - 13 Oct 1814.

DELASHMUTT, Denis. Pvt. under Capt. Daniel Marker, 25 Aug - 27 Oct 1814.

DELASHMUTT, John. 2nd corpl. under Capt. Daniel Marker, 25 Aug - 27 Oct 1814.

DELASHMUTT, Nelson. Pvt. under Capt. Samuel Dawson, 1 May - 5 Jul 1813.

DELASHMUTT, Nelson. Pvt. under Capt. Daniel Marker, 25 Aug - 27 Oct 1814.

DELASHMUTT Otho. Pvt. under Capt. Nicholas Turbutt, 1 Sep - 27 Oct 1814

DELASHMUTT [Delashmitt], Sampson. Pvt. under Capt. Samuel Dawson, 1 May - 5 Jul 1813 and 21 Jul 1814 - 10 Jan 1815.

DELAUTER Frederic. Pvt. under Capt. Daniel Marker 16 Aug - 18 Sep 1813.

DELAWTER Daniel. Pvt. under Capt. Daniel Marker 16 Aug - 18 Sep 1813.

DELAWTER David. 2nd corpl. under Capt. Daniel Marker 16 Aug - 18 Sep 1813. [On 31 May 1794 David Delauder, son of John, was bound to Andrew Low, taylor of Frederick Town to age 21.]

Source: West. Md. Genealogy, 4:3.

DELAWDER, George. Pvt. under Capt. Daniel Shawen; joined 5 Sep 1814; discharged 10 Oct 1815.

DELAWTER [Delawder], Jacob. 3rd corpl. under Capt. Matthew Murray, 25 Aug - 27 Oct 1814; b. c.1795; m. Sarah Brown 31 Aug 1815, Fredericktown, MD; res. Montgomery Co., OH, 1821-1877 (P.O. Germantown in 1871); d. Montgomery Co., OH, 17 Jul 1877. She res. Germantown, OH, in 1878; d. 30 Nov 1880. His children: Alpheus, Ezra, Rebecca, Mary A. (b. Farmersville, OH, May 22, 1822, m. Daniel Hoops, May 26, 1840), Catherine, David, Sarah A., Jacob, Jonas, Lewis and Elizabeth. "Mr. Delawter was for a long time crier at public auctions, was full of wit, and was known throughout the county as Uncle Jake" ... "mbr. and trustee of the Lutheran church."

THE VETERANS

Sources: Bounty land claims, 50-40-52652, 55-120-63195; Pensions, SO12817, SC15996, WO17909; Frank Conover, Ed., **Portrait and Biographical Record of the City of Dayton and Montgomery County, Ohio**, p. 1131.

DELL, Adam. Mbr. of Crawford's "company."

DELL, David. Mbr. of Crawford's "company."

DELOSURE, [Delosier] Ignatius. Pvt. under Capt. William Knox, 26 Aug - 27 Oct 1814; m. 18 Oct 1806 Susanna Nicholson (b. c.1787) (or Nicholas), at Hagerstown, by Rev. Rauhouser, in Ref. Ch. [?]; d. 22 Aug 1850 at Ringgold in Washington Co., MD. Widow res. Washington Co. 1851; Frederick Co, 1855; Ringgold, Washington Co., MD, 1871. Acq.: 1851 - John Fisher and Jacob Bowman, res. Washington Co.; 1871 - Jonathan Harbaugh and Joseph Barkdoll.
Sources: Bounty land claims, 50-40-85619, 55-120-87169; Pension, WO3231, WC1064.

DELPHA, Thomas. Pvt. under Capt. Jacob Alexander, 22 Jul - 19 Sep 1814.

DELPHIA, Thomas. Pvt. under Capt. Matthew Murray, 25 Aug - 27 Oct 1814.

DEMRY, John. Pvt., 38th U.S. Inf.; at enlistment: 5 ft, 7 inches; grey eyes, dark hair, dark complexion; age 22; farmer; b. Fred. Co., MD; enlisted 27 Dec 1814 at Balt., by Lt. Barrett, for the duration of war.

DEMUTH, John. - See Damoot. Pvt. under Capt. Samuel Ogle, 1 May - 5 Jul 1813. [In Henry Young's *Moravian Families of Graceham, Md.*, there is a Johann Demuth who m. Catharine ---; issue: Sophia Theresia b. 23 Aug 1797 at 11:45.]

DENNIS, John. Pvt. from Fredericktown under Capt. Huston/ Capt. Joseph Green, enrolled 23 Jul 1814; deserted 8 Dec 1814.

DERN, Frederick. Pvt. under Capt. Matthew Murray, 25 Aug - 27 Oct 1814.

DERNE, Frederick. Appt'd Capt. in 47th Regt., MM, 1 Feb 1814.

DERNER, George. Pvt. under Capt. Daniel Shawen, 5 Sep - 27 Oct 1814. [See West. Md. Genealogy, 4:2 (descents).]

DERNER, Jacob. 2nd corpl. under Capt. Shawen, 5 Sep - 27 Oct 1814. [See West. Md. Genealogy, 4:2 (descents).]

DERTZBACK, [Dertzbaugh] George. Served under Capt. Henry Steiner, 28 Apr - 29 Jun 1813 and 25 Aug - 27 Sep 1814. Promoted from pvt. to corpl. 16 May 1813; promoted to 3rd Sgt prior to 27 Sep 1814; b. 15 Oct 1790; m. c.1813 Catherine Kregloe (b. 5 Dec 1793); d. at his residence in Frederick, W. 3rd St., 31 Oct 1856, age 66 yrs, 16 days. Catharine Dertzbaugh, d. at residence of her son-in-law, Henry Ziegler, 1 May 1863. Both bur. Frederick Ref. Ch. 1850 census of Fredericktown: George Dartzbaugh, 59, labourer; Catherine, 55; Sophia R., 18. Catherine Dertzbach, eldest dau of George, m. Daniel Derr 21 Sep 1834; Margaret, 2nd dau of George Dertzbach, m. Henry L. Fiegler 31 Mar 1836; Mary Dertzbach, 3rd dau of George, m. Joshua Young 10 Dec 1840.
Sources: **Names in Stone**; (Frederick) **Examiner**, 5 Nov 1856, 19 Nov 1856, 7 May 1863;

FREDERICK COUNTY MILITIA IN THE WAR OF 1812

Bridge in Time; Engelbrecht Diary: 2:128, 200, 400.

DESHNER, Jacob. 3rd sergt. under Capt. Jacob Getzendanner, 9 Aug - 17 Sep 1813.

DEVELBISS [Devilbiss], Charles. Appt'd 13 July 1814, 1st lieut. under Capt. Peter Bankhart, 20th Regt. Served as 1st Lieut., 22 Jul - 3 Oct 1814, temporarily attached to Capt. Magee ("supernumerary by consolidation," 3 Oct 1814).

DEVER, Richard. Pvt. under Capt. Matthew Murray, 25 Aug - 27 Oct 1814.

DEVILBISS, George. Appt'd 12 Jun 1812 as 1st lieut. under Capt. Jacob Eckman, 20th Regt.

DEVITT, David B. Pvt. under Capt. John Brengle, 25 Aug - 19 Sep 1814; b. PA, 28 Nov 1791; m(1) 23 Oct 1821 Miss Ann P. Mantz (d. 17 May 1828); m(2) 19 Jan 1830 Elizabeth Fout (4 Oct 1802 - 10 May 1869), dau of Peter Fout; res. Fredericktown 1850, 1855. 1850 census of Fredericktown: David B. Devitt, 62, tinner, $5,000; Elizabeth, 43; Amelia, 17; Edward J., 15; Margaret, 13; Philip H., 10; Anna M., 7 - all born in MD except David B. He d. 23 Apr 1865. His widow d. at her residence, East Patrick Street after a lingering illness in May 1869.

Source: Bounty land claim, 55-120-6606 (certificate for 40 acres in file); **Bridge in Time; Names in Stone; Frederick-town Herald,** 23 Oct 1821, 26 May 1828, 23 Jan 1830; **(Frederick) Examiner,** 3 May 1865, 12 May 1869; **Md. Union,** 20 May 1869.

DICK, Christian. Pvt. under Capt. Thomas Contee Worthington; joined 17 Aug 1812; deserted 5 Sep 1812.

DICKSON, John. Pvt. under Capt. Daniel Shawen, 5 Sep - 27 Oct 1814.

DILL, Ezra. 3rd corpl. as substitute for John Durst under Capt. George W. Ent, 24 Aug - 30 Sep 1814. [Ezra Dill m. 28 Feb 1819 Miss Margaret Morgan by Rev. Helfenstein. (*Frederick-town Herald*, 6 Mar 1819)]

DILL, Joshua. 1st sergt. under Capt. George W. Ent, 24 Aug - 30 Sep 1814; b. c.1792; res. Fred. Co., MD 1850, 1855; m. Mary Kleinhart c.12 Apr 1817; d. 24 Jul 1868 at his residence at West 3rd St., in Frederick, leaving wife and 4 children. Widow Mary M. Dill d. 14 May 1873, age 79 yrs, 2 mos. 1850 census of Fredericktown: Joshua Dill, 57, farmer, $23,000; Mary, 56; George, 26; Mary M., 17. One-time Judge of Orphan's Court.

Sources: Bounty land claim, 55-160-1870; **FCml; Bridge in Time; (Frederick) Examiner,** 29 Jul 1868, 5 Aug 1868, 21 May 1873; **Md. Union,** 30 Jul 1868.

DINSMORE, Margaret. Wife of War of 1812 veteran. She was b. in Frederick Co., moved to Balt. in 1812; dau of Charles P. Taylor of Charles Co. who served in Rev. War. She d. 23 Aug 1882, res. 77 Albemarle St., Balt, in her 93rd year.

DISCORNEY, Augustis J.(or S.?). From Balt. Town. 4th corpl., later as 3rd corpl., under Capt. George W. Magee, 22 Jul 1814 - 10 Jan 1815.

DITTER, Abraham. Pvt. from Upper Fred. Co. under Capt. James F. Huston; joined 23 Jul 1814; deserted 16 Sep 1814.

THE VETERANS

DIXON, Hezekiah. Pvt. under Capt. Samuel Dawson; joined 14 Oct 1814; deserted 8 Dec 1814.

DIXON, James. Pvt. under Capt. George W. Ent, 24 Aug - 30 Sep 1814; m. 13 Apr 1817 Sophia Ester (b. c.1795) at Middletown, MD, by Rev. Reich, Luth. Ch.; d. near Fredericktown, MD, 25 May 1835. In his diary Engelbrecht noted that James M. Dixon (miller) d. at Johnson's Mill, in the evening of 25 May 1835, in his 45th year. Widow res. Buckeys Town Dist., 1850 with Sophia E., 11; Benjamin F., 16; and Joseph A., 15; d. 5 Aug 1854. In 1855 appeared Joseph A. Dixon, age 20 yrs on 25 Sep 1854, only minor child of James Dixon. Acq.: (1850): Peter Ott; (1855): Richard R. Dixon representing minor son, Joseph A. Dixon; Mason R. Marsh and Joshua J. Zimmerman.

Sources: Bounty land claim, 55-120-19779; Engelbrecht Diary: 2:163; Bridge in Time.

DIXON James. Pvt. under Capt. Henry Steiner, 25 Aug - 27 Sep 1814.

DIXON, James. Pvt., 14 U.S. Inf. under Capt. Samuel Lane. At enlistment: 5 ft 7 inches; grey eyes, dark hair, dark complexion; age 19; b. Fred. Co., MD; enlisted 27 May 1812 at Cumberland by Lt. Nelson until 27 May 1817. Prisoner of war, arrived at Salem from Halifax. At Ft. Independence. Deserted at Schnectady 19 Jan 1815.

DOHERTY [Dougherty, Dockerty], Daniel. At enlistment: 5 ft, 8 inches; grey or blue eyes, brown hair; age 39 or 41; farmer; b. Fred. Co., MD; enlisted 26 Jan or 26 Feb 1814, by Ensign Truax, for duration of war or until May 4, 1815.

Absent sick at Utica, 16 Feb 1815. At Sacketts Harbor 1 March 1815. Discharged at Sacketts Harbor 5 May 1815.

DOLL, Michael. Pvt. under Capt. John Brengle, 25 Aug - 19 Sep 1814; d. 6 Jun, New Philadelphia, OH in his 39th year, leaving a wife and 7 children.

Source: Frederick Herald, 22 Jun 1833.

DOLL, Peter. Pvt. under Capt. John Brengle, 25 Aug - 19 Sep 1814.

DONN, (Dorner?) George. Pvt. under Capt. Samuel Duvall, 3 Aug - 3 Oct 1814.

DORFF, George. Corpl. under Capt. Samuel Dawson, 1 May - 5 Jul 1813.

DORFF, Patrick. Pvt. from Fredericktown under Capt. James F. Huston/Capt. Joseph Green, 23 Jul 1814 - 10 Jan 1815; taken prisoner on 24 Aug at Battle of Bladensburg.

DORSEY, Abraham. Pvt. under Capt. George W. Magee, joined 23 Jul 1814; deserted 1 Oct 1814.

DORSEY, Basil of Evan. Appt'd capt. 12 May 1812, of a company in 13th Regt., MM; served 30 Jul - 27 Sep 1814.

DORSEY, Henry C. Appt'd 27 Apr 1813, 1st lieut. under Capt. Jonathan Norris, 20th Regt., MM.

DORSEY, Michael. Pvt. under Capt. William Knox 26 Aug - 27 Oct 1814.

DORSEY, Otho. Pvt. under Capt. Fonsten, 2 Sep - 27 Oct 1814; b. c.1784; res. Carroll Co., MD, 1851 and 1855.

Source: Bounty land claim, 55-120-44168.

DOUGHERTY, Charles, pvt., 12 U.S. Inf. At enlistment: 5 ft, 9 inches; blue eyes, frosty hair, florid complexion; age

FREDERICK COUNTY MILITIA IN THE WAR OF 1812

36; farmer; b. Fred. Co., MD; enlisted 13 Feb 1813 by Lieut. Fowles, at Strausburgh, for 5 yrs. Mustered at Buffalo 28 Feb and 30 Apr 1815. Mustered under Capt. James Dorman's Company, 8th U.S. Inf., Ft. Osage, 30 Jun, 31 Aug, 1815. Discharged at Camp Jackson 13 Feb 1818.

DOURY [Druery], James. Pvt. under Capt. John Brengle, 25 Aug - 19 Sep 1814.

DOWD, George. From Balt. County. Pvt. under Capt. Galt, 31 Aug - 27 Oct 1814.

DOWDLE, William. Pvt. in the company of Capt. Markey, under Lieut. William Kolb, 13 Oct - 15 Nov 1814.

DOWNEY, John. Pvt. in Capt. Flautt's rifle company, 29 Apr - 29 Jun 1813. [FCml issued to John Downey and Lydia Evans on 6 May 1821.]

DOWNING, Dory. Pvt. under Capt. Barton Hackney, 1 Sep - 27 Oct 1814.

DOYL, Jago(?). Pvt. under Capt. Joseph Wood, 27 Aug - 28 Oct 1814.

DOYLE, Lawrence. Pvt. under Capt. George W. Ent, 24 Aug - 30 Sep 1814; m. 26 Jan 1822 Sarah Gordon (c.1800), in Fredericktown, by Rev. Patrick Davidson, Luth. Ch.; d. Fredericktown 14 Jan 1845. She d. 31 Dec 1873, age 75 yrs, 9 mos., 14 days, native of Parish of Cloughher, Tyrone Co., Ireland. Acq.: 1851 - F. Hawman; 1855 - John Doyle and Margaret Doyle of Fred. Co.

Sources: Bounty land claim (awarded warrant for 40 acres); **Frederick-town Herald**, 2 Feb 1822; **Examiner**, 4 Mar 1874.

DRAPER, William. Appt'd 15 Jun 1813 as ensign under Capt. Jacob Smelser, 28th Regt., MM.

DRONENBURGH, Jacob. Pvt. under Capt. Philip Smith; joined 23 May 1813; deserted 18 Jun 1813.

[Jacob Dronenburg, great-grandfather of Joseph M. Dronenburg, came from Germany in company with two bros. and settled in Frederick County, MD, where he owned a smithy in which he carried on a successful business. He m. and among his children was a son named Jacob. This Jacob Dronenburg was b. in Clarksburg. He m. Mary M. Madery and had: John T.; Jane m. Joseph Brandenburg, farmer and former tax collector of Carroll Co.; Lucay A., widow of James Murray, who was a contractor of Carroll County. From Williams, *Hist. of Fred. Co.]*

DRUMMON, James. 5th sergt. under Capt. William Knox, 26 Aug - 27 Oct 1814.

DUDERAR, George. From New Windsor. Pvt. under Capt. George W. Magee; joined 22 Jul 1814; deserted 1 Dec 1814.

DUFFEY, James. Pvt. under Capt. George W. Magee; joined 22 Jul 1814; deserted 30 Jul 1814.

DUFFIELD, John. Pvt., 25th U.S. Inf., under "Howard." At enlistment: 5 ft, 9 inches, grey eyes; sandy hair, light complexion; age 32(?); cordwainer; b. Fred. Co., MD; enlisted 9 July 1818 for 1 year. Discharged Sacketts Harbor 8 July 1814.

DUGAN [Dougan, Dongan], James. Pvt., 5th U.S. Inf. At the enlistment: 5 ft,

THE VETERANS

10 inches; dark eyes, dark hair, florid complexion; age 25; chair maker; b. Emmittsburg, Fred. Co., MD; enlisted 27 May 1812 in Frederick by Lt. Clarke, for 5 yrs. Prisoner of war, arrived at Salem from Halifax and stationed at Fort Independence. Present at Sacketts Harbor 17 Sep 1814. Appt'd corpl. 2 March 1815. Deserted at Detroit 26 Jun 1816.

DUNAVIN, William. Pvt. from Fredericktown under Capt. James F. Huston/Capt. Joseph Green, joined 23 Jul 1814; deserted 8 Dec 1814; returned 2 Jan 1815; discharged at Annapolis 10 Jan 1815.

DUNN, Edward. Pvt. under Capt. Fonsten, 2 Sep - 27 Oct 1814.

DUNNING, Dora. Pvt. under Capt. Jacob Alexander, 22 Jul - 19 Sep 1814.

DUPLAINT, Dominic. Pvt. from Balt. Town under Capt. George W. Magee, 22 Jul 1814 - 10 Jan 1815. In confinement at Fort McHenry.

DURBIN, William, Jr. Appt'd capt. 4 Apr 1808 of a company in the 20th Regt., MM; served as capt. of a company, 24 Aug - 27 Oct 1814. [*Hornet*, 22 May 1811 - Married Thurs 25th ult. by Rev. Forrester, William Durbin to Miss Elizabeth Reese, all of Fred. Co.; *The Times and Democratic Advocate* - 5 Apr 1838 - Married on Monday morning last by Rev. Jno. L. Pitts, John Blocher, esq., of Cumberland, to Elizabeth, eldest dau of Col. Wm. Durbin, of this place.; *The Visitor* - 29 Oct 1840 - Died at Cumberland, MD, on 13th inst., of pulmonary affection, in her 21st year, Catharine, dau of Col. Wm. Durbin, formerly of this co.]

DURST, Daniel. Pvt. under Capt. George W. Ent, 24 Aug - 30 Sep 1814. FCml issued 1 Oct 1817 to Daniel Durst and Elizabeth Carlin. Mrs. Elizabeth Durst d. 24 Feb 1818 of the smallpox.
Source: **Frederick-town Herald**, 28 Feb 1818.

DURST, John. Furnished substitute, Ezra Dill, who served under Capt. George W. Ent, 24 Aug - 30 Sep 1814.

DUTROW, Henry. Pvt. under Capt. Daniel Shawen, 5 Sep - 27 Oct 1814.

DUTTEROW, David. Appt'd 27 Apr 1813 as capt. of a company in the 20th Regt., MM.

DUVALL, Daniel. Appt'd 28 Dec 1808 as ensign under Capt. Riggs, 13th Regt., MM; served as lieut. under Capt. Philip Smith, 23 May - 8 Sep 1813; m. Ann C. Belt (marr. license issued 18 Dec 1819, Frederick Co); d. 2 Mar 1846, aged 57 yrs; Ann d. 5 Oct 1843, aged 46 yrs. Daniel and Ann C. had five children: Lloyd b. c.1823; Ann E. b. c.1825, d. prior to 19 Jul 1852; Susan V. b. c.1827, d. prior to 19 Jul 1852; Julia [?] b. 24 Mar 1831; Daniel b. 5 Jan 1839. On 27 Aug 1850 Lloyd T. Duvall was appt'd guardian to Daniel B. Duvall. Lloyd T. Duvall res. Fred. Co., 1852 and 1855.
Source: Bounty land claim (awarded warrant for 40 acres).

DUVALL, Elisha. Pvt. under Capt. Denton Darby 3 Aug - 8 Nov 1814. Absent 6 days.

FREDERICK COUNTY MILITIA IN THE WAR OF 1812

DUVALL, John. Pvt., 1st U.S. Inf. under Capt. Hugh Moore, and Col. Jacob Kingsbury. At enlistment: 5 ft, 9 inches; blue or hazel eyes, dark hair, fair complexion; age 21 or 26; blacksmith; b. Fredericktown, MD; enlisted 16 Jan 1812 at Pittsburgh, by Lt. Johnston until 16 Jan 1817. Mustered at Ft. Wayne 16 Feb 1815; promoted to sergt. 1 March 1815. Absent since 13 Apr 1815 at Cincinnati with public dispatch. At Detroit since 13 Jun 1816. Reduced 28 Sep 1816, re-instated 15 Oct 1816. Discharged at Detroit 18 Jan 1817.

DUVALL, Samuel. Appt'd capt. 12 Jun 1812, of a company in 29th Regt., MM; served as capt. of a company, 3 Aug - 3 Oct 1814.

DUVALL, Thomas. Newspaper obit. states he served in the War of 1812; d. 6 Mar 1869 at his residence near Ijamsville, MD, aged 82 yrs, 6 mos, 6 days; bur. Mt. Olivet Cem. She d. 17 Apr 1863 while on a visit to Fredericktown, in her 69th yr.

Source: **(Frederick) Examiner**, 22 Apr 1863, 10 Mar 1869.

EADER, Lazarus. [See Lazarus Atir.] According to Catharine Eader, her husband served under Capt. Darby. [Name apparently written as Atir on the rolls, which likelihood was overlooked by pension authorities.] She stated that he volunteered at New Market, MD; was 5 ft, 7 inches high, had blue eyes, black hair; m. Catharine Carnes [Karnes] (b. 14 Feb 1800), Fredericktown, 26 Jul 1827 [year also given as 1829], by David Shaeffer, Luth. minister; neither m. previously. Lazarus Eader d. 22 Aug 1858, Fredericktown "from being paralyzed," according to the *Examiner;* bur. Mt. Olivet. Catharine moved to Sandy Hook, Washington Co., MD, fol. death of husband; res. there 1879; d. 6 Jan 1880. Acq.: 1879 - Elias W. Bowers, aged 50, Sandy Hook, MD; and F. L. Butler, aged 44, res. Sandy Hook, MD, neighbors for 25 yrs. 1880 - Mary C. Eader, b. 22 Feb 1825; Henrietta E. Eader, now Ward, b. 16 Sep 1836; Sarah Catherine Eader, now Smith, b. 11 Nov 1842. res. of Sandy Hook and Rohrersville, MD, children of Lazarus Eader.

Sources: Pension, WO38345; **Names in Stone**.

EADER, Thomas. Pvt. under Capt. Zacharias, 7 Aug - 10 Sep 1814, 2nd Regt., 1st Cav. Dist. [FCml issued to Thomas Eader and Margaret Weaver 3 Nov 1814. Bur. at Mt. Olivet, Frederick: Thomas Eader, 3 May 1847, age 57; wife Margaret, 28 Aug 1793 - 2 March 1860; dau Susan, 1817 - 1844; son David, 5 Apr 1833 - 28 Apr 1845. 1850 census, Fredericktown: Margaret Eader, 57, $4000; Augustus L. Eader, 30, carpenter; Amelia M. Eader, 22; Anna C. Eader, 13.

Sources: FCml; **Names in Stone**; **Bridge in Time**.

EADER, William. Pvt. under Capt. Philip Smith, May 23 - Sep 8 1813; b. 9 Nov 1791; m. 31 May 1835 Ann Stalling of Fredericktown by Rev. David F. Schaeffer. 1850 census, Fred. E.D.: William Eader, 57, farmer; Laura Eader, 14; Mary Hellen Eader, 12; Ann E. Eader, 9; Alice Eader, 6; Catherine Eader, 3; Savilla Kelley, 40; George Pool, 24, labourer. Also res. Fred. Co.,

102

THE VETERANS

MD, 1855. Acq. (1851) Cornelius Pool. Bur. at Mt. Olivet, Frederick, is William M. Eader; d. 3 Jun 1865.

Sources: Bounty land claim (warrant for 40 acres awarded); **Bridge in Time; Names in Stone; Political Examiner & Public Advertiser,** 3 Jun 1835.

EADOR, Jacob. Pvt. in the company of Capt. Markey, under Lieut. William Kolb 13 Oct - 15 Nov 1814.

EAREHEART, George. From New Windsor; pvt. under Capt. George W. Magee, 22 Jul 1814 - 10 Jan 1815.

EARNST, Abraham. Pvt. under Capt. Philip Smith 23 May - 8 Sep 1813.

EASTERDAY, Abraham. Appt'd 28 Apr 1808, as capt. of a company, 28th Regt., MM.

EATON, Joseph. Pvt. under Capt. Daniel Marker, 25 Aug - 27 Oct 1814.

EBB, Jeremiah. Although from Washington Co. he served in a Fred. Co. company as pvt. under Capt. Samuel Dawson, 14 Oct 1814 - 10 Jan 1815.

EBBERT, Joseph. Pvt. in Capt. Flautt's rifle company, 29 Apr - 29 Jun 1814.

EBBERTS. See Ebert(s).

EBBERTS, Jacob. Pvt. under Capt. George W. Ent, 24 Aug - 30 Sep 1814; b. c.1782; m. 12 Nov 1809 Susanna Stimmel (b. c.1786), in Fred. Co., by Rev. David F. Schaeffer; d. Fred. Co., 13 Jun 1852. [Jacob Eberts, orphan, age 16 yrs on 5 Apr 1796, with consent of mother, Cathrine Eberts, bound to David Levy, Sr., to age 21.] Acq. (1855): John B. Stimmel and James Thomas, res. of Fred. Co.

Sources: Bounty land claim, 55-120-42766; West. Md. Genealogy, 4:4.

EBBERTS, John. Pvt. under Capt. George W. Ent, 24 Aug - 30 Sep 1814. [The following information has been gathered on John Ebbert (Ebert) who may be the same person as subject veteran - John Ebert b. 24 Jul 1772; m(1) --- Hauser; m(2) c.1804, Miss Ann Rebecca Fritchie (21 Jul 1776 - 30 Oct 1822); m(3) 13 Jan 1825 Miss Elizabeth Krug, dau of Rev. John Andrew Krug; John Ebert (Ebbert) d. 1 Apr 1851; Elizabeth Ebert 3d wife of John Ebert, d. 28 Jan 1849, age 70; she was dau of Rev. John Andrew Krug (he d. 1796) and grand dau of Rev. Frederick Handschuh, missionary from Halle Germany to America c.1745.]

Sources: Engelbrecht Diary, 1:317, 2:473, 513; (Frederick) Examiner, 2 Apr 1851; FCml.

EBBERTS, Joseph. Pvt. under Capt. George W. Ent, 24 Aug - 30 Sep 1814; b. c.1779; m. Elizabeth McCormick (b. c.1788), in Fredericktown by Rev. David F. Schaeffer. [The date of the marriage is given by the widow as 1 Apr 1813; but the marr. license was issued to Joseph Ebberts and Elizabeth Carmack on 1 Apr 1817.] Joseph Ebberts d. at Fredericktown 29 Dec 1848; bur. Mt. Olivet Cem., Frederick. She res. Fredericktown, 1852 and 1855. Acq. (1852): John Hanshew, George W. Ent.

Sources: Bounty land claim, 55-120-25882; **Names in Stone.**

EBBERTS, Michael. Newspaper Obit. describes him as one of the "Old Defenders." He m. c.27 Jul 1809 Elizabeth Kelly (b. C.1791); he d. 17

FREDERICK COUNTY MILITIA IN THE WAR OF 1812

Apr 1875. in his 90th year. Both bur. Mt. Olivet Cem.

Sources: (Frederick) Examiner, 5 May 1875; FCml; Bridge in Time; Names in Stone.

EBERT, Eli. Pvt. under Capt. John Brengle, 25 Aug - 19 Sep 1814; b. 23 Dec 1794; res. Liberty, Adams Co., IL, 1853. Source: Bounty land claim, 55-120-50568.

EBERTS, George. From Balt. Pvt. under Capt. James F. Huston/Capt. Joseph Green; joined 23 Jul 1814; deserted 21 Dec 1814; returned 30 Dec 1814; discharged at Annapolis 10 Jan 1815; d. Balt. 22 Jan 1866. [Died in Balt. on 22 Jan 1866, After a long and painful illness, George Ebberts, in his 85th year, "one of the Old Defenders of Baltimore."

Source: (Frederick) Examiner, 31 Jan 1866.

EBY, Samuel. Pvt. under Capt. Philip Smith; joined May 23 1813; deserted 12 Jun 1813.

ECCARD [Eckart, Eckert], Peter. Sergt. under Capt. Daniel Marker, 16 Aug - 18 Sep 1813; b. c.1784; m. Catherina Ambrose (16 Jun 1785 - 13 Sep 1868, at Hagerstown, May 1808; res. Catoctin Dist., Fred. Co. 1850; dau: Sarah Maria b. 15 Mar 1813. Acq.: 1851 - Thomas Bittle, Philip Cline; and Samuel Shipley, from Washington Co., who served in the same company; George Stokes, 1st Sergt. of the company. Peter Eccard d. 22 Dec 1872, age 88 yrs, 10 mos., 23 days; bur. Ellerton Grossnickle's Brethren Ch.

Sources: Bounty land claim, 55-120-12837 (separate from pension file); Pension, SO15978;

Moravian Families of Graceham, Md.; Names in Stone; Bridge in Time.

ECHAR, Christopher. Mbr. of Crawford's "company."

ECK, Peter. Pvt. under Capt. William Knox, 26 Aug - 27 Oct 1814; c.1792; res. Montgomery Co., OH 1852 and 1855.

Source: Bounty land claim, 55-120-66465.

ECKAR, David. Mbr. of Crawford's "company."

ECKER, Christopher. Mbr. of Crawford's "company."

ECKES, Nicholas. Pvt. under Capt. William Knox, 26 Aug - 27 Oct 1814.

ECKHART [Echart], Anthony. Corpl. under Capt. Samuel Duvall, 3 Aug - 3 Oct 1814; b. 6 May 1783; m. Catharine Scheatenhelm (b. c.1787), 6 miles from Fredericktown, Fred. Co., MD, 6 or 13 Sep 1806, each for first time; had five children when they went to Hocking Co. OH. They res. Hocking Co., OH, in 1850, 1855 and 1871 (P.O. address: Logan); he d. 18 Mar 1872 Hocking Co, OH, of asthma; she res. Logan, OH, 1872. Acq.: 1871 - James W. Allen, Adam Giger; 1872 - Susan Keagler, b. 19 Oct 1809, dau of Anthony Eckhart; she res. 14 miles of her parents during her married life; elder sister had then been dec'd. c.20 yrs. Also in 1872 - Hiram Francisco, age 77, living on adjoining farm for past 56 yrs. Letter in the file dated 3 Jan 1932, from Mrs. G. E. Huffman, 1001 Ravinia Road, W. Lafayette, IN, requesting the pension papers of Anthony Eckhart, noting that one of his sisters was named Betsy.

THE VETERANS

Sources: Bounty land claims, 50-40-4724, 55-120-24950; Pensions, SO7007, SC3872, WO8919, WC3542.

ECKIS. See also Eckes.

ECKIS, Peter. Private under Capt. Samuel Ogle, 1 May - 5 Jul 1813; promoted to 4th corpl. 1 Jun 1814.

ECKIS, Samuel. Pvt. under Capt. Samuel Ogle, 1 May - 5 Jul 1813.

ECKMAN, Jacob. Appt'd 16 Aug 1808, as capt. of a company, 20th Regt., MM.

ECKMAN, Jacob. Pvt. under Capt. Daniel Shawen, 5 Sep - 27 Oct 1814.

ECKMAN, John. Pvt. under Capt. Samuel Duvall, 3 Aug - 3 Oct 1814.

ECKMAN, William. Pvt. under Capt. Fonsten, 2 Sep - 27 Oct 1814.

EDMONDSON, Robert. Appt'd 24 Oct 1800 as ensign in the company of Capt. Osb. Hillery, 13th Regt., MM.

EDMUNDSTON, James N. Pvt. under Capt. Samuel Duvall, 3 Aug - 3 Oct 1814.

EDWARDS, James. Pvt. under Capt. Zacharias, 7 Aug - 10 Sep 1814, 2nd Regt., 1st Cav. Dist.

EICHELBERGER, George M. 2nd major, under Lt. Col. Henry Stembel, 3rd Regt., commanding the 2nd Battalion; joined the staff on 1 Sep 1814 and served until c.27 Oct 1814; b. PA; m. Jane Grayson [Greason] c.1813; res. Fred. Co. for 45 yrs; d. 16 Jan 1854, at his residence on West Patrick St., Frederick, age 69 yrs, 11 mos., 5 days. He had suffered from several attacks of paralysis, the last of which was on 26 Dec 1851, from which he lingered until death. He was for many yrs Register of Wills of Fred. Co. His widow, Jane Grayson Eichelberger d. 4 Feb 1876, in her 76th year. Both bur. at Mt. Olivet with other children. 1850 census of Fredericktown: George M. Eichelberger, 65, PA; Jane, 54, PA; William A., 19, MD; Mary Brown, 19 (black). Anne E., wife of Charles A. Gambrill, and oldest dau of Col. George M. Eichelberger, d. 28 Jun 1852, in her 38th year.

Sources: (Frederick) Examiner, 7 Jul 1852, 18 Jan 1854; Names in Stone; Bridge in Time; FCmL.

ELBERTS, George. Pvt. from Balt. under Capt. Joseph Green; joined 14 Oct 1814; deserted 21 Dec 1814; returned 30 Dec 1814; discharged at Annapolis on 10 Jan 1815.

ELDER, Charles. Served under Capt. Thomas Contee Worthington, 17 Aug - 31 Dec 1812. He was promoted from pvt. to 4th corpl. on 19 Dec 1812. [Poss. information on Charles Elder, see *West. Md. Genealogy*, 2:68 (descents).]

ELDER, Charles. 3rd sergt. under Capt. Joseph Wood, 27 Aug - 28 Oct 1814.

ELDER, Henry. Pvt., 2nd Regt., 1st Cav. Dist., 26 Aug - 3 Sep 1814 under 1st Lieut. Upton Reid. [This could be Henry Elder son of Francis Elder. See Edmund Adams and Barbara Brady O'Keefe, *Catholic Trails West, Vol. 2*, p. 382. Henry Elder b. 21 July 1789, son of Francis and Catharine (Spalding) Elder. Francis b. 23 Aug 1755, Fred. Co., MD.]

FREDERICK COUNTY MILITIA IN THE WAR OF 1812

ELDER, Jesse. Pvt., 2nd Regt., 1st Cav. Dist., 26 Aug - 3 Sep 1814 under 1st Lieut. Upton Reid.

ELDER, Nathaniel. Pvt., 2nd Regt., 1st Cav. Dist., 26 Aug - 3 Sep 1814 under 1st Lieut. Upton Reid.

ELKINS, William. According to newspaper obit. he served in War of 1812; m. Mary Keefer c.25 Nov 1819; d. at residence of his dau, North Market St., Frederick, 8 Nov 1869, age c.73 yrs; acting bailiff at the Court House. Widow d. 13 Sep 1873 at residence of her son-in-law, Edward Sinn, in her 73rd year. Service record not located.
Source: (Frederick) Examiner, 10 Nov 1869; .

ELLER, Jacob [of Jacob]. Pvt. under Capt. Barton Hackney, 1 Sep 1814 - 27 Oct 1814; b. c.1795; m. 23 Nov 1826 Elizabeth Grimes (b. c.1806), in Fred. Co, by Rev. John L. Bryan; res. Callaway Co., MO, 1851 and 1855; d. Callaway Co, MO, 7 Dec 1867. She res. Callaway Co., MO, 1878 and 1885 (P.O. Address: Auxvasse); d. 17 Jan 1887, Callaway Co., MO.; bur. on farm where she lived. Acq.: 1853 - Josiah Frazier, Fred. Co. 1878 - Samuel Jesse and Hiram Burt, of Callaway Co., MO.; Elias Eller, age 77, b. and raised in Fred. Co., moved from there to WV near Wheeling and remained there c.12 yrs; moved to Audidin Co., MO where he now res. (1878) since 1838; bro. of Jacob Eller; he states Jacob and Elizabeth Grimes were m. at his father's house (he thinks) in Fred. Co., MD. or at Jacob's own house, that he had just built. Elizabeth's father was living in Montgomery Co., and Elizabeth was visiting at her sister's in the neighborhood "when my big brother made her acquaintance." "Jacob and his family moved to this county about one year before I did. ... my residence being the edge of Audrain and his in the edge of Callaway. .. Elizabeth still lives on the old homested." John Gregg (1878) said that Jacob and Elizabeth settled in northern part of Callaway Co., about 1 mile from Andrain line; he res. same neighborhood and helped to raise first cabin on Jacob Eller's farm, and also the house in which the widow Eller now lives. John T. Eller (1878), son of dec'd. Jacob Eller and Elizabeth, age 37[?], res. with his mother. 1887 - Martha Eller, around age 50.
Sources: Bounty land claims, 50-40-97038, 55-120-74714; Pension, WO22633, WC17980.

ELLIS, John. Pvt. under Capt. Hall, 7 Aug - 10 Sep 1814, 2nd Regt., 1st Cav. Dist.; b. c.1785; m. Anna Maria Fagan (b. c.1799) in Washington, D.C. 12 Dec 1840 by Rev. William Mathews; res. Washington, D.C. 1855; d. 23 Jun 1855, survived by his widow, Anna Maria. Acq. - 1855: Mary Ann Lutz, James Y. Davis, Ralph J. Falconar.
Source: Bounty land claim: 55-120-12364.

ELMS [Elmes, Elema], Joseph. Pvt. under Capt. Denton Darby, 3 Aug - 8 Nov 1814; m. Cena [Sena, Cenett, Asseneth] Nourse [Nouse] (b. c.1790) in Montgomery Co., Nov 1815, by Rev. Desheals; d. 14 Sep 1829 or 1830, Montgomery Co. Cena Elms res. Montgomery Co., MD,. 1855. Acq.: 1851 - George W. Green and Levin

THE VETERANS

Hause; 1855 - William Lee and J. J. Perriog, res. Montgomery Co.
Source: Bounty land claim, 55-120-59626.

ELY, Daniel. Pvt. under Capt. George W. Ent, 24 Aug - 30 Sep 1814; m. Martha Mobberly [Mobley], in Fredericktown, Aug 1815, by Rev. David Shaeffer; d. 23 Feb 1825 in Fredericktown. His remains were interred with military honors by the Frederick Blues, Capt. Ent's company; bur. in the German Reformed graveyard, being one of its parishioners. He was in his 32nd year. She later m. --- Fogler who d. prior to 1 Jan 1851; res. Fredericktown 1851, 1855. Acq.: 1851 - Henry Kelly, Senr, and Rachael Mobly; 1855 - Jane Rebecca Dungan and Maria Dungan.
Sources: Bounty land claim, 55-120-15109; **Fredericktown Herald**, 26 Feb 1825; **Englebrecht Diary**, v.1, p. 327.

ELY, William. Pvt. under Capt. John Brengle, 25 Aug - 19 Sep 1814; m. Miss Sarah Row (b. c.1797), Frederick, MD, 11 Dec 1817 by Rev. David Schaeffer, Luth. Ch., Frederick. At enrollment: 5 ft, 7 inches, 160-170 lbs, dark hair, dark eyes; d. 17 Mar 1840 [or 5 Mar 1841], in Frederick. Widow res. Fredericktown, MD, 1851-1878 (on Patrick St. in 1878); d. 2 Jan 1880, age 83; bur. Mt. Olivet Cem. Acq.: 1851 - Henry Kelly, Senr., and Elizabeth Bender; 1878 - John Lambright, age 72, North Market St.; Ezra Ely, age 77, West 6th St., Frederick. [*Frederick Visiter and Temperance Advocate* - 14 Mar 1839 - Died Monday, 11th inst, Glovenia, infant dau of Wm. Ely, aged 11 months.]
Sources: Bounty land claims, 50-40-80888, 55-120-2414; Pension, WO24205, WC14916.

EMERLY, James. Res. 5 miles of Taneytown; served as pvt. under Capt. Galt, 31 Aug - 27 Oct 1814.

ENGLAND, Andrew. Pvt. under Capt. Samuel Ogle, 1 May - 5 Jul 1813.

ENGLAND, Andrew. Pvt. from New Windsor under Capt. George W. Magee, 22 Jul 1814 - 10 Jan 1815.

ENGLAND, Nathan. No record in the rolls. He m. c.18 Dec 1820, Harriet Root (d. 18 Mar 1857, age 52, bur. Libertytown Lovers Rock Cem.) Obituary in (Frederick) *Examiner* records his death: "old soldier of the War of 1812," at Mount Pleasant on 6 May 1859, age 73 yrs.
Sources: **Names in Stone; FCml; (Frederick) Examiner,** 25 Mar 1857.

ENGLE, David. Mbr. of Crawford's "company."

ENGLE, Frederick. Pvt. under Capt. Jacob Getzendanner, 9 Aug - 17 Sep 1813 and 26 Jul - 21 Aug 1814.

ENGLE, John. Mbr. of Crawford's "company."

ENGLE [Engel], Peter. Pvt. under Capt. Basil Dorsey, 30 Jul - 27 Sep 1814; b. c.1787; res. Richland, Morrow Co., OH, 1850; Jefferson Twp, Noble Co, IN, 1855. Acq.: 1855 - Rodrick [?] Proutz, age 58, and Ezekiel L. Teagarden, age 32, res. same twp. Letter in file dated 6 May 1916, from Mrs. Emma H. Dowlin, Buffalo, Wyoming, asking if heirs were entitled to any unclaimed bounty land due Peter Engle.
Sources: Bounty land claims, 50-40-488, 55-120-44493.

FREDERICK COUNTY MILITIA IN THE WAR OF 1812

ENGLEBRECHT, Michael. From Upper Fred. Co. Principal musician under Capt. James F. Huston, 23 Jul - 13 Oct 1814. [1850 census of Fredericktown: Michl. Englebrecht, 56, tailor; Mary A., 10; Rebecca, 8; Margaret McMullen, 16 - all b. MD. Bur. at Mt. Olivet: Michael Engelbrecht, 1792-1886; wife Rebecca (McMullen), 1802-1847.

Sources: Names in Stone; Bridge in Time; (Frederick) Examiner, 14 Sep 1870.

ENGLEBRECHT [Engelbright, Engelbrecht], William. Pvt. under Capt. Nicholas Turbutt, 2 Sep - 27 Oct 1814; b. 17 Feb 1795; m. Susanna Winter (20 Dec 1801 - 24 Jul 1885), 3 Oct 1830, at Frederick, MD, by Rev. David F. Schaeffer, pastor Luth. Ch. of Frederick; his 1st marr.; he d. Fredericktown 15 Mar 1849, 15 minutes before 7 o'clock, aged 54 yrs, 24 days. At enrollment: 21 yrs old, tailor, dark eyes and hair, b. Fredericktown. 1850 census, Fredericktown: Susan Englebrecht, 49, $1000; Louisa F. Englebrecht, 13. She res. Fred. Co., 1852, 1855, 1878 (Church St., Fredericktown); d. at her residence, E. Church St. 24 Jul 1885; bur. Mt. Olivet Cem; mother of Luther M. and Louisa Englebrecht. Acq.: 1852 - Jacob Engelbrecht, Henry Hilton and A. H. Hunt; 1878 - Michael Engelbrecht, age 85, North Market St., Fredericktown; Joseph M. Ebberts, age 60, East Church St., Fredericktown, acq. 30 yrs; and George Hoskins, Fred. Co.

Sources: Bounty land claims, 50-40-70312, 55-120-7112; Pension, WO13836, WC10955; (Frederick) Examiner, 21 Mar 1849, 5 Aug 1885.

ENGLEMAN, John. Pvt. from New Windsor under Capt. George W. Magee, 22 Jul - 10 Jan 1815.

ENGLER, Philip. Pvt. from New Windsor under Capt. George W. Magee, 14 Oct 1814 - 10 Jan 1815.

ENGLISH, John. Mbr. of Crawford's "company."

ENGLISH, King. 1st sergt. under Capt. Daniel Shawen, 5 Sep - 27 Oct 1814; b. 1790; res. Marion Co., IN, 1850 and 1855.

ENT, George W. From Fredericktown. Appt'd 1 Aug 1814, capt. of a company in the 16th Regt., MM; served as Capt. in 3rd Regt, 24 Aug - 30 Sep 1814; b. c.1778, PA; m. 30 Sep 1806 Miss Margaret Woltz, dau of Dr. Peter and Mary Woltz of Fredericktown; res. Fred. Co., 1850 (in home of Jacob and Anna Hane in Fredericktown), 1855; d 4 Mar 1856 at Cincinnati, OH, age 78 yrs, 3 mos, 6 days. Engelbrecht noted in his diary that Mrs. Mary Woltz, relict of Dr. Woltz of Hagerstown, mother-in-law of George W. Ent, d. 18 Mar 1824; bur. Luth. Graveyard. [See entry for Abraham Blessing.]

Sources: Bounty land claim, 55-120-24031; Bridge in Time; Md. Herald, Oct 1806; The Md. Union, 20 Mar 1856; (Frederick) Examiner, 19 March 1856, 2 Apr 1856 [Memorial poem to Capt. Geo. W. Ent, ... Harrisburg]; Engelbrecht Diary: 2:69.

ENT, John. 3rd corpl. under Capt. Thomas Contee Worthington, 17 Aug - 31 Dec 1812.

ENT, John. [probably the same man as above.] Enlisted in regular army 4 Dec 1812 at Annapolis by Capt. Bernard for 5 yrs. At enlistment: 5 ft 7 1/2 inches, hazel eyes, brown hair, dark complexion, age 27, shoemaker, b. Germantown, PA. Corpl., 16th U.S. Inf. under Capt. J. Baldy; mustered Philadelphia 6 July 1814; discharged at Greenbush on 22 or 25 Apr 1815, wounded.

ERB, John. Pvt. under Capt. Zacharias, 7 Aug - 10 Sep 1814, 2nd Regt., 1st Cav. Dist.

ERBAUGH, Peter. Pvt. under Capt. William Durbin, Jr. 24 Aug - 27 Oct 1814. Absent without leave 25 Oct 1814.

ERHART, George. Pvt. in Capt. Flautt's rifle company, 29 Apr - 29 Jun 1813. [Bur. at New Windsor Presby. Ch. is George Erhard, 1783 - 28 July 1868, age 85, with wife Julia A., 1797 - 16 Apr 1880, age 83 yrs, 5 days; son James, 1821 - 1898; dau Margaret, 1833 - 1908.]

ERVIN, John. Pvt. under Capt. Joseph Wood, 27 Aug - 28 Oct 1814.

ESTERLINE, George. Pvt. from New Windsor under Capt. George W. Magee, 22 Jul - 13 Oct 1814; deserted 1 Oct. In confinement at Fort McHenry.

EVANS David. Mbr. of Crawford's "company."

EVANS, Elisha. Pvt. under Capt. Jacob Getzendanner, 26 Jul - 21 Aug 1814.

EVANS, James. Pvt. under Capt. John Fonsten, 2 Sep - 27 Oct 1814; res. 8 miles from Westminster.

EVANS, Joseph. Pvt. under Capt. George W. Ent, 24 Aug - 30 Sep 1814.

EVERETT, Samuel. Pvt. under Capt. Samuel Dawson, 14 Oct 1814 - 10 Jan 1815.

EVERHART, William. Pvt. under Capt. Daniel Marker, 25 Aug - 27 Oct 1814.

EVERLY, David. His widow stated he was drafted in Capt. Blizzard's company, discharged at Balt. Oct 1814; Elizabeth --- (b. c.1791), 3 Jun 1806, by Rev. Fraider [?], in Fred. Co. She res. Westminster, Carroll Co., MD, 1871. David Everly d. at his residence near Westminster, MD 8 Feb 1866. Acq.: 1871 - Jacob Bankert and David Crowl, res. within 2 miles over 20 yrs.

Source: Pension, WO1701 (rejected for "want of evidence of marriage prior to treaty of peace.")

EVES, Elias. Pvt. under Capt. John Fonsten, 2 Sep - 27 Oct 1814; res. 14 miles from Westminster.

EVITT, George W. Pvt. under Capt. Henry Steiner, 28 Apr - 29 Jun 29 1813 and 25 Aug - 27 Sep 1814; son of Woodward Evitt; d. 8 Nov 1834, Saturday morning, after long and painful illness, in his 48th year [*Herald*], son of Woodward Evitt. Engelbrecht states he d in 46th year; bur. German Ref. graveyard.

Sources: **Frederick Herald**, 15 Nov 1834; **Engelbrecht Diary**: 1:134; 2:134.

EYLER [Eyelor], Henry. Pvt. under Capt. Flautt; 29 Apr - 10 Jul 1813; b. c.1770; m. 15 Aug 1815 Elizabeth Luckabaugh [Luckenbach] (b. c.1800), each for first time, near Emmittsburg, in Fred. Co., MD, by George Flack, [later his widow said G. Plaugh], Moravian preacher. At enrollment: age 43, distiller, b. Fred. Co., MD, 6 ft, 2 inches, fair hair, blue eyes, light complexion; res. Westmoreland Co., PA, 1852, 1855; d.

Burrell Twp, Westmoreland Co., PA, 15 Jul 1857. She res. Westmoreland Co., PA, 1858 (Burrell Twp) and 1878 (P.O. Markle). Children of Henry Eyler: Joseph b. 10 Jun 1816; Elias b. 31 Mar 1818; Henry b. 27 Jul 1820. Acq.: 1858 - Jacob Willery, Lewis Byerly, res. Burrell Twp; 1878 - Andrew Dougherty, J. F. Zimmerman; Thomas Kirkwood, age 59, Greensburg, PA; Mary J. Kirkwood, age 34, Greensburg, PA; both acq. with Elizabeth Eyler, lived on adjoining farms 30 yrs; Peter Luckabugh, age 83 yrs, res. Allegheny Twp, Armstrong Co., PA, present at marriage; William Brisbin, North Huntingdon Twp, Westmoreland Co., PA, res. adjoining farm, became acq. in 1840; 1879 - Stephen Ridinger, Sr., Irwin, Westmoreland Co., PA.

Sources: Bounty land claims, 50-40-87388, 55-120-86414; Pension, WO19769, WC23274; **Moravians in Graceham, Md.**

EYLER, Henry. Pvt. under Capt. Philip Smith; joined 23 May 1813, deserted, returned 25 Jun, discharged 8 Sep 1813.

EYLER, Henry. Pvt. under Capt. Joseph Wood, 27 Aug - 28 Oct 1814.

EYLER, John. Ensign in Capt. George Flautt's rifle company, 29 Apr - 29 Jun 1813; b. 20 Nov 1783; m. 14 Dec 1820 Rebecca Harbaugh (b. c.1798), at Graceham, Fred. Co., MD, by Rev. Charles Klugl, Pastor of Moravian Congregation at Graceham, at her father's residence; res. Fred. Co., MD, 1850 and 1855. John Eyler d. Mechanicstown, MD, 13 Dec 1866; bur. Graceham. Farmer and saw-miller. Widow res. Mechanicstown, MD, 1878; d. 24 Aug 1880, at home of her son, John C. Eyler of Eyler's Valley; bur. Graceham. Their children: Mary Amanda (Catharine) b. 29 Aug 1821, m. David Harbaugh, d. 15 Sep 1899; John Cyrus b. 3 Dec 1823, m. Cecilia Ann Elizabeth ---; Joseph Elizabeth b. 8 Nov 1825, m. Aaron Eyler; Edwin Frederick b. 18 Dec 1826, d. 7 Feb 1855, bur. Graceham 9 Feb 1855; Charlotte Rebecca b. 27 Nov 1828, m. John Adam Williard; Martha Adeline b. 12 Feb 1831, d. 18 Aug 1842; Andrew Jackson b. 15 Aug 1833, m. Sarah ---; Lewis Francis b. 4 Oct 1836, d. 26 Jun 1875 at Reading, PA; Laura Jane b. 23 Nov 1839, m. Milton Harbaugh. Acq.: 1878 - John C. Eyler, Simon W. Harbaugh, John Lantz, age 66; David Harbaugh, age 70.

Sources: Bounty land claims, 50-40-16661, 55-120-35365; Pension, WO18569, WC9135 (admitted 18 Sep 1878); **Moravians of Graceham, Md.; (Frederick) Examiner, 1 Sep 1880; Bridge in Time; Md. Union,** 10 Jan 1867; Md. Union, 10 Jan 1867, 10 Jun 1875.

EYLOR, Henry. Pvt. in Capt. Flautt's rifle company, 29 Apr - 29 Jun 1813.

FAGAN, George. Pvt. from Fredericktown under Capt. James F. Huston, from 23 Jul 1814 until discharged in Balt. by the surgeon (sometime after Capt. Joseph Green assumed command of the company on 20 Sep). George Fagan m. c.27 Aug 1816, Catherine Boly. 1850 census of Fredericktown: George Fagan 60, Penny post, $800; Catherine Fagan 58; Ann Burall 26; George Burall 5; Jane C. Burall, 3; Elizabeth Boli 52 - all b. in MD. George Fagan d. at his residence on W. Patrick St., Frederick, 9 Apr 1855, age 65 yrs. He had been penny post of the Post

THE VETERANS

Office for the prev. 15 yrs and Market Master for several yrs. His eldest dau Elizabeth, m. Henry Fraley (Frolich) 11 Jun 1835.

Sources: FCml; Bridge in Time; (Frederick) Examiner, 11 Apr 1855; Engelbrecht Diary: 1: 157, 2:165, 447, 455, 492, 512, 539, 577.

FAGLER, George. Musician under Capt. Jacob Getzendanner, 26 Jul - 21 Aug 1814.

FAIR, Michael. Pvt. under Capt. Knox; joined 26 Aug 1814; discharged by a doctor at Balt., 8 Sep. 1814; m. Sarah Crouse [Krouse] (b. c.1785), 27 Sep 1803, at Taneytown, Carroll Co., MD, by Valentine Nichademus. At enrollment: 6 ft, 2 inches, dark hair, grey eyes. After discharge they res. Taneytown, MD and Montgomery Co., OH. He d. 25 Sep 1847, Chambersburg, OH. She res. Montgomery Co., OH 1856 and 1878 (Chambersburg); d. 23 Jul 1878. Their children: Volusia, Mary, Elizabeth, Susan, Rebecca, Samuel, Sarah. Acq.: 1856 - Valentine Fair, Joshua Crampton, Samuel Crouse, William Reindollar, Jacob Zumbrun, Samuel Gath; 1878 - Valentine Fair, Joshua Crayton, Samuel Crouse, William Reindollar, Bolzear Stoker, age 78, and Henry Westerman, age 72. [Letter in the pension file from Elisabeth Hutchings regarding expenses for care and nursing for 10 months. Sarah Fair had been blind and confined to bed constantly. No property left after Sarah's death.

Sources: Pension, WO27864, WC14122; Lindsay M. Brien, **Genealogical Index of Pioneers in the Miami Valley, Ohio.**

FAIR, Michael. Pvt. in the rifle company of volunteers of Capt. Daniel Marker, 16 Aug - 18 Sep 1813; b. c.1785; res. Miami Co., OH, in 1851 and 1855.

Source: Bounty land claim, 55-80-7364.

FALCONER, Elisha. Appt'd 21 May 1812 ensign under Capt. Basil Dorsey, 13th Regt., MM; served under Capt. Dorsey, 30 Jul - 27 Sep 1814.

FARQUHAR, William P. Appt'd capt. of a company in 47th Regt., MM on 20 Feb 1813. Served at Battle of Bladensburg. Muster roll lost.

FARST, Michael. Pvt. from New Windsor under Capt. George W. Magee, 22 Jul 1814 - 10 Jan 1815.

FAUBLE - See also Fouble. The following items (edited) taken from Engelbrecht Diary concerning the Fauble family.

(1) Died in Washington City on 18 Sep 1832, Mrs. Catherine Houx, widow of George Jacob Houx ("my cousin") and sister of Messrs. John, Jacob and David Faubel, of Frederick - from cholera.

(2) Married evening of 14 Feb 1839, by Rev. D. Zacharias, Joseph Degrange Faubel, son of Jacob, to Miss Margaret Reynolds, all of Frederick.

(3) Killed - Caspar Faubel, uncle to Messrs. Jacob, John, George and David Faubell. 28 Dec 1841 (date of entry).

(4) Jacob Faubel appointed Postmaster at Frederick town 23 Apr 1849; replaced 11 Apr 1853.

(5) In the Rail Road Excursion on Tuesday, Jun 12, 1877, for Washington and Mount Vernon - a collision - John Faubel nearly 82 "and myself," nearly 80.

FREDERICK COUNTY MILITIA IN THE WAR OF 1812

Source: Engelbrecht Diary: 2:27, 330, 477, 579; 3:511.

FAUBLE, Casper. Pvt. under Capt. Nicholas Turbutt, 1 Sep - 27 Oct 1814.

FAUBLE, George. Pvt. under Capt. Thomas Contee Worthington, 17 Aug - 31 Dec 1812.

FAUBLE [Faubel, Fowble, Fauboe], Jacob. Musician under Capt. Henry Steiner 28 Apr - 29 Jun 1813 and 25 Aug - 27 Sep 1814; d. of pneumonia at his residence W. Patrick St. 24 Jan 1857, age 65 yrs, 9 mos, 24 days; postmaster. Wife Catherine d. 9 Aug 1858, age 64 yrs, 5 mos, 24 days. at her residence in the city of Frederick. Both bur. Mt. Olivet, Frederick with other family members. 1850 census of Fredericktown: Jacob Fauble, 59, postmaster; Catherine Fauble, 56; Ann Fauble, 31; A. Degrange Fauble, 17, carpenter; Margaret Fauble, 18.

Sources: **Bridge in Time; (Frederick) Examiner,** 28 Jan 1857, 11 Aug 1858; **Names in Stone.**

FAUBLE, John. 3d corpl. under Capt. Nicholas Turbutt, 1 Sep - 31 Oct 1814; b. c.1795; m(1) Elizabeth Norris in 1819 (d. 29 Jan 1865); m(2) Mattie E. Metzgar (b. c.1838), 10 May 1870, in Balt. by Rev. John C. Backus; res. Fred. Co., 1851, 1855, 1871 (Fredericktown). 1850 census of Fredericktown: John Faubel 54, tailor, $7,000; Elizabeth 54; Mary Hughes 40 - all b. in MD. John Fauble d. 31 Dec 1882, age 87 yrs, 5 mos., 22 days, in Fredericktown, leaving widow and 2 children; bur. Mt. Olivet Cem., Frederick City; widow res. Fredericktown, 1883; d. 1 Dec 1888. Acq. (1871): Frederick Hawman, Samuel Carmack, res. Fredericktown; 1883 - Rufus E. Faubel, James Bartgis, both res. Fredericktown; Jesse W. Starr, age 45; F. Marion Fauble, age 37, res. Frederick City; Worthington R. Johnson, Justice of the Peace, stated John Fauble was "of a bright, cheerful disposition all his life, and full of fun"; Dr. William T. Wootten, attendant physician of John Fauble. In a statement Mattie E. Fauble said that she firmly believed that when her late husband applied for a marr. license, some persons as a joke put his age at forty yrs when in fact he was near 74 yrs old, that she often afterwards heard him jestingly allude to his age as being forty at the time of their marriage and would playfully tease her about it. In a statement of a clerk of the Court of Common Pleas, in Balt. City, is given date of marriage of 10 May 1870 of John Fauble, res. Frederick, MD, age 40, color white, widower, to Mattie E. Metzgar of Montgomery Co, MD, age 30, color white, single. Pension Office. 1883. "Mr. Webster, From the record of marriage it appears that the John Fauble whom this claimant m. in 1870 was then 40 yrs of age, Such being the fact it would be interesting to know at what age he performed service in the war of 1812-15. It looks as if a Junior John Fauble was trying to step into the old soldiers shoes." [*A bureaucratic joke. Ed.*]

Sources: Bounty land claims, 50-40-64229, 55-120-24550; Pension, SO9511, SC21069, WO42579, WC33540; **(Frederick) Examiner,** Jan 1883; **Bridge in Time.**

FAUNEY, Jacob. Bugler under Capt. William Durbin, Jr.; joined 24 Aug

THE VETERANS

1814; discharged 6 Sep 1814 for "inability."

FEAGA, Frederick. Pvt. from Upper Frederick under Capt. James F. Huston/Capt. Joseph Green; joined 23 Jul 1814; deserted 27 Oct 1814.

FEAGLER, Jacob. Pvt. under Capt. Henry Steiner, 25 Aug - 27 Sep 1814.

FEBUS, Peter. Pvt. under Lieut. William Kolb in det. assigned to guard British prisoners, 13 Oct - 15 Nov 1814.

FECTAR?, Andrew. Mbr. of Crawford's "company."

FELTY, Jacob F. Pvt. under Capt. Thomas Contee Worthington, 17-25 Aug 1812.

FERDON, Charles. Pvt. under Capt. George W. Ent, 24 Aug - 30 Sep 1814.

FERNANDERS, Adam. Pvt. from New Windsor under Capt. George W. Magee; joined his militia company 14 Oct 1814; enlisted in regular army 1 Dec 1814.

FERNANDY [Fernandes?], Thomas. Pvt. under Capt. Samuel Dawson; enrolled 21 Jul; sick on furlough since 26 Sep 1814.

FERRELL, Richard. Stage driver; carried the mail between Washington and Wheeling during the War of 1812; b. Georgetown, Kent Co., MD; moved to Frederick Co., MD, after the war; d. 1833 when cholera raged in the district; m. Margaret Blessing (1 Mar 1795 - 17 Mar 1862) dau of Michael. Children of Richard and Margaret: John, James R., Susan, Abraham, Sarah Virginia and Eliza.

Sources: Williams, Hist. of Fred. Co.; Names in Stone; Bridge in Time.

FESSLER, John. Appt'd 15 July 1814 as 1st lieut. under Capt. Otho Woltz, 16th Regt., MM.

FESTER, Daniel. Pvt. under Capt. Jacob Alexander, 22 Jul - 19 Sep 1814.

FETTERLING, John. Pvt. under Capt. John Fonsten, 2 Sep - 27 Oct 1814; res. 2 miles from Westminster.

FICK, Daniel. Pvt. under Capt. Henry Steiner, 28 Apr - 29 Jun 1813.

FICKEL, Daniel. Pvt. under Capt. Samuel Dawson, 26 Jul - 13 Oct 1814; sick in Balt.

FIELDS, William. Pvt. under Lieut. William Kolb, 13 Oct - 15 Nov 1814, in det. assigned to guard British prisoners at Frederick Barracks.

FILLER, Henry. Pvt. under Capt. Philip Smith, 29 May - 8 Sep 1813.

FILLER, Henry. 3rd sergt. under Capt. Barton Hackney, 1 Sep - 27 Oct 1814.

FILLER, John. Pvt. under Capt. Samuel Dawson, 21 Jul 1814 - 10 Jan 1815.

FILLER, Solomon. Pvt. under Capt. Joseph Wood, 27 Aug - 28 Oct 1814; b. 22 Mar 1793; m. Elizabeth Link (b. 1 Feb 1802), in Frederick Co, MD, at her father's home near Woodsboro, 16 Mar 1820 by Rev. David F. Shaffer, Luth. minister, each for first time; at enrollment: 5 ft, 7 inches, dark hair, dark brown eyes, low in stature; res. Frederick Co., 1850, 1855 and 1871 (Fredericktown); d. 28 Feb 1876, near Liberty, Frederick Co. She res. Liberty, Fred. Co., 1878; d. 22 Nov 1886. Both

FREDERICK COUNTY MILITIA IN THE WAR OF 1812

bur. Libertytown Chapel Luth. Ch. They always res. 5 miles of Woodsboro. 1850 census, Libertytown Dist., household of Ellenore Albaugh 55, and Abraham Albaugh 51: John T. Leakins 15; Solomon Filler 58, labourer, $400; Elizabeth Filler 48; Mary J. Filler 14; Daniel H. Filler 9; Solomon A. Filler 8 - all b. in MD. Acq.: 1871 - Samuel Carmack and George W. Strasberger, res. Frederick Co; 1878 - Adam Link (cousin to Elizabeth), aged 72, Mount Pleasant, MD; and John W. Ogb., merchant, age 71 yrs, acq. 60 and 25 yrs, resp., Lewis Link; 1879 - James Long. A note from Elizabeth Filler, Liberty, MD, "... I am a cripple and in needy circumstances."

Sources: Bounty land claim, 50-40-11590, 55-120-50567; Pension, SO9513, SC5782, WO28907, WC23284; **(Frederick) Examiner,** 1 Dec 1886; **Bridge in Time; Names in Stone.**

FILLER, William. Pvt. under Capt. Joseph Wood, 27 Aug - 26 Oct 1814; on furlough 26 Oct.

FINCH, Adam. Pvt. under Capt. Fonsten, 2 Sep - 27 Oct 1814. [In the bounty land claim 55-160-77091 is the file of an Adam Finch, pvt., who served under Capt. William Ford, 11 May - 17 Jul 1813, in the regt. of Lieut. Colonel Heath. He m. Susanna Atterholt 29 Jul 1823 in Columbiana Co., OH, by a Justice of the Peace, George Brown; and d. there 27 Oct 1854. Acq.: 1857 - Emiline Atterholt and John Atterholt.]

FINCH, John. Pvt. under Capt. Nicholas Turbutt, 2 Sep - 27 Oct 1814. 1850 census, Fredericktown: John Finch 65, labourer; Elizabeth 54; Eliza 17; Rosetta 15; David Ely 25, shoemaker; Julia Ely 21. all b. in MD.

Source: **Bridge in Time.**

FINE, John. Pvt. under Capt. Thomas Contee Worthington, 17-25 Aug 1812. 1850 census, Woodsboro Dist.: John Fine 56, widow, laborer, b. in MD., d. Apr from dropsy, ill for 7 days.

Source: **Bridge in Time.**

FINE, Peter. Pvt. under Capt. Philip Smith; joined 23 May 1813; deserted 14 Jun 1813; returned 2 Jul 1813; discharged 8 Sep 1813 and served under Capt. Basil Dorsey, 30 Jul - 27 Sep 1814.

FIPS, Nathaniel. Pvt. in Capt. Flautt's rifle company, 29 Apr - 29 Jun 1813.

FIRESTONE, Jacob. Pvt. under Capt. John Brengle, 25 Aug - 19 Sep 1814.

FISCHER [Fisher], Adam. Pvt. from Fredericktown under Capt. Thomas Contee Worthington, 17 Aug - 31 Dec 1812, and as 1st Sergt. under Capt. Samuel Dawson, 1 May - 5 Jul 1813. Quarter-master sergt. under Colonel Ragan, beginning on 14 Oct 1814; left service 6 Dec 1814 at Balt.

FISHER, Elisha. Pvt. under Capt. Hall, 7 Aug - 10 Sep 1814, 2nd Regt., 1st Cav. Dist.; b. c.1779; res. Meigsville Twp, Morgan Co., OH 1850, and Morgan Co 1855. [FCml issued to Elisha Fisher and Mary Fowler 25 July 1804.]

Source: Bounty land claim: 55-120-30667.

FISCHER [Fisher], William. From Upper Fred. Co. in 1814. Pvt. under Capt. James F. Huston/Capt. Joseph Green; joined 14 Oct 1814; promoted to quartermaster sergt. on 7 Dec 1814. Served as Quartermaster sergt. under

THE VETERANS

Col. John Ragan, 1st Regt., 7 Dec 1814 - 10 Jan 1815; discharged at Annapolis.

FISH, William. Pvt. under Capt. Matthew Murray, 25 Aug - 27 Oct 1814; m. Helen [Hellen] Joy (b. c.1788), Montgomery Co., MD, 22 Dec 1808, by Rev. William Reed; d. near Middletown, MD, 5 Aug 1822; widow res. Fred. Co. 1852, 1855 and 1856. Acq.: 1852 - Henry Herring, age 58, res. Middletown, ensign in Capt. Murray's company. Henry Michael, res. Fred. Co., age 57, pvt. in Capt. Murray's company. Source: Bounty land claim.

FISHER - See Fischer.

FISHER, Asa. Pvt. under Capt. Denton Darby, 3 Aug - 8 Nov 1814. "Absent 6 days."

FISK, Daniel. Pvt. under Capt. Samuel Duvall, 3 Aug - 3 Oct 1814.

FISTER [Feister, Feaster, Firster, Pfeister], Jacob. Pvt. in U.S. Dragoons. At enlistment: 5 ft 7 or 7 1/2 inches, dark eyes, dark hair, dark complexion; age 23 or 24; farmer; b. Fred. Co., MD; enlisted 22 or 23 Jan 1813 at Frederick Town, by Ens. Clarke, for 5 yrs. Mustered in Capt. Richard Arell's company, 14th U.S. Inf. 16 Feb, 1 March, 30 Apr, 1815. Discharged at Ft. Scott, 22 Jan 1818.

FITZPATRICK, John. Pvt. under Capt. Samuel Ogle, enrolled 1 May 1814; deserted 22 May 1814.

FLANAGAN, Joseph. Pvt. under Capt. Barton Hackney, 1 Sep - 27 Oct 1814.

FLAUTT, George. Appt'd 22 Apr 1808 as capt. of a company in 47th Regt., MM; served as capt. of 1st company (from Fred. Co.), 1st Regt. at Balt. under Col. Miller of Cecil Co.; b. c.1781; res. Perry Co., OH, 1850 and 1855. [FCml issued to George Flautt and Margaret Harbaugh on 31 Dec 1823.] Bounty land claim: 55-120-40606.

FLAUT [Flant], Jacob. Pvt. under Capt. John Galt; joined 31 Aug 1814; sick absent on 19 Sep 1814; b. c.1778; res. Fred. Co., 1851 and 1855. Source: Bounty land claim, 55-120-58110

FLEGAL, David. Pvt. under Capt. William Knox, 26 Aug - 27 Oct 27 1814.

FLICK, Adam. Appt'd 8 May 1812 as 1st lieut. under Capt. Andrew Smith, 47th Regt., MM.

FLOOK, Henry. 4th corpl. under Capt. Daniel Shawen; joined 5 Sep 1814; deserted 15 Oct 1814.

FLEGLE, George. Pvt. under Capt. John Galt, 31 Aug - 27 Oct 1814.

FLENNER, Phillip. Alleged to have served as substitute for John Stoner in the company of Capt. William P. Farquhar and transferred to Capt. Shryock's company; joined c.26 Jul 1814; deserted; b. c.1778; m(1) Catharine Reinhart (d. Adams Co., PA, 1819); m(2) 12 Dec 1827 Elizabeth Felty [Feldy] (b. c.1804), at Cath. Ch. of the Sacred Heart, Abbottstown, Conewago Twp, Adams Co., PA, by Rev. Lewis De Barth; fol. discharge res. Adams co., PA, and Cambria Co. PA; res. Cambria Co., PA, 1852, 1855 and 1872 (Portage, Washington Twp); d. 14 Jan 1878 Portage, PA; bur. Wilmore, PA. Acq.: 1852 - Jacob Heck who served in Capt. Galt's company. Jacob Baumgardner,

FREDERICK COUNTY MILITIA IN THE WAR OF 1812

1st Lieut. 1878 - F. J. Burgoon, age 25 yrs and William Pringle, Jr., age 46, res. Portage, PA. 1879 - N. B. Westbrook, age 36, and Charles Cullen, age 36, both of Portage Twp. 1879 - Rev. H. McHugh, age 43. Letter dated 27 Mar 1879 from Rachael Flenner, Wilmore, PA, dau of Philip and Elizabeth Flenner.

Sources: Pensions, SO28110, SC20147, WO19461 (widow's pension rejected apparently because of desertion, despite the fact he earlier received a pension before his death); Bounty land claims, 50-4082572, 55-120-82367. It appears that while at Baltimore Philip Flenner was transferred from Farquhar's company (when it dissolved) to Schryock's company (from Hagerstown); that a week or two after he was transferred he "went home to see his sick mother, and upon his return met the companies returning home." Shryock's rolls show him as from Frederick Co., "deserted."

FLETCHER, James. Pvt. from Balt. under Capt. Joseph Green, 14 Oct 1814 - 10 Jan 1815; substitute for Thomas Hayes; res. Balt.

FLETCHER, Joseph. Pvt., 38th U.S. Inf. At enlistment: 5 ft, 6 inches; dark eyes, dark hair, dark complexion; age 35; miller; b. Fredericktown, MD; enlisted 22 Feb or 22 Jan 1814 at Petersburg by Capt. Aldridge for duration of war or 5 yrs. Mustered in James H. Belsches' company, 35th Inf., 30 Apr and 30 Jun, 1815, present (sergt.). Discharged 22 July 1816 - furnished substitute.

FLING [Flinn, Flynn], Owen. 4th corpl. under Capt. Nicholas Turbutt, 1 Sep - 29 Oct 1814; m. Jane Boteler (b. c.1798), at Jefferson, Frederick Co., MD, 19 May 1819 [later she gave date as 6 May 1819], by Rev. Shafer, Luth. minister, 1st marr. for both. He d. at Jefferson, Fred. Co., MD, Election day, Nov 1839; he always res. Fred. Co. She res. Washington Co., MD, 1854, 1856 and 1878 (Hagerstown); d. 18 Jul 1879 in Hagerstown. Acq.: 1855 - Ezekiel Cheney, age 70; and Doct. Ed. Boteler, aged 56, res. Washington Co.; 1856 - John French, 42; Elizabeth French, 41, res. Washington Co.; 1878 - William T. Ervin, age 65, Franklin St, Hagerstown; and Henry G. Wiles, 50, Potomac St, Hagerstown, acq. with Jane Flinn 48 and 42 yrs resp.; Joshua D. Wise, age 49 and Sarah E. Wise age 50 of Hagerstown. [Letter from Joshua D. Wise, states he is son-in-law of Jane Flinn.]

Sources: Bounty land claims, 50-40-10032, 55-120-74717; Pension, WO25466, WC14453.

FLUGEL (Fleagle, Flegal, Fleagal), John of Charles. Fifer under Capt. William Knox, 26 Aug - 31 Oct 1814; b. c.1781-1788; m. Susan Newcomer; res. Carroll Co., MD, 1850, 1855, 1871 (P.O. Address: Uniontown). Acq.: 1871 - Abraham Myers, Lewis Harman, of Carroll Co.

Sources: Bounty land claim, 50-40-32944, 55-120-17920; Pension, SO860, SC201.

FLUGLE (Fleagle, Flegle), John. Pvt. under Capt. Fonsten, 2 Sep - 27 Oct 1814; b. 25 Jun 1793; d. 15 Mar 1879; bur. Baust Ch. Cem. In letter on file at Carroll County Historical Society, dictated by S. Franklin Fleagle Sep 1937 is stated, "John Fleagle, Jr. fought in the War of 1812. He was in the Battle of North Point, where he was shot in the leg. The result of this wound was noticeable for the rest of his life, as he always walked lame and carried a cane. He

served in Capt. Fouston's [Fonsten] Company, 3rd Regular, MN, from September 2 to October 28, 1814."
Sources: Scharf, Hist. of West. Md.; Hilda Kuehl, 13000 Glenview Drive, Burnsville, MN 55337.

FOGLE, Abraham. Pvt. under Capt. Samuel Ogle, 1 May - 5 Jul 1813.

FOGLE, David. Res. 11 miles from Westminster; pvt. under Capt. Fonsten, 2 Sep - 27 Oct 1814; m. Mar 1821 Elizabeth Snider (b. c.1793), in Taneytown by Rev. John Grubb; d. near Taneytown 11 Nov 1854; widow res. Carroll Co., MD, 1855. Acq.: 1855 - Jacob Shriver, J. Thomas Shriver, res. Carroll Co.
Source: Bounty land claim, 55-120-9125.

FOGLER, Henry. Pvt. under Capt. George W. Ent, 24 Aug - 30 Sep 1814; m. Miss Martha Dungen [Duncan, Dungan], in Frederick-town, 30 Jun 1840, by Daniel Zacharias; d. Fredericktown, Feb 1842. 1850 census, Fredericktown: Margaret Fogler, 56, $400; William Dungan 22, cigar maker; Jane R. Dungan, 20; Rachael Mobberley, 76. Acq. (1851): Mary Stoner, Rebecca Mobley.
Sources: Bounty land claim, 50-40-21458; The Visiter, Jul 1814; Bridge in Time.

FOLKNER, Peter. Pvt. under Capt. George W. Ent, 24 Aug - 30 Sep 1814.

FORCE, Joseph. Pvt. under Capt. Samuel Dawson, 21 Jul - deserted 23 Aug 1814.

FORD, Edward. Pvt., 14th U.S. Inf., At enlistment: 5 ft 6 inches, grey eyes, light hair, fair complexion; age 37; occupation color maker; b. Fred. Co., MD; enlisted 2 Aug 1814 by Lt. Woodward for duration of war.

FORD, Joseph. Pvt. under Capt. Thomas Contee Worthington, 17 Aug - 31 Dec 1812. 1850 census of Buckeys Town: Joseph Ford 65, labourer; July A. 30; Peter 20, labourer; Ignatius 18, labourer; Clemm S. 10; Stephan 8; John L. 6; Ann M. 8; Jerome 1. all b. in MD.]
Source: Bridge in Time.

FOREMAN, Daniel Pvt. from New Windsor under Capt. George W. Magee, 22 Jul 1814 - 10 Jan 1815.

FOREMAN, David. Pvt. from New Windsor under Capt. George W. Magee, 22 Jul - 10 Jan 1815; b. c.1795; res. Carroll Co., MD, 1851.
Source: Bounty land claim, 50-40-61243.

FOREMAN, Jacob. Pvt. from New Windsor under Capt. Samuel Ogle, 1 May - 5 Jul 1813 and Capt. George W. Magee, 22 Jul 1814 - 10 Jan 1815.

FOREMAN, Valentine. b. 1774, PA, d. 26 Mar 1854 at Mechanicstown. Newspaper obit. describes him as an "Old Defender," mbr. of Capt. Shrim's company of Balt. Volunteers in War of 1812.
Source: (Frederick) Examiner, 5 Apr 1854.

FOREST, Nelson. Mbr. of Crawford's "company."

FOREST, Rezin. Pvt. under Capt. Basil Dorsey, 30 Jul 1814 - 10 Jan 1815.

FORREST, Jeremiah. Pvt. under Capt. Samuel Dawson, 21 Jul - 13 Oct 1814. 1850 census, Hauvers E.D.: Jeremiah Forrest 69, labourer, $1500; Julia 42; Absalom 40; Jeremiah C.34; Washtiann

FREDERICK COUNTY MILITIA IN THE WAR OF 1812

32 female; Henrietta 26; Ann R. 11; W. Catharine 10; Mary S. 4. all b. in Fred. Co.

FORREST, Solomon. Pvt. under Capt. Daniel Marker, 25 Aug - 27 Oct 1814; b. 12 Jan 1789; res. Fred. Co., MD, 1850 and 1855; d. 3 Feb 1869; bur. Garfield, Mt. Bethel Meth. Ch.; m. Elizabeth --- (who d. 6 Nov 1851, age 57 yrs, 10 mos., 1 day). In the 1850 census of Catoctin Dist.: Solomon 60, farmer, Elizabeth 56, Maria 30, Susan 27, Mahlon 20, Hanson 16 and Daniel 14. Acq.: George Strailman, res. Fred. Co. Buried at Garfield, Mt. Bethel Meth. Ch. are: Maria S. (2 Feb 1818 - 3 Nov 1869) and Daniel W. (11 Oct 1908, d. age 71 yrs, 10 mos., 3 days).

Sources: Bounty land claim, 55-120-48176; Names in Stone; Bridge in Time; (Frederick) Examiner, 8 Aug 1855.

FOSTER, James. Served from New Windsor under Capt. George W. Magee, 22 Jul - 10 Jan 1815; 1st Sgt until 1 Oct 1814, then pvt.; discharged at Balt. 25 Nov 1814.

FOUBLE - See Fauble.

FOUT, Christian. Pvt. in Capt. Samuel Duvall's Company, 3 Aug - 3 Oct 1814; substitute for Christian Shenk; b. c.1796-1789; m. Nancy Jackson, Center Co., PA, 8 May 1818; res. Henry Co, IN, in 1856 and 1871 (near Ogden); d. c.1876. Acq. (1871): John P. Pennington, Henry Co., IN, and A. Jackson, Henry Co., IN.

Sources: Bounty land claim, 55-160-73260; Pension, SO4556, SC2288.

FOUT, Peter. Pvt. under Capt. Samuel Duvall, 3 Aug - 3 Oct 1814.

FOWLER, Bartholomew Thomas. Pvt. under Capt. Denton Darby, 3 Aug - 3 Oct 1814, "absent 35 days."; c.1793; m. Eliza Jane Akers, Marshall Co. WV, 29 May 1866; res. Belmont Co., OH, in 1871 (P.O. Address: Dillies Bottom). Acq.: 1871 - James T. Campbell, Albert A. White, res. Montgomery Co., OH.

Source: Pension, SO19894 (rejected by reason of desertion. Auditor states, "on muster roll "deserted" is erased and "drowned" is inserted).

FOWLER, John. Pvt. under Capt. Samuel Dawson, 14 Oct - deserted 23 Oct 1814.

FOX, George. Appt'd 17 Sep 1811 as 1st lieut. under Capt. Philip Smith, 29th Regt., MM.

FOX, John. Pvt. under Capt. Matthew Murray, 25 Aug - 27 Oct 1814 as substitute for Jacob Spoon; b. c.1780; m. Catherine Simon, c.1798. Acq. (1850): Henry Herring, ensign of Murray's company and Leonard Miller, res. Fred. Co. 1850 census, Frederick E.D.: John Fox, 76, pauper, Catherine Fox, 71, and Maria R. What, 14. John Fox d. 24 Aug 1856, at his residence, at Brook Hill, near Frederick, age 86 yrs (according to the *(Frederick) Examiner. Names in Stone* gives his date of death as 22 Aug 1856, age 88 yrs, 6 mos., 28 days with wife Catherine who d. 9 Jan 1869 at age 96 yrs, 1 month, 6 days. Both bur. at Yellow Springs, Brook Hill Meth Ch.

Sources: Bounty land claim, 55-120-14048; Bridge in Time; FCml; (Frederick) Examiner, 27 Aug 1856; Names in Stone.

FOX, Peter. Pvt. under Capt. Daniel Marker, 25 Aug - 27 Oct 1814.

THE VETERANS

FOX, Samuel. Pvt., 1st U. S. Rifles, under Capt. Wm. Smith. At enlistment: 5 ft 8 inches; hazel eyes, fair hair, light complexion; age 19; weaver; b. Fred. Co., MD; enlisted 5 Aug 1812 at Fredericktown or Shepperdstown by Lieut. Swearingen, for 5 yrs. Entered hospital 7 Sep 1814, discharged from hospital 14 Oct 1814. Reduced to pvt. 14 Jun 1816, promoted to sergt. 26 July 1816. Transferred to Capt. Murray's company of Artillery 14 July 1817 and furloughed. New Orleans 31 Dec 1817. Discharged New Orleans 4 Aug 1817.

FRAME, Jacob. Pvt. from Upper Fred. Co. under Capt. James F. Huston, 23 Jul 1814 - 23 Aug 1814; d. 23 Aug 1814.

FRANKFORTHER [Frankfolther, Frankforter, Frankfuther], John. Pvt. from New Windsor under Capt. George Magee, 22 Jul 1814 - 10 Jan 1815, as substitute for David Matthias at Westminster; b. c.1786; m. Mary Witter (b. c.1795), Westminster, MD, 17 Jul 1811, by Rev. Herbst; res. Mahoning Co, OH (Beaver) 1850, Mahoning Co., 1855 and 1871 (North Lima); d. North Lima, OH, 25 [or 27] May 1871. Widow res. Mahoning Co., OH (P.O. Address: North Lima) 1871; d. 22 May 1886. Their children: Elizabeth b. 6 Jun 1812; Daniel b. 12 Nov 1814; John b. 14 Oct 1816; George b. 22 Nov 1818; Catherine b. 19 Aug 1820; Jacob b. 14 Feb 1823; Rebecca b. 4 Jun 1826; David b. 5 Apr 1830; Martha b. 6 Jan 1833; Amos b. 1 Jan 1838. Acq.: 1850 - Philip Houck of Mahoning Co., OH, and John Bennet, of Columbiana Co., OH; 1871 - Samuel W. Gilson, Canfield, OH; David Witter, North Lima; 1872 - John Bennet, age 80, and Sarah Bennet, Ingham Co., MI, present at wedding.

Sources: Bounty land claims, 50-80-41050, 55-80-41780; Pensions, SO4257, SC2025, WO6346, WC5508.

FRANKLIN, Francis. Mbr. of Crawford's "company."

FRANKLIN, Francis. Pvt. from New Windsor under Capt. George W. Magee, 22 Jul 1814 - 10 Jan 1815.

FRANKLIN, Francis. Pvt. under Capt. Samuel Ogle; joined 1 May 1813; deserted 27 Jun 1813.

FRANKLIN, John. Mbr. of Crawford's "company."

FRANKLIN, Thomas. Mbr. of Crawford's "company."

FRAZIER, Fielder. Pvt. under Capt. Matthew Murray; joined 25 Aug 1814; deserted 22 Oct 1814; m. Sarah Ann Phillips at Fredericktown 29 May 1829 by Rev. McElroy, Catholic; d. at Fredericktown 11 Sep 1840, leaving two children, Sarah Ann Frazier (b. 6 Jan 1833) and Cornelius S. (b. 31 Jan 1837, applied for bounty land under his father's service in 1860). Their mother remarried in Washington City, D. C. 15 Mar 1842 to John F. Rhinehart by Rev. Charles A. Davis, Meth. minister.

Source: Bounty land claim, 55-rejected-309842.

FRAZIER, Jeremiah. Pvt. under Capt. Murray; joined 25 Aug; deserted 24 Oct 1814; b. 9 Aug 1785; m. 25 Jan 1816, Catharine Pickins (27 Oct 1797), at Fredericktown; res. Fredericktown, MD, 1871; 1305 9th St., N.W., Washington, D. C. in 1873. He d. 30 Jun 1870 at residence of his son in PA.

FREDERICK COUNTY MILITIA IN THE WAR OF 1812

Catharine Frazier d. at residence of her son, David Frazier, E. Patrick St., Frederick, 7 Nov 1879, in her 83rd year. In bounty land file: letter from Mrs. Charles L. Mason in 1929 and 1930 requesting record of Jeremiah Frazier. Letterhead: Office of Superintendent, The Atchison, Topeka and Santa Fe Railway Co., Marceline, MO; also letters from Louise E. Magruder, 132 Charles St., Annapolis, MD, requesting information on Jeremiah Frazier.

Sources: Bounty land claims, 50-40-568, 55-160-111267 (Bounty land applications separate from pension file); Pensions, SO7030 (rejected 22 Oct 1872 by reason of desertion); **(Frederick) Examiner**, 5 Jul 1876.

FRAZIER [Frazer], Josiah. Enlisted in 27th Regt., at Zanesville, OH, 20 Jun 1813 for 1 year; served under Capt Joseph Carnes, 27th U. S. Inf., Capt. Isaac Van Horne's Company of 19th U.S. Inf. He served under Capt Joseph Carnes until the expiration of a one-year term on 20 Jun 1814. Discharged from 19th Regt. (late of the 27th) at Detroit, MI, age 23, 5 ft, 10 inches, dark hair, dark eyes and fair complexion, by occupation a carpenter. He returned the arms and accoutrements and received: cap and trimmings, a coat, one vest, 4 shirts, 2 woollen overalls, 2 linen, 2 pair of socks, 2 pair stockings, 4 pair shoes, 1 stock, 1 frock, 1 pair trowsers, 1 blanket, 1 pair of gaithers. Afterwards he served in the militia as 2nd sergt. under Capt. Barton Hackney's Company, 1 Sep - 27 Oct 1814 as substitute for Otho Weakly. He was b. c.1791 in MD; m. Eveline ---, Frederick Co., MD Aug 1824, by Parson McConley; res. Fred. Co., MD, 1850; Weverton, MD, 1855; and Poughkeepsie, Dutchess Co., NY, 1871; d. 15 Jul 1875. 1850 census, Petersville Dist: Josiah Frazier 62, carpenter; Eveline 52; Sarah W. 25; Susan A. 20; Josephine 18; George W. 16, carpenter; James L. 13; George Rothery 23 - all b. in MD. except George Rothery b. NJ.

Sources: Bounty land claims, 50-40-48619, 55-120-41375, 50-160-6950; Pension, SO8372, SC5460; **Bridge in Time**.

FREBURGER, Peter. Pvt. under Capt. Henry Steiner, 25 Aug - 27 Sep 1814.

FREDERICK, John. Pvt. under Capt. Matthew Murray, 25 Aug - 27 Oct 1814; b. c.1792; res. Fred. Co. in 1851; witnesses: 1851 - Mary I. Frederick and Joseph Babington, res. Fred. Co.

Source: Bounty land claim, 55-120-40543.

FRESHOUR, Jacob. Appt'd 9 Jun 1809 as capt. of a company in the 16th Regt., MM.

FRESHOUR, Jacob. Pvt., 38th U.S. Inf.; at enlistment: 5 ft, 11 inches; hazel eyes, dark hair, dark complexion; age 26; occupation nailsmith; b. Fred. Co., MD; enlisted 21 Nov 1814, by Ens. Reticker, for duration of war. Discharged from Capt. C. Stansbury's company at Balt. 6 Apr 1815. [FCml issued to Jacob Frushour and Catherine Knouff on 5 May 1809. Jacob and Catherine were divorced in 1817. See Mary K. Meyer, *Divorces and Names Changed in Maryland by Act of the Legislature, 1634-1867.*]

FREY, Michael. Pvt. under Capt. Daniel Shawen, 5 Sep - 27 Oct 1814.

FRIDAY, Henry. Pvt. under Capt. Jacob Getzendanner, 26 Jul - 21 Aug

THE VETERANS

1814; m. Mary Leglider [Lichlider] (b. c.1800), near Fredericktown, 23 Feb 1847, by Meth. pastor; d. Fred. Co., MD Nov 1851. She res. Fred. Co., 1852 and 1855. Acq. (1852): Susanna Relkey, John Green.
Source: Bounty land claim, 55-120-17595.

FRIDAY, Henry. Pvt. under Capt. Barton Hackney; joined 1 Sep 1814; sick, furlough 4 Oct 1814.

FRINGER, George. Pvt., res. 2 miles from Westminster; served under Capt. Fonsten, 2 Sep - 27 Oct 1814; b. 21 Aug 1791 Westminster, MD; m. 6 Nov 1817, Rachel Williams, at her house near Reisterstown by Rev. Richard Neale. She was b. 10 Jul 1794, Balt. Co., dau of John Williams of Balt. Co. George Fringer d. at his residence in Perry Twp, Morrow Co., OH, 28 Sep 1877. She res. Woodview, Morrow Co., OH, 1852 1871 and 1879 ("about 2 miles southwest of Woodbury"). Acq.: 1872 - H. S. Prophet.
Sources: Bounty land claims, 50-40-89642, 55-120-64579; Pension, SO21158 (rejected 11 May 1873 by reason of insufficient service (57 days)); WO36170, WC24003 (admitted 10 May 1879).

FRIZEL, Jacob. Mbr. of Crawford's "company."

FRIZELL, Nimrod. Ensign under Capt. Samuel Dawson, 1 May - 5 Jul 1813.

FRIZIL, Mearad? Mbr. of Crawford's "company."

FRIZILL, Jacob. Appt'd 1 Aug 1814 as ensign under Capt. George W. Magee, 20th Regt., MM.

FRIZZELL, Jacob. Mbr. of Crawford's "company."

FROCK, William. Pvt. under Capt. Fonsten, 2 Sep - 27 Oct 1814; b. 1792 in PA, third son of Michael and Catherine Frock and moved to Maryland with his father prior to 1804. Listed as communicant in St. Mary's Ref. Ch. at Silver Run, beginning in 1814; m. Catherine --- prior to 1819; son, Jacob William b. Oct 1819. William Frock res. Carroll Co., 1851 and 1855.
Source: Bounty land claim, 55-120-52364; The Frocks of Maryland, by Richard Ott, 1979, pub. by author.

FROST, Robert. Servant under Capt. Thomas Contee Worthington, 17 Aug - 31 Dec 1812.

FRUSAR, Adam. Appt'd 1 Jun 1813 as 1st lieut. under capt. George Reinhart, 20th Regt., MM.

FRUSHOUR [Frishouse], Adam. Pvt. under Capt. Samuel Dawson, 1 May - 5 Jul 1813 and 3 Aug - 3 Oct 1814. [Fol. records from Frederick Luth. Ch. may pertain: Children of Adam and Margaretha Froschauer: Sophia b. 8 May 1800; Jacob b. 1 Nov 1801; Fredrich b. 12 Sep 1804; Adam b. 8 Jun 1807; Johannes b. 7 Jan 1810.]
Source: Md. German Ch. Rcds., v.4.

FRUSHOUR, Jacob. Pvt. under Capt. Thomas Contee Worthington, 17 Aug - 31 Dec 1812. [See *Md. German Ch. Rcds.*, v.4.]

FRUSHOUSE [Frushour], Jacob. Pvt. under Capt. Samuel Duvall, 3 Aug - 3 Oct 1814.

FULTON, Robert. Appt'd 23 Apr 1808 as ensign and on 16 March 1812 as 2nd lieut. under Capt. Elie Philips, 2nd Regt., 1st Cav. Dist. On 15 Jun 1813 he was appt'd capt. of the same company. Reference is made by one veteran to active service in Fulton's company during the war. No muster roll has been found.

FUNK, Henry. Served from Upper Fred. Co. as pvt. under Capt. James F. Huston/Capt. Joseph Green, 23 Jul 1814 until he deserted on 30 Oct 1814.

FONSTEN [Funson, Funston], John. Appt'd 27 Apr 1813 as 1st lieut. under Capt. David Dutterow; served as capt. of his own company 2 Sep - 27 Oct 1814.

FURGISON, William. Pvt. under Capt. Samuel Dawson, 1 May - 5 Jul 1813.

FUSS, Conrad. Pvt. under Capt. John Galt, 31 Aug - 27 Oct 1814.

GADULTIG [Geduldig, Gedulig], George. Pvt. under Capt. Thomas Contee Worthington. The company served 17 Aug - 31 Dec 1812 but George Gadultig did not muster. [In Frederick Luth. Ch. records are found fol. births of children of George and Catharina Gedulig: Jacob b. 31 Aug 1796, Wilhelm b. 23 Dec 1810.]

Source: Md. German Ch. Rcds., v.4.

GAITHER, George. Pvt. under Capt. Denton Darby, 3 Aug - 8 Nov 1814.

GAITHER, Lott. Pvt. under Capt. Philip Smith; joined Smith's militia company on 23 May 1813; enlisted in the regular army 27 or 29 Jun 1813 at Craney Island as pvt. in 38th U.S. Inf. under Capt. Miltenberger and John Mowton; he was 5 ft, 9 inches, light eyes, black hair, light complexion, age 23, farmer, b. MD; reenlisted 21 Feb 1814 for duration of war; discharged at Craney Island 15 March 1815.

GALLASPY [Gillaspey], James. Pvt., 14th U.S. Inf.; enlisted Dec 1812 at Fredericktown, MD, by Ens. Clark, for 5 yrs; absent sick at Plattsburgh; discharged at Ft. Hawkins 31 Dec 1817.

GALT - See Gault.

GALT, Moses. Pvt. under Capt. Upton Reid in the 1st Cav. Dist., 26 Aug - 3 Sep 1814.

GALTON, Ignatius. Pvt., 1st U.S. Inf., under Capt. Hook. At enlistment: 5 ft, 6 inches; black eyes, sandy hair, fair complexion; farmer; b. Fredericktown, MD. Tried by Court Martial at New Orleans 24 July 1806, neglect of duty, 25 lashes, remitted. Appears to have re-enlisted 29 Apr 1808 at Ft. Adams by Capt. Swann for 5 yrs at age 18 yrs. Transferred from Capt. Swann's company, 1st U.S. Inf. to Capt. Arbuckles company, 2nd U. S. Inf.; tried while in this company by Court Martial at Columbian Springs, 17 Oct 1809 for deserting 12 Apr and absent until 26 Sep 1809. Sentenced to 50 lashes and to make good time lost; punishment remitted. Appears to have been drummed out of the service from Capt. Ware's company between 1811 and 1814.

GALWITH, John W. Pvt. under Capt. Barton Hackney, 30 Sep - 27 Oct 1814; b. c.1784; m. Elizabeth Fink, Fred. Co., MD, 1 Oct 1815; res. Callaway Co., MO, 1871 (P.O. address: Jones Tan Yard; 6 miles from Fulton).

Sources: Bounty land claim, 55-120-41384 (Application not found); Pension, SO12892 (rejected 23 Mar 1872, insufficient service - 31 days).

THE VETERANS

GAMMER [Grammar, Grammer], Jacob. Pvt. under Capt. Daniel Zacharias, Troop of Horse, 2nd Regt., 1st Cav. Dist., 7 Aug - 10 Sep 1814; m. 15 Feb 1814 Mary Utz dau of Jacob Utz (b. 1795), Westminster, MD, by Rev. John Rudisil, each for first time. At enrollment he was a tailor; b. near Westminster, had black hair and eyes. He d. 6 Apr 1834 in Westminster, MD. His widow res. Carroll Co., MD, 1855, 1871 and 1878 (Westminster). In 1878 correspondence there is a reference to her grandson (name not given). She d. 25 Oct 1884 in Westminster, in her 90th year. Acq.: 1855 - Jacob Grove and Jacob Reese, res. Carroll Co., MD. 1871 - Abraham H. Huber, George A. Reese, res. Westminster. 1878 - William Crouse, age 85, res. Westminster; James Keefer, age 78, res. Westminster, acq. 70 yrs each.

Sources: Bounty land claim, 55-160-29136; Pension, WO326, WC11644.

GAREY, Sabred. Served from Fredericktown as pvt. under Capt. James F. Huston/Joseph Green, 23 Jul 1814; deserted 8 Dec 1814; returned 24 Dec 1814; discharged 10 Jan 1815.

GARLYLE, David. Mbr. of Crawford's "company."

GARRETT, Erasmus. Appt'd 1 Jan 1813 as 1st lieut. under Capt. Burton Philpott, 2nd Regt., 1st Cav. Dist.

GARROTT, Middleton. Pvt. under Capt. Barton Hackney, 1 Sep - 27 Oct 1814.

GARVER, Christian. Pvt. under Capt. Zacharias, 7 Aug - 10 Sep 1814, 2nd Regt., 1st Cav. Dist. [FCml issued to Christian Garver and Mary Morningstar 2 Apr 1803.]

GASSAWAY, Thomas. Pvt. under Capt. Philip Smith; joined 23 May 1813; deserted 18 Jun 1813; and pvt. under Capt. Henry Lowrye, 27 Aug - 28 Oct 1814; prob. rendezvous at New Market with company from Washington Co.

GATES, Robert. Pvt. under Capt. Nicholas Turbutt; joined 2 Sep 1814; deserted 20 Oct 1814.

GAUFMAN, George. Mbr. of Crawford's "company."

GAULT [Galt], John. Appt'd 8 Jan 1808 as capt. of a company in 47th Regt., MM; served as capt. of his own company, 31 Aug - 29 Oct 1814; m. 13 Mar 1805 Sarah Klinehoff [Kleinhoff] (b. c.1778) in Fred. Co., by Rev. Patrick Davidson, Presby. clergyman; d. on his farm near Taneytown c.15 Aug 1820. Widow res. Carroll Co., MD, 1853. Acq.: 1853 - Nicholas Snider, 1st Lieut. of Galt's company.

Source: Bounty land claim, 55-120-51375.

GAULT, Joseph. Served from Upper Fred. Co. as pvt. under Capt. James F. Huston, 23 Jul 1814 - 23 Aug 1814; d. 23 Aug 1814.

GAULT, Samuel. 5th corpl. under Capt. William Knox, 26 Aug - 27 Oct 1814.

GAUSNEL, Beal. Pvt. under Capt. Fonsten; joined 2 Sep 1814; deserted 17 Sep 1814.

GAVER, George. Pvt. under Capt. Daniel Marker 16 Aug - 18 Sep 1813.

GAVER, George. Pvt. under Capt. Samuel Dawson, 21 Jul 1814 - 10 Jan

FREDERICK COUNTY MILITIA IN THE WAR OF 1812

1815. [See Williams, *Hist. of Fred. Co.*, pp. 1605-1606, for additional information on Gaver family.]

GAVER, Henry. Pvt. under Capt. Samuel Dawson, 21 Jul - 13 Oct 1814.

GAVER, John. Pvt. under Capt. Daniel Marker, 16 Aug - 18 Sep 1813. 1850 census, Middletown Dist.: John Gaver 53, labourer, $400; Mary 56; Malinda 17; Martin 16; Ann Cleramer 8 - all b. MD.
Source: **Bridge in Time.**

GAVER, Peter. Pvt. under Capt. Samuel Dawson, 1 May - 5 Jul 1813.

GEARBO, Ignatious. Fifer under Capt. Jacob Alexander, 8 Aug - 19 Sep 1814.

GEAREY, Christopher. Pvt. under Capt. Philip Smith, 23 May - 8 Sep 1813. "Deserted."

GEISENDURF, William. Pvt. under Capt. Daniel Shawen, 5 Sep - 27 Oct 1814.

GEISINGER, David. Commodore, U.S. Navy; native of Frederick; m. Miss Catharine Russell Pearce of Boston 18 May 1816; d. Philadelphia 5 Mar 1860, in his 71st year, native of Fred. Co. Entered Navy in 1809 as midshipman; served on board the Sloop of War, *Wasp*. When the *Wasp* captured the British brig, *Atlanta*, he was placed in command of the prize. Whereas the *Wasp* was lost at sea he survived to participate in the opening of trade with Japan.
Source: **(Frederick) Examiner,** 14 Mar 1860 [long obituary].

GELDZ [Geltz], John. Musician under Capt. Jacob Getzendanner, 9 Aug - 17 Sep 1813 and 26 Jul - 21 Aug 1814.

GERCY(?), Jacob. Appt'd 20 Sep 1813 as ensign under Capt. Thomas Carlton, 16th Regt., MM.

GERNAND, William. Shoemaker, son of Adam and Anna Catharina (Weller) Gernand; b. 26 Nov 1792, Fred. Co., m. Anna Elizabetha Johnson (b. Fred. Co., c.1800), Fred. Co., 18 Jun 1816, by Rev. Gotleib Blech. William Gernand d. at Mechanicstown, MD, 2 Oct 1825; bur. 3 Oct 1825. Their children: Anna Catharine b. 15 Jun 1818, d. of convulsions 14 Mar 1819; Caroline Emilie b. 26 Jun 1820, m. Ephraim Bobletts; Mary Melinda b. 26 Feb 1823; Joseph Alfred b. 27 Nov 1824, m(1) Sarah Ann Elizabeth Waters and m(2) Harriet S. ---. 1850 census of Creagerstown E.D.: Elizabeth Gernand 51, $200; Mary Haspelhorn 27; Henry Haspelhorn 35, blacksmith; Caroline Boblets 29; Ephraim Boblets 7; Joseph Gernand 25, wagonmaker - all b. in MD. Acq. (1855): Leonard Picking.

According to his widow William Gernand was drafted at Mechanicstown, MD Aug 1814, discharged at Camp Hampstead 31 Oct 1814.

John Adam Gernand, tanner, father of William Gernand, b. 15 Jul 1755, Frederick Co; d. 14 Nov 1825; both his parents d. before he m.; he m. near Graceham, MD, 19 May 1789, Anna Catharine Weller (b. 27 Apr 1768 near Graceham, MD, dau of John Jacob and Anna Margaretha (Harbaugh) Weller).

THE VETERANS

Anna Catharine Gernand d. of consumption 29 Oct 1820.

Sources: Bounty land claim; pension; **Bridge in Time**. Much of this genealogy comes from **Moravian Families of Graceham, Md.** by Henry Young. For more information on the Gernand and Weller families see this work.

GETTIER, George. Pvt. on 10 May - 29 Jun 1813 and 25 Aug - 27 Oct 1814, under Capts., Murray and John Kerlinger; b. c.1795; m. 5 Nov 1818 Margurite Kroft (b. c.1795), at Manchester, MD, by Rev. Geiger, each for first time. At enrollment: 22 yrs old, tanner, b. Balt. Co., 5 ft 6 inches, black hair and eyes, dark complexion.res. Balt. 1852 and 1855; d. 6 Aug 1861 Balt., at 102 Druid Hill Ave, near Biddle St.; widow res. Balt. 1878, 44 Druid Hill Ave. Acq.: 1855 - Jacob Gettier and Henry Gettier, res. Balt. City. 1878 - John Garmhausen, No. 40 Druid Hill Ave, age 65, and P. J. Little, No. 38 Druid Hill Ave., age 49, acq. 14 and 10 yrs, resp; Henry Gettier, 279 Biddle St., age 79, and Catharine Stauf, No. 72 E. Lombard St., age 74. Margaret Henly, No. 36 E. Lombard St., age 54; and Mandy J. Jenkins, No. 44 Druid Hill Ave, age 45; and Lewis P. Gettier, No. 44 Druid Hill Ave., age 44 yrs. Mandy J. Jenkins and Lewis P. Gettier were oldest living children of said George and Margaret Gettier (1878).

Sources: Bounty land claims: 50-40-38761, 55-120-66109; Pension, WO19468, WC11766.

GETZ, Henry. Pvt. under Capt. Jacob Getzendanner, 6 Sep - 17 Sep 1813.

GETZENDANNER, Adam. Pvt. under Capt. Getzendanner, 9 Aug - 17 Sep 1813. According to his widow he was also pvt. in the company of Capt. Heater in the 21st Regt of Inf. of Col. Beall, entered at Rockville, MD, around 28 Aug 1814, discharged around 1 Oct 1814. He was b. c.1787; m. Mary Dowden (b. c.1782), in Montgomery Co., MD, 6 Feb 1807, or 6 Feb 1810 [both dates given by widow], by Rev. Blackenridge/Brickenridge, pastor of the English Presby. Ch. Adam Getzendanner d. Fredericktown 15 Mar 1850 at age 63 due to cholera [?], occupation carpenter. Widow res. Fred. Co., MD 1851, in St. Louis City, MO, 1855. Acq. (1851): John Kandale, Peter Ott, Benedick Green who served with Adam in Capt. Heater's company.

Sources: Bounty land claim, 55-120-65424; **Bridge in Time**.

GETZENDANNER, George. 3rd sergt. under Capt. Jacob Getzendanner, 26 Jul - 21 Aug 1814.

GETZENDANNER, Jacob of Adam. Appt'd 26 Jun 1812 capt. of a company in 16th Regt., MM known as the Washington Rifle Greens; served as Capt. of his own company of riflemen in Col. Small's Regt., 9 Aug - 17 Sep 1813 and 26 Jul - 21 Aug 1814.

Jacob Getzendanner, third son of Adam and Elizabeth (Kemp) Getzendanner was b. 25 Jun 1776. On 10 Jan 1797 at the German Ref. Ch. in Frederick, he m. his first cousin Anna Elizabeth Getzendanner (b. c.1777), dau of Balthasar and Anna (Steiner) Getzendanner, by Rev. Runkle, pastor of the Ref. Ch. near Frederick. In later yrs he was appt'd overseer of the Almshouse in Frederick and there d. 18 Apr 1837. Both Jacob and Elizabeth

FREDERICK COUNTY MILITIA IN THE WAR OF 1812

Getzendanner bur. in family cem. now located on the grounds of the VFW Country Club on U.S. 40 outside Frederick. Their children: Henry b. 3 Oct 1797, d. 28 Apr 1826, m. Catharine Kemp 8 Apr 1823; Joseph b 6 Dec 1798; Maria A. b 4 Dec 1799, m. John Berry 8 Apr 1823; Alexander b 16 Jul 1802, m(1) Mary Ann Travers 8 May 1828, m. (2) Anna Maria Hill 23 Feb 1831; Elizabeth b 2 Feb 1804, d 21 Jul 1876, m. (1) George Doll 22 Nov 1823, m(2) George Brown (b. Wash Co., 1800) 1 Nov 1828; Harriet b 20 Jun 1807, m. John Winpegler 10 Dec 1829; Adam H.; Isaac Jacob b 3 Mar 1812; Sophia b 27 Jul 1813, d 11 Jul 1884, m. Joshua Dixon 17 Jun 1835; John Joseph b 2 Dec 1816, d 12 Mar 1875, m. Catherine Keller 25 Sep 1860; Cathrine Maria b 5 Mar 1819, d 4 Nov 1819.

Sources: Bounty land claim, 55-120-14050; Records of Carol L. Porter, 2928 Putty Hill Ave., Balt., MD; **Fredericktown Herald**, 12 Apr 1823, 15 March 1828; **Evan. Reformed Ch. Rcds. of Fred., 1746-1800**; Trustees of the Poor, Proceedings, Fred, 1822-38 (MSA); **Engelbrecht Diary**, v.1. For more details on the ancestry of Jacob Getzendanner, see David C. Getzendanner, **Getzendanner Familie Giezendanner** (Salem, Oregon 1980).

GETZENDANNER, Solomon. Pvt. under Lieut. William Kolb, 13 Oct - 15 Nov 1814, in det. assigned to guard the British prisoners at Frederick Barracks.

GETZENDANNER, Solomon. Drummer and pvt. under Capt Jacob Getzendanner, 9 Aug 1813 - 17 Sep 1813 and 26 Jul - 21 Aug 1814; m. Susannah Spaulding (b. c.1795), in Cath. Ch., Frederick-town, 29 Jul 1822; d. Fredericktown 28 Dec 1841; widow res. Fred. Co. 1850. 1850 census: Susan Getzendenner, age 60 with Solomon J. Getzendenner, age 18. Acq. (1850): Peter Ott, John Randolph, of Fred. Co.

Source: Bounty land claim, 55-120-2735; **Bridge in Time.**

GEYER, Jacob. Pvt. under Capt. John Brengle, 25 Aug - 19 Sep 1814; b. c.1794; res. Allegheny Co., PA, 1855. *The Pittsburg Gazette* announced death of Jacob Geyer at Allegheny City, PA, c.18 Jan 1860. The *Examiner* stated he served as apprentice to the butchering business with Jacob Leab in Frederick "but went West about 40 yrs ago."

Sources: Bounty land claim, 55-160-33523; (**Frederick) Examiner**, 25 Jan 1860.

GEYER, Jonas. Pvt. under Capt. John Brengle, 25 Aug - 19 Sep 1814. In pension application he said he was in the Battle of Balt. in the Battalion of Reserves under Commodore Rogers or Decatur adjacent to the city of Balt. He said he was later commissioned 2nd lieut. in 38th Regt. of U.S. Inf. and "received $200 in advance pay." b. 21 Sep 1794; m. Dorcas Hunter in Washington Co., TN, on 2 May 1826; res. St. Louis Co., MO, 1855 and Douglas Co., KS, 1876 and 1878 (P.O.: Washington Creek); moved to Washington Creek c.1875; d. 11 Jan 1883 age 88 yrs, 3 months, 20 days at res. of son in Sigel, KS, named D.S. Geyer. Acq. - 1878: Robert A. Yeats, age 58, and J. W. Adams, age 39.

Sources: Bounty land claim, 55-160-46776; Pension, SO30635, SC22818.

GHOLSIN, Ambrose. Called into service under Capt. Thomas Contee Worthington but never mustered. The company served 17 Aug - 31 Dec 1812.

GIBBONS, Mathew. Pvt. under Capt. George W. Magee, called into service 22 Jul - deserted 7 Aug 1814.

GIBBONS, Orwell. Pvt. under Capt. Daniel Marker, 25 Aug - 27 Oct 1814.

GIBBS, George. Pvt. under Lieut. William Kolb, 13 Oct - 15 Nov 1814, in det. assigned to guard British prisoners at Frederick Barracks.

GIBBS, John. Pvt. under Capt. Darby, 3 Aug - 8 Nov 1814; b. c.1780; res. Licking Co., OH, 1850.

GIBSON, Thomas. Appt'd 16 Oct 1799 as 1st lieut. under Capt. John Trucks, in a troop of horse of the 9th Brigade.

GILBERT, Jacob. Pvt. under Capt. Fonsten, 2 Sep - 27 Oct 1814; res. 2 miles of Westminster.

GILBERT, John. Pvt. under Capt. Joseph Wood, 14 Oct - 28 Oct 1814.

GILBERT, Michael. Corpl. under Capt. Samuel Duvall, 3 Aug - 3 Oct 1814.

GILBERT, Reuben. Pvt. under Capt. Matthew Murray, 25 Aug - 27 Oct 1814.

GILL, James. From Balt. Pvt. under Capt. Samuel Dawson, 21 Jul - 10 Jan 1815.

GILL, Walter. 4th corpl. under Capt. Barton Hackney, 1 Sep - 27 Oct 1814.

GILLASPY. See Gallaspy.

GILLASPIE [GILLASPY], James. Pvt., 22nd U.S. Inf. At enlistment: 5 ft 7 or 9 inches; grey or brown eyes, dark or black hair and dark complexion; age 27; hatter; b. Middletown, MD; enlisted 14 March 1812 or 14 Apr 1814 at Chambersburgh, by Lieut. J. Culbertson, for 5 yrs. Mustered at Pittsburgh 30 Apr 1814. Discharged at Fort Niagara 14 Apr 1819.

GILLASPY, John [Johannes]. Pvt. under Capt. Samuel Dawson, 21 Jul - 13 Oct 1814; b. 22 Jun 1791, baptized in Zion Luth. Ch. of Middletown.

Source: Md. German Ch. Rcds., v.2.

GILLASPY [Gillespie], Matthew. Pvt. under Capt. Samuel Dawson, 21 Jul 1814 - 10 Jan 1815; b. 10 March 1796 in Middletown, MD, son of Mathew (Mathias) and Mary Gillespie.

Sources: Mary Hitselberger, Fond du Lac, WI; Liber 2, Indentures of Fred. Co., pp. 331-2.

GILLEN, William. 3rd Sergt. from Upper Fred. Co. under Capt. Philip Smith 23 May - 8 Sep 1813 and under Capt. Weaver [succeeded by Capts., Huston and Green], 23 Jul - 13 Oct 1814; b. c.1791; res. Clark Co., IL in 1851.

Source: Bounty land claim, 55-80-5488.

GILLMEYER, Francis. Pvt. in the 1st Cav. Dist., 26 Aug - 3 Sep 1814.

GIRD, William F. Pvt. from Upper Frederick under Capt. James F. Huston, called into service 23 Jul 1814 - deserted 24 Aug 1814.

GIRTY, Samuel. Pvt. under Capt. Samuel Ogle, 1 May - 5 Jul 1813.

GIST, Charles. Pvt., 38th U.S. Inf. At enlistment: 6 ft or 5 ft, 11 1/2 inches; light or blue eyes, light hair, fair complexion; age 30 or 32; cabinetmaker; b. Fred. Co., MD; enlisted 24 Aug or 1 Sep 1814 at Balt. by Lt. Smith or Martin for the duration of war. Discharged at Ft. Covington 31 March 1815.

GIST, John. Corpl., 38th U.S. Inf. under Capt. James H. Hook. At enlistment: 5 ft 4 1/4 inches; grey eyes, light hair, light complexion; age 22; tailor; b. Fred. Co. MD; enlisted 23 Aug 1813 for 1 year. Appears to have re-enlisted 15 Jun 1814 at Balt. by Capt. Hook for duration of war, at age 22. Mustered at Ft. Covington 28 Feb 1815. Discharged 31 March 1815.

GIST, Joshua C. Appt'd 17 Jun 1812 ensign and 27 Apr 1814 as 2nd lieut. under Capt. Francis Hollingsworth, 2nd Regt., 1st Cav. Dist. "Moved away" by 11 May 1824. Mrs. Mary A. Gist, wife of Col. Joshua C.Gist d. near Liberty, age 78 yrs. FCml issued to Joshua C.Gist and Margaret Attley May 1815.

Sources: FCml; Examiner, 2 Jul 1872.

GIST, Thomas. Appt'd 31 May 1813, capt. of a troop of horse, 2nd Regt., 1st Cav. Dist.

GITTINGS, William. Res. Balt. Pvt. under Capt. Joseph Green, 14 Oct 1814 - 10 Jan 1815, a substitute for John Boner.

GLADHILL, John. Pvt. under Capt. Daniel Marker; joined 25 Aug 1814; deserted 12 Oct 1814; b. 14 May 1796; m. 11 May 1823 Sophia Ambrose (14 Sep 1800 - 1 Dec 1876), at her father's house. 1850 census of Middletown E.D.: John Gladhill of G., 53, labourer; Sophia, 50; neither could read or write. John Gladvill res. Myersville, Fred. Co., MD, 1871. John Gladhill d. 24 Feb 1878 at the residence of his son, James S. Gladhill, 1 1/2 miles east of Frederick. He and his wife Sophia bur. Mt. Olivet. Witnesses to pension: Jacob Smith and Jonathan D. English, res. Fred. Co.

Source: Pension, SO12423 (rejected 29 Mar 1872 because of desertion).

GLADHILL, Thomas. Joined his militia company as pvt. under Capt. Flautt 29 Apr 1813; enlisted regular army 15 Jun 1813; in 2nd U.S. Artillery as 4th corpl.; served under Capt. Mowton; enlisted by Lieut. Duncan for 1 year; re-enlisted 21 Feb 1814 at Craney Island by Capt. Mittenberger for duration of war. At enlistment: 5 ft, 6 inches, grey eyes, light hair, light complexion, age 19, farmer, b. MD. Discharged at Craney Island 15 March 1815.

GLADHILL, William. Pvt. under Capt. Flautt; joined 29 Apr 1813; enlisted in regular army 15 Jun 1813 by Lieut. Duncan for 1 year; sent to hospital 22 Sep 1813; 30 Sep 1813 reported sick at Greenleafs Point; transferred to Capt. John Brookes Company, mustered 31 Oct 1813; serving in Major Keeper's detachment on 28 Feb and 30 Apr 1814.

GLISAN, Charles. Pvt. under Capt. Joseph Wood, 27 Aug - 13 Oct 1814; on furlough 26 Oct.

GLISAN [Glison, Glissan], John. Appt'd ensign 16 Jun 1813 under Capt. Thomas Hammond, 29th Regt., MM; served as ensign under Capt. Samuel Duvall, 3 Aug - 3 Oct 1814. 1850 census, Libertytown Dist.: John Glissan 88, $2,900; Harriet England 25. both b. MD.

Source: **Bridge in Time.**

GLOVER, Francis. Pvt. under Capt. Basil Dorsey, 30 Jul - 27 Sep 1814.

THE VETERANS

GODMAN, Jefferson. Served under Capt. Joseph Wood, 2nd Corpl. - 27 Aug - 13 Oct 1814; 1st Corpl. 14 Oct-28 Oct 1814.

GOFF, Richard. Pvt. under Capt. Samuel Duvall, 3 Aug - 3 Oct 1814.

GOGGIN, Thomas. Sergt. under Capt. Denton Darby, 3 Aug - 8 Nov 1814.

GOLDEN, John. Pvt. under Capt. Samuel Duvall, 3 Aug - 3 Oct 1814.

GOLDSBOROUGH, Nicholas W. Pvt. under Capt. Henry Steiner, 25 Aug - 27 Sep 1814; son of William Goldsborough, d. 21 Apr 1840, age 45; bur. at Mt. Olivet. His father res. in Dorchester Co., MD (d. 22 May 1826, age 63), with wife Sarah (13 Aug 1770 - 27 Jul 1854). 1850 census of Woodsboro Dist.: Charles H. Goldsborough, 50, farmer and physician with family, including Sarah Goldsborough, 80. He was the bro. of Drs. Edward Y. and Charles W. Goldsborough.

Sources: **The Visitor**, 30 Apr 1840; **Names in Stone; Bridge in Time; Engelbrecht Diary:** 1:379.

GOMBER, Ezra M. Pvt. under Capt. George W. Ent, 24 Aug - 30 Sep 1814; b. c.1794; m. Miss Margaret Fischer, at Fredericktown, 5 Jul 1832, by Rev. Hammer; d. at Fredericktown 29 Aug 1854, age 59 yrs, 8 mos, 22 days from tetanus from a splinter; res. Fredericktown 1850; she res. Fredericktown 1855. She d. 8 Aug 1860 in her 60th year. Acq. (1855): Richard Harper, George R. Wisong, res. Fred. Co.

Sources: Bounty land claim, 55-120-4626; **(Frederick) Examiner**, 14 Jul 1832, 30 Aug 1854, 29 Aug 1860.

GOMBER, John. Pvt. from Fredericktown under Capts. James F. Huston/Joseph Green, 23 Jul 1814 - 10 Jan 1815.

GONSO (Gonzo, Gonze, Jones), Jacob. Pvt. under Capt. John Brengle, 25 Aug - 19 Sep 1814; m. Margaret Keller, Frederick, MD 5 Sep 1819, by Rev. Shaffer. [The marriage license was issued to Jacob Ganzau and Margaret Keller on 5 Sep 1819.] 1850 census, Fredericktown: Jacob Gonso, age 56, machinist; Margaret Gonso, age 50; Mary Gonso, age 21; Matilda Gonso, age 12. Jacob Gonso d. Fredericktown 22 or 23 Jun 1862; widow d. 17 Oct 1867. Their children: Ann Sophia Gonse b. 8 Jan 1820; William Henry Gonse b. 25 Dec 1822; Mary Elizabeth Gonse b. 21 Mar 1827; Charlotte Keller Gonze b. 26 Mar 1831; Charles Jacob Gonse b. 22 Mar 1835; Catharen Matilda Gonse b. 18 Aug 1839. In 1879 appeared Catharen Matilda Scott, dau of Jacob Jones. Jacob Gonso buried at Mt. Olivet, Frederick, d. 22 Jun 1862. Also bur. there are wife Margaret d. 17 Oct 1867 no age given and Charlotte 26 Mar 1831 - 15 Apr 1909. Acq. of the family (1879): John D. Zieler and Ann S. Zieler, residents of Fredericktown, ages 51 and 50.

Sources: Bounty land claim, 55-rejected-327467; **(Frederick) Examiner**, 9 Jul 1862.

GONSO [Gonzo, Gonso, Jones], John. Pvt. under Capt. Brengle, 25 Aug - 19 Sep 1814.

GOODING, Lampert T. Pvt. from Balt. Town under Capt. George W. Magee, 22 Jul - 10 Jan 1815.

FREDERICK COUNTY MILITIA IN THE WAR OF 1812

GOODLAND [Goodlin], Thomas. Pvt. under Capt. Samuel Ogle, 1 May - 5 Jul 1813 and Capt. Denton Darby (joined 3 Aug 1814, deserted 17 Aug 1814); b. c.1795; m. Elizabeth Finch, 11 Aug 1813, in Loudoun Co., VA. She d. 15 Aug 1858 in Jefferson Co., OH. He res. Jefferson Co., OH, 1855 and Newburgh (P.O. Sloans Station), OH 1871. Acq.: 1871 - William W. Sutton, Ross Twp, Jefferson Co., OH, and Thomas H. Montgomery, Haislet St., Stubenville, OH.
Sources: Bounty land claim, 55-160-81485; Pension, SO7051, SC3847.

GOOKER, Peter. From Balt. County. Pvt. under Capt. John Galt, 28 Sep - 27 Oct 1814.

GORDEN [Gordon], William. Pvt., 2nd U.S. Inf. At enlistment: 5 ft, 7 inches; grey eyes, brown hair, fair complexion; age 29; carpenter; b. Fred. Co., MD; enlisted 2 Sep 1810 at camp of 2nd Regt. by Capt. Piatt or Pratt to serve until 1 Sep 1815. Tried in Capt. Pemberton's company at Fort Stoddert 25 Oct 1811 for overstaying his pass; sentenced to 25 lashes. Ordered to report to Quarter Master of 3rd Inf. 1815.

GORRELL, Samuel. Pvt. under Capt. William Durbin, Jr., 24 Aug - 27 Oct 1814.

GOUGHER, Jacob. Pvt. under Capt. William Knox, 26 Aug - 27 Oct 1814.

GRACE, Charles P. Sergt. under Capt. Samuel Dawson, called into service on 1 May 1813; deserted 25 Jun 1813.

GRACE, Michael. Lieut. under Capt. William Knox, 26 Aug - 27 Oct 1814; b. c.1787; res. Carroll Co. 1850 and 1855.
Source: Bounty land claim, 55-120-1912.

GRACE, William. Pvt. under Capt. Samuel Dawson, 21 Jul - 13 Oct 1814.

GRAFF, George. Appt'd 2nd lieut Oct 1811 in Capt. Henry Steiner's Artillery Company.

GRAFF, George. Lieut. under Henry Steiner 28 Apr - 29 Jun 1813; m. Mary E. Charlton (b. c.1793), Fred. Co., 26 Jun 1811, by Rev. Bowers, Epis. minister; d. Montgomery Co., MD, 10 Dec 1823. She res. Balt. City 1852 and 1855.
Source: Bounty land claim, 55-120-151.

GRAFF, Joseph. Appt'd 21 Apr 1814 as 1st lieut. under Capt. Derne, 47th Regt., MM.

GRAFF, Marcus Y. Corpl. under Henry Steiner, 25 Aug - 27 Sep 1814; b. c.1794; res. Seneca Co., OH, 1850 and 1855.
Source: Bounty land claim, 55-120-75655.

GRAHAM [GRIMES], Ephraim. Pvt., 22nd U.S. Inf. At enlistment: 5 ft 7 or 7 1/2 inches; grey eyes, black hair, dark complexion; age 22; blacksmith; b. Fred. Co., MD; enlisted 16 May 1814 at Pittsburg or Greensborough, PA., by Lt Arrison, for 5 yrs. Ordered to Buffalo 16 Jun 1814. Joined at Buffalo, NY, 30 Sep 1814. Deserted 30 Jun or 10 Aug 1815. Apprehended Aug 1816. Tried by Court Martial at Sacketts Harbor Oct 1816. Sentenced to have his head shaved, deprived of both ears, branded on both cheeks with letter "D," tarred and feathered and drummed out of the service. Deprivation of ears remitted. Discharged and drummed out of the service 28 Oct 1816.

GRAHAME [Graham], Thomas Johnson. Pvt. under Capt. Henry Steiner, 3 Sep - 27 Sep 1814; m. 12 Sep 1822, Miss Caroline Worthington G. Johnson, youngest dau of Col. Baker Johnson by Rev. Johns. She d. 18 Dec 1831 at the house of the bro.-in-law, William Ross, Esq., in Fredericktown. Thomas J. Grahame only son of Major John Colin and Ann Jennings Grahame bur. at Mt. Olivet (21 Nov 1794 - 24 Feb 1827) with wife Caroline Worthington Goldsborough, dau of Col. Baker Johnson (4 Oct 1803 - 18 Dec 1831).]

Sources: (Frederick) Examiner, 14 Sep 1822; Moore, #232; Engelbrecht Diary: 1:37, 174, 435, 674.

GRAMMER, Jacob. Pvt. under Capt. Zacharias, 7 Aug - 10 Sep 1814, 2nd Regt., 1st Cav. Dist.

GRAY, Walter. Pvt. under Capt. Samuel Dawson, 14 Oct - deserted 23 Oct 1814.

GREASON, Nathan. Pvt. under Capt. William Knox, 26 Aug - 27 Oct 1814.

GREEN, Benedict. Pvt. under Capt. John Heeter, Montgomery Co., MD, 4 Aug - 27 Sep 1814. Newspaper obit. states he was soldier of the War of 1812; d. 28 Oct 1869 in Battlestown, western part of Fredericktown. He was a mbr. of the "United Brothers of the War of 1812" in 1859. Bur. with wife Susanna (d. 14 Jan 1882, age 87 yrs, 7 mos) at Mt. Olivet Cem. She d. at residence of her son, John T. Green of Fredericktown.

Sources: (Frederick) Examiner, 14 Sep 1859, 3 Nov 1869 (gives date of death as 29 Oct), 25 Jan 1882; Names in Stone (gives date of death as 28 Oct).

GREEN, Francis. According to his widow he served under Capt. Marker from Middletown. [Muster roll for Marker's company is greatly obliterated and has several entries torn and unreadable.]; m. Elizabeth Easterday (b. c.1774), by Rev. Cline, at Middletown, MD. She res. Fred. Co. (Foxville), MD 1871. Acq.: 1873 - Philip Kline, age 86, Post Office address: Ellerton, Fred. Co., MD, also a militiamen under Capt. Marker.

Source: Pension, WC2737 (rejected for want of proof of sixty days service and presumptive abandonment of the claim, three months having elapsed after sending special circular).

GREEN, George. Pvt. under Capt. Philip Smith; joined 23 May; deserted 29 Jun, returned 30 Jun, deserted 9 Aug. He said he was drafted under Capt. Duvall at Woodsboro around 2 May 1813, but served under Capt. Smith, for 14 days - later said he was absent on leave at Annapolis on 6 or 7 Aug 1813 when the company was discharged; b. c.1788; res. Fred. Co. 1850 and Howard Co., MD 1855.

Source: Bounty land claim, 55-120-28810.

GREEN, Henry. 1st sergt. under Capt. John Gault, 31 Aug - 30 Oct 1814; b. c.1791; res. Washington Co., IN, 1851, 1855, 1871 and 1874 (P.O. Salem); single as of 18 Apr 1871. Acq.: 1855 - George Starbuck and John Colglazier, res. Washington Co., IN.

Sources: Bounty land claim, 50-40-68980, 55-120-9963; Pension, SO10925, SC6696. In the file is a

FREDERICK COUNTY MILITIA IN THE WAR OF 1812

response to P. J. Green, University Station, Grand Forks, North Dakota, 21 Mar 1919.

GREEN, John. Pvt., under Capt. Shawen; joined 1 Sep 1814; deserted 12 Sep 1814.

GREEN, John. Mbr. of Crawford's "company."

GREEN, Joseph. Appt'd 22 May 1812 as 2nd lieut. under Capt. Samuel Ogle; served as 2nd Lieut. from Emmittsburgh under Capt. Samuel Ogle 1 May - 5 Jul 1813; promoted to Capt. 20 Sep 1814; assumed command of Capt. Huston's company; served as capt., 14 Oct 1814 - 10 Jan 1815.

GREEN, Joshua. Pvt. under Capt. William Knox, 26 Aug - 27 Oct 1814; b. c.1794; res. Perry Co., OH, 1850, 1855 and 1871 (Reading Twp, P.O. address: St. Josephs).

Sources: Bounty land claim, 50-40-18426, 55-120-66054; Pension, SO3374, SC1905.

GREEN, Lawrence. Pvt. under Capt. Samuel Duvall, 3 Aug - 8 Nov 1814, as substitute for George Harman; b. c.1788; res. Fred. Co. 1850 and 1855. 1850 census, Catoctin E.D.: Lawrence Green 62, labourer; Mary 55; Benjamin 27, labourer. - all b. in MD.

Source: Bounty land claim, 55-120-83367; Bridge in Time.

GREEN, Lewis. App'd 2nd lieut. 10 Sep 1814 in Capt. Henry Steiner's Artillery company; served under Capt. Henry Steiner, 25 Aug - 27 Sep 1814; m. Eliza Cary, in Fredericktown, 14 Mar 1815, by David F. Schafer; d. Fredericktown 1 Feb 1826. Fol. his death she m. 26 May 1831, in Fremont, Sandusky Co., OH, Platt Brush, who d. 17 Aug 1840; res. Seneca Co., OH, 1851 and 1855 (Cleveland). Acq.: 1851 - Henry C.Brush, Marcus Y. Graff.

Source: Bounty land claim, 55-120-69419.

GREEN, Lewis. 4th sergt. under Capt. John Fonsten, 2 Sep - 27 Oct 1814; drafted at Liberty Town, c.15 Aug 1814; b. c.1790; never married; res. Fred. Co., MD, 1855, Carroll Co., MD, in 1871, 1873 (Taylorsville) and 1878 (Franklin Dist.), and near Reisterstown, MD, in 1878; d. 1 Feb 1879 near Reisterstown under care of George S. Byerly, "his only relative." Acq.: 1871 - Benjamin W. Bennett and George Edward Wampler, res. Westminster, MD. In his claim for expenses, George S. Byerly said, "He fell and hurt his side, coming to my house ..." 1872 - David Buckingham, acq. 20 yrs.

Sources: Bounty land claim, 55-160-44745; Pension, SO1638, SC23351.

GREEN, Samuel. Appt'd 28 Nov 1808 as ensign under Capt. Andrew Smith, 3rd Lieut. under Capt. Samuel Ogle, 1 May - 5 Jul 1813.

GREENAMIRE, William. Appt'd 16 Oct 1799 as cornet in the company of light dragoons under Capt. John Trucks, 9th Brigade.

GREENHALS, John. Mbr. of Crawford's "company."

GREENHOLTZ, Jacob. Mbr. of Crawford's "company."

GREENHOLTZ, John. Mbr. of Crawford's "company."

GREENWALD [Greenwalt], Christian. Sergt. in rifle company of Jacob Getzendanner, 9 Aug - 17 Sep 1813 and

THE VETERANS

26 Jul - 21 Aug 1814; b. c.1785; m. c.28 Apr 1810, Mary Magdalena Smith (d. 11 Jun 1830 in 51st year); m. 28 Nov 1830, Catherine Mottern; res. Fred. Co., MD, 1852 and 1855. 1850 census, Frederick E.D.: Christian Greenwalt 65, carpenter, $1200; Catherine 55; David 17, carpenter; Mary 15; Wilson 13. All b. in MD. Christian Greenwald d. 22 Aug 1865, age 80 yrs, 1 month, res. c.3 miles southwest of Frederick. [Emanuel Greenwald, son of Christian Greenwald m. in New Philadelpha, OH, 17 Dec 1834, Livinia Williams dau of Peter Williams of that place; Susan Greenwald, dau of Christian Greenwald m. 27 Dec 1836, Samuel Zimmerman.]

Sources: Bounty land claim, 55-120-2259; Bridge in Time; FCml; (Frederick) Examiner, 23 Aug 1865; Names in Stone; Engelbrecht Diary: 1:598, 620; 2:143, 234.

GREENWOOD, John. Mbr. of Crawford's "company."

GREY, Zachariah. Pvt. under Capt. Samuel Ogle, 1 May - 5 Jul 1813.

GRIFFIN, Thomas. Pvt., 38th U.S. Inf. At enlistment: 5 ft, 9 inches; black eyes, black hair, dark complexion; age 26; farmer; b. Fred. Co.; enlisted 26 Oct 1814 in Balt. by Capt. Stansbury for duration of war.

GRIFFIN, William. Pvt. under Capt. George W. Magee, entered into militia service on 22 Jul; enlisted 22 Aug 1814.

GRIFFITH, Caleb. Appt'd 15 Apr 1795 as ensign under Capt. Jacob Waters, 13th Regt., MM.

GRIFFITH, John. Appt'd 24 Oct 1800 as 1st lieut. under Capt. Osb. Hillery, 13th Regt., MM.

GRIFFITH, John. Pvt. under Capt. Hall, 7 Aug - 10 Sep 1814, in the 2nd Regt., 1st Cav. Dist.

GRIFFITH, Lemuel. Pvt. under Capt. Joseph Wood, 27 Aug - 13 Oct 1814.

GRIFFITH, Philip. 5th sergt. under Capt. Fonsten, 1 Sep - 27 Oct 1814.

GRIMES, George. From Balt. Town. Pvt. under Capt. George W. Magee; joined 22 Jul 1814; deserted on 25 Sep 1814; c.10 Jan 1815 in confinement at Fort McHenry

GRIMES, Jacob. Musician under Capt. Philip Smith, 23 May - 8 Sep 1813.

GRIMES, Jacob. Pvt., 38th U.S. Inf. At enlistment: 5 ft, 6 inches; black eyes, black hair, fair complexion; age 21; laborer; b. Fred. Co., MD; enlisted 14 Nov 1814 at Fredericktown, by Ensign [sic], for 5 yrs. Mustered at Ft. Covington 30 Apr 1815. Absent left sick at Ft. St. Marks 1819; d. Fort Gadsden 14 or 15 July 1819.

GRIMES, James. Pvt. under Capt. William Durbin, Jr., 24 Aug - 27 Oct 1814; b. c.1790; m. Rebecca Ott, in Fred. Co., MD, 7 Mar 1811; res. Seneca Co., OH, 1855 and 1871 (near Liberty Twp).

Sources: Bounty land claim, 55-120-37015; Pension, SO25554 (rejected 23 Sep 1872; noted "absent without leave")

GRIMES, Nicholas. 14th U.S. Inf. At enlistment; 5 ft 11 inches; blue eyes, dark hair, dark complexion; age 21 or 28; laborer; b. Fred. Co., MD; enlisted 25 May 1812 at Cumberland by Lt. Nelson on 25 May 1817. Mustered at Balt. 3 Apr 1815, sergt. Prisoner of war, returned from England. Deserted 15 Aug and returned 20 Aug 1815. Reduced from Sergt. 20 Aug 1815. At Ft. Hawkins since 2 Nov 1815. Appt'd corpl. 13 March 1816. Sergt. on command at Ft. Jackson in 1817. Discharged 25 May 1817.

GROANER, Andrew. 1st corpl. under Capt. Fonsten, 2 Sep - 27 Oct 1814.

GROFF, John. 3rd sergt. under Capt. Samuel Duvall, 3 Aug - 3 Oct 1814.

GROSHON, Abraham. Abraham Groshon served under Capt. Duvall, according to his widow; record not found; he m. Mary Ann Staup, (b. 11 Apr 1816), c.1838, by Rev. Reuben Weiser, her 1st marr.; at the time of the war he was a plasterer, b. Fred. Co., MD, height about 5 ft, 10 inches, light hair, fair complexion; he d. near Creagerstown 31 Mar 1855. She res. Creagerstown, MD in 1878. Acq.: 1878 - David Staup, age 66, Mechanicstown Dist., and James E. Staup, age 35, res. Fredericktown.

Source: Pension, WO36751.

GROSHON, Elias. His widow said he enlisted in Capt. Baker Johnson's company. He m. Catherine Troxel (b. c.1796), 4 Jun 1813 (or 14), by --- Brown, at Creagerstown, Fred. Co., MD; d. Washington, D. C., 1 Apr 1857; widow res. No. 163 9th St., near Grand, Williamsburg, N.Y. 1871. Witnesses: Emma V. Green and B. Franklin Crabbs, res. 1202 E. St.

Source: Pension.

GROSS, David. Corpl. under Capt. Samuel Duvall, 3 Aug - 9 Nov 1814.

GROSS, John. Pvt. under Capt. Philip Smith; joined 23 May 1813; deserted 29 Jun 1813; returned 30 Jun 1813; discharged 8 Sep 1813.

GROSS, William. Servant to Capt. Samuel Dawson, 14 Oct 1814 - 10 Jan 1815.

GROVE, Jacob. Pvt. in the troop of horse of Capt. Zacharias, 7 Aug - 10 Sep 1814, 2nd Regt., 1st Cav. Dist.; b. c.1790, m. Mary A. Harbolt [Harbold] (b. c.1821), 26 Jan [or 30 Jan] 1843, Westminster, MD; res. Carroll Co. 1852 and 1855; in Adams Co., PA (P.O. Gettysburg) 1878; d. 3 Nov 1874 (or 1873?), Straban Twp, Adams Co., PA. Widow res. Gettysburg, PA, 1878; d. 21 Dec 1895. Acq.: 1871 - Edward B. Buchly and John Winebrenner, res. Gettysburg, PA. 1878 - John Winebrenner, aged 62, Gettysburg, PA, Daniel Trimmer, age 60, Gettysburg, PA, acq. 40 and 20 yrs resp. John Winebrenner said there were 5 children living at the time, all absent from home but one.

Sources: Bounty land claims, 50-40-77650, 55-120-1652; Pension, SO3377 rejected, WO16891, WC10919.

GROVE, John. Appt'd 16 March 1812 2nd lieut. under Capt. Christian Cost, 2nd Regt., 1st Cav. Dist.

GROVE, Leonard S. Pvt. under Capt. Shawen; joined 5 Sep 1824; deserted 24 Oct 1814; m. 29 Jan 1829, Miss Rebecca Fout (b. c.1808), dau of Baltzer Fout of Fred. Co. at Fredericktown, by Rev. David Shafer. At enrollment: c.19 yrs old, farmer, res. Middletown Dist., 5 ft,

THE VETERANS

6 inches high, dark color hair, d. at home near Jefferson 28 Mar 1870. 1850 census, Jefferson Dist.: Leonard S. Grove, 52, farmer, $9,000; Rebecca 42; Greenberry F. 20, farmer; Charles B. 19, farmer; Ellen 17; Ann M. 15; Christianna S. 12; Leonard 10; Edward 6; Mary 4; John 1. - all b. in MD. Acq.: 1878 - Andrew Kessler, age 60; Cornelius Cochran, age 55, acq. 40 and 45 yrs, resp.

Sources: Bounty land claim, 55-160-111403; Pension, WO30159, WC19015 (dropped because he deserted); **Fredericktown Herald**, 7 Feb 1829; **Bridge in Time**.

GROVE, Reuben. Pvt. under Capt. John Brengle, 25 Aug - 19 Sep 1814; b. near Hanover, PA, 25 Mar 1795, where he spent his childhood and youth; moved to MD; settled near Frederick; m. Maria Lantz (15 Oct 1801 - 7 Aug 1874); he d. 7 Feb 1878; mbr. Ref. Ch.; both bur. Mt. Olivet Cem. Their children: Henry, dec'd., farmer of Jefferson Co. WV; Margaret, dec'd., m. George Harrington of Fred. Co., MD; Lydia, dec'd., m. George Ulrich, of Fred. Co.; Catherine widow of late Samuel Hafer of Frederick, MD; David, dec'd., farmer of Frederick Dist., Fred. Co.; Susan, dec'd., m. William Crum, of Martinsburg, WV, engineer on B. & O. R.R.; Harriett, wife of Oliver Young, of Frederick; Elias; Reuben, farmer of Frederick City; Barbara, m. Granison Shook, farmer of Frederick Dist.; Annie, widow of Franklin Stup, of Balt., MD. 1850 census of Buckeys Town Dist.: Reuben Grove 55, farmer; Mariah Grove 49, b. Germany; Catharine 22; David 17; Susan 15; Harriet 14; Elias 12; Barbary 10; Reuben E. 8; Ann M. R. 6; William Smith 27, labourer.

Sources: Bounty land claim, 55-160-9768; **Bridge in Time**; Williams, **Hist. of Fred. Co.**; **Names in Stone**.

GUMP, Benjamin. Pvt. under Capt. Ogle, 1 May - 5 Jul 1813; b. 19 Mar 1793 at 6 a.m.; m. Ester Smith, 20 Dec 1818; she d. 10 Mar 1869. He res. Jackson Twp, Richland Co., OH, 1850, Richland Co, 1855 and 1871. Acq. (1871): William Sweaney. He and Benjamin recalled riding one Patrick Hughes upon a rail for some offence or other. Benjamin Gump was the son of John Gump, farmer, who was the son of John and Elizabeth Juliana (Weller) Gump. John Gump, father of Benjamin, was b. 16 Jul 1769, d. 30 Aug 1804, m. Mar 1793 Anna Maria Williar who was b. Fred. Co., MD, 23 May 1763, and who d. of dropsy 15 Dec 1819. Other children of John and Anna Maria Gump: Elizabeth b. 1 Mar 1795, d. 21 Sep 1797; Elias b. 9 Jun 1797; William b. 19 Jan 1799; Jonathan b. 15 Nov 1802; Elizabeth b. 5 Mar 1805.

Sources: Bounty land claims, 50-40-741, 55-120-84674; Pension, SO8408, SC5665; See **Moravians of Graceham, Md.** for more details on family history.

GUMP, Isaac. Pvt. under Capt. John Galt, 31 Aug - 27 Oct 1814.

GUSEY, Christian. Pvt. under Capt. Samuel Duvall, 3 Aug - 3 Oct 1814.

FREDERICK COUNTY MILITIA IN THE WAR OF 1812

HACKNEY, Barton. App'td. capt. 2 Sep 1811 in 28th Regt., MM. Capt. of his own company from the Middletown/Fredericktown area, 1 Sep - 29 Oct 1814.

HACKNEY, Charles P. Pvt. under Capt. Barton Hackney, 1 Sep - 27 Oct 1814; discharge paper burned in his house c. 1820 in Knox Co.; b. c.1788; m. Elizabeth Levi, Knox Co., TN, 1818; res. 6th Dist., Knox Co., TN.
Source: Pension, SO9314.

HAGAN, Benjamin. Never married; d. Fred. Co. 1821; had bro. Richard and a sister who died in infancy. Acq. - 1858: Benjamin Talbot, cousin of Benjamin and Richard Hagan, res. Washington, D.C., age 56, said that Benjamin Hagan d. at his father's house c.7 miles from New Market. The parents d. c.30 yrs earlier. Daniel Collins, age 77, res. Montgomery Co., 1st sergt.
Source: Bounty land claim, 55-rejected-28901; submitted by Richard Hagan bro. of Benjamin Hagan in 1858, res. Washington, D.C.

HAGAN [Hagon], Francis. Pvt. under Capt. Basil Dorsey, 30 Jul - 27 Sep 1814; res. 8 miles from Fredericktown in 1809; m. c.9 Aug 1827, Matilda Fowler. In Apr 1871 and Apr 1872, Matilda Hagan, widow, was receiving a pension for service of her dec'd. husband in War of 1812 by Special Act of Congress 1832, Chapter 226. She d. 5 May 1874, age 76 yrs, 6 mos., 19 days; bur. Mt. Olivet.
Sources: **Bartgis's Republican Gazette**, 7 Jan 1809; **(Frederick) Examiner**, 12 Apr 1871, 3 Apr 1872, 13 May 1874; **West. Md. Genealogy**, 7:1; FCml.

HAGLEN, Isaac. Pvt. under Capt. Jacob Getzendanner, 9 Aug - 17 Sep 1813.

HAHN, Abraham. Pvt. under Capt. Fonsten, 2 Sep - 27 Oct 1814; b. c.1782; res. Carroll Co., MD, 1850 and 1855.
Source: Bounty land claim, 55-120-54216.

HAHN, Bazil. Pvt. under Capts. Norris and Fonsten; b. c.1792; m. Elizabeth Dell (b. c.1792), at farm of Pipe Creek, Westminster Hundred, now Carroll Co., 13 Jun 1822, by V. Nelson, Meth. preacher. At enrollment: 5 ft, 5 inches, gray eyes, light hair, fair complexion, 22 yrs old; res. Fred. Co., MD c.15 yrs, the rest in Smith Township, Belmont Co., OH (P.O. Address: Warmack); d. 22 Sep 1881, bur. East Richland Cem., Belmont Co; widow res. Belmont Co., OH, 1881. Acq.: 1855 - William Farris and Thomas F. Nichols; 1881 - Samuel C. Lucas, age 50, Alice Hawkinsburg, age 26, res. Smith Township, acq. 35 and 15 yrs, resp.; Hannah E. Noling, res. St. Clarisville, OH, age 28, granddau of Bazil Hahn, stated that Basil Hahn had 10 children, 6 living (in 1881). In 1881 bible records were held by Scott Hawkingburg, husband of granddau; she said that the record had data on 24 mbrs. of family, from 1822 to 1881.
Sources: Pensions, SO518, SC23343, WO41606, WC32440.

HAHN, Benjamin. Pvt. under Capt. Fonsten, 2 Sep - 28 Oct 1814; m. Mary A. Stonebracker (b. c.1821), near Uniontown, Fred. Co., 17 Sep 1840, by Rev Darriel Zollicoffer; formerly from Annapolis, moved to Uniontown as a bachelor. He was a bro. to Basil Hahn;

THE VETERANS

had a sister named Lydia who m. --- Taylor and res. Annapolis in 1879. Benjamin d. 27 Sep 1868 in Carroll Co.; widow res. Carroll Co. 1871; res. with son at Pleasant Valley, Carroll Co. at some times and with her dau at Wakefield, Carroll Co. at other times; she d. 28 Mar 1882. Acq.: 1855 - Solomon Formwalt; 1878 - John Fleagle, 2nd Election Dist. of Carroll Co.; Lewis Green, age 88, res. Balt. Co.

Source: Pension, WO21898, WC23799.

HAHN [Hohn], Daniel. Pvt. under Capt. Philip Smith; joined 23 May 1813; deserted 17 Jul 1813; returned 19 Jul 1813; discharged 8 Sep 1813. [Daniel Hahn of Jacob and Catharina b 7 Mar 1788; bapt. 10 Mar 1790. *Rcds. of Evan, Ref. Ch., Frederick.*]

HAHN, Henry. Pvt. under Capt. Samuel Dawson; joined 26 Jul until he deserted 29 Sep 1814; bur. Taneytown Ref. Ch.: Henry Hawn 10 Dec 1781 - 25 Jan 1867, and wife Anna M. 9 Aug 1859, age 64 yrs, 7 months, 6 days.

Source: **Hist. of West. Md.**

HAHN, Israel. Pvt. under Capt. John Fonsten, as substitute for Conrad Stuller; b. c.1796; m. Elizabeth Manzer, in Columbiana Co., OH, 22 May 1817; res. Elkhart, IN, 1873. Acq.: 1873 - Samuel Hahn, age 83, bro. of Israel Hahn, res. Dark Co., OH.

Sources: Bounty land claim, 55-160-43615; Pension, SO29276.

HAHN, Joseph. Pvt. under Capt. William Knox. He said he served in Capt. Gault's company, joined at Taneytown, Jun 1814 or Aug 1814, discharged because of disability incurred by the service; b. c.1792; res. Finksburgh, Carroll Co., MD, 1854 and 1855.

Source: Pension, SO165539, SC20374.

HAHN, Michael. Appt'd ensign 12 May 1812 under Capt. Jacob Creager, 29th Regt., MM.

HAILEY, John. Pvt., 25th U.S. Inf., under Capt. Edward White. At enlistment: 5 ft, 7 inches; had light or grey eyes, light complexion, age 27, shoemaker and/or wagoner; b. at Winchester, MD. He was enlisted 2 Jul 1814 at Buffalo by Capt. Kinney for the duration of the war. Discharged at Sacketts Harbor 17 May 1815.

HAINER, Andrew. Pvt., 1st Cavalry Dist., 26 Aug - 3 Sep 1814.

HAINES, Daniel. Mbr. of Crawford's "company"; bur. at Johnsville, Beaver Dam Brethren Churches: Daniel Haines, 14 Jul 1793 - 10 Dec 1858; and wife Elizabeth, d. 14 Feb 1846, age 48-10-14; and wife Phebe, d. 15 May 1853, age 40-7-0. 1850 census, Libertytown E.D.: Daniel Haines age 58; Phebea Haines 38, both b. MD. [FCml issued to Daniel Haines and Elizabeth Stem 23 Oct 1815.]

Source: **Names in Stone; Bridge in Time; FCml.**

HAINES [Hines?], Eli. Never joined his company which served under Capt. William Durbin, Jr., 24 Aug - 27 Oct 1814.

HAINES, Henry. Mbr. of Crawford's "company."

HAINES, Henry. Said he was a teamster under Quartermaster Marsteller; "enlisted Sep 1814"; b.

FREDERICK COUNTY MILITIA IN THE WAR OF 1812

c.1790; never married; res. New Windsor 1871.
Source: Bounty land claim, 55-rejected- 329275.

HAINES, Isaac. Never joined his company which served under Capt. William Durbin, Jr., 24 Aug - 27 Oct 1814. [FCml issued to Isaac Haines and Mary Haines 8 Apr 1823.]

HAINES, John. Mbr. of Crawford's "company."

HAINES, John. He said he served as pvt. in John Fonsten's Company, 29th Regt.; that he was drafted at Liberty Town around 15 Aug 1814, discharged at Camp Hampstead 1 Nov 1814. He later amended his statement to say he served under Capt. David Cushwa. There is no record of his serving in Fonsten's company. - b. c.1784; res. Fred. Co., 1851 and 1855. Acq.: 1855 - John Wood and Lewis Green. 1850 census, Libertytown E.D.: John Haines 65, carpenter $150, Susanna 55, Francis 20, labourer, Israel 16 labourer, Jesse 14, Elizabeth 12, David 10, Charles 7 - all b. MD. FCml issued to John Haines and Susanna Deberry 14 Jan 1820. [From Williams: John Haines, grandfather of Albert L. Haines, b. Fred. Co.; settled on the George farm near village of Weldon, Linganore Dist., Fred. Co.; maker of shingles, owned small tract of land near the village.]
Sources: Bounty land claim, 55-120-95252; Williams, History of Fred. Co., Maryland; Bridge in Time; FCml.

HALL, Barruck [Barrock]. Appt'd cornet 22 Dec 1812 under Capt. John Cook, 2nd Regt., 1st Cav. Dist.; served as 2nd Lieut. under Capt. Nicholas Hall, 7 Aug - 10 Sep 1814; m. 4 Jul 1798, Mary Bergee in Fred. Co.; d. at his residence Fredierck Co. 30 Sep 1830. Acq. - 1853: Adam Hagan and Ephraim Davis, res. Fred. Co.
Source: Bounty land claim, 50-40-84975.

HALL, Isaac. Pvt. from Fred. Co. under Capt. Samuel Dawson, 14 Oct 1814 - 10 Jan 1815.

HALL, Joshua. Pvt. from Fred. Co., later corpl., under Capt. Samuel Dawson, 21 Jul - 10 Jan 1815.

HALL, Joshua. Pvt. under Capt. Samuel Dawson, 1 May - 5 Jul 1813.

HALL, Nicholas, Jr. Appt'd lieut. 3 Oct 1807 under Capt. John Cook, 13th Regt., MM. [This may be the same officer as below.]

HALL, Nicholas, Jr. Appt'd 2nd lieut. 16 Mar 1812 under Capt. Cook, 2nd Regt., 1st Cav. Dist., MM, and appt'd capt. in the place of Capt. Cook on 22 Dec 1812 served as capt. of his own company, 7 Aug - 10 Sep 1814.

HALL, Richard. Appt'd ensign 3 Oct 1807 under Capt. John Cook, 13th Regt., MM.

HALL, Thomas B. Appt'd adjutant 8 May 1812 in 2nd Regt., 1st Cav. Dist.

HALLER, Elisha. Pvt. under Capt. James F. Huston/Capt. Joseph Green; entered into the service 23 Jul 1814; on furlough 27 Sep 1814; deserted 8 Dec, returned 27 Dec 1814. [*Frederick Herald*, dated 31 Mar 1832, announced marr. of Elisha Haller, formerly of Frederick, and Miss Fanney Betes, both of New York.]

THE VETERANS

HALLER [Holler], George. Pvt. from Upper Fred. Co. under Capt. James F. Huston and Capt. Joseph Green; joined 14 Oct 1814; deserted 8 Dec 1814.

HALLER [Holler, Hollen, Hallen, Hollar], George William. 3rd corpl. from Fredericktown, later 1st Sergt., under Capt. James F. Huston and Capt. Joseph Green, 14 Oct 1814 - 10 Jan 1815; m. c.4 Apr 1815,Wilhelmina Sinstack (b. c.1794). He res. Middletown Valley, Fred. Co., MD, 1855; d. 17 Aug 1869, age 76 yrs, 3 mos., 18 days, at residence of his son, Samuel M. Haller, in Cumberland, MD. Newspaper obit. states "Capt." Haller was engaged in business in Georgetown, D.C. for over 20 yrs, emigrated to Allegany Co., PA, spent sometime in Somerset Co., PA.; mbr. Masonic Order. His wife d. Cumberland, MD, 23 Feb 1861, age 65 yrs, 11 mos., 2 days. Acq. - 1857: Jacob T. C. Miller, Middletown, MD, says name was spelled Hollen, Hallen or Hollar, yrs ago.
Sources: **(Frederick) Examiner**, 6 Mar 1861, 1 Sep 1869; **Md. Union**, 2 Sep 1860; Bounty land claim, 55-rejected-106093. In this file appears signed discharge paper from Tho. Wm. Morgan, Lieut., 1857, which states, "Frederick Town Jan 22d. 1815. This is to certify that George Holler attchd. to 1st Regt., 11th Brig. D.M. Militia has faithfully performed a six month tour of duty in the Service of the U. States."

HALLER, Henry. Pvt. under Capt. Henry Steiner, 25 Aug - 27 Sep 1814. Probably same Henry H. Haller who d. after 10 Oct 1832 and before 30 Apr 1840. According to *Engelbrecht Diary* he and two sons, Nicholas and Tobias completed a brick wall for Engelbrecht 1830. His wife Sarah M. d. 10 Oct 1832 in her 42nd year. Tobias W. Haller m. Miss Juliann C. Suman, dau of Isaac Suman on 10 May 1838. Margaret Haller, dau of Henry H. Haller m. 30 Apr 1840, William Frazier of Jeremiah.
Source: **Engelbrecht Diary**: 1:607; 2:35, 295.

HALLER [Holler], Jacob. Pvt. from Fredericktown under Capt. Huston/Capt. Green, 23 Jul 1814 - 10 Jan 1815; b. 29 Jun 1794; m(1) c.1816 Mary Daddisman (30 Apr 1797 - 18 Jun 1845); m(2) Ann Michael (17 Oct 1811 - 20 Apr 1874) in Fredericktown; res. Balt. City 1851; Fred. Co. 1855; d. 14 Aug 1873 at his home on S. Market St; in oyster bus.; bur. with wives at Mt. Olivet, Frederick; mbr. of Adam Lodge no. 19, I.O.O.F.; mbr. of the "United Brothers of the War of 1812" in 1859. Acq. - 1871: George Marguart, Frederick Hawman, res. Fredericktown.
Sources: Pension, SO9938, SC7071; **(Frederick) Examiner**, 14 Sep 1859, 20 Aug 1873, 27 Aug 1873, 29 Apr 1874; **Md. Union**, 21 Aug 1873, 28 Aug 1873.

HALLER/HOLER [Hatten?], Jacob. Pvt. under Capt. Nicholas Turbutt, 1 Sep - 27 Oct 1814. [This may be the same Jacob B. Haller of Middletown Valley who m. Miss Elizabeth Bash near New Market in Apr 1813.]
Sources: **FCml**; **Englebrecht Diary**, v.1, 213.

HALLER, Philip. Pvt. under Capt. John Brengle, 25 Aug - 19 Sep 1814; m. Ann Luesa Zeler (or Wilhers), 26 Dec 1830, by Rev Flemmer, Presbyterian minister; d. 1 Sep 1841 in Fredericktown; widow res. Fred. Co. 1851 and Balt. City 1855. Acq.: 1851 - Henry Bot-

FREDERICK COUNTY MILITIA IN THE WAR OF 1812

ler and his wife Ann, present at wedding.

Source: Bounty land claim, 55-120-26408.

HALLER [Holler], Tobias. Appt'd 1st lieut under Capt. Steiner 4 Apr 1808; served as 1st Lieut. under Capt. Henry Steiner, 28 Apr - 29 Jun 1813.

HALLER, William. Pvt. under Capt. Samuel Dawson, 21 Jul 1814 until he deserted 24 Aug 1814.

HAMILTON [Hambleton], John. Ensign under Capt. Basil Dorsey, 30 Jul - 27 Sep 1814. According to his widow he served as lieut. under Capt. Dorsey; m. Catherine Evitt, 30 Apr 1812 (or 30 Mar 1812) by Rev John Helfenstein; d. Balt. 9 Mar 1828. 1850 census, New Market Dist.: Catherine Hamilton age 60; Louisa Plummer 21 and Nelson Plummer 22 carpenter, all b. MD. She res. Fred. Co. 1855. Acq.: 1851 - Rebecca Grove and Louisa Hambleton; 1855 - James Walling and John Hamilton.

Source: Bounty land claim, 55-120-35769; **Bridge in Time.**

HAMILTON, William. Pvt. under Capt. James F. Huston; joined 23 Jul 1814; deserted 23 Aug 1814.

HAMMON, Denton. Pvt. under Capt. Samuel Duvall, 3 Aug - 3 Oct 1814. 1850 census, Libertytown Dist.: Denton Hamond 53, $3275, Rebecca Hammond 55, Jacob Fox 10. all b. MD; FCmls issued to Denton Hammond and Hannah Stoner 9 Sep 1817 and to Denton Hammond and Eliza. M. Hammond 3 Mar 1821.

Sources: **Bridge in Time; FCml.**

HAMMON, James. Pvt. under Capt. John Galt; joined 31 Aug 1814; deserted 21 Oct 1814; first as a drummer, served 4-5 days in that capacity, when position was given to John Durf, "a sickly pvt."; he then hired as a substitute for John McCaliss, a pvt. in same company; b. c.1781; m. Mary Ann Sites, 25 Dec 1817, by Rev Henry Cramer; res. Fulton Co., PA, 1851; d. Fulton Co., PA, 24 Feb 1853; widow res. Greene Co., OH, 1855. She was declared mentally incompetent by Probate Court 1878 and Joshua B. Owsley appt'd guardian; she d. 28 Nov 1878, Jacksonburg, Butler Co., OH. Acq. (1855): Sarah Ann Hammon, Sharlot R. Hammon of Greene Co., OH, late of Fulton Co., PA; Christian Pollack and David Pollack, of Green Co.

Sources: Bounty land claim, 50-40-35608, 55-120-66647; Pension, WO33077, WC21430.

HAMMOND, Carroll. 2nd sergt. under Capt. Fonsten, 2 Sep - 27 Oct 1814.

HAMMOND [Hamond], Hezekiah. Pvt., U.S. Artillery. At enlistment: 5 ft, 9 inches; blue eyes, brown hair, fair complexion; age 34; laborer; b. Fred. Co., MD; enlisted 21 Oct 1810 in Washington by Capt. Beal or Lt. Perkins for 5 yrs. Sent to Ft. Washington 5 Nov 1810; d. 4 Mar 1815 at Fort Nelson.

HAMMOND, James. Pvt. under Capt. John Galt, 31 Aug - 27 Oct 1814.

HAMMOND, Simpson. Sergt. under Capt. Duvall, 3 Aug - 3 Oct 1814, substitute for Daniel Stoner; b. c.1790. On 19 Aug 1809 Zach. Danner, Libertytown, advertised a reward for a runaway apprentice to the harness and saddling business, named Francis Simpson Hammond, 18-19, 5 ft, 8-9 inches.

He said that after the Battle of Bladensburgh they were marched back to Bladensburgh, thence to Washington City and encamped on Windmill Hill between the President's house and the Potomac River, where he was taken sick and unable to do his duty. After a short time in Georgetown he went home last part of Sep 1814. Confined under Doctor's care for more than 6 mos.; crippled with rheumatism, "near death in 1858 but is much better now (1859)." In letter from Simpson Hamond, Overman's Ferry, Muscatine Co., IA, on 10 Jul 1859 he stated that he was planning to move to Kansas Territory in September or October.

Sources: Bounty land claim, 55-160-88429; Fredericktown Herald.

HAMMOND, Thomas. Appt'd capt. 16 Jun 1813, 29th Regt., MM.

HAMMOND, William. Appt'd surgeon, 8 May 1812, 2nd Reg., 1st Cav. Dist.

HANE, Daniel. Pvt. under Capt. John Brengle, 25 Aug - 19 Sep 1814. FCml issued to Daniel Hane and Maria Woltz 8 May 1815.

HANE, David. Pvt. under Capt. John Brengle, 25 Aug - 19 Sep 1814; d. Georgetown, D.C., May 1864; res. Frederick until c.1854 when he moved to Georgetown.

Source: Maryland Union, 5 May 1864.

HANES, William. Pvt. under Capt. Zacharias, 10 Aug - 10 Sep 1814, 2nd Regt, 1st Cav. Dist.

HANICKER, Peter. Pvt. under Capt. Samuel Ogle, 1 May - 5 Jul 1813.

HANIFER, John. Pvt. under Capt. Thomas Contee Worthington, 17 - 31 Dec 1812,

HANN [Haun], Adam. Pvt. from Mechanickstown under Capt. George W. Magee, 23 Sep 1814 - 10 Jan 1815; sergt. until transferred on 23 Sep to Magee's company.

HANN, Henry. Pvt. under Capt. Knox, 26 Aug - 27 Oct 1814; b. c.1784; m(1) Lucy Elder (d. Emmittsburg 12 Aug 1853); m(2) Bridget Maguire, at St. Joseph's Church, Emmittsburg, MD, 23 Nov 1858 [or 25 Nov 1857], by Rev R. Cappessuto, C.M.; res. Balt. City 1855, Adams Co., PA 1872; d. Emmittsburg 29 Dec 1874; widow d. c.Jun 1891. 1850 census, Emmittsburg Dist.: Henry Hann 62, $2500; Lucy 64, Bethilda 24; Monica 22; John Hughs 54; Catharine Elder 45; Lucy Ann Creatin 11; all b. Fred. Co., MD. Bur. Emmittsburg, St. Joseph's Cath. Ch.: Henry Hann, 23 Dec 1873, age 86-2-27; and wife Lucy, 12 Aug 1853, age 68-4-8.

Sources: Pensions, SO28089, SC19932, WO36310, WC25024; **Names in Stone; Bridge in Time.**

HANN, Jacob. Pvt. under Capt. William Knox, 26 Aug - c.30 Oct 1814; on furlough for 10 days on 30 Oct; b. c.1784; m. Mary Magdalene Ocker, in Frederick in 1806. 1850 census, Creagerstown E.D.: Jacob Hann 70 and Mary Hann 68 - both b. MD. He d. Fred.

FREDERICK COUNTY MILITIA IN THE WAR OF 1812

Co. 24 Jan 1855; widow res. Fred. Co. Acq. (1855): Henry Witmar and David Witmar.
Source: Bounty land claim, 55-120-34661.

HANN, William. Pvt. under Capt. William Knox 26 Aug - 27 Oct 27 1814.

HANN, William. Pvt. from New Windsor under Capt. George W. Magee, 22 Jul 1814 - 10 Jan 1815.

HANNAH, Elijah. Pvt. under Capt. John Galt, 31 Aug - 27 Oct 1814; b. c.1792; res. Balt. City 1850.
Source: Bounty land claim, 50-40-83435.

HANSHAW, George. Pvt. under Capt. Daniel Marker, 25 Aug - 27 Oct 1814.

HANSHEW, Henry. Pvt. under Capt. Henry Steiner, 25 Aug - 27 Sep 1814; b. c.1784, son of Frederick Hanshew, grandson of Rev. Handschuh; m. 3 Mar 1825 in Fredericktown, Catharine Susan Stover (b. 10 Dec 1801), dau of John Stover, niece of Barbara Fritchie, by Rev Jonathan Helfenstein. At enrollment: 27 yrs old, a skin dresser, b. Fredericktown, light hair, eyes and complexion; res. Fredericktown 1850, 1851 and 1855; res. West Patrick St. at one time. 1850 census, Fredericktown: Henry Hanshew 65, skindresser, $1,500, Catherine Hanshew 46, Emily E. 21, Fritchie, 20, tailor, George 19, skindresser; Charles A., 15; Daniel S., 13; Julia A., 10; Harriet C., 7; Margaret Stover 70; all b. MD. He d. Fredericktown 8 Mar 1862, at age 77. Widow res. Fredericktown 1878; d. 4 May 1892 at residence of dau, Mrs. Mary Quinn, E. 4th St., Frederick. Henry and Catharine bur. at Mt. Olivet, Fredericktown.

Other surviving children: Emily, Fritchie, Daniel Hanshew and Mrs. John Abbott and Allen Hanshew of Martinsburg, WV. Acq. (1878): G. W. Dertzbaugh, age 52, and R. M. Ramsburg, age 32, of West Patrick St., Fredericktown, each acq. 20 yrs; Henry Nixdorff and George Metzger, acq. with Henry Hanshew 20 yrs; Nicholas D. Hauer and George Markell. John Stover, formerly of Balt. and father-in-law of Henry Hanshew, d. 27 Jun 1825, in his 61st year. Frederick Hanshew, father of Henry and John Hanshew, d. 1 Oct 1832, in his 72nd year. Rev. Hanschuh, grandfather of Henry Hanshew, came from Halle, Germany c.1745.
Sources: Bounty land claim, 50-40-33145, 55-120-2415; Pension: WO13891, WC9098; **Names in Stone; Bridge in Time; Engelbrecht Diary**: 1:329, 349; 2:32; **The Daily News**, 5 May 1892.

HANSHEW, John Frederick William. Citizen of Fredericktown; d. 6 May 1867, age 77 yrs, 2 mos, 16 days, at residence in W. 2nd St.; engaged in lumber business; m. c.1822 Mary Ramsburg; she d. 26 Sep 1826, age 21. Both bur. Mt. Olivet Cem., Frederick. Newspaper obit. stated he served in War of 1812; no record of service in War of 1812 found.
Sources: **(Frederick) Examiner**, 14 Sep 1814, 8 May 1867; FCml; **Frederick-Town Herald**, 30 Sep 1826.

HANSON, Alexander B. Merchant, Fredericktown; pres. Fred. Co. Nat'l Bank; d. 21 Sep 1868, age 78 yrs, 7 mos, 11 days. Newspaper obit. annouced death of Col. Alexander B. Hanson; stated he served in War of 1812. 1850 census, Fredericktown: A.B. Hanson, 60, grocer, merchant, $12,000; Susan H., 48. Wife Susan W. Hanson d. 24 Oct 1864, in her 65th year.

Sources: Bridge in Time; (Frederick) Examiner, 9 Nov 1864, 30 Sep 1868; Md. Union, 3 Nov 1864.

HANSON, John. Pvt., 22nd U.S. Inf. At enlistment: 5 ft, 5 inches; blue eyes, brown hair, dark complexion; age 39; saddler; b. Fred. Co.; enlisted 4 Jul 1814 by Capt. Amberson for duration of war. At Pittsburg, PA, 31 Dec 1814. Discharged 24 or 25 Mar 1815 at Fort Fayette, PA.

HARBAUGH, Alexander. Sergt. under George Flaut, 29 Apr - 29 Jun 1813; tanner of Millerstown (Fairfield, PA); b. 13 Jun 1793 in Fred. Co. son of Christian and Maria Elizabeth (Williar) Harbaugh; m. Miss Rosanna Siess [SGss] (b. 27 Nov 1800 Fred. Co., dau of Godfrey SGss, tanner, and Anna Maria Krmer), by Rev Peter Klugh, at Graceham, MD 4 Apr 1820. At enrollment: age 20, farmer and tanner, 5 ft, 7 inches, light blue eyes, brown hair, fair complexion. He res. Washington Township, Franklin Co., PA, 1850, 1855; d. Mont Alto, PA, 16 Feb 1864, aged 70 yrs, 8 mos, 3 days; bur. Quincy, PA; widow d. c.1896. Acq.(1878): Felix V. Harbaugh, Maria E. Harbaugh, Winfield Harbaugh of Alameda Co, Mrs. Clemtinea S. Hurley of Santa Rosa City, Sonoma Co., CA, the latter two acq. 30 yrs.

Sources: Pension, WO44700, WC35020; Moravian Families of Maryland. See this work for more details on Harbaugh family.

HARBAUGH, Benjamin. Pvt. under Capt. Joseph Wood, 27 Aug - 28 Oct 1814. 1850 census, Hauvers E.D.: Benjamin Harbaugh 57, farmer, $8000; Sarah, 57; Adaline, 23; Anna B., 21; Ephraim, 19; Stansbury, 18; Andrew Coffman, 38, labourer; Joseph Coffman, 29, labourer - all b. Fred. Co., MD. [FCml issued to Benjamin Harbaugh and Sarah Eyler 4 Oct 1826.

Sources: Bridge in Time; FCml.

HARBAUGH [Herbaugh], Elias. Sergt. under Capt. John Galt, 31 Aug - 27 Oct 1814; drafted at Harbaugh's Valley; b. 11 Feb 1789, son of Christian and Maria Elizabeth (Williar) Harbaugh; m. Mary Weaver [Weber], at Chambersburg, 28 Oct 1819; wagon-maker and farmer; son Frederick Alexander b. 2 Jan 1821. Christian Harbaugh, farmer, b. 14 Jan 1753; d. of stroke 23 Mar 1836; m. 6 Nov 1780 Maria Elizabeth Williar, dau of Peter and Elizabeth Magdalena (Schlim) Williar. She was b. 18 Sep 1760 Fred. Co.; d. 28 Sep 1824. 1850 census, Hauvers E.D.: Elias Harbaugh, 66, farmer, $26,000; Sarah, 29; Henry, 27; George 24; Hiram 22; Elias 17; Susan 16; Washington 14; May Ortner 52; Ann Harbaugh 28; George C. Harbaugh 1 - all b. Fred. Co., MD; cash value of farm $11,000, 140 acres of improved land 360 unimproved land, 12 milch cows, 165 animals slaughtered.

Sources: Pension, SO12542, WC7742; Bridge in Time; Moravian Families of Graceham, Maryland.

HARBAUGH, Jacob. Pvt., 2nd U.S. Inf., under Capt. Johnston. At enlistment: 5 ft, 8 inches; hazel eyes, black hair, dark complexion; age 25; farrier; b. Fred. Co.; enlisted 14 May 1808 at New Town or Newton by Lt. Luckett for

5 yrs. Ordered to Columbian Springs 15 Sep 1808. Tried by court martial for sleeping on post 28 Jan 1809 - sentenced to 50 lashes; being drunk - sentenced to 40 lashes; on 15 Dec 1810, for neglect of duty - given 30 lashes - remitted; Jun 1812 for overstaying pass - awarded one week hard labor - remitted; 20 Aug 1812, for being drunk - sentenced to 2 weeks on bread and water. Discharged at Carrys Perdido 14 Mar 1813.

HARDER, Henry. Pvt., 5th U.S. Inf. At enlistment: 5 ft, 7 3/4 or 8 inches; blue eyes, dark hair, fair complexion; age 25; laborer; b. Fred. Co., MD; enlisted 3 or 13 Apr 1812 at Fredericktown by Capt. Johnson for 5 yrs. Deserted 28 Feb 1816 at Detroit.

HARDING, John. Pvt. under Capt. Henry Riggs; b. 7 Dec 1792; m. Hannah Norris (b. 26 Mar 1793) c.25 Mar 1820. In 1850 they res. New Market Dist.; he d. 7 Feb 1872; she d. 20 Feb 1875. Both bur. New London, Central Chapel Meth. Ch. Julia Ann Harding, only dau d. 1837, aged 13 yrs and 23 days.

Sources: Bounty land claim, 55-120-66012; FCml; Bridge in Time; Names in Stone.

HARDING, John. Pvt. under Capt. Henry Lowrye's Washington Co. company, 27 Aug - 28 Oct 1814; joined company at New Market.

HARDING, John. Pvt. under Capt. Denton Darby, 3 Aug - 8 Nov 1814; "deserted"; b. c.1787; res. Shelby Co., MO, 1856.

Source: Bounty land claim, 55-160-60333.

HARDING, John Lackland. Pvt. under Capt. Henry Steiner 9 - 27 Sep 1814; m. c.1804, Eleanor(a) Marshall (d. 31 Mar 1816); m. 30 Mar 1820, Eleanor Mantz, dau of Francis Mantz of Fredericktown by Rev Schaeffer; John L. Harding res. 4 miles from Fredericktown in 1809. Marian Marshall son of John L. and Eleanora Harding, b. 28 Aug 1808. Eleanor Harding d. 2 Oct 1835. Hon. John L. Harding d. at his residence in Frederick 15 Oct 1837 - Chief Justice of the Orphans Court of Fred. Co. - in his 58th year; bur. Epis. burying ground.

Sources: **Fredericktown Herald**, 16 Dec 1809, 1 Apr 1820; FCml; Md. German Ch. Rcds. v. 4; **The Times and Democratic Advocate**, Oct 1837; **(Frederick) Examiner**, Apr 1816; **Engelbrecht Diary**: 1:278; 2:177, 266.

HARDING, Philip. Pvt. under Capt. Denton Darby, 3 Aug - 8 Nov 1814; b. 28 Oct 1794; m. Rebecca Buckey, at Fredericktown, Mar 1844; res. Fred. Co. 1851, 1855, 1872 (P.O. Address: New London); d. 16 Aug 1877; bur. New London, Central Chapel Meth. Church with wife Rachel [according to *Names in Stone*] (she d. 14 Nov 1866, age 59 yrs, 5 mos. 1850 census, New Market Dist.: Philip Harding 54, farmer, $6,000, Rebecca 42, Basil 21, Margaret 18, Lucinda C. 3, Anne V. 1 - all b. MD.

Sources: Pension, 26559, SC20173; **Names in Stone; Bridge in Time.**

HARDING, Solomon. Pvt. under Capt. Denton Darby, 3 Aug - 8 Nov 1814; d. Columbus OH, sentenced on 21 Aug 1835 to state prison, OH, for term of 8 yrs; d. there c.1840-41; wife Jane d. London Twp, Carroll Co., OH, previous to 21 Aug 1835. Acq.: 1851 - Conrad Slates, London Twp, Carroll Co., OH, guardian of Philip Harding, a minor heir of Solomon Harding, dec'd., stated

Philip Harding (b. 26 May 1832) and Martha Harding (b. 26 Apr 1830) were only remaining heirs of said Solomon Harding who were under age of 21 on 28 Sep 1850. Acq.: Peter Simmons, res. London Township Co.; drafted with Solomon Harding; procurred substitute and discharged at Bladensburg 8 Aug 1814.

Source: Bounty land claim, 50-40-47854.

HARDMAN, George. Musician, 5th U.S. Inf. At enlistment: 5 ft, 9 inches; blue eyes, sandy hair, fair complexion; age 26; shoemaker; b. Fred. Co., MD; enlisted 5 Apr 1812 at Hagerstown, MD, by Capt. Miller for 5 yrs. At Pittsburg 30 Aug 1815. Discharged 4 Apr 1817.

HARDY, George. Pvt., 12th U.S. Inf., under Capt. James Paxton. At enlistment: 5 ft, 2 1/2 inches; gray eyes, black hair, light complexion; age 24; laborer; b. Fred. Co., MD; enlisted 31 Dec 1812 or 5 Jan 1813 at Lewisburg, VA, for 5 yrs; d. French Mills 3 Feb 1814.

HARDY, John. Corpl., 12th U.S. Inf. At enlistment: 5 ft, 8 inches, age 22, b. Fred. Co., MD; enlisted 22 Mar 1813 at Wheeling, VA, by Lieut. A. McDonald for 5 yrs. Killed in action 11 Nov 1813 at Williamsburg.

HARDY, Joseph. Pvt. under Capt. James F. Huston, 23 Jul 1814 - 4 Oct 1814; on furlough after 4 Oct; d. while on furlough, 19 Oct 1814 in Balt.; m. 9 Jun 1807 Catherine Ramsburger (b. 6 May 1790, dau of Jacob Ramsberger and Anna Elizabeth Devilbiss, d. 1861). She was bur. at Bethel Lutheran, Frederick, MD. Their children: Ezra Hardy b. 12 Nov 1808; John Caspar Hardy b. 12 Oct 1810; Susanna Hardy b. 4 Oct 1812. After death of Joseph Hardy widow m. George Dutro [Duttero, Duttrow] (1801-1877) and they raised three more children: Lewis, John and Catherine A. Dutro.

Sources: Material submitted by Jeannine M. Hardy, Swanton, OH, a descendant of John Caspar son of Joseph Hardy; records of Frederick Luth. Church, showing birth of Johan Caspar, son of Joseph and Catharina Hardy.]

HARGESHEIMER, Joseph. Pvt. under Capt. Jacob Alexander, 22 Jul - 19 Sep 1814.

HARLAN [Harland], James. Pvt. under Capt. Joseph Wood, 27 Aug - 28 Oct 1814. [Poss. related: James W. Harlan bur. at Woodsboro, Harlan Family Cem., d. 7 Apr 1861, age 67-0-3. James Harlan and Mary Wood m. 13 Apr 1791, wit: Joshua Harlan, James Hall. Also bur. at Harlan Family Cem. is Mary M. Harlan (26 Oct 1793 - 22 Jan 1859). The 1850 census of Woodsboro Dist.: John M. Harlen, 30, wagonmaker; James W. Harlen, 50; Nancy Harlen, 52.]

Sources: Records of Reformed Church of Frederick give date of marriage as 13 Apr 1791 which conflicts with date of FCml (18 Apr 1791); **Names in Stone, FCml, Bridge in Time.**

HARMAN, David. Pvt. under Capt. Thomas Contee Worthington 17 Aug - 31 Dec 1812.

HARMAN [Harmon], Jacob. Pvt. under Capt. Capt. Steiner, 28 Apr - 29 Jun 1813; m. 30 Mar 1799 Margaret Zegler [Zealer] (b. 21 Mar 1771), at Fredericktown by Rev Wagner, German Ref. Church; d. Fredericktown morning of 31 Mar 1839, age 68 yrs, 6

FREDERICK COUNTY MILITIA IN THE WAR OF 1812

months, 4 days, at his residence; bur. Luth. Cem.; widow res. Frederick Election Dist. in 1850, age 75, deaf, in home of Wilson W. Kolb, age 44, physician; Margaret Kolb, age 40 and David Kolb, age 19 and George Kolb, age 12; she also res. Fred. Co. 1855; she d. 5 Mar 1856. Both bur. Mt. Olivet Cem., Fredericktown. Acq.: John Schissler and Wilson Kolb, Jacob Faubel (served May-Jul 1813).

Sources: Bounty land claim, 55-120-1949; Names in Stone; Bridge in Time.

HARMAN, Jacob (or Harmon). Pvt. under Capt. William Durbin, 24 Aug - 27 Oct 1814; b. 26 May 1795; m. Mary Myers, at her father's residence 10 Oct 1819; res. Carroll Co. (P.O. Address: Frizzlesburg) 1871; d. 13 Aug 1871, aged 76 yrs, 2 months, 8 days; bur. Uniontown Pipe Creek Cem.; widow d. 28 Jun 1875, aged 80 yrs, 11 months, 19 days.

Sources: Pension, SO1535; Names in Stone.

HARMAN, John. Pvt. under Capt. William Durbin, 24 Aug - 27 Oct 1814; served with his bro. Jacob Harman; b. 8 Sep 1792; m. Margaret Sell 4 Feb 1819, Carroll Co; d. 7 or 9 Aug 1870; res. Carroll Co. 1851 and 1855; she res. Taneytown, Carroll Co. 1871 and 1878; both bur. Luth. Cem., Taneytown.

Sources: Bounty land claim, 50-40-32943, 55-120-9123; Pension, WO3590, WC12631.

HARNE, Overton. Appt'd lieut. 1 Aug 1814 under Capt. George W. Magee, 20th Regt., MM.

HARNS, Halban. Mbr. of Crawford's "company."

HARRIET, Henry. Pvt. under Capt. John Galt, 31 Aug - 27 Oct 1814; b. c.1796; res. Emmitsburg, MD, for some time; Clear Spring, Washington Co., MD, 1852 and Piedmont, Hampshire Co., VA, 1855.

Source: Bounty land claim, 55-120-66416 (bounty land warrant consumed by fire c.1 Nov 1851, City of Cairo, IL, at Illinois Central Railroad freight house, losing around $500 worth of other property which the Illinois Central Railroad had agreed to pay.

HARRIS, Daniel. 4th Corpl. under Capt. Thomas Contee Worthington, 17 Aug - 31 Dec 1812.

HARRIS, George. Pvt. under Capt. Durbin; joined 24 Aug 1814; discharged 2 Sep for inability; m(1) Nancy Wilson who d. 1 Mar 1858 Uniontown, MD; m(2) 10 Nov 1859 Lydia Slegle of Westminster Dist. (b. c.1808, prev. m. --- Frock?), at Pleasant Valley, Carroll Co., by Rev P. Schewrer, Lutheran Church at St. Mary's. At enrollment: florid complexion, blue eyes, dark hair, 5 ft and 1/2 tall; d. Uniontown, MD, 27 Mar 1876. In 1878 widow was "infirm and sick." Acq. (1878): William N. Martin, age 45, and Emanuel Formwalt, age 43, res. Uniontown, acq. 15 and 10 yrs, resp.; Jesse T. H. Davis and William McCollum, Carroll Co., acq. 15 and 17 yrs as neighbors.

Sources: Bounty land claim, 55-160-97487; Pension, WO21919 (rejected 11 Dec 1878).

HARRIS, John. Pvt. under Capt. Samuel Duvall, 3 Aug - 3 Oct 1814; prob. m. Mary Elder c.1783; d. 7 Feb 1832, age 77; bur. St. Anthony, old Mt. St. Mary's Cath. Cem. Also bur. in same

cem. was Mary Harris, d. 19 Apr 1825, age 70.
Sources: FCml; Names in Stone.

HARRIS, Kinsey. See Kinsey Harrison.

HARRIS, Michael. Pvt. from New Windsor under Capt. George W. Magee; joined 22 Jul 1814; sick on furlough 1 Oct 1814; deserted 6 Dec 1814; b. c.1793; m. Catherine Lloyd, at E. Pike Run, 1847; res. California, Washington Co., PA, 1871.
Sources: Bounty land claim, 55-160-94781; Pension, SO16129 (rejected 25 May 1872 - desertion).

HARRIS, Regin. Pvt. under Capt. Nicholas Turbutt, 1 Sep - 27 Oct 1814.

HARRISON, Kinsey. Pvt. under Capt. Basil Dorsey, 30 Jul - 27 Sep 1814 (listed as Kinsey Harris in the muster rolls); b. MD, c.1796; m. 1 Oct 1841* Margaret Haney (b. c.1802, prev. m. Charles Haney who d. Pittsburg, PA, 1839), in Monroe Co., OH, by Hugh Wayburn, a squire. At enrollment: age 18, farmer, light hair, pale blue eyes, fair complexion; res. Monroe Co., OH, 1850 and Noble Co., OH, 1855 and 1871 (Marion Township, P.O. Address: Summerfield); d. Summerfield, OH, 2 Sep 1873 or 1874; bur. cem. at Summerfield; widow res. Wetzel Co., WV 1879. Acq. (1879): Robert Carpenter, age 42, and Louisa G. Carpenter, 41, res. Wetzel Co, acq, 19 and 22 yrs, resp.; Charles W. Haney, states 1st husband of Margaret d. Pittsburg, PA, bur. Presby. grave yard; Priscilla Harper and Abram Harper (present at wedding); John H. Philpot and Shepherd B. Philpot of Summerfield, OH.

* Date of marriage given by veteran; his widow gave date as 18 Oct 1843.
Sources: Bounty land claim, 55-120-32291; Pension, SO14442, SC16233, WO37195, WC26846.

HARRISON [Harris], Zepheniah. Pvt. under Capt. John Brengle, 25 Aug - 19 Sep 1814; b. 15 Nov 1795. When enrolled: age 19, small heavy set, black hair, fair complexion. FCml issued to Zephaniah Harrison and Mary Bluer 8 Apr 1817. On 4 Sep 1817 a notice was made in the Frederick-Town Herald by Zephaniah Harrison stating that his wife Mary had left his "bed and board." On 12 Apr 1818 Zephaniah Harrison and Mary A. Hallar m. in Frederick City by Rev. D. F. Schaeffer, Luth Church, Frederick. According to the pension application submitted by Mary Harrison in 1878 neither she nor Zephaniah had married prev. [This contradicts a marriage with Mary Bluer. Were there two men named Zephaniah Harrison?] Buried at Mt. Olivet are Zephaniah Harrison (15 Nov 1795 - 28 May 1867) and wife Mary Harrison (14 Jul 1798 - 2 Jan 1882); he d. at his residence on W. Patrick St. 1850 census, Fredericktown: Zephaniah Harrison 54, tanner, $1000; Mary, 52; Edward 18, clerk - all b. in Md. He was a mbr. of the "United Brothers of the War of 1812" in 1859. His widow was living at East Patrick St. in 1878. Acq.: George Hoskins, 73, West 2nd St., Frederick City; Lewis S. Titlow, 32, E. Patrick St., both acq. for 20 yrs. Son Rev. P. L. Harrison res. Frostburg, MD, 1882.
Sources: Bounty land claim, 50-40-80890, 55-120-11410, WO13898, WC11256; Names in Stone; Bridge in Time; FCml; Frederick-Town Herald,

FREDERICK COUNTY MILITIA IN THE WAR OF 1812

4 Sep 1817, 18 Apr 1818; **(Frederick) Examiner**, 14 Sep 1859, 5 Jun 1867, 4 Jan 1882.

HARRY. Servant to Capt. Jacob Getzendanner, 9 Aug - 17 Sep 1813.

HART, Ezra. Pvt. under Capt. Shawen from the Middletown area, 5 Sep - 27 Oct 1814. At enrollment: 5 ft, 8 inches; black hair, grey eyes, fair complexion; laborer; joined at Bedford, PA (according to widow); m(1) in Newry, Blair Co., PA, 6 Dec 1821, Sara Westover dau of Oliver Westover (b. 10 Dec 1746) in Huntingdon Co., PA; she d. 10 Sep 1827. By this marriage he had Liddia b. 24 Oct 1822, Ezra b. 3 Sep 1824, Elizabeth b. 20 Apr 1826, all b. near Newry, Huntington Co., PA. Ezra Hart m(2) 1 Dec 1827 in Newry, PA, Mary Westover (b. 1 Mar 1802), dau of Oliver Westover. By this marriage Ezra Hart had Oliver b. 24 Mar 1828, Theophilus b. 14 Oct 1829, Margaret b. 8 Jun 1831, Sarah b. 13 Mar 1833, Amanda b. 12 Apr 1835, Mary b. 25 Dec 1836, Jerusha b. 16 Oct 1838, Susana b. 18 Jul 1840, Peter S. b. 2 Jun 1842. The last four children were b. at Sugar Run, PA. Ezra res. Little Juniata, PA, in 1823; Mowerys Hill, PA, 1824-4; Kensils Farm, 1825-7; Sugar Run, PA, 1827-53; Eldorado (near Altoona), PA, from 1853 until he d. on 25 Dec 1853; widow continued res. Eldorado until she moved to Altoona in 1861; res. 17th St., between 9th and 10th Avenues in Altoona, PA, 1879; d. 1889. Acq. - 1879: John Loudon, age 55; Catharine Vaughn, 76; James Vaugh, 78 - res. Altoona, PA; and William Burkhart, 66, res. Logan Township, Blair Co., PA. 1856: Samuel Smith, res. Blair Co., PA.

Sources: Pension, WO37194, WC28393; Bounty land claim, 55-160-40123.

HART, Michael. 3rd corpl. under Capt. Daniel Marker, 16 Aug - 18 Sep 1813.

HART, Michael. Pvt. under Capt. Samuel Dawson, from 21 Jul until he deserted 24 Aug 1814.

HARTZACK, Peter. Pvt. under Capt. Joseph Wood, 27 Aug - 28 Oct 1814.

HARVEY, Elisha. Pvt. under Capt. Denton Darby, 3 Aug - 8 Nov 1814; b. c.1794; res. Mount Pleasant Township, Washington Co., PA, 1871 (P.O. Address: Cherry Valley); at that time wife was dead.

Source: Pension, SO9951, SC5717. Pension suspended 11 Nov 1875, because veteran was dependent father of George Harvey.

HASSEFROSS, John. Pvt. under Capt. Nicholas Turbutt, 1 Sep - 27 Oct 1814.

HATCH, Samuel. 1st Sergt. under Capt. Samuel Ogle, 1 May - 5 Jul 1813.

HATTEN, William. Pvt. under Capt. Daniel Marker, 25 Aug - 27 Oct 1814.

HAUER, Adam. Pvt. under Capt. Joseph Green; joined 14 Oct 1814; deserted 12 Dec 1814. [Adam Hauer son of Georg Hauer and Elizabeth Margaret, b. 21 Apr 1790; FCml issued to Adam Hauer and Catherine Lambert 25 May 1817]

Sources: Rcds of Ref. Ch.; FCml.

HAUER, Daniel, Jr. Appt'd capt. 16 Mar 1812, 2nd Regt., 1st Cav. Dist, MM; m. 29 Dec 1812, Miss Margaret Martz, by Rev. Helfenstein.

HAUER, George. Pvt. under Capt. Henry Steiner, 25 Aug - 27 Sep 1814; b. 25 May 1777; m. c.1803 Catherine

THE VETERANS

Shellman (8 Nov 1781 - 2 Feb 1858), dau of Jacob Shellman and sister of William and Jacob Shellman; he d. 22 Oct 1848; both bur. Mt. Olivet, Frederick. Children of George Hauer: (1) William Hauer, b. 3 Jul 1810, apprentice of John Ebert in skin-dressing, 14 May 1827; (2) Elizabeth Hauer, eldest dau, m. Charles P. McMullin, 20 Mar 1832; and (3) Rev. Daniel J. Haurer. Mrs. Hauer's father, Jacob Shellman (son of John who d. 1815, age c.93) d. 29 Nov 1840, in his 91st year. 1850 census of Fredericktown: William Hauer, 38, tanner; Catherine Hauer, 65; Ann C. Hauer, 33; Mary L. Hauer, 27; Susan, 23.

Sources: **Names in Stone; FCml; (Frederick) Examiner,** 17 Feb 1758; **Frederick-Town Herald,** 2 Jan 1813; **Bridge in Time; Engelbrecht Diary,** 1:446; 2:1, 15, 397, 424, 507.

HAUER, Henry. 3rd corpl. under Capt. Henry Steiner, 25 Aug - 27 Sep 1814. [Baptism of Henrich Hauert son of Nicolaus and Catharina b. 7 May 1777, recorded in Ref. Ch. of Frederick. Henry Hauer was a bro. of Daniel Hauer and Mrs. Fritchie, Mrs. Stover, Mrs. Peter Mantz and Mrs. Jacob Steiner and father of Nicholas D. Hauer. 1850 census of Fredericktown: Catherine Hauer, age 60, res. in home of John Watkins, age 39, stage driver and Margaret Watkins, 28. Margaret Ann only dau of Henry Hauer m. 22 Feb 1838, John Watkins.]

Sources: **Recds of Ref. Ch., Frederick; Engelbrecht Diary:** 2:284, 424; **Bridge in Time.**

HAUER, John H. Pvt. under Capt. Henry Steiner, 28 Apr - 29 Jun 1813.

HAUER, John Henry [called Henry Hauer]. 4th Sergt. [and 3rd?] under Capt. Thomas Contee Worthington, 17 Aug - 31 Dec 1812; m. 26 May 1818 Catharine Snider/Snyder (b. c.1785) at New Market, by Rev James S. Higgins; d. Fredericktown 13 May 1847 (or 1848). In 1850 she gave her former name as Snider and in 1855 as Catharine Kiplinger. 1850 census: Catharine Hauer, 60, in home of John Watkins, 39, stage driver; Margaret Watkins, 28; George Hauer, 19, cigar maker; George H. Steel, 22, tanner. Acq.(1850): Jacob Markell and Thomas W. Morgan; (1851): Charles Moor of the same company. Witnesses (1855): Lucretia L. Hauer and Margaret H. Watkins.

Sources: Bounty land claim, 55-80-9526; **Bridge in Time.**

HAUGH, Daniel. Pvt. in the 1st Cavalry Dist., 26 Aug - 3 Sep 3 1814.

HAUGHN, Jonathan. Pvt. under Capt. George W. Magee; joined 22 Jul 1814; discharged 1 Oct 1814 as overage.

HAUKER, John. Pvt. in Capt. Flautt's rifle company, 29 Apr - 29 Jun 1814.

HAUN [Hawn], David. Pvt. under Capt. William Durbin, Jr.; joined 24 Aug 1814; absent without leave 25 Oct 1814.

HAUSAR, Michael. Appt'd capt. of a select company no. 16, on 2 Aug 1799.

HAUSER, William [Wilhelm]. 4th sergt. under Capt. Henry Steiner, 28 Apr - 29 Jun 1813 and 2nd sergt., 25 Aug - 27 Sep 1814; b. 22 Feb 1789 son of Michael and Susanna; d. 15 May 1824 at the home of his father, in Fredericktown; bur. German Refomred Grave yard. Other children of Michael Hauser: Mrs. Louisa Levy consort of

FREDERICK COUNTY MILITIA IN THE WAR OF 1812

John Leonard Levy, d. 6 Jun 1825, in her 25th year; Mrs. Elizabeth Drill, consort of Andrew Drill, d. 20 Dec 1822.
Sources: Recds of Ref. Ch. Frederick; Fredericktown Herald, May 22 1824; Engelbrecht Diary: 1:196, 275, 345.

HAWKINS, James. Pvt. under Capt. Nicholas Turbutt, 1 Sep - 27 Oct 1814.

HAWMAN [HAUMAN], Frederick. Pvt. under Capt. George W. Ent, 24 Aug - 30 Sep 1814; b. 17 Dec 1792; res. Fred. Co., MD, 1851, 1855 and 1871; single in 1871; d. 21 Dec 1877 at the residence of David Ashbaugh; bur. Mt. Olivet, Frederick. 1850 census, Fredericktown: Frederick Hawman, 58, bar keeper, res. household of Benjamin Gilbert, 38, innkeeper. Other occupations: county constable, turnkey at the jail. He was a mbr. of the Frederick delegation of the "United Brothers of the War of 1812" in 1859. He was paralyzed in Jan 1877 and was residing with his bro.-in-law, Wm. T. Duvall on S. Market St. a short time later. He was the last surviving mbr. of Ent's company.
Sources: Bounty land claim, 50-40-395, 55-120-2736; Pension, SO9965, SC5580; Names in Stone; (Frederick) Examiner, 10 Jan 1877, 16 Dec 1877.

HAWN - See Haun.

HAWN, David. Pvt. under Mathew Murray, 25 Aug - 27 Oct 1814; served as substitute for --- McCarty; b. c.1793; m. 20(30?) Mar 1817 Mary Ludwick, at Shepherdstown, VA; res. Jefferson Co., VA, 1851 and 1855 (Shepherdstown). In 1855 a letter to the Commissioner of Pensions stated that "David Hawn is a hard working, rough carpenter, who is entirely illiterate but has been taught by his children to write his name with great difficulty ..." He d. 5 Mar 1875.
Source: Pension, SO23681, SC15143.

HAWN, Isaac. Pvt. under Capt. William Knox, 26 Aug - 27 Oct 1814. [Bur at Emmitsburg St. Elias Luth. Church: Isaac Hahn 14 Jan 1844, age about 78.]
Source: Names in Stone.

HAYDEN, Basil. Pvt. under Capt. Zacharias, 2nd Regiment, 1st Cav. Dist., 7 Aug - 10 Sep 1814; b. c.1785; res. Westminster, MD, 1852.
Source: Bounty land claim, 55-120-53633.

HAYES, Abraham. Pvt. under Capt. William Knox, 26 Aug - 27 Oct 27 1814. [This is prob. Abraham W. Hayes [Hays] son of Joseph and Deborah (Weimer) Hayes; m. c. 1826 Henrietta Musgrave; d. 4 Dec 1836, age 42 yrs, 6 mos, 16 days; she d. 10 Jul 1837, age 42 yrs, 6 days; both bur. Taneytown old cem. on Baptist Rd.]
Sources: Williams, History of Frederick County; Names in Stone; FCmL

HAYNES, Daniel. Mbr. of Crawford's "company."

HAYS, John. Pvt. under Capt. Barton Hackney, 1 Sep - 27 Oct 1814.

HAYS, Thomas. 1st Corpl. under Capt. James F. Huston, 23 Jul - 13 Oct 1814.

HAZLET [Haslet, Hazlett], Jacob. Pvt., 44th U.S. Inf., under Capt. Joseph J. Miles. At enlistment: 5 ft, 11 inches; blue eyes, dark hair, fair complexion; age 24; farmer; b. Fred. Co., MD; enlisted 21 Nov 1814 at New Orleans by Capt. Miles for 5 yrs. Tried by Regtl. Court Martial for conduct unbecoming

THE VETERANS

a soldier; sentenced to receive 30 paddles and whiskey stopped for two weeks. Tried for attempting to pass the guard with whiskey; sentenced to 15 paddles two mornings in succession. On 31 Aug 1816, sick in hospital. Discharged at Baton Rouge 20 or 21 Nov 1819.

HEAD, John. Appt'd 1 Jan 1813, 2nd lieut., under Capt. Baker Johnson, 2nd Regt., 1st Cav. Dist., MM.

HEAD, Zeal (Cecilius). Pvt. under Capt. George W. Ent, 3rd Regt, 24 Aug - 30 Sep 1814; b. 1787; m. c.1816 Catherine Lehr; cabinet maker. Catherine b. 1792, d. 6 May 1876, age 84, 3 mos., 2 days. He d. 2 March 1860, age 72 yrs, 3 mos., 21 days. Both bur. Ref. Ch. Cem.

Sources: FCml; Bridge in Time; (Frederick) Examiner, 7 Mar 1860, 19 Feb 1873, 10 May 1876; Names in Stone; West. Md. Genealogy, 7:1.

HEATER, William. Pvt. under Capt. Samuel Ogle, 1 May - 5 Jul 1813.

HECK, Jacob. Pvt. under Capt. John Galt, 31 Aug - 27 Oct 1814; b. c.1794. At enrollment: res. 3 miles of Taneytown, MD; res. Mountjoy Township, Adams Co, PA, 1851 and 1855. Acq.: 1851 - Jacob Baumgardner, appearing in Adams Co Court house, who was a 1st lieut. in company of Capt. William P. Farquhar.

Source: Bounty land claim, 55-120-558.

HEFNER [Heffner], Daniel. Pvt. under Capt. Joseph Wood, 27 Aug - 28 Oct 1814.

Any of the following (or all three) of the following entries may pertain to Jacob Heffner who d. 22 Jul 1827, in his 45th year and the Jacob Heffner to whom a marriage license was issued with Mary Heffner on 26 Nov 1813.

Sources: FCml; Engelbreght Diary: 1:456.

HEFFNER, Jacob. Pvt. under Capt. Thomas Contee Worthington, 17 Aug - 31 Dec 1812.

HEFFNER, Jacob. Pvt. under Capt. Jacob Getzendanner 9 Aug - 17 Sep 1813.

HEFFNER, Jacob. Pvt. under Capt. John Brengle, 25 Aug - 19 Sep 1814.

HEFFNER, John of Frederick. Appt'd 15 Jul 1814 lieut. under Capt. George Martz, 16th Regt., MM.

HEFFNER [Hefner], Lawrence. Pvt. under Capt. Jacob Getzendanner, 9 Aug 9 - 17 Sep 1813 and 26 Jul - 21 Aug 1814.

[FCml issued to Lawrence Heffner and Charlotte Heffner 19 Dec 1817]

HEFFNER, Michael. Pvt. under Capt. Henry Steiner, 28 Apr - 29 Jun 1813 and 25 Aug - 27 Sep 1814; d. Montgomery Co., OH, 10 Mar 1850; m. Margaret ---; she d. Montgomery Co, OH, 11 Sep 1844. Children of Michael and Margaret Heffner: George W. Heffner, b. 8 May 1819; Harriet Heffner, b. 8 Dec 1827; Julia Ann b. 20 Nov 1829; Lewis H. Heffner, b. 28 Nov 1830; Lavina b. 16 Dec 1835; John Heffner b. 28 Jun 1838; Mary S. Heffner b. 15 Nov 1840. Daniel Kizer, Jr., was appt'd guardian of the minor children. Acq.(1858): David B. Warner, acq. more than 17 yrs, and

FREDERICK COUNTY MILITIA IN THE WAR OF 1812

Samuel Rohrer. Witnesses (1855): George W. Heffner, oldest son of Michael and Margaret Heffner and John T. Kinney, res. Montgomery Co., OH. A letter dated 20 Oct 1939 from Mrs. Ray McDowell, 1804 W. Charles St., Muncie, IN, regarding military and family records of Michael Heffner.
Source: Bounty land claim, 55-160-82365.

HEIM, Andrew. Born 9 Jan 1787; d. 2 Apr 1871; bur. Mt. Olivet, Frederick; d. at residence of his son, William Heim, whom he was visiting at Delaware, OH. Obit. states he was soldier of the War of 1812; no records found. Jacob B. Heim, son of Andrew Heim, d. in his 51st year near Balt. on 26 Jan 1870, mbr. of firm, Heim, Nicodemus & Co., wholesale liquor dealers; bur. Mt. Olivet Cem. His wife d. Balt. while on a visit 1 Dec 1859, in her 70th year.
Sources: (Frederick) Examiner, 5 Apr 1871, 21 Dec 1859; Names in Stone.

HEINER, John. Pvt. under Capt. Reid, 2nd Regt., 1st Cavalry Dist., 26 Aug - 3 Sep 1814.

HEISLEY [Heisely], Frederick Augustus. Pvt. under Capt. James F. Huston, 23 Jul - 13 Oct 1814; b. 3 July 1792 in Fredericktown. He d. at Pittsburg, PA, 12 Jun 1875. He left for PA in 1818 where he resided until his death. His father built the clock in the Reformed Church steeple.
Sources: Englebrecht Diary, v.1, 384; (Frederick) Examiner, 23 Jun 1875.

HEISLEY, John. 2nd Corpl. under Capt. Joseph Green, 23 Jul 1814 - 10 Jan 1815; discharged and continued as substitute for his bro. Frederick Augustus Heisley; b. 30 Nov 1794, Fred., MD; d. 18 Sep 1869 at Harrisburg, PA. Moved to Harrisburg, PA, in 1816, returned to Frederick, studied medicine, grad Md. Medical College in Balt., moved back to Harrisburg c.1835 where he practiced medicine.
Source: (Frederick) Examiner, 29 Sep 1869.

HELDERBRAND - See Hilderbrand.

HELMES [Helms], Samuel. Pvt. from Balt. Town under Capt. George W. Magee, 22 Jul 1814 - 10 Jan 1815.

HELTBYDLE [Heltabidle], Antony Mbr. of Crawford's "company"; m. Maria Favorite c.12 Nov 1814. Issue: Sabina b. 13 Aug 1815; Elizabeth b. 11 Mar 1817.
Source: Moravians Families of Graceham, Md.

HELTIBIDDLE, David. He said he served as pvt. under Capt. William Durbin; said he volunteered at Westminster around 1 Sep 1814, discharged Oct 1814; b. c.1799; res. Carroll Co., MD, 1878 (P.O. Address: New Windsor); fol. discharge he res. near Westminster; at enrollment: 5 ft, 8-9 inches tall, brownish eyes, florid complexion. Acq.: William S. Brown, age 66, Thomas B. Gist, age 54, res. Main St., Westminster, acq. 55 and 35 yrs resp.
Source: Pension, SO33968. Rejected, "no record of the military organization alledged."

HEMPEY [HEMPY], Henry. Pvt. under Capt. Nicholas Turbutt, 1 Sep - 27 Oct 1814, as a substitute; b. c.1792; m. 16 Jan 1816 Catharine (Kitty) Miller (b. c.1799), in Fairfield Co., by Rev John Hite; res. Fairfield Co., OH, 1850, 1855 and 1871 (Walnut Township, 2 miles

THE VETERANS

north of Pleasantville); d. Walnut Township, 27 Mar 1875; widow res. Walnut Township 1878 (P.O. Address: Pleasantville). Acq. (1878): Abraham H. Hite and John Boyer, res. Pleasantville, OH.

Sources: Bounty land claim, 50-40-1294, 55-120-2790; Pension, SO5698 (rejected because of insufficient service of 59 days), WO28808, WC17263.

HENNING, Adam. Pvt. under Capt. John Galt, 31 Aug - 27 Oct 1814.

HENNING, John. Pvt. in the 1st Cavalry Dist., 26 Aug - 3 Sep 1814. [FCml issued to John Henning and Catherine Secrist 4 Dec 1815.]

HENRY, Joseph. Pvt. from Balt. under Capt. Joseph Green, 14 Oct 1814 - 10 Jan 1815; substitute for James Bricket.

HERBAUGH, Jacob. Pvt. under Capt. John Galt, 31 Aug - 27 Oct 1814.

HERBAUGH, Jonathan. Pvt. under Capt. John Galt, 31 Aug - 27 Oct 1814.

HERBERT, Perry. Corpl. under Capt. Samuel Dawson, 1 May - 5 Jul 1813.

HERMAN, John. Privte under Capt. Jacob Getzendanner, 9 Aug - 17 Sep 1813.

HERRING, ... Pvt. under Capt. Jacob Getzendanner, 26 Jul - 21 Aug 1814.

HERRING, Henry. Appt'd lieut. 27 Jan 1814 under Capt. Matthew Murray, 28th Regt., MM; served as ensign under Capt. Matthew Murray, 25 Aug - 27 Oct 1814; b. c.1794; res. Fred. Co., MD, 1850 and 1855.

Source: Bounty land claim, 55-120-27266.

HERRING, Jacob. Pvt. under Capt. Samuel Dawson, 1 May - 5 Jul 1813.

HERRING [HARRIN], Jacob. Appt'd ensign 24 Jul 1814 under Capt. Jacob Alexander, 28th Regt.; served as ensign under Capt. Alexander, 22 Jul - 19 Sep 1814; m. Elizabeth Wirtz (b. c.1793), in Fred. Co., MD, 12 [or 8] Nov 1810, near Point of Rocks [at Trannelsville?], by George Graver, Luth. minister; widow gave three different dates of death: 26 Jul 1831, 26 Aug 1831 and 1 Sep 1831. She moved from Middletown in Apr 1838, and res. Chariton Co., MO, until at least 1852; res. Chariton Co., 1855 and 1871 (on a farm, 1 mile e. of Brunswick). [*Frederick Hornet* - 6 Jan 1807 - Henry Stembel, living in Middletown, offered reward for apprentice, named Jacob Herring, bound to the hatting business; about 5 ft, 19 yrs of age, swaggering walk, freckled in the face, bowlegged.] Acq. - 1852: Jacob Lorentz and John Herring of A. 1856: Elias Turner, Cyrus J. Van Swearingen. 1872: Jasper M. Peery, Samuel Rankin.

Sources: Pension, WO4307, WC3617; Bounty land claim, 50-40-65357, 55-120-83654.

HERSCH, Philip. Pvt., 1st Cavalry Dist., 26 Aug - 3 Sep 1814. [Philip Hersh d. 2 Mar 1815 age 33; bur. Ladiesburg, Haughs (Mt. Zion) Luth. Ch.]

HERSHABARGER, John B. Pvt. under Capt. Barton Hackney, 1 Sep - 27 Oct 1814. Furloughed 20 Oct 1814.

HESS, Charles. Appt'd 22 May 1812 lieut. under Capt. Smith Cornell, 47th Regt., MM.

HESSON, John. Pvt. under Capt. William Knox 26 Aug - 27 Oct 27 1814; b. c.1798; at enrollment: age 19, 5 ft 10 inches, black hair, dark eyes; moved

FREDERICK COUNTY MILITIA IN THE WAR OF 1812

from Maryland in 1820 to live in Union, Montgomery Co., OH; d. Union, OH, 22 Aug 1885. Acq.: 1879 - David K. Boyer, age 67, res. River St., Dayton, OH; David E. Bauer, age 56, res. River St., Dayton, acq. 39 and 22 yrs, resp.; Josiah E. Boyer, acq. 25 yrs. 1880 - Mary Hesson and Eliza Marsteller, res. Montgomery Co., OH.

Sources: Bounty land claim, 55-160-114542; Pension, SO34212, SC25267.

HESSON, Peter. Pvt. from New Windsor under Capt. George W. Magee, 22 Jul - 10 Jan 1815.

HESTAND, Daniel. Pvt. under Capt. Barton Hackney; joined 1 Sep 1814; deserted 23 Oct 1814.

HESTAND, John. Pvt. under Capt. Barton Hackney, 6 Sep - 27 Oct 1814.

HETHYDLE, Jacob. Mbr. of Crawford's "company."

HICHEW - See also Hiteshew.

HICHEW, David. Pvt. under Capt. Fonsten; joined 2 Sep 1814; sick absent 11 Oct, died 23 Oct 1814.

HICKMAN, Isaac. Pvt., Artillery Corps, under Capt. A. G. Williams. At enlistment: he was 5 ft, 6 inches; had blue eyes, dark hair and light complexion; age 20; sailor; b. Fred. Co., MD; enlisted 28 May 1813 at Lewisburg by Capt. Williams for the duration of the war. Mustered at Province Island Barracks 30 Jun 1813. Discharged Buffalo 3 Jun 1815.

HICKS [Hix], Joseph. Pvt. under Capt. Joseph Wood; joined 27 Aug; furloughed 26 Oct 1814; b. c.1787.

HICKSON, Henry H. Ensign under Capt. William Knox, 26 Aug - 27 Oct 1814; b. 16 Mar 1786 son of Thomas and Maria; m. Mary E. Crapster (b. c.1783, dau of John Crapster), Taneytown, Thursday evening, 6 Dec 1810, by W. Rauhauser [Rev A. Grubb?], German Ref. Church; d. Taneytown, 27 Dec 1835; bur. Frederick Ref. Ch. [He d. of pulmonary disease at the residence of his mother in Fredericktown, according to the *Political Examiner*. John Crapster said that Henry Hickson d. 22 Dec 1835;* that they were m. by Rev Runkle.] His widow res. Balt. City in 1852, 1855 (No. 129 N. Eutaw St.). [From Records of the Evangelical Reformed Church in Frederick, Maryland, 1746-1800: Heinrich Hickson son of Thomas and Maria b 16 Mar 1786. spon: Susanna Schr?dter, sister of mother.] Acq.: 1852 - William Crapster, res. Balt. City; 1855 - Louis Lewis, 181 Aisquith St. and William C. Hickson, 129 N. Eutaw St., both Balt. City. 1872 - John Crapster, Evalina L. Shaw, age 71 since 22 Dec 1871. [A divorce was granted to Mary Hickson of Fred. Co., from Henry Hickson, she to have custody of a child. Laws of Maryland chapter 269, 1831 session.]

Sources: Bounty land claim, 50-40-65424; **Names in Stone; Fredericktown Herald**, 8 Dec 1810; Pension, WO7657, WC2696; Mary K. Meyer, **Divorces and Names Changed in Maryland**.

HICKSON, Thomas. Pvt., 14th U.S. Inf., under Capt. D. Cummings. At enlistment: 5 ft, 8 inches; blue eyes, black hair, fair complexion; age 21; merchant; b. Fred. Co., MD; enlisted 23 Nov 1814

THE VETERANS

at Balt. by Capt. Cummings for duration of war. Discharged 16 Mar 1815 at Balt.

HICKSON, Thomas V. Pvt. under Capt. Nicholas Turbutt, 1 Sep - 30 Oct 1814; b. 1794; res. Frederick Co 1855; d. 3 or 4 Nov 1868 at residence of Wm. Albaugh, E. Patrick St., age 74 yrs, 2 mos, 23 days; bur. Ref. graveyard.

Sources: Bounty land claim, 55-120-24548; (Frederick) Examiner, 11 Nov 1868; Md. Union, 12 Nov 1868; WMG, v.7, no.1.

HIDE, Adam. Pvt. under Capt. Samuel Dawson, 1 May - 5 Jul 1813.

HIDER, William. Pvt. under Capt. Joseph Wood, 27 Aug - 28 Oct 1814; rendezvous at Camp Diehl.

HIGH, Frederick. Mbr. of Crawford's "company." [FCml issued to Frederick High and Polly Eckman 31 Mar 1813]

HILARD, Johnson. Pvt. from New Windsor under Capt. George W. Magee, 14 Oct 1814 - 10 Jan 1815.

HILDERBRAND [Helderbrand], George. Pvt. under Capt. James F. Huston, 23 Jul 1814 - until he d. 16 Aug 1814. [Georg Hildebrand of Joseph and Magdalena b 19 Aug 1792.]

Source: Recds Ref. Ch., Frederick.

HILDEBRAND [Hilderbrand, Hildebrant]], John. Appt'd 18 Sep 1812 as ensign in Capt. Jacob Getzendanner's rifle company; served as 2nd lieut. under Capt. Jacob Getzendanner, 9 Aug - 17 Sep 1813 and 26 Jul - 21 Aug 1814; b. c.1775; res. Fred. Co., MD, 1851 and 1855; m. c.1798 Margaret Myers (d. 1 or 10 Jul 1858, age 85); d. 6 Aug 1862, age 86 at residence of his son-in-law, David Thomas; John and his wife bur. Ballenger Creek Pike, St. Matthew's Luth. Church, Church Hill.

Sources: Bounty land claim, 55-120-23259; Names in Stone; (Frederick) Examiner, 28 Jul 1858, 20 Aug 1862; Md. German Church Records, v. 4; Bridge in Time.

HILKEY, George. Pvt. under Capt. Nicholas Turbutt, 1 Sep - 27 Oct 1814; b. c.1789; m. 29 May 1817 Soloma [Siloma, Sarah] Waskey (b. c.1778), Middletown, MD, by Rev McCauly, Meth. minister. George Hilkey res. Ashland,OH, 1850; d. Ashland, OH 23 Feb 1851; widow res. Ashland, OH, 1855. Acq.: 1854 - John Hazlet and Mary Hazlet. 1855 - Elisha Barton and John Hazlett.

Source: Bounty land claim, 55-120-37690.

HILL, Bennet. Pvt. under Capt. Basil Dorsey; joined 30 Jul 1814; reported missing ever since the Battle of Bladensburg, 24 Aug 1814; b. c.1791; res. David Co., KY, 1855.

Source: Bounty land claim, 55-rejected 208985.

HILL, John. Pvt. under Capt. Jacob Getzendanner; 26 Jul - 21 Aug 1814.

HILLERY, James. Pvt. under Capt. Denton Darby; joined 3 Aug 1814; deserted; m. c. 30 Nov 1815 Elizabeth Greenwell. 1850 census, New Market Dist.: James Hilleary 62, carpenter, $500; Elizabeth 53; Louisa 23; Augustus 14; Edward 18 - all b. in Md.]

Sources: Names in Stone; Bridge in Time; FCml

HILLERY, Osborn. Appt'd 24 Oct 1800 as capt. of a company, 13th Regt., MM.

HILLERY, William. Surgeon under Col. John Ragan, 1st Regt, 14 Oct 1814

FREDERICK COUNTY MILITIA IN THE WAR OF 1812

- 11 Jan 1815, b. 25 Mar 1775; d. at his home on the Maryland Tract in his 59th year in 1834; he had labored under a painful disease c. 15 yrs. [In his biography of Thomas Brashear Johnson, Williams mentions, "... Dr. William Hilleary, b. Mar 25, 1775, and d. Mar 15, 1837 ... one of the founders of the Medical and Chirurgical Faculty of Maryland, in 1799. He served as surgeon of Colonel Ragan's regt. in the War of 1812..." Williams' date of death is in error as indicated by the reporting of his death in the *Frederick Herald* in 1834.]

Sourcees: **Frederick Herald**, 1 Feb 1834; Williams, **History of Frederick County, Maryland**, p. 1208.

HILTABYDLE [Hiltabidel, Hiltabidle], George. Mbr. of Crawford's "company." [George Hiltabidel b. 5 Feb 1780; d. 4 May 1869; bur. Wolfsville Ref. Cem. 1850 census, Catoctin E.D.: George Hiltabidle 70, labourer, Mary A. 42; Martha 14; George 8; Serena E. 10.]

Sources: **Names in Stone; Bridge in Time.**

HILTON, Miles. Pvt. under Capt. John Brengle, 25 Aug - 19 Sep 1814; deserted. [1850 census, Middletown E.D.: Miles Hilton, 62, weaver, b. in England in household of Benjamin Ramsburg, 28, wool manufacturer. *Bridge in Time*]

HINER, Harbert. Pvt. under Capt. William Knox, 26 Aug - 27 Oct 1814.

HINES [Haines], Eli. Never joined his company under Capt. William Durbin, which formed 24 Aug 1814.

HINES, Jacob. According to *(Frederick) Examiner* he d. at the residence of James W. Barker, 1106 H St. 31 Nov 1874, in his 97th year; b. Fred. Co., MD, in 1777; came to D.C. about 10 yrs later; his family settled in Georgetown, where he learned the trade of tinner; joined Meth Ch. During War of 1812 he served in the army. His bro., Christian d. 24 Nov 1874.

HINES, John. Pvt. under Capt. William Durbin 24 Aug - 27 Oct 1814, as a substitute for Jacob Repp at Fred. Co. b. c.1765; res. Richland, OH 1851 and Knox Co. 1856. Acq.: 1856 - M. C. McFarland, and W. C. Cooper of Knox Co., OH.

Source: Bounty land claim, 55-120-80865.

HINES [Hynes], John. Pvt. in Capt. Flautt's rifle company, 29 Apr -6 May 1813; enlisted in regular army 20 May 1813 at Baltimore by Capt. Joseph Hook for the period up to 21 May 1814: at enlistment: 5 feet, 8 inches, age 35, b. Fred. Co. MD; served as pvt. in 36th U.S. Inf. Present in Capt. Joseph Hook's company on 30 Apr 1814.

Source: **The Maryland Union**, 3 Dec 1874.

HINES, Michael. Pvt. from New Windsor under Capt. George W. Magee, 22 Jul 1814 - 10 Jan 1815.

HINES, Peter. Appt'd ensign (31 May 1813) under Capt. Thomas Gist, 2nd Regt, 1st Cav. Dist., MM; lieut. (28 Jul 1813) same company.

HINKLE, George. Pvt. under Capt. George W. Ent, 24 Aug - 30 Sep 1814; b. c.1786; d. 21 Apr 1887 at Shookstown; bur. Doubs Cem. He said he served as a pvt. under Capt. Showers; joined at Manchester, discharged at Balt. Dec

1814. Note from 3rd Auditor says he served under Capt. Showers 26 Jul - 11 Sep 1814 when reported as deserted. [Letter from Jacob Showers, Manchester, MD: "Geo. Hinkle of Capt. Adam Showers company of MD mil. comm. by Col Schultz at Balt. on 1814 was reported a deserter. Hinkle was mustered into service about the 26th Jul 1814 and served without intermission until after the battle of Bladensburg, in which battle he participated. After the army was routed he returned home from the field of battle as many others did, and remained there some time." He m. c.13 Sep 1823, Catherine Shafer (4 May 1799 - 8 May 1870); res. Middletown E.D. 1850; both bur. Rocky Springs Cem.

Sources: Bounty land claim, 55-160-21417; **Names in Stone; Bridge in Time; (Frederick) Examiner, 27 Apr 1887.**

HITCHEW, David. 4th Corpl. under Capt. Samuel Dawson, 26 Jul - 13 Oct 1814. [1850 census, Borough of Emmittsburg: David Hiteshew 57, hatter, $400; Mary 55; Amanda 22; Anna Maria 14 - all b. Fred. Co. *Bridge in Time*]

HITER, Abraham. Appt'd 1st lieut. 22 Dec 1812 under Capt. Samuel Thompson, 2nd Regt., 1st Cav. Dist., MM.

HITESHEW [Hiteshoe], Abraham. Pvt. under Capt. William Knox; joined 26 Aug 1814; discharged 21 Oct 1814 at Balt. because of sickness; b. 28 Mar 1789; res. Carroll Co. 1850, 1855, 1857 and 1871 (Union Bridge); d. 1 Aug 1873; bur. Taneytown, Grace Evangelical and Ref. Church with wife Catherine (d. 3 Apr 1858 age 69).

Sources: Bounty land claim, 50-40-34326, 55-120-70725; Pension, SO24085, SC15741; **Names in Stone.**

HITESHEW [Hichew], George. Pvt. under Capt. Samuel Ogle, 1 May 1813 - 5 Jul 1813. 1850 census, Creagerstown E.D.: George Hiteshew 60, labourer, pauper; Rejoiner, female, 54; Emeline 19; all b. MD. George Hiteshew d. 31 Oct 1854 in Adamsville, aged 66 yrs, 6 mos., 29 days. Regina Hiteshew d. prior to 7 July 1875; on that date the appointment of John W. Kolb as administrator of her estate was published in the local newspaper.

Williams, writes that George Hiteshew, grandfather of Capt. Philip L. Hiteshew, was a native of Fred. Co., MD; farmer, all his sons were farmers, and two of them, George and Jacob, served in the War of 1812. [See Jacob Hiteshoe, below.]

Sources: **(Frederick) Examiner, 14 Nov 1855; 7 July 1875; Williams; Bridge in Time; Md. Union, 15 Nov 1855.**

HITESHEW, John. Pvt. in Capt. Flautt's rifle company, 29 Apr - 6 May 1813.

HITESHOE, Gideon. Pvt. under Capt. William Knox, 26 Aug - 27 Oct 1814; b. c.1794; res. Carroll Co. in 1850 and 1855. [Tombstone inscription shows a Gideon Hiteshew d. 9 Apr 1865 age 71; bur. at Taneytown Ref. Cem; wife Mary Ann d. 26 Jun 1879, age 76yrs, 8 mos., 19 days. [FCml issued to Gideon Hitechew and Julian Zumbrum 12 Dec 1820]

Sources: Bounty land claim, 55-120-8110; **Names in Stone; FCml.**

FREDERICK COUNTY MILITIA IN THE WAR OF 1812

HITESHOE, Jacob. Pvt. under Capt. William Knox, 26 Aug - 27 Oct 1814; b. c.1791; res. Bedford Co., PA 1852 and 1855 (Napier Township). [See Hiteshew, George, above.]
Source: Bounty land claim, 55-120-46574.

HITESHOE, John. Pvt. under Capt. William Knox; joined 26 Aug 1814; deserted 23 Sep 1814.

HOBBS, Brice. Pvt., 1st U.S. Inf., Capt. S. Owens. At enlistment: 5 ft, 10 1/2 inches; blue eyes, dark hair, dark complexion; age 35; shoemaker; b. Fred. Co., MD; enlisted 5 Apr 1810 at Chambersburg, PA, by Capt. Owens for 5 yrs. Tried by Garrison Court Martial at Belle Fontaine 21 Sep 1812 for being drunk; fined 1/2 months pay; d. Belle Fontaine 1 Nov 1812.

HOBBS, Rezin [Reson]. Pvt. under Capt. Capt Nicholas Turbutt, 2 Sep - 27 Oct 1814, as substitute; b. c.1790; m. Elizabeth Ramsower, Fred. Co., 27 Dec 1815; res. Montgomery Co., MD, 1850, 1855, 1873 (near Clarksburg).
Source: Pension, SO29088, SC21061.

HOBBS, Samuel. Pvt. and corpl. (30 days) under Capt. Basil Dorsey, 30 Jul - 27 Sep 1814.

HOBBS [Habbs], Warner Mbr. of Crawford's "company." [Dr. Warner Hobbs 1824-1887 bur. in Mt. Olivet, Frederick; FCml issued to Dr. Warner Hobbs and Eliza Ann Dorsey 21 Feb 1816.]
Sources: Names in Stone; FCml.

HOCKINSMITH/HOCKERSMITH, David. Pvt. under Capt. Samuel Ogle, 1 May - 5 Jul 1813 and Pvt. under Capt. John Galt, 31 Aug - 27 Oct 1814. [FCml issued David Hockensmith and Catharine Miller 30 Aug 1819.]

HOCKINSMITH, George. Appt'd lieut. (13 Oct 1807) under Capt. Michael Sluss, 47th Regt., MM.

HOCKINSMITH, John. Appt'd ensign (21 Jan 1812) under Capt. Michael Sluss, 47th Regt., MM.

HOFFMAN, Andrew. Pvt. under Lieut. Kolb, 13 Oct - 15 Nov 1814.

HOFFMAN, Andrew. Pvt. under Capt. John Brengle, 25 Aug - 19 Sep 1814.

HOFFMAN, Casper, son of Henry; d. c.16 Mar 1864, a "soldier of the Second War of Independence," in Frederick Co. Henry Hoffman, father of Caspar, Henry, John, George and Jacob Hoffman d. 16 Nov 1838, in his 82nd year, "near the mountain." He came from Germany with the Hessian Regiments in the Rev. War.
Sources: (Frederick) Examiner, 16 Mar 1864; Engelbrecht Diary, 2:323.

HOFFMAN, George, Senr. Pvt. under Capt. Nicholas Turbutt, 1 Sep - 27 Oct 1814.

HOFFMAN, George W. Appt'd ensign (15 Jul 1814) under Capt. Matthias E. Bartgis, 16th Regt., MM. Served under Capt. James F. Huston from 23 Jul 1814 until 20 Sep when the command was assumed by Capt. Joseph Green, and he was promoted to 2nd Lt.; discharged in Annapolis on 10 Jan 1815.

HOFFMAN, Jacob. According to his widow he served under Capt. William Durbin, drafted at Westminster; at enlistment: 5 ft 11 inches, black hair, black eyes; b. 13 Jan 1790; m. Catharine Hiteshew (b. 11 Jun 1800), at Uniontown, Fred. Co., 13 Apr 1820 by Burgess Nelson, Meth. minister; d. Johnsville, MD, 6 Oct 1864; res. Fred. Co. She res. Johnsville 1881; d. 27 Aug 1887. Both bur. Johnsville, Beaver Dam, Brethren Ch. 1850 census, Fred. Co.: Jacob Hoffman 60, 400, pauper and Sally age 50, in household of Ezra Hoffman 50, upholsterer, Mary 20; Ann 8; Charlotte 5; Ezra 3 - all b. MD. Acq. (1881): Jess Morningstar, age 69, res. Johnsville; Solomon A. Sayler, 31, res. Johnsville, acq. 50 and 20 yrs, resp.

Sources: Names in Stone; Bridge in Time; Pension (rejected because his name does not appear on any rolls of Major Randall's Battalion of Maryland Militia).

HOFFMAN, John. Pvt. under Capt. Samuel Dawson, 26 Jul 1814 - deserted 1 Oct 1814.

HOFFMAN, John. Pvt. under Capt. Joseph Green, later James F. Huston, 23 Jul 1814 - 10 Jan 1815.

HOFFMAN, John. Pvt. under Capt. Joseph Wood, 27 Aug - 28 Oct 1814.

HOFFMAN, John. Appt'd lieut., 12 May 1812, under Capt. Jacob Creager, 29th Regt., MM.

HOFFMAN, Michael. Pvt. under Capt. George W. Ent, 24 Aug - 30 Sep 1814.

HOFFMAN, William. Pvt. from Fredericktown under Capt. Joseph Green and then Capt. James F. Huston, 23 Jul 1814 - 10 Jan 1815.

HOGEN, Ruben. 4th sergt. under Capt. Basil Dorsey, 30 Jul - 27 Sep 1814.

HOHNE, Westol. Drummer under Capt. Alexander, 22 Jul - 19 Sep 1814; b. c.1798; m. Ann S. Cross, at Annapolis in Oct 1820; res. 13 & 15 Gloucester St., Annapolis, MD 1872.

Sources: Bounty land claim, 55-120-66045; Pension rejected for insufficient service (35 days).

HOLBROOK, Thomas. Pvt. from Balt. Town under Capt. George Magee, 23 Jul 1814 - 10 Jan 1815; prisoner at Bladensburgh 24 Aug and paroled 26 Aug, rejoined Regt. 6 Dec 1814.

HOLIGER (Holedger?, Hollinger?), Phillip. Pvt. under Capt. Samuel Duvall, 3 Aug - 3 Oct 1814.

HOLLENBERGER, William. Pvt. under Capt. William Knox, 26 Aug - 27 Oct 1814; m. Elizabeth Stem (b. c.1800), at Uniontown Dist., c.2 miles from Uniontown, 18 Mar 1817, by Rev Williams, Meth. Preacher. At enlistment: 5 ft 9-10 inches, sandy hair, grey eyes, light complexion, blacksmith; fol. discharge res. near Union Bridge 8-10 yrs, then Waynesboro, Franklin Co., PA, for 9 yrs, then Fred. Co., where he d. 28 Sep 1848, c.11 miles east of Fredericktown; widow res. Fred. Co. 1851, Franklin Co., PA, 1855 (Waynesboro), and Franklin Co. 1879 (Chambersburgy Borough). The family record was cut out of the family Bible at the time of the burning of Chambersburg in 1864. Acq. (1879): Wilson Reilly, age 67, Chambersburg, and John W. Shinafield, age 52, Chambersburg, acq. 40 yrs.

Sources: Bounty land claim, 50-40-91480, 55-120-74989; Pension, SO22584, SC19014. Widow also received Civil War pension for service of her son, Joshua - # 172530.

HOLLER. See Haller.

FREDERICK COUNTY MILITIA IN THE WAR OF 1812

HOLLINBERGER, Peter. Pvt. under Capt. William Knox, 26 Aug - 27 Oct 27 1814. [Buried at Uniontown Church of God Cem.: Peter Hollenberger 22 Mar 1860 70-4-22 and wife Magdalena 23 Feb 1862 age 76.]
Source: Names in Stone.

HOLLINGSWORTH, Francis. Appt'd capt. of a company (23 Apr 1813), 2nd Regt., 1st Cav. Dist., MM. and adjutant (23 Apr 1813) of the 2nd Regt., 1st Cav. Dist.

HOLTER/HOLDER Family:
From Williams, *History of Frederick County, Maryland* - The Holter family is of German lineage. The first mbrs of the family in this country, located in Frederick Co, MD. George Holter settled in Fred. Co. c.1768; m. Margaret Arnold on 4 Feb 1776. Their children are: Jacob, Catharine, John, Daniel, Magdalene, Sarah, George, William and Margaret. About 1815 Jacob and Catharine went to Pennsylvania, and went to Pennsylvania, and settled in Centre Co. Jacob walked from Centre Co., PA, and returned, a distance of 220 miles or 440 miles in the trip, to see his bro. and sisters in Fred. Co., MD. George and John settled in Meigs Co., OH, about 1817.

HOLTER [Holder], Daniel. Pvt. under Capt. Henry Steiner 28 Apr - 29 Jun 1813 and 25 Aug - 27 Sep 1814; b. 8 Jan 1783 son of Georg and Anna Margreth Holder.
Sources: See Williams, above; Md. German Church Records, v. 4

HOLTER [Holder], George [Johann Georg]. Pvt. under Capt. Nicholas Turbutt, 1 Sep - 27 Oct 1814; b. 4 Nov 1793 son of Johann Georg and Anna Margretha Holder; m. Anna Maria Ramsburg (dead by 4 Jul 1871), at Fred. Co., 19 Mar 1819; res. Sutton Township, Meigs Co., OH, in 1850 and 1871. [Letter in the pension file dated 9 Sep 1930 from Irma Holter Parrott (Mrs. Dale K. Parrott), 3522 Northampton St., N.W., Washington, D.C., asking about George Holter who m. Margaret Arnold and served in Revolution and his sons, Daniel, William and George Holter, who served in the War of 1812 from Fred. Co.]
Sources: See Williams, above; Bounty land claim, 50-40-32749, 55-120-37238; Pension, SO21504, SC22522; Md. German Church Records, v. 4.

HOLTER, William. Pvt. under Capt. Nicholas Turbutt, 1 Sep - 27 Oct 1814; b. c.1796; m. c.24 Sep 1818 Magdalene Beard; res. Fred. Co., MD, 1851 and 1855; d. 8 Jul 1868 at his residence near Mt. Zion Church, age 72 yrs, 5 mos., 18 days; bur. Feagaville, Zion Church with wife Margaret [?] who d. 20 Aug 1860, age 60 yrs, 4 mos., 4 days. Williams gives names of their children: George B., decd; William; Susan; Mary; Sarah; Peter, decd; Samuel L., decd; John, killed in childhood by being dragged by a horse after becoming entangled in the harness; and Elizabeth, m. to James Heines. All are now decd. 1850 census, Frederick E.D.: William Holter 55, $300, Magdalene 49; Sarah 23; Mary Scarff 21; William Holter 18; Peter Holter 11; Edward Phleger 2. - all b. MD.
Sources: Bounty land claim, 55-120-30222; Williams, History of Frederick County, Maryland, p. 1100, 1103, 1128; (Frederick) Examiner, 29

THE VETERANS

Jul 1868; *The Maryland Union*, 30 Jul 1868; FCml; *Bridge in Time; Names in Stone*.

HOLTZ(?), John. Appt'd ensign (12 May 1812) under Capt. Frederick Barrick, 29th Regt., MM.

HOLTZMAN, John. Pvt. under Capt. Samuel Dawson, 1 May - 5 Jul 1813, as substitute for Abraham Holtzopple; b. c.1790; m. Catherine Hayden (b. c.1807), 23 Jul 1829, by Rev Fairchild; res. Monroe near Uniontown, Fayette Co., PA, 1851; d. at Monroe, PA, 1 Apr 1857. Acq.: 1878 - Joseph Hayden, age 66, and Eliz. Hayden, age 72, res. Uniontown, PA, present at the marriage of John and Catherine, at George Township, PA.
Sources: Bounty land claim, 50-40-70913, 55-120-6524; Pension, WO12558, WC7318.

HOLVER, David. Mbr. of Crawford's "company."

HOMES, James. Pvt. res. 2 miles from Westminster, served under Capt. Fonsten, 2 Sep - 27 Oct 1814.

HONE, Westol. See Hohn.

HOOK [Horn?], Benjamin. Pvt. under Capt. Fonsten, 2 Sep - 27 Oct 1814; sick absent 9 Oct 1814.

HOOK, John. Reference is made in the Adjutant General - Military Papers, dated Apr 6, 1814 "... since Ensigne John Hook of same company [under Capt. Samuel Albaugh] has removed to state of Virginia ..." [Wm. James Hook is recommended to replace him.]

HOOK, William James. Ensign under Capt. Samuel Dawson, 24 Jul 1814 - 10 Jan 1815.

HOOKER, Johnsey. Pvt. from New Windsor under Capt. George W. Magee, 22 Jul 1814 - 10 Jan 1815; sick on furlough 1 Oct 1814.

HOOPER, Barton. Pvt., 12th U.S. Inf.. At enlistment: 5 ft, 11 inches; light eyes, dark hair, dark complexion; age 25; distiller/laborer; b. Fred. Co., MD; enlisted 11 Aug 1812 at Charles Town by Lt. Callis for 5 yrs. Absent sick at Williamsville since 9 Jun 1813. Sent to Gen'l hospital Burlington, entered hospital 5 May 1814. Discharged from hospital 25 or 26 Nov 1814. Discharged at Pittsburgh, PA, 17 Aug 1815, ulcerated leg.

HOOPER, John. Pvt. under Lieut. Kolb 13 Oct - 15 Nov 1814.

HOOPER, John. Mbr. of Crawford's "company."

HOOVER, Daniel. Sergt. in Capt. Flautt's rifle company, 29 Apr - 29 Jun 1813.

HOOVER, George. Pvt. under Capt. Samuel Ogle, 1 May - 5 Jul 1813.

HOOVER, George. Pvt. from Upper Fred. Co. under Capt. James F. Huston/Capt. Joseph Green; joined 23 Jul 1814; deserted 8 Dec 1814.

HOOVER, Henry. Musician under Capt. Daniel Marker, 16 Aug - 18 Sep 1813.

HOOVER, Jacob. Pvt. under Capt. Thomas Contee Worthington, 17 Aug - 31 Dec 1812.

HOPPE, Frederick. Trumpeter under Capt. Zacharias, 7 Aug - 10 Sep 1814, 2nd Regt, 1st Cav. Dist.; m. 27 Sep 1799 Catharine Snouffer (b. c.1778) by Rev. Daniel Shrader, Luth. preacher at

FREDERICK COUNTY MILITIA IN THE WAR OF 1812

General Sherman Tavern on public Road from Balt. to Hanover, York Co. PA.; d. near Westminster, MD, c.25 March 1819; bur. Cryder's Churchyard. Catharine m(2) Frederick Werble c.3 Jun 1824 by Henry Grabers, Luth. preacher near Westminster. Frederick Werble d. Westminster 14 Nov 1852; bur. Cryder's Churchyard. Catharine Werble res. Westminster 1850. Acq. - 1855: Basil Hayden, age 70, res. Westminster; Jacob Mathias, age 71 (pall bearer at Frederick Werble's funeral).

Source: Bounty land claim, 55-160-35620.

HOPPER, Benjamin. Pvt. under Capt. Philip Smith, 23 May 1813; deserted 18 July, returned 19 July, sick leave in Aug/Sep 1813.

HOPPER, Benjamin. Pvt. under Capt. Basil Dorsey, 30 Jul - 27 Sep 1814.

HORKINSON, Norris. Pvt. Capt. Samuel Dawson, 1 May - 5 Jul 1813.

HORN, Abraham. Pvt. under Capt. Barton Hackney, 1 Sep - 27 Oct 1814.

HORN, Basil. Pvt., res. 8 miles from Westminster, under Capt. Fonsten, 2 Sep - 27 Oct 1814.

HORN, Jesse. Pvt. under Capt. Joseph Wood, 27 Aug - 28 Oct 1814.

HORNBLOWER, William. Pvt. under Capt. Basil Dorsey, 30 Jul - 27 Sep 1814. [FCml issued to William Hornblower and Ann Aves 29 Sep 1780.]

HORNBEY, William. Pvt. in Capt. Flautt's rifle company, 29 Apr - 6 May 1813; enlisted in regular army 6 May 1813.

HOUCK, John. Pvt. under Capt. John Brengle, 25 Aug - 19 Sep 1814; b. Aug 1793, d. 1855; bur. Ref. Church, Frederick; m. 24 Mar 1824, Eleanor McCann, at New Market, MD, by Beverly W. Haugh, Meth minister. 1850 census of Fredericktown: John Houck 77; Ellenora 62; Charles 20, Coach maker; Ann 17 - all b. in Md. John Houck d. 21 May 1855 in Frederick City. Widow d. 12 Jan 1874, at the residence of Lewis H. Dill, age 86 yrs, 3 mos. Acq.: 1855 - Henry Shultz, Winchester Clingan, George Houck.

Sources: Bounty land claim, 55-120-12835; **Bridge in Time**; (Frederick) Examiner, 30 May 1855, 28 Jan 1874.

HOUKMAN, Henry. Pvt. under Capt. John Galt, 31 Aug - 27 Oct 1814.

HOUPT [Haupt], Jacob. Pvt. under Capt. Mathew Murray, 25 Aug - 27 Oct 1814; b. c.1792; m. Elizabeth Keller, at Middletown, 24 Mar 1816; res. Washington Co., MD, 1850, 1855 and 1871 (Boonsboro); d. Dec 1888. Acq.: 1855 - Andrew Double, age 58 and George Keafauver, age 31, acq. 18-20 yrs and 8-9 yrs, resp.

Sources: Bounty land claim, 55-120-74989; Pension, SO22584, SC19014.

HOUSER, Henry. Sergt. under Capt. Hall, 7 Aug - 10 Sep 1814; b. c.1787; res. Harrison Co., OH, 1850.

Source: Bounty land claim, 50-rejected-37495. In his application he incorrectly stated his capt. was Thomas Burgee. In fact, Burgee was the lieut.) and consequently the application was rejected.

HOUX, George J. Pvt. under Capt. George W. Ent, 24 Aug - 30 Sep 1814.

THE VETERANS

HOUX, John. Pvt. uner Capt. Joseph Wood, 27 Aug 1814; furloughed 26 Oct 1814. [FCml issued to John Houx and Elizabeth Hufford on 16 May 1812]

HOVIS, Adam. Pvt. under Capt. John Galt, 31 Aug - 27 Oct 1814.

HOWARD, Adam. Pvt. from Upper Fred. Co. under Capt. James F. Huston, 23 Jul 1814 - 13 Oct 1814. 1850 census, Fredericktown: Adam Howard 62, butcher, in household of William Chew 33, livery stable keeper; Ann M. Chew 32; Wm. H. 3 Chew; Charles E. Chew 3; Samuel Chew 2; Mary J. Chew 3/12. all b. MD.
Source: **Bridge in Time.**

HOWARD, Elisha. 5th sergt. under Capt. Hackney, 1 Sep - 29 Oct 1814; b. c.1791; m. 8 Jun 1815 Eleanor Hays (d. 8 Feb 1873, age 81 yrs, 6 mos, 26 days), Barnesville, Montgomery Co., MD; res. Fred. Co. in 1851, 1855 and 1871 (P.O. address: Barnesville, Montgomery Co.). 1850 census, Buckeys Town Dist.: Elisha Howard 66, farmer, $1200; Elenor 59; William S. Hays 10; John O. Hays 8; Charles Jackson 21, black labourer. - all b. in Md. Elisha Howard d. Apr 1874 in Urbana Dist., Fred. Co. Eleanor was the dau of Leonard Hays; she d. without issue; her sisters: Sarah Candler, Abigail Trail; bro.: Abraham Hays.
Sources: Bounty land claim, 55-120-5956; Pension (rejected, having served 59 days); **Bridge in Time**; (Frederick) Examiner, 19 Feb 1873, 29 Apr 1874, 20 May 1874.

HOWARD, Joseph. Pvt. under Capt. Thomas Contee Worthington, 17 Aug - 31 Dec 1812.

HOWARD, Richard. Appt'd ensign (7 Jul 1814) under Capt. Jacob Eckman, 20th Regt., MM.

HOWARD, Thomas. Pvt. under Capt. Thomas Contee Worthington, 17 Aug - 31 Dec 1812; b. 28 Feb 1789; m. 11 May 1830 Eleanor Fleming, dau of Joseph Fleming, in Fredericktown by Rev. David Martin; d. 26 (28?) Sep 1852; both bur. Mt. Olivet, Frederick.
Sources: **Marr. and Deaths of Frederick and Montgomery Cos., 1820-30**; (Frederick) Examiner, 6 Oct 1852; **Engelbrecht Diary**: 1:595.

HOWE, James. Pvt. under Capt. George W. Ent, 24 Aug - 30 Sep 1814.

HUBBARD, William B. Appt'd surgeon's mate (15 Feb 1815), 2nd Regt., 1st Cav. Dist., MM.

HUEY, William. Pvt. from Washington Co. under Capt. Samuel Dawson, 14 Oct 1814 - 10 Jan 1815.

HUFFARD, John. Pvt. under Capt. Joseph Wood, 27 Aug - 13 Oct 1814; furloughed 26 Oct. [FCml ssued to John Huffard and Elizabeth Houcks 28 Mar 1812.]

HUFFMAN, John. Pvt. under Capt. Thomas Contee Worthington, 17 Aug - 31 Dec 1812; d. 12 Nov 1869 near Fairview, age 80 yrs, 10 mos., 12 days.
Sources: (Frederick) Examiner, 22 Dec 1869; **Md. Union**, 23 Dec 1869.

HUGHES, Daniel Boyle. Pvt., 38th U.S. Inf. At enlistment: 5 ft, 2 inches; grey eyes, light hair, fair complexion; age 23; hatter; b. Fred. Co., MD; enlisted 21 Apr or 24 Apr 1814 at Craney Island by Capt. Miltenberger for duration of war. Discharged 15 Mar 1815.

FREDERICK COUNTY MILITIA IN THE WAR OF 1812

HUGHES, Daniel. According to *(Frederick) Examinerk,* Major Daniel Hughes, b. Montreal, Canada, 3 Feb 1773, immigrated to MD in his youth; entered into the U.S. Army; served at the battle of New Orleans, as an officer of Gen. Jackson's staff. Previous to the War of 1812 he had been entrusted with the duty of recovering thirteen American captives who had fallen into the hands of the Mexicans, and was successful in bringing back 12 of them, the other preferring to remain in Mexico. After the war he was appointed Indian Agent to the Cherokee Nation in Georgia, and filled the post for some yrs. The residue of his life was principally spent in this city and its vicinity. He d. a childless widower, but leaves a bro., who is a colonel of the British Army, a sister, resident in Canada. He d. at Temperance Hall in Frederick on 12 Feb 1854, aged 81 yrs, 9 days. Bur. at Mt. Olivet with his wife Elizabeth H., dau of Richard and Elizabeth Potts, d. 3 May 1842, age 64. 1850 census of Fred. Co.: Daniel Hughes, 77, Canada.
Sources: **Names in Stone; Bridge in Time;** (**Frederick**) **Examiner,** 15 Feb 1854.

HUGHES, Hugh. Pvt. under Capt. Thomas Contee Worthington, 17 Aug - 31 Dec 1812.

HUGHES, James. Pvt., 12th U.S. Inf. At enlistment: he was 5 ft, 6 inches; grey eyes, dark hair, dark complexion; age 23; farmer; b. Emmitsburg, MD; enlisted 4 Mar 1813 at Charlestown by Lt. Callis for 18 months. Absent sick at Sacketts Harbor 1814. Discharged at Buffalo at texpiration of enlistment.

HUGHES, James. Pvt. 29th U.S. Inf. At enlistment: 5 ft 4 or 6 inches; grey eyes, dark hair, dark complexion; age 24; laborer; farmer; b. Emmitsburg, MD; enlisted 21 Apr 1814 at Sacketts Harbor by Capt. Rochester. Mustered at Plattsburg 28 Feb, sick in hospital and sick on 30 Apr 1815. Deserted from Fort Stevens 1 Apr 1816. Discharged at Fort McHenry 21 Apr 1819.

HUGHES, Joseph A. Pvt. under Capt. Samuel Duvall, 3 Aug - 3 Oct 3 1814. [FCml issued to Joseph A. Hughes and Eleanor Tricker 3 Apr 1817]

HUGHES, Otho. Pvt. under Capt. Henry Lowrye, 27 Aug - 28 Oct 1814; made rendezvous at New Market with company from Washington Co. [*Fredericktown Herald* - Nov 6 1824 - Died at his sister's (Mrs. Darcus Cookerly) near this place, Thurs last, 28 ult, Otho Williams Hughes, son of Levi Hughes, late of Fred. Co., decd.]

HUGHES, Patrick. Pvt. in Capt. Flautt's rifle company, 29 Apr - 29 Jun 1814.

HUGHES, Patrick. Pvt. under Capt. Fonsten, 2 Sep - 27 Oct 1814; rcs. 8 miles from Westminster.

HUGHES (Hughs), Richard. Corpl. under Capt. Flautt, 29 Apr - 29 Jun 1813. In 1853 the only minor child of Richard Hughes, Hiram Harry Hughes, age 17, was represented by Finly Reeves of Allen Co., OH, in application for a bounty land warrant. Finly Reeves had been appt'd guardian of Hiram and his sister Amanda Cecelia Hughes by Court of Common Pleas, Tuscarawas Co., OH, Dec 1850. Their father,

Richard Hughes d. winter of 1837 in Noble Co., IN. Their mother d. prior to date of bounty land application (16 Nov 1853). Acq. - 1853: William Sweeney, age 64, res. Allen Co., OH. 1855: Finley Reeves guardian of Amanda and Hiram Hughes, res. Allen Co., OH, and heretofore a res. Stark Co., OH, and Putnam Co., OH.
Source: Bounty land claim, 55-160-29147.

HUGHES, Samuel. Pvt., U.S. Artillery Corps. At enlistment: 5 ft, 6 1/2 inches; blue eyes, light hair, fair complexion; age 26; saletree maker; b. Fred. Co., MD; enlisted 18 or 29 Sep 1810 at Washington by Capt. Beal for 5 yrs. Discharged at Fort Nelson 31 Oct 1815.

HUGHS, Edward. Pvt. under Capt. Jacob Getzendanner, 26 Jul - 21 Aug 1814. [FCml issued to Edward Hughes and Sophia Ordner 11 Aug 1836.]

HUGHS, Hugh. Pvt. under Capt. Jacob Getzendanner, 9 Aug - 17 Sep 1813 and 26 Jul - 21 Aug 1814. [FCml issued to Hugh Hughes and Elizabeth Winpigler 2 Apr 1810]

HULL, Andrew. Pvt. res. 4 miles of Taneytown under Capt. John Galt, 31 Aug - 27 Oct 1814.

HULL, Henry. Pvt. from Upper Fred. Co. under Capt. James F. Huston/Capt. Green; joined 23 Jul 1814; deserted 8 Dec 1814.
[FCml issued to Henry Hull and Christianna Iser 19 Mar 1825; *Fredericktown Herald*, May 30 1829 - Died Thursday last, Henry Hull, bricklayer, after a short illness.]

HULL, John. pvt. under Capt. Samuel Dawson; joined 14 Oct 1814; deserted 3 Nov 1814.

HUMBERT, George. Pvt. under Capt. Fonsten, 2 Sep - 27 Oct 1814; drafted from near Union Mills on 25 Aug 1814; joined at Westminster 2 Sep; discharged 27 Oct 1814; b. c.1792; res. Carroll Co., 1855.
Source: Bounty land claim, 55-160-21470.

HUMMEL, John. Pvt. from Upper Fred. Co. under Capt. James F. Huston and Capt. Joseph Green; joined 23 Jul 1814; deserted 8 Dec 1814.

HUMMEL, John. Pvt. under Capt. Thomas Contee Worthington, 17 Aug - 31 Dec 1812.

HUMMOCK, George. Pvt. under Capt. Samuel Duvall, 3 Aug - 3 Oct 1814.

HUNT, John O. Pvt. under Capt. William Knox, 26 Aug - 27 Oct 1814.

HUPPY - See Hoppe.

HURLEY, John. Pvt. under Capt. Samuel Dawson; joined 21 Jul 1814; deserted 24 Aug, returned 10 Sep, deserted 28 Oct 1814.

HURLEY, John. 3rd Sergt. under Capt. George W. Ent, 24 Aug - 30 Sep 1814; m. Sarah Harding (b. c.1786) in Fred. Co. 7 Jul 1811 by Francis Malirrer (Maliner?), a Catholic priest; res. Jefferson Co., KY in 1857; d. Jefferson Co., 7 Jan 1824. Acq.: Hugh Ferguson and Thomas A. Hurley, res, Jefferson Co., KY.
Source: Bounty land claim, 55-160-54322.

FREDERICK COUNTY MILITIA IN THE WAR OF 1812

HURLEY [Henley], Moses B. He said he served as pvt. under Capts. Daniel Marker, Samuel Dawson and Smeltzer. He said he enlisted in Capt. Daniel Marker's Company at Hagerstown, Apr 1812, discharged at Annapolis, Sep 1812, again as substitute in Capt. Smeltzer's Company in May 1813, discharged in Balt. Nov 1813, again went out as substitute in Capt. Dawson's Company in May 1814 from Middletown, discharged at Balt. in Oct 1814; participated in the battles Bladensburg and Balt.; b. c.1790; m. Urilla Ratliffe, at Hagerstown, MD, Oct 1815; res. Union Township, Ross Co., OH (P.O. Address: Chillicothe in the infirmary), in 1871. At that time his wife was dead.

Source: Pension, SO13423 (Rejected - no proof of service).

HUSH, Samuel. Pvt. from Balt. Town under Capt. George W. Magee, 22 Jul 1814; d. 23 or 24 Dec 1814. At enrollment: age 27, shoe maker in Balt. City, 5 ft 10 inches, auburn hair, blue eyes, light complexion; wounded in leg at Bladensburg; 5 days later returned to Balt. where exposed to inclement weather in the entrenchments; given a furlough of 5 days to be removed from Camp to his home in the City of Balt. - d. of typhus fever before furlough expired; m. 27 Mar 1807 Mary Ann Leary (19 Aug 1791 - Mar 1879), by Rev Dr. George Roberts, Meth. Ch. She later m. Joseph Carr on 2 Oct 1818 by Rev Dr. George Roberts; Joseph Carr d. 14 Nov 1818 or 19 Apr 1820 [she gave both dates; grandson gave 14 Nov 1818]. She res. Balt. on Charles St near Balt. St in 1814; afterwards 15 S. Cary St. between Balt. and Holland sts. for 20 yrs; then 743 W. Balt. St., 1873-8. [His date of death of 24 Dec from muster roll; 23 Dec based on widow's application.] She received allowance from government for 5 yrs commencing 19 Jun 1867. Acq.: 1867 - Ellen Powell and Mary Ann Hush (m. William Hush bro. of Samuel Hush), res. Balt. City; Henry Powell and Hannah M. Hush; Samuel F. Primrose, grandson of Mrs. Mary Ann Carr and Samuel Hush, res. same house as his grandmother for 25 yrs. 1878 - Henry Powell, age 77, 29 Aisquith St., Balt.; Samuel C. Hush, son of Samuel Hush the veteran, age 63, 743 W. Balt. St., Balt., acq. 62 and 60 yrs, resp.

Sources: Bounty land claim, 50-40-40923, 55-120-2737; Pension, WO25385 (rejected - because she remarried after death of soldier).

HUSH, William. Pvt. under Capt. Samuel Dawson; joined 14 Oct 1814; deserted 8 Dec 1814.

HUSTON [Houston], James F. From Upper Fred. Co. Appt'd capt. (15 Jul 1814) served as Capt. of his own company beginning on 23 Jul 1814 until Jos. Green took over in a consolidation; made supernumerary officer 20 Sep 1814. He m. Agnes Butler c. 17 Jun 1813. She d. Baltimore 12 Feb 1862, aged 70 yrs; bur. Mt. Olivet Cem.

Sources: FCml; (Frederick) Examiner, 16 Apr 1862.

HUTCHISON, Benedick [Benedict]. Pvt. under Capt. Denton Darby, 3 Aug - 8 Nov 1814; b. c.1795; res. Washington Co., OH, 1855. He said he served once under Capt. Coe in the regt. commanded by Colonel Drewer; enlisted at Annapolis c.1 Apr 1813, discharged Annapolis May 1813; served under Capt. Hinson Marshall and a third time under Capt. Darby. Third Auditor's report states Benedick Hutchinson commenced service under Capt. Darby 4 Oct 1814, was reported 8 Nov as "deserted" and was not on rolls of Capt. Coe.

HUTTON, Enos. 2nd sergt. under Capt. Basil Dorsey, 30 Jul - 27 Sep 1814. [FCml issued to Enos Hutton and Rebeccah Plummer 28 Feb 1808.]

HYATT, Asa. Pvt. under Capt. Hall, 7 Aug - 10 Sep 1814, 2nd Regt., 1st Cav. Dist.; m. 11 May 1812 Mary Ann Phillips (b. c.1795) by Archabald Brawning; d. Hyattstown 20 Aug 1848; widow res. Montgomery Co. 1855.

Source: Bounty land claim, 55-rejected-221569.

HYATT, Jase. Light Dragoons; at enlistment: 5 ft, 7 inches; black eyes, dark hair, dark complexion; age 28; farmer; b. Fred. Co.; enlisted 19 Oct 1812.

HYATT [Hiatts], Joseph [Jase]. Pvt., 14th U.S. Inf. At enlistment: 5 ft, 7 1/2 inches; dark eyes, dark hair, fair complexion, age 42, farmer, b. Fred. Co.; enlisted 1 Oct or 31 Dec 1812 by Lt. Clark for 5 yrs. Prisoner of war; arrived at Salem from Halifax. Stationed at Fort Independence under the command of Capt. George S. Steel. Entered hospital 26 Mar 1814. Joined Regt. at Plattsburg 14 May 1814. Discharged at Greenbush 28 Mar 1815. Disabled by wounds received in right breast at Cooks Mills 19 Oct 1814.

HYATT, WILLIAM. Pvt. under Capt. Hall, 7 Aug - 10 Sep 1814; m. 11 Mar 1814 Margaret Kiney (b. 1794), by George Craver in Fred. Co.; d. Middletown, MD, 17 Feb 1848; widow res. Champaign Co., OH, 1855. Acq. - 1851: James Kinna, John K. Johnson.

Source: Bounty land claim, 55-120-50530.

HYCHEW, David. [See David Hiteshew] Pvt. under Capt. Samuel Dawson; joined 14 Oct 1814; deserted 28 Oct 1814.

HYNSON, John, Sr. From Balt. Co. Pvt. under Capt. John Galt, 31 Aug - 27 Oct 1814.

HYSON, John, Jr. From Balt. Co. Pvt. under Capt. John Galt, 31 Aug - 27 Oct 1814.

INFIELD, George. Pvt. under Capt. Daniel Shawen, 5 Sep - 27 Oct 1814.

INGMAN, Ambrose. Sergt. under Capt. Denton Darby, 3 Aug - 8 Nov 1814; m. 25 Jun 1839 Miss Catharine Louisa Buckey of Frederick [*Fredericktown Herald* - Nov 12, 1831 - d. in the village of New Market on Tues 8th inst, Ambrose Ingman, in his 49th year, leaving widow and children. Funeral with masonic honors, on Sunday 20th inst.]

INLOES, Abraham. Pvt. from Balt. under Capt. Samuel Dawson, 21 Jul - 10 Jan 1815.

IODUM, Daniel. Pvt. under Capt. John Galt; joined 31 Aug 1814; deserted 22 Oct 1814.

IRVINE, John. Served under Capt. Samuel Ogle, 1 May 1813 - 5 Jul 1813; promoted from Cpl to 5th Sgt 1 Jun

FREDERICK COUNTY MILITIA IN THE WAR OF 1812

1813; b. c.1790; m(1) Mary Bigham (d. 21 Dec 1847) and m(2) Amanda M. Seaman (b. c.1810), at Elkhorn Grove [his widow later says at Milledgeville], Carroll Co., IL, 4 Sep 1849, by Rev Silas Jessup. She prev. m. George W. Seaman who d. at Elkhorn Grove, IL, 1 Oct 1845. John Irvin resided in Indiana Co., PA, until 1818, Fayetteville, Franklin Co, PA until 1835, Pittsburg, PA, until 1845, Mt. Carroll, IL, until his death on 21 Jul 1873. Widow res. Mt. Carrol 1878; res. with son in 1887. Acq.: 1855 - David Nelson and Adam Bohn, res. Mt. Carroll, IL; 1871 - Jesse Rapp and Adam Nase, res. of Mount Carroll; 1878 - Joseph P. Allison, age 39 and Samuel J. Campbell, age 57, Egbert T. E. Becker and J. F. Chapman, Nathaniel Halderman, William D. Hughes, Lewis H. Tomkins, all res. Mt. Carroll, IL.; and William B. Rea, citizen of Woodland, Carroll Co, IL.

Sources: Bounty land claim, 50-40-10974, 55-120-5454; Pension: SO43, SC474, WO19386, WC13831.

IRVING, David. Pvt. under Capt. Thomas Contee Worthington 17 Aug - 31 Dec 1812.

ISBELL [ISERMINGER, ISEMINGER], Henry. Pvt. 28th U.S. Inf., 12th U.S. Inf. At enlistment: 5 ft, 10 inches; hazel eyes, brown hair, light complexion; age 25; b. Middletown, MD; enlisted 23 April 1813/19 Jan 1814 at Hagerstown, MD by Capt. Past for 1 year or duration of war. Tried by court martial in Capt. A. L. Madison's company at Buffalo 1 Nov 1814 for desertion; "mentally incapacitated for sentence." Discharged at Buffalo 31 May 1815 at expiration of term.

ISELNAUGEL [Isanogle], Michael. Pvt. under Capt. Joseph Wood, 27 Aug - 28 Oct 1814.

ISER, George. Pvt. under Capt. William Knox; joined 26 Aug 1814; deserted 11 Sep 1814.

ISNOGLE [Icenogal], David. Pvt., 25th U.S. Inf., under Capt. Benjamin Watson. At enlistment: 5 ft, 7 inches; hazel eyes, light hair, fair complexion; age 22; farmer; b. Fred. Co., MD; enlisted 3 April 1813 in Ohio by Ensign Riley for duration of war. As of 30 Sep 1814 in general hospital since 6 July 1814, wounded. At Sacketts Harbor 2 April and 7 May 1815. Discharged at Sacketts Harbor 17 May 1815.

IZOR, Enoch. Pvt. under Capt. George W. Magee; joined 22 Jul 1814; deserted 24 Jul 1814.

JACKSON, Archabald. Pvt. under Capt. George W. Magee, 22 Jul - 13 Oct 1814; mustered in Balt.

JACOBS, Corbin. Pvt. under Capt. George W. Ent, 24 Aug - 30 Sep 1814.

JACOBS, Ignatius. Pvt. from Upper Frederick under Capt. James F. Huston, James F., 23 Jul 1814 - Sick in Frederick Town since 26 Aug 1814. He d. 3 Oct 1883, age 89 yrs, 6 mos., 3 days after a brief illness; bur. Jerusalem Cem. near Myersville along with his wife, Mary Ann (31 Dec 1800 - 30 Aug 1857); dau Martha Jane d. 20 Dec 1856, age 13yrs, 9 days. 1850 census of Catoctin District indicates he was born in the District of Columbia. The enumerator recorded Ignatius, wife Mary and Mary

THE VETERANS

25; Thomas 21, tobacconist; Henry 19, farmer; William, 17, farmer; Helen 15; Francis 13; Jacob 11; Jane A. 7; Susan V. 4. All but Ignatius b. in MD; Ignatius farmed and owned 2 slaves.

Sources: **Names in Stone; Bridge in Time;** (Frederick) Examiner, 7 Nov 1883.

JACOBS, John. Pvt. under Capt. George W. Ent, 24 Aug - 30 Sep 1814; b. c.1790; res. Montgomery Co., OH, 1851, 1855. 1850 census of Buckeys Town Dist.: John Jacobs 55, tailor, $550; Ann E. 60; Rebeccah Kohlhoss 28; George B. Kohlhoss 3; Eliza J. Kohlhoss 1 - all mulatto; all b. MD.

Sources: Bounty land claim, 55-120-33422; **Bridge in Time**; Names in Stone.

JACOBS, Philip. Pvt. under Capt. Nicholas Turbutt, served at Balt. 1 Sep - 27 Oct 1814.

JACOBS, Philip. Pvt. under Capt. Joseph Wood, 27 Aug - 28 Oct 1814.

JACOBS, Philip. Pvt. under Capt. Thomas Contee Worthington 17 Aug - 31 Dec 1812; m. 17 Apr 1812 Jane Watts (b. c.1795) in Fred. Co., MD, by Rev John Welch, Bapt. pastor; d. Oct 1826 from a fall in a well. Acq.: 1851 - Henry T. Keller and Rudy Keller.

Source: Bounty land claim, 55-80-2213.

JAMES, Amos. Pvt. under Capt. Philip Smith, 23 May - 8 Sep 1813; widow said he was drafted under Capt. Quantrell (Washington Co.); m. Harriet --- in Clark Co., OH; d. 6 May 1850. Their children: Jacob H. b. 15 Oct 1842; Charles Wesley b. 6 Aug 1849. She m. Absolem Poland in Champaign Co., 27 Dec 1857 by Rev. William Williams; res. Champaign Co., OH, 1862 with Absolem Poland. Acq.: 1862 - John Smith attended burial of Amos James 6 May 1850.

Source: Bounty land claim, 55-160-103573.

JAMES [Jones?], Amos. 1st Corpl. under Capt. Samuel Dawson, 21 Jul 1814 - 10 Jan 1815.

JAMES, Bazil. Pvt. under Capt. Joseph Wood, 27 Aug - 28 Oct 1814.

JAMES, Isaac. Pvt. under Capt. George W. Magee; joined 23 Jul 1814; deserted 25 Sep 1814.

JAMES, John. Pvt. under Capt. Samuel Ogle, 1 May - 5 Jul 1813. Sick on furlough.

JAMISON, James. Pvt. from Upper Fred. Co. under Capt. James F. Huston, 23 Jul 1814 - deserted 14 Aug 1814.

JAMISON [Jamieson], John. Pvt. under Capt. Henry Steiner, 25 Aug - 27 Sep 1814. "Sick on furlough." [Col. John Jamison d. at his son's residence in Fredericktown 21 Sep 1875, aged 83 yrs; b. Carroll's Manor, Fred. Co.; agent for B&O Railroad at Martinsburg, WV; military storekeeper at Fort Monroe during the Revolution. Participated in the Battle of North Point during War of 1812. His wife d. three mos. earlier; m. c.60 yrs; parents of 14 ch, 7 or 8 still living in 1875.]

Sources: (Frederick) Examiner, 22 Sep 1875; Baltimore American, 20 Sep 1875.

JARVIS, Zadock. Pvt. under Capt. Nicholas Turbutt, 1 Sep - 27 Oct 1814.

JAY [Gray?], William. Pvt. under Capt. Thomas Contee Worthington, 17 Aug - 31 Dec 1812.

JEMISON, James. Reported on 18 Aug 1814 as deserting from Capt. Duvall's company at Bladensburg; described as 22-23 yrs of age; 5 ft, 7-8 inches; deserted the same night he joined as a substitute.

JENKINS, Felix. Pvt. under Capt. Samuel Dawson, 1 Aug 1814 - 10 Jan 1815. [FCml issued to Felix Jenkins and Elizabeth Friar 5 Jan 1808.]

JENKINS, Job. Pvt., 2nd U.S. Inf., under Capt. Arbuckle. At enlistment: 5 ft, 6 inches; hazel eyes, blue hair [sic], fair complexion; age 24; farmer; b. Fred. Co., MD; enlisted 14 Aug 1807 in Fredericktown, MD by Lieut. Chamberlain. Tried by Regt. Court Martial 16 Aug 1810 for insolence; acquitted. Tried by Regt. or Garrison Court Martial 20 Jan 1812 at Fort Stoddart - drunk on guard; sentenced to 45 lashes; remitted. Appears to have again enlisted on 14 May 1812 at Fort Stoddart for 5 yrs. Tried by Regt Court martial at Pass Christian 6 Sep 1815 for disorderly and riotous conduct; ordered to receive 4 cobbs and whiskey stopped 7 days. Deserted 18 March 1816 from New Orleans.

JENKINS, Theodora. Pvt. under Capt. Daniel Marker, 25 Aug - 27 Oct 1814.

JENKINS, William. Sergt. under Capt. Henry Steiner, 28 Apr - 29 Jun 1813 and pvt. 25 Aug - 27 Sep 1814. [*German Ch. Rcds.*, v.4 - Wm. Jenkins son of late Wm. and late Hannah Jenkins b. 12 Jun 1780; bapt 3 May 1795. *Engelbrecht Diary*: 1:364 - death on 14 Oct 1825 of William Jenkins (mason) of Frederick, father of Rev Wm. Jenkins, now of TN, formerly of tihs town.]

JENKINSON, William. Pvt., 32nd U.S. Inf., under Capt. Robert Patterson. At enlistment: 5 ft, 6 inches; blue eyes, brown hair, light complexion; age 19; laborer; b. Fred. Co., MD; enlisted 4 April 1814 in Bedford, PA, by Lt. Hargis for duration of war. Discharged 19 May 1815 at Phila. at expiration of term.

JINKINS, Simon. Pvt. under Capt. Samuel Dawson, 1 May - 5 Jul 1813.

JINKINS, Simon. Pvt. under Capt. Barton Hackney, 1 Sep -27 Oct 1814.

JOHN, servant. From Fredericktown; servant under Capt. Joseph Green, 14 Oct 1814 - 10 Jan 1815.

JOHNS, Thomas. Pvt. under Capt. Samuel Ogle, 1 May - 5 Jul 1813.

JOHNSON, Erasmus. Pvt. under Capt. Nicholas Turbutt, 1 Sep - 27 Oct 1814; m. 9 Sep 1809 Ann Margaret Woodward (b. 1790), in Balt., by Rev Kurtz, Luth. pastor; d. Fred. Co., Oct 1827.

Source: Bounty land claim, 55-120-6232.

JOHNSON, Jacob. Pvt. under in Capt. Marker's Company, 16 Aug - 18 Sep 1813; b. Fred. Co., MD, c.1793; m. Magdalane Vertinbecker, at Hagerstown, MD, 18 Sep 1817; d. 10 Aug 1881. At enlistment: c.20 yrs old, farmer, 5 ft, 11 inches, dark hair, blue eyes, fair complexion. After discharge res. Fred. Co., 11 yrs until 1824; Montgomery Co., OH, 9 yrs; Randolph Co., IN, 45 yrs; Jackson Twp, 1871; 1878 (P.O. Address: "Castle," in Jackson Township). In 1878 he was nearly blind. Witnesses (1855): John Johnson and Adam Smith; 1871 -

THE VETERANS

John Johnson of Randolph Co. and John Neff of Winchester. Acq. (1878) - John Goodman, age 66 and William Goodman, age 82, res. Jackson Township, Randolph Co., IN, neighbors for more than 60 yrs.

Sources: Bounty land claim, 50-40-43537, 55-120-46968; Pension: SO11403, SC24691.

JOHNSON, Jacob. Pvt. under Capt. Daniel Shawen; joined 5 Sep 1814; discharged 19 Oct 1814.

[Williams, *Hist. of Fred. Co.*: Jacob Johnson, grandfather of Charles W. Johnson, one of the early settlers of the upper part of the Middletown Valley, was one of the successful farmers of that section of Maryland. Besides the Johnson homestead, near Ellerton, he owned a valuable farm near Wolfsville, MD Jacob Johnson m. Catherine, dau of the late George Bittle, prominent farmer residing near Bellsville, now Harmony, MD. *Names in Stone* shows Jacob Johnson (19 Aug 1795 - 13 Feb 1867) bur. with wife Catherine (13 Apr 1876 76-2-6.)]

JOHNSON, John Knite. Pvt. under Capt. Barton Hackney, 1 Sep - 27 Oct 1814; drafted at Berlin, Aug 1814; b. 1792; m. 17 Apr 1844, Rebecca Weddle [Weddel] (b. c.1798), at Beallsville (Harmony), Fred. Co., MD, "as contained in the records of the German Baptist Church of Harmony"; res. Fred. Co. 1851, 1855 and Beallstown, Fred. Co, 1871 (P.O. Middletown); d. 19 Aug 1871 in Harmony, MD; widow res. Harmony 1878. Bur. at Hawbottom Johnson Family Cem: (although wrong initial the date of death is same)) John V. Johnson 14 May 1792 - 19 Aug 1871. 1850 census of Middletown E.D.: John K. Johnson 58, no occupation; Rebecca 54; Samuel B. 14. Acq.: 1878 - George Koogle and William B. Taylor, both Fred. Co.; Samuel Kinna, age 68, and Samuel Miller, age 69, of Harmony, MD; acq. 34 yrs.

Sources: Bounty land claim, 50-120-19780; Pension: SO13441, WO32692, WC23888; **Names in Stone; Bridge in Time.**

JOHNSON, Joseph. Pvt. under Capt. George W. Ent, 24 Aug - 30 Sep 1814 [note from 3rd Auditor states "Joseph Johnson's name is on Capt. Ent's rolls from Aug 24 to Aug 29 1814 but he had not joined the co by the 29th of Oct 1814." Joseph Johnson m. Rutha H. Harding in Jamesville, Muskingum Co., OH, 6 Oct 1816 by James Flood, JP; d. Mt. Pleasant, Hocking Co., OH, 26 Mar 1845. Witnesses: 1850 - Richard Johnson and Andrew Darner.

Source: Bounty land claim, 50-rejected-126237.

JOHNSON, Joseph. Pvt. under Capt. Philip Smith; joined 23 May 1813; deserted 26 Jul; returned 14 Aug; discharged 8 Sep 1813.

JOHNSON, Joseph. Ordered to serve as pvt. under Capt. Thomas Contee Worthington, beginning 17 Aug 1812 but never mustered.

JOHNSON, Joseph. 1st sergt. under Capt. Daniel Marker, 25 Aug - 27 Oct 1814.

JOHNSON [Johnston], Joseph. Pvt., 2nd U.S. Inf., under Capt. Wilkinson. At enlistment: 5 ft, 11 inches; grey eyes, fair hair, fair complexion; age 30; laborer; b. Fred. Co., MD; enlisted 1

FREDERICK COUNTY MILITIA IN THE WAR OF 1812

July 1806 by Lieut. G. Russell for 5 yrs and 9 April 1810 at Ft. Stoddert by Capt. Wilkinson to serve until 9 April 1815. Mustered at New Orleans 25 Jan 1813. Discharged at New Orleans 10 April 1815.

JOHNSON, Nathaniel (Colored). Nathaniel Johnson, called "Uncle Nat," d. at age of 104 yrs at residence of John Cook on Carroll's Manor; born a slave; brought to this county in 1820 by Robert Patterson; in 1844 sold by heirs of Alex. H. Brown, to Christian Thomas who was his 18th master. During the War of 1812 he worked on the fortification around Baltimore.

Source: (Frederick) Examiner, 7 Apr 1875.

JOHNSON, Robert. Ensign under Capt. Barton Hackney, 1 Sep - 27 Oct 1814; b. c.1790; m. Malinda Mills in Loudon Co.; res. Loudon Co., VA, 1855, 1871 (Lovettsville).

Sources: Pension: SO23751, SC15578 (admitted 10 Apr 1872); Bounty land claim, 55-160-12401.

JOHNSON, [Johnston] Thomas. Pvt. under Capt. Basil Dorsey, 30 Jul - 27 Sep 1814. He said that he entered the service from Harford Co., MD His widow said he was drafted in Capt. Harper's company in the PA militia, discharged in 1815. Thomas Johnson b. c.1797; m. Catharine Main (b. c.1804) 1 Jan 1824 by Rev. George Lawrence at Beaver Co. PA., each for first time; res. Pittsfield, Pike Co, IL, 1862; d. 6 Apr 1866 Pike Co., IL; widow res. Pike Co., IL 1871; she d. c.1884. Acq.: 1871 - Daniel and Ruth Main, res. Pike Co., IL, acq. 48 yrs. 1880 - Ruthe Main, age 69 and George Main, age 40, acq. 40 yrs, knew them in Beaver Co. PA.

[Letter from D. H. Bodine, Pittsfield, IL, dated 8 Dec 1879, in which he said that Thomas Johnston lived in Hardin Township, about 6 miles from Pittsfield; Johnston sold his bounty land warrant for $40.00 and with the money bought 4 acres of land in Hardin Township of George D. Foot on 16 Aug 1862; lived there several yrs; after his death his widow continued to occupy the same place but in her absence the house took fire and all Johnston's papers were burnt with everything in the house.

Sources: Bounty land claim, 55-160-101296; Pension: WO1733, WC30418.

JOHNSON, Thomas Pvt. from Balt. under Capt. Samuel Dawson, 14 Oct 1814 - 10 Jan 1815.

JOHNSON, Thomas. Pvt. from Fredericktown under Capt. James F. Huston and Capt. Joseph Green; joined 23 Jul 1814.

JOHNSON, Thomas. Pvt. under Capt. Samuel Ogle, 1 May 1813 - 5 Jul 1813.

JOHNSON, Thomas. Pvt. under Capt. Philip Smith, 23 May - 8 Sep 1813; and also under Ely Brashears according to his widow; m. Delila Stallings (b. c.1800), in 1821/22 by Rev. James Martin, Meth. minister; d. near Petersville, Fred. Co., 1848-49; widow res. Fred. Co., MD 1851, Berkley Co., VA 1855. 1850 census, Fred. Co.: Delina Johnson, 51; Sarah E., 20; John T., 18; Crerciller, 16; Caroline, 13; William T., 8; Emanuel Santman, 24, b. VA. Acq.: 1851 - Jacob Santman, Catharine Santman; 1855 - Thomas Duvall and William T. Duvall,

THE VETERANS

res. Fred. Co., acq. 25 yrs; 1856 - Edward Howard, res. Fred. Co. Several discrepancies in widow's applications for bounty land warrants. In 1851 she stated they m. 19 Dec 1821 by Rev. James Martin (Meth. minister) and 1855 she said they m. Nov 1822 by Rev. David Martin, and 1856 she said date of marriage was 11 Dec 1817. In 1851 she said his death of death was 21 Aug 1849; in 1856 she gave date as c.23 Aug 1848.

Source: Bounty land claim, 55-160-28130.

JOHNSON, William. Pvt. under Capt. Denton Darby; joined 3 Aug 1814; deserted 20 Aug 1814 from the camp at Bladensburg. At that time he was described as 33 yrs of age, 5 ft, 8-10 inches; had a dark complexion, a "miller, mason and drunkard."

JOHNSON, William. Pvt. under Capt. Henry Steiner, 25 Aug - 27 Sep 1814; b. 1795; son of Col. Baker Johnson and nephew of the Gov. of MD; m. 17 Sep 1822 Miss Maria Ann Dorsey of Montgomery Co., dau of William H. Dorsey, by Rev. J. Johns; res. Fred. Co., 1850 (Creagerstown E.D.), 1851; d. at his home, "Hay Lands," near Catoctin Furnace, 15 Nov 1862, age 66 yrs, 11 mos, 20 days, leaving a dau. His wife d. 6 Aug 1832, age 39; her child d. a few hours earlier. Both William and his wife bur. Mt. Olivet Cem., Frederick. Mrs. Johnson was the dau of Mrs. Rosetta Dorsey (d. 19 Mar 1831) and sister of Dr. Robert E. Dorsey.

Sources: Bounty land claim, 12-120-58396; (Frederick) Examiner, 19 Nov 1862; Fredericktown Herald, 21 Sep 1822; Names in Stone; Bridge in Time; Engelbrecht Diary: 1:634; 2:20.

JOHNSTON [Johnson], Thomas. Pvt. under Capt. Joseph Wood, 27 Aug -- 28 Oct 1814.

JOLLY, Thomas M. Pvt. under Capt. Henry Steiner, 25 Aug - 27 Sep 1814; m. Rachel Holstein (b. c.1800, d. 16 Oct 1884), Montgomery Co., PA, 9 Jan 1823 by Rev. I. Curtis Clag. At enrollment: age 18, student, 5 ft 6 inches; brown hair, dark eyes, fair complexion; poss. b. Balt. After marriage they lived in Norristown, PA; in 1840 they moved to Clarion, PA; in 1845 they moved to Pottstown, PA.; he d. at Pottstown 11 Jan 1846. She res. Altoona Borough, Blair Co., PA, 1856; Elizabeth St., Osceola Mills, Clearfield Co., PA. 1878. Acq.: 1850 - George Richards and John H. Hobart, acq. over 20 yrs, state Rachel was dau of Mayor M. Holstein, late of Norristown, Montgomery Co.; that Rachel and Thomas have three children yet living. 1855 - Henry A. Sellers and Joshua L. Reifsneider.

Sources: Bounty land claim, 50-40-31947, 55-120-58433; Pension: WO26655, WC14602.

JONES. See also James and Gonso.

JONES, David. Pvt. under Capt. Samuel Ogle, 1 May 1814 - deserted 25 May 1814.

JONES, George. Pvt. under Capt. Samuel Dawson, Samuel, 21 Jul - deserted 24 Aug 1814.

JONES, James. Pvt. under Capt. Barton Hackney, 1 Sep - 27 Oct 1814.

JONES, Jeremiah. Pvt. under Capt. Joseph Wood, 27 Aug - deserted 24 Oct 1814.

JONES, John. Pvt. under Capt. Daniel Marker, 16 Aug - 18 Sep 1813.

JONES, John Pvt. under Capt. Dawson, Samuel; joined 21 Jul 1814; deserted 26 Oct.

JONES, John. Pvt. under Capt. John Galt, 31 Aug - 27 Oct 1814; drafted at Taneytown; b. c.1780; res. Carroll Co., MD, 1852, 1855.

Source: Bounty land claim, 55-120-51376.

JONES, John. 36th U.S. Inf., under Capt. Hardaway. At the enlistment: 5 ft, 6 inches, age 24, b. Fred. Co., MD; enlisted 10 May 1813 at Westminster, MD, by Ens. Philip Fisher for 1 year. Present at muster in Capt. Joseph J. Hook's company 31 Dec 1813.

JONES, John W. Pvt. under Capt. Samuel Dawson, 1 May - 5 Jul 1813.

JONES, John W. Pvt., 22nd U.S. Inf. At enlistment: 5 ft, 10 1/2 inches; age 22; b. Fred. Co., MD; enlisted 14 March 1814 by Lieut. J. Culbertson for 5 yrs. Mustered 30 April 1814 at Pittsburg. Deserted 19 June 1814.

JONES, Nathan. Pvt. under Capt. Samuel Duvall, 3 Aug - 3 Oct 1814.

JONES [Joned?], Richard. Pvt. under Capt. Samuel Dawson, 1 May - 5 Jul 1813.

JONES, Thomas. Pvt. under Capt. Barton Hackney; joined 1 Sep 1814; discharged by surgeon on 4 Oct 1814.

JONES, William. His widow said her husband was drafted at Taneytown, Fred. Co, MD, in 1814, dischharged at Balt; m. Frances Maxwell (b. c.1806), in Cross Creek Township, near Steubenville, Jefferson Co, OH, on 15 Apr 1824, by Thomas Hunt, a Presbyterian clergyman - each for first time. William Jones d. Cross Creek Township 12 Aug 1838. Widow res. Cross Creek Township, OH, 1856 and near Cresswell P.O., OH 1878. Acq.: 1856 - Joseph Reed, Charles M. Jones; Clinkton Porter; John Dougherty; 1878 -Burris Gilkinson, age 56, James Gilkinson age 52, both res. near Holmes Mill, Jefferson Co, OH, acq. 45, 36 yrs resp.

Source: Pension: WO19804, WC10380.

JONES, William. Pvt. under Capt. John Galt, 31 Aug - 27 Oct 1814.

JONES, Zachariah. Pvt., 20th U.S. Inf. At enlistment: 5 ft, 7 inches; light eyes, light hair, fair complexion; age 27; occupation shoemaker; b. Fred. Co., MD; enlisted 4 July 1813 by Lieut. Pendleton for 5 yrs. Mustered at Norfolk, VA, 15 March 1815, sick in Regtl. Hospital; d. in Genl. Hospital 14 May 1815, indisposition.

JORDAN, William. Pvt. under Capt. John Galt, 31 Aug - 27 Oct 1814.

JUDY, Martin. Pvt. from Balt. under Capt. Samuel Dawson; joined 14 Oct 1814; deserted 16 Nov 1814.

JUNKIN. See Younkin.

KALKLOESCHER, Abraham. See Colelasure.

KANE, Jacob. Pvt., 38th U.S. Inf. At enlistment: 5 ft, 6 inches; grey eyes, light hair, light complexion; age 20; prev. occupation wagoner; b. Fredericktown, MD; enlisted 18 Feb 1814 at Craney Island by Capt. Haslett for duration of war. Discharged at Craney Island 15 March 1815.

THE VETERANS

KANODE, Jacob C. b. 30 Dec 1782, d. 11 Dec 1863, age 80 yrs, 11 mos., 27 days; bur. at Mt. Olivet, Frederick. 1850 census of Buckeys Town Dist.: Jacob Kanode, age 65, farmer; David Kanode 34, labourer; Ann A., 28; Catharine M. 18; Jacob C. 18, labourer; John T. 15 all b. in MD]
Sources: **Names in Stone, Bridge in Time, (Frederick) Examiner**, 30 Dec 1863; Williams, **Hist. of Fred. Co.**, p. 1319.

KAUFFMAN [Caffman], Henry. Pvt. under Capt. John Brengle; joined 25 Aug 1814; deserted.

KEATING [Keiting], George S. Resident of Fredericktown. Pvt. from Upper Fred. Co. under Capt. James F. Huston and Capt. Joseph Green; joined 23 Jul 1814; discharged 10 Jan 1815 at Annapolis.

KEEFER. See also Kiefer.

KEEFER, Henry. Pvt. under Capt. Nicholas Turbutt, 1 Sep - 27 Oct 1814.

KEEFER, Lewis. Pvt. res. within 7 miles of Westminster, under Capt. Galt, 31 Aug - 27 Oct 1814.

KEENY, Jacob. Pvt. under Capt. Joseph Wood, entered 27 Aug; deserted 12 Sep 1814.

KEEPERS, Joseph. Pvt. from Upper Fred. Co. under Capt. James F. Huston, 23 Jul - 13 Oct 1814.

KEEPERS, Michell. Pvt. under Lieut. Upton Reid in 1st Cavalry district, 26 Aug - 3 Sep 1814. [*Rep. Gazette* - Dec 21 1822 - Married Sun last by Rev McElroy, Micha (spelled in Micah in New Citizen) Keepers to Mrs. Susan Stevens, all of this co.]

KEITING, George S. See Keating.

KELLER, Charles. Pvt. under Capt. John Brengle, 25 Aug - 19 Sep 1814.

KELLER, Conrad. Pvt., 7th U.S. Inf. At enlistment: 5 ft, 11 inches, dark eyes, dark hair, dark complexion; age 26; occupation tinner; b. Fred. Co., MD; enlisted 5 or 6 Aug 1811 in Washington by Capt Doherty or Lt. Robinson for 5 yrs. Transferred to Lieut. Vails Company at New Orleans 1 Jan 1813. Appt'd corpl. 29 Jan 1814, reduced. Promoted to corpl. 4 March 1814. Promoted to sergt. 24 June 1814. On furlough from 24 Nov to 12 Dec 1815. Discharged 5 Aug 1816.

KELLER, Frederick. Pvt. from Fredericktown under Capt. James F. Huston from 23 Jul - 20 Sep 1814 when Capt. Joseph Green assumed command of the company; deserted 14 Dec, returned 2 Jan 1815; discharged at Annapolis on 10 Jan 1815; b. c.1794; m. Maria Kremer (b. c.1799), 19 Sep 1819, Lancaster, PA, by Rev. Samuel Reineke, of Moravian Ch., each for first time. Affadavit from Moravian church certified marr. of Fredrick Keller, saddler, a single man, son of John Keller and his wife Mary (Blensinger), to Maria Kraemer, dau of John Kraemer, junr and his wife Catharine C. Scheib, by Rev. Saml. Reinke - on 19 Sep 1819. At enlistment (according to his widow): 5 ft 8 inches, fair complexion, dark hair, dark eyes. After marr. they lived at Lancaster and then moved to Litiz where they continued to reside. Frederick Keller d. 9 Sep 1852, at Litiz, PA. She res. Litiz 1878; d. 15 Mar 1884; attended by Dr. Obediah Huebner, Homeopathist of Lancaster. Acq.: 1855

FREDERICK COUNTY MILITIA IN THE WAR OF 1812

- William H. Hall and George T. Greider, res. Lancaster Co. 1878 - T. H. Christ, age 62, Main St, Litiz, PA and Nath. S. Wolle, age 56, Main St, Litiz, PA.; 1885 - Edward Keller, age 63, sadler, Litiz, PA, son of Frederick and Maria Keller.

Sources: Bounty land claim, 50-40-42529, 55-120-61984; Pension: WO30465, WC17519.

KELLER, Frederick. Sergt. under Capt. Philip Smith, 23 May - 8 Sep 1813.

KELLER, Jacob. Corpl. under Capt. Philip Smith, 23 May - 8 Sep 1813; m. Mary Ann Eader (b. c.1786), on 10 Oct 1815 [she later stated 31 Oct 1816, by Rev. David Shaeffer, Lutheran minister], Fredericktown, MD, each for first time. When enrolled: 22 yrs of age, black hair, black eyes, dark complexion, about 5 ft, 7 inches or more. They had several children. Jacob Keller always res. Fred. Co.; d. 30 Sep 1827, Fred. Co. His widow res. Fredericktown, 1850, 1855 and 1878. She was nearly blind in 1872; she d. 26 Mar 1879, Fredericktown, MD.

Acq.: 1850 - Henry T. Keller and Ruben Keller, res. Fred. Co.; 1878 - Polly Hilton and Rubin Keller. Certificate from Mrs. Ann J. Topper [a dau?], owner of 1/2 lot in area C of Mt. Olivet Cemetery, Frederick; says Mary Ann Keller d. 26 Mar 1879. She lists expenses: coffin and care for mother - $30.00; hearse and horses - $5.00; a piece of cord - $.35; line of hacks (6) - $13.00; lot for burying - $13.00; Dr. W. J. Wooten for medical attendance - $50.00. Boarding and nursing Mrs. Mary Ann Keller, 57 months from Mar 1873 when she became blind @ $12.00 per month. Total = $684.00. Nursing and board for 14 months when she was in a helpless condition @ $20.00 per month = $280.00.

Sources: Pension: WO2289; WC9132 (Rejected because marriage was subsequent to the Treaty of Peace); Bridge in Time.

KELLER, John. Fife major under Capt. George W. Ent, 3rd Regt, 24 Aug - 30 Sep 1814.

KELLER, John. Pvt. from Upper Fred. Co. under Capt. James F. Huston and Capt. Joseph Green, called into service 23 Jul 1814; sick in Balt. 30 Aug; deserted 27 Oct.

KELLER, John. Pvt. under Capt. John Brengle, 25 Aug - 19 Sep 1814.

KELLER, Peter. Pvt. under Capt. Nicholas Turbutt, 1 Sep - 27 Oct 1814.

KELLEY [Kelly], Joshua. From Balt. Town, pvt. under Capt. George W. Magee, 22 Jul 1814; deserted 25 Sep 1814.

KELLEY [Kelly], Solomon. 17th U.S. Inf. At enlistment: 5 ft, 7 inches; age 25; b. Fred. Co., MD; enlisted 27 May 1814 by Capt. James Hunter for duration of war. Lexington Barracks 2 June 1814. d. Fort Erie 24 Oct 1814.

KELLEY, William. Pvt. under Capt. George W. Magee; joined 22 Jul 1814; deserted 24 Aug 1814. [*Fredericktown Herald* - 24 Sep 1831 - d. Mon morning last, after a short illness, William Kelley, native of Ireland.]

KELLY, George. Pvt. under Capt. John Brengle, 25 Aug - 19 Sep 1814.

THE VETERANS

KELLY, John. From Balt. Co. Pvt. under Capt. John Galt, 7 Sep - 27 Oct 1814.

KELLY, John. Pvt., U.S. Rifles. At enlistment: 5 ft, 7 or 8 inches; grey or light eyes, light hair, brown complexion; age 24; coach maker and painter; b. Fredericktown, MD; enlisted 1814(?) at Shepardstown, Va by Capt. H. V. Swearingen for 5 yrs. Late Capt. Armsteads Company at Fort Erie 30 Sep 1814. Absent sick at Sacketts Harbor since 16 July 1814. Discharged at Carlisle Barracks 13 July 1815 for disability, as of Lieut. L. Laval's company.

KELTZ, George. Pvt. under Capt. George W. Ent, 3rd Regt, 24 Aug - 30 Sep 1814.

KEMP, ..k [Frederick?] Pvt. under Capt. Jacob Getzendanner, 26 Jul - 21 Aug 1814.

KEMP, Conrad. Mbr. of Crawford's company.

KEMP, John. Pvt. under Capt. Thomas Contee Worthington, 17 Aug 31 Dec 1812.

KEMP, John. Pvt. under Capt. William Durbin; joined 24 Aug 1814; deserted 13 Sep 1814.

KENEDY, William. Pvt. from Balt. Town under Capt. George W. Magee, 22 Jul 1814 - 10 Jan 1815.

KENTNER [probably Kantner], Adam. Pvt. under Capt. Samuel Dawson, 21 Jul 1814 - deserted 16 Nov 1814.

KENWIP, Conrad. Mbr. of Crawford's "company."

KEPHART, David. Pvt. under Capt. John Galt, 31 Aug - 27 Oct 1814.

KEPHART, George. 3rd corpl. under Capt. Barton Hackney, 1 Sep - 27 Oct 1814. His widow stated that he was originally in the company commanded by Capt. Daniel Shawen of Fred. Co. and marched under him to Balt. where he was transferred to the company of Capt. Barton Hackney, both companies commanded by Col. Stemble. George was hired as a substitute for Adam Lawrence in 1814. - m. Catharine Davis (b. c.1795), 16 Mar 1813. George Kephart d. Fred. Co., 11 Sep 1838. His widow res. Allen Co., OH, 1851.

Acq.: 1851 - Henry Brandenburg, res. Montgomery Co., OH, who entered service as substitute for Adam Lorentz of Fred. Co. in Aug 1814 under Capt. Daniel Shawen and transferred to Capt. Hackney's company. Ormand Kephart appeared with copy of the family bible record.

Source: Bounty land claim, 55-120-75653.

KEPHART, George. Pvt. under Capt. Barton Hackney, 1 Sep - 27 Oct 1814; b. c.1784; m. Margaret ---; res. Loudoun Co., VA, in 1857, former res. Fred. Co.; d. 1 Aug 1869 at his residence, "Belmont," in Loudoun Co. Witnesses: 1857 - Benjamin Stewart and Frederick Hawman, residents of Fred. Co., MD.

Source: Bounty land claim, 55-rejected-323200. A letter to the commissioner of pensions from James M. Harding, Justice of the Peace, Fred. Co., referring to a letter stating that Catharine Kephart, widow of George Kephart had already received a land warrant for 160 acres. - "Now my dear sir, there is a very great mistake or a very gross wrong or forgery ... Capt. George Kephart, the applicant ... is now living at "Belmont," near Leesburg, Loudon Co., VA, and has been residing there for some yrs. Previous to that he resided all his lifetime in Fred. Co., MD His wife d. during

FREDERICK COUNTY MILITIA IN THE WAR OF 1812

the late War and her name was Margaret..." [Apparently overlooked was the fact that there were two men named George Kephart who served in Capt. Hackney's company - one as corpl. and the other as pvt. Ed.]

KEPLINGER, John. Pvt. under Capt. Philip Smith, 23 May - 8 Sep 1813. [Fred m.l. John Keplinger and Catharine Bolie 28 Apr 1787]

KESLER, William. Pvt. under Capt. Barton Hackney, 1 Sep - 27 Oct 1814.

KESSELRING [Kelselring], Lewis. Pvt. under Capt. John [Jack] Galt, 31 Aug - 27 Oct 1814; lost his leg owing to exposure to the cold; b. c.1786; res. Huntington Co., PA, in 1855. Acq.: 1855 - James Cowan, Daniel Slates, res. Huntington Co., PA.

Source: Bounty land claim, 55-120-24941.

KESSLER [Kepler?], David. Pvt. under Capt. Nicholas Turbutt, enrolled 8 Sep 1814; went to Balt.; discharged 27 Oct 1814; m. 26 Aug 1808, Araminta Merser in Balt. by Rev. Rossell, Meth. minister; he d. Fredericktown 11 Feb 1839. Acq.: 1850 - Peter Ott and Frederick Clinard.

Source: Bounty land claim, 50-40-12255.

KESSLER, Jacob. Pvt. under Capt. John Brengle, 25 Aug - 19 Sep 1814; m. c.10 Nov 1806 Rachel Goodman (14 Feb 1777 - 4 Apr 1856). She was executor of her husband's estate in 1818. 1850 she res. with Rebecca A. Kessler, age 35, in town of Jefferson. She was bur. Jefferson Union Cem.

Sources: FCml, Frederick-Town Herald, 3 May 1818; Names in Stone, Bridge in Time.

KESSLERING, Lewis. Pvt. under Capt. John Galt, 31 Aug - 27 Oct 1814; res. within 3 miles of Taneytown in 1814.

KETTLE [Kittle], William. Pvt., 22nd U.S. Inf. At enlistment: 5 ft, 5 inches; blue eyes, brown hair, light complexion; age 21; laborer; b. Fred. Co., MD; enlisted 17 Jan 1813 at Carlisle by Lt. Larkins for 5 yrs. Left sick at Williamsville 20 Oct and 26 Oct 1814 - wounded. Joined from Williamsville 27 April 1815. Confined in Watertown jail by civil authority 31 Dec 1817. Sent to state's prison 31 Jan 1818 for 5 yrs. 30 June 1818 dropped.

KHUNTZ, Simeon. Pvt. under Capt. John Galt, 31 Aug - 27 Oct 1814.

KIEFFER (Keeffer), Jacob. Pvt. under Capt. Henry Steiner, 28 Apr - 29 Jun 1813 and 1st corpl., 25 Aug - 27 Sep 1814; b. c.1787; res. Buckeystown District in 1850. 1850 census: Jacob Keefer age 63, farmer; Ann R. Keefer, age 29; Mary C. Keefer, age 27; Charlotte, age 25; Ellen S. Keefer, age 15; Harriet V. Keefer, age 14. He owned a 110-acre farm and two slaves; res. Fred. Co., MD, 1851 and 1855.

Sources: Bounty land claim, 55-120-43975.

KILLIAN [probably Killion], Philip. Pvt. under Lieut. Kolb, 13 Oct - 15 Nov 1814 in guarding British prisoners at Frederick Barracks.

[FCml issued to Philip Killion and Elizabeth Dertzbaugh 31 Aug 1808]

KIMMEL, Anthony. Born Balt. in 1799; m. 19 Oct 1822, Sydney Ann James, only dau of Major Daniel and Margaret James. She was b. 28 Apr 1806; d. 24 Aug 1848. Son Alfred (22 Nov 1833 - 21 Dec 1825); son Hampden (27 Dec 1825 - 20 Aug 1830); son Edmund Clemson (21 May 1831 - 16 Apr 1837); dau

THE VETERANS

Marion Louise (28 Aug 1833 - 1 Apr 1837); son Anthony Zaarr (1836-1897). According to *Scharf,* General Anthony Kimmell entered the militia when a boy. He d. at his residence "Linganore" near New London, Frederick Co... 24 Apr 1871 of paralysis, after lingering illness; bur. "old graveyard on the corner of Lombard and Paca Sts., Balt. Mbr. Free Masons.
Sources: Williams, History of Frederick Co., Scharf's, History of Western Maryland, 461-462, FCml, (Frederick) Examiner, 26 Apr 1871, 3 May 1871.

KINKERLY, John. Pvt. under Lieut. Kolb, 13 Oct - 15 Nov 1814, guarding British prisoners at Frederick Barracks.

KING, Gilbreth [Gilbrith]. Pvt. under Capt. William Durbin, 24 Aug - 27 Oct 1814.

KINKADE [Kingade], Joseph. Pvt. from New Windsor under Capt. George W. Magee; joined 23 Jul 1814; deserted 25 Sep 1814.

KINNA, James. Pvt. under Capt. Nicholas Hall. According to him he volunteered in the cavalry company of Capt. Nick Hall at Fredericktown in 1814, discharged in Washington, Oct 1814. - b. 2 Oct 1789; m. Elizabeth Craft (b. c.1796) 19 Mar 1812, each for first time. At enrollment: black hair, dark brown eyes. He res. Fred. Co. 1851 and 1855; d. near Beallsville, Fred. Co., MD, 2 Jan or 3 Feb 1857; bur. Middletown Ref. Ch. Their children: Mary called Polly (b. c.1814), Sallie called Sarah (b. c.1816), Sampson (b. c.1821), James H. (b. c.1824, dec'd. by 1 Apr 1879), Elizabeth (b. c.1827), Thomas (b. c.1831), William (b. c.1833), David (b. c.1835), Catherine (b. c.1837), Amanda (b. c.1839), Cassiah (b. c.1841) and Deborah (b. c.1843). Their mother res. Fred. Co. up to May 1863 when she moved west to IL. She res. Ogle Co., IL, in 1879, d. c.1881. 1850 census of Middletown E.D.: James Kinna, age 59, farmer, $25,000; Elizabeth 56; Sarah 27; Elizabeth 26; Thomas 24; Catharine 22; David 18; Amanda 15; Cassira 11; Deborah 8; Mahlon Miller 21, farmer, all b. in MD.

Acq.: 1879 - Johnathan Perry, Polo, Ogle Co., IL, acq. with Elizabeth Kinna for 60 yrs, attended the funeral of James Kinna at Middletown, Fred. Co., MD, lived in MD until 1868 when he moved to IL; John Smith, age 67, has known Elizabeth since her arrival in IL; John M. Brandenburg, age 56, b. and reared near James Kinna's old homestead, acq. 20 yrs before James Kinna d.; and George Leatherman, age 52, res. near James Kinna, near Beallsville, Fred. Co.; Martin Perry, age 52, Elizabeth Perry, Debbie Perry, age 22, res. Polo, IL.

Letter dated 15 Jul 1930 to Theresa McGinley, 1023 Magnolia Ave., Bowling Green, KY, regarding James Kinna and Elizabeth Kinna, her great grandparents.
Sources: Bounty land claim, 50-40-34097, 55-120-39368; Pension: WO35620, WC23872; Names in Stone; Bridge in Time.

KINNEY, John W. Served under Capt. John Galt.

KINNY, William. Pvt. under Capt. Philip Smith; joined 23 May 8 1813;

FREDERICK COUNTY MILITIA IN THE WAR OF 1812

deserted 4 Jul 1813; returned 30 Jul; discharged 8 Sep 1813.

KIRFMAN, Christian. See Curfman.

KITTING, John. Pvt. under Capt. Samuel Ogle; joined 1 May 1813; deserted 2 Jun 1813.

KLAY, George. Sergt. under Capt. Denton Darby, 3 Aug - 8 Nov 1814.

KLAY, John. Pvt. under Capt. Denton Darby; joined 3 Aug 1814; drowned.

KLEIN [Kline], Peter. Pvt. under Capt. Nicholas Turbutt, 2 Sep - 27 Oct; b. c.1793; res. Fred. Co., MD 1844; res. Clarke Co., OH 1850, res. with George and Catharine Catrow, also b. MD; res. Miami Co., OH 1855 and Fred. Co. MD, 1870, retired hatter, living with brother Frederick. In application for pension in 1871 he indicated he was not married. Acq.: 1855 - Margaret J. Jacobs and James Furgus. Witnesses: 1871 - Frederick Kline and George Showacre, res. Fred. Co., MD

Sources: Pension: SO7565, SC3917; Jay Lipps, 1539 Sandpiper Ct., Sunnyvale, CA 94087.

KLINE. See Klein.

KLINE, Charles. 1st lieut. under Capt. Daniel Marker, 16 Aug - 18 Sep 1813.

KLINE [Klein], Frederick. 4th corpl. under Capt. Jacob Getzendanner 9 Aug - 17 Sep 1813 and as 3rd corpl., 26 Jul - 21 Aug 1814 and pvt. under Capt. Joseph Wood, 27 Aug - 28 Oct 1814 as substitute for Jacob Larkins; b. c.1792; m. 22 May 1828 Susanna Engle [Engel] (b. Frederick 11 Feb 1803) dau of George (b. c.1771) and Susanna (Young) Engle, in Fred. Co, MD, 22 May 1828; res. Fred. Co. 1851, 1855, 1871. Children: Peter b. 6 Jan 1830; Ruanna Mathilda b. c.1834; Frederick b. 2 Dec 1837; Edward D. b. 22 Nov 1840.

Sources: Bounty land claim, 50-40-36049 cancelled, 50-80-40717, 55-80-17503; Pension: SO7564, SC4980; **Names in Stone; Bridge in Time;** Jay Lipps (see Peter Klein/Kline) who drew from above and addit'l sources: Micro of Evagelical Luth. Ch., Frederick, p. 1342, Weiser, **Baptismal Records of the Evangelical Luth Church, of Frederick, 1780-1811;** Fred. Co., MD Equity Record Liber TG 3, 662f.

KLINE, George. Pvt. under Capt. Daniel Marker, 16 Aug - 18 Sep 1813; m. Elisabeth --- (b. c.1789) in Middletown 1 May 1809 by Rev. George Craver (or Craven). George Kline d. Middletown Valley 13 Apr 1846. Acq.: 1855 - Samuel Weant and Reuben Leaming(?). [*Frederick Herald*, 18 Dec 1830: Married Tues evening 7th inst by Rev. James L. Higgins, George Kline to Miss Sarah Elizabeth, 2d dau of late Frederick Poole, all of this co.]

Source: Bounty land claim, 55-rejected-227375.

KLINE [Klein], Henry. Pvt. under Capt. Jacob Getzendanner, 26 Jul - 21 Aug 1814; b. c.1791; res. Fred. Co., MD, in 1855.

Source: Bounty land claim, 55-120-2260. Jay Lipps (See Peter Klein/Kline) concludes that this is the Henry Klein, who was bound to Nicholas Freydinger, taylor, to age 21, at age of 14 yrs "last June 20, 1800," with the approval of his mother, Margaret Broody/Breedy?. See **Western Md. Genealogy,** 5:2.

KLINE, John. Pvt. under Capt. Jacob Getzendanner, 26 Jul - 21 Aug 1814; b. c.1795; res. Montgomery Co., OH, 1851; d. 12 Jun 1863, Dayton, OH, in his 68th year.

THE VETERANS

Sources: Bounty land claim, 55-120-15795; (Frederick) Examiner, 2 Sep 1863.

KLINE, Philip. Musician under Capt. Daniel Marker, 16 Aug - 18 Sep 1813; served as a substitute for Richard Winpigler. [1850 census of Catoctin E.D.: Philip Kline 63, labourer; Elizabeth 59; Thomas 19; Malinda 17 - all b. in MD.]
Source: Bridge in Time.

KLINK, John Pvt. under Capt. Capt Nicholas Turbutt, 2 Sep - 27 Oct 1814.

KLINK, John. Pvt. under Capt. Jacob Getzendanner, 9 Aug - 17 Sep 1813.

KLISE, William. Pvt. under Capt. Jacob Getzendanner. He said he enlisted at Fred. Co., MD. On the last day of his service he was called on to stand guard duty at Fort Jefferson near Annapolis; b. c.1793; m. Susannah Heffner, Fredericktown, MD, 9 Feb 1817. At enlistment: 23 or 24 yrs old, a carpenter and cabinet maker, from Fred. Co., MD; black hair, blue eyes, light complexion. Fol. discharge he res. Frederick, MD until 1823, res. Germantown, OH, until c.1843, and Miami Co., IN, from 1843 until at least 1878 (P.O. address: Bunker Hill, IN). His wife d. prior to 25 Sep 1878.

Acq.: Levi Klise, age 38 and Larr Klise Smith, age 61, acq. all their lives.
Source: Pension: SO339000-vacated, SO33752; Pension rejected because of lack of evidence of service.

KNAFF, John. Pvt. under Capt. Samuel Ogle, 1 May 1813 - 5 Jul 1813. [*Moravian Families of Graceham, Md.* gives data on the families of two John Knauffs: (1) John Knauff m. Catharine ---; issue Amy b. 5 Sep 1804; d. 20 Feb 1864; m. George Hesser; Mary m. Jeremiah Martin; Catharne m. Benjamin Ogle. (2) John Knauff m. Catharine Biggs. Issue Ellen Rebecca b 11 Mar 1817; Sarah Ann Elisabeth b. Oct 28 Oct 1828. FCml issued to John Knouff and Catherine Biggs 6 May 1803]

KNAUFF [Knouf], Greenbury. See Knouff.

KNIGHT, Peter. Mbr. of Crawford's "company."

KNOT, Caleb. Pvt. from Upper Fred. Co. under Capt. James F. Huston, 23 Jul - 13 Oct 1814; discharged 2 Aug 1814. [Williams - p. 1570 Francis Knott was b. in Emmitsburg, Fred. Co., in 1812, and d. Petersville Dist., Fred. Co in 1881. He was a son of Caleb Knott, also a native Montgomery Co, who was a life long farmer. He m. Ruth Slagle. Names of children given.]
Source: Williams, Hist. of Fred. Co.

KNAUFF [Knuff, Knouff], Jacob. He said he was drafted in the company of Capt. Samuel Dawson at Balt., discharged at Balt. at the close of the war. According to his widow, George Knouff, brother of her husband, was drafted at the same time as her husband. William Smith and John Heighter were members of the same regiment. - b. 1796 in Middletown Valley, MD; m. Eliza W. Warner (b. Fred. Co. 1807), at Fredericktown, 28 Mar 1828, by Rev. David Martin, each for the first time. At enrollment: farmer, medium size, brown hair, blue eyes. Fol. discharge he res. Loudenville, VA, c.15 yrs; Knox Co., OH, 10 yrs; remaining yrs in Morrow Co., OH, making 40 yrs in OH; d.

FREDERICK COUNTY MILITIA IN THE WAR OF 1812

Chester Township, Morrow Co., OH, 12 Jan 1879. Widow res. Morrow Co., OH in 1879 and 1884 (Pagetown). Acq.: 1879 - Major Frost, age 34, Dr. P. F. Cantlebary, age 52, res. Pagetown, acq. 8 and 22 yrs, resp. 1884 - William Johne, age 40, res. Maringo, OH, and John F. Evans, age 77, res. Pagetown, acq. 20 and 5 yrs resp.

Source: Pension: SO32853 - rejected. WO37584 - rejected, no evidence service.

KNOUF, Greenbury. See Knouff.

KNOUF, Jacob. Pvt. under Capt. William Knox, 26 Aug - 27 Oct 1814. He said he was drafted near Taneytown, 26 Aug 1814, into the company of Capt. Knox, 1st Battalion, of Major Beall Randall; discharged at Balt. around 30 Oct 1814. He said his unit was encamped at the Rope Walk on Federal Hill; he served in the capacity of a scout during the Battle of North Point; saw the bombardment of Fort McHenry and witnessed the destruction of the three barges that passed the Fort; after performing duty as a scout he returned to Balt. and encamped on Federal Hill until he was mustered out of service. During the Battle of North Point his regiment marched down on the bayside to prevent the soldiers engaged in battle from being flanked. After the battle his command was employed in guarding Balt. - b. c.1795; m. Eliza Beaver, at Chambersburg, PA, 11 Mar 1851; res. Franklin Co., PA, in 1855 and 1876 (Waynesboro).

Acq.: 1855 - Jacob Zumbrum and James Rodgers, res. Caroll Co., MD, who served in same company. 1876 - Jeremiah Miller, age 39 and M. A. Foltz, age 38, res. Chambersburg, PA.

Sources: Bounty land claim, 55-160-19929; Pension: SO30431, SC21767 (admitted 17 Jun 1876).

KNOUFF [Knouft, Knoufe], George. Pvt. under Capt. Barton Hackney, 1 Sep - 27 Oct 1814; m. 13 Feb 1814, Mary M. Seapley (b. c.1789), at the house of her father, by Parson Hatch, protestant minister. George Knouff d. at his residence in Fred. Co. 20 Feb 1847. His widow res. Montgomery Co., MD in 1855. [She appeared in the courthouse of Loudon Co., VA, to make her application.] Acq.: 1855 - George Kephart, res. Loudoun Co., VA, acq. with George Knoufe and was in the same "mess." Also present at marr. of George and Mary.

Source: Bounty land claim, 55-160-54695.

KNOUFF [Knauf, Knouf], Greenbury. b. c.1792; m. Susan Dertzabaugh (b. c.1796) in Fredericktown on 10 Oct 1815 by Rev. David F. Shaffer, Lutheran minister. Greenbury Knouff d. at Emmitsburgh 5 March 1832 at age 40. His widow res. Fred. Co., MD in 1860. Acq.: 1860 - George Salmon, Daniel Springer, John W. Miller. Pvt. under Capt. John Brengle, 25 Aug - 19 Sep 1814.

Source: Bounty land claim, 55-rejected-311033. Rejected by reason, "Name of Greenbury Knouff is not found on the roll of Captn. J. Brengle's company." [Included in the application was a copy of the muster roll made by Ormond F. Butler. The name on the rolls held by the National Archives reads William Knaup in the same rela

THE VETERANS

tive order as the name Greebury [sic] Knouff on the copy submitted by Ormond Butler.]

KNOUFF [Knauff, Knuff, Kenuff], Jacob. 6th Corpl. under Capt. George W. Ent, 3rd Regt, 24 Aug - 30 Sep 1814; b. c.1790; m. Mary Ann Houck who d. between 1816 and 1822; then m. 4 Sep 1823, Miss Deborah M. Phillips (b. c.1800), at Fredericktown, by Rev. Helfenstein. At enrollment: 24 yrs old, a weaver, c.5 ft, 11 inches tall, light hair, light eyes, light complexion. 1850 census of Fredericktown: Jacob Knauff 60, weaver, $600; Deborah M. 48; Charles E. 23, printer; Lewis H. 21, tailor; Mary A. E. 18; George U. 16, shoemaker; Diana 13; Susan 9; Howard 7; Virginia 4 - all b. MD. Jacob Knouff d. Fredericktown 30 Sep 1867, age 76 years; bur. Mt. Olivet. Widow res. Fredericktown, MD 1878 at 3rd St.; d. Fredericktown 1 Nov 1880, age 79 years, 2 mos., 11 days. Acq.: 1878 - James Kelly and John Rhodes, res. Fred. Co., acq. for 40 and 30 yrs, resp.; Harry C. Keefer, Daniel H. Rohr, Henry K. Hilton and Alice Davison - all res. Fred. Co.

Applying for arrears of pension on 11 Dec 1880 was Jennie Knauff, age 35, res. 4th St., Frederick City, dau of Deborah M. Knauff. Appearing with her were acq., Mrs. Sue Young, age 40 and Edward Young, age 44, both res. 4th St., Frederick City, acq. with Jennie Knauff for 35 and 25 yrs, resp.

A letter dated 25 Jun 1936 from Osee J. Knouf, 229 No. Kensington Ave., La Grange, IL, great, great, granddaughter of Jacob Knouf.

Sources: Bounty land claim, 50-40-56783, 55-120-16120; Pension: WO13028, WC11257; WMG, v.7, no.1; **Republican Gazette**, 13 Sep 1823; **(Frederick) Examiner**, 10 Nov 1880; **The Maryland Union**, 26 Sep 1867; **Bridge in Time.**

KNOUF, John. Pvt. under Capt. John Galt, 31 Aug - 27 Oct 1814.

KNOWER, John. Sea Fencibles, under Capt. M.S. Bunbury. At enlistment: 5 ft, 8 1/4 inches; age 41; b. Middletown, MD, Worcester County [sic]; enlisted 9 Dec 1813; recruit roll at Balt. 11 Dec 1813; d. 26 Dec 1813.

KNOX, William. Capt. of his own company, 26 Aug - 27 Oct 27 1814; d. 19 Oct 1833 at his residence near Taney-town after a lingering illness, age 57 yrs, 10 days, son of John & Jane; bur. Harney, Piney Creek, Presby Ch. with wife Barbara (16 Mar 1793 - 1 Jan 1880); son James (3 Oct 1819 - 27 Jul 1888); son John Robison (16 Oct 1824 - 7 Oct 1888).

Sources: **Carrolltonian**, 26 Oct 1833; **Names in Stone.**

KOCH, John. Pvt. under Capt. Philip Smith, 23 May - 8 Sep 1813.

KOLB. See also Kolp.

KOLB, John F. Pvt. under Capt. Thomas Contee Worthington, 17-25 Aug 1812) [Wms says 25 Aug-31Dec 1812

KOLB, Ramer. Pvt. under Capt. George W. Ent, 3rd Regt, 24 Aug - 30 Sep 1814.

KOLB, William. 2nd Lieut. under Capt. John Brengle, 25 Aug - 19 Sep 1814 and 1st lieut. commanding a det. guarding British prisoners at the Frederick Barracks, 13 Oct - 15 Nov 1814.

FREDERICK COUNTY MILITIA IN THE WAR OF 1812

The Register of the General Society of the War of 1812 gives the following: John William Kolb b. Frederick, 17 Feb 1776; d. Frederick 25 Jan 1835; m. 7 Dec 1797 in Frederick, Eve Maria Ann Miller, b. Frederick 6 Apr 1779; d. Frederick.

Source: **Register of the General Society of The War of 1812.** Descendants of the veteran, William Kolb, who were elected to the General Society of the War of 1812: John Devin Cobb, Jr., elected 1952, living in Washington D.C; David William Kolb, V, elected 1952, merchant, Allen, Wicomico Co., MD; Stanley Denmead Kolb, elected 1947, living in Salisbury, MD and his son Stanley Denmead Kolb, Jr., elected 1951, address: Salisbury, MD.

KOLP [Kulp], Jacob. Pvt., 2nd U.S. Inf., under Capt. Braham. At enlistment: 5 ft, 6 inches; hazel eyes, dark hair and dark complexion; age 24; shoemaker; b. Fred. Co., MD; enlisted 8 April 1808 at Staunton, VA, by Lt. Sevier; d. Mount Vernon 29 Aug 1812 as of Capts. Pemberton's or Carson's companies.

[Williams, *Hist. of Fred. Co.*: Henry Koons came to United States from the Netherlands in 1730, and after short stay in New Jersey came to Fred. County, MD; became acq. with Col. Bruce, of Bruceville, then a part of Fred. Co., and also with Major John Ross Key, who owned a large section of land in same neighborhood. Henry Koons had five sons. Of these John was the grandfather of Rev. Wm. A. Koontz, of the Balt. Conference of the Meth. Episc Ch. Abraham, another son, lived near Keysville; Henry near Bruceville, and George, an expert blacksmith, served in that capacity during Rev. War. At close of war, in 1780, he secured title to farm near Double Pipe Creek bridge, one mile from Middleburg, then Fred. Co., now Carroll Co. George Koons (d. 1817) m. Susannah Shroyer (1760-1848), of near Emmitsburg. They had 11 children, 9 of whom were living when the father d. 1817, viz: Jacob b. 1781; Henry b. 1783; Margaret (Mrs. Hyder) b. 1786; Mary (Mrs. Ogb.) b. 1789; Catharine (Mrs. Stimmell) b. 1792; Peter b. 1795; George b. 1797; Joseph b. 1800; and Susie (Mrs. Dern) b. 1804.

KOON, George. Pvt. under Capt. Daniel Marker; joined 25 Aug 1814; deserted 26 Aug 1814.

KOONS, Henry. Pvt. in the 1st Cavalry Dist., under Capt. Reid, 26 Aug - 3 Sep 1814.

KOONS, Jacob. Pvt. in 1st Cavalry Dist., under Capt. Reid, 26 Aug - 3 Sep 1814.

KOONS, Jacob. Pvt. under Capt. William Knox, 26 Aug - 27 Oct 1814.

KOONS, John. Pvt. in 1st Cavalry Dist., under Capt. Reid, 26 Aug - 3 Sep 1814.

KOONS, William. Pvt. in 1st Cavalry Dist., under Capt. Reid, 26 Aug - 3 Sep 1814. [William Koons 2 Jul 1794 - 18 Dec 1852, bur. Middleburg Meth. Ch, Carroll Co. - *Names in Stone.*]

KOONTZ [Koontze], Jacob. Pvt., 12th U.S. Inf. At enlistment: 5 ft, 7 1/2 inches, dark eyes, dark hair, fair complexion, age 34, bricklayer, b. Fred. Co., MD; enlisted 8 June 1813 at New Market by Lt. Towls for 18 mos. Missing in action on 11 Nov 1813. Roll of Moores company dated Plattsburg, 15 April 1814, present. Prisoner of war, exchanged

THE VETERANS

and received at Chazy, 11 May 1814, and arrived at Plattsburg 1814. Discharged at Buffalo 8 Dec 1814.

KOONTZ, John. Pvt. under Capt. Henry Steiner, 25 Aug - 27 Sep 1814; b. c.1792; m. 5th Oct 1820 Miss Margaret Norris (b. c.1803) by Rev. Griffin. He d. 11 Aug 1863. She d. 4 Nov 1872 in Baltimore City after painful illness of several weeks. Both bur. Mt. Olivet Cem., Frederick. He was employed by B. & O. Railroad for 32 years at the depot in Frederick.

Sources: **Marriages and Deaths of Frederick and Montgomery; Wyandot Pioneer,** U., Sandusky, Ohio, 20 Aug 1862; **(Frederick) Examiner,** 14 Oct 1820, 12 Aug 1863, 13 Nov 1872; **Names in Stone; Bridge in Time.**

KOONTZ, John Pvt. under Capt. Thomas Contee Worthington, 17 Aug - 31 Dec 1812. Not mustered into service?

KORNS, Henry. Pvt. under Capt. George W. Ent, 24 Aug - 30 Sep 1814.

KROUSE, John. Pvt. under Capt. Barton Hackney, 1 Sep - 27 Oct 1814.

KUHN, Peter. Pvt. from Upper Fred. Co. under Capt. James F. Huston and Capt. Green; joined 23 Jul 1814; deserted 5 Dec 1814.

KURBEY, John. Pvt. under Capt. Joseph Wood, 27 Aug - 28 Oct 1814.

KURSMAN, Christian. Pvt. under Capt. Jacob Getzendanner, 4 Aug - 21 Aug 1814.

LAFAVER, John. Pvt. under Capt. Samuel Duvall, 3 Aug - 3 Oct 1814.

LAKIN, John. Pvt. under Capt. Nicholas Turbutt, 1 Sep - 27 Oct 1814. [Bur. at Lakin Family Cem. in the Catoctin Creek area: John Lakin (18 Nov 1790 - 18 Oct 1821).

LAKINS, Benjamin. 2nd lieut. under Capt. Barton Hackney, 1 Sep - 27 Oct 1814.

LAKINS [Lakin], William. Pvt. under Capt. Nicholas Turbutt, 1 Sep - 27 Oct 1814; m. 10 Sep 1827, Susan Ramsberg (b. 4 Sep 1807) near Jefferson, MD by Rev. Jonathan Helfenstein. William Lakin d. near Jefferson 7 Aug 1850, age 56 yrs, 7 mos., 14 days. Susan Lakin d. at her residence near Jefferson, 14 Apr 1877, age 69 yrs, 7 mos., 10 days. Both bur. at Lakin Family cem., Catoctin Creek area with son George P. (11 Sep 1828 - 15 Apr 1830); dau Elizabeth R. (d. 8 Sep 1870, age 36 yrs, 2 mos., 11 days); Susan A. (14 Sep 1842 - 28 Jun 1875). 1850 census of Jefferson Dist.: William H. Lakin, 50(?); Susanna, 40; Elizabeth, 16. Acq.: 1870 - Andrew Kipler and Jona. W. Crum, knew William 30 yrs; William H. Lakin, J.P.

Sources: Bounty land claim, 55-160-111475; **(Frederick) Examiner,** 25 Apr 1877; **Names in Stone; Bridge in Time;** FCmL

LAMAR, Richard. Sergt. under Capt. Jacob Alexander, 22 July - 19 Sep 1814; m. 23 Feb 1812, Mary (Polly) Johnson (b. c.1795), Fred. Co., MD, by Rev. Craver, Luth. Pastor, at her father's house in the Middletown Valley. Richard Lamar d. 18 Jun 1815 in Middletown. His widow res. Middletown Valley, Frederick Co, up to 1871 or later. Acq.: 1856 - John K. Johnson and Bethany Ridgeley; 1872 - Frederick Hawman and William Johnson, res. Fred. Co.

FREDERICK COUNTY MILITIA IN THE WAR OF 1812

Sources: Pension, WO 4077, WC 2039 (admitted 11 Mar 1872); Bounty land claim, 50-40-93828, 55-120-77494.

LAMBERT, David. He never joined his company under Capt. William Durbin, Jr., which served 24 Aug - 27 Oct 1814.

LAMBERT, George. He never joined his company under Capt. William Durbin, Jr., which served 24 Aug - 27 Oct 1814.

LAMBRECHT [Lampbright], George. Pvt. under Capt. George W. Ent, 24 Aug - 27 Oct 1814; b. 4 Nov 1782; res. Fred. Co., 1851 and 1855; d. 13 Feb 1861; bur. Mt. Olivet with wife Rachel (d. 18 Feb 1840). He was keeper of the Tollgate, a mile north of Fredericktown. Acq.: 1855 - Jon. Wise and William Smith. [From *The Frederick Times and Democratic Advocate*, 14 Jun 1838: d. White Hall, IL, 27th May last, Mrs. Sophia Nichols, dau of George Lambrecht, of Frederick, in her 34th year.]
Sources: **Engelbrecht Diary**, v.3., 93; **Names in Stone.**

LAMBRECHT [Lambright], Michael. Pvt. under Capt. George W. Ent, 24 Aug - 30 Sep 1814. [Prob. same Michael Lambright who d. 28 Sep 1851, age 66, bur. Mt. Olivet with Annamary Lambright, who d. 10 Aug 1851, age 61. 1850 census of Fred. Co.: Michl. Lambright, 62, millright; Ann M., 52; Charles O. L., 12. FCml issued to Michael Lambrecht and Mary Metz on 20 Apr 1816.]
Sources: **FCml; Names in Stone; Bridge in Time.**

LAMAN, Jacob. Pvt. under Capt. John Fonsten; joined 2 Sep 1814; deserted 1 Oct.

LANDERMAN (?), Joseph. Pvt. under Capt. Daniel Marker, 16 Aug 16 - 18 Sep 1813.

LANDIS, Jacob. Mbr. of Crawford's "company." [*Frederick-Town Herald*, 18 Jan 1806: m. at Lancaster, 10 Dec 1805, by Rev. Clarkson, Jacob Landes of Fred. Co., to Miss Margaret Skiles of the former place.]

LANE, Joseph. Pvt. under Capt. Galt, 31 Aug - 27 Oct 1814.

LANE, William. Pvt. under Capt. Magee, 22 Jul 1814 - 10 Jan 1815.

LANE, William. Drummer under Capt. Matthew Murray, 25 Aug - 27 Oct 1814.

LANG, Samuel. Pvt. under Capt. Samuel Ogle, 1 May - 5 Jul 1813.

LAPE, Samuel Pvt. under Capt. Jacob Getzendanner, 9 Aug - 17 Sep 1813.

LAPOLE, George. See Leopole.

LARE, Samuel. Pvt. under Capt. John Galt, 31 Aug - 27 Oct 1814, from Balt. Co.; b. c.1781; res. Crawford Co., OH, in 1850.
Source: Bounty land claim, 55-160-50654.

LAREW, William. Pvt. under Capt. Galt, 31 Aug - 27 Oct 1814; res. within 5 miles of Hampstead, MD in 1814.

LARKIN, John. Pvt. under Capt. Murray, 25 Aug - 27 Oct 1814; m. 15 Dec 1814, Margaret Gillaspy (b. 23 Apr 1787, dau of Mathew (Mathias) and Mary Gillespie) at her mother's house in Middletown, MD, by William McCauly, Meth. minister. John Larkin d. at

THE VETERANS

Harpers Ferry, VA, 5 May 1850. His widow res. in Jefferson Co., VA, 1852 (Bolivar) and 1855. Acq. - 1852: John Gillaspy and Thomas C. Gillaspy, bros. of Margaret Larkin, also res. Bolivar, VA. 1855: George Crowl and George N. Smallwood.

Sources: Bounty land claim, 55-120-89845; Mary Hitselberger re the Gillespie family of Middletown.

LARN, William. Pvt. from Balt. Town under Capt. G. W. Magee, 14 Oct 1814 - 10 Jan 1815.

LATE, George Pvt. under Capt. Joseph Wood, 27 Aug - 28 Oct 1814. He d. at Creagerstown Feb 1870, in his 84th year. 1850 census of Creagerstown E.D.: George Late, 63, farmer; Irane Late, 61; Jacob Late, 34; Catherine Late, 31. Bur. at Creagerstown, St. John's Luth. and Reformed Ch.: George Late, d. 11 Feb 1867, age 82 yrs, 7 mos., 30 days; Catherine Late, d. 20 Dec 1854, age 35 yrs, 5 mos., 1 day; Isaac Late, d. 15 Sep 1856, age 67 yrs, 4 mos., 1 day; Jacob Late, d. 20 Aug 1900, age 84 yrs, 1 month, 1 day.

Sources: Bridge in Time; Names in Stone.

LAVARETT [Larovett], Philip. Pvt. under Capt. Samuel Ogle, from 1 May until he left militia to enlist in the regular army on 8 Jun 1813; enlisted by Capt. Joseph Hook for 1 year at Balt. 9 Jun 1813. At enlistment: 5 ft, 6 inches; age 34, b. in Germany. Pvt. in the 36th U.S. Inf. under Capt. Joseph Hook.

LAVORETT, Michael. Pvt. under Capt. Samuel Ogle, 1 May - 5 Jul 1813.

LAWLESS. See LOLLIS.

LAWRENCE, James Pvt. from Upper Fred. Co., under Capt. James F. Huston, 23 Jul 1814. Deserted 16 Aug.

LAYMAN, John Pvt. under Capt. Thomas Contee Worthington,, 17 - 31 Dec 1812.

LAYMAN, John Pvt. under Capt. Jacob Getzendanner 26 Jul - 21 Aug 1814. [*The Times and Democratic Advocate* - 21 Sep 1837. m. Thurs evening last, by Rev. Harkey, John Layman, to Miss Rebecca Blessing, all of this co.]

LEACH [Leech], Benjamin. Pvt., 1st U.S. Inf., under Capt. S. Arvens and T. Hamilton. At enlistment: 5 ft, 8 inches; black eyes, dark hair, dark complexion; age 31; farmer; b. Fred. Co., MD; enlisted 14 Apr 1809 and 8 Jun 1814. 1st enlisted at Winchester for 5 yrs, by Capt Arvens; 2nd enlistment by Capt. Peyton for the duration of the war. Present at Craney Island in 1815; d. 27 Jan 1815.

LEAPLEY, John. Pvt. under Capt. Barton Hackney, 1 Sep - 27 Oct 1814; b. c.1793; m. 18 May 1824, Elizabeth McDaniel (b. c.1807), at Rumley(?), Hampshire Co., VA, by Rev. James Taylor, each for first time. He res. Brown Co., IL, 1850 and 1855; d. Adams Co, IL, 6 Jun 1870. Fol. discharge he res. VA, OH and IL; widow res. Adams Co. IL, in 1879 (P.O. address: Kellerville). Acq.: 1879 - James Gillenwater, age 63; Liberty Courtney, age 58 - res. Adams Co.; Caroline M. Grady, age 53, dau of Elizabeth and John Leapley. From clerk, Hampshire Co, WV - No record of marriage license - Federal soldiers destroyed the records of marriages, 1822-1824.

FREDERICK COUNTY MILITIA IN THE WAR OF 1812

Sources: Bounty land claim, 55-120-66717; Pension, WO 34751, WC 22902.

LEAR, Henry. Reported as deserting on 18 Aug 1814 from Capt. Duvall's company which was camped at Bladensburg; described as a substitute, aged 24-25 yrs, with light complexion, gray eyes, light hair, by profession a hatter. Not shown in the rolls.

LEASER, Peter. Pvt. under Capt. Samuel Dawson, 1 May - 5 Jul 1813.

LECALLEET, John. Mbr. of Crawford's "company."

LECALLUT, George. Mbr. of Crawford's "company."

LEE, Garrett. Never joined his company under Capt. Thomas Contee Worthington, which served 17 Aug - 31 Dec 1812.

LEEMAN [Laman], Isaac. Pvt., 12th U.S. Inf. At enlistment: 5 ft, 7 inches; grey eyes, brown hair, and light complexion; age 19; farmer; b. Fred. Co.; enlisted 5 Feb 1814 by Capt. Past for 5 yrs. Mustered at Staunton 10 May 1814 and mustered in Lieut. William B. Howell's Det., White Hall, on 28 Feb 1815.

LEESE, Philip. Pvt. under Capt. Fonsten, 2 Sep - 27 Oct 1814; res. 7 miles from Westminster.

LEFEVER, George. Pvt. under Capt. Daniel Shawen, 5 Sep - 27 Oct 1814.

LEFEVRE, John. The *Carroll County Democrat* reported death of John Lefevre, "who fought in the defense of this country in the War of 1812 ... a native of France, suddenly stricken by an inscrutable decree of Providence" at Emmittsburg, MD on 3 Jan 1856, while sitting on a fence. 1850 census of 5th E.D.: John Lefever, 69, b. LA; Mary Lefever, 32, b. MD and others.
Sources: (Frederick) Examiner, 16 Jan 1856; Bridge in Time.

LEGG, William. From Balt.. Pvt. under Capt. Samuel Dawson, 14 Oct 1814 - 10 Jan 1815.

LEIZER [Leezer, Lizen, Lezen], Peter. Pvt., 22nd U.S. Inf., under Capt. Joseph Henderson. At enlistment: 6 ft, 1 inch; had grey eyes, dark hair and dark complexion; age 23; laborer; b. Fred. Co.; enlisted 23 March 1814 by Lt. Culbertson for 5 yrs. Mustered at Pittsburg, 30 Apr and Jun 1814. Killed 25 July 1814.

LEMAR, Richard. Pvt. under Capt. Jacob Alexander 22 Jul - 19 Sep 1814.

LEOHR, George. Pvt. under Capt. John Brengle, 25 Aug - 19 Sep 1814; deserted.

LEONARD, Richard. Pvt. under Capt. Samuel Dawson, 1 May - 5 Jul 1813.

LEOPOLE [Leopold, Lapole], George Lewis. Pvt. under Capt. Samuel Dawson 21 Jul - 13 Oct 1814 (absent without leave from 31 Aug to 10 Sep 1814; served from 14 Oct 1814 to ---; remark on pay recipt roll: "Died Dec. 23, 1814." He said he served as pvt. under Capt. Blisson [*There was a Capt. Glisan - Ed.*] and then Capt. Dawson, went out as substitute three times at Berlin, Frederick Co, MD, in 1813, discharged at Bladensburg, North Point and Fredericktown in 1814. Fol. discharge he res. Winchester, Frederick Co, VA; Washington Co, PA for 40 yrs or more

THE VETERANS

(in Burgettstown most of the time). - b. c.1787; res. in Burgettstown, Washington Co., PA, 1878. At enrollment: 5 ft 6 1/2 inches tall, brown hair, gray eyes and fair complexion; stone mason. Witnesses: 1878 - David Pettibon, age 30; and Henry Leopole, 24 - res. Burgettstown.
Source: Pension, SO 33352 (rejected - 3rd Auditor reports on 22 May 1880 that "George Lapole died Dec. 23, 1814)."

LEPPO, Petter. Pvt. under Capt. Samuel Ogle, 1 May - 5 Jul 1813.

LESCALLAT, Richard. Mbr. of Crawford's "company."

LESCALLECH, Richard. Mbr. of Crawford's "company."

LESCALLECT, George. Mbr. of Crawford's "company."

LESCALLEECH, John. Mbr. of Crawford's "company."

LEVY, David T. Pvt. under Capt. Matthew Murray, 25 Aug - 27 Oct 1814; m. 11 Apr 1820, Elizabeth Myers (b. c.1797) in Fred. Co., MD, by Rev. Shaeffer, Presbyterian minister. At enrollment: apprentice in wagon making business with Capt. Murray in Middletown, c.19 yrs old. There was no other David Levy in the area at the time. David Levy d. at Carrolton, Carroll Co., OH, 20 Oct 1839. His widow res. in Carroll Co., OH, in 1857. Acq.: 1857 - Adam Karn, age 73, res. Carrollton, OH, well acq. with David T. Levy in Frederick Co. and also after he removed to Carrollton, OH; stated Levy "was a bro.-in-law of Capt. Matthew Murray and an apprentice to him at the plow and wagon making business." "I worked at the said business for said Capt. Murray, and in the same shop with Levy over eight yrs... I was a soldier in the same war, under Capt. Jacob Alexander..."
Source: Bounty land claim, 55-160-64554.

LEWEN, Paul. Pvt. under Capt. Daniel Marker, 16 Aug - 18 Sep 1813.

LEWIS, John. Pvt. under Capt. Daniel Shawen, 5 Sep - 27 Oct 1814.

LEWIS, William. 5th corpl. under James F. Huston from 23 Jul 1814; 4th corpl. under Capt. Joseph Green, until discharged at Balt. on 6 Dec 1814; res. Frederick Town.
[*Political Examiner* - 9 Mar 1836: m. 3 Mar 1836, by Rev. McGee, William D. Lewis, to Miss Columbia E. Rigdon, all of this city.]

LIDIE [Liday], Jacob. Pvt. under Capt. Samuel Ogle, 1 May - 5 Jul 1813. He said he served under Jacob Creager, as substitute for Frederick Loy, enrolled c.1 May 1813, discharged at or near Spring Garden, Balt., MD, around 4 Jul 1813; later substituted for Daniel Hoover at Fredericktown, MD, c.1 Aug 1814, in company of Jacob Creager, under Col. Hood, discharged at Balt. c.1 Oct 1814; b. 1786; m. 12 Mar 1815, Sarah Sifert (b. c.1791), by Rev. Frederick Rahauser, at Emmitsburg, Fred. Co. He res. Fred. Co., MD, 1850; d. c.16 Jun 1857 at Mechanicstown, MD. Widow res. Mechanicstown, MD 1878; d. 4 Mar 1884. Acq.: 1878 - John B. Gilbert, 68, and Ephraim Carmack, 68, res. Mechanicstown, acq. 30 yrs.
Sources: Bounty land claim, 50-80-21094, 55-80-2212 (widow said that he sold his bounty land

warrant to David Eiker); Pension, WO 21186, WC 16269.

LIDDY. See Lydie.

LIEPLY, Peter. Pvt. under Capt. Brengle, 25 Aug - 19 Sep 1814.

LIGHTLIDER, George. Pvt. under Capt. Joseph Wood, 27 Aug - 28 Oct 1814. Rendezvous at Camp Diehl.

LIGHTNER, George. Pvt. under Capt. Samuel Duvall, 3 Aug - 3 Oct 1814. [Frederick Herald - 3 Aug 1833 - Married Sunday 13th inst., George M. Lightner, of York Pa, to Miss Elizabeth Yost, of New Market, Balt. Co., MD].

LINDSAY, Elisha. Mbr. of Crawford's "company."

LINEBAUGH, William. Pvt. under Capt. Samuel Duvall; joined 3 Aug 1814; discharged in Washington, D.C., 11 Nov 1814; served as substitute for William Pippenger; b. c.1791; m(1) Besty Wise; m(2) 2 Jan 1852, Fanny E. Moore (b. c.1828), Melrose, Rockingham, Co., VA, by Jacob Houck. His first wife d. 22 mos. earlier. Fanny had not m. prev. At enrollment: 5 ft, 5 inches tall, blue eyes, light hair, fair complexion. He res. in Rockingham Co., VA (P.O. Address: Paradise) 1854, Rockingham Co., VA in 1855; Rockingham Co. (P.O. Address: Harrisburg), VA 1871; d. 28 Oct 1881, in Rockingham, VA. His widow res. in Hagerstown, MD, in 1883; d. Hagerstown 13 Apr 1885.

Acq.: (1) 1883 - Henry S. Fox, age 82, Hagerstown, and Jacob Burger, age 57; (2) 1888 - David Boward, Sr., of Hagerstown, age 76 who dug Fanny's grave, John R. Steel, age 50, Hagerstown, Mary E. Black, age 50, knew Fanny for 13 yrs, John D. Lloyd, age 52, Middleburg, acq. with Fanny 18 and 20 yrs resp.; Martha Rimel, age 59, said William Linebaugh d. 29 Oct 1881 c.5 p.m. in her house, signed by her and John J. Rimel; Rev. J. Spangler, age 49, pastor of Zion Ref. Ch. who officiated at Fanny's funeral - said that Fanny d. 13 Apr 1885 age 57 yrs, 5 mos. and 17 days. (3) 1889 - Mrs. Emma Thurston, widow of John Thurston, res. Hagerstown, age 39; knew William and Fannie and their children. One child, Jennie, an intimate friend, d. 1871. She helped prepare the body for burial. During Jun or Jul 1871 Catharine Keenan was b., now wife of Raleigh Hock. Charlotte Hill, widow of Richard Hill of Washington Co., MD, age 53, knew both Fanny and William, Catharine Keenan, the illegitimate child of Mrs. Fanny E. Linebaugh. "Those who were not familiar with her paternity would think that she was one of the Linebaugh children." However she was b. six week before William Linebaugh came back to his wife after being away for over three yrs in the West. She thinks Fanny lived with Keenan because she once heard by letter that William was dead. Sallie Boward, wife of Henry Boward, age 65, said that Catharine was not the child of William; she lived across the street and knew the whole family; that Catharine was the child of Patrick Keenan and Fanny Linebaugh; that Katharine had m. R. H. Hoch of Hagerstown on 24 Dec 1888 under the name of Catherine Keenan. Keenan had been dead several yrs. Charlotte Hill, age 53, washerwoman, Hagerstown, knew that Catharine was b. Jul or Aug 1870 because she had a dau, Anna E. Hill b. 26 Oct 1870. Sarah L. Bonner of Hagerstown, age 42, wife of William F. Bonner, foreman at the Western Maryland Railroad, stated that her son John Andrew Bonner was b. 3 days after Catharine; he was b. 3 Aug 1870. J. R. Spielman, residence of Hagerstown, age 46, undertaker, said Fanny's coffin was paid for by Mrs. Shantz.

In 1878 Mrs. Bessie Shantz, 525 N. Jonathan St., Hagerstown, stated she was dau of Fanny Linebaugh who d., leaving a child under age of 16.

In 1887 Bessie Shantz wrote from Hagerstown that her mother d. over a year ago; that there are 4 children: her bro. who left about 14 yrs ago, never heard of again, her two sisters, Susan and Catharine, who are single. She (Bessie) m. c.5 yrs ago and has three children. Her father was a "diletory old man and never did much for his wife and family." She and her husband took care of her mother and sisters. In 1889 Bessie wrote that she and her husband are "consumpted" and have four small children; that Mrs. Hock (Catherine) is very nervous and her husband's family controls her; that Mrs. Catharine Hock's husband is not yet 21. In 1889 Bessie Shantz, age 29, stated her father was absent from home some yrs before Catharine was b.; he was home afterwards but never stayed much at home and was always moving around from one state to another; that Catharine was b. 30 Jul 1870 or 1871.

In 1889 Susan Linebaugh, age 28 said her mother, on her deathbed told her that Catharine would be 15 yrs of age on 30 Jul of same year (1885).

Special Examiner in 1889 stated that Catharine was b. 30 Jul 1870, baptized under name of Catharine Lymbaugh 23 Jul 1872. Her address was then George St., Hagerstown, MD.

Catharine Hock stated in 1889 that her mother had 3 other living children when she d.: John Limbaugh, Susan Limebaugh and Bessie who m. George Shantz; that her half sister, Susan was c.10 yrs older that Catharine. Her mother told her she was b. 30 Jul 1871.

Source: Pension, SO3192, SC 7533, WO 43106.

LINEWEAVER, Casper. Pvt. under Capt. Daniel Marker, 25 Aug - 27 Oct 1814.

LINGENFELTER, Michael. Pvt. under Capt. Samuel Ogle, 1 May - 5 Jul 1813.

LINN, Abraham. 6th corpl. under Capt. William Knox, 26 Aug - 27 Oct 1814.

LINTON, Zachariah. Pvt. under Lieut. Kolb, 13 Oct - 15 Nov 1814 in a det. which guarded the British prisoners at the Frederick Barracks.

LIPPY [Lippa, Lippie], David. Pvt. under Capt. Fonsten, 2 Sep - 27 Oct 1814; res. 9 miles from Westminster; b. c.1780; m. 16 Jan 1849, Ann Rape (or Nancy Rape, b. c.1790) in Preble Co., OH, by John Holdeman, magistrate of Preble Co., OH. David Lippy d. Darke Co., OH, 8 Apr 1852. His widow res. in Preble Co., OH, 1855.

Source: Bounty land claim, 55-120-87693.

FREDERICK COUNTY MILITIA IN THE WAR OF 1812

LIPSLEY [Lieply?], Peter. Pvt. under John Brengle, 25 Aug - 19 Sep 1814.

LISHURE, John. Pvt. under Capt. Denton Darby; joined 3 Aug 1814; deserted from camp at Bladensburg 20 Aug, age c.22; had sandy complexion, red hair, labourer.

LISHURE, Joshua. Pvt. under Capt. Denton Darby, joined 3 Aug 1814; deserted from camp at Bladensburg on 20 Aug, age c.22; had sandy complexion, red hair, labourer.

LISHURE, Samuel. Pvt. under Capt. Denton Darby, joined 3 Aug 1814; deserted from camp at Bladensburg on 20 Aug, age c.22; had sandy complexion, red hair, labourer.

LITCHLIGHTER [Lichlighter, Lichliter], Conrad. Pvt., 12th U.S. Inf.. At enlistment: 5 ft, 10 inches; had blue eyes, light hair and dark complexion; age 35; prev. occupation sadler; b. Fred. Co., MD; enlisted 23 Sep 1813 at Staunton, VA, by Capt. Page for 5 yrs. At Bay St. Louis since 26 Aug 1817 (as of 31 Aug 1817). On command at Little Escambia beginning 3 Apr 1818; discharged at Pensacola 23 Sep 1818.

LITT, Jacob. Pvt. under Capt. Samuel Duvall; joined 3 Aug 1814; reported as deserting from camp at Bladensburg 26 Aug 1814; described as 20-21 yrs of age, 5 ft 9-10 inches, dark complexion, black eyes, black hair, laborer; b. c.1795; m. 18 Jan 1834, Catharine Caregeir (or Caregur?) (b. c.1797) by William Smith, J.P., of -orox(?) Co., OH. Jacob Litt res. Richland, OH 1850; d. Richland Co. 24 Sep 1852; his widow res. Richland 1855.

Acq.: 1855 - F. M. Fitting and William Walker, res. Richland Co.; 1856 - Jacob Garver (Garber) and Hugh Cowan.
Source: Bounty land claim, 55-120-87108.

LITTLE, David. Pvt. under Capt. George W. Magee; joined 23 Jul; deserted 25 Sep 1814.

LITTLE, John. 2nd sergt. under Capt. William Knox, 26 Aug - 27 Oct 1814.

LITTLE [alias Kline], Peter. Pvt., 14th U.S. Inf., under Capt. Samuel Lane. Poss. b. Fred. Co., (Littlestown?) MD, prisoner of War, exchanged 15 Apr 1814. Discharged 25 Apr 1815, ruptured. (See Peter Kline same company)

LITTLE [Lytle], Peter, Col., 38th U.S. Inf.; present at Balt. 5 Jun, July, Aug, Sept and 11 Oct 1813. Mbr. of Court martial at Washington 18 and 25 Oct 1813. Recruiting at Balt. 1 Nov and 13 Dec 1813. Left for Albany 20 Dec 1813. Craney Island 31 May 1814.

LITTLEJOHN, George W. Pvt. under Capt. George W. Ent, 24 Aug - 30 Sep 1814; m. 4 Aug 1811, Miss Elizabeth Geisinger by Rev. Manlovie; d. 4 Nov 1823.
Sources: **Fredericktown Herald**, 13 Dec 1823; **Hornet**, 7 Aug 1811.

LITTLEJOHN, Leonard J. M. 1st Lieut. under Capt. George W. Ent, 3rd Regt, 24 Aug - 30 Sep 1814; m. 11 Jul 1816, Rebecca Walker (b. 1 Apr 1797) at Mount St. Mary's in Frederick Co, MD, by Rev John Dubois; d. 10 Jul 1824 in Frederick. His widow res. in Fairfield Co., OH 1850, 1852. Acq.: 1850 - Josseph Lilly, age 40, res. Fairfield, OH.

192

THE VETERANS

[Letter from Helen L. Gunther of 3 Apr 1906 inquiring about pension for Leonard Littlejohn's service to which a negative reply was given. Letter dated 7 Jun 1938 from Mrs. Laura Littlejohn Davis to Veteran's Administration, stating that a pension should have been paid to Leonard James Littlejohn, her grandfather, and complaining that she had to take care of her father and mother and had no worldly goods of her own.]
Source: Bounty land claim, 50-40-66030, 55-120-707.

LIVERS, Thomas. Ensign under Capt. Samuel Ogle, 4 Jun - 5 Jul 1813; "reported himself at hdqtrs" Jun 4th. [See Adams, *Cath. Trails West*, vol. 2, p. 404. Listed is Thomas Livers b 25 Oct 1765, d. Washington Co., KY, m. Judith Elder b 25 Oct 1765, Fred. Co., MD, dau of Guy and Eleanor Ogle Elder.]

LLOYD [Loyd], William A. Never reported to his company under Capt. Thomas Contee Worthington, which served 17 - 31 Dec 1812. [*Fredericktown Herald*, 9 Mar 1822: m. at Reading, Feb 26, at residence of late Gen. Swaine, by Rev. Henry Muhlenburg, William Ambrose Lloyd, Esq. of town of Northumberland, PA, to Mrs. Elizabeth Swaine, widow of Gen. Swaine, with fortune of $50,000! *Frederick Herald*, 5 Jul 1834: d Sunday 22d ult., in her 72d year, Mrs. Elizabeth Lloyd, consort of William Lloyd, of the vicinity of Westminster.]

LOBEN [Lowen?], Paul. Pvt. under Capt. Samuel Dawson, 21 Jul - 10 Jan 1815.

LOCK, Abraham. Pvt. under Capt. Joseph Wood, 27 Aug - 13 Oct 1814; deserted 14 Oct.

LOCKE, George. According to Williams, *History of Fred. Co.*, George Locke served under Capt. John Brengle, 25 Aug - 19 Sep 1814. [m. 29th inst., by Rev. D. Zacharias, George W. Lock, to Miss Rebecca Ann Gordon, both of Jefferson, VA.]

LOCKER [Locher], Adam. Pvt. under Capt. George W. Magee, from 22 Jul until missing 24 Aug.

LOGAN, George. Pvt. under Capt. Denton Darby; joined 3 Aug 1814; deserted 30 Aug 1814.

LOGAN, John Pvt. under Capt. Samuel Ogle, 1 May - deserted 26 May.

LOLLIS [Lawless], Phillip. Pvt., 14th U.S. Inf., under Capt. Reuben Gilder. At enlistment: 5 ft, 10 1/2 inches; grey eyes, dark hair, light complexion; age 37; carpenter; b. Fred. Co., MD; enlisted 7 Mar 1814 in MD by Lt. Beale for 5 yrs. 1 May 1815 wounded in left thigh by accident and left at Pitsfield. Discharged at Greenbush 8 Jun 1815, wounded.

LOMAN, Edward. Pvt. under Capt. Samuel Dawson, 14 Oct 1814 - 10 Jan 1815.

LOMAX, Lawson. Pvt., 12th U.S. Inf., under Capt. Sangster. At enlistment: 5 ft, 7 or 8 1/2 inches; blue eyes; age 23 or 25; farmer; b. Fred. Co.; enlisted 15 May 1812 in Alexandria, VA, by Capt. Sangster for 18 mos. Mustered in Burlington 28 Feb 1814. Sick at Sacketts Harbor 30 Apr 1814. Appears to have again enlisted 28 Jan 1815 at Alexandria again enlisted 28 Jan 1815 at Alexandria by Lieut. Randolph for duration of the war. Discharged at Fredericksburg 15 March 1815.

LONG, George. Pvt. under Capt. Joseph Wood, 27 Aug - 28 Oct 1814. He said he served under Capt. John Brown, drafted at Balt. Co., around 1 Jun 1814, discharged at Balt. City Nov 1814. He was b. c.1793; m. Elisabeth Rockney, at Franklin Co., OH, 2 Mar 1817; res. Hancock Co., OH, 1850, 1855 and 1871 (Jackson Township, P.O. Address: Findlay, OH). Acq.: David Garling and George Freese of Hancock Co.

Sources: Bounty land claim, 50-40-76497, 55-120-41868; Pension, SO 19093, SC 11964 (dropped 4 Sep 1883 - failure to claim pension).

LONG, John. Pvt. under Capt. Hackney, 1 Sep - 27 Oct 1814; b. c.1795; res. Guernsey Co., OH, 1851 and 1855.

Source: Bounty land claim, 55-120-60292.

LONG, John. 2nd U.S. Inf., under Capt. P. Willis. At enlistment: 5 ft, 5 inches; light eyes, brown hair and sallow complexion; age 22; laborer; b. Fred. Co., MD; enlisted 24 Oct 1814 at Washington city by Capt. P. Willis for 5 yrs. Deserted 24 or 28 Oct 1814.

LONG, Peter. He said he served under Capt. Norris and Lieut. Fonsten, drafted at Westminster, MD, c.1 Sep 1814 as pvt. in the company of Capt. Norris, discharged at Balt. Sep 1814. - b. c.1796; res. in Taylorsville (P.O. address: Franklinville), Carroll Co., MD, 1879. Witnesses: 1879 - George P. Albaugh, Main St., Westminster, MD, and Alfred W. Buckingham, Taylorsville, MD.

Source: Pension, SO 34427. Rejected - no service record as alleged (no rolls of Capt. Norris's Company and name of Peter Long is not borne on the rolls of Fonsten's company).

LONGMAN, Jacob. Pvt. under Capt. Daniel Marker, 16 Aug - 18 Sep 1813 in Capt. Daniel Marker's company of riflemen; b. c.1788. 1850 census of Middletown Dist.: Jacob Longman, 62; Susanna Longman, 62; Eve Longman, 92. Jacob Longmam res. Fred. Co., 1850, 1851, 1855. Acq. (1851): Thomas Bittle and Philip Cline, who served with him.

Source: Bounty land claim, 55-120-7820.

LONGMAN, Joseph. Ensign under Capt. Daniel Marker in his company of riflemen, 16 Aug - 16 Sep 1813; b. c.1795; m. Matilda Whitmore, in Fred. Co., MD, 15 Aug 1841. 1850 census of Catoctin E.D.: Joseph Longman, 55; Martha A. M. Longman, 48; Jacob Longman, 16; Henry Longman, 8. Jacob Longman res. Fred. Co., 1851, 1854, 1855; Preble Co., OH, 1874 and 1878 (Gratis Township); d. 19 Mar 1887. Acq. (1854): Thomas Bittle, Philip Cline. Thomas Bittle was ensign of Capt. Daniel Marker's company of rifle corps in which Joseph Longman served.

Source: Pension.

LOOKBAUGH, John. Pvt. under Capt. Joseph Wood, 27 Aug - 28 Oct 1814.

LOOKENINBEEL, Samuel. Pvt. under Capt. John Fonsten, 2 Sep - 27 Oct 1814; res. 16 miles from Westminster.

LOON, Michael. Pvt. under Capt. Samuel Duvall, 3 Aug - 3 Oct 1814.

LOUDERSLAGLE, Solomon. Pvt. under Capt. John Fonsten, 2 Sep - 27 Oct 1814.

LOVE, David. Pvt., 12th U.S. Inf., under Capt. T. Moore. At enlistment: 5 ft, 10 inches; age 32; b. Fred. Co., MD; enlisted 22 May 1813 in Wheeling, VA, by Lt. A. McDonald, to serve until 22 May 1818; d. 2 Jan 1814 at French Mills, sickness.

LOW, Jacob Pvt. under Capt. Philip Smith; joined 23 May 1813; deserted 27 Aug 1813.

LOWE, George. Drum major under Capt. George W. Ent, 24 Aug - 30 Sep 1814; d. at his residence in East Fifth St. after brief illness, 8 Aug 1868, age 76 yrs; his eyesight became greatly impaired; bur. Evangelical Luth. graveyard.
Source: **(Frederick) Examiner,** 12 Aug 1868.

LOWE, Jacob. Pvt. under Capt. Thomas Contee Worthington (Aug 17- 25 1812). [See also entry below from *Republican Citizen and Public Avertiser*, 27 Dec 1822.]

LOWE, Jacob. Pvt. under Capt. Samuel Duvall, 3 Aug - 3 Oct 1814.

LOWE, John. 2nd lieut. under Capt. Norris, subsequently Capt. John Fonsten; b. c.1784; m. Mary Glisan (b. c.1794), at Liberty, Fred. Co., 7 Oct 1817, by James L. Higgins, Meth minister. At enlistment: miller, age 29 yrs, 6 ft; dark hair, dark eyes, dark complexion. After discharge res. Bush Creek 20 yrs and town of Liberty; res. Fred. Co., MD, 1851 and 1855; d. at Basil Harding's in MD 21 Sep 1864. Widow res. New London, Fred. Co., 1878. Witnesses: 1855 - Alexander Lowe and Samuel Haller, res. Fred. Co. Acq.: 1878 - W. W. Walker, age 60, res. near New London and Samuel A. Lowe, age 52, res. Woodville, acq. 45 and 40 yrs, resp.; 1879 - Elisea Glisan and William W. Walker, acq. 30 yrs.
Sources: Bounty land claim, 55-120-21867; Pension, WO 34753, WC 21187 (admitted 5 Mar 1879). [See also below.]

From *Republican Citizen and Public Advertiser* dated 27 Dec 1822 - Equity case - George Buckey and Marion his wife, Jacob Houck and Catharine his wife vs. Jacob Low, John Low, Jno. Griar and Sarah his wife - for sale of part of two lots in Fredericktown of Andrew Low who d. intestate leaving fol. children at the time: Jacob Low, Marion Low since m. to Geo. Buckey and two of the complainants, Catharine wife of Jacob Houck.

LOWEN, Paul. See Loben.

LOWERY, Frederick Pvt. under Capt. Samuel Dawson, 21 Jul - 10 Jan 1815.

LOWERY, John. Pvt. under Capt. Samuel Dawson; 21 Jul 1814; deserted 11 Nov 1814.

LOWERY, Joseph. 3rd corpl. from Balt. under Capt. Samuel Dawson, 21 Jul 1814 - 10 Jan 1815.

LOWMAN, John Pvt. under Capt. Samuel Dawson, 1 May - 5 Jul 1813.

LOWMAN, John, Jr. Pvt. under Capt. Fonsten; joined 2 Sep; deserted 14 Sep 1814; said he served as a substitute for John Lowman, Sr, at Fredericktown; b. c.1795; res. Fairfield Co., OH, 1850.
Source: Bounty land claim, 50-80-761.

FREDERICK COUNTY MILITIA IN THE WAR OF 1812

LUCAS, Henry. Pvt. from New Windsor under Capt. George W. Magee, 22 Jul - 10 Jan 1815.

LUCAS, John. Pvt. from Woodsboro area, under Capt. Samuel Duvall, 3 Aug - 3 Oct 1814; m. 1 Dec 1797, Christiana Walters (b. c.1774), by David Martin, Meth. pastor. John Lucas d. at home near New London, MD, 12 Jan 1847. Acq.: 1850 - Frederick Shipley and Peter Boyer, res. Fred. Co.

Source: Bounty land claim, 50-40-44637.

LUCKENBEEL, John. Pvt. in Capt. Peter Snyder's Company of Inf., 2nd Regt., PA militia, 5 Sep - 5 Dec 1814. Rendezvous at York, PA, 5 Sep 1814, res. Schuylkill Co; "sick in hospital." "On furlough since 21 November 1814." This may be the same person as Judge John Lugenbeel who d. Western Star, Medina Co., OH, 28 Dec 1874, after a short illness, from paralysis, aged 82. According to the local newspaper he was b. in Fred. Co., MD, served at Baltimore in 1814; moved to OH in spring of 1833, stopping 8 mos. in Zanesville, moving from thence to Delaware Co., OH, where he remained until the spring of 1861, when he moved to Cleveland, OH; was father of Pinkney Lugenbeel, Col. in Regular Army and D.W.C. Lugenbeel and Mrs. Burnham of Burlington, IA. Mayor of the town of Western Star when he d.

LUCKETT, Otho Holland William. Pvt. under Capt. George W. Ent, 3rd Regt, 24 Aug - 30 Sep 1814; son of Thomas Husey and Elizabeth Lucket (d. c.1817); b. during Rev. War; youth spent in VA and in Fauquier Co. on 27 Nov 1805, negotiated a bond to marry Elizabeth C. Graham. Walter Graham was his surety. In 1806 Otho H. W. Luckett, Nolands Ferry, advertised in the *Frederick-Town Herald* - 700 barrels of corn for sale. In the same newspaper, dated 24 Feb 1810, his petition for benefit under the insolvency act was posted. After service in War of 1812, he moved to Ohio. In 1835, as eldest son, and resident of Chillicothe, he applied for bounty land from the state of Viriginia by right of his father's service in the Rev. War; warrant issued 1838; papers showed his father d. Loudon Co., VA, Dec 1786.

Sources: Harry Wright Newman, **The Lucketts of Portobacco**; Frederick-Town Herald, 24 Feb 1810.

LUCKETT, Valentine Peyton. Commissioned ensign in 14th U.S. Inf. 12 Mar 1812, 2nd lieut. in 1st U.S. Inf. Light Dragoons 9 Oct 1812. Bro. of above Othow Holland Holland Luckett [See above.]

Source: Harry Wright Newman, **The Lucketts of Portobacco**.

LUGENBEEL, Moses. 2nd Lieut. from New Windsor under Capt. George W. Magee, 22 Jul 1814 - 10 Jan 1815; b. 16 Jan 1791; m. c.2 Feb 1826, Maria C. Krammer. She d. 9 May 1862 after illness of 11 weeks, in her 60th year, 32 yrs a mbr. of M.E. Ch. Moses Lugenbeel d. 26 Feb 1868 at residence of his dau, Mrs. Joseph W. L. Carty, in South Market St.

Sources: **(Frederick) Examiner**, 14 May 1862, 4 Mar 1868, 11 Mar 1868; **The Maryland Union**, 12 Mar 1868; **Names in Stone**.

THE VETERANS

LUKINGBEAL, Samuel. Pvt. under Capt. John Fonsten, 2 Sep - 27 Oct 1814; res. 16 miles from Westminster; b. c.1792; m. Mary Fouch, in Fred. Co., MD. She d. prior to 14 Aug 1872. He res. in Montgomery Co., OH, in 1850 and 1855; Appanoose Co., IA in 1872 and in Union, Putnam Co., MO, in 1878 (P.O. Address: Cincinnati, IA.)
Sources: Bounty land claim, 50-40-4806, 55-120-18908; Pension, SO 27946, SC 23898 (rejected 30 Jan 1873 - insufficient service; admitted 10 Aug 1878; dropped 4 Jun 1883 - failure to claim pension).

LUTES, John. Pvt. under Capt. George W. Magee; joined 22 Jul 1814; enlisted 5 Sep 1814.

LUTTON, Henry. Pvt. from Upper Fred. Co. under Capt. James F. Huston, 23 Jul - 13 Oct 1814.

LYDA, James. Pvt. under Capt. Joseph Wood, 27 Aug - 28 Oct 1814.

LYDAY, John. Pvt. under Capt. Philip Smith, 23 May - 8 Sep 1813.

[Mrs. Mary M. Lydey d. Tiffin, OH, 12 Mar 1886, age 86 yrs, 6 mos. The *Seneca Advertiser* said, her maiden name was Mary M. Schroyer, b. Fred Co., MD, 12 Sep 1799; m. John Lydey who d. 6 yrs earlier; they had 6 children (3 sons, 3 daus) 2 still living in 1886: John C. Lydey, Clinton Twp, and Mrs. Mary C., wife of John Beard. John and Mary Lydey went West in 1832 and settled in Tiffin, OH; early mbrs. of Ref. Ch.]

LYDIE [Liddy], John. Enlisted in regular army 14 Feb 1814 by Lieut. Sands, at Hagerstown, for duration of war. At enlistment: 5 ft, 8 inches tall; black hazel eyes, black hair and dark complexion; age 40 or 47; blacksmith; b. Fredericktown, MD. Pvt. in 38th U.S. Inf. under Capt. S. C. Leakin. Mustered at Patapsco Apr 30 and 1 Jun 1814. Mustered at Fort Covington 28 Feb 1815. Discharged at Fort Covington on 31 March 1815.

LYNCH, John. Sergt., 12th U.S. Inf., under Capt. Andrew L. Madison. At enlistment: 5 ft, 10 inches; black eyes, black hair, fair complexion; age 25; hatter; b. Fred. Co., MD; enlisted 5 Aug 1812 at Milwood by Ens. Randolph for 5 yrs. Mustered at Buffalo 28 Feb and 30 Apr 1815. Capt. James Dorman's company, 8th U.S. Inf., Fort Osage, 30 Jun 31 Aug, 1815. Discharged at Ft. Osage 5 aug 1817.

LYNN, John. Pvt. under Capt. John Galt, 31 Aug - 27 Oct 1814; res. within 2 miles of Taneytown in 1814.

LYNN, Joseph. Pvt. under Capt. Samuel Ogle, 1 May - 5 Jul 1813.

MACKEY, William. Pvt. under Capt. Samuel Ogle, 1 May - 5 Jul 1813.

MADARY, Andrew. Pvt. under Capt. Nicholas Turbutt, went to Balt. in 1814, discharged 1 Nov 1814.

MAGEE, George W. Mbr. of Crawford's "company."

MAGEE, George W. From New Windsor. Capt. of his own company, 22 Jul 1814 - 10 Jan 1815.

MAGERS, Laurence. Mbr. of Crawford's "company."

MAGERS, William. Pvt. under Capt. Philip Smith; joined 23 May 1813; deserted 6 Aug 1813.

FREDERICK COUNTY MILITIA IN THE WAR OF 1812

MAGRUDER, Rezin. Lieut. under Capt. Jacob Alexander, 22 Jul - 19 Sep 1814.

MAHUE, James. Pvt. under Capt. Samuel Dawson, 1 May - until he deserted 9 Jun.

MAIN, John Pvt. under Capt. Nicholas Turbutt, went to Balt. in 1814, discharged 1 Nov 1814.

MAIN [Mayn], John Jacob. Pvt. under Capt. J. Getzendanner, 26 Jul - 21 Aug 1814; b. c.1795 in Fred. Co.; m. Sarah Bopst, at his father's house, Fred. Co., MD, Dist. No. 2, 25 Nov 1819, by Rev. Jonathan Helphenstine, minister of German Ref. Ch., each for first time. At enlistment: blue eyes, fair complexion, dark hair, age 19, 5 ft, 6 inches, occupation farmer; res. Fred. Co. 1851, 1855, 1871 (5 miles from Fredericktown). Widow res. Fredericktown 1880; d. 8 Aug 1882. Acq.: 1880 - Edward Routzahn, age 56; and Charles T. Leatherman, age 25, Dist. No. 3 - acq. 35 and 6 yrs, resp.; D. M. Main, Dist. No. 2, Fred. Co. Witnesses: 1880 - Charles T. Leatherman and William F. Main.

Sources: Bounty land claims: 50-40-33717, 55-120-42450; Pension, SO 11820, WO 39884, WC 31609 (admitted 21 Feb 1881).

MAJOR, Laurence. Pvt. under Capt. William Durbin, Jr., 24 Aug - 13 Oct 1814.

MANAHAN, James. Pvt. under Capt. Galt: joined 31 Aug 1814; deserted 15 Sep 1814.

MANAHAN, Thomas. Pvt. under Capt. Upton Norris and John Fonsten; joined 2 Sep; deserted 14 Sep 1814; b. c.1779; res. in Marion Co., OH, in 1851.

Source: Bounty land claim, 50-rejected-123342.

MANN, John. Pvt. under Capt. Samuel Dawson, 21 Jul 1814; enlisted 23 Sep 1814.

MANSFIELD, John. Pvt., 20th U.S. Inf. At enlistment: 5 ft, 4 1/2 inches; age 19; b. Fred. Co., MD; enlisted 12 Aug 1812 by Capt. John Macrae for 5 yrs. Absent sick at Williamsville, May 1813, unfit for duty. Discharged at Greenbush 14 Oct 1813 on surgeon's certificate.

MANTZ, David. Corpl. under Capt. Henry Steiner, 28 Apr - 29 Jun 1813 and as 4th sergt. under Capt. Steiner, 25 Aug - 27 Sep 1814.

MANTZ, Peter. Pvt. under Capt. George W. Ent, 24 Aug - 30 Sep 1814; b. 1793; m. Feb 1822, Elizabeth Mobberly, in Fred. Co., MD. 1850 census of Fredericktown: Peter Mantz, 56, carpenter; Elizabeth, 51; Amanuel 26; Mary E., 21; Margaret 19; Peter, 16; Lewis, 14. Peter Mantz res. in Fred. Co., in 1852, 1855 and 1871 (Fredericktown); d. 4 or 5 Mar 1872, age 78 yrs, 8 mos. at his residence in Frederick, in his 79th year. His wife Elizabeth b. 3 Apr 1798; d. 21 Apr 1874. Both bur. Mt. Olivet. According to Engelbrecht's Diary, Peter Mantz, Jr., m. 6 Jan 1823.

Sources: Bounty land claims: 50-40-60541, 55-120-58399; Pension, SO 10253, SC 8782; **The Maryland Union, 7 Mar 1872; FCml; Bridge in Time; Names in Stone; Engelbrecht Diary: 1:198.**

MARFOOT, Charles. Mbr. of Crawford's "company."

MARFOOT, John. Mbr. of Crawford's "company."

THE VETERANS

MARK, George. Pvt. under Capt. Basil Dorsey, 30 Jul - 27 Sep 27 1814.

MARKELL, Jacob. Ensign under Capt. Thomas Contee Worthington,, 17 - 31 Dec 1812; m(1) Sophia ---; m(2) 23 Feb 1826, Miss Rebecca Miller at Georgetown, D.C.; d. 13 Jan 1867, in Fredericktown, age 80 yrs, 4 mos., 28 days; bur. Mt. Olivet with wife Sophia (17 Apr 1793 - 9 May 1816) and wife Rebecca (14 Jan 1790 - 2 May 1828). Rebecca was dau of Gottlob Miller of Fredericktown. [d. Greensburg, PA, 21 Dec 1825, Ezra Markell, bro. of John, Jacob and Samuel Markell of Fredericktown; d. 23 Sep 1832 of cholera in her 72nd year, Mrs. Mary Markell, mother of John and Jacob Markell.]
Sources: (**Frederick) Examiner,** 16 Jan 1867]; **Frederick-Town Herald,** 11 May 1816, 4 Mar 1826, 10 May 1828; **Names in Stone; Engelbrecht Diary:** 1:373, 381, 494; 2:28, 380.

MARKELL [Markall], John. Quartermaster under Col. John Ragan, 14 Oct - 7 Dec 1814. [Poss. related from *(Frederick) Examiner, 6 Jun 1860*: d. 3 Jun 1860, John Markell at age 78 yrs, 11 mos., 13 days, merchant; b. city of Balt.; moved to local area at age of 10 yrs; bur. Mt. Olivet Cem.]

MARKEN [Markin], Samuel. Pvt. in Capt. Daniel Marker's company of riflemen, from Middletown Valley, 16 Aug - 18 Sep 1813; b. c.1776; m. Margaret Brunner [b. c.1800], 12 Mar 1822, in Hagerstown, by James R. Reiley, German Ref. minister. He res. in Frederick C. in 1851; d. Fred. Co., 12 Jun 1854. Widow res. Fred. Co. 1 mile from Washington Co. in 1855.

Acq.: 1851 - Wesley Marken; 1855 - John Brunner, age 44, and John Dubel, age 27, res. Fred. Co., who knew Samuel Marken 32 yrs and 9 yrs, resp.; 1857 - Jacob F. Miller, age 44, res. Fred. Co., and Dr. William E. Davis, late of Fred. Co., now of Boonsboro, MD, age 27. A letter in 1856 from J. R. Humphries who had power of attorney for Margaret Marken, stated Samuel Markin went by name of Makin and the family was called by this name but the proper spelling is MARKIN.
Source: Bounty land claim, 55-120-92691.

MARKER, Daniel. Capt. of a company of riflemen from the Middletown Valley ordered out by General Winder to serve at Annapolis. Capt. Marker volunteered at Fred. Co. 15 Aug 1813; discharged at Annapolis c.30 Nov 1813; also commanded a company, 25 Aug - 30 Oct 1814, marched to Bladensburgh in Aug and afterwards to Balt. - b. c.1777; m. 26 Nov 1840, Mary Morgan (maiden name, Harkrider?) by Seymour Craig, Baptist minister in Dark Co. Daniel Marker res. in Montgomery Co. in 1850 and Dark Co, OH in 1851; d. Dark Co c.1 Jun (Jan?) 1854. Widow res. in Dark Co., OH 1855.
Acq.: 1850 - John Marker and Jacob Burns who served at same time as Daniel Marker.
Source: Bounty land claim, 55-80-23976.

MARKER, David. Pvt. under Capt. William Durbin, Jr., 24 Aug - 27 Oct 1814; b. c.1792; m. Mary Hiltebridle, 1 Nov 1850 in Carroll Co., MD, by Rev John Winters. He res. Carroll Co; d. at his residence 20 Jan 1855. Acq.: 1855 -

FREDERICK COUNTY MILITIA IN THE WAR OF 1812

Rachel Marker, age 23, and Elizabeth Harman, age 28, res. Carroll Co.

Source: Bounty land claim, 55-120-10674.

MARKER, John. Pvt. in Capt. Daniel Marker's company of "Mountain Rangers," 16 Aug - 18 Sep 1813; b. c.1788; res. in Montgomery Co., OH 1850, 1851, and Miami Co., OH, 1855. Witnesses: Daniel Marker and Jacob Burns who served with him.

Source: Bounty land claim, 55-120-17448.

MARKER, John. Pvt. under Capt. William Durbin, Jr., 24 Aug - 27 Oct 1814.

MARKEY, David. Pvt. under Capt. John Brengle, 25 Aug - 19 Sep 1814; m. 22 Mar 1796, Catharine Feaga (Humel?) (b. c.1783), in Fred. Co., by Rev Schnider. David Markey d. Fredericktown 5 Feb 1820; bur. by David F. Shaffer, Luth. minister.

Source: Bounty land claim, 55-120-38622.

MARLIN, Thomas. Pvt. under Thomas Marlin, 1 Sep - 27 Oct 1814.

MARLOW, Hanson. Pvt. under Capt. Nicholas Turbutt, 1 Sep - 27 Oct 1814; b. c.1796; m. Louisa Young, in Petersville Dist., 20 May 1824. He res. in Fred. Co., MD, 1852, 1855 and 1871 (Petersville Dist., P.O. Address: Barry, res. near Berlin; d. 13 Feb 1880, age 83 yrs, 1 month, 20 days; bur. Petersville St. Mark's Episc. Ch. with wife Louisa who d. 20 Aug 1859, age 56 and with son Henry Frazier, who d. 14 Feb 1843, age 14 yrs, 6 mos., 14 days.

Sources: Bounty land claim, 55-120-56004; Pension, SO 22009, SC 15700; (Frederick) Examiner, 25 Feb 1880, 3 Mar 1880.

MARQUERT, George. Pvt. under Capt. John Davidson, Union Light Inf., 1st Regt., District of Columbia, 15 Jul - 26 Jul 1813 and 19 Aug - 8 Oct 1814. According to tombstone, at Mt. Olivet, Frederick, b. Frederick 11 Mar 1793, d. 13 Feb 1884 from general debility; an inmate of Montevue Hospital for a number of yrs.

Sources: (Frederick) Examiner, 20 Feb 1884; Names in Stone.

MARS.., Robert Mbr. of Crawford's "company."

MARSHALL, Augustus. Pvt. under Capt. Barton Hackney, 1 Sep - 27 Oct 1814.

MARSHALL, Henry. Pvt. under Capt. William Durbin, 24 Aug - 27 Oct 1814.

MARSHALL, Robert. Mbr. of Crawford's "company."

MARTIAL, Thomas. Pvt. under Capt. Daniel Shawen; joined 5 Sep 1814; deserted 15 Sep 1814.

MARTIN, Anthony. Pvt. under Capt. John Fonsten; sick absent 29 Sep 1814, d. Balt. 21 Oct 1814; m. Robina Addlesperger [earlier application says Ensberger] (b. c.1790) in Westminster, MD, on 4 or 24 Feb 1810 [both dates given by the widow] by Rev. Zockey. Widow res. Balt. City, 1850 and 1855. Acq: 1850 - Elizabeth Bittinger and Peter Clantice. 1855 - Peter Kreis and Basil Root, res. Balt. City.

Source: Bounty land claim, 55-120-37692.

MARTIN, David. Pvt. under Capt. William Knox 17 Sep - 27 Oct 1814.

MARTIN, Ezra. Major on staff of 16th Regt. under Lieut. Colonel Steiner.

THE VETERANS

MARTIN, Jacob. Pvt. under Capt. Daniel Marker, 25 Aug - 27 Oct 1814.

MARTIN, John. Corpl. under Capt. Philip Smith, 23 May - 8 Sep 1813; said he also served as sergt. major in the comapny commanded by Samuel Duvall in regt. commanded by Col. Jacob Cramer from early part of Jul 1814 and discharged in city of Washington 14 Nov 1814; b. c.1777; res. in Fredericktown in 1852.
Source: Bounty land claim, 50-80-48481.

MARTIN, John. Pvt. under Capt. Joseph Wood, 27 Aug - 28 Oct 1814.

MARTIN, Peter. Pvt. under Capt. Samuel Dawson, 17 May - 5 Jul 1813.

MARTZ, George. Apppt'd Capt. of a militia company in 16th Regt, MM, 15 Jul 1814; d. 23 Feb 1868 at his res near Fredericktown, age 81 yrs, 11 mos., 23 days. Catherine, wife of Major George Martz, d. 20 Jan 1858, age 79 yrs, 10 mos., 12 days.
Sources: Md. Union, 3 Feb 1858, 5 Mar 1868.

MASAW, John. Pvt. under Capt. Daniel Shawen, 5 Sep - 27 Oct 1814.

MATHIAS, Griff. Pvt. under Capt. Philip Smith, 29 May - 8 Sep 1813. [Prob. same Griffith Mathias bur. at Creagerstown, St. Johns Luth. and Ref. Ch., d. 2 Nov 1851, age 64 with Susan Mathias who d. 16 Dec 1875, age 96. 1850 census of Creagerstown Dist.: Griffith Mathias, 60, b. PA, pauper; Susan, 70; Mary Hepper, 67.]

MATHIAS, John. 1st sergt. under Capt. John Fonsten, 2 Sep - 27 Oct 1814; b. c.1782; res. Carroll Co., MD, 1850. Witnesses: 1855 - Jacob Mathias and James L. Switzer, res. Carroll Co.
Source: Bounty land claim, 55-120-60527.

MATTERN, Peter Pvt. under Capt. Nicholas Turbutt, went to Balt. in 1814, discharged 1 Nov 1814.

MATTHEWS, Lewis. He said he volunteered as a fifer in the company of Capt. Samuel Ogle in Fred. Co., MD, c.1 Apr 1813; b. c.1792; m. --- who d. at Slipping Rock, PA, 9 Aug 1869. He res. in Slipping Rock, Lawrence Co., PA, in 1871.

[*Moravian Families of Graceham, Maryland* - Louis Matthews (Matthus) son of Philip Matthews b. in Fred. Co., m. 21 Dec 1814 Sarah Leinbach who was b. 11 Aug 1791 in Fred. Co., dau of Christian and Anna Rosina (Paus) Leinbach. Christian Leinbach, son of Frederick and Elizabeth Leinbach, b. at Skippack 13 Feb 1739; d. 13 Jul 1792; m. 30 Apr 1782, Anna Rosina Paus, dau of Christian and Magdalena (Frey) Paus. Christian Paus b. 5 Oct 1710 in Bergord, Lower Hungary. For more details on Leinbach and Paus families see *Moravian Families of Graceham, Md.*]
Sources: Pension, SO 23245 - rejected 12 May 1874 by reason of presumptive abandonment.

MATTINGLEY, Gabriel J. Pvt. under Capt. John Brengle, 25 Aug - 19 Sep 1814.

MATTINGLY, Gabriel. Pvt. under Lieut. Kolb, 13 Oct - 15 Nov 1814 in a det. which guarded British prisioners at the Frederick Barracks.

MATTINGLY, Thomas. Pvt. under Capt. Daniel Marker, 25 Aug - 27 Oct 1814.

MATZENBAUGH, Daniel. Pvt. under Capt. Samuel Dawson. He said he and his capt. lived in Funkstown at the time, both blacksmiths. His widow thought that he entered into service at Hagerstown in Jun, served 3 weeks, when he hired substitute, Joseph Zimmerman, and paid him fifty dollars per month. Zimmerman was a shoemaker in Balt. Daniel Matzenbaugh m. Barbary Zimmerman (b. c.1790), 29 Nov 1812, in Hagerstown, by Rev. Shaffer; d. Franklin Square, Franklin, Columbiana Co., OH, 6 Jun 1840. His widow res. Washingtonville, Columbiania Co., OH. Acq.: 1860 - Samuel Matzenbaugh, fifer, and John Matzenbaugh, pvt. - both served in same company; 1872 - Jacob Bossert and John Ryan. 1873 - Susanna Bossert dau of Barbary Matzenbaugh.

Sources: Bounty land claim, 55-160-99841; Pension, WO 4807, WC 2193 (admitted 23 Mar 1872).

MAY, Benjamin. Pvt. under Capt. Jacob Getzendanner, 9 Aug - 17 Sep 1813.

MAY, Charles. Pvt. under Capt. Samuel Dawson, 21 Jul 1814 - 10 Jan 1815; b. c.1792; m. Henrietta May, in Fred. Co., MD; res. Pickaway Co., OH, 1851, Grove City, Franklin Co., OH, 1871. Henrietta May d. c.1844. He d. Friday, 5 Aug 1881, at home of his dau Elisabeth Newton (wife of Mahlon A. Newton) with whom he had lived since 1875; bur. Mt. Pulaski Cem., Mt. Pulaski, Logan Co., IL. Acq.: 1881 - M. P. Pinney, M.D., who treated Charles May several times in last 3 yrs.

Source: Bounty land claim, 50-80-24525 (admitted 22 Jun 1871).

MAY, John. Pvt. under Capt. Barton Hackney, 10 Sep - 27 Oct 1814; b. c.1795; m. Magdalena Rohrer at Washington Co., MD, May 1817; res. Pickaway Co., OH, in 1851, 1855 and 1871 (near East Ringgold).

Sources: Bounty land claim, 55-120-37501; Pension, SO 7216, SC 23146 (rejected - insufficient service).

MAYBERRY, Israel. Pvt. under Capt. George W. Ent, 24 Aug - 30 Sep 1814; b. 1793; res. Allegany Co, MD, 1851 and Hampshire Co, VA, 1855.

Source: Bounty land claim, 55-120-59565.

MAYERS, Lawrence. Mbr. of Crawford's "company."

McALROY - See McUlroy.

McATEE, Leonard. 2nd U.S. Light Dragoons, under Capt. J. R. Stokes. At enlistment: 5 ft, 11 3/4 inches, age 24; b. Fred. Co., MD; enlisted 27 Dec 1812 for 18 mos. Mustered at Salisbury, NC, 29 Dec 1812.

McBARE, Charles. Pvt. under Capt. George W. Magee, from 22 Jul until he enlisted 25 Jul 1814.

McBEE, William. Pvt. under Capt. Joseph Wood, 27 Aug - 28 Oct 1814.

McCAHAN - See Mechan.

McCALLEY, John James. 1st Sergt. under Capt. Thomas Contee Worthington,, 17 - 31 Dec 1812 and Ensign under George W. Ent, 24 Aug - 30 Sep 1814; b. 27 Apr 1793; d. 15 Apr 1825; m. Elizabeth Brunner (16 Aug 1795 - 8 Dec

THE VETERANS

1867). [Mrs. Elizabeth McCulley d. in her 72nd year at residence of her son-in-law, John C. Hardt in Frederick.]

Sources: Engelbrecht Diary: 1:267, 337; Names in Stone; FCml; (Frederick) Examiner, 18 Dec 1867.

McCANN, John. Mbr. of Crawford's "company."

McCARTY, Anthony. Pvt., 3rd U.S. Inf., under Capt. Moore. At enlistment: 5 ft, 5 inches; had grey eyes, light hair and light complexion; age 28; prev. occupation boatman; b. Fred. Co., MD; enlisted 8 Aug 1808 at Fredericktown by Lieut Bowie, for 5 yrs. Appears to have re-enlisted 30 Apr 1813 at English Turn by Capt. Dinkins for duration of war. At Fort Pierce 18 Jan 1814. Tried by Regt. Court Martial 4 Aug 1814 for fighting - acquitted. New Orleans 16 Feb 1815.

McCARTY, Joseph. Pvt., U.S. Artillery. At enlistment: 5 ft, 8 inches; grey eyes, black hair, dark complexion; age 33; laborer; b. Fredericktown, MD; enlisted 23 Oct 1813 at Savannah by Capt. Robinson for 5 yrs. Discharged 22 Oct 1818.

McCAY [McCoy?], Samuel. 3rd sergt. under Capt. Samuel Dawson, 21 Jul 1814 - 10 Jan 1815.

McCLAIN, George. Pvt. under Capt. Henry Steiner, 25 Aug - 27 Sep 1814.

McCLAIN, James. Pvt. under Capt. George W. Magee; joined 22 Jul 1814; deserted 30 Aug 1814.

McCLASKEY, William. Pvt. from Balt. under Capt. Samuel Dawson, 21 Jul - 10 Jan 1815.

McCLEAN (McLeane), Charles. Pvt. under Capt. Samuel McDonald, 6th Regt., Baltimore City; d. 27 Oct 1863, native of Baltimore City, age 73 yrs, 10 mos., 24 days, 41 yrs; res. Fred. Co.; bur. Mt. Olivet with wife Julia A., who d. 23 Jul 1870, age 62 yrs, 4 mos., 21 days; 1850 Census of Liberty Dist.: Charles McLain, 60, cooper; Julianna, 40; Margarett E., 9; Charles A. 8; George E., 5; Fanny B., 3.

Sources: Names in Stone; Bridge in Time; (Frederick) Examiner, 3 Aug 1870; The Maryland Union, 4 Aug 1870.

McCLEERY, Robert. Pvt. under Capt. George W. Ent, 24 Aug - 30 Sep 1814.

McCLOUD, Thomas. Pvt. under Capt. Joseph Wood, 27 Aug - 28 Oct 1814; "sick in hospital."

McCOLEN, Samuel. Pvt. under Capt. Samuel Dawson, 14 Oct 1814 - 10 Jan 1815.

McCONLEY, Samuel. Pvt. under James F. Huston from 23 Jul 1814 and later under Capt. Joseph Green, from 14 Oct 1814 until he enlisted on 3 Nov 1814.

McCORMICK, George. Pvt. under Capt. Nicholas Turbutt, joined 1 Sep 1814; discharged 1 Nov 1814; b. 1796; res. Fred. Co. 1855.

Source: Bounty land claim, 55-120-3920.

McCOY, Samuel. Pvt. under Capt. Samuel Ogle, 1 May - 5 Jul 1813.

McCRAY, James. Fifer under Capt. Samuel Dawson, 26 Jul 1814 - deserted 29 Sep 1814.

McCRAY, William. Pvt. under Capt. Samuel Dawson, 26 Jul - 10 Jan 1815.

McCUMSAY, William. Mbr. of Crawford's "company."

McDANEL, George. Pvt. under Capt. Samuel Dawson; joined 21 Jul; deserted 25 Jul 1814.

McDANIEL, Jacob. Pvt. under Capt. Philip Smith; joined 23 May 1813; deserted 27 Aug 1813.

McDANIEL, John. Pvt. in Capt. George Flautt's rifle company, 29 Apr - 29 Jun 1813; discharged at Fort McHenry Jul 1814; said he stood guard at Ft. McHenry for about 3 weeks; b. c.1790; m. Mary McDaniel. She d. c.1840. He res. in Fairfield Co., OH, 1850, 1855, 1871 (Liberty St, P.O. address: Basil). [Enquiry dated 12 Feb 1906, Basil, OH, from Sherman McDaniel asking about John McDaniel.]

Sources: Bounty land claim, 50-40-2900, 55-120-76550; Pension, SO 3206, SC 1391.

McDANIEL, Joseph. Pvt. under Capt. John Fonsten, 2 Sep - 27 Oct 1814; RES. 15 miles from Westminster; m. 3 Jan 1811, Mary Evers (b. c.1791) in Fred. Co., MD, by Joshua Jones. Joseph McDaniel d. Knox Co., OH, 23 Aug 1847. Widow res. Knox Co., OH, 1854. Acq.: 1854 - David McDaniel, present at the wedding; William P. Crain and William Lefever.

Source: Bounty land claim, 50-40-99983.

McDAVITT, Peter. Pvt. under Capt. Barton Hackney; joined 1 Sep 1814; deserted 23 Oct 1814.

McDAVITT, William. Pvt. under Capt. Samuel Dawson, 1 May - 5 Jul 1813.

McDERMOT, Richard. Pvt. under Capts. James F. Huston and Joseph Green, from 23 Jul 1814 until he deserted 16 Dec.

McDERMOT, Richard. Pvt. from Upper Frederick under Capt. James F. Huston, 23 Jul 1814 - 13 Oct 1814.

McDEVITT, John. Pvt. under Capt. George W. Ent, 24 Aug - 30 Sep 1814.

McDEVITT, Peter. Pvt. under Lieut. Kolb, 2 Nov - 15 Nov 1814 in a det. assigned to guard the British prisoners at the Frederick Barracks.

McFARLAN, Peter. Pvt. under Capt. Joseph Wood, 27 Aug - 28 Oct 1814; sick absent with leave 12 Oct.

McFARLAND, Peter. Pvt. under Capt. Henry Steiner, 25 Aug Aug - 27 Sep 1814.

McGEE, James. Pvt. under Capt. John Fonsten, 2 Sep - 27 Oct 1814; sick absent 24 Sep 1814.

McGINIS, Thomas. Pvt. under Capt. Samuel Ogle, 1 May 1813 - 5 Jul 1813.

McGINNISS, Henry. Pvt. under Capt. Samuel Dawson, 1 May - 5 Jul 1813.

McGRAW, John. 5th U.S. Inf. At enlistment: 5 ft, 7 inches; blue eyes, dark hair and dark complexion; age 27; laborer; b. Fred. Co., MD; enlisted 18 Oct 1814 at Lancaster by Lt. Rea for 5 yrs. Mustered at Harrisburgh, PA, 31 Oct 1814. Deserted 21 or 24 Oct 1814 from Lancaster.

McGRAW, John. 36th U.S. Inf.; b. Fred. Co., MD(?); enlisted 2 Mar 1814 at Annapolis by Capt. Deneal for duration of war. Mustered at Georgetown, D. C. March 1814. Deserted 10 Jun and taken 17 Nov, 1814. Confined by order of court martial at Ft. McHenry for

THE VETERANS

desertion 10 Jun 1814. Discharged 30 March 1815 at contonment near Fort Covington.

McHENRY, Benjamin. 4th sergt. under Capt. Samuel Ogle, 1 May - 5 Jul 1813, and 4th sergt. under Capt. Joseph Wood, joined 27 Aug; furloughed 4 Oct, returned 16 Oct; discharged 13 Oct 1814.

McINTIRE, James Pvt. under Capt. Samuel Duvall, 3 Aug - 3 Oct 1814.

McINZIE [McInsey, McKinsey, McKinzie], Austin [Augustine]. Pvt. under Capt. Fonsten, 2 Sep - 27 Oct 1814; res. 3 miles from Westminster; m. 31 Jan 1820, Mary Ford (b. c.1799) in Fred. Co. by Rev. Graver. Marr. license reads Augustine McKinzie and Mary Ford. Austin McInsey d. 8 Aug 1849 Seneca Co., OH. Widow res. Seneca Co., OH, 1851 and Allen Co., OH, 1855.

Source: Bounty land claim, 55-160-21450.

McKINNEY, John. Pvt. under Capt. John Galt, 31 Aug - 27 Oct 1814; res. within 5 miles of Taneytown in 1814.

McKINSTREY, Joseph. 2nd sergt. from New Windsor, under Capt. George W. Magee, later 1st sergant under Capt. Magee, 22 Jul 1814 - 10 Jan 1815.

McKISSIC, James. Pvt. under Capt. John Galt; joined 31 Aug 1814; sick absent 14 Oct 1814.

McKLEY, George. Pvt. under Capt. John Fonsten, 2 Sep - 27 Oct 1814; enlisted in the regulary army 27 Sep 1814.

McKNITT, William. 3rd sergt. from New Windsor, later 2nd sergt., under Capt. George W. Magee, 22 Jul 1814 - 10 Jan 1815.

McMAHAN, Jerry. Pvt. under Capt. Samuel Dawson, 1 May - 5 Jul 1813.

McMILLAN, Thomas. Pvt. under Capt. Nicholas Turbutt, 1 Sep - 27 Oct 1814; b. c.1788; res. Marshall Co., WV in 1871 (P.O. address: Henry Fork), Roane Co., WV; lives in Marshall Co., WV.

Sources: Bounty land claim, 55-120-66648; Pension, SO 22982 (rejected because of insufficient service - 1 mo., 29 days).

McMULIN, James. Pvt. under Capt. Jacob Alexander, 22 Jul - 19 Sep 1814.

McMULIN, William. Pvt. under Capt. Jacob Alexander, 22 Jul - 19 Sep 1814.

McMULLEN, Samuel. Pvt. under Capt. Daniel Marker 16 Aug - 18 Sep 1813.

McMULLIN, John. Pvt. under Capt. Samuel Dawson, 1 May - 5 Jul 1813.

McMULLIN, Samuel. Pvt. under Capt. Samuel Dawson, 13 Sep - 13 Oct 1814.

McMULLIN, Thomas. Pvt. under Capt. Nicholas Turbutt, went to Balt. in 1814, discharged 1 Nov 1814.

McOYE, Henry. Pvt. under Capt. John Fonsten, 2 Sep - 27 Oct 1814; res. 15 miles from Westminster.

McPHERSON, Robert Grier. Pvt. under Capt. Henry Steiner, 28 Apr - 29 Jun 1813 and under 1st lieut. under Capt. Henry Steiner, 25 Aug - 27 Sep 1814; b. 22 Mar 1788; d. (Major Robert Grier McPherson) in his 37th year, 19 Aug 1824, at Belle Air, son of Col. John McPherson. His widow, Maria, b. 5 Dec 1792 in PA; m. 18 May 1827, Dr. William Bradley Tyler; she d. 29 Oct 1866. Both bur. Mt. Olivet Cem.

Sources: **Frederick-Town Herald**, 21 Aug 1824; Englebrecht Diary, 1: 290, 447; Names in Stone; Bridge in Time.

McPHERSON, William. Pvt. under Capt. Samuel Ogle; joined 1 May 1813; enlisted 2 Jun 1813.

McPHERSON, William. Pvt. under Capt. Henry Steiner, 3 - 27 Sep 1814.

McPHERSON, William Smith. Pvt. in 1st artillery, under Capt. Henry Steiner, 25 Aug - 27 Sep 1814; said he acted as corpl. at Battle of North Point; stationed on Loudenslayers Hill in charge of a battery of 6 guns; b. c.1794; m(1) Catharine C. David dau of John N. David of Phila.; she d. 20 Mar 1832 in her 35th year. Three of their children d. of scarlet fever: Howard d. 14 Dec 1832 in his 5th year; Sarah Ann d. 15 Dec 1832, age c.13 yrs; Henry, age 3 yrs, on 24 Dec 1832. Dr. William S. McPherson m(2) 21 Jul 1835 at Annapolis, Mrs. Harriet Neth (b. c.1809), dau of Samuel, by Rev. George McElhenney. Harriet prev. m. Louis Neth who d. 10 Oct 1832 in Annapolis. At enrollment: 5 ft, 9 inches tall, age 20 yrs; brown hair, gray eyes, light complexion; physician and farmer. He res. City of Balt., 1854, 1877, 1878 (317 Park Ave.). After marriage they res. Fred. Co. 8 yrs at Prospect Hill; moved to Balt. in 1843; res. 112 Franklin St., Balt.; 63 Green St., Balt.; Woodfoud(?) Hall, Howard Co., MD; and then in Balt. City: 56 Carey St., 227 Druid Hill Ave, 169 and 175 Hoffman St., 338 & 317 Park Ave. Harriet res. No. 57 N. Carrollton, Balt. (P.O. Address: 23 N. Calvert St.) in 1880.

Acq.: 1878 - John W. Kennedy, age 67, res. Hagerstown, MD, acq. 45 yrs; 1879 - John G. Proud and Robert M. Proud of Balt. 1880 - Mary R. Brooke, age 66, 303 Park Ave., Balt.; and Elizabeth Worthington, age 65, 177 No. Stricker St., Balt., both acq. with Harriet 50 yrs. In 1880 Rev. Osb. Ingle stated the Ch. records of All Saints Parish, Fred. Co., showed that Catharine McPherson d. 20 Mar 1832.

Sources: Bounty land claim, 55-160-1143211; Pension, SO 30767, SC 22524, WO 39272, WC 29904 (dropped 17 Jun 1885); Williams, **History of Fred. Co.**; Engelbrecht Diary: 2:46, 59, 169.

McULROY/McALROY, James. Pvt. under Capt. Joseph Wood, 10 Sep - 28 Oct 1814.

McVAY, John. Pvt. under Capt. John Galt, 31 Aug - 27 Oct 1814; b. c.1794 in Ireland; m. Jane McVey, at Greenfield, Wayne Co, MI, 5 Aug 1827, each for first time, by John Burbank, J.P. At enlistment: 5 ft, 8 inches tall, light complexion, light brown hair, blue eyes, farmer. John McVay d. at Brownstown, Wayne Co., 14 Nov 1863. After his death his widow lived with son, John McVay at Waterloo, Jackson Co., MI (P.O. address: Grass Lake, P.O. Box 250), except for two yrs which she spent in IL. By 1878 she was too infirm to travel; d. 17 Nov 1879.

Acq.: 1878 - Jackson Simpson, age 62 and Sarah Simpson, age 57, res. Waterloo, acq. 24 yrs; 1879 - John McVay, requests reimbursement for coffin $26.00, digging grave $2.00 and physician $9.00.

Sources: Bounty land claim, 50-40-46403, 55-120-4822; Pension, WO 26024, WC 16364.

McVICKER [McViker], David. Pvt. under Capt. John Brengle, 25 Aug - 19 Sep 1814.

McVICKERS, David. Pvt. under Lieut. Kolb, 13 Oct - 15 Nov 1814, in det. assigned to guard the British prisoners at Frederick Barracks.

McVAY. See McWay.

McWILLIAMS, Clement. Pvt. in 1st Cav. Dist., 26 Aug - 3 Sep 1814.

McWILLIAMS, James. Pvt. under Capt. John Fonsten, 2 Sep - 27 Oct 1814; res. 6 miles from Westminster.

MEARLE, Nicholas 3rd sergt. under Capt. Daniel Marker 16 Aug - 18 Sep 1813.

MEASLE, Daniel. Pvt. from Upper Fred. Co., under Capt. James F. Huston and under Capt. Joseph Green, from 23 Jul 1814, until he deserted 4 Dec 1814.

MEASLE [Measell], Jacob. Pvt. under Capt. Nicholas Turbutt, 1 Sep - 27 Oct 1814. A few yrs after discharge, his house was robbed and certificate of discharge stolen - b. Oct 1790; m. Mary Heffner (b. c.1793), in Frederick, MD, by Rev. Shafer, c.12 Jun 1814; res. Scipio Twp, Seneca Co, OH 1871. He d. 31 Jul 1873 at Scipio. Widow res. Scipio Township (P.O. address: Republic) in 1873.

Acq.: 1873 - Dr. H. K. Spooner res. Republic 13 yrs, family physician of Jacob Measle 13 yrs; stated Mary Measle is very aged and infirm, being corpulant diseased in her ft and limbs. Frederick Wadams and John A. Smith, res. Scipio Township, each lived 10 or more yrs near neighbor to Jacob Measle. Mrs. Catharine Strong, age 78, last Apr, b. and raised Fred. Co., MD, knew Jacob and Mary Measle when children; she and Jacob Measle were cousins; knew them in MD and past 25 yrs in OH; said they raised a large family. Michael Heffner, age 74, bro. of Mary Measle; states that when Jacob was enrolled in the militia his sister, Mary, came home to her father's home where he also still lived.

Sources: Pension, SO 9561, SC 5420 (admitted 26 Sep 1871), WO 10415, WC 5857 (admitted 20 Dec 1873, dropped 4 Sep 1876 for failure to claim pension).

MEASLE [Meazle, Missell], Valentine. Pvt. under Capts. James F. Huston and under Joseph Green, 23 Jul 1814 - until he left to enlist in regular army 28 Nov (according to militia company muster roll). Army enlistment register indicates he enlisted 5 Nov 1814 at Balt., served in 26th U.S. Inf. as pvt. At enlistment: 5 ft, 6 inches, black eyes, dark hair, dark complexion, 21 yrs of age, shoemaker, b. Fred. Co., MD. Discharged from Capt. William Bezean's det. at Philadelphia 23 March 1815 at end of enlistment.

MECHAN/McCAHAN, John. Pvt. under Capt. Joseph Wood, 27 Aug - 28 Oct 1814; lost cartridge box.

MEDARY, John. Pvt. under Capt. Denton Darby, 3 Aug - 8 Nov 1814. Absent 6 days.

MEDCALF, Thomas. Pvt. under Capt. William Durbin, Jr.; joined 24 Aug 1814; left militia to enlist in regular army 15 Sep 1814. Army enlistment register indicates he served as pvt. in 14th U.S. Inf.; enlisted at Balt., 15 Oct 1814 by Capt. Cummings for 5 yrs. Promoted to sergt.; served in Capt. D. Cummings' det. at Balt. At enlistment: 5 ft, 10 1/2 inches, dark eyes, brown hair, dark complexion, 37 yrs of age, blacksmith, b. Tawney [Taneytown?], MD.

MEDLEY, Thomas. Pvt. under Lieut. Kolb, 13 Oct - 15 Nov 1814, in det. assigned to guard British prisoners at Frederick Barracks.

MEDTART, Lewis. Pvt. under Capt. George W. Ent, 24 Aug - 30 Sep 1814; b. 24 Jan 1791; res. Fred. Co., MD, 1855; d. 15 Nov 1862; postmaster of Fredericktown; bur. Mt. Olivet Cem. by Adam Lodge No. 35 I.O.O.F.

Source: Pension, 55-120-14934; **(Frederick) Examiner** 19 Nov 1862.

MELAND, Edward. Pvt. under Capt. Jacob Getzendanner, 26 Jul - 21 Aug 1814.

MERCIER (Mercer), Cornelius. Pvt. under Capt. Dennis Barnes, Nace's Regt., Balt. Co., 18 Aug - 10 Sep 1813; b. 1794, Fred. Co. son of Richard Mercier; m. 17 Dec 1829, Miss Sarah Gaither, dau of Major Samuel and Ruth (Shipley) Gaither; d. Fred. Co.

Sources: Williams, **History of Fred. Co.**; **Frederick-Town Herald**, 19 Dec 1829.

MERRITT, James. Pvt. under Capt. Samuel Dawson, 14 Oct 1814 - deserted 29 Oct 1814.

MERRITT, James. Pvt. from Upper Frederick under James F. Huston and Capt. Joseph Green, Joseph, 23 Jul 1814 - 10 Jan 1815; res. Fredericktown in 1814.

MERTINA, Jacob. Pvt. under Capt. Matthew Murray; joined 25 Aug 1814; absent from 4 Oct 1814.

MESSINGS, John. Corpl., 17th U.S. Inf. At enlistment: 5 ft, 10 inches; blue eyes, sandy hair, fair complexion; age 40; blacksmith; b. Fredericktown, MD; enlisted 9 Apr 1814 at Chillicothe, OH, by Lieut. Carney for duration of war. Discharged at Chillicothe, OH, 9 Jun 1815.

MESSLER, John. Pvt. under Capt. John Fonsten, 2 Sep - 27 Oct 1814; res. 12 miles from Westminster.

METCALF, Hezekiah. Reported by Capt. Duvall as deserting from camp at Bladensburg 24 Aug 1814; substitute, aged 45-50 yrs; dark complexion, gray eyes, dark hair, about 5 ft, 7-8 inches, a "collier, laborer or drunkard." Not on muster rolls.

METCALF, Mordecai. Corpl., 22nd U.S. Inf. At enlistment: 5 ft, 11 inches; black eyes, black hair, dark complexion; age 20; miller; b. Fredericksburg, MD [sic]; enlisted 7 or 17 Jun 1814 by Lieut. Morrow for 5 yrs. Mustered in Lieut. J. R. Guy's Det., Fort Fayette, 16 Jun 1814. Ordered to Buffalo 16 Jun 1814. Joined at Buffalo from Lieut Guy's Det. 30 Sep 1814. Absent at Buffalo since 2 Oct 1814 by reason of sickness. At Shomac Bay 31 Dec 1816 and 28 Feb 1817. Confined at Watertown jail by civil authority. Sent to state prison for 5 yrs 31 Jan 1818. Dropped from rolls.

METCALF, Thomas. Pvt., 14th U.S. Inf. At enlistment: 5 ft, 10 1/2 inches; dark eyes, brown hair, dark complexion; age 37; prev. occupation blacksmith; b. Tawney [Taneytown?], Fred. Co., MD; enlisted 15 Oct 1814 in Balt. by Capt. Cummings for 5 yrs. Mustered by Capt. D. Cummings's Det., Balt. 16 Feb, 31 Mar and 30 Apr 1815, present as sergt.

METCALF, William. Pvt. under Capt. Joseph Wood, 10 Sep - 28 Oct 1814.

METZ, George. Pvt. under Capt. Samuel Dawson, joined 14 Oct 1814; deserted 6 Dec 1814.

METZ, John William (William John?). Pvt. from Upper Fred. Co., MD, under Capt. James F. Huston/Capt. Joseph Green, 23 Jul until he deserted on 12 Dec 1814. (prob. same William Metz who d. 5 Dec 1860 in his 86th year at his residence in Frederick; native of Germany; bur. Mt. Olivet; mbr. of "United Brothers of the War of 1812.")
Source: (Frederick) Examiner, 12 Dec 1860.

MICHAEL, Andrew. Pvt. under Capt. Samuel Dawson; joined 21 Jul 1814; enlisted 5 Nov 1814.

MICHAEL, Charles W. Fifer under Capt. Fonsten, 2 Sep - 27 Oct 1814; b. c.1788; m. 12 May 1825, Maria C. Scott at Bedford Co., PA. He res. in Lewistown, Fulton Co., IL, 1850, 1871.

Acq.: 1852 - John Beaver recalled that Charles Michael had presented him with a fife gemmet 1 or 2 days before the discharge of the company. According to Beaver, Charles Michael played his fife with the fife major for a short period of the tour. 1871 - Henry L. Bryant and Martin Eichelberger, res. Lewistown, IL; Reuben R. McDowell and Lewis W. Ross, both state that Charles W. Michael had lived in the neighborhood c.25 yrs.
Source: Pension, SO 7429, SC 20348 - initially rejected as insufficient service under Capt. Fonsten but later approved after earlier service under Capt. Kerlinger was also proved.

MICHAEL, Henry. Pvt. under Capt. Mathew Murray, 25 Aug - 30 Oct 1814; d. 23 Mar 1863, at residence of John Crone, Middletown, in his 79nd year.
Source: (Frederick) Examiner, 1 Apr 1863.

MICHAEL, John. Fifer under Capt. William Durbin, Jr., 24 Aug - 27 Oct 1814.

MICHAEL, John. Pvt. under Capt. Barton Hackney, 10 Sep - 27 Oct 1814; b. c.1791; res. Fred. Co. in 1855.
Source: Bounty land claim, 55-160-22113.

MICHAEL, Lewis. Pvt. under Capt. Samuel Dawson, 1 May - 5 Jul 1813.

MICHAEL, Lewis. Pvt. under Capt. Matthew Murray, 25 Aug - 27 Oct 1814.

MICKLE, Conrad. 2nd sergt. under Capt. Daniel Marker 16 Aug - 18 Sep 1813.

MILES, William. From Washington Co., pvt. under Capt. Samuel Dawson, 14 Oct 1814 - 10 Jan 1815.

MILLEN, Jacob. Pvt. under Capt. Samuel Ogle, 1 May - 5 Jul 1813.

MILLER, Charles. 1st sergt. under Capt. Matthew Murray, 25 Aug - 27 Oct 1814; b. c.1793; res. Clermont Co., OH, 1851, 1855.
Sources: Bounty land claims, 50-40-20935, 55-120-3846.

MILLER, Christian. Pvt. under Capt. Barton Hackney, 1 Sep - 27 Oct 1814.

FREDERICK COUNTY MILITIA IN THE WAR OF 1812

MILLER, Frederick. Pvt. under Capt. Philip Smith, 23 May 1813; enlisted 10 Jul 1813.

MILLER, Frederick. 4th corpl. under Capt. Joseph Wood, 27 Aug - 13 Oct 1814. and 3d corpl., 14 Oct - 28 Oct 1814.

MILLER, George. Pvt. under Capt. Jacob Getzendanner, 26 Jul - 21 Aug 1814.

MILLER, George. Pvt. under Capt. Philip Smith, 23 May - 8 Sep 1813; b. 9 Oct 1791; d. 14 Jan 1861 of dropsy; 1850 census of Creagerstown Dist.: George Miller, 58; Catherine, 44; Manerva A., 19; George W., 15; Jacob L., 14; William H., 12; John I., 10; Lewis E., 8; Thomas E., 6; Charles, 3; Martha Metcalf, 20. He owned farm of 200 acres. Catharine Miller d. 14 Mar 1875, age 68 yrs, 5 mos., 5 days. Dates on her tombstone: 10 Oct 1806 - 15 Mar 1875. Both George and Catherine Miller bur. Creagerstown, St. John's Luth. and Reformed Ch..

Sources: Bounty land claim, 55-120-19007; **Bridge in Time; (Frederick) Examiner,** 25 Mar 1875; **Names in Stone.**

MILLER, George. Pvt. under Capt. Thomas Contee Worthington, 17 - 31 Dec 1812; sick on leave when the company was discharged; b. c.1790; res. Fred. Co., 1850, 1855. Acq.: 1854/1855 - Charles Moore, res. Frederick City, served in Worthington's company; Jacob Markel, ensign of same company.

Source: Bounty land claim, 55-80-6944.

MILLER, George. Pvt. under Capt. Daniel Shawen; joined 5 Sep 1814; sick absent 6 Oct 1814.

MILLER, Henry. Pvt. under Capt. Samuel Duvall, 3 Aug - 3 Oct 1814.

MILLER, Jacob. Pvt. under Capt. Daniel Marker, 16 Aug - 18 Sep 1813.

MILLER, Jacob. 36th U.S. Inf., under Col. Henry Carberry. At enlistment: 5 ft, 5 inches; age 27; b. Fred. Co., MD; enlisted 18 May 1813 at Frederick, MD, by Lieut. Thos. Ritchie for 1 year. Mustered by Capt. C. C. Randolph's company 30 Sep and 31 Oct 1813. Capt. Hugh W. Deneale's company 1 March 1814.

MILLER, John. "Col. John Miller ... of Sabillasville, in Fred. Co., died rather suddenly at his residence a fortnight ago, in the 78th year of his age. ... responded to his country's call in the War of 1812 and did noble service in the tented field." He d. 15 Dec 1867 of Dropsey, aged 77 yrs, 8 mos., 22 days. His wife Polly (b. 27 Feb 1802, d. 16 Nov 1875). 1850 census of Fred. Co.: John Miller, 60, saw miller; Mary, 48; Hiram, 17; Elizabeth J., 15; Thomas J., 12; Washington, 10.

Source: **The Maryland Union,** 2 Jan 1868. [Because of his being a commissioned officer it appears likely that this is same John Miller who served as 2nd Lieut. under Capt. Samuel Dawson.]

MILLER, John (hatter). The fol. information appears to relate to one person named John Miller, occupation hatter: b. 14 Aug 1774; d. c.22 Aug 1827. He had three wives; his last wife, Sarah Miller d. 11 Apr 1827. Perhaps he is one of the veterans named John Miller in the following entries. David Miller son of John Miller (hatter) m. 26 Sep 1839,

THE VETERANS

Miss Christiana Haller dau of Joshua Haller.
Source: **Engelbrecht Diary**: 1:433, 461; 2:357.

MILLER, John. 2nd Lieut. under Capt. Samuel Dawson, 21 Jul 1814 - 10 Jan 1815.

MILLER, John. Pvt. under Capt. George W. Ent, 3rd Regt, 24 Aug - 30 Sep 1814.

MILLER, John. Pvt. under Capt. Henry Steiner; could not join because of sickness for period company served, 25 Aug - 27 Sep 1814.

MILLER, John. Corpl. from Mechanickstown; transferred to Capt. George W. Magee, on 23 Sep 1814; discharged 10 Jan 1815.

MILLER, John. Pvt. under Capt. Samuel Dawson, 1 May - 5 Jul 1813.

MILLER, John. Pvt. under Capt. Daniel Shawen; joined 5 Sep 1814; d. 9 Oct 1814.

MILLER, John. 1st corpl. under Capt. Daniel Shawen, 5 Sep - 27 Oct 1814. [Note that there were two men named John Miller serving in Capt. Shawen's company.]

MILLER, John W. Pvt. under Lieut. William Kolb 13 Oct - 15 Nov 1814, at Frederick Barricks on special service to guard the British prisoners; b. ca 1795; m. Ann Catharine Kolb, in Fredericktown 24 Feb 1812 (?). He res. Fredericktown 1872; d. Jul 1873.

Letter dated 7 May 1886 from son of John Miller, Currensville, Clearfield Co., PA, stated his father's pension was put aside in Aug 1871. He kept his father 15 yrs before he died.

Source: Bounty land claim, 55-160-2046; Pension, SO 28017 (rejected by reason of insufficient service - 34 days).

MILLER, Leonard. Pvt. under Capt. Samuel Dawson, 1 May - 5 Jul 1813.

MILLER, Leonard. 4th sergt. under Capt. Matthew Murray, 25 Aug - 27 Oct 1814; b. c.1783; res. Fred. Co., MD, 1852. Acq.: 1852 - Henry Herring, ensign of Capt. Murray's company, and Jeremiah Frazier, pvt. same company.
Source: Bounty land claim, 50-rejected-160004. [no apparent reason for the rejection. Ed.]

MILLER, Martin. Pvt. under Captian Samuel Dawson, 1 May - 5 Jul 1813 and 21 Jul - 10 Jan 1815.

MILLER, Peter. Pvt. under Capt. Samuel Duvall, 3 Aug - 3 Oct 1814.

MILLER, Philip Pvt. under Capt. Samuel Dawson, 21 Jul until he deserted on 1 Oct 1814.

MILLER, Valentine. Pvt. under Capt. William Durbin; joined 24 Aug 1814; discharged 9 Sep 1814 for inability.

MILLS, Ezra. Pvt. under Capt. Samuel Dawson, 1 May - 5 Jul 1813.

MILTIN, William. 1st lieut. under Capt. William Durbin, Jr., 24 Aug - 13 Oct 1814.

MILTON, John. Mbr. of Crawford's "company."

MINNICK, George. Pvt. under Capt. Matthew Murray, 25 Aug - 27 Oct 1814.

MINOR, William. Pvt. under Capt. Denton Darby, 25 Aug - 8 Nov 1814.

MISSELL See Measle.

MISSINGER, Daniel. Listed as a deserter from Capt. Duvall's company in the local newspaper, *Engine of Liberty*, although not shown in Duvall's muster rolls; described as substitute, having dark eyes, dark hair, one forefinger off at the first joint, by profession a laborer.

MITCHELL, Leonard. 1st corpl. under George W. Ent, 3rd Regt, 24 Aug - 30 Sep 1814.

MITTEN, William. Pvt. under Capt. George W. Ent, 24 Aug - 30 Sep 1814; b. c.1785; m. 1812, Mary Goslin at Fredericktown. He res. Hagerstown, MD, 1851; Washington Co., MD 1855; Mt. Morris, Ogle Co, IL, 1871.

Sources: Bounty land claim, 50-40-406744, 55-120-71627; Pension, SO 20163, SC 12403 (admitted 7 Feb 1872).

MITTER, John. Mbr. of Crawford's "company."

MIXELL (Meixel), Jacob, Sr. Pvt. under Capt. John Brengle, beginning on 25 Aug; later deserted. [Prob. same Jacob Meixel who d. Balt. 2 Jan 1872 in his 79th year; m. Elizabeth (Betsy), dau of Joseph and Dorcus Howard; FCml issued to Jacob Mixel and Betsy Howard on 15 Feb 1814. Elizabeth Meixsel d. 6 Apr 1868, in her 76th year.]

Sources: FCml; (Frederick) Examiner, 15 Apr 1868, 31 Jan 1872.

MOBLEY [Mobly], Basil. Pvt. under Capt. John Brengle, beginning on 25 Aug; later deserted.

MOBLEY [Mobberly], Eli [Ely]. Pvt. under Capt. George W. Ent. He said he volunteered at Fredericktown c.22 Aug 1814, discharged at Balt. Oct 1814. At time of enrollment in company of Capt. Ent, he was bound by the Orphan's Court of Fred. Co. to said George W. Ent, and "had no rights except such as might be granted by his master." He further said, "As the holder of his indentures his master could receive all pay coming to him and not account for anything." - b. Oct 1800; m.c.15 Apr 1824, Sophia Mayberry; moved to Hagerstown in 1833; res. Hagerstown, MD, 1855. She d. 1863. He d. 6 Aug 1885 of diarrhea and exhaustion induced by it, at residence of son-in-law, Martin L. Byers. At date of death he had 5 children still living, all res. Hagerstown.

Acq.: 1855 - Abraham Crum, age 58 and William Biershing, age 60, both of same company of Capt. Ent, both res. Washington Co. - both dead by 22 May 1872. Peter Mantz d. shortly prior to 22 May 1872. 1887 - Dr. J. McPherson Scott, MD, age 37, attending physician at time of death of Eli Mobley; Martin L. Byers, age 49, druggist, res. Hagerstown, and son-in-law of Eli Mobley.

Sources: Bounty land claim, 55-160-54516; Pension, SO 11184-rejected, SC 23679; FCml; (Frederick) Examiner, 12 Aug 1885.

MOBLEY, Elias. Pvt. under Capt. Fonsten, res. 2 miles from Westminster, 2 Sep - 27 Oct 1814; m. 15 Sep 1825, Rachel Hill (b. c.1809) in Jefferson Co., IN, by Steven Gudgel, J.P. of Jefferson Co. Elias Mobley d. Jefferson Co., IN, 8 Sep 1840. Henry P. Lee made the coffin. Acq: 1856 - Littelton Hill, Squire S. Hill. 1857 - William F. Hill; John E. Stretcher, Agt., Greenwood P.O., refers to widow Moberly as destitute.

THE VETERANS

Source: Bounty land claim, 55-160-64088.

MOBLEY, Isaac. Pvt. and for a while as 4th sergt., under Capt. Samuel Dawson, 21 Jul 1814 - 10 Jan 1815.

MOBLEY, John. Pvt. under Capt. Samuel Dawson, 1 May - 5 Jul 1813.

MOCK, Peter. Pvt. under Capt. Fonsten; joined 2 Sep 1814; deserted 14 or 24 Sep 1814; b. c.1778; res. Darke Co., OH, 1855.

Source: Bounty land claim, 55-rejected-211975 (rejected, "deserted 24 Sep 1814").

MOLING, Edward. Pvt. under Capt. Jacob Getzendanner, 9 Aug - 17 Sep 1813 and Capt. Nicholas Turbutt, 2 Sep - 27 Oct 1814; b. c.1783; m. 1810 Susanna Bevins at Fredericktown, MD, by Rev David Martin. Edward Moling d. Fred. Co. 30 May 1852.

Source: Bounty land claim, 55-120-14205. On reverse is recorded "for value received I William Moling, executor of Edward Moling, sen, decd, ..."

MOLING, Noble. Pvt. under George W. Ent, 24 Aug - 30 Sep 1814; m. 26 Dec 1817, Sarah Bevans (b. 1791), in Fredericktown, MD, by Rev. David Shaffer, Luth. pastor. Noble Moling d. Fred. Co., 22 Apr 1822. Widow res. Fred. Co. 1851, 1855. Acq.: 1851 - Joseph Routzahn, res. adjoining farm.

Source: Bounty land claim, 55-120-4873.

MONDAY, Dadies [Dahdeus, Daddeus]. Pvt. under Capt. Alexander, 22 Jul - 19 Sep 1814; b. ca.1784; res. Richland Co., OH 1852 and 1855.

Source: Bounty land claim, 55-120-54544.

MONTGOMERY, James. Sergt. under Capt. Basil Dorsey, 30 Jul - 27 Sep 1814; b. c.1795; m. 31 Dec 1818, Caroline E. Sedwick, (b. c.1797) at her father's house near Port Republic, Calvert Co., MD, each for first time, by Rev John P. Bozman, Rector of Christs Prost. Epis. Ch.. At enlistment: 5 ft 8 inches, weighed 160 pounds, red hair, and light blue eyes; res. Fred. Co. 1851, 1855; d. 14 Nov 1867, age 72 yrs, 9 mos., 29 days, near Urbana, Fred. Co. Widow res. Frederick Co (P.O. Address: Urbana) 1878; d. Frederick Co, 19 Mar 1879. They had no children. He was bro. of Col. John Montgomery of Fredericktown.

Extract from Family Bible Records of John Sedwick. John Sedwick b. 13 Sep 1775; Elizabeth Rawlings b. 26 Dec 1779; m. 1 Dec 1796. Caroline Elizabeth Sedwick b. 28 Sep 1797. James Montgomery and Caroline E. Sedwick m. 31 Dec 1818. Rebecca Prisciller Sedwick b. 17 Jun 1805. Sophia Jane Sedwick b. 22 Apr 1826. "We, the undersigned, daus. of John & Elizabeth Sedwick & sisters to Caroline E. Montgomery, herby certify that the foregoing is a true and correct extract from the Family Bible Records of our late father John Sedwick, who d. Monroe Co., IN. Dec 5 1849. /signed/ Rebeca P. Monson and Sophia J.

Acq.: 1855 - Uriah S. Bantz and George Kantner, res. Fred. Co. 1878 - William McPherson(?), age 72, res. Fred. Co, and Thomas A. Smith, age 53, res. Urbana, Fred. Co., MD, acq. c.37 yrs; Thomas A. Smith, of Fred. Co., acq. 38 yrs; and Philip Reich, age 82, and Andrew J. Delashmut, age 53, res. Fredericktown.

Application for reimbursement by Dr. E. E. Mullinix: $46.50; Susan A. Bennet for nursing and care: $20.00; C. C. Carty for burial expenses: $6.71.

Sources: Bounty land claim, 55-120-30455; Pension, WO 29347, WC 20827; **(Frederick) Examiner**, 20 Nov 1867; **The Maryland Union**, 21 Nov 1867.

MONTGOMERY, JOHN. d. 14 Jan 1879 at residence of his son-in-law, Robert Dean, 5 miles east of Fredericktown, in his 86th year; some yrs prev. Judge of Orphans' Court. [Prob. Capt. John Montgomery who served in 1st Artillery Regt., Baltimore City, 19 Aug - 30 Nov 1814. Mary Montgomery, widow of Col. John Montgomery d. 24 Jul 1884 at residence of her son James, near Reich's Ford, in her 88th year; bur. Mt. Olivet.]

Sources: **(Frederick) Examiner**, 15 Jan 1879, 22 Jan 1879, 30 Jul 1884.

MOONY [Mooney], Daniel. Pvt. under Capt. Galt, 31 Aug - 27 Oct 1814.

MOORE, Charles. Pvt. under Capt. Nicholas Turbutt, 2 Sep - 27 Oct 1814; b. 1790; res. Fred. Co., 1851, 1855; res. Washington, D.C. 1869.

Source: Bounty land claim, 55-rejected-16946 (rejected because of desertion on "20 Oct 1813")

MOORE, Charles. Pvt. under Capt. Thomas Contee Worthington,, 17 - 31 Dec 1812; said he was substitute at Balt. for James Moore in Sep 1814; b. c.1794-1797; res. Fred. Co., MD, 1851, 1855.

Source: Bounty land claim, 55-80-1155.

MOORE, James. According to the *(Frederick) Examiner* he was a soldier of War of 1812; d. 18 Aug 1870 at his residence in Urbana Dist., Fred. Co., after a week's illness, age about 83 yrs. 1850 census of Buckeys Town Dist.: James More, 56, farmer, MD; William, 33; Mary A., 24.

Sources: **(Frederick) Examiner; Bridge in Time.**

MOORE, John. Pvt. under Capt. Jacob Getzendanner 26 Jul - 15 Aug 1814.

MOORE, Thomas. Pvt. from Balt., under Capt. Joseph Green, 23 Jul 1814 - 10 Jan 1815; substitute for Ignatius Jacobs.

MOORE, William. 1st sergt. under Capt. William Knox, 26 Aug - 27 Oct 1814; b. 1774; res. Antrim Township, Wyandot Co., OH 1850 and Edenville, Wyandot Co., OH, 1855.

Source: Bounty land claim, 55-120-12824.

MORAN, William. Pvt. under Capt. Denton Darby 3 Aug - 8 Nov 1814. Absent 8 days.

MORGAN, Thomas W. 3rd corpl. under Capt. Thomas Contee Worthington until 4 Dec when promoted to quartermaster sergt.; served 17 Aug - 31 Dec 1812; served under Capt. Huston and Capt. Joseph Green, 23 Jul 1814 - 10 Jan 1815, as 2nd lieut. until promoted to 1st lieut. on 20 Sep 1814; b. c.1790; res. Fred. Co., 1814, 1850; d. by paralysis 9 Jun 1862; elected Sheriff of Frederick Co. 1821 for 3 yrs; served as magistrate and at length an officer in Farmers and Mechanics Bank; bur. Evan. Ref. Ch. Cem. 1850 census of Fredericktown: Thomas W. Morgan, bank cashier, 59; Mary A., 54; Ellen W., 24; George, 21; Virginia D., 15; Thomas, 13; Mary, 11; Ellen Fowler, 30. Mary Morgan d. 14

THE VETERANS

Oct 1868 at her residence in East Church St., age 68 yrs, 1 month.

Acq.: 1850 - Jacob Markell, who was Lieut. and Ensign of the company. Joseph Conrad and George Fagan who were pvts. in same company.

Sources: Bounty land claim, 50-160-11293; **Bridge in Time; Names in Stone;** (Frederick) Examiner, 11 Jun 1862, 21 Oct 1868.

MORGAN, William. Pvt. under Capt. George W. Ent, 24 Aug - 30 Sep 1814.

MORIARTY [Moryatta], John. Pvt. from Balt. under Capt. Samuel Dawson, 21 Jul 1814 - 10 Jan 1815.

MORRISON, James. Pvt. under Capt. Samuel Dawson, 26 Jul 1814 - deserted 29 Sep 1814, returned 8 Oct 1814, deserted 8 Dec 1814.

MORT, George. Pvt. under Capt. Samuel Ogle, 1 May - 5 Jul 1813; b. c.1794; m. Nov 1820 Mary Craig, in Bedford Co, PA; m. 19 Jul 1871, Sarah E. Houtzer (b. c.1818) by Rev. A. R. Krebs, at Lima, OH. He res. Allen Co., OH 1855, in Monroe Township, Allen Co., OH, 1871; d. West Cairo, Allen Co, OH, 30 Aug 1876. Expenses submitted by John Mort, West Cairo, OH: coffin and funeral expenses $30.00; medical services $5.25; clothing $9.50. John Mort was administrator of estate of George Mort. His widow Sarah Mort, res. West High St., Lima, OH, 1878, 1880; d. 18 Oct 1894.

Acq.: 1871 - William Smith, Jane Smith, Solomon Drew, Channcy E. Curtis, Philip Keil and Levi Williams, all res. Monroe Township, Allen Co., OH. 1878 - Sarah M. Curtis and Mary R. Bryan, of Lima, OH.

Sources: Bounty land claim, 55-160-13780; Pension, SO 11857, SC 7260, WO 18925, WC 15313.

MORT, William. Pvt. under Capt. Philip Smith; joined c. 23 May 1813; deserted 18 Jun, found 4 Aug 1813; discharged c. 8 Sep 1813.

MOSBURG [Mosburgh], Abraham. Pvt. from Fredericktown under Capt. Samuel Dawson, 1 May - 5 Jul 1813 and Capts. James F. Huston and Joseph Green, 23 Jul 1814 - 10 Jan 1815.

MOSBURG [Mosbury?, Moxbury?], John. Pvt. under Capt. Jacob Getzendanner, 9 Aug - 17 Sep 1813.

MOSBURGH [Mossburgh], Daniel. Pvt. under Capt. Samuel Dawson, 1 May - 5 Jul 1813 and 2nd sergt. under Capt. Dawson, 21 Jul - 13 Oct 1814.

MOSBURY, Abraham. Light Dragoons, under Capt. Littlejohn. At enlistment: 5 ft, 11 inches; grey eyes, fair hair, dark complexion; age 21; miller; b. Fred. Co., MD; enlisted 14 Sep 1813 at Leesburg by Capt. Littlejohn for 5 yrs. Alexandria, D. C. 12 May 1814. Discharged.

MOSER [Mosser], Henry. Pvt. under Capt. Samuel Duvall, 3 Aug - 3 Oct 3 1814; b. c.1795; m. 18 Aug 1826, Ann [Anna] Hartsock (b. 1808) at Fredericktown, MD, by Rev. Dr. Shaffer [she also gave minister's name as Helfenstein, German Ref. preacher]. [Marr. license gives name as Susanna Hartsock in error, according to her. She being unable to write her name, did not realize the error until later.] Henry Moser res. Fred. Co., MD, 1850; d. 18 or 19 Jul 1853 in Mechanicstown Fred.

Co., MD. She res. in Catoctin Furnace, Fred. Co., 1878; d. c.1885. Acq.: 1850 - Lawrance Green, age 62 yrs, res. Frederick Co. served in same company as Henry Moser. 1855 - James David Smith and Anna C. Moser, res. Fred. Co. 1878 - Caleb J. Peddicord and Ephraim Carmack, res. Mechanicstown; W.S. McPherson, age 55, and Solomon Frailey, age 75, res. Dist. of Mechanicstown. 1878 - Thomas Pearl, age 76, res. Lewistown, Fred. Co.; later said that about a week after the marriage of Henry Moser and Ann Hartsock he, Thomas Pearl, was m. to Susannah Hartsock the sister of Ann Moser and lived with her till her death which occurred about 2 yrs earlier.

Source: Pension, WC 20446, WC 18580.

MOSER, John. Pvt. under Capt. Samuel Dawson, 5 May - 5 Jul 1813.

MOSLER [Mosier?], John. Pvt. under Capt. George W. Ent, 3rd Regt, 24 Aug - 30 Sep 1814.

MOSSITER, Christopher. Appt'd lieut. under Capt. Henry Riggs, 13th Regt., 26 Jun 1804. "Moved away."

MOUNT, George. Pvt. under Basil Dorsey, 30 Sep Jul 27 Sep 1814.

MOWERY, Henry. Pvt. under Capt. Samuel Dawson, 21 Jul - 10 Jan 1815.

MOXBURY, John. See Mosburgh.

MOZER [Mazer, Moser], Leonard. Pvt. under Capt. Jacob Creager. He said he was drafted at Woodsboro, MD, in Jul 1814, discharged at Balt. 30 Sep 1814; b. 17 Sep 1785; m. Nancy Woolford at Jacob Wellcos(?)'s house, Creagerstown Dist. He res. Fred. Co. 1851, 1855, 1871 (Mechanicstown); d. 30 Jun (or 1 Jul) 1872 at home of his son, Leonidas Moser; bur. with wife Nancy (d. 7 Oct 1867, age 72 yrs, 9 mos., 12 days) at Thurmont, United Brethren and Blue Ridge Cem. Witnesses (1871): George Stokes and Frederick Hawman. 1850 census of 10th E.D.: Leonard Moser, 65, labourer; Nancy Moser, 66; E. Leonard Moser, 16 - all b. Fred. Co. [*Moravian Familes of Graceham, MD* - Leonard Moser, farmer, bapt. 5 Mar 1820, m. Lydia Anna Wolfart who was b. 25 Dec 1794. Issue: Anna Margaret b. 15 May 1812, had an illegitimate son by William Brown; Lyvina b. 12 Nov 1814; Henry b. 20 Oct 1817; Daniel b. 31 Mar 1820; Frederick Arnold b. 31 Dec 1822, d. 4 Jan 1823; Angelina b. 14 Jul 1825; Sarah Elizabeth b. 17 Jun 1829; Leonard Ephraim b. 7 May 1833.]

Sources: Bounty land claim, 50-40-25651, 55-120-3549; Pension, SO 10166, SC 5660; **Moravian Families of Graceham, MD; (Frederick) Examiner,** 10 Jul 1872.

MUCK, Frederick. Pvt. under Capt. Matthew Murray, 25 Aug - 27 Oct 1814; m. 29 Oct 1805, Margaret Fryman (b. c.1786), in Hagerstown, MD, 29 Oct 1805, by Rev. Rauhauser. Frederick Muck d. Fred. Co., 15 Apr 1823, within 2 1/2 miles of Middletown and 1/4 mile of residence of Daniel Kaugle of C. Widow res. Fred. Co., MD, 1851, 1855, 1856. Acq.: 1851 - Henry Herring and David Boileau; 1856 - Henry Muck, present when Frederick Muck and Margaret Fryman were married; Daniel Kaugle (?), present when Frederick Muck d.

Source: Bounty land claim, 55-160-23762.

MUCK, Henry. Pvt. under Capt. Matthew Murray, 25 Aug - 27 Oct 1814; b. c.1781; res. Fred. Co., MD, 1852, 1855. Acq.: 1852 - Henry Herring, ensign of Capt. Murray's company. Leonard Miller, pvt. in said company.

MUCKELFRESH, David. Mbr. of Crawford's "company."

MULINIX, Rezin. Pvt. under Capt. Basil Dorsey, 30 Jul - 27 Sep 1814.

MULNIX, John. Pvt. under Capt. John Fonsten, 2 Sep - 27 Oct 1814; res. 16 miles from Westminster.

MURDOCK, George W. Sergt. under Capt. Henry Steiner, 28 Apr - 29 Jun 1813.

MURDOCK, John B. Pvt. under Capt. John Galt; joined 31 Aug; dead 18 Oct 1814.

MURDOCK (Modock), Richard B. Pvt. in Capt. Henry Steiner's Artillery company, 25 Aug - 27 Sep 1814; b. c.1793; m. 19 May 1825, Sarah R. Howard (b. c.1796) in Fred. Co., by Rev. Armstrong. Richard Murdock res. in Fred. Co. 1851; d. Fred. Co. 15 Apr 1855. 1850 census of Buckeys Town Dist.: Richard B. Modock, 58, farmer; Sarah R., 40; Richard H., 24; Susan L., 23; Sarah R., 21; July A., 21; Lorra, 9; Augustus, 8; Horris B., 5; Lydia H., 4; Eliza, 40; Elizabeth R. Howard, 34. Acq.: 1855 - John Markell and Louis Markell, res. Fred. Co. Bur. at Urbana Zion Episc. Ch.: Richard B. Murdoch, d. 15 Apr 1855, age 63 yrs, 21 days; wife Sallie B., 26 Sep 1872, age 68 yrs, 3 mos.; and other mbrs. of family.

Source: Bounty land claim, 55-120-71259; **Bridge in Time; FCml; Names in Stone; Frederick-Town Herald, 28 May 1825.**

MURFEY, John. Pvt. under Capt. George W. Magee, from 22 Jul 1814 until he enlisted on 5 Sep 1815.

MURPHY, James. Pvt. under Capt. Daniel Marker; joined 25 Aug 1814; deserted 28 Sep 1814.

MURPHY, Thomas. Pvt. under Ogle, Samuel, 1 May - 5 Jul 1813.

MURPHY, Thomas. Pvt., 16th U.S. Inf. At enlistment: 5 ft, 6 1/2 inches; blue eyes, fair hair, fair complexion; age 19; b. Fred. Co., MD; enlisted 7 Jan 1814 at Lancaster by Lieut Bryan for 5 yrs. Left sick at Plattsburgh 28 Aug 1814. Deserted near Buffalo, 1 Jun 1815.

MURPHY, Thomas, Jr. Pvt. under Dawson, Samuel from 26 Jul 1814, until he deserted 8 Dec 1814.

MURPHY, Thomas. Pvt. under Capt. Samuel B. Dawson, 1 May - 5 Jul 1813 and 26 Jul 1814 - 10 Jan 1815; b. c.1786; m. 12 Dec 1816, Jane Downey (b. c.1790), at Fredericktown, MD, by Rev. Sheffer, each for the first time. He res. in McLean Co., IL, in 1850 and 1855; d. Putnam Co., IL, 3 Feb 1857 (res. Padua Co., IL). His widow res. City of Peoria, IL in 1879. Pension was dropped 4 Sep 1880 due to her death. Acq.: 1879 - Sabra S. Michael, age 40, and Hezekiah Murphy, age 45, dau and son of Jane and Thomas Murphy, both res. Peoria, IL; William Guss, age 51 and Elizabeth Guss, his wife, age 51, currently in Taylor Co., IA, who lived in Putnam Co., IL when Thomas Murphy d.

FREDERICK COUNTY MILITIA IN THE WAR OF 1812

Sources: Bounty land claim, 55-80-10261, 55-80-26627; Pension, WO 37094, WC 28497; FCml.

MURRAY, Basil [Bazil]. Pvt. under Capt. Jacob Alexander, 22 Jul - 19 Sep 1814; m. 9 Sep 1822, Mary Shawen [Shauen, Shanen] (b. c.1800), in Fred. Co., MD, by Rev John McCauley. Basil Murray d. Fred. Co., 25 Nov 1824. Widow res. Marion Co. MO, 1855. Acq.: 1855 - Doct. Lloyd Dorsey, Joseph Cartzendafner(?), res. Fred. Co.

Source: Bounty land claim, 55-160-5532.

MURRAY, James. Pvt. under Capt. Basil Dorsey, 30 Jul - 27 Sep 1814; m. 26 Aug 1813, Anna Boyer (b. c.1798), in Fred. Co., by David Martin. James Murray d. at Bidsoll, Allegheny Co., NY, 5 Feb 1833. Anna Murray res. in Huron, Eni Co., OH, 1871. Acq.: 1873 - Mary A. Porter and Ann C. McLaughlin, appear at Eaton Co., MI, courthouse, who heard that their father, now dead, was present at the marriage of James and Anna Murray.

Sources: Bounty land claim, 55-120-61225; Pension, WO 7244 (rejected 21 Apr 1873 for want of proof of marriage and presumptive abandonment of claim).

MURRAY [Murry], Joshua. Pvt., later as sergt., under Dawson, Samuel, 21 Jul 1814 - 10 Jan 1815.

MURRAY, Matthew. Capt. of his own company from the Middletown area; served 25 Aug - 27 Oct 1814.

MURRAY, Thomas. 1st sergt. under Capt. William Durbin, 24 Aug - 27 Oct 1814.

MURRY, James. Mbr. of Crawford's "company."

MURRY, John. Mbr. of Crawford's "company."

MURRY, Mathias. Pvt. under Capt. Jacob Getzendanner, 26 Jul - 21 Aug 1814.

MURRY, Samuel. Mbr. of Crawford's "company."

MURRY, Solomon. Mbr. of Crawford's "company."

MUSSER, John. Pvt. under Capt. Jacob Getzendanner, 9 Aug 9 - 17 Sep 1813 and 4th sergt., 26 Jul - 21 Aug 1814.

MUSSETER, Christopher. 1st lieut. under Capt. Samuel Duvall, 3 Aug - 3 Oct 3 1814. [Bur. at Mt. Olivet: Christopher Mussetter (15 Aug 1772 - 6 Jun 1852) with wife Ruth (13 Nov 1783 - 16 Dec 1870) dau of Plummer and Jemima Ijams. FCml issued to Christopher Mussetter and Ruth Ijams, 17 Dec 1799. 1850 census of New Market Dist.: Christopher Mussetter, 79, farmer; Ruth Mussetter, 67; Elizabeth Mussetter, 46; Christopher Mussetter, 37; Ann Mussetter, 27. Mrs. Ruth Mussetter, d. 16 Dec 1870, at her residence near Ijamsville, age 87 yrs, of pneumonia. Her dau, Mrs. Ellen A. Ijams was connected with the Deaf and Dumb Institution of Frederick.]

Sources: FCml; Names in Stone; Bridge in Time; The Maryland Union, 29 Dec 1870, 10 Jan 1871.

MUSZ [Nusz?], Michael. Pvt. under Capt. Samuel Dawson, 1 May - 5 Jul 1813.

MYERHEIFER, John. Corpl., 38th U.S. Inf. At enlistment: 5 ft, 9 inches; brown/black eyes, black hair and a brown complexion; age 30; saddler; b. Fredericktown, MD; enlisted 1 March

THE VETERANS

1814 at Craney Island by Capt. Rothrock for duration of war. Absent in General Hospital at Norfolk 15 March 1815. Discharged at Craney Island, 15 March 1815.

MYERLY, Benjamin. Pvt. under Capt. John Fonsten; joined 2 Sep 1814; deserted 28 Sep 1814; b. c.1795; m. 10 Jun 1812, Catharine Crowel, by Rev. M. Harpst. Benjamin Myerly d. at his residence 11 Jan 1853. Widow res. in or near Westminster, MD, in 1871.

Source: Pension, WO 511 (rejected - insufficient service).

MYERLY, David. Pvt. under Capt. John Fonsten; joined 2 Sep 1814; deserted 25 Sep 1814; drafted near Westminster; said he was taken sick while in service; b. c.1789; res. Pipe Creek Hundred, Carroll Co. 1851; res. Carroll Co. 1855.

Source: Bounty land claim, 55-rejected-111783 (rejected - desertion).

MYERLY, Jacob. 2nd corpl. under Capt. Fonsten, 2 Sep - 27 Oct 1814.

MYERLY, Solomon. Pvt. under Capt. John Fonsten, 3 Sep - 27 Oct 1814; res. 3 miles from Westminster; b. May 1795; m. Sally Byers, in Fred. Co., 10 Jun 1817; res. Westminster, Carroll Co., MD, 1871.

Source: Pension, SO 1353 (rejected 23 Jun 1871 - insufficient service).

MYERS, Jacob. Mbr. of Crawford's "company."

MYERS, Jacob. Pvt. from upper Fred. Co., under Capt. James F. Huston, 23 Jul - discharged 3 Aug 1814.

MYERS, Jerry. Pvt. from Balt., later a servant, under Capt. Samuel Dawson, 5 Aug 1814 - 10 Jan 1815.

MYERS, John. Pvt. under Capt. Joseph Wood, 27 Aug - 28 Oct 1814.

MYERS, John. Pvt. under Capt. John Fonsten, 2 Sep - 27 Oct 1814; res. 6 miles from Westminster; b. c.1791; res. Crawford Co., OH, 1851 and 1855. Witnesses: 1855 - Henry Snyder and George W. Myers, res. Crawford Co., OH.

Source: Bounty land claim, 55-120-31118.

MYERS, John of Peter. Pvt. under Capt. John Fonsten, 2 Sep - 27 Oct 1814.

MYERS, Martin. Pvt. from Upper Fred. Co., under Capt. James F. Huston and Capt. Joseph Green, beginning on 28 Aug 1814 - deserted 8 Dec 1814.

MYERS, Michael. Pvt., 20th U.S. Inf., under Capt. John P. Duval. At enlistment: 5 ft, 6 inches; light eyes, sandy hair, light complexion; age 34; shoemaker; b. Fred. Co., MD; enlisted 19 July 1814, by Lieut. Ligon for duration of war. Mustered at Camp Defiance 15 March 1815. Discharged at Norfolk 20 March 1815.

MYERS, Peter. See Myres.

MYLES, James. From Balt. Co. Pvt. under Capt. John Galt, 31 Aug - 27 Oct 1814.

MYRES, Peter. Pvt. under Capt. Barton Hackney, 1 Sep - 27 Oct 1814.

FREDERICK COUNTY MILITIA IN THE WAR OF 1812

NAIL [Naille], Peter. Served under Capt. Daniel Zacharias in the Cav. of 2nd Regt., under Col. Kemp in Fred. Co. Aug 1814, discharged Oct 1814; b. c.1794; m. Mary Harman (b. MD c.1792), 25 Dec 1815, in Taneytown, MD, by Rev. Grubb; res. Fred. Co. 1850 (8th E.D.), 1851, 1856, 1871 (Oak Orchard). He d. 29 Sep 1872 Oak Orchard, MD. Widow res. Oak Orchard, MD 1878; d. c.6 May 1882. Acq: 1856 - Michael P. Galligher, Mark Bishop, res. Fred. Co.; 1871 - Upton Roop and Solomon Ecker, res. near New Windsor, Carroll Co.; 1878 - Luke C. Ensor and Jeremiah Greenwood of Fred. Co., acq. 14 yrs; William Ecker, age 36, and Luther J. Mason, age 27, acq. 25 and 28 yrs, resp.

Sources: Bounty land claim, 50-40-48706, 55-120-88019; Pension, SO17849, WO28351, WC15159 (pension claim rejected by reason of insufficient service, 7 Aug - 10 Sep, 1814); Bridge in Time.

NAILE, William. Pvt. under Capt. William Knox, 26 Aug - 27 Oct 1814.

NAILLE [Naile], Samuel. Pvt. under Capt. William Knox, in 1st Battalion, under Major Beale Randall 26 Aug - 27 Oct 1814; b. c.1790; res. Carroll Co. MD 1855; m. c.24 Dec 1827, Elizabeth Norris Clabaugh (d. 28 Aug 1826(?), age 34 yrs, 9 mos., 28 days); he d. 19 Oct 1869, age 83; both bur. Taneytown, Trinity Luth. Ch.

Sources: Bounty land claim, 55-120-3615; Names in Stone; FCml.

NAILOR, John. Pvt., 20th U.S. Inf., under Capt. Charles Gee. At enlistment: 5 ft, 5 inches, blue eyes, black hair, ruddy complexion; age 23; occupation saddle tree maker; b. Fred. Co., MD; enlisted 5 Jan 1814 by Lt. S. [sic] for duration of war. Discharged at Norfolk 20 March 1815.

NASH, Archibald. Mbr. of "Crawford's company."

NATT, Joseph. Pvt. under Capt. Daniel Shawen, 5 Sep - 27 Oct 1814.

NEAD, Henry. Pvt. in 1st Cav. Dist., 26 Aug - 3 Sep 1814.

NEAFF [Neff], Abraham. Pvt. under Capt. Henry Steiner, 25 Aug - 27 Sep 1814. [Shown in Luth. Ch. records of Middletown is Daniel Jacob son of Abraham and Dorothe Neff b. 18 Nov 1820; bapt. 7 Jul 1822. FCml issued to Abraham Neff and Margaret Amelia Murray 28 May 1814.]

NEAL, Samuel, Sr. *(Frederick) Examiner*, 19 Jun 1872, noted death of Samuel Neal, a prominent and respectable colored man who d. at his res. in Fredericktown, "Saturday last, aged about 80 yrs. ... served his country with fidelity during the War of 1812," bur. Cath. grave-yard. 1850 census of Fredericktown: Samuel Neil, 50, labourer, $500; Ellen, 50; Rebecca, 24; Sophia, 9 - all mulatto.

Source: (Frederick) Examiner, 19 Jun 1872.

NEFF, Andrew. Pvt. in Capt. Daniel Marker's company, 16 Aug - 18 Sep 1813, in regt. of riflemen of Col. Small; b. c.1792. 1850 census of Catoctin E.D.: Andrew Neff, age 60, laborer, in the home of Henry Bower. Also res. Fred. Co. 1851, 1852. Acq: Thomas Bittle, Ensign of Capt. Marker's company, and Philip Cline, who served with Andrew Neff.

THE VETERANS

Source: Bounty land claim, 55-120-76702.

NEFF [Nafe], George. Pvt. under Capt. Daniel Shawen, 5 Sep - 27 Oct 1814. At enrollment: dark complexion, dark hair, brown eyes, 5 feet, 10 inches; m. 12 Dec 1820, Margaret Hesson [Hessong] (b. c.1804), Fredericktown, MD, by Rev. Henry Sheaffer, Luth. minister, each for first time. George Neff res. Fred. Co., MD, 1820, 1845; d. 26 Feb 1846 near Fredericktown in almshouse [admitted 13 Dec 1845]. Widow res. Middletown, Fred. Co., MD, 1852, 1855, 1881 and OH, 1864-65; d. 24 Mar 1891, Middletown, MD. George Washington, son of George and Margarett Neff b. 25 Nov 1828; bapt. 10 Aug 1837 in Ref. Ch. of Middletown. Acq: 1852 - Margret Hessong, mother of Margaret Neff, and Catherine Hessong, sister of said Margaret Neff; 1881 - Lawson Alexander, age 68, Main St, Middletown, MD, and Joseph Lorentz, age 57, Main St., Middletown, MD, acq. 50 and 30 yrs, resp.

Sources: Bounty land claim, 50-40-86130, 55-120-79835; Pension, WO41357, WC32154; **Western Maryland German Ch. Records**, v.4, v. 1.

NEFF, Jacob. Pvt. under Capt. Daniel Marker, 16 Aug - 18 Sep 1813; b. c.1793; m. Magdelena Shipley (b. c.1793) in Washington Co., 8 Dec 1816 by Rev John Rowkausand. [According to the widow. A marriage license was issued in Washington Co., MD, for Jacob Neff and Mag. Shipley on 21 Aug 1817.] Jacob Neff d. 10 Mar 1826 of a shipwreck, drowned at age 27, in Lake Erie "while riding in a small boat which was oversett." All passengers were drowned but eight among whom were William and John Lightway [see acq. below]. Magdelana res. Jackson Co., MI, in 1855. Susanna, dau of Jacob and Magdalena Neff b. 18 Jan 1822; bapt. 8 May 1822 and Elizabeth dau of Jacob and Magdalena Neff b. 25 Dec 1816; bapt. 1 Aug 1821 - both baptized in Luth. Ch., Middletown, MD. Acq: 1855 - Elizabeth Swope, age 35, and John Brawn, age 50, res. Springport, Jackson Co., MI; knew their children; 1859 - William Lighteway, age 71, and John Lighteway, age 63, res. Detroit, MI. .

Sources: Bounty land claim, 55-rejected-233317; **Md. German Ch. Rcds.**, v.2.

NELSON, Arthur. Surgeon's mate under Capt. Col. John Ragan, 1st Regt., 14 Oct 1814 - 10 Jan 1815; discharged at Annapolis.

NELSON, John. Served under Capt. Henry Steiner, 28 Apr - 29 Jun 1813; promoted from pvt. to corporal 16 May. He served as corporal in Steiner's co and 1st Lt and Aid de Camp in the 11th Brigade; 2nd Lt. of Capt. Matthew Murray's company 25 Aug - 27 Oct 1814; b. c.1794; res. Balt. City 1852.

Source: Bounty land claim, 55-80-66.

NESMITH [Nussmith], Thomas J. Pvt. under Capt. Matthew Murray, 25 Aug 1814 - Oct 1814. "When I left Maryland in 1815, I left my discharge [paper] which was lost." He was b. c.1795; m. Nancy Dorsey, at Uniontown, PA, 28 Jul 1816; res. Fayette Co., PA, 1850, 1851, 1855; York Twp., IA, 1872; d. c.Sep 1886. Acq: 1872 - John H. Nesmith, res. York Twp, Iowa Co., and

FREDERICK COUNTY MILITIA IN THE WAR OF 1812

James H. Nesmith, res. York Twp., Iowa Co.
Sources: Bounty land claim, 55-120-10360; Pension, SO26317, SC16572.

NEUSBAUM, John. Pvt. under Capt. Fonsten, 2 Sep - 27 Oct 1814; res. 15 miles from Westminster.

NEWCOMER, John. Pvt. under Capt. William Knox; joined 26 Aug 1814; deserted 15 Sep 1814. On 5 Sep 1855 appeared George Jekes(?), res. Bedford Co, PA, guardian of William Newcomer, minor child of John Newcomer, whose mother, then a widow was issued warrant for 40 acres. [Note from 3rd Auditor refers to bounty land warrant issued to Mary Newcomer, widow of John Newcomer].
Source: Bounty land claim (55-rejected-210880).

NEWINS, Thomas. Pvt. under Capt. Henry Steiner, 28 Apr - 29 Jun 1813.

NEWPORT, David. Pvt. under Capt. George W. Ent, 3rd Regt., 24 Aug - 27 Oct 1814; b. MD c.1794; res. Fred. Co., MD, 1850, 1851. 1850 census of Fredericktown: David Newport, age 52, laborer and Mary Newport, age 54.
Sources: Bounty land claim, 50-40-43746; **Bridge in Time**.

NEWRY, John. Pvt. under Capt. John Galt, 31 Aug - 27 Oct 1814.

NICADEMUS, Andrew. Served in Crawford's "company." Bur. at Nicodemus-Nusbaum Family cem. in New Windsor: Andrew Nicodemus 9 Oct 1787-8 Jul 1853; bur. with Rachel Nicodemus (dates missing from broken stone). FCml issued to Andrew Nicodemus and Rachel Cassell on 26 Oct 1809.
Source: Names in Stone; FCml.

NICADEMUS, Henry. Served in Crawford's "company." FCml issued to Henry Nicodemus and Catherine Cassell 7 Dec 1810.
Source: FCml.

NICHOLLS [Nichols], Jacob. 1st Lieut. under Capt. Samuel Dawson, 1 May - 5 Jul 1813 and 2nd Lieut. under Capt. George W. Ent, 24 Aug - 30 Sep 1814; b. c.1789; res. Montgomery Co., MD, 1851, 1855. [Jacob Nicol son of Johann and Philippina b. 20 Oct 1788; bapt. 11 Mar 1789 at Ref. Ch. in Frederick. FCml issued to Jacob Nichols and Sarah Rawlin on 2 Jun 1818.]
Sources: Bounty land claim, 55-160-36855; Records of Reformed Ch. of Frederick; FCml.

NICHOLLS, Raphael. Pvt. under Capt. Samuel Dawson, 1 May - 5 Jul 1813. [FCml issued to Raphael Nicholls and Sarah Grimes on 19 Jul 1814.]
Source: FCml.

NICHOLS, Adam. Pvt. under Capt. Henry Steiner, 25 Aug - 27 Sep 1814; m. 24 Aug 1814, Maria O. Kelley (b. c.1799), by Selah Bunn(?), Meth. minister. Adam Nichols d. Somerset, OH, 1 Feb 1855; widow res. Somerset Co., 1871. Acq: 1871 - George Henricks and W. G. Brickner, res. New Lexington, Perry Co., OH.
Source: WO1766 (rejected 7 Dec 1871, only served 34 days).

NICHOLS, Benjamin. See Nickles.

NICHOLS, John. Pvt. under Capt. Daniel Marker, 25 Aug - 27 Oct 1814;

m. 28 Mar 1833, Rebecca Padgett (b. c.1814), in Fred. Co., MD, by Rev. David Shaffer, Luth. Pastor. John Nichols d. Fred. Co., 17 Oct 1843. Acq: 1852 - Mary Padgett and B. F. Gattan, both at wedding; 1853 - Walter B. Kemp and David Hergesheimer.
Source: Bounty land claim, 55-120-24401.

NICHOLS, Ralph. 1st corporal under Capt. BArton Hackney, 1 Sep - 27 Oct 1814.

NICKEM, Peter. 1st corporal under Capt. Matthew Murray, 25 Aug - 27 Oct 1814.

NICKUM [Nickem], Joseph. Pvt. under Capt. Matthew Murray, 25 Aug -27 Oct 1814; b. 4 Jul 1793; m. c.31 Aug 1839 Amy Walker (b. c.1823), in Jefferson Co., IN. When enrolled: age c.20 yrs, 5 feet 8-9 inches, dark complexion, dark hair, dark eyes. After the war he res. Jefferson Co., IN, Lee and Wayne Cos., IA.; d. 18 Jul 1864 New York, IA. Widow res. New York, Wayne Co, IA, 1878; d. New York, IA, 5 Jun 1894. In 1894 Joseph Nickum, son of Joseph Nickum and his wife, Amy, res. New York, IA. Acq: 1878 - J. M. Bennett, age 30, res. New York, IA, and Lernira (?) Mason, 50, res. New York, IA, acq. 21 yrs; Ely Sticker, age 58, res. Linn Co., MO., present at wedding of Joseph and Amy Nickum; 1879 - David M. Clark, Elias Jackson and A. Hutchison, res. New York, IA.
Source: Bounty land claim, 50-40-20235, 55-120-72749; Pension, WO27927, WC25246; FCmL

NICKLES, Benjamin. Pvt. under Capt. Barton Hackney, 1 Sep - 27 Oct 1814.

NICODUMUS, Henry. Served in Crawford's "company.

NIHART [Nehart], Jacob. Pvt., 38th U.S. Inf. At enlistment: 5 feet, 8 1/2 inches; age 40; b. Fred. Co., MD; enlisted 29 Dec 1813 at Cumberland by Lieut. Jones for 1 year. Mustered at Cumberland on 3 Jan 1814. Mustered in Capt. J. H. Hook's company near Covington 31 Dec 1814. Discharged 29 Dec 1814.

NILES, John. Pvt. under Capt. Nicholas Turbutt, 1 Sep - 27 O(ct 1814.

NIXDORFF, Henry. Pvt. under Capt. Henry Steiner, 28 Apr - 29 Jun 1813 and 25 Aug - 27 Sep 1814; b. 25 Dec 1780; m. c. 10 Feb 1814 Susanna Medtart (b. 29 Jul 1788, d. 27 or 29 Sep 1870). He d. 4 May 1859 at his res. on W. Patrick St. after protracted illness; bur. Mt. Olivet Cem., Frederick. Also bur. Mt. Olivet: son Henry M., merchant of Frederick (10 Jan 1830 - 1 Aug 1908); son Rev. George A. Nixdorff (20 Aug 1823 - 5 Nov 1907), "for 40 yrs an active minister of Luth. Ch."; Lewis M. Nixdorff, merchant, b. c.1827, d. 1908, bur. with wife Eliza (Miller) at Mt. Olivet; she d. 1908. Other children of Henry and Susan: Mary E. m. George Smith; Susan m. Samuel Hinks; Julia M. m. Charles M. Miller. [Records of Luth. Ch. of Frederick reveal Henrich Nixdorff son of Samuel and Barbara Nixdorff b. 27 Dec 1780; bapt. 11 Feb 1781. Also b. to same parents were Samuel, Susanna, Magdalena, Elisabeth, Georg and Tobias.] d. 5 Dec 1830, Godfrey Medtart, bro. of Jacob Medtart and Mrs. Nixdorff.

FREDERICK COUNTY MILITIA IN THE WAR OF 1812

Sources: Bounty land claim, 55-120-13294; Names in Stone (gives incorrect year of death for Henry as 1839); **Maryland German Ch. Records**, v. 4.; FCml; **Williams, History of Fred. County, Maryland; Bridge in Time;** (Frederick) **Examiner,** 11 May 1859, 19 Oct 1870; **The Maryland Union,** 20 Nov 1870; **Engelbrecht Diary:** 1:621; 2:165.

NOBLE, John. Pvt., 26th U.S. Inf., under Lieut. P. Callan. At enlistment: 5 feet, 5 inches; blue eyes, light hair and fair complexion; age 23; occupation shoemaker; b. Fredericktown, Fred. Co., MD; enlisted 13 Nov 1814 at Balt. by Lt. J. Whelpley for duration of war. Discharged from Capt. Bezeau's Det. on 23 March 1815 at Philadelphia at expiration of his term.

NOEL, Blazon. Pvt. under Capt. Ogle, Samuel, 1 May - 5 Jul 1813.

NOGGLE, Joseph. Pvt. from New Windsor under Capt. George W. Magee, 22 Jul - 10 Jan 1815.

NOLEN [Nolin], Barnabas. Pvt., 25th U.S. Inf., under Capt. Ben. Watson. At enlistment: 5 feet, 8 inches; hazel eyes, sandy hair, light complexion; age 19; occupation laborer; b. Fred. Co., MD; enlisted 12 Feb 1815 in OH, by Lt. See for duration of war. At Sacketts Harbor, 26 Feb, 24 March, Jun and 25 Dec 1814. Mustered in Capt. Burbridge's Company, 16 Feb 1815. Discharged at Sacketts Harbor 17 May 1815.

NORRIS, Henry. Pvt. under Capt. Jacob Alexander, 22 Jul - 19 Sep 1814.

NULTON, John. 3rd sergt. under Capt. Matthew Murray, 25 Aug - 27 Oct 1814.

NUSBAUM, Jacob. Pvt. under Capt. Joseph Wood, 27 Aug - 28 Oct 1814. Records of Ref. Ch. of Frederick show Jacob Nussbaum of Johannes and Margaretha b. 28 Jul 1773.
Source: **Rcds. of Ref. Ch. Frederick.**

NUSBOM, Henry. Served in Crawford's "company." [FCml issued to Henry Nusbaum and Sarah Snyder 28 Nov 1808.]

NUSSEAR, Jesse W. Pvt. in Balt. City company of Capt. Henry Myers, serving 19 Aug - 18 Nov 1814; d. 28 July 1874, age 79 yrs, 6 mos., 29 days, near Mt. St. Mary's College, Fred. Co.; bur. Mt. St. Mary's Cath. Cem. with his wife, Mary A. (6 July 1877, age 75 yrs, 11 mos., 7 days). 1850 census of Emmittsburg area: Jesse Nurser, 54, shoemaker; Mary Ann, 49; Mary Ann, 25; Elizabeth C., 15; Louisa, 12; Ann Margaret, 8; Mary Capoote, 91 (b. Phila., PA).
Sources: **Md. Militia, War of 1812** (Balt.), v.2; **Names in Stone; Bridge in Time; The Maryland Union,** 6 Aug 1874.

NUSSER, John. Pvt., 36th U.S. Inf., under Capt. Jos. Hook. At enlistment: 5 feet 7 or 7 1/2 inches; gray eyes, dark hair, dark complexion; age 33 or 38; occupation carpenter; b. Fred. Co.; enlisted 23 or 24 July 1814 at Balt. by Capt. Jas. Hook for duration of war. Mustered at Ft. Covington 31 Dec 1814, absent sick in Genl. Hospital at Balt. since July 1814. Deserted 21 March 1815. Discharged at Ft. Covington 30 March 1815.

NUSSMITH. See Nesmith.

NUSZ, Jacob. Pvt. under Capt. George W. Ent, 3rd Regt., 24 Aug - 29 Oct 1814; m. Mary Cantner (b. c.1793) in Fredericktown 13 Aug 1814 by Rev. David F. Shaffer, Luth. minister. Jacob

THE VETERANS

Nusz d. 10 Mar 1843. Widow res. Fred. Co. 1851. Acq: 1851 - Jacob Rease, Henry Shultz, Jacob Knoux and Michael Lambright.
Source: Bounty land claim, 50-40-41510.

NUSZ, Michael. Pvt. from Upper Fred. Co. under Capts. Joseph Green and James F. Huston, 14 Oct 1814 - 10 Jan 1815; deserted 2 Dec 1814. [FCml issued to Michael Nusz and Elizabeth Esther 2 May 1809.]

O'BRYAN [O'Brian], Mashac [Meshack]. Sergt., 17th U.S. Inf. At enlistment: 6 feet, blue eyes, brown hair, fair complexion; age 40; occupation blacksmith; b. Fred. Co., MD; enlisted 1 Oct 1813 for duration of war. Mustered in Capt. Martin L. Hawkins' Company 16 Feb 1815. At Erie, PA, 28 Feb 1815, Capt. Jas. Herron's Det., Chilliocothe, 7 Jun 1815; discharged Chillicothe 9 Jun 1815.

O'NEAL, William. Pvt. under Capt. Denton Darby, 3 Aug - 8 Nov 1814.

OBRIEN, Edward. Pvt. from Mechanickstown under Capt. George W. Magee, 23 Jul - 10 Jan 1815.

OCKER, Henry. Pvt. under Capt. John Galt, 31 Aug - 27 Oct 1814; b. c.1795; res. Miami Co., OH, 1851, 1855, 1871 (Newbury Twp); had not m. by age 77. In 1871 he res. with friends (P.O. address: North Clayton). Acq: 1871 - Wm. Fenfrock and John G. Schaefer, res. Miami Co., OH.
Sources: Bounty land claim, 50-40-44831, 55-120-49843; Pension, SO23011, SC15023.

OCKS, Jacob. Pvt. under Capt. Samuel Dawson, 14 Oct 1814 - deserted 1 Nov 1814.

ODONAL, James. Pvt. under Capt. John Galt, 31 Aug - 27 Oct 1814.

ODONALD, John. Pvt. under Capt. Samuel Ogle, 1 May 1813 - 5 Jul 1813.

OGLE, Eli. 2nd sergt. under Lt Kolb Oct 13- 15 Nov 1814).

OGLE, Samuel V. Capt. of his own company, 1 May 1813 - 5 Jul 1813; d. 1852; bur. Frederick Ref. Cem. Mary J. C. Hobbs, wife of Louis J. Hobbs and dau of Capt. Ogle, d. 11 Dec 1866, age 63; bur. Frederick, St. John's Cath. Cem.
Sources: **Names in Stone**; (Frederick) Examiner, 9 Jan 1867.

OLER, John. Pvt. under Capt. John Galt, 28 Sep - 27 Oct 1814.

OLER [Ohler], Joseph. Pvt. under Capt. Samuel Dawson, 26 Jul - deserted 29 Sep 1814.

OHLER (Oler), Peter. Pvt. under Capt. Samuel Ogle, 1 May - 27 1813; b. c.1784; m. c.20 Feb 1815, Elizabeth Wyant (d. prior to 17 Mar 1871), at Chambersburg, TN. He res. Walker Twp, MI (P.O. address: Grand Rapids).
Source: Pension, SO2510 (rejected 18 Sep 1871 because of insufficient service).

OILER, George. 14th U.S. Inf., under Capt. Samuel Lane. At enlistment: 5 feet, 7 inches; sandy eyes, brown hair, brown complexion; age 30; b. Fred. Co. MD; enlisted 16 or 18 May 1812, to serve until 16 May 1817; d. Halifax prison 19 Sep 1813 while prisoner of war.

ORENDORF, John. Pvt. under Capt. William Knox, 26 Aug - 27 Oct 1814.

ORNDERF, Joseph [Jacob?]. Pvt. under Capt. Samuel Dawson, 26 Jul 1814; deserted 29 Sep 1814.

ORPERT [Ospert?], John. Never joined company under Capt. William Durbin, which served 14-27 Oct 1814.

ORPIT, John. Mbr. of Crawford's "company."

ORPIT, Thomas. Mbr. of Crawford's "company."

ORTNER, John. Pvt. under Capt. John Brengle, 25 Aug - 19 Sep 1814; m. c.24 Dec 1818, Sophia Shoup [Shope] (b. c.1798); he d. 10 May 1827 in his 31st year - painter and chairmaker; bur. Luth. grave yard. His widow m. c.11 Aug 1836, Rev. Edward Hughes; she res. Fredericktown 1850.

Sources: Engelbrecht Diary: 1:261, 446; 2:216; FCml; Bridge in Time.

OSPERT, John. See Orpert.

OTT, Frederick. Pvt. from Upper Fred. Co. Capt. Joseph Green and Capt. James F. Huston, 23 Jul 1814 - sick in Frederick Town 25 Aug - deserted 8 Dec 1814. [Friedrich, son of George and An. Marg. Ott b. 9 Mar 1789; bapt. 3 May 1789. Catherine Ott wife of Frederick (12 Aug 1786 - 21 Feb 1815); bur. Creagerstown St. John's Lutheran and Reformed Ch.. FCml issued to Frederick Ott and Catherine Martin 18 Apr 1808.]

Sources: Md. German Ch. Rcds., v.7; Names in Stone; FCml.

OTT, George. Pvt. under Capt. Galt, 31 Aug - 27 Oct 1814; res. within 7 miles of Taneytown 1814.

OTT, Michael. Pvt. under Capt. William Knox, 26 Aug - 27 Oct 1814; b. c.1794; m(1) Polly Hahn; m(2) Mary Reaver at Taneytown 1 May 1833. He res. Carroll Co. 1852, 1855, 1871 (near Taneytown); d. 20 May 1872. Witnesses: 1871 - Aloysius F. Orndorff, Washington Reaver, res. Carroll Co.

Sources: Bounty land claim, 50-40-71071, 55-120-3956; Pension, SO12312, SC7599 (admitted 4 Nov 1871). Note on envelope: "Jun 14, 1872 - Per agt. Returning vochers for p'mt. of arrears to decedent's ex'g - for the benefit of one child."

OTT, Peter. Pvt. under Capt. Capt Nicholas Turbutt, 1 Sep - 24 Oct 1814; b. MD, 8 Dec 1785 son of Barnhardt and Anna Elisabeth Ott; bapt. 7 May 1786; m. Sarah Ann Bruner c.4 Oct 1815 (FCml). 1850 census Fredericktown: Peter Ott, 63, labourer; with Sarah A. Ott, 50 and William A. Hopper, 14. Peter Ott res. Fred. Co. in 1855; d. 29 Jan 1858, age 73 yrs, 29 days; bur. Frederick Reformed Cem. with wife Sarah Ott who d. 30 Mar 1869, age 76. Acq: 1850 - John Fauble and John Finch who served in the same company.

Sources: Bounty land claim, 55-120-514; Names in Stone; Md. German Ch. Rcds., v. 4; Bridge in Time.

OURENT, Daniel. Pvt. under Capt. Fonsten, 2 Sep - 27 Oct 1814; res. 15 miles from Westminster.

OWEN, Isaiah. Pvt. under Capt. Samuel Duvall, 3 Aug - 3 Oct 1814.

OWEN, John. Pvt. under Capt. Denton Darby, 3 Aug - 8 Nov 1814. [FCml is-

THE VETERANS

sued to John Owen and Abigail Cullom 4 Sep 1783.]

OYSTER, George. 2nd lieut. under Capt. William Knox, 26 Aug - 27 Oct 1814. [FCml issued to George Oyster and Polly Houck on 13 Nov 1815.]

OYLER, George. Pvt. under Capt. John Galt, 6 Sep - 27 Oct 1814.

OYLER, John. Pvt. under Capt. John Galt, 31 Aug - 27 Oct 1814.

PACKWOOD, John. Pvt. under Capt. Fonsten; joined 2 Sep 1814; deserted 9 Oct 1814.

PADGET, Allison. Pvt. under Capt. Daniel Shawen, 5 Sep - 27 Oct 1814.

PADGETT, John. Pvt. under Capt. Samuel Dawson, joined 1 May 1813; deserted 3 Jun; returned 12 Jun 1813l; enlisted in regular army 28 or 29 Jun 1813 at Balt. by Capt. J. Hook. At enlistment: 5 feet, 9 inches; age 21, b. Charles Co., MD; served in 36th U.S. Inf.; mustered 30 Sep and 31 Oct 1813 by Capt. Jos. Hook's company (as corporal). He d. 7 Feb 1814.

PADGETT, Solomon. Pvt., 2nd U.S. Inf. At enlistment: 5 feet 8 1/2 inches; hazel eyes, brown hair, fair complexion; age 30; farmer; b. Fred. Co., MD; enlisted 4 Sep 1807 at Fredericktown MD by Lt. Luckett for 5 yrs. Ordered to Columbian Spring 15 Sep 1808. Assigned to Capt. Bonyer's company. Deserted; sentenced 50 lashes; corporal punishment remitted. Sentenced 50 lashes for drunkeness 15 Aug 1810. Ordered to Baton Rouge, 9 Feb 1811. Transferred to Capt. Lawrence's company; d. 26 Apr 1811 at Fort Stoddert.

PAIN, James. Pvt. under Capt. Samuel Ogle, 1 May 1813 - 5 Jul 1813.

PAINE, James. 5th U.S. Inf. At enlistment: 5 feet, 11 inches; gray eyes, light hair, fair complexion, age 33, farmer; b. Fred. Co., MD; enlisted 5 Jun 1815 at Balt. by Lt. Fendall for 5 yrs. At Harrisburgh, PA, 30 Apr 1814. Sent from Harrisburgh to Phila 30 May 1814 in company under Lt. W. C. Bird.

PAINE, John. Pvt. under Capt. George W. Ent, 3rd Regt., 24 Aug - 30 Sep 1814. [FCml issued to John Pain and Catherine Keller on 17 Oct 1816.]

PALMER, Matthew. Pvt. from Washington Co. under Capt. Samuel Dawson, 14 Oct 1814 - 10 Jan 1815.

PAPE, William. Pvt. under Capt. Matthew Murray, 25 Aug - 27 Oct 1814.

PARKER, Samuel. Pvt. under Capt. Jacob Getzendanner, 9 Aug - 17 Sep 1813.

PARKS [Park], William. Pvt. from New Windsor under Capt. George W. Magee, 22 Jul - 10 Jan 1815.

PARR, Henry. Pvt. under Capt. Samuel Ogle, 1 May - 5 Jul 1813.

PATRICK, Robert. Pvt. from Upper Fred. Co. under Capt. James F. Huston, 23 Jul 1814 - 13 Oct 1814.

PAUL, Michael. Pvt., U.S. Artillery. At enlistment: 5 feet, 6 inches; blue eyes, black hair, dark complexion; age 29; occupation tailor; b. Fredericktown, MD; enlisted 10 March 1812 in Dist. of Columbia for 5 yrs. Present at Wiliamsville 21 Dec 1814. Plattsburgh 30 Apr, 30 Jun, 1815. Discharged at Ft. Independence 13 March 1817.

PAXTON, John. Pvt. under Capt. William Knox, 26 Aug - 27 Oct 1814; b. c.1779; res. Carroll co., MD, 1850, 1855. [Bur. Emmetsburg Presby. Cem. was John William Paxton; he d. 24 May 1860.]
Source: Bounty land claim, 55-120-18124; Names in Stone.

PEACOCK, Jacob. Pvt. under Capt. Samuel Dawson, 1 May - 5 Jul 1813.

PEACOCK, William. Pvt. from Upper Fred. Co. under Capt. Joseph Green/Capt. James F. Huston; joined 23 Jul 1814; deserted 27 Oct 1814. [FCml issued to William Peacock and Sarah Hines 13 Jan 1820.]

PEARCE, Lemuel. Mbr. of Crawford's "company."

PEARCE, William. Member of Crawford's "company."

PENNYBAKER, Samuel. Pvt. under Capt. Samuel Ogle, 1 May 1814; enlisted 7 Jun 1814 in regular army by Capt. Miltenberger for 1 year. Pvt. in 38th U.S. Inf.; transferred to Capt. Rothrock's company prior to 30 Apr 1814; absent in Richmond with "QM Wadon" (?) in late Dec and late Feb 1813/1814. [FCml issued to Samuel Pennybaker and Susannah Plunck 25 Jul 1783.]

PEPPER, Abraham. Pvt. under Capt. William Knox, 26 Aug - 27 Oct 1814, absent without leave 24 Oct 1814.

PEPPLE, Abraham. Enrolled in PA militia at Gettysburg, 26 Feb 1814; discharged 26 Aug 1814 Buffalo, NY; b. c.1790, in now Carroll Co.; res. Emmitsburg Dist. with David Koffman, 40, and Nancy Koffman in 1850. The *Examiner* noted Abraham Pepple had large tumor removed from left hip at Shank's National Hotel in Fredericktown in May 1856. It was stated that he had served "in the War of 1812, at Lundy's Lane and most of the frontier battles." Bur. at Friends Creek, Ch. of God, is Caroline Pepple dau of Abraham and Maria who d. 1 Apr 1854, age 13 yrs, 10 mos., 17 days. On 22 Sep 1894 Eliza Seifert, widowed dau of Abraham Pepple sought land warrant based on father's service. [Letter was sent from the Office of Deputy State Supervisors of Election, Fairfield Co., OH.]
Sources: Bounty land claim, 55-80-1062; Bridge in Time; (Frederick) Examiner, 7 May 1856; Names in Stone.

PERDUM, Mordecai. Pvt. under Capt. Basil Dorsey 30 Jul - 27 Sep 1814. "furloughed 9 Sept. until well."

PERKINS, John. Pvt. under Capt. John Galt; joined 31 Aug 1814; deserted 26 Sep 1814; b. c.1781; res. Fred. Co., MD, in 1851.
Source: Bounty land claim, 50-rejected-63581.

PETERMAN, Jacob S. Pvt. under Capt. John Galt, 31 Aug - 27 Oct 1814; b. 15 Jan 1782; m. 4 Jan 1814, Martha Caster (b. 16 Dec 1790) in Emmittsburgh, Fred. Co., MD, by Rev. Rauhauser, "German Presby. Ch." [Martha stated that no marr. license issued; bans were published in said ch.] Jacob and wife res. Franklin Co., OH 1851, 1855. Jacob S. Peterman d. 28 Jul 1867 in Pickaway Co., OH; bur. Truso Ch., Truso Twp., Franklin Co., OH;

THE VETERANS

1872. Widow res. Columbus, Franklin Co., OH 1871. Acq: 1871 - John Miller and James Taylor, acq. with Jacob Peterman for 25 yrs; W. H. Morrison and M. H. Taylor; William E. Peterman, son of Jacob and Martha Peterman. Family record is included in pension file and includes dates of birth of Jacob S. and "Marthew" Peterman and their date of marriage and dates of birth of fol.: dau Maryan (Nov 16, 1814); son William Alja(?) (Jan 17, 1817); Lizze Amanda (Apr 9, 1820); son Georg Washington Golden(?) (March 15, 182-); son Simson Thomas (February 10, 1827); dau [blank] (Nov 30, 1830).

Sources: Pension, WO4424, WC2219; Bounty land claim, 50-40-23645, 55-120-66060.

PETERMAN, John. Pvt. under Capt. Samuel Ogle, 1 May - 5 Jul 1813. [Bur. at St. Anthony, old Mt. St. Mary's Cath. Cem. was Mary Blackburn, wife of John Peterman and Isaac Shafer 4 Jun 1847, age 56. - *Names in Stone*]

PETERS, Charles. Pvt. under Capt. John Brengle, 25 Aug - 19 Sep 1814. [FCml issued to Charles Peters and Polly Stewart 6 Apr 1816.]

PETERS, John. From Fred. Co. as corpl. and pvt. under Capt. Samuel Dawson, 26 Jul - 10 Jan 1815. He stated he was wounded at the Battle of North Point, the ball cutting the flesh above the left knee. - b. c.1792-1794; m. --- who d. in 1869; res. Belmont Co., OH 1850, 1853, 1855, 1871 (Wayne Twp, P.O. address: Pilcher). Acq: 1853 - Phillip Reed, res. Franklin Co 1853, also mbr. of Capt. Dawson's company.

Sources: Bounty land claim, 50-40-7913, 55-160-16743; Pension, SO16515, SC10431 (admitted 29 Dec 1871).

PETERS, Michael. 2nd sergt. under Capt. George W. Ent, 24 Aug - 30 Sep 1814. [FCml issued to Michael Peters and Ann Grabell 28 Sep 1816. Bapt. at Luth. Ch., Middletown, MD: Anna Cecilia dau of Michael and Anna Peters, b. 1 Mar 1823, and Mary Margaret dau of Michael and Anna Peter, b. 9 Sep 1820.]

Sources: FCml; Md. German Ch. Rcds., v.2.

PETERS, Samuel. Pvt. under Capt. Fonsten, 2 Sep - 27 Oct 1814; res. 1 mile from Westminster; b. c.1795; m(1) 15 Aug 1830, Elizabeth Zepp (d. Williamsport, MD, c.1850) at Westminster, MD; m(2) 15 May 1870, Sarah Prudence (b. c.1813), by Rev William T. Maupin [Moppin], in Macon Co., IL. Samuel Peters res. Washington Co., MD, 1850, 1851, 1855; and Decatur Twp, Macon Co., IL, 1871, 1875; d. c.15 Oct 1876; bur. Greenwood Cem., Decatur, IL. Acq: 1878 - Jonathan Carrier, Macon Co., IL; 1879 - William Young, Macon Co., IL, knew Samuel Peters and first wife.

Sources: Bounty land claims, 50-40-34211, 55-120-54058 (rejected - insufficient service); Pensions, SO15814, WO32267, WC26557 (admitted 7 Aug 1879).

PEUSEY [Pewsey], George. Never joined his company under Capt. William Durbin, Jr., which served 24 Aug - 27 Oct 1814.

PEUSEY [Pewsey], Joel. Never joined his company under Capt. William Durbin, which served 14-27 Oct 1814.

PHARES?, Williams. Pvt. in the 1st Cav. Dist., 26 Aug - 3 Sep 1814.

PHEBUS, Peter. Pvt. under Capt. Capt Nicholas Turbutt, 1 Sep - 27 Oct 1814; m. 3 Aug 1820, Elizabeth Gardner (b. PA 1802), at St. Johns' Ch. in Fredericktown, by Rev. Francis Maleve, Pastor of the Cath. Ch.; witnessed by Mrs. Wittington and family. Peter Phebus d. Frederidcktown 16 Jun 1839. 1850 census of Fredericktown: Elizabeth Phebus, 47, b. PA; Ann R., 17; Elizabeth 16; Benjamin F., 14; Catherine A., 11. All children b. in MD. Acq: 1851 - Peter Ott, sergt. of company in which Peter Phebus served; and Frederick Clinard, both res. Fred. Co.
Source: Bounty land claim, 55-120-13293.

PHELPS, Charles. Pvt. from Washington Co. under Capt. Samuel Dawson, 14 Oct 1814 - 10 Jan 1815.

PHILLIPS, Elie. Capt. of a company in 2nd Regt., 1st Cav. Dist. [Elie Phillips m. 27 May 1806, Mrs. Catherine Stallings. FCml issued to Elie Phillips and Catherine Harris on 22 Feb 1796.]
Sources: **Republican Advocate**, 30 May 1806; FCml.

PINTER, Thomas. Servant under Capt. Samuel Duvall, 3 Aug - 3 Oct 1814.

PIPER, Jacob. Pvt. under Capt. Daniel Shawen, 25 Aug - 27 Oct 1814.

PIPER, Michael. Pvt. under Capt. Samuel Duvall, 3 Aug - 3 Oct 1814.

PITT, Thomas. Pvt. from Upper Fred. Co. under Capt. Joseph Green/Capt. James F. Huston; joined 23 Jul 1814; deserted 27 Oct 1814.

PLESTER, Stephen. Pvt. under Capt. Thomas Contee Worthington, 17 Aug - 31 Dec 1812.

PLICKENSTEMER [Plickenstarve?], Christian. Pvt. under Capt. Daniel Shawen, 5 Sep - 27 Oct 1814.

PLUMMER, William. Pvt. under Capt. Daniel Shawen; joined 5 Sep 1814; deserted 2 Oct 1814.

POBST, John. See Bopst. Pvt. under Capt. John Brengle, 25 Aug - 19 Sep 1814. [FCml issued to John Pobst and Lydia Shucke 21 Jun 1818.]

POLE, Thomas. Mbr. of Crawford's "company." [Bur. at Sams Creek, Bethel Methodist Ch. was Thomas Pole; d. 31 Aug, age 37.]
Source: **Names in Stone.**

POLMAN, John. Pvt. under Capt. Barton Hackney; joined 10 Sep 1814; deserted 21 Oct 1814.

POLMAN, Michael. Pvt. under Capt. Barton Hackney, 10 Sep - 27 Oct 1814.

POOL, Basil. Pvt. under Capt. Fonsten; joined 2 Sep 1814; sick absent on 3 Oct 1814.

POOL [Poole], Cornelius. Pvt. under Capt. Philip Smith, 23 May - 8 Sep 1813; b. 1792; res. Fred. Co, MD, 1850, 1855. [Bapt. at Frederick Luth. Ch. were: Cornelius b. 24 Feb 1794; Susanna b. Aug 1792; Eleonora b. 18 Jun 1790; Wilhelm b. 21 Oct 1787 - all children of Conrad and Magdalena Pul.] Acq: 1851 - William Eader; 1855 - Jacob Smith, Samuel S. Simmons.
Sources: Bounty land claim, 55-120-5758; **Maryland German Ch. Records,** v. 4.

THE VETERANS

POOL [Poole], Henry M. Pvt. under Capt. Samuel Ogle, 1 May 1813 - 5 Jul 1813 and pvt. under Capt. George W. Magee - joined 23 Jul 1814; deserted Oct 1814.
[The following may apply: (1) d. 8th E.D. Jan 1850 was Henry Poole, age 54, farmer, from consumption, ill for 10 days; (2) bapt. in Frederick Luth. Ch. was Henry son of Henry and Mary Poole, b. 15 Jan 1796, bapt. 27 Sep 1796; (3) FCml issued to Henry Poole and Polly Mahaney 9 Mar 1811.]
Sources: **Bridge in Time** (mortality schedule); **Records of the Evangelical Reformed Ch. in Frederick, Maryland, 1746-1800**; FCml.

POOL, John. Pvt., 16th U.S. Inf. At enlistment: 5 feet, 9 inches; black eyes, black hair and dark complexion; 36; occupation comb maker; b. Fredericktown, MD; enlisted 25 July or 27 Aug 1812 at Phila., PA by Lt. Powers for 5 yrs. Joined Regt. from the hospital. Mustered in Capt. Alex. McEwen's company 1 May 1815.

POOL, John. 30th U.S. Inf. At enlistment: 5 feet, 9 inches; age 37; b. in Fredericktown, MD; enlisted 8 Apr 1814 at Burlington by Capt. Barney for the duration of the war.

POOLE, Frederick. Pvt. under Capt. John Brengle, 25 Aug - 19 Sep 1814.

POOLE, Jacob. Pvt. under Capt. Samuel Dawson, 1 May - 5 Jul 1813.

POOLE, William. Pvt. under Capt. George W. Ent, 3rd Regt., 24 Aug - 30 Sep 1814; b. c.1790; m. 6 May 1811, Catharine Alrick (b. c.1795) in Frederick by Jonathan Hefferstine, German Reformed minister. William Poole d. at Frederick on 3 Feb 1855. 1850 of Fredericktown: William Poole, 66, blacksmith; Catherine Poole, 50; Hanson, 29; Lucretia L. Poole, 17; Martha H. Poole, 14; William Poole, 12 - all b. in MD. Acq: 1855 - George Straitman(?) and Frederick Lambert, res. Frederick; 1856 - John Poole and Stephen J. Kline, res. Fred. Co. [FCml issued to William Poole and Catherine Abrecht 30 Apr 1814.]
Sources: Bounty land claim, 55-120-89513; **Names in Stone.**

POBST, John. - See John Bopst.

PORTER, James. Pvt., 2nd U.S. Inf. At enlistment: 5 feet, 9 inches; dark eyes, dark hair, dark complexion; age 33; farmer; b. in Fred. Co., MD; enlisted 7 or 17 July 1807 in Washington by Lt. Bowie for 5 yrs. Absent since 5 Sep 1807 at Ft. Dearb. Tried by court martial for desertion; sentenced to 50 lashes. Sentenced 19 Jun 1809 for theft; sentenced 40 lashes. Tried for selling blanket and sentenced 25 lashes. In hospital at Washington 5 Dec 1810. Discharged for disability.

PORTER, John A. Pvt. under Capt. John Brengle, 25 Aug - 19 Sep 1814; b. c.1792; m. c.21 Jul 1818, Mary Ann Watt, who d. 30 Jun 1830; he later m. 5 Sep 1851, Catharine Baer, in Fredericktown by Rev. Daniel Zacharias. John A. Porter res. Fred. Co., 1851; for many yrs a constable and policeman; d. Fredericktown 20 Apr 1855 after protracted illness. 1850 census of Fredericktown: John A. Porter, 48 [58?], laborer; Catherine Bear, 39; William Bear, 23, cooper; Henry Bear, 16;

FREDERICK COUNTY MILITIA IN THE WAR OF 1812

George, 14; Caroline, 12; John, 11; Jane, 8; Frances, 6; Charles A., 4 - all b. MD. Catherine Porter d. 13 July 1866 in her 58th year. Acq: 1855 - Michael Rowe and Sarah Ely, res. Fred. Co. In a letter from Catharine Porter, wife of Jno. A. Porter, dated 17 Dec 1855, Frederick she said that she had given bounty land warrant to Mr. James Harding and that she had a house full of small children and needed the money.

Sources: Bounty land claim, 50-40-85338, 55-120-9527 (canceled), 55-120-59134 (Certificate for 120 acres in the file); **(Frederick) Examiner,** 5 Nov 1851, 2 May 1855, 22 Aug 1866; **Bridge in Time; FCml.**

PORTER [Parter?], Reason. Pvt. from Balt. Co.; joined 5 Sep 1814; deserted 22 Sep 1814.

POTTER, William. Pvt. under Capt. Samuel Duvall, 3 Aug - 3 Oct 1814.

POTTS, Philip T. Pvt. under Capt. Henry Steiner, 25 Aug - 27 Sep 1814. Philip Thomas Potts son of Richard and Elizabeth Potts, d. 15 Jan 1818, 25; bur. Mt. Olivet, Frederick.

Source: **Names in Stone.**

POWDER, Jacob. 2nd corpl. under Capt. William Durbin, 24 Aug - 27 Oct 1814; b. c.1795; res. Carroll Co., MD 1855. [FCml issued to Jacob Powder, Jr., and Elizabeth Byers 25 Apr 1818. Elizabeth Pouder is shown in 1860 census of Westminster area of Carroll Co.]

Sources: Bounty land claim, 55-160-11789; **FCml; Carroll County, Maryland 1860 Census Index.**

POWEL, George. Pvt. under Capt. Fonsten, 2 Sep - 27 Oct 1814; res. 6 miles from Westminster.

POWEL [Powell], Jacob. Pvt. under Capt. John Fonsten, 2 Sep - 27 Oct 1814 (drafted at Uniontown); res. 8 miles from Westminster; b. c.1780; m. 13 Nov 1802, Elizabeth Wantz (b. c.1780) by Daniel Shrader, Luth. minister. He res. Carroll Co. in 1850; d. Carroll Co. 21 Apr 1855. Acq: John Flegle, age 61, and Frederick Wants, age 78, res. Carroll Co.

Source: Bounty land claim, 55-120-54057.

POWEL, Nathan. Mbr. of Crawford's "company."

POWELL, Jonathan. 2nd sergt. under Capt. Matthew Murray, 25 Aug - 27 Oct 1814.

POWELL, Samuel. 1st Sergt. under Capt. Samuel Dawson, 21 Jul 1814 - 10 Jan 1815.

POWERS, Thomas. Pvt. from Washington Co. under Capt. Samuel Dawson, 14 Oct 1814 - 10 Jan 1815.

PROBY [Praby], John. Pvt. under Capt. William Durbin, Jr., 24 Aug - 27 Oct 1814.

PRATHER, James. Pvt. from Mechanickstown as under Capt. George W. Magee, 23 Jul - 10 Jan 1815. [*Md. Herald and Hagerstown Advertiser* - Sep 2 1808 - Distiller wanted - James Prather living near Mr. Harbnine's Tavern at the Big Spring.]

PRAUGH, Abner. Mbr. of Crawford's "company."

PRAUGH, John. Mbr. of Crawford's "company."

PRESTON, John. Pvt. under Capt. Fonsten; joined 2 Sep 1814; furloughed from 21 Oct 1814 for 7 days.

THE VETERANS

PRETZMAN [Pretsman], George. Pvt., 38th U.S. Inf., under Capt. Jno. Buck. At enlistment: 5 feet 10 1/2 inches; gray eyes, brown hair and dark complexion; age 23; occupation carpenter; b. Fred. Co., MD; enlisted 9 Jun 1814 by Ens. Martin for duration of war; d. at Genl. Hospital at Balt. on 2 Dec 1814.

PRICE, George. Pvt. in the 1st Cav. Dist., under Capt. Upton Reid, 26 Aug - 3 Sep 1814. [FCml issued to George Price and Catherine Coale on 6 May 1816.]

PRIESTMAN, George. Pvt. under Capt. Philip Smith 23 May - 8 Sep 1813.

PROTZMAN [Prutzman, Pretzman, Pristman], Jacob. Pvt. under Capt. Creager; drafted at Creagers Town, served near Washington City and at battle of North Point and Balt. He m. Feb 1808,* Elisabeth Ringer (b. c.1787) at Creagerstown, MD. (FCml issued 7 Feb 1807 to Jacob Sprutzman and Elizabeth Ringer.) Jacob d. 1 Mar or 1 Apr 1832 at Hagerstown. His widow res. Seneca Co., OH, 1854; Hagerstown, MD 1855. Acq: 1854 - Daniel Young, of lawful age, former res. Fred. Co., MD, first acq. in 1811; 1855 - John Ringer and David J. Barr, res. Hagerstown; 1871 - Joshua Wilson and Benjamin Brown; 1873 - Peter Eichelberger and Harriet Leonard, acq. for 25 yrs.

Sources: Bounty land claims, 55-40-100905, 55-120-7774; Pensions, WO4432, WC5273 (admitted 2 Jun 1873).

* This date taken from Elizabeth's first application for bounty land; later she gave date of marriage as 22 Dec 1803.

PRUTZMAN [Pratzman?], Christian. Pvt. under Capt. Daniel Shawen, 5 Sep - 27 Oct 1814.

PRYAR, John. Pvt. under Capt. Samuel Dawson; joined 26 Jul 1814; deserted.

PUMPHREY, William of Samuel. Pvt. under Capt. Samuel Duvall, 3 Aug - 3 Oct 1814. He said he entered service at Fredericktown as a substitute for John Cremer, son of the colonel, around 1 Aug 1814; discharged at Washington, D.C. around 10 Nov 1814; b. c.1783; res. Montgomery Co., MD, in 1852 and in St. Mary's Co. in 1859.

Source: Bounty land claim, 55-120-95588.

PURDY, Henry. Pvt. under Capt. Samuel Ogle, joined 1 May 1813, deserted but enlisted 15 or 16 Jun 1813 in regular army according to militia rolls by Lt. Fendell for 5 yrs.

PYFER, John. Pvt. under Capt. Henry Steiner, 28 Apr - 29 Jun 1813.

PYFER, Philip, Jr. Pvt. under Capt. Henry Steiner, 28 Apr - 29 Jun 1813 and 25 Aug - 27 Sep 1814; m. 16 Aug 1812, Rachel Brengle (b. c.1789) in Frederick by Rev Jonathan Helfenstein, of the German Ref. Ch., Frederick. FCml issued to Philip Pyfer, Jr. and Rachel Brengle on 15 Aug 1812. Philip Pyfer d. in Balt. on 27 Mar 1830. 1850 census of Fredericktown: Rachael Pyffer, 62; Margaret M. Pyffer, 25; Ann C. Pyffer, 22. Rachael owned one slave. Bur. at Mt. Olivet, Frederick: Rachel wife of Philip (22 Oct 1787 - 16 Nov 1857); and son Philip Henry (10 Aug 1824 - 4 May

FREDERICK COUNTY MILITIA IN THE WAR OF 1812

1881). Bur. at the Frederick Ref. Cem. was Philip Pyfer (27 Oct 1744 - 7 Oct 1819), b. Freuden Stadt, Germany. Warner Pyfer, youngest son of Philip Pyfer, d. 1929 at Michael Buckey's, his bro.-in-law (husband of Catherine Buckey). Acq: 1852 - Catharine Brengle (sister-in-law) and Margaret Harman.

Sources: Bounty land claim, 55-120-13294; FCml; Names in Stone; Bridge in Time; Engelbrecht Diary: 1:556, 589, 678.

PYLE, John Pvt. under Capt. Samuel Dawson; joined 26 Jul 1814; deserted 21 Aug 1814.

PYOTT, James. Pvt. under Capt. Creger. He said he served under Capt. Worfle (or similar name) and then Capt. Greegle. He was drafted at Fredericktown latter part of Jul 1814, he thinks, discharged at Balt., latter part of Sep 1814, he thinks; participated in Battle of Bladensburg and the Battle of Balt. - b. c.1783; m. Susannah Beckwith, at Fredericktown, about 1809 [according to him]. FCml issued to James Pyott and Susanna Beckwith 11 Jul 1809. She d. prior to 27 May 1871. He res. Roane Co., TN, 1851, 1855, 1871 (P.O. address: Post Oak Springs), on Emery Road about 10 miles west of Kingston; d. 26 Dec 1871; had no children. Acq: 1851 - Samuel Pyott and Isaac Eblen, both served in VA regt. at same time as James Pyott was in the service, having frequently seen him at that time; 1855 - Samuel Owings and James T. Shelley, res. Roane Co.

Sources: Bounty land claim, 55-120-50094; Pensions, SO20286, SC21498.

QUEEN, William. Pvt. under Capt. Hackney, as a substitute, 1 Sep - 27 Oct 1814. He said he served under a Capt. Bruner for about a month, then transferred to Capt. Hackney - b. c.1788; m. 20 May 1816 (or 25 May 1817?), Elizabeth Fowler (b. c.1798), at Muskingum Co., OH, by E. S. Rishey. At enrollment: about 5 1/2 feet tall, light complexion, light or hazel eyes; res. Scioto Co., OH, 1850, 1855; d. Bloom Switch, OH, 20 Feb 1869. His widow res. Scioto Co., OH, 1880, infirm from age; she had res. Bloom Twp the last 45-50 yrs. Acq: 1880 - Washington C. Richart, 66 and Asaph Bennett, 56, acq. 45 and 30 yrs, resp.; John Phillips, 63, all res. Bloom Twp.

Sources: Bounty land claim, 55-120-14225; Pensions, WO39499, WC30428.

QUYNN, Patrick. Pvt. in the company of Lieut. Upton Reid, 1st Cav. Dist., 26 Aug - 3 Sep 1814.

QUYNN, William. Pvt. under Lieut. Kolb, 6 - 15 Nov 1814.

RADER, Michael. Pvt. under Capt. John Galt, 31 Aug - 27 Oct 1814.

RAFESNIDER, John. Pvt. under Capt. William Knox, 26 Aug - 27 Oct 1814.

RAGAN, John. From Washington Co. Lieut. Colonel of the 24th Regt. and specially formed 1st Regt. in service of U. S., consisting of companies from Western Maryland. This regt. served 21 Jul 1814 - 10 Jan 1815. He was captured by the British at the Battle of Bladensburg but released.

RAINEY, John. Pvt. under Capt. Samuel Duvall, 3 Aug - 3 Oct 1814.

RAIT, Hammond. Never joined his company under Capt. William Durbin, which served 24 Aug - 27 Oct 1814. [FCml issued to Hammond Raitt and Eleanor Norris 30 Oct 1797.]

RAMER, John. Pvt. under Capt. Jacob Getzendanner, 6 - 17 Sep 1813. [Frederick Luth. Ch. records show a William Perry Ramer son of John and Susannah Ramer b. 4 Dec 1818; bapt. 4 Mar 1821.]

RAMSBURG, Frederick. Pvt. under Capt. Nicholas Turbutt, 1 Sep - 27 Oct 1814; m. 24 May 1818, Lydia Snook by Rev. Jonathan Helfenstein, of German Ref. Ch. Frederick Ramsburg d. 29 Jun 1836. Frederick J. Ramsburg, son of Frederick and Lydia, d. 25 Jul 183?; bur. at Bethel Luth. Ch. (between Mountaindale and Yellow Springs). Acq: 1851 - Urias Ramsburgh, Simon Snook and John Reese, res. Fred. Co.; 1855 - Dennis Ramsburgh and Jacob Zimmerman, res. Fred. Co.

Ramsburg family came here from Germany, first settled in PA but afterwards moved to MD, settling near Charlesville, Fred. Co. A mbr. of the third generation of family was Frederick Ramsburg.

Sources: Bounty land claim, 55-120-55322; Williams, **History of Fred. Co.**; **Names in Stone.**

RAMSBURG [Remsberg], Joseph. Pvt. under Capt. Daniel Shawen, 5 Sep - 27 Oct 1814; b. 26 Mar 1796; m. 25 Dec 1820, Magdalene Bowlus (b. 5 Sep 1798), at Middletown, MD. [According to him; however the FCml issued to Joseph Ramsburg and Magdalena Bowlus 24 Dec 1821.] 1850 census of Middletown Dist.: Joseph Ramsburg, 53; Magdalen Ramsburg, 51; and Edward Ramsburg, 21, labourer - all b. in MD. Joseph res. Middletown, Fred. Co., 1871; d. Middletown 27 Aug 1873. His widow res. Middletown in 1875; d. 30 Aug 1883 at her res. on West Main St., Middletown, of paralysis; bur. Middletown Lutheran Cem. Three children survived her: Joseph and Edward Ramsburg and Mrs. Joseph Gaver, widow. Family Record: Joseph Ramsburg b. 26 Mar 1796; Magdalene Ramsburg b. 5 Sep 1798; Ann Catharine Ramsburg b. 5 Sep 1821; Josephus Ramsburg b. 3 Jun 1823; Levi Ramsburg b. 24 Mar 1825; Ann Rebekah b. 25 Feb 1827; Edward Ramsburg b. 10 Feb 1829; Ann Eliza Ramsburg b. 28 Jul 1831. Acq: 1875 - Jacob Smith served with Joseph Ramsburg in company of Capt. Shawen; Lewis Roderick, res. Fred. Co., who served in same company. 1878 - Josephus Remsburg and Edward Ramsburg, children of Joseph Ramsburg, aged 55 and 49, resp.; John Derr, 65, and Lawson Alexander, 65, res. Middletown res. in community and town of Middletown.

Sources: Bounty land claims, 50-40-56643, 55-120-32792; Pensions, SO12173 (rejected 1 Apr 1872 due to insufficient service), WO11382, WC16779 (Admitted 18 Jan 1879); **Names in Stone; Bridge in Time;** FCml; (Frederick) Examiner, 22 Aug 1883, 5 Sep 1883.

RAMSBURG, Lewis. Pvt. under Capt. Thomas Contee Worthington 17 Aug - 31 Dec 1812; b. 3 Jun 1798, m. Charlotte, dau of Col. S. Steiner of Fredericktown. She d. Jan 1824, in her 27th year leaving husband and parent. His wife Susan B., b. KY 21 Feb 1812, d. 28 Oct 1855 leaving a husband and 7 children. Lewis d.

5 Jan 1865 in 67th year, connected c.23 yrs with Frederick-Town savings institution as its secretary. Both bur. Mt. Olivet Cem. 1850 census of Fredericktown: Lewis Ramsburg, 52; Susan B., 38, b. KY; Jane B., 15, b. KY; Wm. E., 13, b. KY; Mary A., 11, b. MD.

Sources: (Frederick) Examiner, 31 Oct 1855; 11 Jan 1865; Names in Stone; Bridge in Time; Frederick-Town Herald, 17 Jan 1824.

RAMSOUR [Ramsower], Henry. Pvt., 5th U.S. Inf., under Capt. James Dorman. At enlistment: 5 feet, 6 1/2 inches; hazel eyes, light hair, fair complexion; 22; farmer; b. Fred. Co., MD; enlisted 26 May 1812 at Fredericktown by Lt. Clarke for 5 yrs. Hospital guard on 28 Apr 1814. Joined his regt. 4 May 1814. Sent to hospital at Plattsburgh [NY] 1 Aug 1814. Absent sick at Plattsburgh since 1 Aug 1814. Buffalo [NY] 1 March and 30 Apr 1815. Discharged at Greenbush 10 May [or 1 May] 1815, ulcerated leg.

RANDALL, Mordacai. Pvt. under Capt. George W. Ent, 24 Aug - 30 Sep 1814.

RANDELL, Robert. Pvt. from Upper Fred. Co. under James F. Capt. Huston and Capt. Joseph Green; joined 23 Jul 1814; deserted 27 Oct 1814.

RANDLE, Nicholas. Mbr. of Crawford's "company."

RAPP, Samuel. Pvt. under Capt. Alexander, 22 July - 19 Sep 1814; b. in MD, m. Barbara Schu [Schur] (b. c.1802), at York, PA, 13 Mar 1817, by Rev George Geistweit, each for first time. Record of marr. held by Trinity Ref. Ch., Reading. At enrollment: carpenter, dark brown hair, grey eyes, dark complexion. Fol. discharge he res. in York, PA; d. York 1838. After his death his widow lived in Reading, PA; in 1878 res. at 1036 Penn St., Reading, PA; d. 27 Feb 1887. [In the records of Frederick Luth. Ch. appear baptism of Samuel son of Philipp and Susanna Rapp, b. 25 Aug 1793; bapt. 3 Apr 1794.] In Reading, PA in 1878: Jacob Rapp, 52, son of Samuel and Barbara Rapp, res. 1027 Greenwich, Reading, PA; and Mary J. Barrett, dau of Samuel and Barbara Rapp, age 42, res. 1036 Penn St., Reading, PA. Mrs. Maggie Glase, granddau of Samuel Rapp, age 36 and her husband Capt. Jacob W. Glase, tinsmith, age 39, residing at 213 S. 4th St., Reading, PA. Miss Annie C. Simmons, granddau of Samuel Rapp, age 26, housekeeper, 518 Cedar St., Reading, PA. Mrs. Mary Stahr, granddau of Samuel Rapp, age 36, housekeeper, 923 Green St., Reading, PA. Mrs. Susan Getrost, dau of Samuel Rapp, age 67, housekeeper, 726 10th St., Reading, PA. Jacob Rapp, son of Samuel Rapp, age 60, butcher, and Barbara Ann Rapp, dau-in-law of Samuel Rapp, age 56, housekeeper, res. 436 Mulberry St., Reading, PA. Isaac R. Fisher, no relation, age 64, alderman, 237 North 8th St., Reading, PA. John Simmons, son-in-law of Samuel Rapp, age 62, laborer, 518 Cedar St., Reading, PA. Samuel Berret, son-in-law of Samuel Rapp, age 72, retired merchant, 1036 Penn St., Reading, PA.

Sources: Bounty land claim, 55-120-56768; Pensions, WO17219, WC11479.

THE VETERANS

RATTLE [Rattler], William. Pvt. under Capt. John Brengle, 25 Aug - 19 Sep 1814.

RAWLINS, Wilson. Pvt. under Capt. Samuel Dawson, 21 Jul 1814 - deserted -- Nov 1814.

RAY, John. Pvt. under Capt. George W. Magee, 23 Jul - 13 Oct 1814; sick absent 27 Aug. [FCml issued to John Ray and Elizabeth Roop on 2 Jan 1809.]

REAM, George. Pvt., U.S. Artillery. At enlistment: 5 feet, 7 inches; brown eyes, brown hair and fair complexion; age 21; occupation shoemaker; b. Fred. Co., MD; enlisted 5 July 1814 at Youngstown, PA, by Lt. Nevell for duration of war. Buffalo 28 Feb & 20 Apr 1815. Ft. Niagara 30 Jun 1815. Discharged at Buffalo 3 Jun 1815.

REAMS, John. Pvt., 28th U.S. Inf. At enlistment: 5 feet, 10 inches; black eyes, black hair and fair complexion; age 20; shoemaker; b. Fred. Co., MD; enlisted 3 May 1814 in KY, by Capt. Stockton for duration of war. Mustered in Lt. T. Edmondson's company 5 Apr 1815. Discharged at Detroit on 30 Jun 1815 from Capt. Stockton's company.

REASER, Jacob. Native of Fred. Co.; in his youth he engaged in the Marchant Marine which traded in the West Indies and England. He joined Capt. Stile's Balt. company of marine artillery 29 Aug 1814. (listed as Jacob Razor in muster roll.) Company discharged 30 Nov 1814. He d. in his 79th year in 1860 near Frederick-town. [Poss. related: 1850 census of Frederick-town: Jacob Reese, 55, farmer; Catherine, 52. FCml:

Jacob Reese and Catherine Derr on 6 Jun 1822.]
Sources: (Frederick) Examiner, 5 Dec 1860; Bridge in Time, FCml.

RECRUIT, Richard. Pvt. under Capt. Barton Hackney, 1 Sep - 27 Oct 1814; "sick in hospital 22 Oct."

REDENOUR, John. Deserted from Capt. Duvall's company at their Bladensburg camp on 16 Aug 1814 and described as: drafted man, 21-22 yrs old, 5 feet 8-9 inches, dark complexion, dark eyes, dark hair, by profession a blacksmith.

REED, Benjamin. Pvt. under Capt. Barton Hackney; joined 1 Sep 1814; deserted 24 Oct 1814.

REED, George. Pvt. under Capt. Samuel Ogle, 1 May - 5 Jul 1813. He said he volunteered in Capt. Ogle's company at Emmittsburg in 1813, discharged at the Patapsco Encampment near the city of Balt. Their regt. was at Fort McHenry for one week; b. c.1791; m. Nancy Lomdon, in Gettysburg, PA, in 1824 or 25. He res. Guilford Twp, Franklin Co., PA, 1871 (P.O. address: Chambersburg). Acq: 1871 - Henry Hockersmith and William M. Rupert, acq. 50 and 15-20 yrs, resp. Pension, 2677, SC1171 (admitted 13 Jul 1871).

REED, James. Pvt. under Capt. Basil Dorsey, 30 Jul - 27 Sep 1814; m. 20 Dec 1819, Susan Smith [b. c.1788], in Fred. Co., by Rev. George Rozell. James Reed d. at Fredericktown, Knox Co., OH, 16 Sep 1844. [FCml issued to James Reid and Susan Smith 22 Dec 1818.]
Source: Bounty land claim, 55-160-38083.

REED, John. Pvt. under Capt. Samuel Dawson, 1 May - 5 Jul 1813; he said that he also volunteered in Capt. Nicholas Osb.'s company of VA cavalry at Loudon Co., VA, in fall of 1813 and discharged at Norfolk, VA, in Mar 1814. Afterward entered Capt. John Stevens' company of VA militia in Loudoun Co., Va, discharged at Norfolk, VA in 1814, and was in Capt. P. M. Goggins's company of VA militia at Norfolk; in the service c.2 yrs. Received bounty land warrant for 160 acres - b. c.1794; m. Elizabeth Miller, at Morgan Co., OH, 4 Oct 1860; res. Morgan Co., OH, 1871 (P.O. address: Pennsville).

Sources: Pension, SO5531, SC2908. Admitted 17 Aug 1871.

REED, Philip. Pvt. from Fred. Co. under Capt. Samuel Dawson, 21 Jul - 10 Jan 1815; m(1) 17 Apr 1817, Mary Weakly (d. Columbus, OH, 19 Apr 1839) of Fred. Co.; m(2) 5 May 1841, Sarah Pursell (b. c.1785), at Jackson Twp, by Rev. P. Peirce. Philip Reed came to Columbus c.1827 from Fredericktown, MD. She res. Columbus, OH, in 1878 (20 East Boon St.). At enlistment: about 5 feet, 7 inches high, fair complexion, light hair, blue eyes; d. Columbus, OH, 26 Jul 1861. Sarah Reed d. 1 Sep 1893. Acq: 1878 - B. F. Martin, age 58, res. 79 E. Friend St., Columbus, and Nathan Cole, age 62, E. Friend St., Columbus, acq. 35 and 40 yrs, resp.; John R. Coo, No. 432 E. Rich St., Columbus, George McDonald, 191 E. Broad St., Columbus, acq. 26 yrs.

Sources: Bounty land claims, 50-80-21082, 55-80-15511; Pensions, WO1511, WC8571 (admitted 28 Aug 1878).

REED, Philip. Pvt. under Capt. Samuel Ogle, 1 May - 5 Jul 1813.

REEDER, James. Pvt. under Capt. Barton Hackney, 1 Sep - 27 Oct 1814; "sick in hospital 17 Oct."

REES, Benjamin. Pvt. under Capt. Fonsten, 2 Sep - 27 Oct 1814; res. 6 miles from Westminster.

REICHART, Christian. Pvt. under Capt. Fonsten, 2 Sep - 27 Oct 1814; res. 13 miles from Westminster.

REID, James. Pvt. under Capt. Thomas Contee Worthington 17 Aug - 31 Dec 1812. See James Reed.

REID, Upton Scott. Lieut. and Capt. in 1st Cav. Dist., 26 Aug - 3 Sep 1814.

REINICKER, Paul. Pvt. under Capt. John Galt, 31 Aug - 27 Oct 1814.

REITZELL, Philip. 4th Sergt. under Capt. Capt Nicholas Turbutt, 1 Sep - 27 Oct 1814; m. 1 Sep 1819, Maria Straigle(?) by Benjamin Keller at borough of Carlisle. Philip Reitzel d. at Lancaster 27 Apr 1848. Widow res. Lancaster Co., PA, 1852. Acq: 1852 - Frederick Keller, now of Lancaster Co., PA, age 58; served as a drafted militiaman and knew Philip Reitzel then of Fredericktown; was a quartermaster or a quartermaster sergt. in the company of Capt. Turbutt.

Source: Bounty land claim, 50-rejected-128544.

RELIEN, Jacob S. Pvt. under Capt. Barton Hackney, 1 Sep - 27 Oct 1814.

REMSBURG, Ezra. Pvt. under Capt. Daniel Shawen, 5 Sep - 27 Oct 1814.

RENSBERT, Joseph. Pvt. under Capt. Daniel Shawen, 5 Sep - 27 Oct 1814.

THE VETERANS

REVELL, James. Pvt. under Capt. Samuel Duvall, 3 Aug - 3 Oct 1814.

REYNOLDS [Reynold], Horatio. Pvt. from Fredericktown under Capt. James F. Huston/Capt. Joseph Green; joined 23 Jul 1814, deserted 8 Dec, returned 30 Dec 1814; discharged in Annapolis c.10 Jan 1815.

RHINECHER, Peter. Pvt. under Capt. George W. Magee; joined 22 Jul 1814; deserted 12 Aug 1814.

RHODES, Samuel. m. Anna Catsdeafler at Fred. Co., MD, Dec ---- (FCml issued on 23 Nov 1822 to Samuel Roads and Ann Cartzdaffner). Anna d. c.1867. He res. Lancaster, Fairfield Co., OH, in 1877 (Lancaster); said he served under Capt. Barton Hackney, drafted Sep 1814, discharged 1814.
Source: Pension, SO30725. Rejected 22 Sep 1880 - no evidence of the service in alleged company.

RHODERICK. See Roderick.

RHYNE [Rine], John. Pvt. under Basil Dorsey, 30 Jul - 27 Sep 1814; b. c.1790; res. Pike Twp, Coshocton Co., OH (P.O. address: West Carlisle) 1871.
Source: Pension, SO12675, SC7732 (admitted 7 Nov 1871).

RICE, Philip. Pvt., 38th U.S. Inf., under Capt. S. C. Leakin. At enlistment: 5 feet, 8 inches; gray eyes, brown hair and fair complexion; occupation wheelwright; b. Fred. Co., MD; enlisted 21 Oct 1813 by Lt. Janes for 1 year. Re-enlisted 11 March 1814 by Capt. Buck for duration of war, age 23 or 33. Balt. 1 Jun 1814. Deserted 15 July 1814. Absent at Camp South River; sentenced by court martial to hard labor at Ft. McHenry. Released 11 Jan 1815.

RICHARDS, John. Pvt. under Capt. William Knox, 26 Aug 1814; deserted 28 Aug 1814.

RICHARDS, John. Pvt. under Capt. Samuel Dawson, 1 May - 5 Jul 1813.

RICHARDS, John. Pvt. under Capt. Matthew Murray, 25 Aug - 27 Oct 1814. He said he served under Capts. Murry and Shryock; b. c.1795; m. Ann Richards (b. c.1795), in Clermont Co., OH, 23 Apr 1818, by Rev. William Thompson. John Richards d. in Clermont Co. 3 Aug 1849. In 1851 she res. Clermont Co., OH. Acq: Michael Richards, age 59 (1851), res. Clermont Co., OH.
Source: Bounty land claim, 55-120-43775.

RICHARDS, Michael. Pvt. under Capt. Barton Hackney, 1 Sep - 27 Oct 1814.

RICHARDS, William. Pvt. under Capt. Capt Nicholas Turbutt, 1 Sep -27 Oct 1814; b. c.1796; m. Charlotte Fowler, 1820. FCml issued to William Richards and Charlotte Fowler on 15 Dec 1820. He res. Hyattstown, Montgomery Co., MD, in 1871.
Sources: Bounty land claim, 55-120-63095; Pension, SO3973 (rejected 28 Sep 1871 - insufficient service); FCml.

RICHARDS, William W. Pvt. under Capt. Denton Darby, 3 Aug - 8 Nov 1814, as substitute for John Richards; b. c.1797; m. 8 May 1821, Rebecca Stone (b. c.1805), at Harrison Co., OH, by Charles Chapman, J.P. William W. Richards res. Guernsey Co., OH, 1851, 1855, 1871 (Middlebourne); d. Washington, OH, 9 Sep 1881. Widow d. 13 Mar 1889. Acq: 1882 - S. Potts, age

75, res. Cambridge, OH, and Henry Young, age 66, res. Washington, OH, acq. 44 and 42 yrs, resp.; Hezekiah Clements, age 80, res. Washington, OH; Elias Burdett, age 79, res. Washington, OH; James McDowell, age 36, res. Washington, OH; Alfred Skinner, age 61, res. Washington, OH.

Sources: Bounty land claim, 55-120-69772; Pensions, SO6497, SC4223, WO42041, WC32704 (admitted 23 Aug 1882, dropped 16 Oct 1891).

RICHARDS, Zachariah. Pvt. from Balt. under Capt. Joseph Green, 14 Oct 1814 - 10 Jan 1815.

RICHARDSON, Elijah. Mbr. of Crawford's "company." [FCml issued to Elijah Richardson and Elizabeth Brawner on 21 Sep 1807.]

RICHARDSON, Joseph. According to his widow he served as a pvt. in the Indian Wars under Anthony Wayne and afterward a volunteer in the War of 1812; he m. Susannah Southgate (b. c.1776), in Fred. Co., 19 Sep by Lewis Brown. Joseph Richardson d. Marshall Co., VA, 3 Jul 1835.

Source: Bounty land claim, 50-rejected-152287.

RICHARDSON, Zachariah. Pvt. from Upper Fred. Co. under Capt. James F. Huston, 23 Jul - 13 Oct 1814.

RICHMOND [Richment], Francis. 1st Lieut. in Capt. Matthew Murray's company, 25 Aug - 27 Oct 1814; b. c.1801; m. Catherine Powell (she being his 2nd wife), 6 Mar 1827, by Rev. Martin, at Middletown, Fred. Co., MD. Francis Richmond d. at Hannibal, Marion Co., MO, 3 Oct 1844. Widow res. Marion Co., MO, 1879; d. 22 Jun 1881 (note from George Richmond, her son, dated 16 Mar 1886). [Appearing in the records of the Ref. Ch., Middletown: Daniel, son of Francis and Sussan Richmend, b. 12 Jan 1807, bapt. 5 Apr 1807.] Acq: 1879 - Joseph Richardson, age 65, res. Louisiana, Pike Co., MO, 42 yrs and res. Fred. Co., MD, 23 yrs, acq. when res. Fred. Co.

Sources: Bounty land claim, (pending) 55-334450; Pension, WO37528, WC29564 (admitted 20 May 1880); Md. German Ch. Records, v.1.

RICHTER, Frederick. Pvt. under Capt. Barton Hackney, 1 Sep - 27 Oct 1814.

RICHTER [Rector], John. Pvt. under Capt. John Brengle, 25 Aug - 19 Sep 1814. At enrollment: c.5 ft, 10 inches, auburn hair, blue eyes, fair complexion. Fol. discharge he res. several yrs in Fredericktown; in Perry Co., OH since 1831; b. c.1797; res. near Ferrara, Perry Co., OH in 1878. [Records of the Frederick Evan. Ref. Ch. show Johannes, son of Henrich and Catharina Richter, b. 3 Apr 1796, bapt. 4 Apr 1796. FCml issued to John Richter and Catherine Cookerly 23 Jun 1829.] Acq: 1878 - Arthur T. McArter, age 42 and Berman H. Bentley, age 54, both res. near Ferrara, acq. 30 and 20 yrs resp.

Sources: Bounty land claim, 55-160-42195; Pension, SO33568, SC24321 (admitted 10 Sep 1878; dropped 1 Feb 1883 due to death).

RICKETS, Bazel. b. in Montgomery Co. in 1800; m(2) Alina Smith (widow) at Roscoe, Coshocton Co., OH, 13 Apr 1835. At enrollment:, age 14, blue eyes, light brown hair, fair complexion, 5 ft, 4 inches. He res. Fredericktown until c.1822 when he m. and moved to Middletown. There he lived two yrs, then

THE VETERANS

moved to Cass Twp, Muskingum Co. (P.O. address: Dresden), OH, res. there 1871, 1878. Acq: Henry W. Kipp, age 34, res. Cass Twp, and John Hoopes, age 65, res. Zanesville, OH, acq. 25 yrs.

He said he was drafted under the orders of Capt. Darby. He was in Fredericktown, MD, with his father's team of two horses and wagon when word came that the enemy was in Washington and coming toward Frederick, res. with his father in Fred. Co., MD, c.12 miles from Fredericktown. Commanded by military authorities he proceeded to Fredericktown Barracks and took on load of knapsacks, muskets and provisions and hauled them to Tennellytown under guard of four men, thence to Washington on the Georgetown Road; continued hauling under orders for 18 days, then he placed under control and orders of Campbell Nichols, and aided him in the delivery of 16 or 17 prisoners at Fredericktown Barracks.

Sources: Bounty land claim, 55-160-112729; Pension, SO26553 (rejected 28 Jul 1874 - presumptive abandonment).

RICKETTS, Benjamin. Pvt. under Capt. John Galt, 31 Aug - 27 Oct 1814.

RICKETTS, Hezekiah. Corpl. under Capt. Darby. He said he was at the Battle of Bladensburg; b. c.1791; m. Sarah ---, at Hanady Town, MD. [FCml issued to Hezekiah Ricketts and Sally Poole on 12 Nov 1819.] He res. c.6 miles west of Hopkinsville, KY, 1871, 1872 with wife Sarah; he was nearly blind. Acq: 1871 - B. M. Ricketts, age c.24, res. Christian Co., KY, and D. S. Hays, age over 70, res. Hopkinsville, KY, acq. with Hezekiah Ricketts for c.50 yrs; William M. Shipp res. Christian Co., OH, acq. c.38 yrs. 1872 - John T. Ricketts, son of Hezekiah Ricketts.

Sources: Bounty land claims, 50-40-53812, 55-120-22598; Pension, SO6495, SC15871 (admitted 15 Apr 1872).

RIDDLEMOSER, Abraham. Pvt. from Upper Fred. Co. under Capt. Huston, James F.; joined 23 Jul 1814; deserted 11 Sep 1814.

RIDER, Frederick. Pvt. under Capt. Joseph Wood, 27 Aug - 28 Oct 1814.

RIDER, George. Pvt. under Capt. Joseph Wood, 27 Aug - 28 Oct 1814. [FCml issued to George Rider and Ann McDaniel on 12 Mar 1819.]

RIDGELY [Ridgly], Alfred. From Fredericktown - 2nd Corporal and later as 3rd sergt. under Capt. James F. Huston and Capt. Joseph Green, 23 Jul - 10 Jan 1815.

RIDGELY, Henry. Pvt. under Capt. Samuel Dawson, 21 Jul - deserted 4 Oct 1814.

RIDGELY [Ridgley], Joshua. Pvt. under Capt. Jacob Alexander, 22 Jul - 19 Sep 1814; b. 9 Jun 1793; res. Middletown, Fred. Co., MD, 1850, 1852, 1855. 1850 census of Middletown Dist.: Joshua Ridgley, 55, laborer, with Margaret Ridgely, 50; Asa Ridgeley, 12; John Koogle, 18 - all b. MD. Bur. at Middletown Luth. Cem.: Joshua Ridgely (9 Jun 1793 - 30 Jan 1864) and Margaret Ridgely (22 Jul 1798 - 1 Mar 1877).

Sources: Bounty land claim, 55-120-26778; **Bridge in Time; Names in Stone.**

RIDGLEY, Frederick. Pvt. under Capt. Samuel Duvall, 3 Aug - 3 Oct

1814; b. c.1777-81; res. Montgomery Co., Ohio 1850.
Source: Bounty land claim, 55-120-62591.

RIDGLEY, Richard. Pvt. in Capt. Matthew Murray's company, 25 Aug - 27 Oct 1814; b. c.1774; m. 28 Aug 1798, Mary Hymes (b. 10 Dec 1780) by Rev. Phillip Snider, Presby. preacher, in Fred. Co. Rev. Snyder d. c.1842. Richard Ridgley d. 20 Dec 1863; widow res. Luken Town, Lawrence Co., IL (P.O. address: Sumner).

Family Records of Richard and Mary Ridgley - Richard Ridgley and Mary Hymes m. 20 Aug 1798. Births: George William Ridgley b. 3 Oct 1799; Westall Ridgley b. 14 Aug 1801; Ana Ridgley b. 26 Aug 1803; Daniel Ridgley b. 3 Oct 1805; Sarah Ridgley b. 8 Mar 1808; Rebecca Ridgley b. 6 Jun 1810; Richard Ridgley b. 18 Jul 1812; Elias Ridgley b. 6 Oct 1814; Elizabeth Ridgley b. 8 Aug 1817; Ezra Eligah Ridgley b. 21 Jun 1820; Mary Ann Martha Ridgley b. 4 Mar 1823; John Lawrence Ridgley b. 8 Oct 1825. Deaths: Anna Basord 23 Sep 1837; Richard 21 Jul 1841; Westall 27 Mar 1847; Richard Sen 24 Dec 1863 (or 20 Dec 1863); Ezra E. 28 Oct 1865 (or 24 Oct 1868); George William Ridgley 15 Mar 1863; Sarah Doan 1 Feb 1849.

Acq: 1871 - Edward N. Moore and Ann M. Moore, res. Lawrence Co. 1872 - Henry Sherraden and Anner Sherraden, res. Lawrence Co., IL, acq. with Richard and Mary Ridgley since 1832.

Several letters in pension file dated 1932 and 1934 from Mrs. John W. Noble, No. 50 Petersboro, Detroit, MI, asking about Richard Ridgley of Fred. Co., MD.
Sources: Bounty land claim, 50-40-9996, 55-120-84173; Pension, WO7278, WC3872 (admitted 3 Sep 1872).

RIDINGER, Peter. Pvt. under Capt. Samuel Ogle, 1 May - 5 Jul 1813. His widow said he was drafted in Capt. Knox's Company in Aug 1814, discharged at Balt. Nov 1814. He was b. 28 Oct 1793; m. Catharine Shriver (b. c.1797) at Taneytown in 1813 by Mr. Grub. Peter Ridinger d. 11 May 1841/11 May 1842. [The date of 1841 was given by his widow in her application for bounty land; the 1842 date is shown on the tombstone.] He was bur. at Taneytown, Grace Evangelical and Reformed Ch. His widow res. Taneytown in 1871.
Sources: Pension, 1326 (rejected 30 Dec 1872 - no proof of service in Capt. Knox's company and presumptive abandonment of claim); Names in Stone.

RIEHL, Jacob. Pvt. under Capt. John Brengle, 25 Aug - 19 Sep 1814. [Frederick Luth. Ch. records show Jacob son of Georg and Elisabeth (Schneider) Riehl b. 5 Oct 1795, bapt. 6 Dec 1795. Other children of George and Elisabeth were bapt. in this ch.: Johannes, b. 25 Jan 1793; Anna b. 15 Apr 1791; Sophia b. 6 Jul 1789.] Jacob m. Miss Catharine Boswell Dec 1821, by Rev. D. F. Schaeffer. Jacob Riehl served as Court House keeper. 1850 census of Frederick-town: Jacob Riehl, 54; Catherine, 48; John H., 26, plasterer; Carlene Haller, 10. Catharine Riehl d. 1 Jan 1873 at her res. on West Patrick St., leaving aged husband; bur.

THE VETERANS

Mt. Olivet Cem. He d. at his res. W. Patrick St. on 28 Aug 1876.
Sources: Bridge in Time; (Frederick) Examiner, 8 Jan 1873, 30 Aug 1876;

RIFE, Abraham. Pvt. under Capt. John Galt, 31 Aug - 27 Oct 1814, res. 5 miles from Taneytown.

RIFE, Daniel. Pvt. under Capt. George W. Magee, 23 Jul - 10 Jan 1815, res. Mechanickstown. [FCml issued to Daniel Rife and Elizabeth Sumbrun 8 May 1811.]

RIFLE, John. Pvt. under Capt. Duvall, 3 Aug - 3 Oct 1814.

RIFFLE, John. Pvt. under Capt. Jacob Getzendanner, 9 Aug - 17 Sep 1813. [FCml issued to John Riffle and Sophia Derr 31 Mar 1828.]

RIGGLE, Adam. Pvt. from New Windsor under Capt. George W. Magee, 22 Jul - 10 Jan 1815.

RIGGS, Henry. Capt. of his own company, 27 Aug - 2 Oct 1814. His widow said he was drafted at New Market c.15 Aug 1814; m. 30 Jan 1821, Mary Hobbs (b. c.1792), in Fred. Co., by Rev Joseph H. Jones, Bapt. minister. Henry Riggs d. Fred. Co. 7 Jan 1849. Widow res. Fred. Co. 1851, 1855. Acq: 1851 - John Harding, pvt. in company of Henry Riggs; Nathan Nelson present at wedding; Nathan Maynard of Thomas and H. G. Maynard, present at burial of Capt. Henry Riggs.
Source: Bounty land claim, 55-120-62454.

RIGGS, Osha [Asha]. Pvt. under Capt. Samuel Dawson; joined 21 Jul 1814; deserted 22 Dec 1814.

RIGISON, James C. Pvt. under Capt. George W. Magee, 23 Jul - 13 Oct 1814.

RILEY, Charles. Servant under Capt. Samuel Duvall, 10 Sep - 3 Oct 1814.

RILEY, Daniel. Mbr. of Crawford's "company.

RINEDOLLER, John. Pvt. under Capt. William Knox, 26 Aug - 27 Oct 1814; b. c.1782; res. Carroll Co., MD, 1851.
Sources: Bounty land claims, 50-40-24860, 55-120-17966.

RINEHEART, Daniel. Pvt. from New Windsor under Capt. George W. Magee, 23 Jul 1814; prisoner at Bladensburgh 24 Aug, rejoined regt. 10 Nov 1814.

RINEHEART [Rinehart], John. Pvt. under Capt. George W. Magee, 22 Jul 1814; enlisted in regular army 19 or 21 Aug 1814 by Capt. Smith in Balt. 19 Aug 1814 for 5 yrs. At enlistment: 5 ft, 9 inches, blue eyes, brown hair, light complexion, age 38 or 28, laborer, b. Balt. Pvt. in 38th U.S. Inf. The Recruiting return shows him at Fort McHenry on 16 Feb and 28 Feb 1815. Serving in Capt. Thomas Sangston's Det., Ft. Covington on 30 Apr 1815.

RINER, George. Pvt. under Capt. Philip Smith 23 May - 8 Sep 1813. He said he was 2nd lieut., volunteered at Woodsbury, Fred. Co. - b. 3 May 1782; m. Abigail Jones c.16 May 1814. 1850 census of New Market Dist.: George Riner, 68, farmer; Abigail Riner, 62; Catherine Riner, 25; Mary Riner, 22 - all b. MD. George Riner d. 20 Mar 1871; bur. at Walkersville, Glade Ref. Cem. as Capt. George Riner; also wife Abigail;

FREDERICK COUNTY MILITIA IN THE WAR OF 1812

dau Catey, 11 Jul 1863, age 16 yrs. Catharine Riner 2nd dau of George and Abigail d. 14 July 1846, 46 yrs and 1 day.

Sources: Bounty land claim, 55-120-36677; (Frederick) Examiner, 30 July 1863, 19 Apr 1871; Names in Stone; FCmI.

RINER, William. Pvt. under Capt. Thomas Contee Worthington 17 Aug - 31 Dec 1812.

RINNER, John. Pvt. under Capt. George W. Ent, 3rd Regt., 24 Aug - 30 Sep 1814.

RIPPEN, William. Pvt. under Capt. Denton Darby, 3 Aug - 8 Nov 1814; b. c.1778; res. Loudoun Co. VA, in 1855.

Source: Bounty land claim, 55-160-24396.

RIPPIN [Rippen], Thomas. See Thomas Rippon below. He served as pvt. in 36th U.S. Inf. At enlistment: 5 feet, 11 inches; age 25; b. Fred. Co., MD; enlisted 17 May 1813 at Fredericktown, MD by Lt. Thomas Ritchie for 1 year; mustered at Frederick 23 May 1813. In Capt. Randolph's company on 30 Sep and 31 Oct 1813.

RIPPON, Thomas. Pvt. under Capt. Lowrye, Henry, joined militia 27 Aug; enlisted in regular army 25 Oct 1814. [1850 census of Fred. Co.: Thomas Rippen, miller, 64; Henry Rippin, 34, cooper; Margaret Rippin, 25; John T. Rippin, 3; William Rippin, 2; Josephine Rippin, 1 - all b. MD.]

RISE, William. Pvt. under Capt. Daniel Shawen; joined 5 Sep 1814; sick absent 21 Oct 1814.

RITCHIE, Thomas. 1st Lieut. in 36th U.S. Inf.; recruiting at Frederick on 23 May and 24 Jun 1813; recruiting at Waynesburg, PA, July, Aug and Sep in 1813; recruiting at Richmond, VA, May and Jun 1814; recruiting at Jerusalem; recruiting at Norfolk.

ROACH, Gustavus. Pvt. under Capt. Denton Darby, 3 Aug - 8 Nov 1814. The following was apparently mistakenly filed under name of Gustavus Roach - pertaining to his alleged father Dennis Roach, a pvt.. "Army Pay Office Washington, Decr. 8th 1815. I hereby certify that it appears from documents on file in this office that Dennis Roach late a pvt. of Capt. Robt. W. Kents' company of the late 14th Regt. of Infy. of U. States Army, enlisted on the sixth day of July 1812 to serve for the period of five yrs and that he d. in the service on the 22nd day of November 1812. And further that Gustavus Roach the bearer hereof appears from said documents to be the son and one of the heirs at law of said Dennis. Given under my hand Robert Balns(?)." Orlando Cook, Ignatius Edelin and John Cunningham made oath that Gustavus Roach is the reputed son of the late Dennis Roach - as above states. James M. Varnum, J.P.

ROADPOUCH, Peter. Pvt. under Capt. Fonsten, 2 Sep - 27 Oct 1814; res. 7 miles from Westminster; b. c.1773; m. 14 Feb 1797, Elizabeth Yingling (b. c.1775) by Rev. Kobrecht. He res. Pipe Creek Hundred, Carroll Co., MD, in 1850; d. near Union Mills 19 May 1852. Widow res. Carroll Co. 1855.

Source: Bounty land claim, 50-80-93918.

ROBERTS, Benjamin. Pvt. under Capt. Thomas Contee Worthington 17 Aug - 31 Dec 1812.

THE VETERANS

ROBERTS, William. Pvt. under Capt. Daniel Marker, 25 Aug - 27 Oct 1814. His discharge paper was destroyed by fire in his own dwelling, 1835. - b. c.1778; res. Jefferson Co., OH, 1850, 1855.
Source: Bounty land claim, 55-120-29918.

ROBERTSON, Alexander. 1st sergt. under Capt. John Brengle, 25 Aug - 19 Sep 1814; b. Scotland in 1793; m. Mary Mantz, in Fredericktown, 1 Sep 1818 by Rev. Patrick Davidson. Alexander Robertson d. Fredericktown 28 Dec 1822, age 29; bur. Mt. Olivet Cem., Frederick. His widow res. Fred. Co., 1855. Acq: 1855 - Thomas W. Morgan, William Baer and Ezra Houck, res. Fred. Co.
Sources: Bounty land claim, 55-160-4483; Names in Stone; FCmL

ROBERTSON, George. Pvt. under Capt. Joseph Wood, 27 Aug - 13 Oct 1814; absent 28 Oct.

ROBERTSON [Robinson], John. Pvt. under Capt. William Durbin, joined 24 Aug; absent without leave 29 Sep 1814. He said he was furloughed at City of Balt., being sick and unfit for service in Oct 1814; b. c.1794; m. 1851, Susan Smith (b. c.1823) in Fred. Co. He res. Balt. City 1850 and Carroll Co. MD, 1855; d. Carroll Co. 15 Jul 1855. Acq: 1852 - William Sullivan, Jacob Powder and John Beaver.
Source: Bounty land claim, 55-120-20156.

ROBERTSON, William. Pvt. (corporal until transferred on 23 Sep) under Capt. George W. Magee, 23 Jul - 13 Oct 1814.

ROBINETT, Richard. Pvt., 42nd U.S. Inf., under Capt. G. W. Barker. At enlistment: 5 feet, 6 1/2 inches; blue eyes, dark hair, dark complexion; age 25; occupation cooper; b. Fred. Co., MD; enlisted 28 Oct 1814 at ? Castle by Capt. Barker for 5 yrs. Mustered 1 Jan and 16 Feb 1815 at Philadelphia. Capt. Isaac Roach's company of U.S. Artillery, Ft. McHenry on 30 Jun 1815. Deserted at Ft. McHenry 24 aug 1815.

ROBINS, Benjamin. Pvt. under Capt. Joseph Wood, 27 Aug - 28 Oct 1814.

ROBINSON, Charles. From Balt. County. Pvt. under Capt. John Galt, 31 Aug - 27 Oct 1814.

ROBINSON, George. From Balt. County. Pvt. under Capt. Galt, 31 Aug - 27 Oct 1814.

ROBINSON, John. Pvt. under Capt. William Durbin, Jr., 24 Aug - 13 Oct 1814. Absent without leave 29 Sep 1814.

ROBINSON [Robertson], Joshua. Pvt. under Capt. William Durbin, Jr., 24 Aug - 27 Oct 1814.

ROCK, John. Corporal under Capt. Samuel Duvall, 3 Aug-3 Oct 1814.

ROCKWELL, Tolbert. Pvt. under Capt. George W. Magee, 14 Oct 1814 - 10 Jan 1815 - Hancock, Wash Co.

RODERICK (Rhoderick, Rhodruc, Rothrock, Rodhrick, Rodrock, Rotruck, Rodrick), Lewis. Pvt. [appears in the muster rolls and on the bounty land application as Rothrock] under Capt. Shawen; joined 5 Sep 1814; deserted 24 Oct 1814. His son, J. S. L. Rodrick, said that when British had left, his father and several others, left his company, and went home before a discharge was issued, with no idea of desertion, that the nights were cool and his clothing thin, and he wished to get warmer clothing.

Lewis Roderick b. 15 Jan 1796 in Washington Co.; m. 15 Mar 1821, Margaret Flook (b. 12 Jul 1801), at Fredericktown, by Rev. J. C. Bucher, each for first time. At enrollment: 18 yrs old, miller, c.5 feet and 8 inches, dark hair, dark eyes, white complexion. Fol. discharge he res. in Middletown and Jefferson Dist., in Fred. Co. 1850 census of Jefferson Dist.: Lewis Rhodruc, 54, R.R. agent; Margaret A., 50 [and family]; res. Fredericktown in 1872; suffered stroke of paralysis in fall of 1877 and d. Fred. Co., 8 or 12 Aug 1879, leaving widow and seven children. Widow res. near Jefferson, Fred. Co (P.O. address: Lander) in 1880.

In Middletown Ref. Ch. records: Jacob Randolph, son of Lewis and Margaret Rodrick, b. 4 Jan 1822, bapt. 14 Apr 1822; also Mary Ann Magdaline, dau of Lewis and Margaret Roderick, b. 22 Nov 1823, bapt. 9 May 1824. Margaret Rhoderick d. 2 Aug 1883, age 82 yrs, 20 days. Both Lewis and Margaret bur. Jefferson Union Cem.

Acq: 1873 - Frederick Hawman and Jacob Hallar who also served at the same time. Letter from J. S. L. Rodrick, son of Lewis Rodrick. 1875 - Jacob Smith, res. Fred. Co who was mbr. of Capt. Shawen's company. 1876 - Letter from J. S. L. Rodrick, son of Lewis Rodrick; says that the name on the rolls is Rotruck because the sergt. was a Dutchman. J. S. L. Rodrick was the fifth child, in his 49th year in 1878. 1880 - John A. Lynch, age 54, West Second St.,

Fredericktown, and Daniel T.Laking, age 38, West Patrick St., Fredericktown, acq. 40 and 30 yrs, resp.

Sources: Pension, SO26019 (rejected by reason of insufficient service; also charged with desertion); WO39612 (rejected 30 Apr 1881 - because of desertion); Bounty land claim, 55-160-110205 (application was made in 1870); FCml; Maryland German Ch. Records, v. 1; (Frederick) Examiner, 20 Aug 1879; Names in Stone; Bridge in Time.

ROGERS, James. 4thh corpl. under Capt. William Knox, 26 Aug - 27 Oct 1814.

ROHR, George. Orderly Sergt. under Capt. George W. Ent, 24 Aug - 30 Sep 1814; merchant; b. c.1793; m. 24 Dec 1816, Miss Catharine Koontz, at Fredericktown by Rev. J. Helfenstein. She d. 22 Feb 1822, leaving her husband and a child. He res. St. Louis, MO, 1871, a widower.

Sources: Bounty land claim, 55-160-63123; Pension, SO2313, SC2325 (admitted 3 Aug 1871); Frederick-Town Herald, 28 Dec 1816, 2 Mar 1822.

ROHR, Peter. Pvt. from Fredericktown, under Capt. James F. Huston/Capt. Joseph Green, joined 23 Jul 1814; furloughed 23 Sep - discharged Balt, 6 Dec 1814 by surgeon.

ROLLINS, John C. Pvt. under Capt. Samuel Duvall, 3 Aug - 3 Oct 1814.

ROOSS or ROOP, Jacob. Mbr. of Crawford's "company." [Jacob Roop, a farmer whose land lay along Sams Creek just across the line in Carroll Co., MD; m. Sarah Hartsock. Their children: Joseph; Daniel; Samuel; Jesse; Joel; Kitty (Mrs. Linn); Jacob; Elizabeth (Mrs. Bonebrake). Jacob

THE VETERANS

Roop is bur. Uniontown Pipe Creek Cem., 4 Sep 1785 - 19 Jan 1860 with his wife Sarah, 20 Jun 1866, aged 79 yrs, 2 months, 22 days.]
Sources: Williams, History of Fred. Co.; Names in Stone.

ROPP, Samuel. Pvt. under Capt. Jacob Alexander, 22 Jul - 19 Sep 1814 and pvt. under Capt. Capt Nicholas Turbutt, 1 Sep - 27 Oct 1814.

ROSS, Frederick. Pvt. under Capt. Joseph Wood, 27 Aug - 13 Oct 1814.

ROSS, James. 3rd sergt. under Capt. William Knox, 26 Aug - 27 Oct 1814.

ROTHROCK. See Roderick.

ROUTSON, John. Pvt. under Capt. Samuel Ogle, 1 May-5 Jul 1813.

ROUTSONG, John. Pvt. from New Windsor under Capt. George W. Magee, 22 Jul - 10 Jan 1815. [FCml issued to John Routsong and Catherine Biser on 26 Sep 1816.]

ROW, Frederick. Pvt. from Upper Fred. Co. under Capt. James F. Huston, 23 Jul - discharged 3 Aug 1814.

ROW, John. Pvt. under Capt. Samuel Dawson, 21 Jul - 13 Oct 1814.

ROW, John. Pvt. under Capt. Thomas Contee Worthington 17 Aug - 31 Dec 1812.

ROW, Michael. Pvt. under Capt. Jacob Alexander, 22 Jul - 19 Sep 1814.

ROW, Michael. Pvt. under Capt. John Galt, 31 Aug - 27 Oct 1814.

ROW, Samuel. Pvt. under Capt. John Galt, 31 Aug - 27 Oct 1814; b. c.1795; res. within 6 miles of Taneytown in 1814; Franklin Co., PA, in 1850 and 1855 (Washington Twp). Acq: 1844 - Daniel Mickley, William Shinefield, res. Washington Twp, Franklin Co., PA.
Source: Bounty land claim, 55-120-25231.

ROWE, George. Ensign under Capt. Thomas Blair, Allegany Co., 23 Jul - 28 Oct 1814.

ROWE, Michael. Pvt. under Lieut. Kolb, 13 Oct - 15 Nov 1814.

ROWE [Row], Michael. Pvt., 38th U.S. Inf. At enlistment: 5 feet, 3 1/2 inches; black eyes, black hair, dark complexion; age 19; occupation chairmaker; b. Fred. Co., MD. Enlisted 11 Jan 1815 at Fredericktown by Lt. Reticker for duration of war. Mustered in Capt. Charles Stansbury's company 3 Apr 1815. Discharged at Balt. 6 Apr 1815.

ROWE, William. Pvt. under Capt. John Brengle, 25 Aug - 19 Sep 1814.

ROWHAM, Jacob. 4th corporal under Capt. Matthew Murray, 25 Aug - 27 Oct 1814.

ROWSEN, Jacob. Pvt. under Capt. Fonsten, 2 Sep - 27 Oct 1814; res. 9 miles from Westminster.

RUBERT, Jacob. Pvt. under Capt. Samuel Ogle, 1 May - 5 Jul 1813.

RUDY, Christopher. Pvt. under Capt. Samuel Dawson, 17 Sep - 13 Oct 1814?? [The entry appears to read, "Joined the service 17 Sept." This wording is somewhat unusual and might mean that he enlisted in the regular army on this date.] [From the Middletown Reformed Ch. records - Christianus, son of Dieterich and Suss. Rudy b. 13 Nov 1796, baptised 23 Apr 1797.]
Source: Maryland German Ch. Records, v. 1.

FREDERICK COUNTY MILITIA IN THE WAR OF 1812

RUSH, William. Pvt. under Capt. Samuel Dawson, joined 14 Oct; deserted 1 Nov 1814.

RUTTER, Thomas. Pvt. under Capt. John Fonsten, 2 Sep - 27 Oct 1814; said he served under Capt. Starret of the City of Balt.; drafted at City of Balt. and entered into service at the City of Annapolis c.1 Sep 1812; discharged at Annapolis last of Dec 1812; pvt. in company of Capt. John Bond of Balt. Co., drafted at Balt. Co., entered service around 6 May 1813, discharged Balt. City c.10 Jul 1813; b. c.1790; res. Balt. Co., in 1850.

Source: Bounty land claim, 50-40-81669.

RYAN, James. Pvt. under Capt. Philip Smith 23 May - 8 Sep 1813.

RYE, Henry. Pvt. under Capt. Henry Steiner, 25 Aug - 27 Sep 1814. [FCml issued to Henry Rye and Anne Smith on 7 Dec 1814.]

Source: FCml.

SACKER, John. Pvt. from New Windsor under Capt. George W. Magee, 22 Jul - 10 Jan 1815.

SAFFELL [Safill], Orlando [Orlander]. Pvt. under Capt. Joseph Wood, 27 Aug - 13 Oct 1814; furloughed 27 Sep. Widow recalled that he served under Capt. Durbin as sergt.; m. c.29 Sep 1813, Deborah Saffell (b. c.1794), by Parson Reed, Montgomery Co., MD. Orlando d. New Lexington, OH, 20 Mar 1838. Acq.: 1872 - Samuel Saffell and Mary Rebecca Saffell, near New Lexington, Perry Co., OH.

Source: Pension, WO 8512 (rejected).

SALLERS, Ellett. Pvt. under Capt. George W. Ent, 3rd Regt, 24 Aug - 30 Sep 1814.

SALMON, Charles. Pvt. under Capt. Henry Steiner, 25 Aug - 27 Sep 1814.

SALMON, George. Pvt. under Capt. John Brengle, 25 Aug - 19 Sep 1814; m. 6 Apr 1819, Catherine Smith dau of Capt. Daniel Smith of Smithfield by Rev. Hause. "Capt. Smith was an old Revolutionary hero," of Harbaugh's Valley. Catherine was sister of Charles Smith who m. Miss Rebecca Motter of Emmittsburg. His son Charles D. Smith, res. St. Joseph, MO (1877). Mrs. Salmon was mbr. of M.E. Ch. 1850 census of Fredericktown: George Salmon, 54, chairmaker; Catherine Salmon, 49. George Salmon d. at his residence, E. Second St., 20 Aug 1867, age 72 yrs, 25 days. Bur. with him at Mt. Olivet was his wife Catherine 28 Oct 1877, age 77. He was mbr. of Adam Lodge, No. 35 I.O.O.F. When she d. she res on East Second St., Frederick.

Sources: (**Frederick**) **Examiner**, 19 Nov 1862, 31 Oct 1877; **Frederick-Town Herald**, 10 Apr 1819; **Names in Stone**; **FCml**; **Bridge in Time**.

SAMSEAL [Samsell, Sampsell], Peter, son of Devalt; fifer under Capt. Jacob Alexander, 22 Jul - 19 Sep 1814; b. 17 Mar 1741, d. 19 Sep 1804; m. 6 Aug 1800, Mary [Maria] Gillespie. Their dau Mary [Maria] b. 31 July 1801 and bapt. in Middletown Ref. Ch.. According to Mary Hitselberger, "It looks as if Peter d. after 9 February 1827 on his way back to Tennessee after the settlement of the land in Middletown." His sons traced his return as far as North Carolina where they lost his trail. His wife d. near

248

THE VETERANS

Bean Station, Grainger Co., TN. According to Mrs. Joan J. Schooler, of Carlisle, Iowa, descendant of Peter Sampsell, the children of Peter were Mary, John, Elizabeth, Serena, Peter II, Isaac, Hiram and perhaps others. According to Mrs. Schooler, Devalt Sampsell came from Bucks Co., PA. Mentioned in the will of Devalt Sampsell were his wife, Anna Mary, son John. Named in a later transfer of his property were his children, Peter, John and Jacob Sampsell and two daus, Mrs. Elizabeth Broy and Mrs. Catherine Shovalter, both of Beaver Co., PA.

Sources: **Maryland German Ch. Records**, vol. 1; correspondence from Mary Hitselberger, Fond du Lac, WI; George C. Rhoderick, Jr., **The Early History of Middletown Maryland**.

SANDERS [Saunders], Thomas. Pvt. under Capt. Basil Dorsey, 30 Jul - 27 Sep 1814. [He said he was ensign in company of Capt. Basil Dorsey] b. 1783; m. Henrietta Trunnel c.15 Apr 1816; res. Fred. Co. 1850, 1855. 1850 census of Buckeys Town Dist.: Thomas Sanders, 65, blacksmith; Henrietta Sanders, 55.

Source: Bounty land claim, 55-120-13292; FCmL

SANDS, George. From Fredericktown. Principal musician under Capt. Joseph Green, 14 Oct 1814, until he deserted on 5 Nov 1814.

SANDS [Sans], Richard. 1st corpl. under Basil Dorsey, 30 Jul - 27 Oct 1814; b. c.1789 in Balt. Co., MD, farmer; when enrolled: dark hair, blue eyes, light complexion; m(1) c.7 Apr 1817, Rebecca Harrison; m(2) 30 May 1867, Ann Shannon (b. c.1825), at Perry Co., OH, by Benjamin F. Starer, J.P., she for the first time. Rebecca D. Sands, d. in Union Township, 20 Feb 1866. Fol. discharge res. Balt. Co., MD; and Harrison, Coshocton, Perry and Morgan Counties, OH; res. Morgan Co., OH, in 1871; d. 13 Dec 1871 in Union Township. Ann Sands res. Union Township, Morgan Co, OH, in 1878 (P.O. address: Ringgold). Acq.: 1855 - Augustus D. Havener, Morgan Co., OH; 1871 - Samuel Harrison and Otho H. Williams, res. Union Township, Morgan Co, OH; 1878 - Otho H. Williams, age 57, and William Harrison, age 41, res. Ringgold, OH. William Harrison was a nephew of said Richard Sands and often visited at his uncle's house, about a mile distant. Otho H. Williams lived about 1/4 mile from the family residence.

Sources: Pensions, SO 32947, SC 21743; WO 7527, WC 5663; FCmL

SANS, William. Pvt. under Capt. Basil Dorsey, 30 Jul - 27 Sep 1814.

SANSENY, John. Mbr. of Crawford's "company."

SARGEANT, Jacob. Pvt. under Capt. Samuel Duvall, 3 Aug - 3 Oct 1814.

SARGENT, Jacob. Pvt. under Capt. Philip Smith, joined 23 May 1814 - deserted 23 Aug 1814.

SAVOY, Samuel. Capt.'s servant under Capt. Joseph Wood, 27 Aug - 13 Oct 1814.

SAYLOR, John Frederick. Drafted in Capt. Creager's company, at Creagerstown, Fred. Co., MD, in 1814; the regt. was mustered in at Annapolis, MD, and from there went to Norfolk [according to him]; participated in Battle of Bladensburg, as a drummer. After

tle of Bladensburg, as a drummer. After the Battle of Bladensburg he went with his regt. to Montgomery Court House and then to Balt. where the regt. was placed in the intrenchments and was there during the battle of North Point.

John Frederick Saylor m(1) Susan Thumb (d. 1824); m(2) 28 Jul 1828, Susan (Susanna) Frantz (b. c.1804), at Hagerstown, MD (according to him). His widow later stated they m. in town of Fairfield in Adams Co, PA, on 28 Jul 1828, by David Busler, minister of the Ref. Ch., she for first time. They res. Fairfield from the time of marr. to 1870 and thereafter in Cumberland Township, Adams Co., PA; raised 13 children; he d. in Cumberland Township, 26 Jan 1877; bur. c.4 miles from Gettysburg. She res. Cumberland Township (P.O. Gettysburg), PA in 1878; d. 1 Dec 1887; bur. 3 Dec. Undertaker was Daniel Trimmer. Her attending physician was T. T. Tate, M.D. Acq.: 1878 - William B. Meals, aged 50, Gettysburg, and John W. McGinley, aged 79, Fairfield, Adams Co., acq. 35 and 55 yrs, resp. William B. Meals is 1st cousin of Mrs. Saylor. Annie E. Beecher wife of John Beecher; stated Frederick Saylor lived at her house at the time of his death. George W. Wolf was a neighbor who witnessed death of Frederick Saylor. Letter dated 9 Dec 1878, Galveston, Cass Co., IN, from Em Saylor, dau of John Frederick Saylor and Susan Saylor.

Sources: Pensions, SO 24251, SC 17985; WO 26293, WC 18411.

SCAGGS, Richard D. Served in 38th U.S. Inf. At enlistment: 5 ft, 10 inches; dark eyes, gray hair, light complexion; age 39; tailor; b. Fred. Co., MD; enlisted 29 Jun 1814 at Norfolk, VA by Lt. Duncan for duration of war. Discharged at Craney Island 15 Mar 1815.

SCHAFFNER, George. Sergt. under Capt. Dawson, Samuel, 1 May - 5 Jul 1813.

SCHAFFNER, Jacob. Pvt. under Capt. Henry Steiner, 25 Aug - 27 Sep 1814.

SCHELL, Charles, Jr. Pvt. under Capt. Capt Nicholas Turbutt, 1 Sep - 27 Oct 1814.

SCHELL, Ezra. Sergt. under Capt. Dawson, Samuel, 1 May - 5 Jul 1813.

SCHELL, Ezra. Pvt. under Capt. George W. Ent, 3rd Regt, 24 Aug - 30 Sep 1814; m. Margret Deshan [Dashon] (b. c.1805) at Balt. by Rev. Kurtz, Luth. minister on 16 Nov 1815. Ezra Schell d. Fredericktown 30 May 1840. Widow res. Fred. Co. 1850, 1855. [based on bounty land applications; however, her name does not appear in 1850 census of Fred. Co., i.e. not shown in *Bridge in Time*.] Acq.: 1850 - Frederick Hawman, res. Fred. Co. and Henry Hilbert, res. Balt. City. 1855 - John Lambright and Ormond F. Butler, res. Fred. Co.

Source: Bounty land claim.

SCHELL, Jesse. 3rd sergt. under Capt. Thomas Contee Worthington, 17 Aug - 31 Dec 1812; reduced to 4th corpl. on 1 Dec and 3rd corpl. on 19 Dec. [d. 5 Apr 1827, Jesse Schell, son of "the late Charles Schell of this city." d. 21 Sep 1827, in her 67th year, Mrs. Mary Schell, widow of "the late Mr. Charles Schell of this city." *Engelbrecht Diary*: 1:440, 466.]

THE VETERANS

SCHEPLEY, Frederick. Servant to Capt. Daniel Marker, 16 Aug - 18 Sep 1813.

SCHISSLER, John. Pvt. under Capt. Henry Steiner 28 Apr - 29 Jun 1813 and 25 Aug - 27 Sep 1814; b. 1789; m. Catherine Smith (b. c.1796), in Anne Arundel Co., Feb 1816 [widow gave this date in 1853; later gave date 14 Feb 1814] by Rev. James Day. John Schissler (shoemaker) d. 14 Jan 1831, in his 41st year; bur. at Frederick Evan. Luth. Ch. Cem. 1850 census of Fredericktown: Catherine Schisler, 54; Hiram Schisler, 32, physician; Margaretta R. M. Schisler, 25; Catherine S. Schisler, 3, b. in PA; Ann M. Schisler, 1. All except three-year old Catherine b. in MD. Catherine res. Fred. Co. in 1855. Acq.: 1853 - Joseph M. Ebberts and James Brunner, res. of Frederick; 1855 - Margaretta R. M. Schissler and Margaretta Engelbrecht, res. Fred. Co.

Sources: Bounty land claim, 55-120-5811; FCml; (Frederick) Examiner, 12 Aug 1874; Frederick-Town Herald, 22 Jan 1831, 12 Feb 1831; Bridge in Time; Names in Stone; Engelbrecht Diary: 1:625.

SCHIVALLER, John. Pvt. under Capt. John Brengle, 25 Aug - 19 Sep 1814.

SCHLEICHK, Isaac. Pvt. under Capt. Philip Smith, 23 May - 8 Sep 1813.

SCHLEY, Henry. 3rd Lieut. under Capt. Samuel Duvall, 3 Aug - 3 Oct 1814.

SCHLEY, Henry. Pvt. under Lt. Col. Jacob Cramer. He said he acted as Adjutant by brevet to a det. of drafted militia commanded by Lieut. Colonel Jacob Cramer. He was drafted at Woodsborough, Fred. Co., in 1814; discharged in Washington City c.14 Nov 1814. After the war he organzied the celebrated "Warren Greens" Rifle Company. On death of his father, in 1835, he succeeded to the office of Clerk of Fred. Co. Court; later cashier of Fred. Co. Bank. - b. c.1794; res. Fred. Co., 1850, 1855. 1850 census shows him res. Fredericktown, 56, clerk with Sarah M. Schley, 53; Clarence, 11; Charles, 28, lawyer; Harriet, 18; Louesa, 8 mos.. Major Henry Schley d. at home of his son, Dr. Fairfax Schley in Frederick 1 Apr 1871, 78 yrs, 14 days; bur. at Mt. Olivet with his wife Sarah Maria who d. 18 Feb 1867, 69 yrs, 5 days after a brief illness of pneumonia. He was bro. of William Schley, lawyer of Balt. City. In 1862 he was vice-president of the "United Brothers of the War of 1812," in Fred. Co.

Sources: Bounty land claim, 55-120-4648; Names in Stone; Bridge in Time; (Frederick) Examiner, 15 Jan 1862, 20 Feb 1867, 5 Apr 1871; The Maryland Union, 6 Apr 1871.

SCHNYDER, John. Corpl. under Capt. Dawson, Samuel, 1 May - 5 Jul 1813.

SCHOLL, Henry. Pvt. under Capt. John Brengle, 25 Aug - 19 Sep 1814. [In records of Luth. Ch. Frederick: Henrich son of Christian and Catharina School b 23 Sep 1778. FCml issued to Henry Scholl and Christena Fiega 21 Dec 1811.]

Sources: MD German Ch. Rcds, v.4.

SCHRIVER, Jacob. Pvt. under Capt. Henry Steiner, 25 Aug - 27 Sep 1814. [d. Westminster, MD, 15 Oct 1840, in his 62nd year, Jacob Shriver, bro. of

FREDERICK COUNTY MILITIA IN THE WAR OF 1812

Messrs. Abraham and Isaac Shriver. *Engelbrecht Diary*: 2:426]

SCHROYER [Shroyer, Shrawyer], Frederick. Pvt. under Capt. Fonsten, 2 Sep - 27 Oct 1814; m. Rachel Esterline (b. c.1800), at Hanover, PA, in 1837 or 1838 by Rev. Rotroff. He m. prev. (name unknown). At enrollment: spoon maker, yellowish hair, grey eyes. Fol. discharge he res. Balt. and Carroll Cos.; 1879 P.O. address: Westminster, MD; d. near Manchester, MD, 1843. Widow res. Carroll Co., 1855 - said that her house had burned down consuming everything including marr. certificate. She said her husband's children by his first marr. objected to second marr. In 1879, she res. Carroll Co., destitute and feeble. Acq.: 1856 - William Weckley who served with Frederick Shroyer under Capt. Magee; 1858 - Michael Lynch; Lewis Wampler; Sebastiana Trump; res. 1/2 mile of Frederick and Rachel Schroyer; 1879 - J. William Earhart, age 54, res. Union Mills, Carroll Co.; Joseph Lippy, age 56, res. 7th Dist. of Carroll Co.

Sources: Bounty land claim, 55-160-84343, under name of Shrawyer; Pension, WO 37475, WC 27851, under name of Shroyer.

SCHUANTIEGEL [Snowtickel], George. Pvt. under Capt. John Brengle, 25 Aug - 19 Sep 1814.

SCHULTZ, David. Pvt. under Capt. Joseph Green, entering service on 14 Oct 1814 - deserted 8 Dec 1814.

SCHULTZ, David. Pvt. under Capt. Thomas Contee Worthington, 17 Aug - 31 Dec 1812.

SCOTT, Joseph. 3rd corpl. under Capt. Daniel Shawen, 5 Sep - 27 Oct 1814.

SCOTT, Thomas. Pvt. under Capt. Henry Steiner, 25 Aug - 27 Sep 1814.

SEABOLD. See Sebold.

SEABROOKES, Samuel. Pvt. under Capt. Fonsten, 2 Sep - 27 Oct 1814.

SEBOLD [Seabold, Seapold], Peter. Pvt. under Capt. Farquhar, 1st Regt.; drafted at or near Teneytown around 26 Jul 1814; discharged at Balt. c. 30 Sep 1814; b. c.1777-1784; m. 1809. Catharine Deetering[?] in Berks Co, PA. Catherine b. Berks Co., PA, 11 Jul 1786, d. 27 Dec 1827, bur. at Catholic Cem., Taneytown. 1850 census of Emmitsburg Dist: Peter Seapolt, 67, farmer, b. Germany; Isabel Seapolt, 50, b. Germany; William Seapolt, 20; Joseph Seapolt, 18; Andrew Seapolt, 10; Anastasia, 9. All children b. Fred. Co. Peter Seabold res. Emmittsburg Dist., 1871. Acq.: 1856 - William Mooney, Jacob Baumgardner; Sebastian Addelsperger, of Frederick Co, aged 66 yrs.

Sources: Bounty land claim, 55-160-77353; Pension, SO 12687; **Bridge in time.**

SEARLY, Joseph. 1st corpl. under Capt. Daniel Marker, 16 Aug - 18 Sep 1813.

SECRIST, Jonas. Pvt. under Capt. John Galt, 31 Aug - 27 Oct 1814; res. within 4 miles of Taneytown in 1814.

SEERLY, Joseph. Pvt. under Capt. Samuel Dawson, 21 Jul 1814 - 10 Jan 1815.

SEERS [Siers], Alexander. Pvt. under Capt. James F. Huston/Capt. Joseph

THE VETERANS

Green, entering service on 23 Jul 1814; deserted 29 Oct.; res. Upper Fred. Co.

SEFER, Joseph. 36th U.S. Inf. At enlistment: 5 ft, 11 inches; age 40; b. Fred. Co., MD; enlisted 18 Apr 1813 at Balt. by Capt. Jos. Hook. Mustered on 24 Apr 1813.

SEGRUFF [Synuff], Michael. Never joined service. His company served under Capt. William Durbin, Jr., 24 Aug - 27 Oct 1814.

SEIZE [Seis], George. Pvt. under Capt. John Brengle, 25 Aug - 19 Sep 1814. [FCml issued to George Seis and Peggy Renner 1 May 1818.]

SELBY, Henry. He said he served as pvt. under Capts. Barns, 18 Aug - 10 Sep 1813; as pvt. under Capts. Dorsey and Timanus, 30 Jul - 27 Oct 1814, as substitute for Ezekiel Picket; entered at Balt. Co., c.27 Aug 1814; discharged at Balt. c.27 Oct 1814; b. c.1794; moved to OH c.2 yrs fol. discharge, leaving his discharge papers with his bro., Larkin Selby. Henry Selby res. Ross Co., OH, 1850, 1851 and 1855.

Sources: Bounty land claims, 50-40-1524, 50-40-63915, 55-80-2665.

A letter dated 14 Aug 1928, 16 Taylor St., Chevy Chase, MD, from Catherine C. (Mrs. Lee R.) Pennington, asking for records of Henry Selby, of Maryland, whose wife or widow was Susan or Susannah Boteler Selby. "I believe that he died in the Dist. of Columbia. His wife died in 1874 aged about 88..."

SELBY, Obadiah. Pvt. under Capt. John Fonsten, 2 Sep - 27 Oct 1814 as substitute for John E. Thomas who was drafted at Uniontown; b. c.1795; m. 25 May 1817, Elisabeth Ferree (b. c.1782) at home of her mother (Mary Ferree) in Fred. Co., MD, by Rev. Patrick Davidson; res. Seneca Co., OH, in 1850; d. at his residence in Seneca Co., OH, 26 Sep 1855. Acq.: Nancy Ingrm, acq. 40 yrs.

Source: Bounty land claim, 55-120-81944.

SELL, Lewis. Pvt. under Capt. Galt, 31 Aug - 27 Oct 1814.

SELLERS, Jacob. Pvt. under Capt. William Knox, beginning on 26 Aug 1814 - deserted 27 Aug 1814.

SELLMAN, William. Lieut. under Capt. Riggs; said he entered service in Fred. Co. Aug 1814; discharged at Balt. Oct 1814; b. c.1785; res. Montgomery Co., MD, 1855.

Source: Bounty land claim, 55-rejected-212858.

SENIOR, Jacob. Pvt., U.S. Rifles, under Capt. B. Harrison. At enlistment: 5 ft, 6 inches; blue eyes, dark hair, dark complexion; age 21; hatter; b. Fred. Co.; enlisted 24 Aug 1814 at Lancaster by Lt. Stockton for duration of war. Discharged at Detroit 30 Jun 1815.

SENSE, Peter. Pvt. under Capt. William Durbin, Jr., 24 Aug - 27 Oct 1814.

SENSENEY, John. Mbr. of Crawford's "company."

SENSENY, Isaac. Mbr. of Crawford's "company."

SERGEANT, John. Pvt. under Capt. Philip Smith, 29 May - 8 Sep 1813.

SERGENT, George. Pvt. under Capt. Shryock, George, 14 Oct 1814 - 10 Jan 1815; "deserted."

FREDERICK COUNTY MILITIA IN THE WAR OF 1812

SERGENT, James. Pvt. under Capt. Shryock, George, 14 Oct 1814 - 10 Jan 1815; "deserted."

SEWELL, Charles B. Pvt. under Capt. Samuel Duvall, 3 Aug - 3 Oct 1814.

SEWMAN, Isaac. 4th sergt. under Capt. Daniel Shawen, 5 Sep - 27 Oct 1814.

SHADE, George. From Upper Fred. Co.; musician under Capt. Henry Steiner, 28 Apr - 29 Jun 1813 and musician under Capt. James F. Huston, 23 Jul 1814 - 13 Oct 1814.

SHAEFFER [Shafer], George. Pvt. under Capt. Ent, 24 Aug - 30 Sep 1814; b. c.1795; m. Betsey Flintin, at Henrietta, NY, 11 Sep 1817; res. Somerset, Niagara, NY, in 1871; he d. 26 Jan 1879. Letter in pension file from Moses Breckon of Somerset, NY, stating he is husband of only dau of George Shaeffer; requests reimbursement for coffin ($20.00), digging grave ($2.00), cloth for shroud ($1.80), Physician, Henry H. Fouts ($2.00); stated that the last sickness continued uninterruptedly 24 Jan til death.

Source: Pension, SO 11930, SC 7472 (admitted 2 Nov 1871).

SHAFER, Daniel. Pvt. under Capt. Joseph Wood, 27 Aug - 28 Oct 1814.

SHAFFER, Daniel. Appearing in the *(Frederick) Examiner* was an article taken from the *Catoctin Clarion*. It stated that Daniel Shaffer d. 16 Jan 1880, age 88 yrs and 4 mos.; served as sergt. in war of 1812 in Capt. Creager's company, raised in this locality, Col. Hood commanding. After having served the time, for which he volunteered, he went as substitute for John Smith. He was at the battle of Bladensburg and after the retreat, was transferred to Baltimore. He was on guard at Fort McHenry the night the British vessels passed there. ... appointed gate keeper on the Frederick and Emmittsburg Pike and served in that position 19 yrs." 1850 census of Creagerstown Dist.: Daniel Shafer, 59, shoemaker; E. Elizabeth, 17; Heneretta A., 15, Washington L., 13. Bur. at Thurmont United Brethren and Blue Ridge Cem.: Daniel Shaffer (1791-1880).

Sources: **(Frederick) Examiner,** 21 Jan 1880; **Names in Stone; Bridge in Time.**

SHAFER, Frederick. Pvt. under Capt. Samuel Ogle, 1 May 1813 - 5 Jul 1813.

SHAFER, Frederick. Pvt. under Capt. Fonsten; joined c.Sep 1814; deserted 4 Oct 1814.

SHAFER, George. Pvt. under Capt. George W. Ent, 3rd Regt, 24 Aug - 30 Sep 1814.

SHAFER, Jacob. Pvt. under Capt. John Galt, 31 Aug - 27 Oct 1814.

SHAFER, John. Pvt. under Capt. Fonsten, 2 Sep - 27 Oct 1814; res. 4 miles of Westminster.

SHAFFER, George. Pvt. from Washington Co. under Capt. Samuel Dawson, 14 Oct 1814 - 10 Jan 1815.

SHAFFER [Shafer], Jacob. Pvt. under Capt. Galt.

SHAFFER, John. Pvt. from Upper Fred. Co. under Capt. James F. Huston/Capt. Joseph Green; entered 23 Jul 1814; deserted 15 Oct.

THE VETERANS

SHAFFNER, Jacob. Pvt. under Capt. Philip Smith, 23 May - 8 Sep 1813. [FCml issued 28 Dec 1816 to Jacob Shaffner to Harriet Smith.]

SHAFNER, Peter. Pvt. under Capt. Matthew Murray, 25 Aug - 27 Oct 1814.

SHAMER (Sharner?), John. Drummer under Capt. William Durbin, joined 24 Aug - absent without leave on 25 Oct 1814.

SHAMHART, Henry. The pension file shows he served under Capt. Williams; m. 28 Nov 1820, Catherine Overly; d. 19 Dec 1858, age 63 yrs, 16 days. In 1879 her P.O. address was Quaker City, Guernsey Co., OH; Noble Co., OH in 1884. She d. prior to 19 Aug 1896. Acq.: 1879 - Asbury Knauff and George J. Long of Galesville, OH, who knew Catherine and Henry Shamhart since 1835; 1884 - William Forsyth, age 71, and Mrs. Nancy Forsyth, age 70, res. 2 miles of Henry and Catharine Shamhart.

The family bible contains fol.: Henry Shamhartt and Katharine m. 28 Nov 1820. William Henry Shamhart and Rachel Williams m. 30 May 1857. John Shamhart and Mary Catharine Brill m. 27 Apr 1857. George Bolton and Amanda Catharine Shamhart m. 1 Aug 1858. Henry Shamhartt b. 2 Dec 1794. Katharine his wife b. 24 Jul 1804. Children - George Shamhartt b. 13 Jul 1821; Fovina [?] Shamhartt b. 27 Mar 1823; Martha Shamhartt b. 1 Dec 1824; Henry Shamhartt b. 25 Oct 1826, d. 27 Oct 1826; John Shamhartt b. 28 Oct 1827; Elisabeth Anne Shamhartt b. 24 Dec 1829; Emily Caroline Shamhartt b. 9 Apr 1831; Mary Shamhartt b. 15 Mar 1833; William Henry Shamhartt b. 28 Jan 1835; Ephraim Shamhartt b. 5 Jul 1837; Amanda Katharine Shamhartt b. 18 Aug 1839; Pheby Shamhartt b. 20 Feb 1842, d. 17 Mar 1842; Jane Shamhartt b. 11 Feb 1843, d. 25 Mar 1843; Tompson Luther Shamhartt b. 2 Jul 1846; David Shamhart b. 7 Jan 1849, d. 15 Feb 1849; Reason Shamhartt b. 27 Apr 1852 at 10:04 a.m. The father d. age 63 yrs, 16 days. William Henry Shamhart d. 27 Apr 1863, aged 28 yrs, 3 mos.. Rezin Shamhart d. 7 Mar 1873, aged 20 yrs, 10 mos., 10 days.

Source: Pension, WO 35364, WC 33724.

SHANABROOKE, Casper. Pvt. under Capt. John Fonsten; joined 2 Sep 1814; deserted 1 Oct 1814.

SHANER, Melcher. Pvt. under Capt. Dawson, 26 Jul 1814 - 10 Jan 1815. He said he was drafted into Capt. William Faulker's [prob. meant Farquhar] Company at Taneytown, Md, in 1812; b. c.1796; m. Elizabeth Mark [or Marks], at Taneytown, MD, 1825. In 1871 he res. Frankfort, Pike Co., MO. 1850 census of Woodsboro Dist.:, Melki Shaner, 54, shoemaker; Elizabeth Shaner, 49, b. PA; Mary J. Shaner, 27, b. PA; Luvina M. Shaner, 18, b. PA; Julean A. Shaner, 11, b. MD; Moses Found, 1, b. MD. FCml issued on 16 Dec 1819 Melcher Shaner and Elizabeth Marks.

Sources: Pension, 25606, SC 19454; **Bridge in Time**; FCml.

SHANEYBROOK, Jacob. Pvt. under Capt. Samuel Ogle, 1 May 1813 - 5 Jul 1813.

FREDERICK COUNTY MILITIA IN THE WAR OF 1812

SHANK, John. Appointed 1st Lieut. 23 Apr 1808 under Elie Phillips of the Light Dragoons, attached to the 7th Brigade (Fred. Co.).

SHANK, Peter. Pvt. under Capt. Matthew Murray, 25 Aug - 27 Oct 1814. He said he volunteered to serve in the place of his bro. who had been drafted; b. c.1793; res. West Dayton, Montgomery Co., OH, 1871 (not m. at that time); living with two unnamed daus who supported him, in Dayton, OH, in 1887; d. 13 Oct 1889.

[In the 1850 census there is in the Woodsboro Dist, Peter Shank, 67, carpenter; Susan Shank, 40.] [FCml issued on 5 Jun 1819 to Peter Shank and Mary Miller and FCml issued 6 Mar 1839 Peter Shank and Susan Stull]

Sources: Pension, SO 12120, SC 7304 (admitted 27 Oct 1871); **Bridge in Time.**

SHANK, Philip. Pvt. under Capt. Shawen, 5 Sep - 27 Oct 1814; b. c.1789; m. Barbara Beckerbaugh, at Fred. Co. c.27 May 1813; res. Montgomery Co., OH, 1851, 1855 and in Liberty, Montgomery Co., OH, 1872. Acq.: 1851 - Jacob Burns.

Sources: Bounty land claim, 55-120-11265; pension, 26356, SC 18634 (admitted 19 Aug 1872); FCml.

SHANKEL, Philip. Pvt. under Capt. George W. Ent, 3rd Regt, 24 Aug - 30 Sep 1814.

SHANNABROOKE, Casper. Pvt. under Capt. Fonsten; joined 2 Sep 1814; deserted 1 Oct 1814.

SHARAN, Jacob. Never joined his company under Capt. William Durbin, which served 14-27 Oct 1814.

SHARNER, John. See Shamer, John.

SHARRAH, William. Pvt. under Capt. William Knox, 26 Aug - 27 Oct 1814.

SHARRAR [Sharrah, Sharrer, Sharer], George. Pvt. under Capt. William Knox, 26 Aug - 27 Oct 1814; m. 21 Mar 1814, Mary Frey(?) (b. c.1795) in Fred. Co., by Rev John Grub. George Sharrer d. Fred. Co., MD, 20 Aug 1821. Widow res. Miami Co., OH 1855. Acq.: 1855 - Henry Ocker and John Nichodemus, res. Miami Co., OH, acq. 15-20 yrs prev. to death of George Sharrer.

Source: Bounty land claim, 55-160-15533.

SHARRAR, Jacob. Never joined service under Capt. William Durbin, Jr., whose company served 24 Aug - 13 Oct 1814. [FCml issued 20 Aug 1813 to J. Sharer and Ruth Carr.]

Source: FCml.

SHARTZ, Daniel. Served under Capt. Creeger, 1 Aug - 27 Sep 1814. He said he was drafted in Fred. Co., Jun 1814, discharged at Balt. around 1 Sep 1814. He was engaged in the Battle of Bladensburg and present at the Battle of North Point. He was b. c.1794; m. c.23 Dec 1819, Catharine Ringer, in Fred. Co., MD; res. near Indianapolis, IN (Lawrence Township), in 1871.

Sources: Pension, SO 1068, SC 94099 (admitted 6 Dec 1871); FCml.

SHAUM, John. Pvt. under Capt. Samuel Duvall, 3 Aug - 3 Oct 1814.

SHAWBAKER, Jacob. See Showacre.

SHAWEN, Daniel. Capt. of his own company, called into service on 5 Sep 1814; the company discharged by him on 27 Oct 1814.

THE VETERANS

Mentioned in Millard Rice, *New Facts and Old Families*, is the tavern of Daniel Shawen in Jefferson, Fred. Co. Reference is made in the 1831 Act of the Legislature to a "house occupied as a tavern by Daniel Shower [Shawen]."

SHAWEN/SHAWN, James. Ensign under Capt. Daniel Marker, 25 Aug - 27 Oct 1814; m. 1 Feb 1802, Catharine Temple (b. c.1784), in Fredericktown. James Shawn d. Fred. Co., 7 Dec 1831. 1850 census of Fredericktown: Catharine Shawen, 65, in home of Samuel T. Shawen, 40, huckster, Mary Shawen, 26, Lucretia M. Shawen, 7, Edward M. Shawen, 5, Samuel Shawen, 3.

Sources: Bounty land claim, 50-40-46598, 55-120-15651; Names in Stone.

SHAWEN, Joseph. Allegedly served under Capt. Nicholas Turbutt; m. Catharine Baker (b. c.1791) in Fred. Co., near town of Jefferson, in 1811 [- according to widow. However FCml issued on 19 Jun 1813 in Fred. Co.], by Rev. David Martin. At enrollment (according to widow): c.26 yrs old, farmer, res. Fred. Co., 5 ft, 8 inches tall, black hair, black eyes, fair complexion. Fol. discharge res. Middletown and Fredericktown; d. at Fredericktown, 28 Oct 1844. 1850 census of Fredericktown: Catherine Shawen, 59, living at the home of Cornelius Shawen, 33, who operated a livery stable; Isabella Shawen, 22; Oscar S. Shawen, 2; Joseph Shawen, 27; Andrew J. Shawen, 23, barr keeper; Mary Shawen, 18; and Francis T. Harper, 10; and Jacob Walling, 15, laborer. P.O. address of Catharine Shawen in 1878 was Frederick City. Acq.: 1878 - Godfrey Koontz, 75, Court St., Fredericktown; and Henry Lorentz, 66, West Third St., Fredericktown, both acq. for 55 yrs; Col. Samuel Carmack, 85, res. Fred. Co., acq. for past 50 yrs.

Source: Pension, WO 15145 (rejected 23 Dec 1879 - no evidence of alleged service).

SHAWN, James. See Shawen.

SHAWN/SHOWN (Williams lists as Sohwen), John. Pvt. under Capt. Thomas Contee Worthington, 17 Aug - 31 Dec 1812. "Not mustered into service." "Substitute for William Crew."

SHEELEY [Shealy], Andrew. Pvt. under Capt. William Knox, 26 Aug - 27 Oct 1814. He said he served under Capt. Knox and Capt. William Piper; b. Fred. Co., MD; m. Hannah Bottomfield (b. c.1808, dau of Peter Karns of Prividence Township), at Bloody Run (now called Everett), Bedford Co., PA, 28 Feb 1841, by Henry Messersmith. She prev. m. Jacob Bottomfield and he prev. m. Anna Davis; both Jacob Bottomfield and Anna Davis d. near Bloody Run. Andrew Sheely d. Bloody Run, PA, 28 Jun 1856. At enrollment: age 16, stone mason, 5 ft, 11 inches tall, dark hair, black eyes, dark complexion. Hannah Sheeley res. Everett Borough, PA, 1878, Acq.: 1879 - Catharine Sparks, res. Providence Township, acq. with Hannah Sheeley 50 yrs; Philip C. Messersmith of Everett Borough, son of Henry Messersmith who was a J.P.

Source: Pension, WO 28149, WC 28689. Widow thinks land warrant may have been awarded to Baltzer Sheeley, son of Andrew.

SHEELY, John. Res. 3 miles of Taneytown in 1814. Pvt. under Capt. John Galt, 31 Aug - 27 Oct 1814.

FREDERICK COUNTY MILITIA IN THE WAR OF 1812

SHEETENHELM, Jacob. Pvt. under Capt. Samuel Duvall, 3 Aug - 3 Oct 1814; m. 2 Oct 1798, Mary Walters (b. c.1774) in Fred. Co., by Rev. David Martin. [FCml issued to Jacob Shetinghellern (Sheetinghellum?) and Mary Walter on 25 Sep 1798.] Jacob Sheetenhelm d. Fred. Co., 1 Jan 1836; widow res. Fred. Co., MD, 1851. Acq.: 1851 - Rezen Stevens and Joseph Kiens, res. Fred. Co.; 1855 - Washington Hammond and Charles Lease, res. Fred. Co.; 1869 - Reuben Sheetenhelm, son of Jacob Sheetenhelm. (FCml issued 29 Oct 1838 to Reuben Sheetenhelm and Elizabeth Lease.)
Sources: Bounty land claim, 55-160-110113; FCml.

SHEETS, Jacob. Pvt. under Lieut. Upton Reid, 1st Cav. Dist., 26 Aug - 3 Sep 1814. 1850 census, 5th E.D.: Jacob Sheets, 60, b. MD; Ann M. Sheets, 44, b. PA; Mary J. Hawk, 14; Daniel Hawk, 10; Hannah E. Sheets, 7. [Jacob Sheets bur. in cem. of the Taneytown, Trinity Luth. Ch. (d. 11 Mar 1866 - age 76 yrs, 4 mos., 6 days)].
Sources: Bridge in Time; Names in Stone.

SHEETS, Samuel. Pvt. under Capt. Fonsten, 2 Sep - 27 Oct 1814; res. 6 miles of Westminster.

SHEICY?, Henry. Mbr. of Crawford's "company."

SHELLMAN, Jacob. Pvt. under Capt. Henry Steiner, 25 Aug - 27 Sep 1814; b. c.1798; m. Sarah Hamler (b. c.1821), in Sommersett, OH, 1 Jun 1842; had a dau b. in 1844. When enrolled: 17 yrs old, farmer, Fred. Co., MD, 5 ft, 6 inches tall, dark hair, black eyes, dark complexion.

They res. Franklin Co., OH 2 yrs; Marion Co., OH, 7 [4?] yrs; Henry Co., OH 31 yrs - Gilead, Morrow Co., OH, in 1850; Henry Co., OH, 1855; and Bellemore, Putnam Co., OH, in 1871. He d. 24 Aug 1882 Marion Township, Henry Co, OH.

Witnesses to their wedding d. of cholera in summer of 1850. She was in ill health at age 61. She knew little of her late husband's first marr.; they lived in MD. She gave date of marr. as 5 Apr 1842 [different from husband's information given above.], marr. performed by Rev Shafer.

Williams, *History of Fred. Co.*, states Jacob Shellman, Sr., and Jacob Shellman, Jr., served in War of 1812. Jacob Shellman, Jr. was tanner and farmer; he moved to Indiana; m. 20 Dec, Charlotte Whip. [1850 census of Frederick E.D.: Solomon J. Zimmerman, 27, farmer; Catherine, 20; Charlotte Shellman, 50.]
Sources: Bounty land claim, 50-40-13077; 55-120-66606; Pension, SO 21871, SC 23190, WO 42450, WC 33217; Williams, Hist. of Fred. Co.; FCml; Engelbrecht Diary: 1:312.

SHELTON, Thomas. Pvt. under Capt. Fonsten; joined 2 Sep 1814; deserted 14 Sep 1814.

SHEPHERD, Thomas. Never joined service. His company served under Capt. William Durbin, Jr., 24 Aug - 27 Oct 1814. [FCml issued 18 Dec 1816 Thomas Shepherd and Nancy Wilson. There is a Thomas Shepherd bur. at Union Bridge Pipe Creek Friends Cem. in Carroll Co. (d. 12 Nov 1875, age 87)].
Sources: FCml; Names in Stone.

THE VETERANS

SHILLING, John. Pvt. under Capt. Fonsten; joined 2 Sep 1814; deserted 1 Oct 1814.

SHILLING, Michael. From Balt. Co.. Pvt. under Capt. John Galt, 31 Aug - 27 Oct 1814.

SHILLING, William. Pvt. under Capt. Shawen; joined 5 Sep 1814; deserted 18 Sep 1814; m. 30 Jan 1812, Hannah Martin (b. 1794) at her father's house in Fred. Co., by Rev. Carver, Luth. minister. William Shilling d. Columbus, OH, 18 Feb 1839. Widow res. Columbus, OH, 1851; Miami Co., OH, 1855; Troy, Miami Co., OH, 1860. In 1860, she stated that her husband while on tour at Balt. was sent on furlough on 18 Sep 1814 to return home to see his gravely ill wife and child, she having given birth to her first born, a son, David Shilling (still living in 1860). When she had partly recovered her husband started back to his post but met his company returning home. Acq.: 1851 - Elsa Heaston, sister of Hannah Shilling, said William and Hannah raised a family of children; 1852 - David Martin, a relative of Hannah Shilling; 1855 - Jesse Shilling and Isaac Hauser.

Source: Bounty land claim, 55-rejected-129971.

SHINDLER, John. Pvt. under Capt. John Brengle, 25 Aug - 19 Sep 1814. [1850 census, Petersville Dist., Frederick Co: John Schindler b. Germany, 56; Hannah 51; Louisa 15; Oliver Cramer 14. FCml issued 3 Nov 1818 John Shindler and Hannah Leatherman.]

Sources: FCml; Bridge in Time.

SHINN, Joseph. Pvt. under Capt. Jacob Getzendanner, 26 Jul - 21 Aug 1814.

SHIPLEY, Elias. Pvt. under Capt. Samuel Ogle; enrolled 1 May 1813 - deserted 4 Jun 1813; b. c.1789; res. Marshall Co., VA, in 1852. [Williams, p.1292, mentions a Elias Shipley son of Denton Shipley.]

Sources: Bounty land claim, 55-rejected-13916. [Williams, Hist. of Fred. Co., p. 1292, writes about Denton Shipley, b. Sykesville, 1st Lieut., in War of 1812; owned land near Westminster.]

SHIPLEY, Isaac. Pvt. under Capt. Lowrye, Henry; enrolled 27 Aug - deserted 1 Oct. [FCml issued 22 Feb 1834 Isaac Shipley and Mary Ann Boyer.]

SHIPLEY, Samuel. Pvt. under Capts. Samuel Ogle and Dunn. He served under Capt. Ogle, 1 May - 5 Jul 1813, substitute for John Hartsock; enrolled at Balt. c.1 May 1813, discharged at Balt. 10 Jul 1813. On 1 Aug 1813 at Balt. he was enrolled as a substitute for Nehemiah Hall in company of Capt. Dennis Barnes. - b. c.1790; res. Madison Co., IN, 1850, 1855.

Source: Bounty land claim, 55-120-16898.

SHIPLEY, Samuel. 4th corpl. under Capt. Daniel Marker, 16 Aug - 18 Sep 1813. Also said he served in company of Capt. Dennis Osb_e [O'burns?], 3rd Regt., as substitute for Joseph Keplinger at Boonsboro, c.28 Aug 1814, discharged at Camp Hampstead 31 Oct 1814; b. c.1792; res. Washington Co., MD, 1851, 1855.

Source: Bounty land claim, 55-120-85585.

SHIVERS, Cornelius. According to widow he was drafted under Capt. Murray at Middletown and discharged in Balt. City, in 1814. He m(1) 20 Sep 1821; m(2) Jul 1853 Micha Smith (b. c.1803), at New London, Fred. Co., MD, by Rev Nicholas Dorsey. At enrollment: age 19 yrs, short and heavy in stature, light hair and complexion. Micha m. prev. James Smith who d. c.17 Apr 1851. Fol. discharge Cornelius res. New London rest of his life. 1850 census of Fred. Co.: Cornelius Shivers, carpenter, 53; Susanna Shivers, 54; Clara Shivers, 20; Washington Shivers, 9. Cornelius Shivers d. at New London 7 Apr 1861, in his 65th year. At the time of his death he was mbr. of Linganore Mounted Guard. Widow res. New London in 1878. Acq.: 1878 - William W. Walker, 60, New London; and James S. Walker, 29, Fredericktown - both acq. 20 yrs; also acq. was B. J. F. Simpson.

Sources: Bounty land claim, 55-120-3145 (not in pension file); Pension, WO 13775, WC 12156 (admitted 16 Nov 1878, dropped due to death, 29 Mar 1892); FCml; (Frederick) Examiner, 13 Mar 1861.

SHOCKNEY, John. Pvt. from New Windsor, in Capt. Flautt's company of riflemen, 29 Apr - 29 Jun 1813 as substitute for David Taney, and under Capt. George W. Magee, joined 22 Jul 1814; deserted 6 Dec 1814. He also said he was substitute for Solomon McHenry [later identifies him as Solomon McKinney of Balt. Co.], in Capt. Blizzard's Company, Aug or Sep 1813, discharged after less than a month; he was a substitute for Henry or Robert Smith in Capt. Magee's Company around 1 Aug 1814 and served until he contracted measles about four mos.

later, about the time the "Regt. started to winter quarters at Annapolis." He was b. c.1791; m. Jerusa Anderson, in Balt. Co, MD, between Christmas and New Yrs, 1820; res. Randolph Co., IN 1851 and Wayne Township, Randolph Co, 1871. Acq. - 1871: Jeremiah Smith, Thomas W. Coffin.

Sources: Bounty land claim, 55-80-37373; Pension, SO 16109.

SHOE, John. Mbr. of Crawford's "company." [*History of Montgomery Co.*, OH - John Shoe b. Fred. Co., MD, 1783, d. 1862 in Montg Co.; a bro. Philip settled in Miami Co.; (sons of Jacob Shoe); John m. Mar 29, 1806 in MD, Charlotte Loy].

SHOEMAKER, Christopher [Christoph on muster roll]. Pvt. under Capt. Fonsten; joined 2 Sep 1814; deserted 14 Oct 1814; b. c.1768; res. Belmont Co., OH, in 1851 and 1853 (Fairview).

Source: Bounty land claim, 50-rejected-166104. "Fairview October 12th 1858. To the Bounty land office - Gentlemen I am informed that I deserted from my post. It is absolutely not so that when I got sick Capt. John Funston went with me from camp to the west end of Howard Street to the wagon to send me home then returned me deserted whitch is false. When I valuntered I was one year and five mos. over forty five yrs of age. That makes me now Eighty six yrs of age. After I got home I lay sick for more than one year. I esteem Capt. John Funston not a man of truth as he was a whig and I a democrat. He tried to ..(?) me all he could. I sent an affidavit some time last spring and got no answer from it. Christopher Shoemaker."

SHOEMAKER, John. Pvt. under Capt. John Galt, 31 Aug - 27 Oct 1814.

SHOEMAKER, Nicholas. Pvt. under Capt. Philip Smith, joined 23 May - deserted 4 Jul - 1813. [FCml issued 22

THE VETERANS

May 1810 to Nicholas Shoemaker and Elizabeth Roads.]

SHOLL, Christian. Pvt. under Capt. Jacob Getzendanner, 9 Aug - 17 Sep 1813.

SHOLL, Henry. Pvt. under Capt. John Brengle, 25 Aug - 19 Sep 1814.

SHOOK, Adam. Pvt. from Balt. Town and later as 4th corpl. under Capt. George W. Magee, 23 Jul - 10 Jan 1815.

SHOPE [Shoup], George Brengle. Pvt. under Capt. John Brengle, 25 Aug - 19 Sep 1814; b. 1796; m. c.11 Feb 1818, Elizabeth Dofler (b. 1802), dau of George Dofler; she d. 14 Jan 1829 in her 28th yr; bur. Meth. Grave yard. He later m. c.15 Aug 1829 Louisa Keller (b. 1810); she d. of apoplexy on 28 Jan 1873, age 62 yrs, 1 mo., 27 days. He was one of two who were captured by John Brown on his raid on Harpers Ferry; mbr. of Independent Fire Company; d. at his residence on East Patrick St., 6 Jun 1871, age 74 yrs, 5 mos., 25 days. Bur. at Mt. Olivet Cem.: George Brengle Shope 1796-1871; wife Louisa (Keller) 1810-1873; son Augustus K. 1831-1831; dau Marie Louise 6 Sep 1833-13 May 1917; son Milton W. 1837-1865; son Horace A. 1840-1876; dau Alice Ellen 7 Nov 1845-20 July 1921; son Ernest R. 1846-1871. Also bur. in Mt. Olivet is Elizabeth Shope (1802-1829). 1850 census of Fredericktown: George B. Shape [sic], 53, cabinet maker, Louesa, 38 [plus other family mbrs.].

Sources: **Frederick Herald**, 17 Jan 1829; (Frederick) **Examiner**, 14 Jun 1871, 5 Feb 1873; FCml; Name in Stone; West. Md. Genealogy, v.7, 1.

SHORB, [Shurp] Conrad. Pvt. under Capt. Knox, 26 Aug - 27 Oct 1814; joined 17 Sep; m. 13 Apr 1818, Catharine Forney (b. c.1795), by Rev. Runkles at Emmittsburg, Fred. Co. At enrollment: 5 ft, 9-10 inches, dark hair, light eyes, florid complexion. After discharge res. Fred. Co. [now Carroll Co.], MD remainder of his life; d. 16 Oct 1862; bur. at Taneytown Trinity Luth. Ch. Cem. Widow res. Taneytown, Carroll Co., MD, 1879, unable to travel because of infirmity. Acq. (1879): Benjamin Poole, Samuel Angell, Double Pipe Creek, MD.

Sources: Bounty land claim, 55-120-8109; Pension, WO 37149, WC 27515; FCml.

SHORB, John A. Pvt. in Capt. George Flaut's company, 29 Apr - 29 Jun 1814; b. c.1793; never m.; res. Shippensburg, Cumberland Co., PA, 1871.

Source: Pension, SO 18690, SC 17201.

SHORL [Shorb?, Sholl?], John. Pvt. in 1st Cav. Dist., 26 Aug - 3 Sep 1814. [John Shorb bur. in St. Anthony, old Mt. St. Mary's Cath. Cem. (near St. Mary's College); d. 31 May 1870.]

Source: Names in Stone.

SHORTS, Jacob. Pvt. under Capt. John Galt, 31 Aug - 27 Oct 1814.

SHOTZ [Shots], Henry. Pvt. under Capt. George W. Ent, 24 Aug - 30 Sep 1814. [FCml issued 12 Dec 1820 to H. Shots and Elizabeth Miller and 21 Mar 1833 to H. Shotts and Mary Susan Myers]

SHOTS [Shoto], John. Pvt. under Capt. John Brengle, 25 Aug - 19 Sep 1814.

FREDERICK COUNTY MILITIA IN THE WAR OF 1812

SHOUP, Baltzer. Pvt. under Capt. John Galt, 6 Sep - 27 Oct 1814, res. 2 miles from Hampstead in 1814.

SHOUP, Jacob. Pvt., 1st Cav. 26 Aug - 3 Sep 1814.

SHOVER, Adam. Pvt. under Capt. Barton Hackney, 1 Sep - 27 Oct 1814.

SHOWACRE [Shabaker, Shawbaker, Showbaker], George. Pvt. under Capt. George W. Ent, 24 Aug - 30 Sep 1814; b. 11 Oct 1795; m. Matilda Keefer (b. 12 Sep 1819 in Bavaria, Germany according to pension, b. 7 Sep 1820 according to tombstone), at Frederick, MD, 24 Dec 1844 by Rev. Daniel Zacharias, D.D. At enrollment: 5 ft, 10 inches tall, weighed c.160 lbs, dark sandy hair, light eyes or blue. After discharge res. near Fredericktown until 1769 when he moved to a home 3 miles northeast of Fredericktown where he d. 3 May 1873. Widow d. 7 Mar 1924! Both bur. Mt. Olivet. 1850 census of Fredericktown: George Shabaker, 54, plasterer, b. MD; Matilda, 29, b. Germany; George W., 4; Jacob, 1. Son George W. Showbaker, never m., served Union army at 16, Co. E, 7th MD Inf. Vol., d. 1869 of consumption. Other son had large family.

Sources: Pension, 7377, SC 3920, WO 17715, WC 14337; **(Frederick) Examiner**, 7 May 1873; **The Maryland Union**, 8 May 1873; **Names in Stone; Bridge in Time**.

SHOWACRE, Jacob. Pvt. under Capt. George W. Ent, 3rd Regt, 24 Aug - 30 Sep 1814. Jacob Shawbaker, mbr. of "United Brothers of the War of 1812," celebrated defense of Balt. with fellow Frederick veterans in 1859.

Source: **(Frederick) Examiner**, 14 Sep 1859.

SHRADER, John. Pvt., 17th U.S. Inf. At enlistment: 5 ft, 9 inches; blue eyes, dark hair, dark complexion; age 40; occupation farmer; b. Fred. Co.; enlisted 27 Oct 1813 at Hamilton, OH, by Lt. Stall for duration of war. In Featherstone's company, Chillicothe, OH, 31 May 1815; discharged at Chillicothe, OH 9 Jun 1815.

SHRINER, George. Pvt. under Capt. John Galt, 31 Aug - 27 Oct 1814; m. 17 Mar 1798, Anna Hollenberger [Hollenberry?] (b. c.1781) by Georg Nicademus; res. 3 miles of Hampstead in 1814. George Shriner d. near Taneytown 7 Oct 1824. Widow res. Carroll Co., MD, 1851. Acq.: 1851 - Henrietta Shoemaker and John Shoemaker.

Source: Bounty land claim, 50-40-75477.

SHRIVER. See also Schriver.

SHRIVER, Benjamin. Mbr. of Crawford's "company."

SHRIVER, Isaac. Quartermaster, 2nd Regt., 1st Cav. Dist.

SHRIVER, John. Pvt. under Capt. Fonsten, 2 Sep - 27 Oct 1814.

SHRIVER, Samuel. Pvt. under Capt. Fonsten, 2 Sep - 27 Oct 1814; res. 8 miles from Westminster.

SHRIVER, Thomas. Capt. of rifle company from PA, took part in battle of North Point; his company (from York, PA) was acknowledged on 10 Oct 1814 by the Committee of Vigilance and Safety of Baltimore as having performed service on the Fortifications - b. Carroll Co., 2 Sep 1789; d. New York City 18 Apr 1879; after the war he res. Frederick and Balt. counties; moved to

THE VETERANS

Cumberland, MD, c.1855; became one of the owners of Good Intent State Company and in May 1843, elected Mayor of Cumberland. In 1853 he moved to Phila. and started an omnibus line; later established with his son Walter the firm of T. Shriver & Co in New York.
Source: (**Frederick**) **Examiner,** 27 Apr 1879; **Md. Hist. Mag.,** v.XL:1, 11-12.

SHROTES, John. Pvt. under Capt. Samuel Dawson, 26 Jul - 13 Oct 1814; "sick in Balt..."

SHROYER, Frederick. Pvt. under Capt. John Fonsten, 2 Sep - 27 Oct 1814; res. 8 miles from Westminster.

SHROYER, William. Pvt. under Capt. Joseph Wood, 27 Aug - 28 Oct 1814.

SHRYOC, John. From Balt. Pvt. under Capt. Joseph Green, 14 Oct 1814 - 10 Jan 1815; discharged Annapolis. He deserted 27 Dec, returned 30 Dec 1814.

SHRYOC, John. Pvt. from Upper Fred. Co., under Capt. James F. Huston, 23 Jul 1814 - 13 Oct 1814.

SHRYOCK, Henry. 4th corpl. under Capt. Joseph Wood, 27 Aug - 28 Oct 1814; b. 10 Jan 1795; m. 20 Mar 1828, Catharine M. Guisebert [Gisbert, Geisbert] (b. 31 Mar 1810, d. 18 Feb 1885) at Creagerstown, by Rev. Michael Wachter, each for first time. At enrollment: age 18 or 19, worker in a factory; about 6 ft tall; black hair, gray eyes. He res. Creagerstown, Fred. Co., fol. discharge; d. Myers' Mill near Creagerstown 18 Jul 1875; both bur. Utica, St. Paul's Evangelical Luth. Ch. Catharine was dau of Jonathan Geisburt of Creagerstown Dist. Their children were Mary E. who m. John J. Valentine; Rebecca; Henry V. of Waynesboro, PA; George W.; Sarah A.; John J. Henry Shryock owned and managed a fulling mill known as Myers Mill on Hunting Creek. Henry was son of Valentine and Christina Shryock. 1850 census of Cragerstown Dist.: Henry Shryock, 55, farmer; Catherine, 41; Mary H., 41; Rebecca C., 19; Henry V., 17; George W., 14; Sarah A. D., 10; James W., 7; John J., 4. Acq.: 1850 - George Late and Solomon Filler who served with Henry Shryock; 1878 - Sarah Shryock, 38; H. J. Krise, 38, both res. Fred. Co. Appeared on 23 Sep 1878 was Maria Lathgiver (Sathgiver?), dau of dec'd Rev. Michael Wachter, pastor of the Luth. Congregation at Creagerstown. She had his diary in which there was entry of marr. of Henry Shryock and Catharine Geisbert.
Sources: Pension SO 9462, SC 5380, WO 32438, WC 19599 (widow's pension last paid 4 Dec 1884); Bounty land claim, 55-120-15077; **Bridge in Time;** (Frederick) **Examiner,** 28 July 1875, 25 Feb 1885; Williams, **History of Fred. Co.;** FCmL

SHUE, Jacob. Pvt. under Capt. George W. Magee, 22 Jul - 13 Oct 1814; also served under Capt. Showers?

SHUEY, Daniel. Pvt. under Capt. Fonsten, 2 Sep - 27 Oct 1814; res. 2 miles of Westminster.

SHULTZ, David. Pvt. from Upper Fred. Co. under Capt. James F. Huston, 23 Jul - 13 Oct 1814.

SHULTZ, George. Orderly sergt. in Capt. Markey's company, under Lieut. Kolb, 13 Oct - 15 Nov 1814, guarding the British prisoners at the Frederick Barricks. He said that he served under Lt.

FREDERICK COUNTY MILITIA IN THE WAR OF 1812

William Kolb by order of Morris Jones, marshall of the dist. of Frederick who had charge of the prisoners at the Barrick at Fredericktown during the war. He said he was drafted at Fredericktown around 15 Sep 1814 and continued as one of the guards until discharged at Fredericktown c.23 Oct 1814. He was b. c.1786; m. c. 24 May 1814, Sophia Kemp. 1850 census of Frederick E.D.: George Shultz, 63, farmer, b. PA; Sophia, 57; Theadore, 23; Mary M., 34; Carline A., 19; Lewis H., 17 - all except George b. in MD. George Shultz res. Fred. Co., MD, 1855; d. 6 Oct 1874, age 88 and bur. Mt. Olivet Cem.; mbr. of Ref. Ch. Bur. same plot: wife Sophia (1 Jan 1876, age 83); dau Mary M. (5 Apr 1908, age 92); dau Caroline A. (19 Mar 1915, age 84). Acq.: John W. Miller and Henry Shultz. Sophia d. at her residence on West Third St., Frederick.

Sources: Bounty land claim, 55-160-2048; FCml; (Frederick) Examiner, 14 Oct 1874, 5 Jan 1876; Names in Stone; Bridge in Time.

SHULTZ, Henry. Pvt. in Capt. Markey's company, serving under Lieut. Kolb, 13 Oct - 15 Nov 1814, guarding the British prisoners at the Frederick Barracks.

SHULTZ, Martin. 2nd sergt. under Capt. James F. Huston and Capt. Joseph Green, 23 Jul 1814 - 10 Jan 1815, res. Frederick Town. "On furlough since 8 Oct"; b. Apr 1796; blind and res. York Co., PA, 1851. Acq.: 1855 - Marcus Carroll and Samuel Keyser.

Source: Bounty land claim, 50-80-57802, 55-80-1117.

SIAS, Nicademis. Mbr. of Crawford's "company."

SIDNEY, Edward. 29th U.S. Inf. At enlistment: 5 ft, 7 inches; black eyes, black hair, dark complexion; age 21; prev. occupation sailor; b. Fredericktown, MD; enlisted 17 Nov 1814 at New York by Capt. Spencer for duration of war; mustered 30 Apr 1815 as sergt. Discharged at Plattsburgh 29 Jun 1815.

SIER [Sears], John. Pvt., 14th U.S. Inf., under Capt. Samuel Lane. At enlistment: 5 ft, 7 inches; dark eyes, brown hair, dark complexion; age 38; b. Fred. Co.; enlisted 19 May 1812 at Westminster by Lt. Gist for 18 mos. Prisoner of war, exchanged on 10 Apr 1814; in Boston 2 May 1814. Discharged at Greenbush 20 Jun 1814.

SIERS, Alexander. Pvt. from Upper Fred. Co. under Capt. James F. Huston, 23 Jul - 13 Oct 1814.

SIGLER, Peter. Pvt. under Capt. Samuel Dawson, 21 Jul - deserted 6 Aug 1814.

SILING, J. Andrew. Pvt. under Capt. Daniel Shawen, 5 Sep - 27 Oct 1814; b. c.1798; res. Huntington Co., IN, 1850.

Source: Bounty land claim, 50-40-26003.

SILVERTHORN, William. Pvt. under Capt. Samuel Dawson; joined 14 Oct 1814; deserted 2 Nov 1814.

SIMMONS, Daniel. 3rd corpl. under Capt. Basil Dorsey; joined 30 Jul 1814; discharged 24 Sep 1814; discharged at Balt. by furlough on 25 Sep 1814; b. c.1789; res. Jefferson Co., OH, 1850 and in Harrison Co., OH in 1855. Acq.: 1855 - John Epley and William R. Stewart. [FCml issued 24 Apr 1813 Daniel Simmons and Elizabeth Burkhardt]

THE VETERANS

Sources: Bounty land claim, 55-120-68931.

SIMMONS, George. Pvt. under Capt. Basil Dorsey, 30 Jul - 20 Sep 1814; m. 1815 Susan [Susannah] Engle (b. c.1785) by Rev. James Day, Meth. minister. George Simmons d. Fred. Co., 8 Oct 1838, age 59; bur. with wife at Kemptown, Simmons-Engle Family cem. ("on Roughton farm off Bill Moxley Road.") Widow res. Fred. Co. 1850, 1855; d. 5 Nov 1856 at age 72. Acq.: 1850 - Joseph Kemp and Ezekiel Moxley; 1856 - Jacob Engle, bro. of Susannah Simmons, states that George Simmons d. 1837 and bur. on his (Jacob Engle's) farm; Isaac Burke, groomsman at their marr.

Sources: Bounty land claim, 55-120-58165; FCml. [issued 28 Oct 1815]

SIMMONS, Isaac. Pvt. under Capt. Basil Dorsey, 30 Jul - 20 Sep 1814. [FCml issued 21 Nov 1815 to Isaac Simmons and Mary Kain.]

SIMMONS, James. 1st Lieut. under Capt. Barton Hackney, 1 Sep - 27 Oct 1814; m. 11 Mar 1823 Sophia Simpson (b. c.1797), in Fred. Co., MD, by Rev. James Reid. James Simmons d. Fred. Co., 8 Mar 1843. Acq.: 1855 - William Ricahrdson and Charles S. Simmons, res. Fred. Co. Witnesses: 1852 - Mary R. Simmons and Jacob Kessler, res. Fred. Co.

Source: Bounty land claim, 55-120-75119.

SIMMONS, John. Corpl. under Capt. Daniel Marker, 25 Aug - 27 Oct 1814; b. c.1783; res. Fred. Co. 1852, 1855. [There was a Col. John Simmons (d. 2 Sep 1857, age 74) bur. in Catoctin Creek area, Lakin Family cem., east of Fry Road.

Also bur. there was Serena Simmons 4 Aug 1792 - 16 Feb 1874. 1850 census of the Jefferson Dist. of Fred. Co.: John Simmons, age 67 and Serena Simmons, 54.]

Sources: Bounty land claim, 55-120-68586; Names in Stone; Bridge in Time.

SIMMONS, Thomas. Pvt. under Capt. Basil Dorsey, 30 Jul - 27 Sep 1814. [FCml issued 21 Mar 1821 to Thomas Simmons and Kezia D. Cain.]

SIMMONS, Zachariah. From Fredericktown - Alledged deserter by Capt. Getzendanner, described as small man, taylor by trade. According to Simmons, in an advertisement in *Fredericktown Herald*, he had volunteered earlier under Capt. Christian Cost in a troop of horse. Capt. Cost later confirmed this.

Source: **Frederick Herald**, dated 28 Aug 1813.

SIMPSON, Benjamin. Pvt. under Capt. Fonsten, 2 Sep - 27 Oct 1814; "sick absent" on 14 Oct; b. 1774; res. Washington Co., MD, 1851, 1855.

Source: Bounty land claim, 55-120-4519.

SIMS [Simms], John. Pvt., 14th U.S. Inf., det., Capt. D. Cumming. At enlistment: 5 ft, 11 inches; blue eyes, light hair, light complexion; age 24; occupation farmer; b. Fred. Co. Mustered on 29 Oct 1814 at Balt. by Lt. Gale for duration of war. At Balt. on 16 Feb and 14 Mar 1815. Discharged 18 Mar 1815.

SIMS, Patrick. Pvt. under Capt. Basil Dorsey, 30 Jul - 27 Sep 1814.

SIX, George. Pvt. in 1st Cav. 26 Aug - 3 Sep 1814. 1850 mortality census shows that George Six d. Creagerstown Dist.

FREDERICK COUNTY MILITIA IN THE WAR OF 1812

of Fred. Co., MD, Jan 1850; stone mason; had been sick for 4 yrs with cholera(?).] His tombstone shows George Six (6 Apr 1785 - 23 Nov 1851), bur. at the Creagerstown St. John's Luth. and Ref. Ch.]

SIX*, John. Pvt. in 1st Cav. 26 Aug - 3 Sep 1814.

SIX*, John. The following two entries represent a single file at the National Archives; it appears that the applications of two different persons named John Six have been mistakenly merged: one who enlisted in 1812 for 5 yrs and submitted his bounty land claim for the first time in 1871 while res. Seneca Co., OH.; and the second one who volunteered into the militia in 1814 and res. Carroll Co., MD 1850, 1855. [Fred m.l. 21 Feb 1816 John Six and Mary Morrison and 7 Aug 1819 John Six to Catherine Stull. *Names in Stone* lists John Six bur. in the Taneytown, Grace Evan. and Ref. Ch., 5 May 1791 - 15 May 1869 with wife Sarah A. 11 Mar 1809 - 26 Mar 1874.]

(1) SIX*, John. He said he volunteered at Bruceville, Frederick Co, MD, c.15 Aug 1812 for term of 5 yrs; discharged at Fredericktown, MD, on 15 Aug 1817. He was a pvt. [and Ensign?] in the company of Capt. John Trux (or Trucks); b. c.1790; res. Tiffin, Seneca Co., OH, in 1871.

Source: Bounty land claim, 55-120-22906 (submitted in 1871).

(2) SIX*, John. 3rd corpl. under Capt. William Knox, 26 Aug - 27 Oct 1814; b. c.1790-1792; res. Carroll co., MD, 1850, 1855.

Source: Bounty land claim, 55-120-22906 (see above).

SIX, Leonard. Cornet in the 1st Cav. Dist., 26 Aug - 3 Sep 1814.

SLACK, James. Pvt. from Balt. under Capt. Joseph Green, 14 Oct 1814 - 10 Jan 1815 as substitute for Joseph Keepers. He said he served as pvt. under Capts. Stewart and Green. He said he was drafted as a pvt. under Capt. Coats at Balt. Co., around 1 Aug 1813; discharged at Balt. around 10 Sep 1813; also a pvt. under Capt. Stewart, drafted at Balt. around 18 Aug 1814; discharged at Balt. around 18 Nov 1814. Also a pvt. under Capt. Green as a substitute for Joseph Keipers around 20 Nov 1814; discharged at Annapolis around 31 Jan 1815. Widow said he was drafted at Ellicot Mills.

He was b. c.1777; m. Elizabeth Gardiner in Adams Co, PA, in 1819 by Rev. John Hinch; d. Ashland, OH, 4 Jun 1854; widow res. Ashland Co., OH, 1855. Acq.: 1855 - Henry Whiteman and James Gardiner, res. Ashland Co., OH.

Source: Bounty land claim, 55-80-3743.

SLAGLE, Charles. Pvt. under Capt. Barton Hackney, 1 Sep - 27 Oct 1814.

SLAGLE, Jacob. Pvt. under Capt. Samuel Dawson; joined 1 May 1814; deserted 16 Jun 1814.

SLAGLE, Jacob. Pvt. under Capt. Barton Hackney, 1 Sep - 27 Oct 1814.

SLARRAP, Jacob. Pvt. under Capt. William Durbin, 14-27 Oct 1814.

SLATER, James B. From Balt. Town. 4th sergt. and later as 3rd sergt. under Capt. George W. Magee, 22 Jul - 10 Jan 1815

SLAUGENHEPT, John. Pvt. under Capt. Samuel Ogle; joined 1 May 1813; deserted 2 Jun 1813.

SLICE, Michael. Pvt. under Capt. Philip Smith; joined 23 May 1813; deserted 18 Jun 1813.

SLICK, Frances. Pvt. under Capt. George W. Magee; joined 23 Jul 1814; deserted on 20 Sep 1814. [Francis Slick bur. at the Taneytown, Grace Evan. and Ref. Ch., 8 Feb 1857, age 63.]
Source: Names in Stone.

SLICK, John. 1st lieut. under Capt. William Knox, 26 Aug - 27 Oct 1814.

SLIDER, Jacob. Pvt. under Capt. William Knox, 26 Aug - 27 Oct 1814. [FCml issued 30 Sep 1819 to Jacob Slider and Sophia Kreise.]

SLIFE [Schlife], Henry. Pvt. under Capt. William Durbin, joined 24 Aug; deserted 30 Sep 1814; b. 1794; res. Reynoldsburgh, Franklin Co., OH, 1852; Franklin Co., OH, in 1855.
Source: Bounty land claim, 55-120-36473.

SLIFE [Shlife], John. Pvt. from New Windsor under Capt. George W. Magee; joined 22 Jul 1814. "Sick absent 18 Sep." "Deserted" 20 Nov 1814. - m. Jun 1810, Mary Magdalena [McElener?] Krisher? [Chrinher?] (b. c.1792) in Fred. Co., by Rev Grubb in Taneytown. John Shlife d. Fairfield, OH, 21 Jan 1845 [or 22 Jan 1844]. Widow was res. Fairfield Co., OH, in 1852. Acq.: 1852 - Henry Shlife, age 57, past res. Fairfield Co.; states John Shlife and his wife were parents of 10 children; he and John Shlife served in the war at Balt.; William Raven, age 64, res. Violet Township, Fairfield Co., OH.
Source: Bounty land claim, 55-120-36476.

SLOAN, John. 4th corpl. under Capt. John Brengle, 25 Aug - 19 Sep 1814.

SLOTHOUN [Slothour?], Francis. Pvt. under Capt. Samuel Ogle, 1 May - 5 Jul 1813.

SLUSSER, Andrew. Pvt. under Capt. Daniel Shawen, 5 Sep - 27 Oct 1814.

SMEETHE, Peter. Pvt. under Capt. Fonsten; joined 2 Sep 1814; discharged by certificate 8 Oct 1814.

SMELTZER, Jacob. Never joined his company which served under Capt. William Durbin, Jr., 24 Aug - 27 Oct 1814.

SMEY, Daniel. Pvt. under Capt. Daniel Shawen, 5 Sep - 27 Oct 1814.

SMITH, Caspar. See Gaspar Smith.

SMITH, Benjamin. Res. Emmitsburgh. Pvt., later 3rd corpl., under Capt. James F. Huston/Capt. Joseph Green, 23 Jul 1814 - 10 Jan 1815.

SMITH, Charles. Pvt. under Capt. John Galt, 31 Aug - 27 Oct 1814.

SMITH, Christian B. 27th U.S. Inf. At enlistment: 5 ft, 8 inches; gray eyes, fair hair, fair complexion; age 27; occupation shoemaker; b. Emmittsburg, MD; enlisted 18 Apr 1814 at Newark by Capt. Spencer for duration of war; discharged as drum major at Zanesville, OH, 27 Mar 1815.

FREDERICK COUNTY MILITIA IN THE WAR OF 1812

SMITH, Elijah. Pvt. under Capt. Samuel Dawson, 26 Jul 1814 - 10 Jan 1815; b. c.1794; res. Balt. City 1850, 1855 [sick in head?, too sick to answer questions].
Source: Bounty land claim, 55-80-1945.

SMITH, Felix. 3rd corpl. under Capt. Samuel Ogle, 1 May 1813 - 5 Jul 1813.

SMITH, Frederick. Pvt. under Capt. Philip Smith, joined 23 May 1813; deserted 12 Jun 1813.

SMITH, Frederick. Pvt. under Capt. John Galt, 31 Aug - 27 Oct 1814.

SMITH, Gaspar. Pvt. under Capt. Jacob Criggers (Creager); m. 24 Mar 1825, Rachel Hampton (b. c.1805), by George Burkert, J.P. in Sullivan Co., TN; neither m. prev. At enrollment: 6 ft, 1 inch, about 140 lbs., blacksmith, black hair and eyes, fair complexion, b. c.4 miles from Fredericktown. Fol. discharge Gaspar Smith res. MD 4 yrs, then Sullivan Co., TN; he d. at Hiltons, TN, 30 Nov 1858. Acq.: 1878 - Peter Yoakley, 48, and Geo. W. Fonce, 28, acq. 27 and 21 yrs, resp.; William Beard, Calvin M. Rader, 57, Joseph E. Spurgin, 47.
Source: Pension, WO 32732, WC 22937.

SMITH, George. Mbr. of Crawford's "company."

SMITH, George. Pvt. under Capt. Joseph Wood, 27 Aug - 13 Oct 1814; furloughed 26 Oct.

SMITH, George. Pvt. under Capt. John Fonsten; joined 2 Sep 1814; deserted 4 Oct 1814.

SMITH, George. Pvt. under Capt. Robert Fulton, Aug - Sep 1814; m. 22 Sep 1822, Catharine Gibson in Emmittsburg, MD; he d. Woodsboro, 11 Aug 1837. Catharine d. 20 Sep 1855. Their children: Mary Jane Smith b. 2 Aug 1823; George Gibson Smith b. 23 Jun 1825; Harriet E. Smith b. 18 Oct 1827; Annie M. Smith b. 25 Jan 1829; Hellen S. Smith b. 30 Jun 1832; Loretta C. Smith b. 10 Feb 1834; George W. Smith b. 11 Jul 1837. Acq. (1870): Adam Holbruner [Holburner], res. Woodsboro, pvt. who served in Fulton's company; and John A. Baker, res. Woodsboro, pvt. in same company; also Frank Donnely and Mary Jane Donnelly of Fred. Co. George W. Smith (b. c.1838) son of George Smith res. Woodsboro 1870.
Sources: Bounty land claim, 55-160-110147; Pension.

SMITH, George M. Pvt. under Capt. George W. Magee, 22 Jul 0 13 Oct 1814.

SMITH, Henry. Pvt. under Capt. N. Turbutt, 1 Sep - 30 Oct 1814; m. 14 Jan 1801, Mary Zimmerman (b. c.1776), in Fred. Co., by Rev. W. Mahler, Luth. minister. [She stated in 1850 they m. 1801; however FCml issued 9 Jan 1802.] Henry Smith d. Fredericktown 7 Apr 1816. 1850 census of Fredericktown: Mary Smith, 74; Harriet McDaniel, 45; and Cammilla, 19. Acq.: 1850 - Margaret Powel, age 71, sister of Mary Smith. 1855 - Harriet McDaniel and Theresa Smith.
Sources: Bounty land claim, 55-120-4038; **Bridge in Time.**

SMITH, Henry. Pvt. under Capt. John Galt, 31 Aug - 27 Oct 1814.

THE VETERANS

SMITH, Isaac. Pvt. under Capt. Thomas Contee Worthington, joined 17 Aug; deserted 18 Oct 1812.

SMITH, Jacob. Pvt. under Capt. William Knox, 26 Aug - 27 Oct 1814; b. c.1785; m. Isabela Dugen in Washington Co., MD, c.25 Jun 1825, by Rev. Jeremiah Mason. Res. Knox Co., OH, 1851; d. Huntington Co., IN, 10 Jul 1854. Acq.: 1855 - L. C. Pomeroy, M.D., and Julius Gotsch, res. Huntington Co.
Source: Bounty land claim, 55-120-2902.

SMITH, Jacob. Pvt. under Capt. Daniel Shawen, 5 Sep - 27 Oct 1814; b. c.1796; res. Fred. Co., MD, 1851, 1855. [Appears to be same Jacob Smith who m. Rebecca Horine c.27 Feb 1821. 1850 census of Middletown E.D.: Jacob Smith, 54, farmer; Rebecca, 56; Daniel W., 10; Jonas H., 8; Jacob S., 6; Sarah C., 9 mos. Bur. Myersville Luth. ch. yard: Jacob Smith of M., d. 13 Jun 1880, age 84 yrs, 17 days, with Rebecca Smith, who d. 23 Sep 1873, age 81 yrs, 7 days. - *Examiner.* The *Maryland Union* states she d. 2 Oct 1873.]
Sources: Bounty land claim, 55-120-18352; (Frederick) Examiner, 8 Oct 1873, 16 Jun 1880, 23 Jun 1880; Bridge in Time; Names in Stone; FCmI; The Maryland Union, 9 Oct 1873.

SMITH, Jacob. Corpl., 18th U.S. Inf., under Capt. Wm. C. Taylor. At enlistment: dark eyes, dark hair, dark complexion; occupation tailor; b. Fred. Co.; enlisted 15 Aug 1814 Charleston, S.C. by Lt. Bruton. 14 Aug 1819 resigned as sergt. Court martial sentence at Ft. Hawkins, GA 30 Apr 1816. Absent sick at Ft. Gadsden. Discharged 14 Aug 1819.

SMITH, James. Pvt. under Capt. Samuel Dawson, 21 Jul - 13 Oct 1814.

SMITH, John of M. Newspaper stated (later rescinded), Capt. John Smith of M., "soldier of the War of 1812," d. 20 Jan 1874 in Woodsboro, age c.85 yrs. Corrected made stating Mr. Smith appeared to be recovering. He was father-in-law of Thomas M. Holbrunner, mayor. He d. 22 Mar 1875. 1850 census of the Woodsboro Dist.: John Smith of M., 58, farmer and limeburner, $7000; Elizabeth, 38; Susan, 21 and others. [Uncertain which of below named soldiers this might be.]
Sources: (Frederick) Examiner, 11 Feb 1874, 18 Feb 1874; Md. Union, 26 Mar 1875; Bridge in Time.

SMITH, John. Sergt. under Capt. Philip Smith, 23 May - 8 Sep 1813; b. c.1790; res. Fred. Co. 1851 and 1855.
Source: Bounty land claim, 55-120-24402.

SMITH, John. Pvt. under Capt. George W. Ent, 24 Aug - 30 Sep 1814; b. c.1795; res. Greene Co., TN, in 1850 and 1855. Acq.: 1855 - Joseph H. Earnest and Matthew C. Hundley, res. Greene Co., TN.
Source: Bounty land claim, 55-120-51043.

SMITH, John. From Upper Fred. Co. Pvt. under Capt. James F. Huston/Capt. Joseph Green; joined 23 Jul 1814 - deserted 8 Dec 1814.

SMITH, John of John. On the existing rolls he served as pvt. under Capt. Samuel Duvall, 3 Aug - 3 Oct 1814. However, the third auditor reports that he served as pvt. under Capt. Samuel

Duvall, 3 Aug - 6 Nov 1814 during which time he is reported on the rolls "Absent without leave 6 days." He m. 20 Jun 1817, Susannah Fogle (b. c.1802), by Rev Hause, Luth. minister. John Smith d. 7 Jul 1846 in Fred. Co.; widow res. Fred. Co. 1851. 1850 census of Dist. 8: Susanna Smith, 70; Michael Smith, 44; Susan Smith, 34. Bur. at Woodsboro St. Peter's Rocky Hill Luth. Ch. are John of John Smith 28 Jan 1792 - 8 Jul 1845 and wife Susannah 31 Aug 1800 - 26 Aug 1872. Acq.: 1851 - John M. Fogle and Matthias Fogle who said that Susannah Fogle "was married at our house ..."

Sources: Bounty land claim, 50-40-49974; **Bridge in Time; Names in Stone; FCml.**

SMITH, John. From Mechanickstown, 1st lieut. under Capt. George W. Magee, 23 Jul 1814 - 10 Jan 1815.

SMITH, John. Pvt. under Capt. Joseph Wood, joined 27 Aug 1814; deserted 24 Sep.; b. c.1788; res. Fred. Co., MD, 1850 and in Martinsburg, VA, 1855.

Source: Bounty land claim, 55-120-37507.

SMITH, John Dinsmore. Corpl. under Capt. John Brengle, 25 Aug - 19 Sep 1814. [FCml issued 30 Jun 1822 to John D. Smith and Ann C. Gomber.]

SMITH, Joseph. Pvt. under Capt. William Knox, 26 Aug - 27 Oct 1814.

SMITH, Joseph. Sergt. under Capt. Philip Smith, 23 May - 8 Sep 1813 and Capt. Joseph Wood, 27 Aug - 28 Oct 1814; m. 10 Apr 1817, Mary Ebbarts (b. c.1793) in Fred. Co., by Rev. R. Hammond, Meth. minister. Joseph Smith d. Fred. Co., 29 Mar 1849. Mary Smith res.

Fred. Co. 1851, 1855. Acq.: 1851 - Hezekiah Bernard served in same company as Joseph Smith; Joseph M. Smith. 1855 - Ephraim Smith.

Sources: Bounty land claim, 55-80-9698; FCml.

SMITH, Michael. Pvt., 2nd U.S. Inf., Det. of Invalids under Lt. J. Brants. At enlistment: 5 ft, 5 inches; blue eyes, brown hair, light complexion; age 56; baker; b. Fredericktown, MD; enlisted 1 Feb 1813. Discharged at Sacketts Harbor 17 Sep 1816 by surgeons certificate of old age; served 3 yrs, 7 mos. and 17 days.

SMITH, Philip. Capt. of his own company; served 23 May - 8 Sep 1813.

SMITH, Randolph. Pvt., U.S. Artillery, under Capt. J. S. Peyton. At enlistment: 5 ft, 9 1/2 inches; blue eyes, brown hair, dark complexion; age 28; sailor; b. Fred. Co.; enlisted 7 Jun 1814 at Winchester by Capt. Peyton for duration of war. At Craney Island on 15 Mar 1815.

SMITH, Robert. Servant under Capt. Thomas Contee Worthington, 17 - 31 Dec 1812.

SMITH, Robert. 1st corpl. under Capt. William Durbin, Jr., 24 Aug - 27 Oct 1814; b. c.1793; res. Hancock Co., IN, 1850, 1855. Acq.: 1855 - Prestley Guymon and James H. Carr, of Hancock Co.

H. J. Williams, Postmaster, Hancock Co, IN, stated on 30 Sep 1874 that he had just learned that Robert Smith is dead long since and that his son James H. Smith resides in Moral, Shelly Co., IN.

Source: Bounty land claim, 55-120-25716.

THE VETERANS

SMITH, Samuel. Musician under Capt. Philip Smith, 23 May - 8 Sep 1813.

SMITH, Samuel. Pvt. under Capt. Philip Smith, 23 May - 8 Sep 1813. [Name of Samuel Smith appears twice in the rolls of Capt. Philip Smith, once as pvt. and once as musician.]

SMITH, Samuel. Pvt. under Capt. Daniel Marker, 25 Aug - 27 Oct 1814.

SMITH, Samuel Price. Dr. Samuel Price b. near Frederick, 21 Dec 1795; graduated Doctor of Medicine; practiced medicine at Taneytown; moved to Cumberland in 1820; served in War of 1812, present at Battle of North Point. Surgeon in Union Army.

Source: (Frederick) Examiner, 7 Dec 1881.

SMITH, Solomon. Pvt. under Capt. Denton Darby, 30 Aug - 8 Nov 1814.

SMITH, Solomon. Pvt. under Capt. Creager and Capt. Philip Smith, 23 May - 8 Sep 1813 and Capt. Creager, as substitute for Mathias Fogle, c.1 Aug 1814 - 1 Oct 1814; m. May 1812, Sarah Ann Fogle (b. c.1790) in Frederick Co., by Rev David Shaffer, Luth. minister. Solomon Smith d. Fred. Co., MD, 13 Aug 1823. His widow res. Fred. Co., MD 1851. Acq.: 1851 - John M. Fogle and Solomon Fogle; 1855 - Jacob Beard; Solomon Ernest and William Andes, res. Fred. Co., MD.

Sources: Bounty land claim, 55-80-39392. FCmL

SMITH, Thomas. Pvt. under Capt. Samuel Dawson, 14 Oct 1814 - 10 Jan 1815.

SMITH, William. Pvt. under Capt. Samuel Dawson; joined 21 Jul 1814 - deserted 24 Aug.

SMITH, William. From Upper Fred. Co. Pvt. under Capt. James F. Huston and Capt. Joseph Green; joined 23 Jul 1814 - deserted 8 Dec 1814.

SMITH, William. Pvt. under Capt. Thomas Contee Worthington, 17 Aug - 31 Dec 1812; promoted to 3rd corpl. 22 Sep 1812.

SMITH, William. Pvt. under Capt. Samuel Dawson, 1 May - 5 Jul 1813.

SMITH, William. Pvt. under Capt. Stone. According to Casper Smith, b. c.1798, William Smith was in the Battle of Bladensburg, that he entered the service of U.S. in Fred. Co., MD, in 1814. William Smith m. Elizabeth Hulstine, in Sullivan Co., TN, 21 Nov 1816, by George Burkheart, J.P. After close of war William Smith moved to TN, res. Sullivan Co. William Smith d. Tallapoosa Co., AL, 21 Mar 1847. Acq. (1852): John S. Cash, who knew William Smith in Tallapoosa Co.

Source: Bounty land claim, 55-rejected-274212.

SMITH, William. 14th U.S. Inf. At enlistment: 5 ft, 11 inches; age 21; b. Fred. Co., MD; enlisted 30 Mar 1813 at Fredericktown by Lt. J. S. Nelson for 18 mos. In Capt. Montgomery's company, Plattsburg, pvt. Discharged Mar 1814. Reenlisted.

SMITH, William. Served under Capt. D. Cummings. At enlistment: 5 ft, 8 inches; blue eyes, light hair, fair complexion; age 21; laborer; b. Fred. Co.; enlisted 6 Jan 1815 at Balt. by Lt. A. Woodward for duration of war. Dis

FREDERICK COUNTY MILITIA IN THE WAR OF 1812

charged 18 Mar 1815. Substitute for John C. Richards, citizen of Balt.

SMITH, William. Pvt., 22nd U.S. Inf. under Capt. D. McFarland. At enlistment: 5 ft, 7 1/2 inches; blue eyes, black hair, dark complexion; age 25; occupation nailor and hatter; b. Fred. Co., MD; enlisted 13 Aug 1812 at Fayette by Capt. Foster for 5 yrs. On extra duty at Niagara 11-24 Dec 1812. Discharged at Burlington 19 Apr 1814 by surgeon's certificate, of asthma.

SMITHY, John. Pvt. under Capt. Matthew Murray, 25 Aug - 27 Oct 1814.

SMUR, Jacob. Pvt. under Capt. Matthew Murray; joined 25 Aug 1814; deserted 21 Oct 1814.

SNAVELY, John. Pvt. from Upper Fred. Co. under Capt. James F. Huston/Capt. Joseph Green; joined 23 Jul 1814; deserted 4 Dec 1814; b. c.1793; res. Balt. City in 1851.

Source: Bounty land claim, 50-rejected-64379.

SNECK, Henry. Pvt. under Capt. Fonsten, 2 Sep - 27 Oct 1814; res. 9 miles from Westminster.

SNECK [Snack], John. Pvt. under Capt. Fonsten, 1 Sep - 27 Oct 1814; res. 9 miles from Westminster. According to him he served in the companies of Capts. Shower, Murray and Fonsten, 10 May - 7 Jul 1813, 26 Jul - 29 Aug 1814 and 2 Sep - 28 Oct 1814; b. c.1779; res. Carroll Co., MD, 1851, 1853 and 1855. Witnessess: 1855 - George Zepp and Daniel Matthias, res. Carroll Co.

Source: Bounty land claim, 50-80-48447, 55-80-23717.

SNEEMAN, William. 2nd corpl. under Capt. Jacob Alexander, 22 Jul - 19 Sep 1814.

SNERR, Charles. Pvt. under Capt. Daniel Marker, 16 Aug - 18 Sep 1813.

SNIDER, Jacob. Pvt. under Capt. George W. Magee, 22 Jul - 13 Oct 1814.

SNIDER, Joseph. From New Windsor. Pvt. under Capt. George W. Magee, 14 Oct 1814 - 10 Jan 1815.

SNIDER, Nicholas. 1st Lieut. under Capt. Galt, 18 Aug - 29 Oct 1814. According to reference cited below, he was also appt'd paymaster just before Battle of North Point. He was b. 9 May 1786 at Chambersburgh, PA; m. 1 Sep 1807, Margaretta (b. 14 Feb 1786), dau of Hugh and Jane (Boyd) Thomson of Taneytown; entered dry goods business at early age; partner with Cornelius Howard at Pikesville, MD, where he lived until 1814 when he and his family moved to Taneytown; appt'd Judge of Orphans' Court for Fred. Co. 1830; served 6 yrs as U.S. Marshall for Dist. of MD in Balt.; retired near Graceham, Fred. Co. where he d. 11 Jun 1856. Widow d. Emmittsburgh, MD, 20 July 1865. Both bur. at Taneytown. Their children: Amelia b 13 July 1808, m James Reindollar; Catherine Elizabeth b 3 Jan 1810, m Zebulon Kuhn; Caroline Rebecca b in Balt. 3 Sep 1812, m George W. Sharpe of York Co., PA; Anna Mary b 29 May 1813, m Thomas Rudisil; Jeremiah b in Taneytown 23 Nov 1815, m at Xenia, OH, Angeline Tiffany (St. Louis, MO); Ellen Margaret b 3 Feb 1818; Louisa b 16 Dec

THE VETERANS

1819; Samuel Thomson b 2 May 1822, d 8 Apr 1831.

Sources: Handwritten notebook purchased by Virginia Stenley, Taneytown, MD, at an antique show, entitled, "An Account of William Thomson, The first of the name in America and His Children." A portion of the account regarding Margaretta Snider was attributed to her dau Ellen M. Snider. The latest entries date around 1878. Copy of this account placed in Filing Case A, Md. Hist. Society. The Maryland Union, 26 Jun 1856. (Frederick) Examiner, 2 July 1856.

SNOOK, Henry. Pvt. under Capt. Philip Smith, 23 May - 8 Sep 1813.

SNOWDAGLE, George. Pvt. under Capt. Samuel Dawson, 1 May - 5 Jul 1813.

SNOWTICKEL, George. Pvt. under Capt. Brengle, 25 Aug - 19 Sep 1814.

SNUR, Henry. Pvt. under Capt. Daniel Shawen, 5 Sep - 27 Oct 1814.

SNYDER, Abraham. Pvt. under Capt. Matthew Murray, 25 Aug - 27 Oct 1814.

SNYDER, Christian. Pvt. under Capt. Basil Dorsey, 30 Jul - 27 Sep 1814; entered as substitute at New Market, MD; b. c.1780. 1850 census of New Market Dist.: Christian Snyder, age 75, farmer, living by himself. Res. Fred. Co. in 1851.

Source: Bounty land claim, 50-40-49803.

SNYDER, George. Pvt. under Capt. Matthew Murray, 25 Aug - 27 Oct 1814.

SNYDER, Henry. Pvt. under Capt. John Brengle; joined 25 Aug 1814; deserted. [Bur. at Woodsboro St. John's Ref. Ch.: Henry Snyder 18 Jul 1852, age 60 yrs, 5 mos., 27 days; wife Ann Mary 6 Sep 1823, age 47 yrs, 7 mos., 26 days, mother of Jacob, Elizabeth, Margaret and Ann E. Snyder.]

Source: Names in Stone.

SNYDER, Jacob. Pvt. under Capt. Samuel Dawson, joined 14 Oct 1814; deserted -- Nov 1814.

SNYDER, John. 2nd corpl., later as pvt., under Capt. Samuel Dawson, 21 Jul 1814 - 10 Jan 1815.

SOHWEN See Shawn.

SOLLERS, Sabritt. Major of 1st Battalion, 20th Regt. under Lt. Col. Wampler; apparently not called into service; b. 24 Aug 1772, son of Thomas and Ariana (Dorsey) Sollers and grandson of Sabritt Sollers who m. Mary Heighe dau of James Heighe of Calvert Co and great grandson of John Sollers who d. Calvert Co. in 1699. Our subject Sabritt Sollers m. Mary Dorsey 25 Dec 1806. She d. 26 Feb 1820; he d. 17 Jul 1834.

Thomas Sollers was Major of the Gunpowder Battalion in MM in the Rev. War.; J.P. Balt. Co. 1774; mbr. of the Committee of Correspondence in 1776; Naval Officer of the Port of Balt.

Sources: Mrs. Thomas S. George, 1941, Sollers and Allied Families, copy held by the Md. Historical Society. This information was furnished by descendant, Charles L. Cassidy, D.V.M., 16410 Yeoho Rd., Sparks, MD 21152. These George notes give vital data on Thomas and Ariana Sollers and their children.

SOLOMON, negro. Servant under Capt. Samuel Duvall, 3 Aug - 3 Oct 1814.

SOMERS, John. Pvt. under Capt. Samuel Dawson, 1 May - 5 Jul 1813 Pvt. Returned from Balt.

SOMERVILL, James. Pvt. under Capt. Henry Steiner, 25 Aug - 27 Sep 1814.

FREDERICK COUNTY MILITIA IN THE WAR OF 1812

SOUDER, Conrad. Pvt. under Capt. Fonsten; joined 2 Sep 1814; deserted 16 Sep 1814.

SOWERS, Jacob. Pvt., U.S. Dragoons. At enlistment: 6 ft, grey eyes, brown hair, ruddy complexion; age 35; farmer; b. Fred. Co.; enlisted 26 Mar 1814 by Capt. Burd for 5 yrs. At Chambersburg, PA, on 30 Mar 1814. Mustered in Capt. Hites' company on 20 Jan 1816.

SPALDING, Basil. Pvt. under Lieut. Upton Reid, 1st Cavalvry, 26 Aug - 3 Sep 1814.

SPALDING, Henry. Pvt. in the 1st Cav., 26 Aug - 3 Sep 1814. [FCml issued 25 Oct 1819 to Henry Spalding and Sarah M. Hughes.]

SPEAKER, John. Pvt. under Capt. Joseph Wood; joined 27 Aug 1814; deserted 13 Sep 1814; m. 1795(?) Magdelena Young (b. c.1777) by Jonathan Rauhauser, German Ref. minister. John Speaker d. Lisbon, OH, c.1840. Witnesses: 1859 - George Stokes and Henry Young.
Source: Bounty land claim, 55-rejected-303919.

SPEALMAN, Andrew. Mbr. of Crawford's "company."

SPEELMAN, Andrew. From New Windsor. Pvt. under Capt. George W. Magee; joined 22 Jul 1814; sick on furlough 1 Oct; "3 weeks sick," discharged in Balt. by surgeon 1 Dec 1814.

SPONSALER, Jacob. [See Jacob Sponseller below.] Pvt. under Capt. Fonsten; joined 2 Sep 1814; sick absent on 7 Oct 1814.

SPONSELLER, Frederick. Pvt. under Capt. Capt Nicholas Turbutt; 1 Sep - 27 Oct 1814; b. c.1795; res. Washington Co., MD, in 1852.
Source: Bounty land claim, 50-40-78049, 55-120-17778.

SPONSELLER, Jacob. Pvt. under Capt. George W. Ent, 24 Aug - 30 Sep 1814; b. c.1788; m. c.6 Dec 1814, Catherine Shape (d. 1 Sep 1870, age 77 yrs, 6 mos., 20 days). 1850 census of New Market Dist.: Jacob Sponseler, 59, farmer; Catherine, 57; Arthur, 19; George, 17; Anna, 15. Williams states that Jacob Sponseller was father of 8 children. Jacob d. 23 Nov 1873, age 82 yrs, 5 mos., 18 days; both bur. Mt. Olivet, Frederick.
Sources: Bounty land claim, 50-40-29946, 55-120-14971; Williams, **History of Fred. Co.**; **Bridge in Time**; **Names in Stone**; **The Maryland Union**, 4 Dec 1873; **(Frederick) Examiner**, 10 Dec 1873.

SPONSELLER, William. Pvt. under Capt. Philip Smith, 23 May - 8 Sep 1813.

SPONSLER, David. From New Windsor. Pvt. under Capt. George W. Magee, 22 Jul - 10 Jan 1815. [FCml issued 3 Apr 1816 to D. Sponseller and Patience Buckman]

SPONSLER [Sponsaler], William. Pvt. under Capt. Samuel Duvall, 3 Aug - 3 Oct 1814; his widow said he was discharged on account of sickness; m. 14 May 1815, Elizabeth Sowers by Rev. James Higgans, Methodist minister in Fred. Co. William Sponsler d. Tuscarawas Co., OH, 18 Aug 1841. Widow res. Tuscarawas Co., OH, 1856. Acq.: 1856 - Jess Sponsler and Sarah Ann Kennedy, res. Tuscarawas Co; Anthony Eckhart, age 73, 3rd sergt. in Capt. Duvall's company, also drafted at town of Woodbury around Jul 1814 into same

company as William Sponsler; Jacob Sponsler, age 69 on 6 May, bro. of William Sponsler, pvt. in the company of Capt. Upton Norris and afterwards John Fonsten; was drafted at Sans Creek(?), town of Liberty.
Source: Bounty land claim, 55-160-60089.

SPRENGLE, David. Pvt. under Capt. Nicholas Turbutt, 1 Sep - 27 Oct 1814; d. 9 Sep 1832, in his 37th year, "of the prevailing epidemic." He m. c.2 Oct 1823, Caroline Mary Ann Ruth; she d. Ashland, OH, 14 Mar 1882, age 75 yrs, 9 mos., 24 days; immigrated to Ashland Aug 1835; she was niece of Lewis Medtart and Henry Nixdorff of Frederick; mbr. of Evan. Luth. Ch.
Sources: **Frederick Herald**, 15 Sep 1832, 22 Mar 1882; FCmL

SPRINGER, Daniel. Pvt. under Capt. John Brengle, 25 Aug - 19 Sep 1814; b. c.1798; m. Elizabeth Rose. She was b. 24 Feb 1799, d. 16 Mar 1828 at 7 a.m., "dau of Mrs. Rose." 1850 census of Fredericktown: Daniel Springer, hatter, 52; and Mary Carmack, 38. He res. Fred. Co., MD, 1850, 1851, 1855; bailiff to Circuit Court; d. at his residence, West Patrick St., 23 Mar 1871 age 75 yrs, 7 mos., 18 days; bur. Ref. graveyard.
Sources: Bounty land claim, 50-40-85569, 55-120-12847; **(Frederick) Examiner**, 29 Mar 1871; **Engelbrecht Diary**, v.1, 535; **West. Md. Gen.**, v.7, 1.

SPRUTTSMAN, Jacob. Pvt. under Capt. Joseph Wood, 27 Aug - 28 Oct 1814; rendezvous at Camp Diehl.

SPURRIER, Lancelot. 14th U.S. Inf. under Capt. Samuel Lane. At enlistment: 5 ft, 11 inches; black eyes, dark hair; age 21; b. Fred. Co.; enlisted 21 May 1812 at Westminster, MD, by Lt. Gist. On 21 Nov 1813 he was at Boston. Prisoner of war, exchanged 15 Apr 1814. Reenlisted 30 Apr 1814. 2 May 1814, sergt. Discharged 6 Jun 1815.

SPURRIER, Green [Greenbury]. Pvt. under Capt. Fonsten, 2 Sep - 27 Oct 1814; res. 16 miles from Westminster; while in service called Greenbury, but true Christian name is Green; b. c.1794; res. Balt. City, 1852, 1855.
Source: Bounty land claim, 55-120-2157.

SQUIRE, Thomas. Pvt. under Capt. Barton Hackney, 1 Sep - 27 Oct 1814.

STAHL [Steahl], Henry. Pvt. under Capt. John Brengle, 25 Aug - 19 Sep 1814.

STALEY, Abraham. Pvt. under Capt. Capt Nicholas Turbutt, 1 Sep - 27 Oct 1814; b. c.1783; res. Fred. Co., 1851, 1855. 1850 census of Frederick Dist.: Abraham Staley, 67; and Catherine, 68. Abraham Staley, bur. Frederick Ref. Cem. *[(Frederick) Hornet* announced marr. of Abraham Staley to Miss Elizabeth Shaffer, on 26 Feb 1811.]
Sources: Bounty land claim, 50-40-27197, 55-120-15650; **Names in Stone; Bridge in Time; The (Frederick) Hornet**, 27 Feb 1811.

STALEY [Staly], Moses. Pvt. under Capt. Jacob Getzendanner, 9 Aug - 17 Sep 1813. 1850 census of Fred. E.D.: John A. Staley, 28, farmer; Ann E. Staley, 53; Henry Staley, 31, labourer; Phebe A. Staley, 18; Lewis Staley, 16; John A. Staley, 1 mo. On 21 Jun 1855 in Fred. Co. appeared Lewis Edward Staley, age 20 yrs on 31 Jan 1855; and his bro. Josiah Oliver, age 17 on 1 Jul 1855 - the sons of Moses Staley, dec'd. Their

FREDERICK COUNTY MILITIA IN THE WAR OF 1812

father, Moses Staley d. near Frederick in 1840; their mother remarried and was still living. Acq.: 1855 - Christian Steiner and Cornelius Staley, res. Fred. Co. [FCml issued 18 Sep 1816 to Moses Staley and Ann Elizabeth Stull.]
Sources: Bounty land claim 55-rejected-178036; FCml.

STALEY, Peter. Pvt. under Capt. Capt Nicholas Turbutt, 1 Sep - 27 Oct 1814. 1850 census: Peter Staley, 52, farmer; Margaret, 52; Sarah, 18; Abraham T., 15; Anne S., 13; John W. Creager 11. Peter Staley, no dates, bur. Frederick Ref. Cem. FCml issued on 22 May 1818 to Peter Staley, Jr. and Margaret Albaugh.
Sources: FCml; Names in Stone; Bridge in Time.

STALL, Andrew. From Upper Fred. Co. Pvt. under Capt. James F. Huston and Capt. Joseph Green, 23 Jul 1814; sick in Balt. from 20 Sep until 27 Oct 1814 when he deserted.

STALL, Henry. Pvt. under in Capt. Markey's company under Lieut. Kolb, 13 Oct - 15 Nov 1814, guarding British prisoners at the Frederick Barracks.

STALL, Jacob. Pvt. under Capt. Fonsten; joined 2 Sep 1814; deserted 15 Sep 1814.

STALLINGS, Charles T. Lieut. of U.S. Navy, served in War of 1812, "fell victim to the yellow fever, contracted at Cuba." Native of Frederick; entered navy c.1810, as a midshipman."
Source: **Frederick-Town Herald**, 9 Nov 1822.

STALLINGS, Otho. Lieut., U.S. Navy, d. at Key West 12 Jan 1824.
Source: Frederick-Town Herald, 19 Feb 1825.

STALLINGS, Richard. Pvt. under Capt. Nicholas Turbutt, 1 Sep - 27 Oct 1814; drafted at Buckeystown; b. c.1793; res. Fred. Co., MD 1850. 1850 census of New Market Dist.: Richard Stallings, age 57; William H. Stallings, 19; Delilah R., 17, b. VA; Mary A. M., 14, VA; Fanny Cobelance, 65, b. MD.
Source: Bounty land claim, 50-40-15476.

STALY, Malachiah. Pvt. under Capt. Fonsten; joined 2 Sep 1814; deserted 14 Sep 1814.

STAM, Nathan. Mbr. of Crawford's "company."

STAMP, George. Pvt. under Capt. Samuel Dawson, 1 May - 5 Jul 1813. [FCml issued on 13 Feb 1815 to George Stamp and Elizabeth Padgett]

STANSBURY, Isaac. Pvt. under Capt. Fonsten, 2 Sep - 27 Oct 1814, res. within 4 miles of Westminster.

STARNER [Sterner], Jonathan. Pvt. under Capt. George W. Magee, 22 Jul - 13 Oct 1814.

STARRY, George. Pvt. under Capt. William Durbin, Jr., joined 24 Aug; absent without leave 25 Oct.

STATES, John. Pvt. under Capt. Samuel Dawson; joined 21 Jul; deserted 29 Sep 1814.

STAUB [Staup], Jacob. Pvt. under Capt. Joseph Wood, 27 Aug - 28 Oct 1814; d. Petersville, 3 Jan 1872, age 81; bur. Petersville St. Mary's Cath. Ch.; native of PA according to his obit. in *The Maryland Union;* however the 1850 census indicates b. in MD. The obit. also states he served as a PA volunteer in the defense of Balt. contrary to the

THE VETERANS

in the defense of Balt. contrary to the fact that the muster roll of Capt. Wood carries a Jacob Staup. Obit. states he moved to Fred. Co. after his service at Balt. 1850 census of Frederick E.D.: Jacob Staub, 59, labourer; Catherine Staub, 59; Francis J. Staub, 30; Jerome Staub,28, labourer; Edward T. Staub, 27, teacher; Lucinda Staub, 25; Andrew J. Staub, 23, labourer; Ann E. Staub, 20. Bur. at Frederick, St. John's Cath Cem.: Andrew J. Staub (7 Apr 1828 - 14 Jan 1873 with wife Mary E. (23 Apr 1834 - 24 Jan 1900).

Sources: Names in Stone; The Maryland Union, 11 Jan 1872; (Frederick) Examiner, 21 Mar 1877; Bridge in Time.

STAUB, John. Pvt. under Capt. Joseph Wood, 27 Aug - 28 Oct 1814; b. c.1788; m. Margaret Hawman in Fred. Co., near PA in Jun 1811 by Rev. John Dubois. John Staub res. Adams Co., PA, 1850; d. Littlestown, PA, 30 Jun 1852. Widow res. Adams Co., PA, 1855. Acq.: 1855 - Ephraim A. Stonesifer and Jacob Wilt [Dilt?], res. Littlestown.

Sources: Bounty land claims, 50-40-20670, 55-120-6160.

STAUFFER, George. From Upper Fred. Co. Pvt. under Capt. James F. Huston/Capt. Joseph Green; joined 23 Jul 1814, deserted 17 Dec, returned 24 Dec 1814, discharged Annapolis 10 Jan 1815. [*German Ch. Rcds.*, v.4 - Georg son of Daniel and Christina Stauffer b 29 Apr 1788.]

STAUFFER, John. From Upper Fred. Co. Drummer under Capt. James F. Huston and Capt. Joseph Green, entered service 23 Jul 1814, deserted 25 Sep, returned 24 Oct, deserted 8 Dec, returned 24 Dec; discharged Annapolis 10 Jan 1815.

STAUP, Adam. Pvt. under Capt. Joseph Wood, 27 Aug - 28 Oct 1814; rendezvous at Camp Diehl.

STAUP, Eli. Pvt. under Capt. Joseph Wood; joined 27 Aug; deserted 26 Oct 1814.

STAUTON [Stanton], John. Pvt. in 17th U.S. Inf. At enlistment: 4 ft, 10 inches; hazel eyes, light hair, fair complexion; age 14; shoemaker; b. Manchester, Washington Co., MD [sic]; enlisted 1 Jan 1814 at Maysville, Lexington, KY, by Capt. B. W. Saunders for 5 yrs. Marched to Detroit, 14 May 1814. 28 Feb 1815, drummer. Detroit 31 Dec 1815.

STEAHL, Henry. Pvt. under Capt. John Brengle, 25 Aug - 19 Sep 1814.

STEEL, Daniel. Pvt. under Capt. Philip Smith, joined 29 May - deserted 29 Jun; returned 30 Jun; deserted 6 Aug - 1813; b. c.1791; res. Belmont Co., OH, in 1855. Witnesses: 1855 - John T. Steel and James Moore. [FCml issued 9 Oct 1812 to Daniel Steel and Sussana Ader.]

Sources: Bounty land claim, 55-rejected-15840; FCml.

STEEL, Joseph. Pvt. under Capt. Philip Smith, 23 May - 8 Sep 1813.

STEEL, Joseph. 4th corpl. under Capt. William Durbin, Jr., 24 Aug - 27 Oct 1814.

STEERS, John. 2nd sergt. under Capt. Jacob Alexander, 22 Jul - 19 Sep 1814. "Sick on furlough."

STEGNER, George. Pvt. under Capt. Fonsten, 2 Sep - 27 Oct 1814, res. 12

FREDERICK COUNTY MILITIA IN THE WAR OF 1812

Carroll Co., MD, 1871 near post office at Union Mills.

Source: Pension, SO 2158, SC 23831 (rejected 9 Mar 1872 - insufficient service, admitted 1 Aug 1878).

STEGNER, Jacob. Pvt. under Capt. Fonsten, 2 Sep - 27 Oct 1814, res. 12 miles of Wesminster; b. c.1779; res. Manchester, MD, in 1851.

Source: Bounty land claim, 55-120-82385.

STEINER, Henry. Capt. of artillery company, served 28 Apr - 29 Jun 1813 and 25 Aug - 27 Sep 1814; m. 20 May 1806, Miss Rachel Murray. In 1815 he was appt'd Register of Wills; d. 18 May 1825, in his 50th year, leaving wife and 7 infant children. Rachel Rebecca, 3rd dau of Capt. Henry Steiner, d. 27 Feb 1835 in her 16th year. Mrs. Elizabeth, relict of Henry Steiner, d. morning of 17 Apr 1833, at her residence in Frederick.

Sources: **Frederick-Town Herald**, 24 May 1806; 21 May 1825; 27 Apr 1833, 28 Feb 1835.

STEINER, John Thomas. Pvt. under Capt. Henry Steiner, 28 Apr - 12 May 1813 and 25 Aug - 27 Sep 1814. [John Thomas Steiner, son of Jacob Steiner, Esqr., d. 27 Jun 1820, 9 o'clock, age 31 yrs, 1 month, of consumption. - *Engelbrecht Diary*: 1:23.]

STEINER, Stephen. Lieut. Col. of the 1st Regt. under Capt. Col. John Ragan, 1st Regt, 14 Oct 1814 - 10 Jan 1815; discharged at Annpolis; m. Barbara --- who d. 9 Mar 1819 at age 43; later m. 4 May 1821, Elizabeth Bausman, in Fredericktown, MD, by Rev. Helfenstein, minister of Ref. Ch. He had at least two children; George eldest son b. 1798, d. 21 Oct 1817; dau Charlotte, wife of Lewis Remsberg, b. c.1797, d. 1824. Stephen Steiner d. Fredericktown 8 Sep 1829. Widow res. Balt. City 1853, 1855. Acq.: 1853 - Lewis A. Bierly and Frederick B. Steiner, res. City of Balt.

Sources: Bounty land claim, 50-40-52369, 55-80-34529; FCml; **Frederick-Town Herald**, 25 Oct 1817, 11 Mar 1819, 12 Sep 1829.

STEINER, William. 2nd corpl. under Capt. Henry Steiner, 25 Aug - 27 Sep 1814; d. 13 Feb 1835, of lingering pulmonary disease, in his 41st year, "for the last 15 yrs chief clerk in the office of the Register of Wills in this county ..." Son of Jacob Steiner who prev. died.

Sources: **Frederick Herald**, 21 Feb 1835; **Engelbrecht Diary**: 1:129.

STEMBLE, Henry. Lieut. Colonel of the 28th Regt. of MM.

STEMP, George. Pvt. under Capt. Daniel Shawen, 5 Sep - 27 Oct 1814.

STEPHENS, Charles. Pvt. under Capt. Basil Dorsey, 30 Jul - 27 Sep 1814. [FCml issued 29 Aug 1820 to C. Stevens and Catherine Snyder]

STEPHENS, James. Pvt. under Capt. Daniel Marker; joined 25 Aug 1814; deserted same day.

STEVENS, Joseph. Pvt. under Capt. Daniel Shawen, 5 Sep - 27 Oct 1814.

STEVENS, Reason. Mbr. of Crawford's "company." [FCml issued 23 Nov 1811 to Renzin Stevens and Polly Durbin.]

STEVENSON, Abelard. 3rd sergt. under Capt. Fonsten, 2 Sep - 27 Oct 1814; b. c.1795; res. Knox Co., OH, 1855. Witnesses: 1855 - Henry Shields and Edward T. Getzendanner.

THE VETERANS

Source: Bounty land claim, 55-160-7877.

STEVENSON, David. From New Windsor; 3rd corpl., later 4th sergt., under Capt. George W. Magee, 22 Jul - 10 Jan 1815.

STEVENSON, Levi L. Widely known in VA and NC, d. 30 Aug at the residence of his son-in-law, Col. M. G. Harman, near Staunton, VA; b. Liberty, Fred. Co., MD, 11 Nov 1787; Capt. in War of 1812; came to Staunton in 1813; mbr. of Masonic Lodge.
Source: **The Maryland Union**, 4 Sep 1873.

STEVENSON, Wesley. Pvt. under Capt. George W. Ent, 3rd Regt, 24 Aug - 30 Sep 1814.

STEWARD, David. Pvt. under Capt. Joseph Wood, entered into service 27 Aug 1814; deserted 1 Oct 1814.

STEWART, Daniel. Pvt. under Capt. Daniel Marker, 25 Aug - 27 Oct 1814.

STEWART, William. Pvt. under Capt. Philip Smith, 23 May - 8 Sep 1813; d. 17 Apr 1824 in his 31st year; bur. Bapt. Ch. yard with military honors.
Source: **Frederick Herald**, 24 Apr 1824.

STICHER, George. Pvt. under Capt. Philip Smith, 23 May - 8 Sep 1813.

STICHER, Peter. Pvt. under Capt. Jacob Getzendanner, 9 Aug - 17 Sep 1813. [Peter Stitcher d. 8 Jun 1838, after a severe and protracted illness, age 54 yrs; to be bur. family burial grounds, Balt. City.]
Source: **Republican Citizen**, 22 Jun 1838.

STICHER [Sticker], Solomon. Drummer under Capt. Samuel Duvall, 3 Aug - 3 Oct 1814; b. 1796; res. Carroll Co., MD, in 1851 and 1855. [Married Sunday 2 Jun 1811 by rev. Welsh, Solomon Stickel, cordwainer, to Miss Mary Dull, both of Frederick. *Frederick Hornet*]
Sources: Bounty land claim, 55-120-34330; **(Frederick) Hornet,** 5 Jun 1811. In the file is letter from Solomon Sticker: "Carrollton, May 10, 1851 - Dear Sir; I received your communication informing me that you could find no such man as Solomon Sticher in Capt. Duvals Co. of Drafted men from Fred. Co, Md. I was enrolled in Capt. Joseph Woods Co. for three mos. afterwards exchanged my place with Enoch Chinoth in Capt. Duval's Co. for 6 mos so that his co. could have my services as drummer. The roll may have been burnt at the time the capitol was burnt."

STIMMEL, John B. According to (Frederick) Examiner, he was a soldier in the War of 1812. b. 7 Jul 1791; m. c. 17 Feb 1816, Elizabeth Smith; res. Mount Pleasant, 1881. He d. 17 Feb 1883; bur. with wife Elizabeth (25 Jun 1794 - 16 Dec 1876) at Woodsboro St. Johns Ref. Cem. 1850 census of Woodsboro Dist.: John B. Stimmel, 59, farmer; Elizabeth, 55; John, 23; Henrietta J., 18; John Anders, 50.
Sources: FCml; (Frederick) Examiner, 21 Dec 1881, 21 Feb 1883, 28 Feb 1883; **Names in Stone; Bridge in Time.**

STINCHACOMB Vachel. From Frederick Town. 4th sergt. under Capt. James F. Huston/Capt. Joseph Green, from 23 Jul 1814 until discharged Balt 6 Dec 1814 by surgeon.

STINCHCOMB [Stinchecome], Nathaniel. From Fredericktown, pvt. under Capt. William Knox, 26 Aug - 27 Oct 1814; m. 27 Mar 1816, Elizabeth Blair (b. c.1795), in Fred. Co., by Rev. Green, Presby. minister. [FCml issued to Nathaniel Stinchicum and Elizabeth

FREDERICK COUNTY MILITIA IN THE WAR OF 1812

Willard on 4 Aug 1815.] Nathaniel d. at or near Jeromeville, Richland Co., OH, 16 Sep 1826. In 1852, John Blair stated "I was an eye witness to the marr. of my sister Elizabeth to Nathaniel Stinchacomb." Elizabeth res. Richland Co., IL, 1852, 1855. Acq. (1852): William W. Wise, William Kidd, res. Richland Co., IL.

Source: Bounty land claim, 55-rejected-68267.

STINE, Patrick. Pvt. under Capt. Galt.

STINER, John. Pvt. under Capt. William Knox; joined 26 Aug - deserted 15 Sep 1814. [On Jan 20, 1807 - A reward was offered for an apprentice to the house carpenter's and joiner's business, John Stiner, age c.20, 5 ft, 10-11 inches tall; had dark complexion, dark brown hair, large lump on his left hand.]

Source: Maryland Herald, 20 Jan 1807.

STOKES, George. 1st sergt. under Daniel Marker in regt. of riflemen; b. c.1786; m. Hannah Ambros, at Hagerstown, 10 Dec 1810. He res. Fred. Co., 1850, 1855, c.1871; d. 11 Oct 1873, age 86 yrs, 7 mos., 3 days. 1850 of Creagerstown Dist.: George Stoykes, 65, cooper; Hannah, 64; Susan, 20. His wife Hannah d. at Mechanicstown, 7 Apr 1878, age 89 yrs, 5 mos., 22 days. Both bur. at Thurmont, United Brethren and Blue Ridge Cem. Their son Henry Stokes res. Emmittsburg. Acq.: 1851 - Thomas Biddle and Philip Cline belonged to same company; c.1871 - Frederick Housman and Leonard Mozer, res. Fred. Co.

Sources: Pension, SO 9472; Bounty land claims: 50-40-35432, 55-120-3550; Names in Stone; (Frederick) Examiner, Oct 1873, 17 Apr 1878;

The Maryland Union, 11 Apr 1878; Bridge in Time.

STONE, George. Pvt. under Capt. Fonsten, 2 Sep - 27 Oct 1814; res. 9 miles from Westminster.

STONE, Jacob. Pvt. under Capt. John Fonsten, 2 Sep - 27 Oct 1814; res. 7 miles from Westminster; b. 1788; m. Hannah Bower, at her father's residence in 1808. Res. Carroll Co., MD, 1850, 1855. Acq.: 1871 - Joseph Hesson, Jacob Knipple, res. Westminster.

Sources: Pension, SO 1730, SC 7350 (admitted 31 Oct 1871); Bounty land claim: 55-120-41036, 50-40-22254.

STONE, James. Pvt. under Capt. Denton Darby, 14 Aug - 8 Nov 1814.

STONE, John. Pvt. under Capt. Fonsten; joined 2 Sep 1814; deserted 14 Sep 1814.

STONER - See Steiner.

STONER, Christian. Pvt. under Capt. George W. Ent, 3rd Regt, 24 Aug - 30 Sep 1814.

STONER, David. Pvt. under Capt. Joseph Wood, 27 Aug - 28 Oct 1814. [FCml issued 27 May 1812 to David Stoner and Catherine Bell.]

STONER, Ezra. 2nd corpl. under Capt. George Ent, 24 Aug - 30 Sep 1814; m. 27 Aug 1814, Mary Fogler (b. c.1794), by Rev Jonathan Helfenstein, in Fredericktown, MD. He d. 23 May 1828 Fredericktown; widow res. Fredericktown, MD, 1851, 1855, 1877. Acq.: 1855 - Sarah Ely and William Stoner, res. Fred. Co.; 1871 - Edward H. Dyer and Franklin M. Lease, res. Frederick. Michael Eberts and Frederick Hawman.

THE VETERANS

Sources: Bounty land claim, 50-40-26457, 55-120-3146; Pension, WO 1631, WC 965.

STONER, Jacob. Pvt. under Capt. George W. Ent, 3rd Regt, 24 Aug - 30 Sep 1814.

STONER, John. Never joined his company under Capt. William Durbin, Jr., which served from 24 Aug to 27 Oct 1814.

STORM, James. 2nd corpl. under Capt. Galt.

STORM, Peter. 5th corpl. under Capt. George W. Ent, 24 Aug - 30 Sep 1814. [Name recorded in Family record as John Peter Storm.] He was b. 21 Jan 1787, son of Jacob and Julianna Storm; m. 13 Jan 1811, Mary Magdalene Haller (15 Feb 1784- 2 Nov 1862) at Fredericktown, MD, by Rev. David F. Schaeffer, Luth. pastor. Peter Storm d. Fredericktown 28 Apr 1821 between hour of 5 and 6 p.m., age 34 yrs, 3 mos., 7 days.; widow res. Fred. Co. 1851, 1855 (Fredericktown). Both bur. Mt. Olivet Cem. Acq.: 1851 - P. L. Storm, certified Family Record; 1855 - Allen M. Young and George D. Miller, res. Fred. Co.

Sources: Bounty land claim, 50-40-73073, 55-120-5812; **Names in Stone; MD German Ch. Rcds, v.1.**

STORRAP, Jacob. Pvt. under Capt. William Durbin, Jr., 24 Aug - 13 Oct 1814.

STORRAP, John. Pvt. under Capt. William Durbin, Jr., 24 Aug - 13 Oct 1814.

STOTELMYER, John K. 4th corpl. under Capt. Jacob Alexander, 22 Jul - 19 Sep 1814. [Fcml issued 25 Aug 1828 to John Stottlemyer jr. and Mary Hay.]

STOTELMYER, Joseph. Pvt. under Capt. Jacob Alexander, 22 Jul - 19 Sep 1814.

STOTLEMIRE, David. Pvt. under Capt. Daniel Marker; joined 25 Aug 1814; deserted 20 Oct 1814.

STOTTLEMEYER [Stoulemyer], Joseph. Pvt. under Capt. Daniel Shawen, 5 Sep - 27 Oct 1814.

STOTTLEMYER [Stotelmyer, Stotlemyer], David. Pvt. under Capt. Samuel Dawson, 1 May - 5 Jul 1813 and 1st corpl. under Capt. Jacob Alexander, 22 Jul - 19 Sep 1814; first served as a substitute for Christian Harshman; then volunteered at Middletown, wounded at Bladensburg on 24 Aug 1814. - b. c.1795; res. Fred. Co. 1850 and 1855.

[Williams states that David Stottlemyer, Jr., son of David and Margaret Stottlemyer was b. and grew up on a farm near Middletown. He farmed and owned a mill, the Keller Mill. He m. Margaret Magruter. They had fol. children: Jacon and Johns, twins; David; Daniel; Joseph; Margaret who m. George Lizer. David, Jr. and Margaret were mbrs. of German Ref. Ch.]

Sources: Bounty land claim, 55-80-23718; Williams, **Hist. of Fred. Co.**

STOTTLEMYER, George. Pvt. in Capt. Flautt's rifle company, 29 Apr - 29 Jun 1813; b. c.1793; m. 8 Feb 1814, Susan Stottlemyer, at Hagerstown. 1850 census of Catoctin Dist.: George Stottlemyer, 57; Susanna, 54 [and others]. Bur. at Wolfsville United Brethren Cem: George Stottlemyer 6 Oct 1871, age 78 yrs, 3 mos., 2 days - with wife Susan 5 Jun 1872, age 77. Witnesses -

FREDERICK COUNTY MILITIA IN THE WAR OF 1812

1850: Daniel Stottlemyer, Joseph Stottlemyer, res. Fred. Co.

Sources: Bounty land claim, 55-120-59303; Names in Stone; Bridge in Time; Pension, SO 24321, SC 18775.

STOTTLEMYER [Stotlemyer], Jacob. 3rd corpl. in Capt. Jacob Alexander's company, 22 Jul - 19 Sep 1814; b. c.1794; m. Nov 1814, Barbara Protzman, by Rev Rauhauser, at Hagerstown, MD; res. Fred. Co., MD, 1851, 1855. Jacob Stottlemyer d. near Wolfsville, 20 Jan 1865. In 1873 widow res. with their son John R. Stottlemyer near Wolfsville, Fred. Co., MD. She d. prior to 7 Dec 1876. Acq.: 1873 - John A. Wilson and Hezekiah Cline, res. near Wolfsville.

Sources: Bounty land claim, 55-120-41041; Pension WO10537 (separate from bounty land claim); Bridge in Time.

STOTTLEMYER, John. Pvt. under Capt. Samuel Dawson, 1 May - 5 Jul 1813.

STOTTLEMYER [Stotelmyer], John of D. 4th corpl. under Capt. Jacob Alexander, 22 Jul - 19 Sep 1814; b. c. 1794.

Source: Bounty land claim, 55-120-54203.

STOUB [Stoup], Adam. Pvt., 36th U.S. Inf. At enlistment: 5 ft, 8 inches; age 43; b. Fred. Co.; enlisted 16 Jun 1813 at Frederick by Lt. Thomas Ritchie for 1 year; mustered by Capt. H. W. Deneal's company 1 Mar 1814.

STOUFER, Henry. Pvt. under Capt. John Galt, 31 Aug - 27 Oct 1814.

STOUFFER [Stoufer], David. Pvt. under Capt. Fonsten, 2 Sep - 27 Oct 1814; res. 8 miles from Westminster.

STOUFFER [Stoufer], Jacob. Pvt. under Capt. Fonsten; joined 2 Sep 1814; deserted 7 Oct 1814.

STOUFFER, John. Musician under Capt. Henry Steiner, 25 Aug - 27 Sep 1814. [John Stouffer of Joseph m. 15 Mar 1825, Miss Elenor Stoner, dau of Abraham Stoner.]

Source: Engelbrecht Diary: 1:331

STOVER, Daniel. Pvt. under Capt. George W. Ent, 3rd Regt, 24 Aug - 30 Sep 1814.

STOVER, George. Pvt. under Capt. Barton Hackney, 1 Sep - 27 Oct 1814.

STOVER, William. 2nd corpl. under Capt. Barton Hackney, 1 Sep - 27 Oct 1814.

STRAILMAN, George. Pvt. under Capt. Daniel Marker; joined 25 Aug 1814; deserted 20 Oct 1814.

STRICKSTROCK [Strickstruck], Jacob. Pvt. under Capt. John Brengle, 25 Aug - 19 Sep 1814; b. 3 Sep 1794, son of Adam and Ottilia Strickstrock; d. 11 Jul 1840, in his 46th year in Fredericktown. Jacob's sister Catharina bapt. same ch. 11 May 1787. 1850 census: Catherine Strixtruck, age 50, res. Fredericktown.

Sources: (Frederick) Visitor, 16 Jul 1840; German MD Ch. Rcds, v.4; Bridge in Time.

STRINE, Peter. Pvt. under Capt. Samuel Duvall, 3 Aug - 3 Oct 1814; b. c.1785; res. Richland Co., OH, 1851 and 1855.

Source: Bounty land claim, 55-rejected-115667. "Peter Strine entd. Capt. Saml. Duval's co 3 Aug 1814 and is reported deserted on rolls from 3 Oct to 8 Nov 1814."

STRINE, William. Pvt. under Capt. John Galt; joined 31 Aug 1814; deserted 15 Sep 1814; res. 5 miles from Taneytown.

STUDAY, Henry. Mbr. of Crawford's "company."

STUDY, Jacob. Mbr. of Crawford's "company."

STULL, Benjamin. Mbr. of Crawford's "company."

STULLER, Conrad. Pvt. under Capt. Fonsten, 2 Sep - 27 Oct 1814; res. 8 miles from Westminster.

STULLER, Ulerich. Pvt. under Capt. Fonsten; joined 2 Sep 1814; deserted 9 Oct 1814.

STULTS [Stultz], James. Pvt. under Capt. John Galt, 31 Aug - 27 Oct 1814; res. 3 miles of Hampstead in 1814; d. 24 Dec 1861 in Carroll Co., in his 94th year.

STYERS, Cornelius. Pvt., 5th U.S. Inf. At enlistment: 5 ft, 8 inches; grey eyes, dark hair, ruddy complexion; age 47; occupation shoemaker; b. Fred. Co.; enlisted 22 (or 27) Mar 1812 in VA by Lt. Saunders for 5 yrs. At Fort Crawford. Discharged 22 Mar 1817.

SUIT, Nathaniel. Pvt. under Capt. Denton Darby, 3 Aug 8 Nov 1814; b. c.1794; res. Bladensburg, MD, Prince George's Co., 1850, 1855.
Source: Bounty land claim, 55-120-23960.

SUITZER, John. Drummer under Capt. Samuel Dawson, 1 May - 5 Jul 1813.

SULLIVAN[Sulivan], Abraham. Lieut. under Capt. William Durbin, Jr., entered active service 24 Aug 1814; discharged 3 Sep for "inability"; m. 1823, Sarah Fouble (b. c.1805), by Abr. Green, Bapt. minister. Abraham Sullivan d. 1846; widow res. City of Balt. 1855. Acq.: 1855 - William Witten(?) and John Krous, res. Carroll Co.
Source: Bounty land claim, 55-rejected-196855.

SULLIVAN, Daniel. 2nd sergt. under Capt. William Durbin, Jr., 24 Aug - 27 Oct 1814; promoted to 1st sergt. 10 Sep. He said he was a 2nd lieut. under Capt. William Durbin and after he arrived at the City of Balt. he was placed under the command of Colonel Henry Stemple and in the course of about two weeks was placed under the command of Major Randall. - b. c.1794; m. 6 Oct 1816, Mary Loara [Loran] (b. c.1793) by Rev. Burgess Nelson; res. Uniontown, Carroll Co. MD, 1851; d. at his residence in Carroll Co. 31 Jan 1853. Widow res. Carroll Co. 1855. Acq.: 1855 - David Fout and John Smith, res. Carroll Co.
Sources: Bounty land claim, 55-120-18049; FCmL

SULIVAN, David. 3rd sergt. under Capt. William Durbin, Jr., 24 Aug - 27 Oct 1814.

SULIVAN, Jacob. Pvt. under Capt. William Durbin, Jr., 24 Aug - 27 Oct 1814.

SULIVAN, William. 4th sergt. under Capt. William Durbin, Jr., 24 Aug - 27 Oct 1814.

SUMAN, Isaac. 12th U.S. Inf. At enlistment: 5 ft, 7 inches; gray eyes, brown hair, light complexion; age 19; farmer; b. Fred. Co.; enlisted 5 Feb 1814 at Hagerstown by Capt. Post for 5 yrs; pvt. under Capt. Post; entered hospital 7

FREDERICK COUNTY MILITIA IN THE WAR OF 1812

Sep 1814 and discharged from same 28 Oct 1814. Left sick at Lake George 5 Sep 1814. Discharged at Buffalo 6 Jun 1815, injury of his right thigh received before enlistment.

SUMAN, John. Pvt. under Capt. Daniel Shawen, 5 Sep - 27 Oct 1814.

SUMBRUM, David. Pvt. under Capt. John Galt; joined 31 Aug 1814; deserted 15 Sep 1814.

SUMBRUM, John. Pvt. under Capt. John Galt, 31 Aug - 27 Oct 1814; res. within 5 miles of Taneytown in 1814.

SUMMER, Jacob. Pvt. under Capt. Daniel Shawen, 5 Sep - 27 Oct 1814. [Jacob Summers, b. 24 Nov 1791, d. 5 Oct 1868 at his residence in Middletown Valley, bur. with wife Catherine 3 Apr 1845, age 49 yrs, 2 mos., 22 days and wife Elizabeth who d. 24 Mar 1875, age 75 yrs, 2 mos., 20 days, bur. at the Summers Family Cem, near Ch. Hill, Ellerton. 1850 census of Catoctin Dist.: Jacob Sommers, 58, farmer; Elizabeth, 49.]
Sources: Williams, History of Fred. Co.; FCml; Names in Stone; Bride in Time.

SUMMERS, William. Pvt., 2nd U.S. Inf. At enlistment: 5 ft, 9 inches; brown eyes, brown hair, fair complexion; age 31; occupation coppersmith; b. Fredericktown, MD; enlisted 8 Apr 1808 by Col. John Bowyer for 5 yrs. Drunk on guard - sentenced 50 lashes 19 Feb 1811. Appears to have reenlisted by Capt. Lawrence on 8 Jan 1813 at Mt. Vernon for 5 yrs. Reenlisted 12 Dec 1817.

SUTLZ, Nicholas. Pvt. in the 1st Cav. Dist., 26 Aug - 3 Sep 1814.

SUTTON, Henry. Pvt. under Capt. Joseph Green, entering into service on 14 Oct 1814; deserted 29 Oct 1814.

SWAN, William. Pvt. under Capt. Denton Darby, joined 3 Aug; deserted 19 Aug 1814.

SWARTZ, Daniel. 1st corpl. under Capt. Capt Nicholas Turbutt, 1 Sep - 27 Oct 1814.

SWEARENGAN, Van. Pvt. under Capt. Jacob Alexander, 22 Jul - 19 Sep 1814, b. 28 Apr 1792; m. c.1817, Elizabeth Herring; d. 6 Apr 1846; bur. with wife Elizabeth (6 Jan 1797 - 8 Apr 1862) at Middletown Luth. Cem.
Sources: Names in Stone; FCml.

SWIGERT, John. Never joined his company which served under Capt. William Durbin, Jr., 24 Aug - 27 Oct 1814.

SYBERT, David. Pvt. under Capt. Samuel Dawson, 14 Oct 1814 - 10 Jan 1815.

SYCAFOOSE [Sickafoose, Sigafoos, Sigafoose, Sigenfoos], Henry. Pvt. under Capt. Samuel Dawson, 21 Jul 1814 - 10 Jan 1815.

SYER, Nichodemus [Nickodemus]. From New Windsor. Pvt. under Capt. George W. Magee; joined 22 Jul 1814; deserted 6 Dec 1814.

SYMS, John. Pvt. in 36th U.S. Inf. under Capt. Jas. Hook. At enlistment: 4 ft, 7 1/2 inches; grey eyes, light hair, fair complexion; labourer; shoemaker; b. Fred. Co.; enlisted 2 Jun 1814 at Frederick by Lt. Zahn for duration of war. Rendezvous 1 Dec 1814. Dis-

THE VETERANS

charged at Ft. Covington on 30 Mar 1815.

SYNUFF, Michael. See Segruff.

SYPHER, Henry. Pvt. under Capt. William Knox, 26 Aug - 27 Oct 1814. [FCml issued to Henry Sypher and Catherine Wagner 20 Apr 1811.]

TABLER, Christian of William. 2nd sergt. under Capt. Marker, 25 Aug - 27 Oct 1814; m. 18 Apr 1847 [or 19 Apr 1848], Sarah R. Lyeth [In pension file her former name is given as Sarah H. Ridgely] (b. c.1808), by Rev. Bernard C. Wolff at Balt. He res. Berkely Co., VA 1850, 1855. Christian Tabler d. Martinsburg, WV, 6 Apr 1854. Widow res. Philo, Champaign Co., IL, 1878; d. at home of her son, Benjamin L. Tabler, Philo, IL, 22 Aug 1885, with whom she res. c.19 yrs; bur. Lucas Grove Cem., near Philo. Her son was merchant in Philo. Witnesses: 1855 - Benjamin S. Lyeth and Henry F. McSherry, res. Berkely Co., VA. [Query in pension file from Mrs. Stella Barnes Simmons, dated Oct 1921, re Christian Tabler.]

Sources: Bounty land claim, 55-120-33233 (separate from pension file); Pension, WO 13618, WC 9977 (admitted 18 Sep 1878).

TABLER, William. Pvt. under Capt. Nicholas Turbutt, 1 Sep - 27 Oct 1814.

TACWELL/TARWELL/TASWELL, Robert. 3rd sergt. under Capt. Samuel Ogle, 1 May 1813 - 5 Jul 1813.

TALBOTT. See Tolbott.

TALBOTT, David. Pvt., U.S. Artillery under Capt. J. Gibson. At enlistment: 5 ft, 8 inches; brown eyes, brown hair; age 24; wheelwright; b. Fred. Co.; enlisted 4 or 5 March 1812 at Lancaster by Capt. Gibson for 5 yrs. At Charlestown 20 Feb 1813. Captured at Queenstown and paroled 25 March 1813. Promoted to sergt. on 20 Apr 1814. Discharged 5 March 1817.

TALBOTT, Wilson. Pvt. under Capt. Nicholas Turbutt; 2 Sep - 27 Oct 1814.

TALHELM, Peter. Pvt. under Capt. Samuel Duvall, 3 Aug - 3 Oct 1814.

TALL, Walter. Pvt. under Lieut. Kolb, 13 Oct - 15 Nov 1814 in det. assigned to guard the British prisoners at the Frederick Barracks.

TALLHAMMER, Mathias. Pvt., 38th U.S. Inf. At enlistment: 5 ft, 6 inches; hazel eyes, dark hair, dark complexion; age 36; farmer; b. Fred. Co.; enlisted 18 Aug 1814 at Balt. by Lt. Cochrean for duration of war [or 1 year]. 31 Dec 1814 absent in arrest at Ft. Covington for desertion. Ft. McHenry 28 Feb 1815 - Deserted 6 Feb 1815, off his post.

TALLHELM [Talhelm], Peter. Pvt. under Capt. Philip Smith, 23 May - 8 Sep 1813; m. 16 Dec 1821 Mary Logan, in Greencastle, Franklin Co, PA, by Rev John Ruthrauff. Peter Tallhelm d. near Johnstown 2 Jul 1850. She res. Antrim Township, PA, in 1856. Acq.: 1856 - William Matten and David Bennsburgh, res. Franklin Co, PA, and Washington Co. MD. Letter from Mary Tallhelm, State Line, P.O., Franklin Co., PA in 1859.

Source: Bounty land claim, 55-160-57991.

TALLHELM, Peter. See Talhelm.

TAMAN, Aquilla. Pvt. res. 5 miles of Westminster, under Capt. Fonsten, 2 Sep - 27 Oct 1814.

FREDERICK COUNTY MILITIA IN THE WAR OF 1812

TANEY, Ethelbert. Pvt. under Capt. Knox, 26 Aug - 27 Oct 1814; b. c.1796; res. Hancock, Washington Co., MD, 1851, 1855.
Source: Bounty land claim, 55-120-30020.

TANEY, Felix B. 3rd corpl. under Capt. Galt, 31 Aug - 27 Oct 1814; b. c.1788; m. 12 Jun 1864, Mary C. Cretin, at Mount St. Mary's College Ch.; he res. Fred. Co., MD, 1851, 1855, 1871 (near Emmittsburg).
Sources: Bounty land claim, 50-40-43286, 55-120-60403; Pension, SO 12751 (rejected by reason of insufficient service - 30 days) - Letter in pension file from Mrs. Charles Silverson, 2655, Lake of the Isles Blvd., Minneapolis, MN.

TANNEHILL [Taneyhill], Carlton. Pvt. under Capt. Basil Dorsey, 30 Jul - 27 Sep 1814; b. c.1790; res. St. Charles Co., MO, 1851.
Source: Bounty land claim, 50-40-38736 (certificate in file), 55-160-39574.

TANEYHILL, Samuel. Pvt. under Capt. Joseph Wood, 9 - 28 Oct 1814.

TANNER, Jacob. Pvt. under Capt. Samuel Ogle, 1 May 1813 - 5 Jul 1813.

TANNER, Jacob. Sergt., 38th U.S. Inf. At enlistment: 5 ft, 7 inches; light or gray eyes and light hair; age 28 or 25; tailor; b. Emmittsburg, MD; enlisted 21 Jun 1814 by Lt. Martin. Discharged at Ft. McHenry 28 March 1815.

TANNER, James. Pvt. under Capt. Philip Smith; joined 23 May 1813; deserted 29 Jun 1813.

TAPMAN, Obediah. Pvt., 5th U.S. Inf. under Capt. Leroy Oxie. At enlistment: 5 ft, 7 1/2 inches; gray eyes, brown hair, light complexion; age 22; cordwainer; b. Allegany Co., MD; enlisted 7 Jun 1813 at Balt. by Lt. Bird for 5 yrs. Cantonment near Buffalo on 28 Feb and 30 Apr 1815.

TARLTON, Elisha. From Balt. Co. Pvt. under Capt. John Galt, 31 Aug - 27 Oct 1814.

TARREYHILL. See Taneyhill.

TAUNEY [Tourney], John. Pvt. under Capt. William Durbin, Jr., 24 Aug - 27 Oct 1814.

TAYLOR, Frederick. Pvt., 22nd U.S. Inf. under Capt. D. McFarland. At enlistment: 5 ft, 10 inches; gray eyes, brown hair, fair complexion; age 24; shoemaker; b. Fred. Co.; enlisted 12 Jun 1812 at Uniontown, PA by Lt. Johnson for 5 yrs. Deserted from Williamsport 4 Oct 1812. Deserted 24 Jan 1814 from French Mills.

TAYLOR, Hezekiah. From New Windsor. Pvt. under Capt. George W. Magee, 23 Jul - 10 Jan 1815.

TAYLOR, Isreal Pvt. under Capt. Denton Darby, 3 Aug - 8 Nov 1814. "Absent 6 days."

TAYLOR, Israel. Pvt. under Capt. Basil Dorsey, 30 Jul - 27 Sep 1814; b. c.1791; res. Chester Co., PA 1855.
Source: Bounty land claim, 55-160-29975.

TAYLOR, Jesse. Pvt. under Capt. Philip Smith, 23 May - 8 Sep 1813; said he was pvt. in company of Capt. Eli Brashear and transferred to Capt. Smith; b. c.1792; res. Fred. Co., 1851, 1855. 1850 census of New Market: Jesse Taylor, age 56, labourer; Phoebe, 43.
Source: Bounty land claim, 50-40-53190, 55-120-24824; **Bridge in Time.**

THE VETERANS

TAYLOR, John. Pvt. under Capt. Denton Darby, 3 Aug - 8 Nov 1814.

TAYLOR, John. Pvt. under Capt. George W. Ent, 3rd Regt, 24 Aug - 30 Sep 1814.

TAYLOR, John. Pvt., 14th U.S. Inf. At enlistment: 5 ft, 6 inches; dark eyes, dark hair, dark complexion; age 35; weaver; b. Fred. Co.; enlisted 1 Apr 1814 at Williamsport by Capt. McDonald for 5 yrs. Sick at Plattsburg. Discharged 1 Jun 1815 at Greenbush, disability (Capt. McDonald's company).

TAYLOR, William. Pvt. under Capt. Nicholas Turbutt, 1 Sep - 27 Oct 1814; received certificate of discharge but it became worn out by his carrying it in his pocket; b. c.1796; res. Greene Co., OH, 1855.

Source: Bounty land claim, 55-120-5894.

TELLER, Aquila. Pvt. under Capt. Denton Darby, 3 Aug - 8 Nov 1814. "Wounded in Action" at the Battle of Bladensburg.

TENER, David. Pvt. under Capt. Joseph Wood, 27 Aug - 28 Oct 1814; rendezvous at Camp Diehl.

TENER, Philip. Pvt. under Capt. Joseph Wood, 27 Aug - 28 Oct 1814; rendezvous at Camp Diehl.

TESHNER, Jacob. 2nd sergt. under Capt. Jacob Getzendanner, 26 Jul - 21 Aug 1814.

TESHNER, Jacob. 2nd sergt. under Capt. Nicholas Turbutt, 1 Sep - 27 Oct 1814.

THOMAS, Archibald. Pvt. under Capt. Daniel Marker, 25 Aug - 27 Oct 1814.

THOMAS, Benjamin. Pvt. under Capt. Philip Smith, 23 May - 8 Sep 1813.

THOMAS, Benjamin. 1st lieut. under Capt. Samuel Dawson, 21 Jul 1814 - 10 Jan 1815; b. 25 Jan 1781; m. 1 Apr 1819, Martha Casey (b. c.1796) in Belmont Co., OH, by Rev Vachel Hall. Benjamin Thomas res. Mason Township, Laurence Co., OH, 1850; d. Lawrence Co. 22 Jan 1852, age 70 yrs, 11 mos. and 28 days. Widow res. Lawrence Co., OH, 1862. Acq.: 1862 - Mrs. Eleanor Rucker, Robert Massey, John Rapp and Walter Rose, res. Lawrence Co., OH.

Source: Bounty land claim, 55-80-49187.

THOMAS, David. 36th U.S. Inf. At enlistment: 5 ft, 6 inches; age 44; b. Fred. Co.; enlisted 11 Aug 1813 at Waynesburg, PA by Lt. Thomas Ritchie for 1 year. Discharged 25 Sep 1813, having obtained a substitute, John Harcushimer.

THOMAS, Elijah. Mbr. of Crawford's "company."

THOMAS, Otho. 1st lieut. under Capt. Daniel Marker, 25 Aug - 27 Oct 1814; b. c.1789; res. Fred. Co., MD, 1852 and 1855.

Source: Bounty land claim, 55-120-24403.

THOMAS, Samuel. Pvt. under Capt. George W. Ent, 24 Aug - 30 Sep 1814.

THOMAS, William. Pvt. under Capt. Daniel Marker; joined 16 Aug 1813; deserted 25 Aug 1813.

THOMPSON, George. Pvt., 12th U.S. Inf. under Capt. Madison. At enlistment: 5 ft, 10 1/2 inches; gray eyes, dark hair, fair complexion; age 19; occupation miller; b. Fred. Co.; enlisted 10 Oct

FREDERICK COUNTY MILITIA IN THE WAR OF 1812

1812 at Harpers Ferry by Lt. Wager for 5 yrs. Absent at Niagara on 31 Aug 1813. Present on 28 Feb and 30 Apr 1814. Discharged 10 Oct 1817.

THOMPSON, Henry K. m. 27 Mar 1818, Parmelia Jacobs (b. c.1805), at her bro's. house (Philip Jacob), in Fred. Co., by Rev Samuel L. Higgins, Meth. minister, each for first time. Fol. discharge he res. Middletown, Beallsville, Rocky Springs and Fredericktown; d. Rocky Springs, Fred. Co., 18 (or 19) Jun 1857. Widow res. South St., Fredericktown, 1878; d. 21 Apr 1882.

Parmelia Thompson said that she never knew her husband to have a middle name. They knew each from childhood, went to school together - "don't know whether we fell in love with each other when we were children or not..." In her letter of 11 Dec 1878 she said that by her marr. to Henry Thompson she had the fol. children: John, c.54; Elizabeth, c.52.

Deposition from Charles F. Fleming, superintendant of Mount View Hospital, of Fred. Co., stating hospital is used for keeping the poor and insane of co., certifies that "Henry Thompson was admitted Jun 17, 1857; d. Jun 19, 1857; bur. in grave yard of house by Daniel Ellis." At that time the institution was called the Almshouse. Acq.: 1878 - James J. English, age 57, Market St., Fredericktwon; Horatio Waters, age 45, South St., Fredericktown, acq. 30 and 22 yrs, resp.; Richard J. Lamar and Stephen Jacob Kline, acq. since 1837.

Sources: Bounty land claim, 55-120-90096; Pension, WO 17022, WC 17026 (admitted 28 Jan 1879).

THOMPSON, Richard. In U.S. Dragoons under Capt. John Burd. At enlistment: 5 ft, 9 3/4 inches; blue eyes, sandy hair, light complexion; age 21; laborer; b. Fred. Co.; enlisted 14 May 1812 for 5 yrs. 1812-1814 proved to be a minor.

THOMPSON, Thomas. Pvt., U.S. Artillery. At enlistment: 5 ft, 10 inches; gray eyes, black hair, dark complexion; age 24; harnessmaker; b. Frederick City, MD; enlisted 19 Apr 1812 at Washington City by Lt. Hight for 5 yrs. Discharged 18 Apr 1817.

THOMPSON, William B. Never joined his company under Capt. Thomas Contee Worthington, which served 17 Aug - 31 Dec 1812.

THOMSON, Bithy. From Balt. Servant to one of the officers of the company of Capt. Daniel Marker, 25 Aug - 27 Oct 1814.

THOMSON, Hugh. 2nd lieut. under Capt. Henry Lowrye, 27 Aug - 28 Oct 1814. Wounded at Bladensburg; discharged at Annapolis. He said he was ensign under Capt. Farquhar and Lieut. under Capt. Henry Lowery, 26 Jul - 14 Oct 1814. - b. c.1788; m. 5 Feb 1811 Elizabeth Sponsellar (b. c.1791) at Taneytown, Carroll Co., MD, by Rev. Rauhouser. He res. Taneytown, MD 1814, 1850, 1851; d. Taneytown 18 Dec 1852. She res. Carroll Co. 1855. Acq.: 1871 - John Thomson and Benjamin Shunk; 1878 - Aloysius F. Orndorf and Edward Spalding, res. Carroll Co., MD.

Sources: Pension, WO 397, WC 378; Bounty land claim, 50-80-8833, 55-80-7718.

THE VETERANS

THRALLS, John. Pvt. under Capt. Daniel Marker; joined 25 Aug 1814; deserted 25 Sep 1814.

TIER, John. Pvt. under Capt. Philip Smith; joined 23 May 1813; deserted 7 Jun 1813.

TILGHMAN, John. Servant under Capt. Samuel Duvall, 3 Aug - 3 Oct 1814.

TINGSTRUM, Peter. Pvt. under Capt. James F. Huston, 23 Jul - 13 Oct 1814. "Sick in Frederick Town since 30 Sep."

TITLOW, Adam. 4th corpl. under Capt. George W. Ent, 24 Aug - 30 Sep 1814; m. 3 Nov 1811 (or 12 Dec 1813), Rebecca Hull in Fredericktown by Rev. David F. Shaffer, Luth. minister. Adam Titlow d. Fredericktown 10 Jul 1834. Widow res. with one of her daus near Frederick in 1851. Acq.: 1851 - Barbara Brengle, John Hauck and Cecilius Head. Letter dated 7 Feb 1868 from Frederick MD, to Court of Pensions, Washington, D.C., requesting opinion on land warrant of Rebecca Titlow who had d., leaving 4 children as her only heirs.
Source: Bounty land claim, 50-41511.

TITLOW, Daniel. Pvt. under Capt. Nicholas Turbutt, 1 Sep - 27 Oct 1814.

TITLOW, George. 1st sergt. under Capt. Samuel Dawson, 1 May - 5 Jul 1813; promoted to Sergt. Major 8 May 1813; b. 20 (or 30) Sep 1790; m. c.1817, Elizabeth Young (11 Mar 1800 - 17 Apr 1872). George Titlow d. 1 Feb 1842. His widow, formerly of Middletown, d. Georgetown, D.C.; sister of Miss Sophia Young who d. Balt. City 16 Jan 1872 and sister of Mrs. Catharine Keafauver, wife of Capt. John Keafauver of Balt. City who d. 19 Apr 1872. Both bur. Middletown Reformed Cem. with 3rd dau Mary Catherine (1 Jul 1824 - 5 Mar 1887); 4th dau Sophia S. (20 Apr 1826 - 12 Nov 1906); 5th dau Ophelia C. Y. (28 Feb 1831 - 5 Jul 1875).
Sources: FCml; Names in Stone; (Frederick) Examiner, 24 Apr 1872; Maryland Union, 27 Jan 1872, 18 Apr 1872.

TOHAY, John. Pvt. under Capt. Samuel Dawson, 26 Jul - 10 Jan 1815.

TOLBOTT, Benjamin. Pvt. under Capt. Daniel Marker, 25 Aug - 27 Oct 1814.

TOLL, Walter. Pvt. under Capt. Jacob Alexander, 22 Jul - 19 Sep 1814.

TOM, negro. Servant to Dr. Nelson under Capt. Col. John Ragan, 1st Regt, 14 Oct 1814 - 10 Jan 1815.

TOOPHORN, George. Waiter to Major Eichelberger, from Capt. Galt's company, 31 Aug - 27 Oct 1814. According to Nicholas Snider, 1st lieut. in Galt's company, George Toophorn was waiter to Major Eichelberger by the Major's selection of him from the ranks for that purpose; b. c.1795; res. Allegheny Co., PA, in 1855.

TOOSONG, Francis T. Pvt. under Capt. George W. Magee, 22 Jul - 13 Oct 1814; enlisted in regular army 8 or 15 Aug 1815 by Lt. Martin at Balt. At enlistment: 5 ft, 3 3/4 inches tall, had gray eyes, brown hair, dark complexion, age 20, shoemaker, b. Jacquemee, St. Domingo; served in 38th U.S. Inf. as corl. and promoted to sergt. He was serving in Major George Keyser's Det. on 30 Sep 1814 and in Capt. Stansbury's

FREDERICK COUNTY MILITIA IN THE WAR OF 1812

company on 3 Apr 1815 when discharged at Balt. City.

TORRENCE [Tarrence], James. Pvt. under Capt. Daniel Shawen, 5 Sep - 27 Oct 1814.

TOURNEY, John. See Tauney.

TOWNSEN, Samuel. Mbr. of Crawford's "company."

TOWNSON, Thomas. Mbr. of Crawford's "company."

TRACEY, Basil. From New Windsor. Fifer under Capt. George W. Magee, 22 Jul - 10 Jan 1815.

TRESLER, Henry. Pvt. under Capt. John Galt, 31 Aug - 27 Oct 1814.

TREXLER, Peter. Pvt. under Capt. Samuel Ogle, 1 May 1813 - 5 Jul 1813.

TRIC, Thomas. 2nd corpl. under Capt. Samuel Ogle, 1 May 1813 - 5 Jul 1813.

TROMBO, George. Pvt. from New Windsor under Capt. Magee, 24 Jul 1814 - 7 Jan 1815; b. c.1783; res. Carroll Co., MD, 1851 and 1855. Acq.: 1853 - Charles Devilbiss, lieut. in Magee's company; also William Weekly.
Source: Bounty land claim, 55-80-28080.

TRONBERGER, Frederick. Pvt. under Capt. John Galt, 31 Aug - 27 Oct 1814, res. 2 miles of Taneytown in 1814.

TROUT, John. Corpl. under Capt. Getzendanner, 20 Jul - 21 Aug 1814. He said he also volunteered c.31 Jul 1813; discharged at Annapolis on 10 Sep 1813; volunteered again under the same officer at Fredericktown around 26 Jul 1814. - b. c.1783; m. c.13 Apr 1805 Margaret Shown. He and Margaret res. Fred. Co., MD, 1850 with William G. Brown, a whitesmith, and his family. At that time he was age 67 and Margaret was 74 yrs old.
Source: Bounty land claim, 50-40-15477.

TROUTMAN, Peter. Pvt. under Capt. Turbutt, 1 Sep - 29 Oct 1814. Left certificate of discharge with his mother MD c.1825. She d. prior to his application for bounty land in 1855. He was b. c.1786; m. Christina Reynold, in Fredericktown. [FCml issued to Peter Troutman and Christena Runner on 8 Aug 1809.] Res. Cape Girardeau Co., MO, 1855 and Grant Co., KY, 1872 (P.O. address: Zion Station).
Sources: Bounty land claim, 55-120-50473; Pension, SO 27301 (rejected 28 Aug 1872 - insufficient service).

TROXEL, George. 2nd lieut. under Lieut. Upton Reid, 1st Cav. Dist., 26 Aug - 3 Sep 1814. [George Troxel d. 20 Jul 1832; bur. at Emmitsburg, St. Elias Luth. Ch.. Age on stone ?8-10-23; wife Elizabeth 2 Jul 1850, age 69 yrs, 10 mos., 6 days.]
Source: Names in Stone.

TROXEL, Jacob. Pvt. under Lieut. Upton Reid, 1st Cav. Dist., 26 Aug - 3 Sep 1814. [Jacob Troxel bur. Emmitsburg, St. Elias Luth. Ch., d. 9 May 1831, age 46 yrs, 8 mos., 7 days.]
Source: Names in Stone.

TROXEL [Troxell], Jacob. Pvt. under Capt. Ogle, 1 May - 5 Jul 1813; b. c.1794; m. Elizabeth Green, in 1838; res. Carroll Co., MD, 1851, 1855, 1871 (P.O. address: Piney Creek). Witnesses: Josiah Adlesperger and James Adlesperger, res. Carroll Co.

THE VETERANS

Sources: Pension, SO 3115, SC 3430 (admitted 25 Aug 1871); Bounty land claim, 55-120-17968.

TROXEL, Peter. Pvt. in 1st Cav. Dist., 26 Aug - 3 Sep 1814. [1850 census of Fred. Co.: Peter Troxel, age 82, b. Fred. Co., living with Joshua Motter, age 49, merchant, and other mbrs. of Motter family; also Felix J. Troxel, age 21, clerk. Bur. at Emmitsburg, St. Elias Luth. Ch.: Peter Troxell, son of Peter, 23 Oct 1768 - 4 Dec 1856. Also bur. there was Peter Troxell (26 May 1816, 39 yrs, 19 days) and wife Magdalene (23 May 1850, age 68).]

Sources: **Bridge in Time, Names in Stone.**

TRUMBO - See Trombo.

TRUMP, Casper. Pvt. under Capt. Funsten; joined 2 Sep; deserted 24 Sep 1814; b. c.1791; m. Christena Bucher (b. c.1791) at Manchester 11 May 1812 by Jacob Geiger, preacher of the German Ref. Ch. Casper Trump d. Carroll Co. 17 Aug 1845. She res. Carroll Co., MD, 1855.

Source: Bounty land claim, 55-rejected-146267.

TSCHUDY, Martin. From Upper Fred. Co. Pvt. under Capt. Thomas Contee Worthington, 17 Aug - 31 Dec 1812 and pvt. under Capt. James F. Huston, joined 23 Jul 1814; enlisted 4 Sep 1814.

TUDOR, James. Drummer under Capt. Samuel Dawson; joined 21 Jul 1814 - deserted 24 Oct 1814.

TUDOR, John. Pvt. under Capt. Nicholas Turbutt, 2 Sep - 27 Oct 1814.

TULLEY, Aquila. Pvt. under Capt. Darby in service of the U.S.; m. Mrs. Margaret Glisan [Gleson], Sunday evening, 30 Dec 1821, by Rev. Davidson. Letter to the Secretary of War dated 3 Jan 1818, from Aquilla Tulley, states he was drafted into service of U.S. in fall of 1814, marched from Fredericktown, MD, in the company of Capt. Darby, near the beginning of Aug 1814, severely wounded in the left arm by a musket ball, by which his arm was broken, so as to disable him to perform manual labor. According to Aqulla Tulley Capt. Darby had by this date, moved to the western country. Depositions of Richard Clarke and Jacob Cramer concur with his statement. Also statement of Dr. John Wootton, Montgomery Co., dated 6 Feb 1818. From 5th Military Dist. Washington, 7 Feb 1818, ... "gunshot wound in his left arm which has weakened and partly disabled it."

Sources: Pension, SO 25892; **Republican Gazette,** 5 Jan 1822; FCmI.

TURBUTT, Nicholas. Capt. of his own company, served 1 Sep - 27 Oct 1814; d. in Fredericktown at age 68. On 12 Sep 1826, Miss Maria, dau of Capt. Nicholas Turbutt of Fredericktown m. William Small.

TURFIEL [Turvill], Lewis. From New Windsor. Pvt. under Capt. George W. Magee, 22 Jul 1814 - 10 Jan 1815. In "confinement at Fort McHenry."

TURNER, Benjamin. Pvt. under Capt. William Durbin, Jr., 24 Aug - 27 Oct 1814. Absent without leave.

TURNER, Jesse. Pvt. under Capt. William Durbin, Jr., 24 Aug - 27 Oct 1814.

TURNER, Joshua. b. 1776; res. Belmont Co., OH, in 1855 and 1858.

FREDERICK COUNTY MILITIA IN THE WAR OF 1812

Appointed Lieut. under Capt. Ely Brashears [appointment papers from the state of MD in his file, signed by Governor Winder]. He served as lieut. in the company of Capt. Henry Riggs, 13th Regt from Aug to Oct 1814. He said that he he was permitted to return to his home after the Battle of North Point and Bombardment of Fort McHenry. The first order he received was at Hyats Town, Montgomery Co., Md, to bring in the Recruits, to New Market. Before arriving at Hyats Town the order was countermanded, a new order to bring the men to Fredericktown, MD, to Capt. Snyder, marched a few miles from New Market then he was ordered to take sargeant Gabriel Duval to go to Carrolls Manor, then took with him six men and joined Capt. Ely Brashears's Company at Balt. boarded with Nicholas Hart a cooper, near Loudenstagus (Loudenslager's?] dwelling, paid my own board, last week in August 1814 joined the Company was on duty during the Bombardment and 30 days or more in actual service, I was stationed on Capt. Pringle's left under Col. Stiner, or Stoner, also I the said Joshua Turner in 1794 was ordered out with the army against the Whiskey Boys in Pennsylvania, marched from Fredericktown, MD, under the ordres of Capt. Henry Brothers and continued the whole term of actual service until discharged...

In a letter from his agent, George A. Buckaway "...although he may have been cashiered in 1814 his services in Capt. Henry Brothers's company in 1794 against the Whiskey Boys deserves a land warant and I beg of you to have the affair investigated ..."
Source: 55-rejected-294916.

TURNER, Solomon. Pvt. under Capt. William Durbin, Jr., 24 Aug - 27 Oct 1814, a substitute for George Smellser who was drafted from Fred. Co. He was paid several hundred dollars by Smellser. He said that Capt. Durbin commanded a volunteer company that met at their rendezvous at Sulphur Springs, Fred. Co., c.23 Aug 1814. On fol. day the company marched from Sulphur Springs to Washington City, but on their arrival at Frederick the company was ordered to Balt. City.

He was b. c.1785; res. Fairfield Co., OH 1850 (Rushville), 1855. Letter dated 12 Oct 1905 from Edward H. Cooper, Paulding, OH, asked for the whereabouts of Solomon Turner at the time of his death. The letter was answered to the effect that no information was known on the death of Solomon Turner.
Source: Bounty land claim, 55-120-45087.

TWIG [Twigg], Thomas. Pvt. under Capt. Samuel Dawson, 21 Jul - until the end of August. He prob. joined Dawson's company at Balt.; enlisted in regular army 30 Aug 1814 at Balt. by Lt. Spicknall. At enlistment: 5 ft, 9 inches, dark eyes, dark hair, dark complexion, age 26 or 29, shoemaker, b. Somerset Co., MD; b. c.1776; res. Balt. city in 1856.

Discharge papers given by order of Brigadier General W. Winder, 10th Mil. Dist., to Thomas Twigg, pvt. of Capt. Sheppard C. Leakins, 38th Regt.

THE VETERANS

of Inf. "who was enlisted 30 Aug 1814 is discharged from army of the United States." Given at Fort McHenry, Balt., 28 Mar 1815.
Source: Bounty land claim, 12-160-251.

TWINER, Daniel. Pvt. under Capt. Samuel Dawson; joined 21 Jul; deserted 26 Jul 1814.

UHLER, David. Pvt. under Capt. George W. Magee, 22 Jul 1814 - 10 Jan 1815. "On furlough 21 days." He said he served as substitute for James Blanchford; res. New Windsor 1814; b. c.1794; m. 11 Feb 1819, Harriet Dell; res. Hancock Co., IL, 1854, 1855, 1871 (Appanoos). Witnesses: 1871 - Jacob Holmes and William S. Brown, res. Carroll Co. [Pension application submitted by David Uhler while in Carroll Co.]
Sources: Pension, SO 1661, SC 734 (admitted 29 Jun 1871); Bounty land claim, 55-120-12960.

UMBAUGH, John. Pvt. under Capt. Barton Hackney, 1 Sep - 27 Oct 1814; drafted at Trap Town; b. c.1794; res. Loudoun Co., VA, in 1855.
Source: Bounty land claim, 55-16-42593.

UMBERGER, Michael. 4th corpl. under Capt. Lowrye, Henry, 27 Aug - 28 Oct 1814. [FCml issued to Michael Umberger and Nancy Wood 4 Apr 1794.]

UNGLEBEE [Unglesby], Zachariah. Pvt. under Capt. Basil Dorsey, 30 Jul - 27 Sep 1814; b. c.1790; m. 26 Feb 1828, Mary Ann Engle (Bethel?) (b. c.1790) by J.P. He res. Guernsey Co., OH, 1850; d. c.7 Nov 1851. Acq.: 1850 - Andrew Rodgers and Jacob Heiner, res. Muskingum OH; 1851 - John Rogers, L. D. Rogers, res. Guernsey Co., OH.

UNGLESBEE, Erasmus. Pvt. under Capt. Basil Dorsey, 30 Jul - 27 Sep 1814.
Source: Bounty land claim, 55-120-69498.

UPDEGRAFF, David. Pvt., 14th U.S. Inf. At enlistment: 5 ft, 10 1/2 inches; age 30 or 36; b. Fred. Co., MD; enlisted 20 May 1814 at Sharpsburg, MD, by Ens. Carr for duration of war; d. Manlins, NY 7 or 17 Nov 1814 of flux.

UPHOLD, Sebastian. Pvt. under Capt. John Galt, 31 Aug - 27 Oct 1814.

UPRAFT, Thomas. Pvt., 38th U.S. Inf. At enlistment: 5 ft, 10 1/2 inches; brown eyes, dark hair, light complexion; age 28; farmer; b. Fred. Co., MD; enlisted 9 Apr 1814 by Lt. Duncan for duration of war. Mustered by Capt. S.C. Leakins company, Patapsco [Balt.] on 30 Apr and 1 Jun 1814. Mustered with Capt. Jno. Buck's company at cantonment near Balt. on 31 Jan and 28 Feb 1815; d. 27 Jan 1815 in Regt. hospital.

URVIN, James Pvt. under Capt. Denton Darby, 3 Aug - 8 Nov 1814.

URVIN, James of James. Pvt. under Capt. Denton Darby, 27 Sep - 8 Nov 1814.

VANBLARCUM [Vanblarkeum], Evert. Pvt. from Upper Fred. Co. under Capt. James F. Huston/Capt. Joseph Green; joined 23 Jul 1814; deserted 5 Nov 1814.

VANPHERSON, Nathaniel. Pvt. under Capt. Philip Smith, 23 May - 8 Sep 1813. [FCml issued to Nathan Vanferson and Jemima Stevens on 1 Nov 1811.]

VANZANT, John. Pvt. under Capt. William Knox, 26 Aug - 27 Oct 1814.

FREDERICK COUNTY MILITIA IN THE WAR OF 1812

VARLEE, Henry. Fifer under Capt. Samuel Dawson, joined 1 May; deserted 28 Jun 1813.

VAUGHN, Thomas. Pvt. under Capt. William Durbin, Jr., 24 Aug - 27 Oct 1814.

VERNON, Nathaniel. Served under Capt. Butler in Pittsburg Blues, present at battle of Mississineway and seige of Fort Meigs under General Wm. H. Harrison. In 1829 he made application for the chair of mathematics in Frederick College. Receiving the appointment he spent 40 yrs in the position. - b. Goshen Township, Chester Co., PA, 10 Aug 1790; d. 11 May 1880 at residence of his son, Col. George W. F. Vernon, West Third St.; bur. Mt. Olivet Cem. with wife Charlotte L. (21 Jul 1891, age 89 yrs, 5 mos, 12 days).

VILE, Peter. Pvt. under Capt. Samuel Duvall, 3 Aug - 3 Oct 1814.

VILE, William. Pvt. under Capt. Samuel Duvall, 3 Aug - 3 Oct 1814.

VORE, William. Drummer under Capt. Basil Dorsey, 30 Jul - 27 Sep 1814.

W..., George. Mbr. of Crawford's "company."

WADKINS [Wodkins], John. 2nd U.S. Inf. under Lt. T. F. Thomas; discharged at New Orleans on 9 Apr 1815; enlisted at Washington by Lt. Thomas for duration of war on 3 Apr 1814. At enlistment: 5 ft, 8 inches, blue eyes, dark hair, light complexion, age 31, farmer, b. Fred. Co., MD.

WADSWORTH [Watson], Samuel. Pvt. under Capt. Matthew Murray, 25 Aug - 27 Oct 1814; b. c.1795; res. Muskingum Co., OH, 1853.

Source: Bounty land claim, 50-40-92341.

WAGERS, Henry. Pvt. under Capt. Basil Dorsey, 30 Jul - 27 Sep 1814.

WAGGONER, John. Pvt. under Capt. Joseph Wood, 27 Aug - 28 Oct 1814.

WALKER, Andrew. Drummer under Capt. William Knox, 26 Aug - 27 Oct 1814.

WALKER, George B. Pvt. under Capt. Samuel Dawson, 1 May - 5 Jul 1813; b. c.1790; res. Champaign Co., OH, 1850; d. Champaign Co. 21 Sep 1851. In 1855 George B. Walker, Jr., son of George B. Walker, appeared in Greene Co. Court to state that he was bro. and next friend of Mary Jane Walker, res. Champaign Co, OH, age 12 yrs, b. 15 Nov 1842, only minor heir of George B. Walker dec'd. Acq.: 1855 - John W. Walker and Samuel L. Walker, res. Greene Co.

Source: Bounty land claim, 55-160-20297.

WALKER, Jonathan. From Upper Fred. Co. Pvt. under Capt. James F. Huston and Capt. Joseph Green; joined 23 Jul 1814; deserted 20 Nov 1814.

WALKER, Stephen. Pvt. under Capt. Samuel Dawson; joined 21 Jul 1814; deserted 25 Jul 1814. [FCml issued to Stephen Walker and Margaret Steward 8 Dec 1809.]

WALKER, William. Pvt. under Capt. William Knox, 26 Aug - 27 Oct 1814.

WALKER, William. Mbr. of Crawford's "company."

WALLACE, Joseph. Pvt. under Capt. Samuel Dawson; joined 21 Jul 1814; en-

THE VETERANS

listed regular army 20 or 22 Aug 1814 by Capt. Stansbury in Balt. At enlistment: 5 ft, 7 inches, age 27, b. Buckingham, PA; pvt. in 38th U.S. Inf.; mustered by Capt. S.C. Leakins' company at Fort McHenry, Balt., 10 Sep 1814. Absent deserted 25 Sep 1814. In arrest at Washington for desertion 31 Dec 1814 and Jan 1815.

WALTER [Walton], Christian. Pvt. under Capt. William Durbin, Jr., 24 Aug - 27 Oct 1814. Absent without leave 25 Oct 1814.

WALTER, Jacob. From New Windsor. Pvt. under Capt. George W. Magee, 22 Jul 1814 - 10 Jan 1815.

WALTER, Jacob. Pvt. under Capt. Fonsten; joined 2 Sep 1814; deserted 21 Sep 1814.

WALTER, Joseph. Pvt. under Capt. John Fonsten, 2 Sep - 27 Oct 1814; res. 12 miles from Westminster; b. 26 Jan 1786; m. 11 May 1812, Susanah Wampler in Fred. Co., by Curtis William, Meth. minister. Joseph Walter d. Wayne Co., IN, 8 Oct 1823; widow m. c.4 Mar 1824, Samuel McMullen who d. St. Joseph Co., IN, c.8 Sep 1838. Witnesses: 1855 - William McMullen, age 43; and Isaac Miller, 39; Solomon Miller, 41.

Source: Bounty land claim, 55-160-48122.

WALTER, William. Pvt. under Capt. John Fonsten, 2 Sep - 27 Oct 1814; res. 12 miles from Westminster. Samuel Lookinbeal, John Yokey and his bro., Joseph Walter, were his mess mates. - b. c.1793; res. Preble Co., OH, 1851, 1855.

Source: Bounty land claim, 55-160-8800.

WALTERSON, John. Pvt. under Capt. John Fonsten; joined 2 Sep 1814; deserted 20 Sep 1814.

WALTON, Christian. See Walter.

WAMPLER, Abram. Pvt. under Capt. Fonsten; b. c.1792; res. Carroll Co. MD, 1852.

Source: Bounty land claim, 55-120-1460.

WAMPLER, Lewis. Pvt. under Capt. Fonsten, 2 Sep - 27 Oct 1814; b. 1794; res. Carroll Co., MD, 1850, 1855. Witnesses: 1855 - Abner Neal and Geo. Edw. Wampler.

Source: Bounty land claim, 55-120-52457.

WANDLE, David. Pvt. under Lieut. Kolb, 13 Oct - 15 Nov 1814 in a det. assigned to guard the British prisoners at the Frederick Barracks.

WARCK, Andrew. Pvt. under Capt. Samuel Dawson; joined 21 Jul; discharged 18 Sep 1814; m. Dec 1811, Sarah McIntire (b. c.1773) by Rev Dr. Glendy, Presby. minister. Andrew Warck d. Balt. Sep 1815; widow res. Balt. 1859. Acq.: 1859 Col. Wm. Stansbury who res. opposite side of the street and James Darling who lived but two squares off, were her near neighbors.

Source: Bounty land claim, 55-160-91541.

WARD, Edward. Pvt. under Capt. Nicholas Turbutt; joined 1 Sep 1814; enlisted in regular army at Balt. 5 Sep 1814 by Lt. Cochran for duration of war. At enlistment: 5 ft 11 inches, grey eyes, dark hair, fair complexion, age 22 yrs, occupation cooper, b. Ireland - pvt. in Samuel C. Leakin's company at Fort McHenry. On 31 Dec 1814 he was reported as absent sick in the General Hospital; deserted from the General Hospital 1 Jan 1815.

WARE, William. One of three men whom the British Navy claimed had deserted from the British frigate, *Melampus,* and enlisted on the United States frigate *Chesapeake.* Commodore Barron, in a letter to the Secretary of the Navy, dated Apr 7, 1807, gave the fol. account,

"William pressed from on board the brig *Neptune,* Capt. Crafts, by the British frigate *Melampus,* in the Bay of Biscay, has served on board the said frigate fifteen mos..

"William Ware is a native American, b. on Pipe Creek, Fred. Co., State of MD, at Bruce's Mills, and served his time at said mills. He also lived at Ellicott's Mills near Balt., and drove a wagon several yrs between Hagerstown and Balt.. He also served eighteen mos. on board the United States frigate *Chesapeake,* under the command of Commodore Morris and Capt. James Barron. He is an Indian-looking man."

Source: J. Thomas Scharf, **History of Western MD.**

WARFIELD, John. Mbr. of Crawford's "company."

WARMAN, Noah. Mbr. of Crawford's "company."

WARNER, Abraham. Never joined his company under Capt. William Durbin, Jr., which served 24 Aug - 27 Oct 1814.

WARNER, Daniel. Pvt. under Capt. Samuel Duvall, 3 Aug - 3 Oct 1814.

WARNER, George. Never joined his company under Capt. William Durbin, Jr., which served 24 Aug - 27 Oct 1814. [Bur. at Uniontown Ch. of God Cem.: George Warner d. 18 Jun 1862, age 79.]

Source: **Names in Stone.**

WARNER, Henry. Pvt. under Capt. Samuel Dawson; joined 21 Jul 1814; deserted 5 Nov 1814.

WARNER, William. Pvt. under Capt. Samuel Dawson, 14 Oct 1814 - 10 Jan 1815.

WARNON, Noah. Mbr. of Crawford's "company."

WARTHEN, Benjamin. Pvt. under Lieut. William Kolb, 13 Oct - 15 Nov 1814.

WARTHEN, John. Pvt. under Capt. George W. Ent, 24 Aug - 30 Sep 1814. [FCml issued to John Warthen and Henrietta Shirley 20 Jan 1817.] Henrietta Warthan, age 55 res. 5th E.D. of Fred. Co. in 1850, b. MD; res. with family of James D. Hickey, 38, prof. of Drawing, b. MD; Catharine H. Hickey, 24, b. MD; Mary J. Hickey, 5, b. MD; James F., 2 b. MD; John Sherley, laborer, b. MD.]

Sources: **FCml; Bridge in Time.**

WARTHEN, Nicholas. Pvt. under Capt. Hackney, 1 Sep 1814 until 29 Oct 1814; b. c.1785; m. Heneretta Mitchell in Fred. Co., MD; res. Chickasaw, IA, 1871. Acq: 1871 - M.C. Ayres, C.A. Harris, residents of New Hampton, Chickasaw Co., IA.

Source: Pension, SO613 (rejected because of insufficient service). There is reference to his bounty land warrant, 55-120-10795. However the bounty land application was not in the pension

THE VETERANS

file nor was a separate bounty land file located by the National Archives staff.

WASKEY, Christian. Pvt. under Capt. Barton Hackney, 1 Sep - 27 Oct 1814.

WATKINS, John. [See also John Wadkins.] Enlisted in regular army 16 March 1808 by Lt. Luckett 5 yrs. At enlistment: 5 ft, 10 inches, blue eyes, brown hair, light complexion, age 27, farmer, b. Fred. Co., MD; pvt. in 2nd U.S. Inf. under Capt. Reubin Chamberlain.

WATT, Robert. Pvt. under Capt. Thomas Contee Worthington, 17 Aug - 31 Dec 1812. [FCml issued to Robert Watt and Mary Row on 10 Mar 1806.]

WATTS, John. Pvt. under Capt. Joseph Wood, 27 Aug - 13 Oct 1814; deserted 14 Oct, "musket not delivered up."

WAY, Jacob. Pvt. under Capt. Barton Hackney, 10 Sep - 27 Oct 1814.

WAYS, Basil. Pvt. under Lieut. Kolb, 1 - 15 Nov 1814, in det. assigned to guard the British prisoners at the Frederick Barracks.

WAYS, Basil J. Pvt. under Capt. Nicholas Turbutt, 1 Sep - 27 Oct 1814; b. c.1783; m. 2 Spr 1804, Cecila Driskol (b. c.1788), in Anne Arundel Co., MD, by Rev. Dawsey [Dorsey] of Meth. Ch. Basil Ways d. 21 May 1844 at Fredericktown; bur. at St. John's Catholic Cem. at 3rd and East Streets, Frederick; widow res. Allegany Co., MD, 1850, 1855. Acq.: 1850 - Frederick Clinard and Peter Ott who knew that Basil and Cecila Ways raised a family of children.

Sources: Bounty land claim, 55-80-19511; **Names in Stone.**

WAYS, Thomas. Pvt. under Capt. John Fonsten; joined 2 Sep 1814; deserted 14 Sep 1814.

WEAVER, Jacob. Enlisted in regular army by Ensign Philip Fisher 2 or 6 May 1813 at Westminster, MD for 1 year. At enlistment: 5 ft, 6 inches, age 36, b. Fred. Co., MD; pvt. in Capt. Joseph Hook's company; on 30 Apr 1814 he was reported as sick.

WEAVER, Lewis. Capt. of his own company. His company was activated c.23 Jul 1814. According to one veteran, Capt. Lewis Weaver commanded the company at the battle of Bladensburg and after that he took the company to Baltimore. They arrived at camp on 4 September outside Baltimore. At some point he was cashiered and succeeded by Capt. James F. Huston who in turn was succeeded by Capt. Joseph Green [from Emmitsburg] who remained in command until the company was discharged on 10 January 1815 at Annapolis.

WEAVER, Michael. Pvt. under Capt. Henry Steiner 28 Apr - 29 Jun 1813; b. c.1787; res. Georgetown, D.C. 1851, 1855.

Source: Bounty land claim, 55-120-11289.

WEAVER, Philip. Pvt. under Capt. Samuel Dawson, joined 21 Jul 1814; deserted 25 Jul 1814.

WEAVER, Phillip. Pvt. under Capt. Funsten, 2 Sep - 27 Oct 1814; b. c.1793; res. 6 miles from Westminster in 1814; res. New Windsor, Carroll Co., MD, 1855.

Source: Bounty land claim, 55-160-41700.

FREDERICK COUNTY MILITIA IN THE WAR OF 1812

WEBB, John. Pvt. under Capt. Samuel Ogle, 1 May 1813 - 5 Jul 1813; enlisted in regular army 14 or 15 Jun 1813 for 1 year; pvt. in 38th U.S. Inf. until discharged on 14 Jun 1814.

WEBSTER, David. Pvt. under Capt. John Brengle, 25 Aug - 19 Sep 1814.

WEBSTER, Samuel. Pvt. under Capt. John Brengle, 25 Aug - 19 Sep 1814

WEDDLE, George. Pvt. under Capt. Barton Hackney, 1 Sep - 27 Oct 1814.

WEDELLE [Weddle], John. Pvt. under Capt. Samuel Dawson; joined 21 Jul - deserted 28 Oct 1814.

WEEKLEY, William. From New Windsor. Pvt. under Capt. George W. Magee, 22 Jul - 10 Jan 1815.

WEIST [Wiest], John. Pvt. under Capt. Thomas Contee Worthington 17 Aug - 31 Dec 1812.

WELCH, Henry. From Upper Fred. Co. Pvt. under Capt. James F. Huston and Capt. Joseph Green; joined 28 Aug 1814 - deserted 8 Dec 1814.

WELCH, Jacob. Pvt. under Capt. John Galt, 31 Aug - 27 Oct 1814.

WELK, George. Pvt. under Capt. Fonsten, 2 Sep - 27 Oct 1814; res. 10 miles from Westminster.

WELLER, Henry. Pvt. under Capt. John Galt; joined 31 Aug 1814; sick absent 19 Sep 1814.

WELSH, William. Pvt. under Capt. Samuel Dawson; joined Jul 1814 - enlisted 21 Sep 1814.

WENRICK, John. Pvt. under Capt. Nicholas Turbutt, 1 Sep - 27 Oct 1814.

WEST, Abiham [Abraham]. New Windsor. Pvt. under Capt. George W. Magee; joined 22 Jul 1814; sick absent 1 Sep; discharged 26 Dec by surgeon.

WEST, Abraham. Mbr. of Crawford's "company."

WEST, Isaac. Enlisted in regular army 9 Apr 1814 by Lt. Duncan at Libertytown, MD for duration of war. At enlistment: 5 ft, 7 inches, grey eyes, brown hair, light complexion, age 22, occupation cooper, b. Fred. Co.; pvt. in Lt. Beech's company; discharged near Balt. 30 March 1815.

WEST, Joseph. 1st sergt. under Capt. Hackney, 1 Sep - 27 Oct 1814. In 1851, Fred. Co., MD, appeared Levin West, res. Fred. Co., guardian and uncle of fol.: Joseph West, b. 18 Sep 1833; Mary Elizabeth West, b. 21 Jan 1835; and Eugene West, b. 24 Apr 1839 - only minor children of Joseph West, dec'd, who d. Fred. Co. 11 May 1842 with no widow now surviving him.
Source: Bounty land claim, 55-120-49641.

WEST, Joshua. Mbr. of Crawford's "company."

WEST, Joshua. Pvt. under Capt. Fonsten; joined 2 Sep 1814; deserted 15 Sep 1814.

WEST, Nathaniel. From New Windsor. Pvt. under Capt. George W. Magee, 22 Jul - 10 Jan 1815.

WEST, Stephen. Pvt. under Capt. Basil Dorsey, 30 Jul - 27 Sep 1814.

WEST, William. Pvt. under Capt. Fonsten; joined 2 Sep 1814; deserted 13 Sep 1814; said he was drafted Cromers

THE VETERANS

Tavern, Fred. Co., MD; b. c.1780; res. Amboy, Hillsdale Co., MI, in 1856.
Source: Bounty land claim, 55-rejected-237837.

WETZEL, Daniel. Pvt. under Capt. Knox, 26 Aug - 27 Oct 1814; b. c.1793; laborer, res. Fred. Co. 1850 in 5th E.D. with Betty Ann Wetsel, age 24, insane; Margaret Wetsel, age 16; Jacob Wetsel, age 10; Samuel Wetsel, age 14 - all b. Fred. Co. Daniel Wetzel d. Jul 1853; his wife d. 1842. His sons, Samuel (age 18) and Jacob (age 16) res. Emmitsburg, Fred. Co. 24 May 1855, represented by their next friend, Josiah Weitsel. Acq.: 1855 - Andrew Annan and Joseph Welty, res. Fred. Co.
Sources: Bounty land claim, 55-120-62745; Bridge in Time.

WETZEL, John. Pvt. under Capt. William Knox, 26 Aug - 27 Oct 1814; b. c.1794; m(1) 20 Jun 1849, Eliza Sheets (b. 17 Sep 1820) at Millerstown (later called Fairfield), at Schnievley's Tavern, Adams Co., PA, by Rev. Robinson, minister of German Ref. Ch. She was b. Eliza Shrader (?) at Gettysburg, Adams Co., PA. At enlistment: black hair and black eyes; he d. near Emmitsburg, MD, Jul 1861 (hanged himself in garret of his house), c.80 yrs old. Eliza res. with her father, Jacal Shrader near Gettysburg, PA, in 1838; she had a dau by Washington Collison but was never m. to him. Eliza Shrader m(1) Henry Sheets Dec 1840 [or 1841] by Squire Rhodes at Gettysburg, PA; he cut his throat in winter of 1843. Eliza res. Blue Ridge Mountain, near Emmitsburg, in Fred. Co., MD, from 1840 to 1885.

Letter from Josephine Byard, Emmittsburg, MD, dated 4 Mar 1885 - regarding her father, John Wetzel. "... my mother Eliza Wetzel ... her first husbon was Henry Sheats he cut his throat. Her second husbon was Washington Collasson and he run away from her and is liveing near Cashtown, Addams Co., PA. ... third hosbon was John Wetzel wich was my father it was said he hung himself but he did not it was don for him for he was stone blind at the time."

Fol. this letter a Special Examination was made to determine whether Eliza Wetzel was the legal widow of John Wetzel. The examiner concluded that Washington Culison m. only once, then to Mary Rogers at Taneytown, Carroll Co., in 1842. Widow res. with her married dau, wife of Henry Underdarzk, at Balt. Her father and the dau by Cullison, were dead. When Culison was about twenty yrs of age he had an illegitimate girl child by pensioner, then residing with her father, Jacal Shrader near Gettysburg, PA. Said Calison not married to pensioner. About the time of birth of child said Calison came to reside with Joseph Bowers husband of deponent to learn the trade of cabinet making. The examiner concludes that letter was written by Josephine Byard at the instigation of her husband, John Byard who has been in jail ... on complaint of the pensioner for making a murderous assault on her with a shot gun.

Acq.: 1879 - James A. Elder, age 49, res. Emmittsburg, MD, and John H. Wetsel, age 27, res. near Emmittsburg, MD. 1885 - Andrew Auman b. 29 Apr 1805 at Emmitsburg, MD, remembered when Eliza came with her father to reside in the neighborhood. Josiah Wetzel, son of Daniel Wetzel, b. near Emmittsburg, MD, 22 Feb 1816 and res. near his place of birth all his life, farmer at Emmittsburg, MD, nephew of John Wetzel, gave evidence regarding below testimony. Daniel Wetzel, b. Aug 1833 near Emmittsburg, MD. Anthony McBride b. 15 Jul 1810 at Balt., came to Emmitsburg in 1845; states that John and Eliza Wetzel had two children. Elizabeth Bowers (maiden name Elizabeth Calison.), age 67, b. in York, PA, widow of Joseph Bowers and sister of Washington Colison b. at Oxford, 9 miles from Gettysburg, PA, in 1819, and d. Sandy Mount, Carroll Co., MD, May 1882, age 63; Daniel Wetzel, age 51, farmer, Emmittsburg, bro. of preceding witness. Anthony McBride, age 74, Emmittsburg.

1850 census of 5th E.D., Fred. Co.: John Wetsel, 75, laborer, b. PA; Elizabeth Wetsel, 30, b. MD; Margaret Wetsel, 9, b. MD; Annie Wetsel, 7, b. MD.

Sources: Pension, WO 35557, WC 24557 (dropped 18 Mar 1901); **Bridge in Time.**

WHARTON, Ralph [Ralphael]. Pvt. under Capt. John Galt, 31 Aug - 27 Oct 1814; said he was drafted at Smiths Tavern; b. c.1773; res. Fred. Co. 1851. Acq.: 1851 - Nicholas Snider, Graceham, MD, 1st lieut. under Capt. John Galt stated, Ralph Wharton is "mainly supported by the sisterhood at Emmitsburg who employ him to keep their gate of public entrance to their institution."

Source: Bounty land claim, 50-40-68694

WHEELER, Edward. Mbr. of Crawford's "company."

WHERRITT, Bennett. Pvt. under Capt. Nicholas Turbutt, 1 Sep - 27 Oct 1814.

WHETSEL, William. Pvt. under Capt. John Galt; joined 31 Aug 1814; discharged 5 Sep 1814.

WHETTER, Leonard. Pvt. under Capt. Basil Dorsey, 30 Jul - 27 Sep 1814.

WHETTLE, John. Pvt. under Capt. Samuel Dawson, 1 May - 5 Jul 1813.

WHIFFEY [Whiffery], Andrew. Enlisted in regular army at Norfolk, by Capt. Nelson on 23 Nov 1814; pvt. in 36th U.S. Inf.; reported as deserted on 16 Feb 1815. At enlistment: 5 ft, 9 1/2 inches tall, age 27, b. New Market, Fred. Co., MD.

WHIPP, George. Pvt. under Capt. George W. Ent, 24 Aug - 30 Sep 1814; substitute for a Lend. Sterm; b. c.1792; res. Franklin Co., OH, 1851 and 1855. [According to query in Fred. Co. Gen. Society Newsletter, 1991, of Katherine Mary Strohm, 3472 Grinnell Drive, Columbus, OH 43231, George Whip b. 13 May 1792, VA, m. 1816 Mary Lashorn, immigrated to Franklin Co., OH, 1833, d. Columbus OH.]

Source: Bounty land claim, 55-120-724.

WHITE, Joseph. Pvt. under Capt. Philip Smith, 23 May - 8 Sep 1813.

WHITE, Thomas. Pvt. under Capt. Samuel Dawson; joined 21 Jul; deserted 7 Nov 1814, substitute for John Getzendanner in the company of Capt. Dawson, until the Battle of Bladensburg and

THE VETERANS

afterwards by Col. Stephen Steiner; b. c.1797; res. Lima, IN, in 1851.
Source: Bounty land claim, 50-rejected-86308.

WHITE, Walter. Pvt. under Capt. Denton Darby, 3 Aug - 8 Nov 1814, as substitute for Adam Sponsellar; company discharged when he was at his home on furlough; b. c.1794; res. Fred. Co., MD, 1851, 1855; res. Cedar Rapids, Linn Co, IA, 1871; wife d. 20 Feb 1863 to whom he m. at Bertram, Linn Co., IA, 31 Oct 1861. At enlistment: black hair, brown complexion, height c.5 ft, 6 inches; res. Cedar Rapids, IA 1871 and Araby, Frederick Co, MD 1878; fol. discharge res. Iowa c.18 yrs and before and since in Fred. Co., MD.

Acq.: 1871 - J. J. Snouffer and William Stick, both of Cedar Rapids. 1878 - Samuel Carmack, age 85, Patrick St., Fredericktown, and Adolphus Feashake(?), age 83, Patrick St., Fredericktown, acq. 65 and 75 yrs, resp. 1879 - Ignatius Jacobs, age 85, res. Jackson Dist., Fred. Co., mbr. of Capt. Weaver's company; remembers that White obtained a furlough and returned home, his mother being very ill. 1879 - Samuel Carmack recalls that Walter White having been a sergt. in Capt. Duvall's company; that said Walter White having been a fifer, when in action at the Battle of Bladensburg; that White threw away his fife, obtained arms and accoutrements and stood his ground manfully to the end of the contest.
Source: Pension, SO 15938, SC 25214; Bounty land claim, 55-160-13100.

WHITLOCK, John. Pvt. under Capt. Joseph Green, 14 Oct 1814 - 10 Jan 1815; res. Balt.

WHITMIER, Simon. Pvt. under Capt. John Fonsten, 2 Sep - 27 Oct 1814; res. 12 miles from Westminster.

WHITMORE, Frederick. Pvt. under Capt. John Galt; joined 31 Aug 1814; discharged 5 Sep 1814.

WHITMORE [Witmer], James. Pvt. in 22nd U.S. Inf.; enlisted 28 Oct or 1 Nov 1814 at Mt. Pleasant. At enlistment: 5 ft, 7 inches, gray eyes, fair hair, fair complexion, age 32, occupation hatter, b. Fredericktown, MD; at Pittsburg 31 Dec 1814, serving under Capt. Jacob Carmack 16 Feb and 28 Feb 1815; in Capt. M. Swett's company U.S. Arty 1 Oct 1815; joined from Capt. Sproull's company 2nd U.S. Inf. 19 Sep 1815. In Capt. J.T. B. Romayne's Company 31 Dec 1815 and 29 Feb 1816. Reported as deserted 1 or 15 Jun 1816. In confinement on "Gov. Isld."

WHITTER, Leonard. According to the *(Frederick) Examiner* he was a soldier of the War of 1812; d. at Alms house of spotted relapsing fever on 21 Apr 1870, age about 65 yrs. Well-known, he lived between Frederick City and Hagerstown and spent most of his time in jail; addicted to drinking to excess.
Source: (Frederick) Examiner, 27 Apr 1870.

WIAND, Henry. Pvt. under Capt. Daniel Marker, 25 Aug - 27 Oct 1814.

WIAND, John. Pvt. under Capt. Daniel Marker, 25 Aug - 27 Oct 1814.

WICKAM [Wickham], Andrew. Pvt. under Capt. Philip Smith; joined 23

May 1813; deserted 19 Jun 1813 and served as pvt. under Capt. Samuel Duvall, 3 Aug - 3 Oct 1814. [See Andrew Wickham] [FCml issued to Andrew Wickham and Elizabeth Sticker 25 May 1807. Note: Andrew Wickham bur. in Creagerstown, St. John's Luth. and Reformed Ch.]

Sources: FCml; Names in Stone.

WICKARD, Adam. Pvt. under Capt. George W. Magee, joined 22 Jul; deserted 1 Oct 1814.

WICKARD, Philip [Phillip]. Pvt. under Capt. William Knox, 26 Aug - 27 Oct 1814; b. c.1790; res. Gettysburg, PA, 1851, 1855. Acq.: 1851 - Patrick Burk, sergt. in Capt. Knox's company.

Source: Bounty land claim, 55-120-666.

WICKHAM, Andrew. [See Andrew Wickam.] Pvt. in 38th U.S. Inf.; enlisted by Lt. Reticher at Fredericktown on 11 or 20 Dec 1814. At enlistment: hazel eyes, light hair, age 33, a distiller, b. Fred. Co., MD; discharged from Capt. Stansbury's Co. at Balt. 6 Apr 1815 at end of enlistment.

WICKHAM, Jacob. Pvt. under Capt. Philip Smith, 23 May - 8 Sep 1813. Said he acted as substitute for John Wickham in the company commanded by Capt. Saml. Duvall, c.19 Aug 1814 - discharged at Bladensburg around 24 Aug 1814. Also a substitute for Michael Creager in the company commanded by Robt. Fulton called to proceed to Balt. around 9 Sep 1814. -b. c.1787; res. Washington Co., MD, in 1852.

Source: Bounty land claim, 50-rejected-149223. 3d auditor's office states that name of Jacob Wickham not found on rolls of Capt. S. Duvall; and "There are no rolls of Capt. Samuel Smith of Md. Mil. [Note that Jacob Wickham served under Capt. Philip Smith not Samuel Smith, as he incorrectly stated in his application.]

WIDRICK, Christian. Pvt. under Capt. Nicholas Turbutt, went to Balt in 1814, discharged 1 Nov 1814.

WIDRICK, John. Pvt. under Capt. Jacob Getzendanner, 9 Aug - 17 Sep 1813 and 26 Jul - 21 Aug 1814. [Bur. at Mt. Olivet Cem. in Frederick are John Widerick, 18 May 1781 - 20 Jul 1850; wife Elizabeth, 11 Mar 1791 - 13 Dec 1868. *Names in Stone.*

WIGLE, Frederick. Corpl. under Capt. Samuel Dawson, 1 May - 5 Jul 1813.

WILCALIDEL, Jacob G. Mbr. of Crawford's "company."

WILEY, Ephriam. Pvt. under Capt. George W. Ent, 3rd Regt, 24 Aug - 30 Sep 1814.

WILHIDE, 2nd, Jacob. Pvt. under Capt. Samuel Duvall, 3 Aug - 3 Oct 1814.

WILLHIDE [Willhite], George. Pvt. under Capt. Philip Smith, 23 May - 8 Sep 1813.

WILHIDE [Wilhite], Jacob, Jr. Pvt. under Capt. Samuel Duvall, 3 Aug - 3 Oct 1814; b. 9 Sep 1793; d. 17 Jan 1862; m. Margaret Late c.13 Nov 1813. Margaret b. 13 Apr 1784; d. 13 Sep 1862. He res. Woodsboro Dist. 1850. 1850 census of Woodsboro Dist.: Jacob Wilhide, 55, farmer, $24,000; Margaret Wilhide, 65; Reuben Wilhide, 26; Catharine Wilhide, 20; Niles Wilhide, 7; Daniel Renner, 26, laborer. He res. Carroll Co., MD 1855 and the family is shown in the 1860 census of Carroll Co. Jacob Wil-

THE VETERANS

hide and his wife Margaret and their dau Catherine Ann are bur. at Meth. Protestant Cem., Detour, MD.
Sources: Bounty land claim, 55-120-86150; Names in Stone, Bridge in Time.

WILKINSON, Liner W. Res. Frederick Town in 1814. Pvt. under Capts. James F. Huston/Joseph Green, 23 Jul 1814 - 10 Jan 1815.

WILLHIDE, Henry. Pvt. under Capt. Joseph Wood, 27 Aug - 28 Oct 1814. [1850 census of Creagerstown Dist.: Henry Wilhide, 55, farmer; Mary A. Wilhide, 30; Elizabeth, 22; Henry Willhide, 68; Susan, 24, dumb and deaf; Henry, 28; John, 27, deaf.

WILLHIDE, Jacob. Pvt. under Capt. Philip Smith, 23 May 1813; deserted 19 Jun 1813.

WILLHITE, George. See Willhide.

WILLIAM. From Upper Frederick. Capt.'s servant under Capt. James F. Huston/Capt. Joseph Green; joined 23 Jul 1814; discharged 8 Dec.

WILLIAMS, David. Pvt. under Capt. Nicholas Turbutt, 1 Sep - 27 Oct 1814.

WILLIAMS, Eli. Pvt. under Capt. Nicholas Turbutt, 1 Sep - 27 Oct 1814; b. c.1791; res. Botetourt Co., VA, 1853, 1855.
Source: Bounty land claim, 55-180-24450.

WILLIAMS, James. Never joined his company under Capt. William Durbin, Jr., which served 24 Aug - 27 Oct 1814.

WILLIAMS, John. Pvt. under Capt. Samuel Dawson, 14 Oct 1814 - 10 Jan 1815.

WILLIAMS, John B. Pvt. under Capt. Philip Smith; joined 23 May 1813; deserted 19 Jun 1813. [FCml issued to John B. Williams and Nancy Smith 3 Jun 1808. Bur. at St. Paul's Luth. Ch. in Uniontown was John B. Williams, d. 23 Jul 1861, age 66 and wife Temperance, 19 Nov 1872, age 69 yrs, 7 days.]
Sources: FCml, Names in Stone.

WILLIAMS, Lilburn. Pvt. under Capt. Basil Dorsey; joined 30 Jul 1814; discharged by General Foreman on 24 Sep 1814.

WILLIAMS, Lilburn. Pvt. under Capt. Fonsten, 2 Sep - 27 Oct 1814; res. 17 miles from Westminser.
[FCml issued to Lilben Williams and Deborah Plummer on 26 Jul 1819.]

WILLIARD [Willard], Elias. Pvt. under Capt. Hackney, 30 Sep - 27 Oct 1814; drafted at Middletown; b. c.1779; m. 1808, Magdalena Baker (b. c.1786) by Rev Getith(?), Washington Co., MD. He res. Columbiana Co., OH, 1852, 1855; d. Millport, OH, 9 Jul 1862. She res. Millport, Columbiana Co., OH, 1871; d. 24 May 1871. Witnesses: 1855 - Samuel Williard and Henry Williard, res. Franklin Township, Columbiana Co., OH. Acq.: 1871 - William Laughlin and Thomas McKarns, Franklin Township, Columbiana Co., OH.
Sources: Pension, WO 2605 (rejected - insufficient service); Bounty land claim, 55-120-62833.

WILLIS, Henry. Mbr. of Crawford's "company."

WILLSON, Edward J. Pvt. under Lieut. Upton Reid, in 1st Cav., 26 Aug - 3 Sep 1814.

WILLYARD, John. Pvt. under Capt. John Galt; 31 Aug 1814; deserted 10 Sep 1814.

WILLYARD, Lawrence. Pvt. under Capt. John Galt, 3 - 27 Oct 1814.

WILSON, Andrew. Pvt. under Capt. Denton Darby, 3 Aug - 8 Nov 1814.

WILSON, Aquilla. Pvt. under Capt. Barton Hackney, 1 Sep - 27 Oct 1814.

WILSON, John. From Upper Fred. Co. Pvt. under Capt. James F. Huston/Capt. Joseph Green; joined 23 Jul; deserted 7 Dec 1814.

WILSON, John. Never joined his company under Capt. Thomas Contee Worthington, which served, 17 Aug - 31 Dec 1812.

WILSON, John. Corpl. under Capt. John Brengle, 25 Aug - 19 Sep 1814; b. c.1797; res. Winchester, VA, 1853.

Source: Bounty land claim, 50-rejected 168935.

WILSON, John of Alexander. Res. Frederick Town in 1814. Pvt. under Capt. James F. Huston/Capt. Joseph Green, 23 Jul 1814 - 10 Jan 1815; discharged 6 Dec by surgeon.

WILSON, Otho. Never joined his company under Capt. Thomas Contee Worthington, which served 17 Aug - 31 Dec 1812.

WILSON, Otho. Pvt. under Capt. George W. Ent, 24 Aug - 30 Sep 1814.

WILSON, William. Pvt. under Capt. Basil Dorsey, 30 Jul - 27 Sep 1814. Acted as corpl. for 30 days.

WILSON, William. Pvt. making a rendezvous at New Market with the company of Capt. Henry Lowrye, from Washington Co., 27 Aug - 28 Oct 1814.

WILSON, William. Pvt. under Capt. John Fonsten; joined 2 Sep; deserted 14 Sep 1814.

WINBIGLER, John. Pvt. under Capts. Shawken (Shawen?) and Matthew Murray, 25 Aug - 27 Oct 1814; m. 22 Dec 1822, Mary Maudy, at Jeromeville, Ashland Co, OH, by Rev Shew, Luth. minister, each for first time. At enrollment: 22 yrs old, farmer, b. near Fredericktown, 5 ft, 8 inches tall; black hair, eyes, dark complexion. Fol. discharge res. Fred. Co., MD until 1817; then Ashland Co. OH until he d. at Jeromeville, 2 Apr 1848.

Acq.: 1878 - Henry Winbigler, age 70, Jeremeville, OH; William Remley, age 64, Jeremeville, OH, acq. 56 and 34 yrs resp. Children of Mary Winbigler: John J, 57 yrs, Richard 44(?) yrs, Mary Winbigler, 46 yrs.

Sources: Bounty land claim, 50-40-19477, 55-120-30866; Pension, WO 31120, WC 17272.

WINCEL, John. Pvt. under Capt. James F. Huston and Capt. Joseph Green; joined 23 Jul 1814; deserted 7 Dec 1814.

WINDPIGLER [Winpigler], George. Pvt. under Capt. Thomas Contee Worthington; joined 17 Aug 1813; deserted 29 Aug 1812. [George Windpigler m. c.17 Aug 1822, Mahala Scaggs, dau of Leonard Scaggs (d. c.4 Oct 1821), leaving heirs, among whom was Mahala wife of George Winpigler. See Fred. Co. equity records.]

WINE, Jacob. Pvt. under Capt. Fonsten; joined 2 Sep 1814; deserted 14 Sep 1814.

WINEBRENER FAMILY - Philip Winebrener came to MD from Pennsylvania. He first located at Hagerstown, and later removed to Fred. Co. Here he settled on a tract of 212 acres, which is now included in the "Self Defense" property, owned by his grandson. Here he spent the rest of his days. The name of his wife was Eve. They were the parents of four children: John, well known as the founder of the Ch. of God; Jacob who d. aged about thirty yrs; Christian; and a dau who m. Ezra Cramer. - Williams, *History of Frederick County, Maryland.*

WINEBRENNER [Winebrunner], Jacob. 2nd lieut. under Capt. Joseph Wood, 27 Aug - 28 Oct 1814. [*Frederick Herald*, dated 21 Dec 1822 reported a fire which destroyed the house of Jacob Winebrener near Woodsborough. Four small children and a young woman were sound asleep. Neighbors discovered the blaze; all were saved.]

Source: **Frederick Herald**, 21 Dec 1822.

WINEBRENNER [Winebrener], Peter. Enlisted at Richmond by Capt. Isaac F. Preston for 1 year on 10 Aug 1813. At enlistment: 20 yrs old, b. Fred. Co., MD. 6 March he was reported sick in hospital.

WINFIELD, Lawrence. Pvt. under Capt. Daniel Marker, 25 Aug - 27 Oct 1814; b. c.1796; res. Warren Co., OH, 1850, 1852 [town of Morrow] and 1855.

Source: Bounty land claim, 55-120-10638.

WINGIFAIR, John. Mbr. of Crawford's "company."

WINK, George. His widow said he served under Capt. Shower (prob. Capt. Adam Shower of Balt. Co.; m. Susan Sentz (b. c.1797), m. 1813 at her father's residence. She res. Manchester, Carroll Co., 1871. Acq.: 1871 - William L. Tracy, George K. Frank, res. Carroll Co.

Source: Pension, WO 2606 (rejected).

WINPIGLER, George. Pvt. under Capt. Daniel Marker, 25 Aug - 27 Oct 1814.

WINPIGLER [Windpigler], John. Pvt. under Capt. Daniel Marker, 25 Aug - 27 Oct 1814; b. c.1795; m. 10 Dec 1829, Harriett Getzendanner (b. c.1812), by Rev. Smaltz, German Ref. minister of Fredericktown. John Winpigler res. Fred. Co., 1850; d. near Fredericktown 31 Aug 1851; bur. 1 Sep 1851 on Getzendenner's grave yard near Frederick [certified by David Zacharias, pastor of said ch., 28 Sep 1852]. Witnesses: 1855 - John J. Getzendanner and John H. Fout, res. Fred. Co.

Source: Bounty land claim, 55-120-22904.

WINPIGLER [Winbigler], Michael. Pvt. under Capt. Jacob Getzendanner, 26 Jul - 21 Aug 1814. He said the company was organized to guard the Governor at Annapolis, MD. - b. c.1795; m. Miss Elizabeth Goodman, 21 Apr 1822 at Fredericktown, MD, by Rev. Schaeffer; res. Warren Co., IA, 1855 and Coffey Co., KS (near LeRey, Lekey?), 1875. Acq.: 1855 - Jury Todhunter and Isaac N. Todhunter, of Warren Co., IA. 1875 - William B. Parsons, Burlingtere(?),

FREDERICK COUNTY MILITIA IN THE WAR OF 1812

KS and Manuel(?) Winpigler, LeKey (Lekoy?) KS,

Sources: Bounty land claim, 55-160-17666; Pension, SO 28275, SC 2335.

WINRAT [Winratt], John. Mbr. of Crawford's "company."

WINTER, Jacob. From Balt. Co.. Pvt. under Capt. John Galt, 31 Aug - 27 Oct 1814.

WINTERS, Frederick. Mbr. of Crawford's "company."

WINTERS, Ignatious. Pvt. from Upper Fred. Co. under Capt. Huston and Capt. Green, 25 Aug - 28 Sep 1814; m. Margaret Hartz (b. c.1790), at Fredericktown c.Aug 1813 by Rev. Mallaway. Margaret Conroy, widow of Ignatious Winters first said he d. at Fredericktown Jul 1824 but later said he d. in KY on 7 Jul c.1821. She later m. --- Conroy; res. Fredericktown 1851, 1855. Acq.: 1851 - Henry Kelly and Mrs. Margarett Newport, res. Fred. Co., MD; 1855 - Ezra Rowe and Hillary Haller, res. Fred. Co.

Source: Bounty land claim, 55-120-2494.

WINTERS, John. Drummer from New Windsor, under Capt. Magee, 22 Jul - 10 Jan 1815. - m. Sep 1810, Elizabeth Wampler (b. c.1786). John Winters d. in Fredericktown, 1820 (the widow gives 1820 as the year of death in her application in 1852 and year of 1830 in her application in 1855. [bur. in Winter's Luth. and Ref. Cem., New Windsor: John Winter, 3 Jun 1827, age 43 yrs, 5 mos., 26 days.] Acq.: 1855 - Abraham Wampler and Benjamin Yingling.

Source: Bounty land claim, 55-120-24032. Note below that John Winters serving under Magee as drummer would likely be the same John Winters who served as drummer under Ogle.

WINTERS, John. Drummer under Capt. Samuel Ogle, 1 May 1813 - 5 Jul 1813.

WISE, James. Pvt. under Capt. Daniel Marker; joined 25 Aug 1814; deserted 29 Aug 1814.

WISSINGER, George. Pvt. under Capt. Brengle, 25 Aug - 19 Sep 1814; b. c.1784; m(1) c.1807, Elizabeth Leab; m(2) 30 Sep 1845, Harriet Winkler [Winkley], in Georgetown, Washington, D. C., by Rev Stephen Ceazaway(?), Episc. minister. George Wissinger res. Washington, D. C. 1852, 1855; d. 27 Feb 1862, Georgetown, D. C. Elizabeth Leab was sister of Jacob Leab; she d. 27 Jan 1838, in her 54th year; bur. Luth. Grave Yard. Harriet Wissinger, his widow, res. Washington, D.C. in 1878 (at No. 411 Ridge St.); d. of pneumonia 21 Dec 1886 Washington, D. C., age 84 yrs, 6 mos, 27 days, res. D.C. 70 yrs, sick for 6 days; bur. Oak Hill; undertaker was John R. Wright. Grace Roberts, M. D. was attending physician. Acq.: 1852 - David Hane pvt. in Capt. Brengle's company; 1878 - Samuel Wise and Annie M. Pumphry; Sophia Speacht, dau of Mrs. Elizabeth Wissinger; Daniel Derr, res. Fredericktown; Joseph Duvall, res. Balt. City. William A. Ridgely, age 34, No. 35 H. St. N.W., Washington, D.C. and Annie Pumphrey, age 51, res. No. 411 Ridge St., Washington, D. C., acq. 30 and 50 yrs resp.

Sources: Bounty land claim, 55-120-29; Pension, WO 13932, WC 10528; Wash D.C. marr. lic.;

THE VETERANS

Engelbrecht Diary, v.2, 279; FCml; Names in Stone; **(Frederick) Examiner,** 12 Mar 1862.

WISSINGER, Leonard. From Upper Fred. Co. Pvt. under Capt. James F. Huston, 23 Jul 1814 - 13 Oct 1814. [FCml issued to Leonard Wisinger and Catherine Winpeagler 20 Mar 1804. 1850 census of Middletown Dist.: Leonard Wissinger, 75; Catharine Wissinger, 64; Solomon Wissinger, 27, cooper; Leonard Wissinger, 9 - all b. MD.]

Sources: Bounty land claim, 55-120-21492 (widow's application - cancelled - no applications in file); **FCml; Bridge in Time.**

WISSINGER, Peter. Pvt. under Capt. John Brengle, 25 Aug - 19 Sep 1814; b. c.1793; res. Fred. Co., MD, 1850 and 1855. 1850 census of Middletown Dist.: Peter Wissinger, 54, b. MD, with the family of Isiah Mealey, 49, miller. [In Luth. Ch. of Fredericktown were bapt. on 2 Feb 1794, Peter and Catharina, twins b. to Peter and Maria Susanna Wiesinger on 1 Sep 1793.]

Sources: Bounty land claim, 55-120-513; **Md. German Ch. Records,** v.4; **Bridge in Time;** Engelbrecht Diary.

WITMER. See Whitmore.

WIVEL, John. Pvt. under Capt. John Galt, 31 Aug - 27 Oct 1814; b. c.1784; res. 5 miles of Taneytown in 1814, near Emmitsburg in 1851 and 1855.

Source: Bounty land claim, 55-120-39886.

WOLFE FAMILY [Williams, *Hist. of Fred. Co.* - The American progenitor of the Wolfe family was a native of England. He emigrated to America about 1770, and settled in Pennsyvlania. He enlisted in the American army in the War of Independence, and served throught that struggle, being a participant in a number of engagements. After the close of the war, he returned to Pennsylvania, and was soon afterward married. He became the father of seven sons. Three of these sons, after reaching maturity, came to MD; two settled in Washington Co. and another in Carroll Co. The third of these was named Jacob. Jacob Wolfe, son of the emigrant was b. near York, PA. He accompanied his two bros. to MD, and located in the Middletown Valley, Fred. Co. He took up his residence about one mile from the present village of Wolfsville, and served in the War of 1812. He saw lots of hard fighting. He was m. but the name of his wife is unknown. They were the parents of six children, the oldest son being named Jacob, after his father. [Ed. note - It seems Williams is confused. Jacob Wolf (below) who served in War of 1812 is the one who m. Catharine Main.]

WOLF [Wolfe, Woolf], Jacob. Pvt. under Capt. D. Shawen, 5 Sep - 27 Oct 1814; b. 1788; m. 1810, Catharine Main at George Town, D.C. 1850 census of Catoctin area: Jacob Wolf, 61, farmer; Catharine Wolf, 78; both b. MD. He res. Wolfsville, Fred. Co., MD, 1871. Acq.: 1871 - Jacob Smith and Joseph Ramsberg, res. Fred. Co., MD. Jacob Wolf d. 5 (or 6) Mar 1872, age 84 yrs, 16 days; his wife Catherine d. 12 Jul 1855, age 83 yrs, 6 mos., 31 days; both bur. Wolfsville Ref. Cem. When he d. Jacob Wolfe was father of three children, 18 grandchildren, 60 great grandchildren and 3 great-great grandchildren.

FREDERICK COUNTY MILITIA IN THE WAR OF 1812

Sources: Pension, SO 11639 (rejected by reason of insufficient service); **Names in Stone; Bridge in Time; (Frederick) Examiner,** 13 Mar 1872.

WOLF [Wolfe], John. Sergt. under Capt. Samuel Duvall, 3 Aug - 6 Oct 1814 (according to the rolls but see below); drafted at Woodsboro; b. 18 Apr 1789; m. c.7 Mar 1815, Mary Holtz (b. c.1794), in Fred. Co., c.7 Mar 1815, by Rev. Helphenstine, Presby. clergyman. John Wolfe d. 17 Apr 1855 Fred. Co.; bur. Johnsville Meth. Protestant Ch. with wife Mary (29 Oct 1792 - 9 Feb 1879).

Sources: Bounty land claim, 55-120-79783; **Names in Stone; FCml.** In the bounty land application file is signed slip saying, "John Wolf a Draughted Soldier under My Command in the United States Service is hereby Discharged as sick from this Day November 9th 1814. /s/ Cap Samiel Deuval.

WOLFE, George. Also see Woolfe. Pvt. in the 1st Cav. dist., 26 Aug - 3 Sep 1814.

WOLGAMOTT, Joseph. From Washington Co. Pvt. under Capt. Samuel Dawson, 14 Oct 1814 - 10 Jan 1815.

WOLTZ, Otho. 3rd lieut. under Capt. Samuel Dawson, 1 May - 5 Jul 1813.

WOOD, Aaron. Enlisted in regular army on 25 or 27 Jun 1813 at Fredericktown by Ensign Philip Fisher for 1 year. Pvt. in 36th U.S. Inf. under Capt. Jos. Hook; reported as deserted 12 July 1813.

WOOD, Bennet. Pvt. under Capt. Fonsten; joined 2 Sep 1814; deserted 28 Sep 1814; he said he was taken sick near Balt. and sent home on furlough. - b. c.1774; res. Harrison Township, Perry Co., OH, 1850 and 1853.

Source: Bounty land claim, 50-rejected-159921.

WOOD, Joel. 1st corpl. under Capt. Samuel Ogle, 1 May 1813 - 5 Jul 1813.

WOOD, Joseph. 1st lieut. under Capt. Philip Smith, 23 May - 8 Sep 1813 and capt. of his own company, 3 Aug - 28 Oct 1814; m. 1 Jun 1804, Nancy Grable (b. c.1785) near Woodsboro, MD, by Rev Lewis Browning, Meth. minister. Joseph Wood d. near Woodsboro 14 Oct 1849. A note dated 30 May 1855, Woodsboro, from Charles Wood son of Nancy Wood, regarding his mother's certificate for bounty land. Acq.: 1850 - James Harlin; 1855 - James W. Harlan and Geo. M. Shaw, res. Fred. Co.

Source: Bounty land claim, 55-80-23420.

WOODARD, Nathaniel. Pvt. under Capt. Daniel Marker; joined 25 Aug; furloughed 11 Oct 1814.

WOODS, Michael. Pvt. under Capt. Fonsten, 2 Sep - 27 Oct 1814; res. 10 miles from Westminster. [In 1837 a divorce was granted to Mary Woods of Frederick from Michael Woods.]

Source: Mary K. Meyer, **Divorces and Names Changed in MD.**

WOODWARD, Branton. Pvt. under Capt. George W. Ent, 3rd Regt, 24 Aug - 30 Sep 1814.

WOODWARD [Woodard], Nathaniel. Pvt. under Capt. Jacob Getzendanner, 9 Aug - 17 Sep 1813 and 26 Jul - 26 Aug 1814 under Capt. Marker. He said he enlisted as a substitute for Perry Hillery at Fredericktown around 15 Sep 1813; b. c.1776; m. c.30 May 1801, Mary Colours [Culler] (b. c.1784), near Fredericktown by Rev David Shaffer.

[He gave the date of marr. as 1801; however the date of the marr. license was 25 May 1805.] He res. Franklin, Warren Co., OH, 1851; d. Franklin, OH, 31 Oct 1854. Records of Luth. Ch. in Frederick show Susannah (b. 29 Jan 1808, bapt. 13 Aug 1808) dau of Nathaniel and Marg. Woodward and Lewis son of Nathaniel and Marg. Woodward (b. 25 Feb 1811, bapt. 1 Jun 1811).
Acq.: 1852 - John Bankard, res. Warren Co., OH, who volunteered with Nathaniel Woodward c.9 Aug 1813; Jacob Bankard, res. Preble Co., OH who served in same company. 1855 - Alexander Ross and D. L. Crider, res. Franklin, OH. who knew them to raise a family. Barbary Albought and Catherine Baker, res. Montgomery Co., OH, who res. near Frederick at time of their marr.

Source: Bounty land claim, 55-120-55815.

WOOLARD, John. 4th sergt. under Capt. Daniel Marker; joined 25 Aug 1814; furloughed 23 Oct 1814.

WOOLF, Jacob. Pvt. under Capt. Daniel Shawen, 5 Sep - 27 Oct 1814.

WOOLFE, George. Pvt. under Capt. Barton Hackney; joined 1 Sep 1814; deserted 23 Oct 1814.

WOOLTZ, Hezekiah. 2nd sergt. under Capt. Thomas Contee Worthington, 17 Aug - 31 Dec 1812.

WOOLTZ, Otho. Pvt. under Capt. Thomas Contee Worthington, 17 Aug - 31 Dec 1812.

WOOLTZ, Otho. 2nd lieut. under Capt. Nicholas Turbutt, 5 Sep - 27 Oct 1814.

WOONDER, John. New Windsor. Pvt. under Capt. George W. Magee, 22 Jul - 10 Jan 1815.

WOOTTON, Richard. Pvt. under Capt. Thomas F. W. Vinson, Extra Battalion, Montgomery Co., MD, 1 Aug - 27 Sep 1814; b. son of Richard in Rockville, MD c.1792; res. Fred. Co. 1850, 1871; grad. Dickinson College, Carlisle, PA, studied law under Benjamin S. Torrance; gave it up and retired to the farm he inherited from his father, containing c.1600 acres; left Prot. Episc. Ch. for Roman Cath Ch.; gave up his wordly possessions; d. 4 Sep 1877 in Frederick, MD.

Sources: Bounty land claim: 55-120-21489; Pension, SO 10724, SC 7349; (Frederick) Examiner, 12 Sep 1877.

WORTHINGTON, Thomas Contee. Commanded a company at Balt. and Annapolis, 17 Aug - 31 Dec 1812. Appt'd Aid de Camp to Brigadier General Henry Barrick, 7th Brigade prior to 20 Nov 1813. Later commissioned Brigadier General of the Ninth Brigade. - b. 25 Nov 1782, son of William and Jane (Contee) Worthington of Mt. Ida on the Chesapeake Bay and Maggothy River in Anne Arundel Co.; moved to Frederick to practice law; elected to House of Delegates; elected to Congress in 1824; d. Frederick 12 Apr 1847, unmarried; bur. Mt. Olivet. William Worthington, father of Thomas C. Worthington, d. 14 Jan 1822, in his 75th year.

Sources: Williams, Hist. of Fred. Co.; Names in Stone; Engelbrecht Diary: 1:117.

WRIGHT, Benjamin. 1st sergt. under Capt. Basil Dorsey, 30 Jul - 27 Sep 1814.

FREDERICK COUNTY MILITIA IN THE WAR OF 1812

[Bur. St. John's Cath. Cem. in Frederick is Benjamin Wright (b. 29 Aug 1790 - d. 16 Jan 1827). Annoucement in *Frederick Herald* stated Lieut. Col. Benjamin Wright d. at residence of William Wirtenbaker in New Market in his 36th year.]
Source: **Frederick Herald**, 27 Jan 1827.

WRIGHT, James. Pvt. under Capt. Thomas Contee Worthington; joined 17 Aug 1812; deserted 18 Oct 1812.

WRIGHT FAMILY - John Wright, grandfather of John H. Wright, b. in 1781; emigrated from north of Ireland to U.S. and took up residence at Frederick City, MD. Occupation unknown; d. 26 Jul 1850; m. Polly Talbot. They were parents of Lewis, Henry, Sarah, Ann Rebecca and John A. - Williams, *History of Frederick County, Maryland*.

WRIGHT, John. Pvt. under Capt. Samuel Ogle, beginning on 1 May 1813 - deserted 26 Jun 1813.

WRIGHT, John of David. Pvt. under Capt. Samuel Ogle, 1 May - 5 Jul 1813.

WRIGHT, Reuben. Enlisted in regular army on 25(?) March 1814 in KY by Ensign Ewing for duration of war. At enlistment: 5 ft, 11 inches, grey eyes, dark hair, fair complexion, age 24, occupation wagon maker, b. Fred. Co., MD; corpl. in 17th U.S. Inf. under Capt. Benjamin W. Sanders; discharged in Chillicothe, OH, 7 Jun 1815.

WRIGHT, Samuel. Lieut. under Capt. Basil Dorsey, 30 Jul - 27 Sep 1814.

WYMAN, John. Pvt. under Capt. John Galt, 31 Aug - 27 Oct 1814.

YACKE, Peter. Pvt. under Capt. Barton Hackney; joined 1 Sep 1814; deserted 23 Oct 1814.

YAGER, Charles. Pvt. under Capt. George W. Ent, 24 Aug - 30 Sep 1814; bur. at Mt. Olivet: Charles Yager (b. in Denmark, d. 12 Mar 1836, age 60); wife Caroline (b. in Germany, d. 13 Apr 1836, age 55).
Source: **Names in Stone.**

YANDES, George. Mbr. of Crawford's "company." [Bur. at St. John's Reformed Ch., Woodsboro, was George Yantis (26 Feb 1826, age 46 yrs, 6 mos., 13 days).]

YANTIS [Yentes], Christian. Pvt. under Capt. Thomas Contee Worthington, 17 Aug - 31 Dec 1812. [Elizabeth dau of Christian and Susannah Yantiz b. 23 Jan 1810, bapt. 30 May 1811 - Luth. Ch., Frederick]

YANTIS [Yentes], William. Pvt. under Capt. Daniel Shawen, 5 Sep - 27 Oct 1814. He said he was drafted in Capt. Isaac Wilson's company at Emmittsburgh MD, spring of 1812, discharged at Balt. in the Fall. Afterwards, he said, in Aug 1813 he volunteered at Frederick, MD, in George Flaut's company of militia. About last of July 1814 he again enlisted as a substitute in Capt. Daniel Shawen's company. - b. c.1792; m. Elizabeth Sisler, in Fairfield Co., OH, 12 Jul 1816. His address changed to Hope, Franklin Co., OH, in 1871 (care of D. S. Wilder). Acq.: H. B. Alben, George Wagner, res. Columbus and Plain Township, resp.
Source: Pension, SO 18847, SC 18319.

THE VETERANS

YATES, Charles. Pvt. under Capt. Samuel Dawson, 21 Jul - deserted 26 Jul 1814. [FCml issued to Charles Yates and Catherine Minick on 14 Jan 1818. 1850 census of Petersville Dist.: Catharine Yates, 58, b. MD and Georgetta Yates, 16, b. MD.]

YEISER, Daniel. Pvt. under Capt. Samuel Ogle, 1 May - 5 Jul 1813; b. c.1788; m. Oct 1813, Barbara Kepelring, near Taneytown; res. Carroll Co., MD, 1852, 1855 and 1871 (Union Mills). Sources: Bounty land claim, 55-120-54202; Pension, SO 11548, SC 7128.

YEONITS, Christian. Pvt. under Capt. Samuel Duvall, 3 Aug - 3 Oct 1814.

YERK [Yirk], James. Pvt. under Capt. James F. Huston, Capt. Lewis Weaver/Capt. Joseph Green, beginning 23 Jul 1814; "Sick in Quarters since 2 Oct 1814." Res. Emmittsburgh 1814. On 28 Jan 1856 appeared James S. Yerk, res. Tiffin, Seneca Co., OH, who declared he was guardian of Margarett Ann Yerk, minor child and heir of James Yerk who d. c.Aug 1840, Mercer Co. His widow d. 6 Mar 1841. Margarett Ann Yerk was only surviving child of James Yerk under the age of 21 yrs, age 19 on 3 Mar 1855. Acq.: 1856 - Thomas Brundage and Aaron Case, res. Tiffin, OH.

Letter dated 2 Oct 1888, saying that Miss Margaret M. Yerk, dau of James Yerk is quite destitute and that the land warrant issued to her may have been used by her dissipated bro. Letter from Department of the Interior stated that the land warrant issued to Margaret A. Yerk was located at Fargo, Dakota, July 18, 1883, by Joseph W. McGregor. Source: Bounty land claim, 55-160-52544.

YINGLING, David. Pvt. under Capt. Basil Dorsey, 30 Jul - 27 Sep 1814; b. c.1794.

YINGLING, David. From New Windsor. 2nd corpl. under Capt. George W. Magee, 22 Jul - 10 Jan 1815, as substitute for Wm. McCumsty; b. c.1784; m(1) Mary Leicster who d. in 1813 and m(2) 11 Jan 1816, Rachel Stone (b. c.1795), in Westminster, by Rev Forester. At enrollment: age 31 yrs, painter in Westminster, MD, 5 ft, 9 inches tall, black hair, dark complexion, dark eyes. David and Rachel res. Westminster 6 or 7 yrs after date of their marr. and then for 55 yrs in Reisterstown where he d. 17 Nov 1852. Rachael Yingling res. Balt. Co. in 1855 and 1878 (Reisterstown). Acq.: 1855 - George L. Shipley and Philip D. Thomas, res. Balt. Co.; 1878 - William M. Berryman, age 71, and Henry Baker, age 59, both of 4th E.D. of Balt. Co.; George R. Stone, age 59, of Balt. Co. of Reisterstown and John Gies, age 69, of Reisterstown. Sources: Bounty land claim, 50-80-11263, 55-80-30696; Pension, WO 25264, WC 15320. Note dated 24 Jan 1852 from David Yingling regarding his son David G. Yingling to pick up land warrant from E. Beaty Graff.

YINGLING, Henry. Pvt. under Capt. Fonsten; joined 2 Sep 1814; deserted 3 Oct 1814. He said he was drafted at Fred. Co. by Adam Feiser in Sep 1814; took sick and was discharged Oct 1814 at Balt.; b. c.1781; res. Tuscarawas Co., OH, in 1855; acq.: 1857 - Daniel Hibbert res. Defiance Co., OH, who slept same place as Henry Yingling one night while in service in a rope yard while the company was destitute of tents. Jacob Shilling, res. Harrison Co., OH, also in company of Capt. Funston.

Source: Bounty land claim, 55-rejected-162888.

YINGLING, John. 2nd sergt. under Capt. William Durbin, Jr., 24 Aug - 27 Oct 1814.

YINGLING, John. Pvt. under Capt. John Galt, 31 Aug - 27 Oct 1814; res. within 5 miles of Taneytown in 1814.

YINGLING, John. Pvt. under Capt. Fonsten; joined 2 Sep 1814; deserted 20 Sep 1814; b. c.1786; m. 1807, Ellen Eck (d. prior to 20 March 1871); res. Carroll Co., MD, 1855 and 1871. Acq. - 1871: J. William Earhart, Ira E. Crouse, res. Carroll Co.

Source: Bounty land claim, 55-rejected-7427 (rejected -desertion).

YINGLING, Philip. Pvt. under Capt. Basil Dorsey, 30 Jul - 27 Sep 1814.

YIRK - See Yerk.

YONILS, Christian. Pvt. under Capt. Samuel Ogle, 1 May 1813 - 5 Jul 1813 Pvt.

YORK, John. Pvt. under Capt. George W. Ent, 3rd Regt, 24 Aug - 30 Sep 1814.

YORKEE [?], John. Pvt. under Capt. John Fonsten, 2 Sep - 27 Oct 1814.

YOUNG, Andrew. Pvt. under Capt. John Brengle, 25 Aug - 19 Sep 1814. [Bur. at St. John's Catholic Cem., Frederick: Andrew Young, d. 29 Jan 1828, age 49. - *Names in Stone*]

YOUNG, Andrew. Pvt. under Captin John Galt, 31 Aug - 27 Oct 1814.

YOUNG, Charles. Acting corpl. for 30 days under Capt. Basil Dorsey, 30 Jul - 27 Sep 1814; b. c.1790; m. 29 Oct 1816, Ann [Nancy/Nancy Ann] Dorsey, in Frederick Co.; res. Jefferson Co., OH, 1850, 1855, 1871 (Sloans Station, Knox Township).

Sources: Bounty land claim, 55-120-62750; Pension, SO 10732, SC 7434.

YOUNG, Conrad [Conrod]. Pvt. under Capt. Samuel Dawson, 21 Jul - 10 Jan 1815; said he was a substitute; on furlough at time his company was discharged; b. c.1787; d. 25 Apr 1856; m. Margaret --- who d. 9 Sep 1853, age 67 yrs, 4 mos., 2 days. They were bur. at Mt. Olivet, Frederick.

Source: Bounty land claim, 50-rejected-92876.

YOUNG, Davault (Dewalt). Pvt. under Capt. Samuel Dawson, 1 May - 5 Jul 1813; deserted 5 Jun; returned 25 Jun 1813; d. 25 Jan 1877, at residence of his dau in Locust Grove, Washington Co., MD, in his 88th year; former resident of Middletown Valley; father of Joseph E. Young of Frederick Co.

Source: (**Frederick**) **Examiner**, 7 Feb 1877.

YOUNG, David. [Prob. the same David Young of the fol. two entries.] d. 31 Jul 1825; bur. in Cath. burying ground with military honors by Capt. Houck's company of which he was a mbr.. He left a widow and children.

Source: **Frederick-town Herald**, 5 Aug 1825.

YOUNG, David. Pvt. under Capt. John Brengle, 25 Aug - 19 Sep 1814.

THE VETERANS

YOUNG, David. Pvt. under Lieut. William Kolb, 13 Oct - 15 Nov 1814 in a det. assigned to guard the British prisoners at the Frederick Barracks.

YOUNG, George. Mbr. of Crawford's "company."

YOUNG, Jacob. Pvt. under Capt. Ogle, 1 May 1813 - 5 Jul 1813; b. c.1786; m. 12 Jan 1811, Elizabeth Price (b. c.1792) in Fred. Co., MD, by Rev. Frederick Rauhauser. Jacob Young d. Fountain Co., IN, 23 Jan 1853. Widow res. Fountain Co., IN, in 1855. Acq.: William Crumpton and Daniel Young, res. Fountain Co., IN.
Source: Bounty land claim, 55-120-61449.

YOUNG, John. Pvt. under Capt. Thomas Contee Worthington, 17 Aug - 31 Dec 1812. Absent without leave.

YOUNG, John. Pvt. under Capt. James F. Huston and Capt. Joseph Green, 23 Jul 1814 - 10 Jan 1815; res Frederick Town in 1814.

YOUNG, John. Pvt. under Capt. William Knox, 26 Aug - 27 Oct 1814.

YOUNG, John. Pvt. under Capt. John Galt, 31 Aug - 27 Oct 1814.

YOUNG, John. Pvt. in U.S. Dragoons; enlisted 5 Sep 1812 at Carlisle, PA, by Capt. Hayne for 5 yrs. At enlistment: 5 ft, 6 inches, grey eyes, dark hair and dark complexion, age 33, occupation saddler, b. Fredericktown, MD. From Capt. Hayne's company he joined Capt. S. Halsey's company 15 Apr 1813; in Capt. Hopkins' company at New York on 18 Nov 1813, "absent sick at Schlasser." In Capt. G. Haig's co. 16 Feb and 30 Apr 1815. Hospital return dated New York Harbor, 11 July 1815, reported as unfit for service, old age and infirmity, age 37.

YOUNG, Thomas. Pvt. under Capt. John Brengle, 25 Aug - 19 Sep 1814; "deserted."

YOUNG, William. Pvt. under Capt. Samuel Dawson, joined 26 Jul 1814; enlisted in regular army 28 Sep 1814 by Lt. Whelpley in Balt. At enlistment: 5 ft, 5 inches, grey eyes, dark hair, dark complexion, age 25, laborer, b. Fredericktown, MD; served in 26th U.S. Inf. until discharged at Phila. 23 March 1815.

YOUNGMAN, William H. Pvt. under Capt. Thomas Contee Worthington, 17 Aug - 31 Dec 1812.

YOUNKIN, John. Claimed to have served in Capt. Samuel Dawsey's company from Middletown. [Based on the other names of officers and men that he named in the company it is obvious he is referring to the company of Capt. Samuel Dawson. However Younkin's name is not on the muster rolls of 13 Oct 1814 or 10 Jan 1815] He said he hired a substitute after serving 6 weeks. - b. 27 Jul 1791; m. Feb 1820, Margaret (also known as Elizabeth?) Trout (b. Loudoun,k VA) at York Twp, Morgan Co., OH. He said he moved to Lancaster Co., VA, c.2 yrs fol. discharge. In Apr 1817 moved to Bearfield Township, OH and continued to live there until 18 Jun 1879 when he moved to Morgan Co., near Deavertown. Acq: 1880 - James Bagley, 58, Deavertown; Thomas Longstreth, 69, Deavertown, both acq. 50 yrs. Research by Donna Logan determines John Younkin to be the son of Rudolph Younkin and Elizabeth Hockman. Children of John Younkin: Susanna, b. c.1821, William, b. c.1828, Elizabeth b. c.1834, Lydia b. 1836, Amos b. 9 Feb 1837, Isaac b. 21 Apr 1840, d. 19 Dec 1938, Burlington, KS., Ephraim P., b. Sep 1842, Margaret b.21 Apr 1845, Eli b. c.21 Apr 1845.

Source: Pension, SO 30744; Donna Younkin Logan, 12109-A Old Frederick Rd., Thurmont, MD 21788.

YOUTZ [Yountz], John. Pvt. in 36th U.S. Inf.; Capt. Samuel C. Leakin's Company at Balt. 30 Apr 1814; Capt. John Buck's Company, 31 Dec 1814 (absent at that time at Camp Woodyard); recruiting duty from 27 Jan 1815; discharged near Balt. City 30 March 1815. Enlisted at Hagerstown or Creagerstown on 20 Feb 1814 by Lt. Flecher or Ensign Sands for duration of war. At enlistment: 6 ft, dark eyes, dark hair and fair complexion, age 21, occupation laborer, b. Fred. Co., MD.

YOWLER, George. Pvt. under Capt. Samuel Dawson, 1 May - 5 Jul 1813.

YOWLER, George. Pvt. from Fredericktown under Capt. James F. Huston/Capt. Joseph Green; joined 23 Jul 1814; deserted 8 Dec 1814 returned 2 Jan 1815; discharged 10 Jan 1815: m. Oct 1818, Elizabeth Boners (b. c.1797), at Hagerstown in Oct 1818 (according to the widow in 1852) or 1829 (according to the widow in 1855), by Rev. Benjamin Kurtz. George Yowler d. Chewsville, Washington Co., MD, 8 May 1842 (according to widow in 1852) or 1843 (according to widow in 1855). Widow res. Washington Co., MD, 1852 and 1855. Acq.: 1852 - James Hurley and Maria Hurley, res. Washington Co.; 1855 - W. N. Hamm and H. H. Gaither, res. Hagerstown, MD.

Source: Bounty land claim, 55-120-76704.

YOWLER, Michael. Pvt. under Capt. Jacob Getzendanner 9 Aug - 17 Sep 1813 and 26 Jul - 21 Aug 1814. [FCml issued to Michael Yowler and Catherine Shafer on 16 Sep 1809.]

ZACHARIAS, Daniel. Capt. of a Troop of Horse, 2nd Regt., 1st Cav. Dist. In her brief compilation of *The Zacharias Family of Carroll Co. MD*, Cora Schaefffer Massey gives the fol. information: John Daniel Zacharias b. 6 Apr 1777 on farm in now Carroll Co., d. 24 Apr 1815; m. 16 Jan 1810 Susanna Sherman (b. 2 Apr 1786, d. 5 Feb 1852, dau of Brig. Gen. Conrad Sherman and Helene Schlagle Sherman of York, PA. According to Massey they had fol. children: Helen, Appolonia and Daniel.

Source: Cora Schaeffer Massey, Pen Mar, PA, The Zacharias Family of Carroll Co. MD.

ZACHARIAS, Mathias. Pvt. under Capt. John Galt, 31 Aug - 27 Oct 1814.

ZACKARY, John. Pvt. under Capt. Samuel Dawson; joined 21 Jul; deserted 26 Jul 1814.

ZEALER, Adam. Pvt. under Capt. Thomas Contee Worthington, 17 Aug - 31 Dec 1812.

ZEISO, George. See Seize.

ZILHART [Zeilert], Frederick. Enlisted 26/27 Apr 1813 at Hagerstown by Capt. Miller for 5 yrs. At enlistment: 5 ft, 7 inches, dark eyes, dark hair, dark complexion, age 27, occupation blacksmith, b. Funkstown, MD; served as ar-

THE VETERANS

tificer in 5th U.S. Inf. under Capt. R. H. Bell. On "extra duty" at Plattsburg, NY from 1 Aug 1814. Serving in det. of Ensign E. Upham at Plattsburg 31 Oct 1814.

ZIMMERMAN, George. Fifer under Capt. Turbutt, 1 Sep - 27 Oct 1814; m. 29 Dec 1831, Mary Ann Martz (b. c.1814, d. Sep 1895), in Fred. Co., by Rev Swarlt(?), of German Ref. Ch. George Zimmerman manufactured paper; d. in Fred. Co. 23 Oct 1843. Widow res. Fred. Co. 1851 and 1855. Acq.: 1855 - Charles H. Burkhart, Joseph Brown, res. Fred. Co. Mary Ann Martz was dau of Major George Martz (b. 31 Mar 1786) who m. Catherine E. Reese, dau of John Reese, farmer and miller who res. northwest of Frederick-Town.

Sources: Bounty land claim, 55-120-13895; Williams, **Hist. of Fred. Co**, p. 1592.

ZIMMERMAN, Henry. Pvt. under Capt. Denton Darby; joined 3 Aug 1814. Taken prisoner on 24 Aug 1814.

ZIMMERMAN, Valentine. Pvt. under Capt. Nicholas Turbutt, 1 Sep - 27 Oct 1814. [In the records of Luth. Ch. of Frederick is the birth of Georg Valentin, son of Johannes and Barbara Zimmerman, b. 27 Oct 1792, bapt. 5 Jul 1792.]

Source: **MD German Ch. Rcds**, v.4.

ZOLLINGER, George. Pvt. under Capt. William Knox, 26 Aug - 27 Oct 1814; b. c.1791; m. Oct 1819, Catharine Myers (b. c.1796) at Hagerstown, MD [marr. license issued in Washington Co. 21 Oct 1819], each for first time. When enrolled: 23 yrs of age, farmer, 6 ft high, black hair, grey eyes and fair complexion. Fol. discharge until 1848 George Zollinger res. Fred. Co. and then until his death he res. Cooper Co., MO; d. Cooper Co., Mo, 16 Sep 1871. Widow d. 16 Feb 1881.

[The Moravian records show George Zollinger, farmer in the mountains, son of --- and Sevilla (Machhold) Zollinger, m. Catharine Meyer, dau of --- and Catharine (Maus) Meyer. Their children - Margaret Sivilla b. 4 Sep 1820; Susanna Angelica, b. 3 Jun 1823; Lewis Augustus, b. 30 Aug 1825; Mary Catharine b. 25 Nov 1827; Anne Elizabeth b. 3 Apr 1830; Eleonora Francisca b. 27 Mar 1835; Benton George b. 30 Apr 1838.]

Acq.: 1878 - John H. Windsor, age 46; and Elenor Windsor, age 42; res. Cooper Co.; 1879 - James F. Adams, Cooper Co., MO, who officiated at the burial of George Zollinger in absence of a minister; and David B. Gibson, Boonville, Cooper Co., MO.; John H. Zollinger. Letter from Mrs. E. H. Harris, 615 West Broadway, Sedalia, MO, dated 19 Nov 1923, asking for information on her ancestor, George Zollinger of Fred. Co., MD.

Letter from Mrs. A. L. Ferguson, 109 So. 9th St., Columbia, MO. [Heading of letter: A. L. Ferguson, Druggist], dated 21 Feb 1921, asking for information regarding her grandmother, Catherine Meyers Zollinger who received a pension from war of 1812, questioning whether it came by virtue of service of her husband George Zollinger or from service of her bro. Calvin Meyers.

Sources: Bounty land claim, 50-40-44812, 55-120-57750; Pension, SO 18852, SC 13115, WO 22254, WC 20298; **Moravians of Graceham Md.**

ZUMBRUN (Zumbren), George. Pvt. under Capt. William Knox, 26 Aug - 27 Oct 1814.

ZUMBRUN, Henry. Pvt. under Capt. Philip Smith; joined 23 May 1813; deserted 9 Jul; returned 30 Jul; discharged 31 Jul 1813; b. c.1782; res. Montgomery Co., OH, 1850. Acq.: 1850 Henry Kinzy, age 69.

Source: Bounty land claim, 55-rejected-74863.

ZUMBRUN [Zumbren, Zumbrum], Jacob. Pvt. under Capt. William Knox, 26 Aug - 27 Oct 1814; b. c.1794; m(1) Margaret Carnell [Cornell] (d. Taneytown 16 Jan 1852); m(2) Sarah Claybaugh (d. c.17 Jan 1855); m(3) 8 Nov 1855 Sarah Hann (b. c.1814), by Robert W. Dunlap, pastor of Ch., Hagerstown, MD. Jacob Zumbrun res. Carroll Co., MD, 1850, 1855; d. near Taneytown 13 Sep 1868. His widow res. Taneytown, MD, 1882. Acq.: 1882 - Robert J. Jemison and Mrs. Sarah C. Martin, both res. near Graceham, Fred. Co., MD; 1883 - William Kiser, age 52 and Margaret M. Kiser, age 59, Taneytown, MD.; Daniel and Martha A. Hess of Taneytown.

Sources: Bounty land claim: 55-120-4028; Pension, WO 42485, WC 33237. In this file for unknown reasons is a release given by John Thomas Ohler to his guardian Jacob Zumbrun, in which John Thomas Ohler on 1 Aug 1853 acknowledges receipt of $241.63 as final settlement made with the orphans Court of Carroll Co on 25 Jul 1853.

APPENDIX B: ADJUTANT GENERAL PAPERS

1. List of Persons recommended to Gov. and Council for Appointments in the Frederick Regiment. July 5, 1794 by John McPherson. [This is probably the the 16th Regiment. Editor]
Town Battalion.
1st Comp. John Graham, Valentine Brother, Abner Ritchie
2d John Ritchie, Thoms. Hickson, Jacob Houser
3d George Bare, Jr., Casper Shaaff, Laurence Bringle, Jr.
4th Henry Brother, Allen Quinn, Rezin Davidge
5th Henry Garhheart (Garnheart?), Jacob Meddart, Stephen Stoner.
Country Battalion.
1st Peter Stilly, Jacob Ketzenturner, Jacob Holtz.
2d George Wedrick, Conrad Shaffer, Nicholas Holtz.
3d Jacob Baltzell, George Shaffer, Nicholas Zimmerman.
4th Arthur Fleming, Patrick McGill, Adam Freshour.
5th Wm. Beckwith Head, Tobias Butler, Jr., Alexr. Ogle.

2. 15 Oct 1794. Volunteers for a cavalry company from Taneytown area.
"We the subscribers being desirous of forming a troop of Light Dragoons in and about Taney Town in the County of Frederick do hereby severally promise and Engage to Equip ourselves as privates in the said troop on or before the first day of January next on which day we will proceed to Elect the officers we wish to command said company and we do further promise and agree to obey the orders of the officers so Elected in Every Respect as such and agreeable to the act for the regulation of the militia of the state. Witness our hands this 15th day of Octr. 1794 -John Trucks, Captn.
Thos. Gibson, First Lieutenant.
Bernard McSherry, Second Lieutenant
Joseph Little, Coronet.
David Keppart, Andrw(?) Young, Samuel Thomson, Christian Flaut, Jacob Fletcher, Adam Welsh, Francis Jimmison, David Henry, Adam Good. Harmand Raitt, John Honniwatt, Matthias Shroyer, Thos. Harris., Jacob Cress, Joseph Black, Jacob Sherman, Abm. Berier, Joseph Hughes, Jacob Troxel, Jacob Tanner, David Cooper, John Ramsey, Thos. Livers. Nathaniel Elder, John Golt, Jesse Martin, George Wolf, Henry Swope, Robert Bigham, Abm. Rouser, Michael Coskery, Henry Stimmel, Coonrade Hersh, James Curnel, John Havener, William Walker, William McCrea. Joseph McCrea, Thos. Fisher, John McCalister, Daniel Renner.
Agreed to by Messrs. D. B. & K. Commissd. the 25th 1795.

3. MILITIA FINES
"At the meeting of my company of maletia on the 28th of November 1795, at Roll call the following persons were absent to wit (each fined 50 cents) John Miller, George Shoup, John Wardeck, George Hinklie, Adam Densmore, Lewis Fout, Thomas McCarlin, Jacob Fout, Baltzer Smith, Jacob Schlyock, Peter Frans, Godig(?) Grammer, Anthony Woodward, John Marloy, Jonathen Ballet, Peter Hoff, Benjamin Ireland, John Gaston, Jacob Staley of Joseph, Elias Bruner, John Staley, Joseph Staley Jr., Thomas Weirs. Arthur Fleming, Capt."

4. Jan 10, 1798. Lt. Robert Cumming to Gov. "...that an association has been entered into by a number of respectable inhabitants of Frederick County for the purpose of forming a Troop of Volunteer Horse after inroling themselves they have proceeded to nominate their officers. I informed Brigadier General Crab of their circumstances with a request that he would be pleased to make known to your favorable approbation agreably to the Militia law: which I presume he has done. At the time I wrote General Crab the nominating of Captain only was complete since which time the three officers have been nominated. The who nomination is a follows viz. Mr. John Flemming

FREDERICK COUNTY MILITIA IN THE WAR OF 1812

Captain, Mr. Richard Winchester first Lieutenant. Mr. Daniel Renner, second and Mr. Barnhart Gilbert Cornet. Mr. Flemming has been particularly active and zealous promoting the subject. ... Inclosed you will receive the enrolment as it was delivered me by Mr. Flemming and the other Gentlemen. ..."
[Enclosed is the following]
"We whose names are under written having enrolled ourselves as horsemen in the 29th Regiment of Maryland Militia by the name of the Buckskin Troop have made choice of the following officers. John Fleming Capt., Richard Winchester 1st Lieut., Daniel Renner, 2d Lieut., Barnhart Gilbert, Cornet. Joseph Browning, Thomas Beatty, Daniel Deleplane, Solomon Barrick, Eli Phillip, William Cookerly, Jacob Shoemaker, Jeremiah Browning, John Stull, John Shank, Robert Fulton, Henry Yantis, John McGary, William Barrick, John Crum, John Huffman, Jacob Schriner, Michael Cryner, John Cookerly, Christion Crall, Michael Zimmerman, Joseph Ogle, John Schryock, Joseph Spooner, Ceceliour Head, Lewis Smith, Peter Smook, Elias Lefever, Jacob Cookerly, Abraham Andrews, George Hape, Peter Engle, John Miller, Michael Morningstar, Henry Fox, George Zimmerman, George Freise."

5. From Major Jo Swearingen to Gov. 1798 Sept. 10, Frederick Co.
"The Petition of Sundry Inhabitants of Lower Kottocton Hundred in the 28th Regiment of Militia, Gentlemen finding that in the Other Regiments in the Brigade the vacancies haveing beeing filled and finding that no order haveing been issued in the 28th Regt. we supposed to be owing to the Col. Haveing Resigned, After Viewing the critical situation of our country, and haveing a wish to be prepared in case of danger, we being destitute of officers to command our company, we haveing resigned and the other resideing out of the county, we beg leave - Gentlemen to solicit you attention to our Company and the Regiment. Also we recommend the following persons as Officers to command us, Jacob Grove, Captn.; Conrad Young of Jacob, Lieut.; George House, Ensign, they being persons of good characters resideing within the bounds of the company and who we have a desire to be commissioned.
"John House, John Lambeth, Caleb(?) House, Jacob Coleman, Peter Flook, Henry Shrayer, ...[unable to read]; Henry Burkitt, Canrode Wissman, George Bealer, David Muldore, John Mearty, Daniel Eagenbroad, Philip Hoershman, William Hardista, Jacob Metzger, Casper Young, Cunrade Falks(?), Philip Willyard, John Forgason, John Willgerd, Jacob Willyard, Voluntine Wisman, Richard House, Steven House, George Young, Jacob Cuntz, Jon. Shomel, Frederick Murry, Samuel Slifer (Flifer?), Devid Slifer (Flifer?), George Wisman, Jacob Wisman, John Fink, Solamon Fink, John Willyard son Eline (?), Jacob Reedy(?), Peter Willyard, Henry Ashaman, Philip Keefar, Peter Wisman, James Chorin, Jon. Gephard, Willam Tucker, James Castle, Cornelus Grinel, Henry Eseberger, Jacob Riser, Christean Wine."

6. Nov 18th 1799. 28th Regt.
"...That in consiquence of a resignation of the Captain belonging to their company in said regiment they proceeded on the 16th day of Nov. inst. with the consent of the Colonel to elect another in his place when to the great astonishment of nearly two thirds of the company Elias Botelar offered to fill the vacancy and a large majority of the company being over anctious to prevent his election opposed him with three candidate which so divided the intrests against him that he was elected. we thing it not necessary here to give Mr. Botelars general caracter as we believe Ather Shaff Esqr. one of your Honorable is sufficiently acquainted with it to give the necessary information on that head. ...Wm. Luckett, Pat. McGill, Elias Thrasher, Geo. Groves, James Summons, Junr, Christian Coat, George Gease, Jacob Martin, Georg

APPENDIX B: ADJUTANT GENERAL PAPERS

Lutan, William Johnson, Henry Haines(?), Jacob Harris, Samuel Batzin(?), George Fultone, Francis Warthing, David Ban..(?)_, Geo. Bargen, Valintine Bargen, Frederick Bergan, Abraham Birckhead, Benjn. Rice, Martin Worthen, Abraham Lakin, Daniel Lakin, Sam.(?) Grof, ..., Conrad Kemp, Wm. Thomas, Benj. Thrasher, Sen., Benj. Thrasher, Jun, Andrew Stage, Thomas Thrasher Junr, Eli Thrasher, Walter Tall, Solomon Vickers, Zachariah Simm.., Jacob ..., ..., James Hook..."

7. 1801 Oct 28, Frederick Co.
"We the subscribers being desirious of enroleing our selves in Select Company of Infantry Under the Command of Thomas Burk, Abraham Sandes and William Pole whom we have chosen for our officers, viz. Thomas Burk Capt., Abraham Sandes Lieut. and William Pole, Ensign., Now we the under signed do hereby pledge ourselves to and for each other and to our country that we will at anytime when cald on by the Executive of the State, come forward (to a man) Quell any insurrection or invation that shall or may be offered against the Peace and dignity of the State of Maryland, and we hold our selves bound to go out of the State on a simlar action, and we further agree and pledge our selves that we will equip our selves with such uniforms as our said officers shall direct, and that we will conform to all Rules and Regulations that may be adopted by our said officers for the policy of said Company and our Country. 12 October 1801.
[Signed] "George Prugh, Dennis Ensey, Abraham Gundy, John Winters, John Isenbarg, Jacob Keefer, David Haines, Daniel Haines, Thomas Mannahan, Wm. Malahan, James Pain, David Fishburn, Emal. Brawer Junr, David Brower, Jacob Brawer, Ludwick Greenwood, Wm. Hager, John P. Albaugh, Jacob Wampler, Joseph Poole, John Ungeefehn(?), Thomas Pole, Richard Stevenson, James(?) Meguohan(?), Jonathan West, Dorsey Barnes, John Orr..?, George Kiefer, Peter Isintiarg(?), Evan Crawford, Christn. Haas, Henry Demmil, Ja.. Staly(?), Henry Staly, Jacob Sargent, ..., Peter Sentman(?), Georg ..., John Myers, Charles Murry, Benjamin Sriver(?), Wm. Conner, Thos. West, Shadrick West, John Swigard, George Bosley, George Haynes Jur., Christian Swigard, Wm. Crawford, Thomas Tawnsend, John Murray, William Ewing, Dorsie Williamson, James Fawlan, John Malloner, John Kelley, Henery Prugh, Jacob ..eaddey, Jesse Lucas, Benjamin Myers, David ..., Joseph Cale, John Messter, Archibald Barnes, Zachariah Barnes, John Baxter, Thomas Barnes, Henry Stoufer, Aolser Conrad, ----."

8. 1802, Oct. 5, Frederick Co.
Thos. Gibson, Taney Town, to John Gwinn, Junr, Esqr,, Annapolis. Respecting Troop of Horse, Frederick Co. "...our troop shortly after you left this place held an election for the dift. officers who had or intended to Resigne, I expect mine & Mr. Truxes are Returned and I presumne Mr. Little Intends sending his by Mrs. Gwinn. Mr. Greenemeyer the coronet has died since the election took place, and of course there will be some one appointed in his stead on the next day of peraid, the Regiment to which we are attachd peraids on the sixteenth Instant which makes the company anxious that the commisions shoud be here before that time, and I know my neglecting to send for them has causd some dissatisfaction but if they can be sent on before that day all things will yet go Right, the Troop did me the honour to give myself the Captaincy, Mr. Josias Clements first Lieutenant, Mr. John Galt, second Lieutenant, the Coronet is not yet elected but will be on the next day of ...[remainder of letter has been cut out.]..."

9. 1808, June. Petition "That the Battallion to which they belong composing a part of the 13th Regiment of Maryland Militia in Frederick County is commanded by Major John S. Hall, who formerly resided within the bounds thereof but has since the date of his commission removed to

FREDERICK COUNTY MILITIA IN THE WAR OF 1812

Frederick Town where he now resides, a considerable distance from the whole of the men composing the said Battallion... That the said Major John S. Hall is much given to intoxication, in deed he is never sober scarcely if he can procure liquor enough to make him drunk, and besides he is by no means proper character to be trusted with any monies that may come into his hands, in virtue of his officers, having lately cleared out by the insolvent law, after having been confined for a length of time in the common jail of Frederick County....
[Signed] Henry Snyder, Captn Volunteer compy.; Silas Baily, Lieutenant; John Smith, first sergant; Arthur Tanzey; Jesse Wright, Ensign; Nickls. Hall, Jun.; James Wa...; Hugh Seman, second sergant; David Way; Jacob Grove; Joseph James Captn, militia; Alter Dorsey, fourth sergant volunteer company; Michael Armberger 3 sergent; George Philps; John Burckhartt; Wm. Vore; Jon Warfield, genl.; Thomas Ogle; Enos Hutton."
[Subsequently John S. Hall's commission was revoked and Joab Watters appointed.]

10. 5 June 1814. In a letter of June 5, 1814, from Lt. Col. John Ritchie to Governor and Council, Lt. Col. Ritchie gives a recapitulation of the resignations and vacancies at that point, "Town Battalion -
1st Company - David Markey, resigned.
2d Company - (under Captain Matthias E. Bartgis) - "William Baer of Henry who was commissioned as Lieut. sd. company - I believe has never taken the oaths required nor acted under his commission and I was informed by him, he did not mean to accept."
Frederick A. Heisley the Ensign in said company, has resigned.
3d Company - Bene T. Pigman, Capt. resigned; Raymond Sanderson, Lieut., resigned.
4th Company - Thomas C. Worthington, Capt., resigned.
5th Company - Stephen Steiner, Captain, promoted to Major. John M. Beatty, Lieut., has removed out of the District.
Uniform Company - Stephen Steiner, Captain of the 5th and also Captain of this company promoted, as afsd., to Major.
In the second or country Battalion.
1st Company - (under Capt. Nicholas Turbott) - James Shawhan, Ensign, has removed out of the District and commission considered vacated.
2d Company - (Commanded by Capt. Jacob Gitzendanner of Adam, who is also Capt. of a rifle company,) George Zealer, Ensign, in the District Compy., has resigned
4th Company - John Feagler, Captain, resigned.

11. FIRST FREDERICK TROOP OF CAVALRY
"Frederick Town, June 11, 1812. Daniel Hauer Junr., enclosed list of First Frederick Troop of Cavalry - tendering their services."
Daniel Hauer, Junr., Capt.
David Kemp, 1st Lieut.
Nicholas Brengle, 2nd Lieut.
Nicholas Buckey, Acting Cornet
Peter Brengle, 1st Sgt.
William Michaels, 2d Sgt.
David Eader, 3d Sgt.
John Leather of John, 4th Sgt.
Josep. L. Huhn, 1st Cpl.
Samuel Fleming, 2nd Cpl.
George Erter, 3d Cpl.
John Hauffman, 4th Cpl.

Privates:
George Baltzell
Christian Kemp
George Creager, Jr.
John Markell
Peter Fout
Henry Sinn

David Buckey
William Geisendarf
Joel Mearsh
Samuel Reynalds
Adam Schissler
Daniel Stimmel
Richard P. Thomas

Thomas Howard
Jacob Houck
Christian Getzendoner
John Leather of George
Michael Rowe

APPENDIX B: ADJUTANT GENERAL PAPERS

Peter Nicholas   Wm. Shellman   Conrad Shafer

12. No date. A List of names who are formed in a "company of malisha commanded by Capt. Evan L. Crawford, Lieut. Willis, Ensign Abraham Bail."

John Hooper	Jacob Helbydle(?)	Samuel Townson
John Lescalleech	Jacob Wyers	Henry Sheicy(?)
Jacob Frizel	Ludwick Bail	Jesse Baring
George Heltbydle	Edward Wheeler	Andrew Fectar(?)
Richard Lescallech	Charles Marfoot	John English
John Angle	Nathan Powel	Peter Bond
William McCumsay	John Wingafair	David Dell
John Greenholtz	Nicholas Randle	Georg Gaufman
Jacob Greenholtz	George Lecallert	David Holver...(?)
Peter Knight	Robert Dadds	John Franklin
John Murry	Lawrance Magers	Francis Franklin
David Evans	Elijah Richardson	Joseph Cail
Lloyd Benitt	George Yandes	George Smith
Robert Benitt	Richard Davis	John Senseney
George Young	Benjamin Stull	James Murry
Daniel Haines	Joshua West	Antony Heltbydle
John Haines, Cpl	Thomas Pole	Henry Clay
Michael Crawell	Henry Nicademus	Nicademus Sias
John Haines	Andrew Nicademus	John Milton
Emanuel Brawer	Nelson Forest	William Brawner
Wm. Walker	Reason Stevens	Elish Lindsay
Thomas Townson	John Winratt	Wm. Pearce
Michael Bartholow	Joshua Barthalow	Elijah Thomas
Jacob Landis	John Canaday	Henry Studay
Abner Praugh	William Bail	Abraham West
Conrad Kenwip	John McCann	Solomon Murry
Robert Marshall	Warner Habbs	Daniel Riley
Christopher Eckar	Antony Aranald	Adam Dell
George W. Magee	Isaac Angle	Epheriam
John Shoe	Balser Caugh	Buckingham
Frederick Winters	John Marfoot	David Engle
Jacob Caugh	Elijah Band	John Engle
David Caugh	Nathan Stam	Jacob Roop
Henry Haines	Mearad(?) Frizil	(Rooss?)
John Greenwood	Halban Harns	Benjamin Shriver
Thomas Orpit (?)	John Warfield	John Dagan
Noah Warman	John Praugh	

13. Formation of a company under Captain Evan Crawford [Apparently this company was never accepted, because of the opposition of the regimental commander to the election of Evan Crawford as captain.] "April 1812. We the undersigned ... having met last summer to choose officers to command us in our company which belongs to Major Sollers's Battalion of Frederick Co. which officer did wright for commissions for the officers which as yet has not been received..."
Signatures:

John Dagen	Henry Nusbom	Joshua Bond
Lemuel Pearce	George Hiltabydel	Jacob G.Wilcalidel
George Yandis	Henry Clay	Conrad Kenwip
Emanuel Brow,	John Hooper	(Kemp?)
Junr.	David Mackelfresh	John Shoe
Archabald Nash	John Lecalleet	Richard Lescallat
Anthony Heltbridle	Ludwick Bail	Jacob Cough
George W. Magee	Thomas Townson	John Sanseny
------	Frederick Winters	John Coomes
John Mitter	Thomas Orpit	Jacob Study

FREDERICK COUNTY MILITIA IN THE WAR OF 1812

John Orpit
Frederick High
Daniel Haynes
Michael Bartholow
John Green
Basil Buckingham
John Haines
David Caugh
J. Bartholow
Adam Dell
Laurence Magers
Samuel Townsen
John Winrat
 (Winsat?)

Peter Bond
Christopher Echar
Robert Mars ...
David Eckar
George Lescallect
Benjamin Shriver
Isaac Senseny
George Smith
Samuel Murry
John Angle
Robert Bennett
William Bail
Jacob Frizzell
David Dell

Andrew Spealman
Abraham West
George Young
John Greenwood
Peter Knight
John Greenhals
Nicholas Randle
Henry Nicademus
Andrew Nicademus
Noah Warnon
David Garlytle
Thomas Franklin
Joseph Caoshing

14. RETURN OF DRAFTS OF MAJOR JAMES, 13TH REGIMENT
"A Return of Infantry draughted from the 13th Ridgment ... agreeable to the orders of Major General Joseph Wilkison of 15 July 1812..."

From Capt. Ely
 Brasher's Comp.:
John S. Tracy
George Gray
Caleb McElfresh
Stephen Murry
James Macketee
Seth Harvy
Amos Pigeon
John B. Williams
Edward Walker
From Capt. Henry
 Snyder's Company:
James Armstrong
Thomas Gasway
John Keplinger
Nathan Macferson
Christian Snyder
Daniel Buzzard,
 Junr.
John Smith

From Capt. Basil
 Dorsey's Company:
Henry Webb
Ephraim Cain
Amos Nelson
Jacob Butcher
James Murry
Hugh Leamon
Henry Cutsail
Samuel Guyer
Peter Cartnail
Richard Clark
Joseph White
William Cain
David Fishburn
Peter Fine
From Capt. Henry
 Riggs' Company:
Isaac Scligh
Mordica Fore(?)
Jacob Keller Junr

Thomas Ratliff
Jessy Taylor
William Plummer of
 Jacob
William Yardly
Levy Thompson
Edin Hammond
Thomas Johnson
Ormond Hammon
From Capt. John H.
 Simmons' Company:
Barton Fisk
John Darnall
William Wills
Abraham Coons
Benjamin Hopper
Hilleary Williams
Robert Davison
Jacob Dioneburgh
Walter Simpson
Charles Morse
Marsh Dewvall

Submitted by Joseph James, Major, July 31, 1812. Commandant.

15. "A Muster Roll of a detachment of the Militia of the State of Maryland required to be held in readiness for actual service as the quota ordered from the 9th Brigade of Maryland Militia by the division order of the 8th May 1812. The five companies of Infantry are organized into a battallion under the command of Major Ezra Mantz."

Capt. Daniel Hauer Trooop of Cavalry:
Daniel Hauer, Jr.
David Kemp, 1st Lieut.
Nicholas Brengle, 2d Lieut.
Michael Buckey, Cornet
Peter Brengle Sgt.
William Michael, sgt.
David Eader, sgt.

John Leather of Jno., sgt.
Joseph Kuhn, cpl.
Samuel Fleming, cpl.
George Erter, cpl.
John Kaufman, cpl.
William Gisenderfer, trumpeter.

APPENDIX B: ADJUTANT GENERAL PAPERS

Privates:
Christian Kemp
George Creager, Junr
John Markell
Peter Fout
Henry Sim
David Buckey
Joel Marsh
Samuel Reynolds
Adam Shisler
Daniel Stemmell
Richard Thomas
Thomas Howard
Jacob Houck
Christian Getzendanner
John Leather of Geo
Michael Rowe
Conrad Shafer
Peter Nichols
William Shellman
George Baltzell
Henry Showy(?)
Christian Garver(?)

Captain Henry Steiner's Company of Artillerists
Henry Steiner, Capt
Tobias Haller, 1st Lieut
George Graff, 2nds Lieut
George Shade, Drummer
Jacob Fouble, fifer
John Buckey, sgt
William Jenkins, sgt
George W. Murdock, Sgt
Lewis Green, Sgt
George Carey, Cpl
William Hauser, Cpl
John Nelson, Cpl
James Scott, Cpl
Privates:
William Baer
Leonard J. Boone
George Dertzbaugh
Robert G McPherson
Philip Pyfer, Jr
Jacob Keafer
Samuel Barrick

David Boyd
Daniel Holler
John Pyfer
Thomas Rewings
Jacob Harman
George W. Evitt
Peter Ambrose
John J. Steiner
Daniel Burkhart
Michael Baer of Jno
John Brengle of Christian
Vachel Stinchecumb
Michael Heffner of Fredk
David Mantz of Peter
Thomas Scott
Samuel Smith
William Cassell
Henry Nixendorff
John D. Smith
Michael Weaver
John Schisler
Benjamin Waters

Capt. Flaut's company of riflemen: George Flaut, Capt
Abraham Blessing, Lieut
John Oyler, Ensign
John Wisman (Wibman?)
Privates:
Peter Haver
Archibald McAfee
Jacob Summers
Barney Swope
Jacob Miller
George Haver of Peter
George Stottlemyer of George
John Size
Francis Fuller
George Gaver
Jacob Lorentz
John Tombs
Philip Rough
George Main
John S.(?) Marlow
Abraham Hergert
Arthur Boteler
George Titlow
John Hilleary
Thomas West

John Arnold
John Damond
Daniel Hoover
Elias Willyard
Nathaniel Fubbs (Tubbs?)
Alexander Harbaugh
William Swaeny(?)
Jacob Yandiss
Philip Morningstar
Christian Sheely
Jacob Hammer
Peter Kimpey
John Shorb
James Morrison
Joseph Shorb
John Forney
William Yandiss
George Whitmore of Geo
William Biggs of Ben
Henry Oyler
John McDaniel
Richard Hughes
Henry Herbaugh
Andrew Willyard
Jacob Grau
Danial Sell
John Little
Michael Blessing
William Rowe
John C. Adams
William Wetzell
Ignatius Brawner
George Martin
George Rupirt
Beale Sellman
Henry Tawney
George Harman
Thomas W. Durbin
David Tawney
Samuel Haines of Jo
John Cooe, Jr
David Yingling
John Metcalf
Isac Norris
Joseph Harris of Mord
David Freeze
James Sergiant
Ulrick Switzer
Abraham Wolfe
William Strine
Daniel Rinchart(?)
John Adams
Thomas Wood

FREDERICK COUNTY MILITIA IN THE WAR OF 1812

Thomas Mumford Capt.
Worthington's Company of Infantry
Thomas C Worthington, Capt
Thomas Carlton, Lieut
Jacob Markell, Ensign
Richard W. Batter, Sgt
Humphrey Coale, Sgt
Joshua Davis, Sgt
William H. Youngman, Sgt
Hezekiah Woltz, Cpl
Henry Hower, Cpl
Jacob Hoover, Cpl
Isaac Heges, Cpl
George Fouble, Drummer
George Boyer, Fifer
Privates:
John Houng
Henry Hall
William Smith
David Shultz, Jr
Jacob Lowe
Robert Watt
George Whipp
Daniel Ely
Peter Keefer
Abraham Neff
Philip Jacobs
Isaac Wysong
Peter Doll
Christopher Yonitz
William Thomas
William A. Lloyd
Otho Woltz
Otho Wilson
David B. Devitt
Jacob Reed
Ambrose Goslin
George Doyle
Jesse Schell
John Koontz
John J. McCully
Adam Fischer
Jacob Markell
John Fritrchie
George Bruner
Casper Mantz

Joseph Ford
Henry Thomas
Joseph Johnson
Adam Zealer
William B Thompson
John Wilson
Thomas Morgan
Thomas B. Johnson
Jacob Browman
Lewis Ramspey
John Renner
George Thomas, Jr
George McClain
Marcy Brighley
Hugh Hughes
John Layman
George Whitmore
Adam Bankert
Charles Moore
Isael [Israel?] Myers.
John Shown, Jr
David Irving
George Miller
Frederick Staley of Jacob
John Hemp
Garrett Lee
John Heffner of Fredk
Joseph Fry
Daniel Holtzapple
John Boyer
Daniel Harris
Samuel Craner (Craver?)
William Ellis
George Gawultig

Capt. Hobbs's Company of Infantry:
William C. Hobbs, Capt
Elijah (?) ... and
...[one name was apparently crossed through causing the obliteration and above was written Elijah(?), both Lieut.
Samuel Green, Ensign
George Warner, Sgt
Joseph Stottlemyer, Sgt
James Hartley, Sgt

Samuel Girty, Sgt
George Koontz, Cpl
Samuel McKullen(?), Cpl
Samuel Panabaker, Cpl
Jacob Foreman, Jr., Cpl
Privates:
Samuel Garver
William Ferguson
Frededrick Main
Jacob Routzawn
John Young
John Biser
Solomon Miller
Benjamin Moser
Solomon Bradshaw(?)
John Coy
John Reinecker
Thomas Gilbert
Henry Houpt
John Willey
Jacob Koogle
Lewis Michael
Samuel Castle
John K Stottlemyer
Jacob Doub
Christian Hershman
John Doub
Stephen West
Daniel Martz
William Hobbs
John Cochran
Samuel T. Dorsey
John Clarey
John Engle
Charles Pickett
John Buxton
Walter Beavin
Ely C. Dorsey
John Hartsock
Daniel Yantis
Resin Hopkins
Otho Dorsey
Isaac Lyon
David McDaniel
Adam Myers
John Miller
Jacob Haines
David Haines
David Marsh
Joshua Franklin
Daniel Shipley
Levin Geslin
Peter Crapster
Samuel Southgate

APPENDIX B: ADJUTANT GENERAL PAPERS

Jacob Troxall
John Mooring
John Sowers
Solomon Renner
John Weddle
Gabriel Hennyman

Captn. Ogle's
company of
Infantry:
Samuel Ogle, Capt
Joseph Green,
 Lieut
Thomas Levers,
 Ensign
James Matthews,
 Drummer
Lewis Matthews,
 Fifer
Benjamin Ogle,
 Sgt
Privates: Jacob
Farner (Tarner?)
Francis Stottshour
 (Slottshour?)
George Oyster
Samuel Agnew
Samuel Hatch
Felix Smith
John Ogle
William Witherow
Frederick Loy
Mordecai Beall
Casper Cumming
Peter
 Kellenberger
Henry Baucher
Benjamin Gump
Henry Green
William Smith
John Demoth(?)
Peter Kuhn
Jonas Matthews
Erhart Hamn(?)
Philip Diel
David Jones
Robert Tupple
George Reed
David Hockersmith
Jacob Flegle
Henry Starner
William Macky
Peter Hornicker
John Kelten(??)
Jacob Young
John Irwin
Jacob Walter
Joel Wood
George Troxall of
 Jacob
George Keller

Robert Brotherton
Joseph Lynn
Thomas Wilson
James Clabaugh
Joseph Link
Jacob Shaneybrook
George Zimbran
 David Bonder
Jacob Eline
Peter Fair
Abraham Hesson
Philip Slick
John James
William Clingan
Jacob Pepple
John Slangenhoupt
Joseph Crouse
Jacob Turner
William Gibson
Alexander Davis
Elijah Currens
 (Currun?)
Samuel Echiss
Luke Davis
William Lindsey
John Dugan
Jacob
 Slangenhoupt

Capt. McGee's
Compay of
Infantry:
George W
 McGee, Capt
Miles Mitten,
 Lieut
Nimrod Firzzle,
 Ensign
John Winters,
 Drummer
John Yingling of
 Jacob, Fifer
Jacob Shaeffer,
 Sgt
Henry Crumrine,
 Sgt
Peter Bayer, Sgt
John Funson, Sgt
Peter Boring, Cpl
John Crout, Cpl
Henry Klink, Cpl
Jacob Earhart,
 Cpl
Privates:
James Head
David Brower
David Wampler
William Carter
John Craul
George Colegate
Abraham Kurtz

Jacob Snouffer
Jacob Casner
Peter Hawk
Henry Hawk
John Brown
Michael
 Linganfelter
John Baumgartner
Jacob Humbert
Abraham Kine
Peter Leppo
Danuel Yeiser
Peter Bixler
Jacob Miller
George Rumler
Joseph Matthias
John Flickinger
George Rinedollar
David Leister
John Jones
Samuel Long of
 Jacob
Andrew Engle
Abraham Curtz
Abraham Appler
Jacob Yingling
Abraham Fogle
Herbert Smith
Michael Garver
George Heichew
Peter Myers
Abraham Derr
Thomas Boyer
Benjamin Ogbum
Dan Durbin
Joshua Smith
John Lutz
Nathaniel Weeber
Nicholas Corbin
William Pearce
Francis Franklin
Elisha Lindsey
Henry Willis
Jacob Roope
Jacob Landiss
George Lescolade
Elijah Thomas
Andrew Speelman
Evan Crawford

Capt. Dawson's
Company of
Infantry
Samuel Dawson,
 Capt
John S. Brownley,
 Lieut
John Simmonds,
 Ensign
David Furney,
 Drummer

FREDERICK COUNTY MILITIA IN THE WAR OF 1812

Abraham Holtzapple, Fifer
Perry Herbert, Sgt
Richard Scaggs, Sgt
Dewault Young, Sgt
Levin West, Sgt
George Stump, Cpl
Jacob Blessing, Cpl
James Berry, Cpl
John Holler, Cpl
Privates:
Jordan Stewart
Richard Leonard
George B. Walker
William Smith
Ignatius Briggs
John Sultzer
Hezekiah Trundle
Thomas Noland
Nathan Crum

John Cain
Peter Tritt
Andrew Hughes
Izrael Mills
Stoffel Long
Peter Martin
Henry Crum
Ralph Nicholas
Henry Groce
Richard Padget
Simon Jenkins
John Jones
Fielder Turton
John Easterday
Prewsley Warfield
Thomas Bell
George Wissinger
George Herring
Francis King
Jacob Richards
Valentine Hide
Jacob Thomas
George Youtsey
John Richards
Richard Templin

Christian Niswanger
George Motter
Daniel Routzawn
Jacob Windpigler
George Backenbaugh
John House
David Mullendore
Richard Jones
Peter Ganer (Gaver, Gauer?)
James Mayhue
Jacob Biser
Henry Rumspark
David Kellar
Henry Smeltzer
Henry Beeckely
John Goddard
George Wackter
Jacob Jackson
Peter Shank
John Whilhoup

Field and Staff Officers:
Major Ezra Mantz
Adjutant John Rigney
Paymaster William Tyler
Quarter Master John Markle
Surgeon John Fischer

"The foregoing muster roll contains a true return of the detachment of militia required from the 9th Brigade by the division order of the 8th May 1812. which detachment is organized into companies and Battallion and the field and other officers thereto designated as required by the Division Order of the 16th Sepr. 1812. By order of Brigadier General. Joseph Swearingen.
Richard Brooke, Inspector of the 9th Brigade M.M. Oct 5 1812. "

APPENDIX C: THE COMMISSION BOOKS

During the War of 1812 the brigade and regimental staffs pertaining to Frederick County were manned by the following men. (Dates of appointment to the position are given, followed frequently by reasons for leaving the position.)[1]

7th Brigade - Robert Cummings, Brigadier General, Nov 7 1801; Henry Barrick, Dec 28 1812
Inspector - Leonard Watkins, Oct 15, 1801
Aid de Camp - James Boyle, Aug 5 1814 [In the Nov 20 1813 issue of --- was announced that James Johnson, was appointed Aid de Camp to Brig. General of the 7th Brigade of Md. Militia - Henry Barrick, Brig. Gen. 7th Brigade]

13th Regiment - Lieutenant Colonel - Philip Mackelfresh, Sep 16 1797
Major - Joal Waters, June 28 1808
Major - Joseph Jones, Apr 4 1812
Adjutant - William Hall, Oct 1807, resigned; John James Jr, Mar 5 1813
Quartermaster - Henry Wood, Oct 3 1807, resigned; Henry McElfresh, May 31 1813, resigned; Upton Wagers, Sep 10 1814
Paymaster - Joel Waters, 24 Oct 1808; removed on board (?); John Cook, March 11 1811; Promoted Otho Sprigg, Jun 26 1812
Surgeon - Bett Brashear, Jun 26 1812; Warner Hobb, May 31 1813
Surgeon's Mate - none

28th Regiment - Lieutenant Colonel - Henry Stembel, Jan 6 1812
Major - Peter Cobbretz, Apr 30 1812
Major - Jacob Grove, Jan 6 1812
Adjutant - John Shafer, May 2 1808, resigned; John Stembel, Apr 23 1813, moved away
Quartermaster - Frederick Stemble, Jr, Jan 5 1812
Paymaster - Jonathan Levy, Apr 18 1808 dead
Surgeon - William Hillery, 15 Oct 1801
Surgeon's Mate - Lewis Creager, Apr 18 1808 removed; Arthur Nelson, Sep 5 1812, resigned; Lewis Creager, Sep 13 1814

29th Regiment - Lieutenant Colonel - Henry Barrick, Apr 3 1802; Jacob Cramer, Dec 28 1812
Major - Middleton Smith, Mar 14 1804
Major - Jacob Cramer, Oct 5 1801; William Bookerly, Apr 27 1813
Adjutant - Joseph Hedges, 20 Sep 1802
Quartermaster - William More, Sep 12 1807

FREDERICK COUNTY MILITIA IN THE WAR OF 1812

Paymaster - Sabastian Graff, Nov 5 1801
Surgeon - Henry Baker, 15 May 1800, resigned; Samuel Johnson, Aug 22 1812
Surgeon's Mate - None

9th Brigade
[Names of staff not available, except for Richard Brooke. Ed.]
Richard Brooke, Inspector, 9th Brigade.

16th Regiment - Lieutenant Colonel - John Ritchie, Apr 30 1812; Stephen Steiner, Feb 1 1814
Major (1st Battalion, Town Battalion) - Ezra Martz Apr 30 1812
Major (2nd Battalion, Country Battalion) - Jacob Firestone, Jun 6 1812
Adjutant - Henry R. Warfield, Sep 16 1799, resigned; James F. Huston, Jun 26 1812, resigned; John Rigney, July 20 1812
Quartermaster - Richard Brook, Oct 13 1807
Brigade Major - John Markle, Aug 23 1812
Surgeon - John Fisher, Apr 15 1795, resigned; John Baltzell, Feb 14, 1815.
Surgeon's Mate - John Baltzell, Sep 3 1799, promoted; Jack Baer, Feb 14 1815

20th Regiment - Lieutenant Colonel - John Wampler, Mar 4 1808
Major - Sobret Sollers, Apr 4 1808
Major - Joshua Stevenson, Oct 17 1797
Adjutant - Benjamin Yingling, Dec 4 1810,, resigned; John Matthias, Jul 8 1813, resigned; Benjamin Yingling, Aug 1 1814
Quartermaster - John Fisher, May 2 1808
Paymaster - Richard Cockey, Apr 15 1811, resigned; Jacob Matthias, June 1 1813
Surgeon - George Colegate, Dec 2 1809, resigned; Robert Dods, June 12 1812
Surgeon's Mate - George Colegate, Nov 15 18098

47th Regiment - Lieutenant Colonel - John Huston, Apr 30 1812
Major - John Huston, Jul 8, 1808; Geo. M. Eicleberger, Jun 5 1812
Major - John Anstee, Dec 26 1810; Hugh Shaw, Jul 6 1812
Adjutant - William Knox, June 23 1808 promoted; James Moore, Apr 21 1814
Quartermaster - Peter Troxel of Peter, Jan 8 1808, resigned; Lewis Motter, Oct 31 1812
Paymaster John (es)? Gibbeny, Jan 8 1808

APPENDIX C: THE COMMISSION BOOKS

Surgeon - Robert L. Annon, Jan 8 1808, resigned; Richard Wells, Oct 31 1812 removed; Daniel M. Moore, Feb 1814
Surgeon's Mate - Richard Wells, Jan 8 1808 promoted.

1st Regimental Cavalry District was comprised of Washington and Frederick Counties.
On the staff were the following officers:

Lieutenant Colonel - Frisby Tilghman, Feb 13 1812; Henry Kemp, May 8 1812, resigned Dec 20 1814.
Major [1st Regiment, Washington Co.] Otho H. Williams (1784-1852), Feb 13 1812
Major [2nd Regiment, Frederick Co.] - Henry Kemp, Feb 13 1812; Daniel Hanes, Jr., May 13 1813
Adjutant - Thomas B. Hall, May 8 1812
Quartermaster - Henry Strause; Isaac Shriver, Apr 23 1813
Paymaster Jno. Hanson Thomas, Jul 14 1814
Surgeon - Wm. Hammond, May 8 1812. [An ad appeared in the Hagerstown Week Advertiser, of 2 Nov 1814, stating that "Dr. Hammond informs the public that he has returned from his Military tour, and is again ready to attend those who may require his professional services."]
Surgeon's Mate -

APPENDIX D: MUSTER ROLLS OF ACTIVE UNITS

During the course of the war it frequently became necessary to reorganize and consolidate units. Many companies arrived at their destination under strength and were merged with other companies. Such consolidations created a surplus of officers who were carried as supernumerary and dismissed. The several regiments of Frederick County came to be reorganized with the regiments of Washington and Allegany Counties into the First, Second and Third Regiments, notwithstanding the existance of regiments in other parts of the State also designated as First, Second and Third.

Field and Staff of the First Regiment.
The service covered the period, 14 October 1814 through 10 January 1815. On the staff were the following officers: Regimental commander, John Ragan, Col., resident of Hagerstown; Stephen Steiner, Lt. Col., Fredericktown;
John Blackford, Major of the 1st Battalion;
Benjamin G. Cole, Major of the 2nd Battalion;
Charles Christian Fechtig, Adj, joined on 10 Nov;
Nathan Cromwell, Adj, discharged on 9 Nov 1814;
William Hillery, Surgeon, discharged on 11 Jan 1815, resident of Fredericktown;
George W. Boerstler, Paymaster, resident of Hagerstown;
John Thomas, Quartermaster, joined 8 Dec, resident of Baltimore;
John Markall, Quartermaster, discharged 7 Dec 1814, resident of Fredericktown;
Arthur Nelson, Surgeon's Mate, resident of Fredericktown;
Daniel Fitzhugh, Surgeon's Mate, resident of Hagerstown;
Joab Dagett, Hospital Steward(?), joined 23 Dec;
Adam Fisher, Quartermaster Sergeant, discharged in Dec 1814, resident of Fredericktown;
William Fisher, Quartermaster Sergeant, joined 7 Dec, resident of Fredericktown;
William Harvey, Sergeant Major, resident of Hagerstown;
George Shade, Drum Major, resident of Hagerstown;
Fredrick Hinsill, Fife Major, resident of Hagerstown;
Sam, negro, servant to Col. Ragan, resident of Hagerstown;
Charles, negro, servant to Lt. Col., resident of Fredericktown;
Ned, negro, servant to Major Blackford, resident of Hagerstown;
Daniel, negro, servant to Major Cole, resident of Hagerstown;
Tom, negro, servant to Dr. Nelson, resident of Fredericktown;
Robert, negro, servant to Fitzhugh, resident of Hagerstown.

All were discharged at Annapolis except Nathan Cromwell at Baltimore on 9 Oct 1814; John Markill who left the service on 7 Dec at Baltimore; Adam Fisher who left the service on 6 Dec 1814 at Baltimore; Charles Christian Fechtig.

The following dates of promotion appearing in the muster roll used for pay purposes, do not agree with the book of commissions found in the Maryland Adjutant General file. Perhaps these are dates of appointment and promotion within the service of the United States.
Charles Christian Fechtig was appointed adjutant on 10 Nov. William Fisher was appointed Quartermaster on 7 Dec.
John Ragan was appointed Colonel on 21 Jul; promoted from Lt. Col. on 25 Aug 1814.
Stephen Steiner Lt. Col. 20 Jul promoted from Major on 25 Aug
John Blackford 1 Major 21 July
Benjamin G. Cole 2 Major, 20 Jul, promoted from Captain 25 Aug 1814.

APPENDIX D: MUSTER ROLLS OF THE ACTIVE UNITS

Nathan Cromwell, adjutant 21 Jul
John Markall, Quartermaster, 20 Jul
George W. Boerstler, 1 Lt. and Paymaster 24 Aug
William Hilleary, Surgeon 21 Jul
Arthur Nelson, Surgeon's Mate 21 Jul
Daniel Fitzhugh, Surgeon's Mate 23 Jul
Christian Baker, Sergeant Major, 21 Jul
Adam Fischer, Quartermaster Sergeant, 21 Jul.
William Buttler servant to Col. Ragan 21 Jul
Charles 20 Jul to Lieut Col. Steiner
Edward Cook 21 Jul, servant to Major Blackford
John on 21 Jul to Dr. Hilleary
Daniel 21 Jul to Major Cole
John Carnes 20 Jul, Quartermaster Markall
Robert Creek 23 Jul to Dr. Fitzhugh
John 21 Jul to Adj. Cromwell
Dr. Hilleary's servant mustered up to 19 Sep 1814, since then sick absent.

Field and Staff of the Third Regiment. All members were from Frederick Co. except John Reynolds who resided in Washington Co. The dates shown are the dates when the members began their duty.
Henry Stembel, lt. col., 25 Aug
John Reynolds, 1st major, 20 Aug, commanding the 1st Battalion
George M. Eichelberger, 2nd major, 1 Sep, commanding the 2nd Battalion

Benjamin Jones, 1st lt., adjutant, 14 Sep
Leonard J. M. Littlejohn, 1st lt., paymaster, 25 Aug
Frederick A. Schley, 1st lt., quartermaster, 25 Aug
Jacob Baer, surgeon, 25 Aug
Michael Baer, surgeon's mate, 1 Sep
William Bantz, surgeon's mate, 4 Sep
Robert McCleery, sgt. major, 25 Aug
Caspar Shaffner, quartermaster, 25 Aug

Servants of the 3rd Regimental Staff -
Jack, 25 Aug servant to Lt. Col. Stembel
Watt, 25 Aug servant to Lt. Col. Stembel,
Philip, 25 Aug servant to Major Reynolds
Charles, 25 Aug servant to Major Eichelberger
Matilda, 26 Sep servant to Adjutant Jones
Jacob, 26 Sep servant to Quartermaster Schley
Mentor, 26 Sep servant to Surgeon Baer
Mary, 26 Sep servant to surgeon's mates, Bantz and Baer

The company of Captain Thomas Contee Worthington was one of the first to serve. Worthington's company was stationed at Fort Severn under the command of Lieutenant Colonel Jacob Small. Members of Worthington's company served at intervals betweeen 17 Aug and 31 Dec 1812.
Thomas Contee Worthington, capt.
Thomas Carleton, lt., promoted to quartermaster
Jacob Markell, ens.
John J. McCalley, 1st sgt.
Hezekiah Wooltz, 2nd sgt.
Jesse Schell, 3rd sgt., reduced 22 Sep, 4th cpl. 13 Dec, 3rd cpl. 19 Dec
Henry Hauer, absent on duty, sick
Richard Butler, 1st cpl., reduced to private 22 Sep
Cary Cyrus, 2nd cpl., 4th sgt. 22 Sep

FREDERICK COUNTY MILITIA IN THE WAR OF 1812

Ent, John, 3rd cpl., reinstated 1st cpl 1 Oct, enlisted 3 Dec
Daniel Harris, 4th cpl., discharged Henry Biershenk, fifer
Privates:
Atkins, Charles of William
Atkins, James
Byer/Boyer, George, 4th cpl. 22 Sep, died 13 Dec
Brown, Francis, sick
Boyer, John, deserted 12 Oct
Cole, Humphrey
Carter, Joseph, deserted 5 Sep
Clarke, Hugh
Craver, Clements, deserted 3 Sep
Crew, William, joined 16 Oct as substitute for Wm. B. Thompson
Dick, Christian, deserted 5 Sep
Davis, Joshua, did not muster
Elder, Charles, 4th cpl. 19 Dec
Frushour, Jacob, 1st cpl. 9 Sep
Fine, John, deserted 10 Sep
Fischer, Adam
Ford, Joseph, on furlough
Felty, Jacob F., enlisted 12 Nov
Fauble, George, deserted 27 Dec, absent without leave
Ghoslin, Ambrose, did not muster
Gadultig/Gadultick, George, did not muster
Harman, David
Hanipin/Hanifer, John, enlisted 9 Nov
Hughes, Hugh
Hooffman/Huffman, John
Hummell, John
Heffner, Jacob, furloughed
Howard, Thomas
Howard, Joseph, substitute for Jacob Hoover, died 26 Dec
Jay/Gray, William, discharged
Johnson, Joseph, did not muster
Irving, David, did not muster
Jacobs, Philip
Kolb, John F.
Kemp, John
Koontz, John, did not muster
Lowe, Jacob
Layman, John
Loyd, William A., did not muster
Lee, Garrett, did not muster
Moore, Charles
Miller, George, discharged for inability
Morgan, Thomas W., appt'd quartermaster sgt., 3rd cpl. 4 Dec
Plester, Stephen
Reid, James, appt'd 2nd cpl. 22 Sep
Ramsburg, Lewis, deserted 29 Aug Lewis
Riner, William, sick, furloughed, deserted 21 Dec
Row, John
Smith, Isaac, deserted 18 Oct
Smith, William, 3rd cpl. 22 Sep
Schultz, David
Shawn/Sohwen, John, did not muster, substitute for Wm. Crew
Tschudy, Martin
Thompson, William B., did not muster
Watt, Robert
Wiest/West, John
Winpigler/Windpigler, George, deserted 29 Aug
Wright, James, deserted 18 Oct
Wooltz, Otho
Wilson, Otho, did not muster
Wilson, John, did not muster
Young, John, absent without leave
Yantis, Christian
Youngman, William H.
Zealer, Adam
Smith, Robert, servant
Frost, Robert, servant
Roberts, Benjamin, servant

Captain George Flautt's company of riflemen was called up on 29 April 1813 and placed in the service of the United States. Many of the men came from the Emmittsburg area. They served as a detachment under the command of Lieut. Col. William C. Miller of Cecil County at Baltimore. The regiment was sometime referenced as the First Regiment. Several veterans said they stood guard at Ft. McHenry for about 3 weeks. They were discharged on 29 June 1813.

George Flautt, Capt.
Abraham Blessing, Lieut.
John Eylor, Ensign
George Mytinger, Sgt.(1)
Archable Jackson, Sgt.(2)
Daniel Hoover, Sgt.
John Little, Sgt.
Elixander Harbaugh, Sgt.

APPENDIX D: MUSTER ROLLS OF THE ACTIVE UNITS

Elijah Curence, Cpl.
Michael Burk, Cpl.

William Pope, Cpl.
Richard Hughes, Cpl.

Privates:
John Arnold(3)
John C. Adams(4)
James Blanchford
Peter Boham
Jacob Blessing
John Burkhart
Mathew Call
George Creak(5)
James Cuningham
John Downey
Henry Eylor
Joseph Ebbert
George Erhart
Nathaniel Fips
William Gladhill(6)

Thomas Gladhill(7)
John Hiteshew
Patrick Hughes
John Hines(8)
John Hauker
William Hornbey(9)
Joseph Kinkade
Baltzer Loud(10)
John Long(11)
John Myerheffer(12)
Jacob Miller
John McDaniel
Clemmen Peers
Daniel Rinhart
Joseph Rutter

Peter Rimpey
Nathan Size
Beal Selman
James Sargent
John Shorb
George Stottlemyer
George Stouffer
John Shockney
William Sweeney
William Thomas
David Wood
Jacob Walter
William Wettzel
Jacob Winters
Jacob Yantis

1. Appt'd sgt. major 8 June 1813.
2. Appt'd sgt. major 8 June 1813.
3. Deserted 15 May 1813.
4. Deceased 11 May 1813.
5. Deceased 30 May 1813.
6. Enlisted 6 June 1813.
7. Enlisted 15 June 1813.
8. Enlisted 6 May 1813.
9. Enlisted 6 May 1813.
10. Enlisted 11 June 1813.
11. Enlisted 8 June 1813.
12. Enlisted 14 June 1813.

In response to the threat on Baltimore Captain Henry Steiner's artillery company was called into service. The company was formed in Fredericktown on 1 May 1813. Seven days later they left for Baltimore where they were placed in the "service of the United States." This unit served from 28 April through 29 June 1813. They returned home, having received praise for their conduct.

Henry Steiner, capt.
Tobias Holler, 1st lt.
George Graff, 2nd lt.
John Buckey, sgt.
William Jenkins, sgt.
George W. Murdock, sgt..
William Hauser, sgt., promoted from cpl. 16 May

John Nelson, cpl., promoted 16 May from private
John Brengle, cpl., promoted 16 May from private
George Dertzback, cpl., promoted 16 May from private
David Mantz, cpl.
Jacob Fauble, musician
George Slade, musician

Privates:
Ambrose, Peter
Baer, Michael
Baer, William
Barrick, Samuel
Boyd, David
Burkhart, Daniel
Cossell, William

Dean, Thomas
Evitt, George W.
Fick, Daniel
Harman, Jacob
Hauer, John H.
Heffner, Michael
Holter, Daniel

Kieffer, Jacob
McPherson, Robert G., 4 June assistant aid and private... Brig. Gen. Miller.
Newins, Thomas

FREDERICK COUNTY MILITIA IN THE WAR OF 1812

Nixdorff, Henry
Pyfer, Philip

Pyfer, John
Schissler, John

Steiner, John T.
Weaver, Michael

This company served 1 May - 5 July 1813 in the 2nd Regiment under Lieut. Col. Richard K. Heath at Baltimore.

Samuel Dawson, capt.
Jacob Nicholls, 1st lt.
Mat. E. Bartgis, 2nd lt.
Otho Woltz, 3rd lt.
Nimrod Frizell, ens.
Geo. Titlow, 1st sgt., promoted to sgt. major 8 May
Adam Fischer, 1st sgt.
Ezra Schell, sgt.
Geo. Schaffner, sgt.

Charles P. Grace, sgt., deserted 25 June
Perry Herbert, cpl.
Geo. Dorff, cpl.
John Scnyder, cpl.
Frederick Wigle, cpl.
John Suitzer, drummer
Henry Varlee, fifer, deserted 28 June

Privates:
Alexander, Jacob
Alexander, Henry
Alsop, Joseph, deserted 5 June, returned 25 June
Bennett, John
Beall, Thomas
Bradshaw, Solomon
Briggs, Asa
Craver, Clem.
Chaney, Charles J.
Chew, Wm.
Cr..., Nathan
Carlin, Cornelius
Calhoon, Robert L.
Collins, Elijah
Delashmutt, Sampson
Delashmutt, Nelson
Furgison, Wm.
Frushour, Adam
Gaver, Peter
Holtzman, John
Herring, Jacob
Hall, Joshua

Horkinson, Norris
Hide, Adam
Jones, John W.
Jones, Richard
Jinkins, Simon
Leaser, Peter
Leonard, Richard
Lowman, John
Miller, John
Moser, John, joined 5 May
Martin, Peter, joined 17 May
Michael, Lewis
McMahan, Jerry
Murphy, Thomas
Mobley, John
Mahue, James, deserted 9 June
McGinniss, Henry
Mills, Ezra
Mosburgh, Daniel
Miller, Martin
Miller, Leonard
McDavitt, Wm.
McMullin, John

Mosburgh, Abm.
Musz, Michael
Nicholls, Raphael
Padgett, John, deserted 3 June, returned 12 June, enlisted 28
Peacock, Jacob
Poole, Jacob
Richards, John
Reed, John
Stottlemyer, David
Stottlemyer, John
Slagle, Jacob, deserted 16 June
Snowdagle, George
Stamp, George
Smith, William
Somers, John
Walker, Geo. B.
Whettle, John
Yowler, Geo.
Young, Devault, deserted 5 June, returned 25 June

Captain Samuel Ogle's company, from the Fredericktown and Emmittsburgh area was called up on 1 May 1813 and marched to Baltimore and joined the new formed 2nd Regiment under Lieut. Col. Richard K. Heath. Private Benjamin Gump said the company was stationed at the "Old Orchard." They were discharged on 5 July. Some said they were discharged at Spring Gardens in Baltimore; some said the place of discharge was Federal Hill; others recalled they had been dismissed at the Patapsco Encampment near the city of Baltimore.

Samuel Ogle, capt.
Elijah Bond, 1st lt.
Joseph Green, 2nd lt.
Samuel Green, 3rd lt.
Ormond F. Butler, 3rd lt., transferred to Capt. Mathew's company, 15 June

Thomas Livers, ens, reported himself at hdqtrs 4 June
Samuel Hatch, 1st sgt
Samuel Agnew, 2nd sgt.
Robert Tacwell/Tarwell/Taxwell, 3rd sgt.
Benjamin McHenry, 4th sgt

APPENDIX D: MUSTER ROLLS OF THE ACTIVE UNITS

John Irvine, 5th sgt., promoted from cpl. to 5th sgt. 1 June
Joel Wood, 1st cpl.
Thomas Tric, 2nd cpl.
Felix Smith, 3rd cpl.
Peter Eckis, 4th cpl., promoted to 4th cpl. 1 June
Silas ..., 5th cpl., promoted to 5th cpl. 1 June
John Winters, drummer

Privates:
Andrews, Adam, deserted 8 June
Alcot, Joel
Andrew, Herbert
Boher, Henry, deserted 25 May
Bennet, David
Baroll, Lewis
Bayer, Abraham
Brooner, John
Boring, Peter
Boring, Zachariah
Border, David
Barnover, David
Crouse, Joseph
Cain, Jacob, enlisted 6 June
Clineferburck, Cornelius
Crumrine, Henry
Carbin, Nicholas
Crout, John
Cassner, John
Cassner, Jacob
Crouse, John
Carter, William
Davis, Alexander
Demuth, John
Dailey, Archibald
Eckis, Samuel
England, Andrew
Fogle, Abraham
Franklin, Frencis, deserted 27 June
Fitzpatrick, John, deserted 22 May
Foreman, Jacob
Gump, Benjamin
Girty, Samuel
Grey, Zachariah
Goodland, Thomas
Hanicker, Peter
Hoover, George
Heater, William
Hockinsmith, David
Hichew, George
James, John
Joners, David, deserted 25 May
Johnson, Thomas
Johns, Thomas
Kitting, John, deserted 2 June
Knaff, John
Lynn, Joseph
Liday, Jacob
Leppo, Petter
Lavarett, Philip, enlisted 17 June
Lavorett, Michael
Lingenfelter, Michael
Lang, Samuel
Logan, John, deserted 26 May
Mackey, William
McGinis, Thomas
McPherson, William, enlisted 2 June
Murphy, Thomas
Mort, George
Millen, Jacob
McCoy, Samuel
Noel, Blazon
Odonald, John
Oler, Peter, discharged 27 May
Parr, Henry
Poole, Henry M.
Peterman, John
Pain, James
Pennybaker, Samuel, enlisted 7 June
Purdy, Henry, deserted and enlisted 16 June
Routson, John
Reed, Geo.
Rubert, Jacob
Ridingen, Peter
Reed, Philip
Slaugenhept, John, deserted 2 June
Slothoun, Francis
Shaneybrook, Jacob
Shafer, Frederick
Shiply, Elias, deserted 4 June
Shiply, Samuel
Trexler, Peter
Tanner, Jacob
Troxell, Jacob
Wright, John, deserted 26 June
Wright, John of David
Webb, John, enlisted 15 June
Yonils, Christian
Young, Jacob
Yeiser, Daniel

Captain Smith's Company - During the period, 23 through 29 May, 1813, a company of milita was drafted from the Woodsboro area [about 83 members] and formed under Captain Philip Smith. They were ordered into service by Brigadier General H. Barrick. When they reached Annapolis they were placed under the command of Col. Gassaway Watkins who was in charge of the Annapolis Harbor. The company was discharged verbally around 8 September 1813 at the State House.

During the period the company was active there were 31 desertions; several others returned before the company was discharged. On 5 June 1813 rewards were offered for "Christian Geary, living near Christian Harman's, south mountain, draughted in Captain Willhide's rifle company, 29th regiment Md. militia, aged about 23 yrs, 5 ft 6-7 inches, had on long blue coat, linen pantaloons and white hat; and

FREDERICK COUNTY MILITIA IN THE WAR OF 1812

Thomas Gasaway, aged 28 yrs, 5 ft 8-9 inch, living about 4-5 miles from New Market near Reel's mill on Bush creek; and Nathan Vanpherson living in New Market, aged about 23 yrs, 5 ft 7-8 inch, had on blue chambray cotton coat, black-corded pantaloons and took with him one blue cloth coat. The two latter persons are from the extra battalion, 7th brigade, Md. militia - Philip Smith, Capt Commandt., 3rd company Md. Militia, stationed at Fort Severn, Annapolis Harbor."

Philip Smith, capt.
Joseph Wood, 1st lt.
George Riner, 2nd lt.
Daniel Duvall, ens.
Joseph Smith, sgt.
Frederick Keller, sgt.

John Smith, sgt.
Jacob Keller, cpl.
Richard Clark, cpl.
John Martin, cpl.
Jacob Grimes, musician
Samuel Smith, musician

Privates:
Armstrong, James
Barnerd, Hezekiah
Burkard, Jacob
Williams, John B.,
  deserted 19 June.
Bussard, Daniel,
  deserted 29 June
Clants, Charles
Cain, Thomas
Condon, Thomas
Carr, Thomas
Curry, James,
  deserted 15 Aug,
  returned 26 Aug
Campbell, John
Darnell, Benedick,
  deserted 20 July
Dronenburgh,
  Jacob, deserted
  18 June
Earnst, Abraham
Eader, William
Eyler, Henry,
  deserted 14 June,
  returned 25 June
Eby, Samuel,
  deserted 12 June
Fine, Peter,
  deserted 14 June,
  returned 2 July
Filler, Henry
Gearey,
  Christopher,
  deserted
Green, George,
  deserted 29 June,
  returned 30 June,
  deserted 9 Aug
Gaither, Lott,
  enlisted 29 June
Gillen, William
Gassaway, Thomas,
  deserted 18 June

Gross, John,
  deserted 29 June,
  returned 30 June
Hopper, Benjamin,
  deserted 18
  July, returned 19
  July, sick leave
  in Aug/Sep
Hohn, Daniel,
  deserted 17 July,
  returned 19 July
Johnson, Joseph,
  deserted 26 Aug,
  returned 14
James, Amos
Johnson, Thomas
Koch, John
Kinny, William,
  deserted 4 July,
  deserted 30 July
Keplinger, John
Lyday, John
Low, Jacob,
  deserted 27 Aug
McDaniel, Jacob,
  deserted 27 Aug
Miller, George
Mort, William,
  deserted 18 June,
  found 4 Aug
Magers, William,
  deserted 6 Aug
Miller, Frederick,
  enlisted 10 July
Mathias, Griff
Pool, Cornelius
Priestman, George
Ryan, James
Smith, Frederick,
  deserted 12 June
Sticher, George
Sponseller,
  William
Smith, Solomon

Steel, Daniel,
  deserted 29 June,
  returned 30 June,
  deserted 6 Aug
Snook, Henry
Smith, Samuel
Shoemaker,
  Nicholas,
  deserted 4 July
Shaffner, Jacob,
  deserted 23 June,
  confined
Stewart, William
Slice, Michael,
  deserted 18 June
Schleichk, Isaac
Steel, Joseph,
  deserted 23 Aug
Sergeant, John
Thomas, Benjamin
Tanner, James,
  deserted 29 June
Tallhelm, Peter
Tier, John,
  deserted 7 June
Thomas, Benjamin
Taylor, Jesse
Vanpherson,
  Nathaniel
Wickham, Andrew,
  deserted 19 June
Wickham, Jacob
Willhite, George
White, Joseph
Zumbrun, Henry,
  deserted 9 July
  and returned 30
  July
Willhide, Jacob,
  deserted 19 June
Sargent, Jacob,
  deserted 23 Aug

APPENDIX D: MUSTER ROLLS OF THE ACTIVE UNITS

Captain Jacob Getzendanner's rifle company, called variously as the First Company, Washingtonian Rifle Greens, or Washingtonian Green Volunteers was attached to the 16th Regiment of Maryland Militia. The company drilled at "Dean's old field," and at "John Getzendanner's lower meadow spring" - sometimes in "full uniform with arms and twenty rounds of blank cartridges." They were called into active service with a notice appearing in the Frederick Herald on 31 Jul 1813 and left for Annapolis around 9 August 1813 with a total of about 44 men. On Sept. 17, 1813, Capt. Getzendanner's company of Washington Rifle Greens, returned to Frederick from Annapolis, the British fleet having nearly all left the Chesapeake Bay. They announced their arrival in Frederick by firing a volley.

Jacob Getzendanner, Capt.
John A. Dean, 1st lt.
John Hildebrand, 2nd lt.
Christian Greenwald, 1st sgt.
Jacob Bankard, 2nd sgt.
Jacob Deshner, 3rd sgt.

Adam Getzendanner, 4th sgt.
James Dean, 1st cpl.
Robert Dean, 2nd cpl.
William Albert, 3rd cpl.
Frederick Kline, 4th cpl.

Privates:
Atkins, Charles
Klink, John
Getzendanner
  Solomon, musician
Geltz John,
  musician
Privates:
Heffner, Lawrence
Engle, Frederick
..., ...
Herman, John
Aubert, Jacob
Bready, John

Mosburg, John
Woodward,
  Nathaniel
Widrick, John
Bankard, John
Staly, Moses
Parker, Samuel
Musser, John
Carlin, Cornelius
Moland, Edward
..., ...
Lape, Samuel
Cursman, Christian
May, Benjamin

Yowler, Michael
Heffner, Jacob
Hughs, Hugh
Sticher, Peter
Riffle, John
Haglen, Isaac
Ramer, John, 6 -
  12 Sep
Getz, Henry, 6 -
  12 Sep
Sholl, Christian
Harry, Negro
  servant, 17 Aug -
  15 Sep

Captain Marker's Company - On Monday evening, the 16th of August, 1813, "a company of the mountain boys of this county, commanded by Capt. Marker, reached town on their march to Annapolis, for which place they proceeded next morning. This company is composed of a fine, hardy, healthy set of men, accustomed to labour and fatigue - They were all armed with their own rifles, in the use of which they are very expert, and are perhaps the best company of sharp shooters in the State." The rifle company of Captain Marker (28th Regiment) was from Middletown; they were called Mountain Rangers, and served at Annapolis, until September 1813.

Daniel Marker, capt.
Charles Kline, 1st lt.
Thomas Biddle, ens.
... ...
Conrad Mickle, 2nd sgt.
Nicholas Mearle, 3rd sgt.
Peter Eccard, 4th sgt.

Joseph Searly, 1st cpl.
David Delawter, 2nd cpl.
Michael Hart, 3rd cpl.
Samuel Shipley, 4th cpl.
Philip Kline, musician
Henry Hoover, musician

Privates:
Marker, John
Gaver, George
Markin, Samuel

Neff, Andrew
Fair, Michael
Landerman, (?)
  Joseph

Gaver, John
Longmon, Jacob
Johnson, Jacob
Delawten, Daniel

FREDERICK COUNTY MILITIA IN THE WAR OF 1812

Delauten, Frederic
Kline, George
Neff, Jacob
Bootman, Jacob
McMullen, Samuel
Lewen, Paul
Miller, Jacob

Bond, Alexander
Cearly, Joseph
..., John
Jones, John
Snerr, Charles

Thomas, William,
  deserted 25 Aug
Schepley,
  Frederick,
  captain's servant

The Company of Samuel Dawson was called into service a second time from 21 Jul (many didn't join until the 26th) 1814 until 10 January 1815 when the company was discharged at Annapolis. They participated in the Battle of Bladensburg and the defense of Baltimore in the 2nd Regiment. There are two consecutive rolls below.

Roll (1) 21 Jul - 13 Oct 1814:
Sam Dawson, capt.
Benj. Thomas, 1st lt.
John Miller, 2nd lt.
James Hook, ens.
Sam Powell, 1st sgt.
Danl. Mossburgh, 2nd sgt.
Samuel McCoy/McCay, 3rd sgt.
Isaac Mobberly, 4th sgt.

Amos James/Jones, 1st cpl.
John Snyder, 2nd cpl.
Joseph Lowery, 3rd cpl.
David Hitchew, 4th cpl.,
  26 July - 13 Oct
Tudor James, drummer
James McCray, fifer,
  deserted 29 Sep

Privates:
Anders, John, 26
  July to ?
Alexander, Henry
Anthony, Henry
Bennett, John B.,
  deserted 6 Aug
Boyle, Charles,
  deserted 23 Aug
Boroughs, Isaac,
  sick in Baltimore
  12 Oct
Carney, Patrick
Clark, John,
  joined 10 Sep
Conly, James
Castle, Elijah
Clark, Josiah
Casey, Jason
Cook, John, joined
  26 July, sick in
  Baltimore
Delushmutt, Basil
Davis, Nathan,
  absent without
  leave 19-28 Aug
Davis, John, sick
  in Baltimore
Davis, Paris,
  deserted 23 Aug
Delushmutt,
  Sampson
Davis, Jonathan
Filler, John
Forest, Jeremiah

Ford/Force,
  Joseph, deserted
  23 Aug
Fernundy,
  [Fernandy,
  Fernandz?]
Thomas, to 26
  Sep, sick on
  furlough since 26
  Sep
Fickle, Daniel,
  joined 26 July,
  sick in Baltimore
Gaver, Henry
Gillaspy, John
Gaver, George
Gill, James
Hart, Michael,
  deserted 24 Aug
Haller, William,
  deserted 24 Aug
Hall, Joshua
Hurly, John,
  deserted 24 Aug,
  returned 10 Sep
Hahn, Henry,
  joined 26 July,
  deserted 29 Sep
Hoffman, John,
  joined 26 July,
  deserted 1 Oct
Jones, John
Jones, George,
  deserted 24 Aug
Jenkins, Feliz,

joined 1 Aug
Inlows, Abraham
Kentner, Adam
Laban, Paul
Lowery, Frederick
Lowery, John
Lapole, George,
  absent without
  leave 31 Aug - 10
  Sep
Mowery, Henry
Murry, Joshua
McDaniel, George,
  deserted 25 July
Miller, Martin
May, Charles
Mann, John,
  enlisted 23 Sep
McMullin, Samuel,
  joined 13 Sep
Moriarity, John
Murphy, Thomas,
  Jr.
McKlasky, William
Murphy, Thomas,
  Senr., joined 26
  July
Michael, Andrew
McCray, William,
  joined 26 July
Miller, Philip,
  joined 26 July,
  deserted 1 Oct
Morrison, James,
  joined 26 July,

338

APPENDIX D: MUSTER ROLLS OF THE ACTIVE UNITS

deserted 29 Sep,
returned 8 Oct
Oler, Joseph,
joined 26 July
deserted 29 Sep
Orndurff, Jacob
[Joseph?], joined
26 July, deserted
29 Sep
Pryor, John,
deserted
Peter, John
Pyle, John,
deserted 21 Aug
Rudy,
Christiopher,
"joined the
service 17 Sep"
Ridgely, Henry,
deserted 4 Oct
Reed, Philip
Riggs, Osha
Row, John
Rawlins, Wilson

Sigler, Peter,
deserted 6 Aug
Seerly, Joseph
Smith, William,
deserted 24 Aug
Smith, Thomas
Smith, Elijah
Smith, James,
joined 26 July
Slates/States,
John, joined 26
July, deserted 29
Sep
Shower, Melcher,
joined 26 July
Shrotes, John,
joined 26 July,
sick in Baltimore
Sycafoose, Henry
Turner/Twiner,
Danl., deserted
26 July
Twig, Thomas,
enlisted 1 Sep
Tohay, John,
joined 26 July

Weddle, John
Warner, Henry
White, Thomas
Warck, Andrew,
discharged 18 Sep
Welch, William,
enlisted 21 Sep
Weaver, Philip,
deserted 25 July
Wallace, Joseph,
enlisted 22 Aug
Walker, Stephen,
deserted 25 July
Yates, Charles,
deserted 26 July
Young, Conrad
Young, William,
enlisted 28 Sep
Zachary, John,
deserted 26 July
Gross/Grace,
William
Myers, Jerry, 3
Aug - 13 Sep,
from Baltimore

Roll (2) 14 Oct 1814 - 10 Jan 1815
Samuel Dawson, capt.
Benjamin Thomas, 1st lt.
John Miller, 2nd lt.
James Hook, ens.
Samuel Powell, sgt.
Samuel McCoy, sgt. Joshua
Joshua Hall, sgt.

Amos Jones, sgt.
Joseph Lowery, cpl., resident of Baltimore
John Peters, cpl.
Joshua Hall, cpl.
Tuder James, drummer, deserted 24 Oct

Privates:
Anthoney, Henry
Buroughs, Isaac,
discharged 27 Oct
Beard, Richard,
deserted Dec
Bertin, Benjamin,
deserted 24 Oct
Boovey, Jacob,
resident of
Hagerstown
Booth, Robert,
deserted 24 Oct,
resident of
Hagerstown
Carney, Patrick,
resident of
Hagerstown,
deserted 26 Oct
Clark, John,
resident of
Hagerstown,
deserted 29 Oct

Cowley, James,
resident of
Hagerstown,
deserted 29 Oct
Castle, Elisha
Clark, Josiah,
resident of
Baltimore
Carnes, Thomas,
died 30 Dec
Casey, Jason,
deserted 8 Dec
Cross, Thomas,
deserted 8 Dec
Crandle, James,
deserted 8 Dec
Cole, William,
resident of
Baltimore
Coss, Peter,
resident of
Washington Co.

Davis, John,
resident of
Baltimore
Davis, Nathan,
resident of
Baltimore,
deserted 8 Dec
Delashmitt, Samson
Davis, Jonathan
Dixon, Hezekiah,
deserted 8 Dec
Ebb, Jeremiah,
resident of
Washington Co.
Everett, Samuel
Filler, John
Forrest, Jeremiah
Fernandes, Thomas
Fowler, John,
deserted 23 Oct
Gillaspy, Mathew
Gaver, George

FREDERICK COUNTY MILITIA IN THE WAR OF 1812

Gill, James, resident of Baltimore
Gray, Walter, deserted 23 Oct
Hull, John, deserted 3 Nov
Hush, William, deserted 8 Dec
Huey, William, resident of Washington Co.
Hall, Isaac
Hurley, John, deserted 28 Oct
Jones, John, deserted 26 Oct
Jenkins, Felix
Inloes, Abraham, resident of Baltimore
Johnson, Thomas, resident of Baltimore
Judy, Martin, resident of Baltimore, deserted 16 Nov
Kentner, Adam
Loben, Paul
Lowery, Frederick
Lowery, John, deserted 11 Nov
Lapole, George, died 23 Dec
Legg, William, resident of Baltimore
Loman, Edward, resident of Baltimore
Mowery, Henry
Miller, Martin
May, Charles
Mobley, Isaac
McColen, Samuel
Moryatta, John, resident of Baltimore
Murphy, Thomas, deserted 8 Dec
McClaskey, William, resident of Baltimore
Murphy, Thomas
Michael, Andrew, enlisted 5 Nov
McCray, William
Morrison, James, deserted 8 Dec
Miles, William, resident of Washington Co.
Meritt, James, resident of Washington Co., deserted 29 Oct
Metz, George, resident of Washington Co., deserted 6 Dec
Ocks, Jacob, resident of Washington Co., deserted 1 Nov
Powers, Thomas, resident of Washington Co.
Palmer, Matthew, resident of Washington Co.
Phelps, Charles, resident of Washington Co.
Rush, William, deserted 1 Nov
Reed, Philip
Ridgely, Henry, joined 21 July
Riggs, Asha, deserted 22 Dec
Rawlins, Wilson, deserted Nov
Silverthorn, William, deserted 2 Nov
Shaffer, George, resident of Washington Co.
Snyder, Jacob, deserted Nov
Sybert, David, resident of Baltimore
Smith, William, joined 21 July
Seerly, Joseph
Smith, Thomas
Smith, Elijah, resident of Baltimore
Snyder, John
Shaner, Melcher
Sycafoose, Henry
Tohay, John
Weddle, John, deserted 28 Oct
Warner, Henry, deserted 5 Nov
White, Thomas, deserted 7 Nov
Wolgamott, Joseph, resident of Washington Co.
Warner, William
Williams, John
Young, Conrad
Gross, William, servant
Myers, Jerry, servant, resident of Baltimore

A Detachment from the 32nd Regiment attached to Lt. Col. Hood's Regiment. In July 1814, Captain Jacob Alexander's Company of volunteers left Middletown Valley for Annapolis. Their service covered 22 July to 19 Sept, participating in the Battle of Bladensburg on 24 August, where one of their company, James Bryant, died on the field of battle. David Stotelmyer of the same company was wounded. This company continued on to Baltimore and participated in its defense. They departed Baltimore around 20 September, arriving home in about three days, marching a total of 53 miles.

Jacob Alexander, Capt.
Rezin Magruder, Lt.
Jacob Harrin, Ens.
Lenore Beckworth, 1st sgt, sick on furlough
John Steers, 2nd sgt, sick on furlough
John K. Stotelmyer, 3rd sgt.

APPENDIX D: MUSTER ROLLS OF THE ACTIVE UNITS

Daniel Barkman, 4th sgt.
David Stotelmyer, 1st cpl.,
 wounded 24 Aug.
David Wm. Sneeman, 2nd cpl.
Wm. Jacob Stotelmyer, 3rd cpl.
Jacob John Stotelmyer, 4th cpl.
John Westol Hone, drummer,
 joined at Annapolis
Peter Samseal, fife major,
 previously in the service of
 U.S. with Dawson
Ignatious Gearbo, fifer

Privates:
Alexander, Jacob
Alexander, Valuntine
Bryant, James
Beard, John
Carty, James
Carty, John
Carne, Adam
Conner, James
Conner, James
Conner, Aquila
Dunning, Dora
Delpha, Thomas
Fester, Daniel
Hargesheimer, Joseph
Lemar, Richard
McMulin, James
McMulin, William
Monday, Dodies
Murray, Bazil
Norris, Henry
Ridgely, Joshua
Row, Michael
Ropp, Samuel
Swearengan, Van
Stotelmyer, Joseph
Toll, Walter
Officer's waiter

The company of George Washington Magee was from the New Windsor area;
they served 22 Jul 1814 - 10 January 1815, in the 1st Regiment in the
service of the United States. Most of the company went on to
Baltimore from Bladensburg and after the Battle of Baltimore, were
sent to Annapolis. At Battle of Baltimore the company was positioned
in the entrenchments at Hampstead Hill. The last members of the
company on active duty were discharged at Annapolis in January 1815.

Muster roll (1) 22 July - 13 Oct 1814:
George W. Magee, capt.
Charles Develbiss, 1st lt.,
 supernumerary by consolidation
 on 3 Oct
John Smith, 1st, lt.
Moses Lugenbeel/Lugen, 2nd lt.
David Barnover, ens.
William Coomes, sgt.
Joseph McKinstrey, sgt.
William McKnitt, sgt.
James B. Slater, sgt.
Coonrod Crisher, sick on
 furlough to 1 Oct
Peter Boreing, cpl.
David Yingling, cpl.
David Stevenson, cpl.
Augustis P.[J?] Discorney, cpl.
Basil Tracey, fifer
John Winters, drummer

Privates:
Henrey Blufford,
 sick absent 24
 Aug
Bond, Charles
Blewbaugh, John
Bricker, David
Bricker, Henry
Banker, John,
 deserted 1 Oct
Blizard, Beal
Black, Isaac,
 missing 22 Aug
Butler, James,
 discharged 1 Sep
 by surgeon
Cole, Enzer
Casner, John
Coaker, Walter
Call, Mathias
Copenheaver,
 William
Coosix, Joseph
Carrol/Carvel,
 William, deserted
 29 July
Crosbury, James
 B., deserted 20
 Aug
Condon, Thomas,
 corporal "until
 transferred to me
 on 23 Sep"
Cooper, John
Crumage,
 Frederick,
 deserted 30 July
Dehoof, John,
 deserted 1 Oct
Duplaint, Dominick
Duderar, George
Duffey, James,
 deserted 30 July
Dorsey, Abraham,
 deserted 1 Oct
England, Andrew
Earhart, George
Easterline,
 George, deserted
 1 Oct
Engler, Phillip
Engleman, John
Foster, James, 1st
 sgt. until 1 Oct
Franklin, Francis
Frankforter, John
Farst, Michael
Foreman, Jacob
Foreman, Danial
Foreman, David
Grimes, George,
 deserted 25 Sep
Gibbons, Mathew,

FREDERICK COUNTY MILITIA IN THE WAR OF 1812

deserted 7 Aug
Griffan/Griffin,
 William, enlisted
 22 Aug
Hines, Michael
Hooker, Jonsey,
 sick on furlough
 1 Oct
Harris, Michael,
 sick on furlough
 1 Oct
Hann, William
Haughn, Jonathan,
 discharged 1 Oct,
 overage
Hesson, Peter
Helm, Samuel
Hush, Samuel
Haughn/Hann, Adam,
 sgt. "until
 transferred to me
 23 Sep"
Jackson,
 Archibald,
 mustered in
 Baltimore
James, Isaac,
 deserted 25 Sep
Izor, Enoch,
 deserted 24 July
Kinkead, Joseph,
 deserted 25 Sep
Kelly, Joshua,
 deserted 24 Aug
Kelly, William
Kenedy, William
Little, David,
 deserted 25 Sep
Lutes, John,
 enlisted 5 Sep
Loerher/Locher,
 Adam, missing 24
 Aug
Lucas, Henry
Miller, John, cpl.
 until transferred
 23 Sep
Murfey, John,
 enlisted 5 Sep
McBear, Charles,
 enlisted 25 July
McClain, James,
 deserted 30 Aug
Noble, Joseph
O'brien, Edward
Phrater, James
Pool, Henry M.,
 deserted Oct ...
Parks, William
Ray, John, sick
 absent 27 Aug
Robison, James C.
Robison/Robertson,
 William, cpl.
 "until trans-
 ferred 23 Sep"
Rigle, Adam
Rife, Daniel
Routsong, John
Rineheart, John,
 enlisted 21 Aug
Rhenicher, Peter,
 deserted 12 Aug
Slick, Francis,
 deserted 10 (20?)
 Sep
Shook, Adam
Smith, George
 N.[M?]
Sheu, [?] Jacob,
 "mustered under
 Capt. Showers"
Snider, Jacob,
Shock, John
Syer, Nichodimus
Sterner, Jonathan
Speelman, Andrew,
 sick on furlough
 1 Oct
Sponsler, David
Slife, John, sick
 absent 18 Sep
Sacker, John
Taylor, Hezekiah
Trumbo, George
Turfiel, Lewis
Gooding, Lambert
 T.
Toosang,
 Francis T.,
 enlisted 15
 Aug
Uler, David
Wickart, Adam,
 deserted 1 Oct
West, Abraham,
 sick absent 1 Sep
Weekly, William
West, Nathaniel
Woonder, John
Walter, Jacob
Burket, Jacob,
 waiter
Black, Philip,
 servant,
 discharged 12 Oct

Muster roll (2) 14 Oct 1814 - 10 Jan 1815:
George W. Magee, capt.,
 New Windsor
John Smith, 1st lt.,
 Mechanickstown
Moses Lugenbeel, 2nd lt.,
 New Windsor
David Barnover, ens.
Joseph McKinstrey, 1st sgt.,
 New Windsor
William McKnitt, 2nd sgt.
James B. Slater, 3rd sgt.,
 Baltimore Town

David Stevenson, 4th sgt.,
 New Windsor
Peter Boreing, cpl.,
 New Windsor
David Yingling, 2nd cpl.
Augustus P. [S?] Discorney,
 3rd cpl., Baltimore Town
Adam Shook, 4th cpl.
Basil Tracey, fifer,
 New Windsor
John Winters, drummer

Privates:
Amick, George,
 Baltimore Town
Bond, Charles,
 New Windsor
Blewbough, John,
 in confinement at
 Fort McHenry
Bricker, David,
 New Windsor
Bricker, Henry,
 New Windsor
Blizzard, Beal,
 deserted 6 Dec
Burket, Jacob,
 deserted 6 Dec,

APPENDIX D: MUSTER ROLLS OF THE ACTIVE UNITS

Mechanickstown
Cole, Enser, deserted 6 Dec
Casner, John, New Windsor
Coaker, Walter, New Windsor
Call, Matthias, New Windsor
Copenhaver, William, deserted 6 Dec
Crisher, Conrod, joined 22 July, sick last muster, furloughed 15 days
Coosix/Coosin, Joseph, Baltimore Town
Condon, Thomas, Mechanickstown
Cooper, John, discharged Baltimore 25 Nov, over age, Mechanickstown
Dupliant, Dominic, Baltimore Town, in confinement at Fort McHenry
Duderar, George, New Windsor, deserted 1 Dec
England, Andrew, New Windsor
Eareheart, George, New Windsor
Esterline, George, New Windsor, in confinement at Fort McHenry
Engler, Philip, New Windsor
Engleman, John, New Windsor
Foster, James, New Windsor, discharged Baltimore 25 Nov
Franklin, Francis, New Windsor
Frankforter, John, New Windsor
Farst, Michael, New Windsor
Foreman, Jacob, New Windsor
Foreman, Daniel
Foreman, David, New Windsor
Fernanders, Adam, to 1 Dec,, New Windsor, enlisted 1 Dec
Grimes, George, joined 22 July, Baltimore Town, in confinement at Fort McHenry
Holbrook, Thomas, Baltimore Town, joined 23 July, prisoner at Bladensburgh 24 Aug, paroled 26 Aug and joined regiment 6 Dec
Hines, Michael
Hooker, Johnsey, joined 22 July
Harris, Michael, deserted 6 Dec
Hann, William
Hesson, Peter
Helms, Samuel, Baltimore Town
Hush, Samuel, Baltimore Town, dead 24 Dec
Hann, Adam, Mechanickstown
Hilard, Johnson, New Windsor
Kinkade, Joseph, New Windsor
Kelly, Joshua, joined 22 July, Baltimore Town
Kenedy, William, Baltimore Town
Lane/Larn, William, Baltimore Town
Lucas, Henry, New Windsor
Miller, John, Mechanickstown
Noggle, Joseph, New Windsor
O'Brien, Edward, Mechanickstown
Prather, James, Mechanickstown
Parks, William, New Windsor
Rineheart, Daniel, joined 23 July, prisoner at Bladensburgh 24 Aug, joined regiment 10 Nov
Riggle, Adam, New Windsor
Rife, Daniel, Mechanickstown
Rockwell, Tolbert Hancock, MD
Routsong, John, New Windsor
Snider, Joseph, New Windsor
Shockney, John, New Windsor, deserted 6 Dec
Syer, Nichodemus, New Windsor, deserted 6 Dec
Sponsler, David, New Windsor
Speelman, Andrew, New Windsor, 3 weeks sick, discharged in Baltimore by surgeon 1 Dec
Slite/Slife, John, New Windsor, deserted 20 Nov
Sacker, John, New Windsor
Taylor, Hezekiah, New Windsor
Trumbo, George, New Windsor
Turfiel, Lewis, New Windsor, in confinement at Fort McHenry
Gooding, Lambert T., Baltimore Town
Uhler, David, New Windsor, on furlough 21 days
West, Abraham, New Windsor, joined 22 July, discharged 26 Dec by surgeon
Weekley, William, New Windsor
West, Nathaniel, New Windsor
Woonder, John, New Windsor
Walter, Jacob, New Windsor
Black, Sam, servant, joined 17 Oct, Balt. Town, discharged at Balt. 8 Dec

FREDERICK COUNTY MILITIA IN THE WAR OF 1812

The company of Captain Lewis Weaver (Emmitsburg area) served from 23 July 1814 until 10 January 1815. They served at Bladensburg, Annapolis and Baltimore. According to one veteran, Captain Lewis Weaver commanded the company at the battle of Bladensburg and after that he took the company to Baltimore. They arrived at camp on 4 September outside Baltimore. At some point he was cashiered and succeeded by Captain James F. Huston who in turn was succeeded by Captain Joseph Green [from Emmitsburg] who remained in command until the company was discharged on 10 January 1815 at Annapolis. Private Martin Shultz stated that when Capt. Huston was taken sick he returned to Fredericktown and never rejoined the regt. From that point the company remained under the command of Lt. Thomas W. Morgan until Capt. Green took command and retained it until the company was discharged. A reference is made in the *Frederick-town Herald* to the departure of a company "from town, commanded by Captain Huston" during the last week in July, 1814. From this item we would conclude that Huston first commanded the company followed by Weaver, perhaps Morgan and Green, in that order. On December 31, 1814 a reward was posted in the Frederick-Town Herald for deserters from this company. Fifty had deserted at Baltimore, three had deserted at Annapolis and two had deserted at Bladensburg. Capt. Green offered $550 for the return of the men, "at my quarters at Annapolis."

Roll (1) 23 July - 13 Oct 1814:

James F. Huston, capt., supernumerary officer on 20 Sep
Joseph Green, 2nd lt., promoted to capt. 20 Sep
Henry Smith, 1st lt., discharged 2 Oct
Thomas W. Morgan, 2nd lt., promoted 1st lt. 20 Sep
George W. Hoffman, ens., promoted 2nd lt. 20 Sep
John Boner/Beoner, 1st sgt.
Martin Shultz, 2nd sgt., on furlough since 8 Oct

William Gillen, 3rd sgt.
Vachel Stinchacomb, 4th sgt.
Thomas Hays, 1st cpl.
Alfred Ridgely, 2nd cpl.
George W. Haller, 3rd cpl.
Levi Davis, 4th cpl.
William Lewis, 5th cpl.
Michael Englebrecht, musician
George Shade, musician
John Stouffer/Stauffer, drummer, deserted 25 Sep

Privates:
Ankrum, George
Aldworth, John
Beall, Thomas N.
Brooke, Richard
Brish, David
Britten, John
Beard, John
Becket, James
Burk, Daniel
Baldwin, Nicholas, deserted 2 Aug
Burns, James D., enlisted 12 Aug
Conner, Thomas, furloughed since 4 Oct
Crumbecker, David
Conradt, Joseph
Carnes, Jacob
Cox, William
Cooley, Joseph, missing since 24 Aug, battle of Bladensburg
Crilly, Michael
Cochran, James
Dorf, Patrick, made prisoner 24 Aug
Dehoff, Andrew
Dunavin, William
Ditter, Abraham, deserted 16 Sep
Dennis, John
Eberts, George
Feaga, Frederick
Fagan, George
Fisher, William, 16 Aug - 13 Oct
Funk, Henry
Frame, Jacob, died 23 Aug
Gomber, John
Gault, Joseph, died 23 Aug
Gird, William F., deserted 24 Aug
Garey, Sabred
Haller, George
Hull, Henry
Hoffman, John
Hoffman, William
Howard, Adam
Haller, Elisha, on furlough since 27 Sep
Heisley, Frederick A., substitute for John D. Heisley
Haller, Jacob
Hummell, John
Hardy, Joseph, on furlough since 4 Oct
Hoover, George
Hamilton, William, deserted 23 Aug
Hildebrand, George, died 16 Aug

344

APPENDIX D: MUSTER ROLLS OF THE ACTIVE UNITS

Johnson Thomas
Jacobs, Ignatius, sick in Frederick-Town since 26 Aug
Jamison, James, deserted 14 Aug
Kuhn, Peter
Keller, Frederick
Keeting, George S.
Keller, John, sick in Baltimore 30 Aug
Knott, Caleb, discharged 2 Aug
Keepers, Joseph
Lutton, Henry
Lawrence, James, deserted 16 Aug
McConley, Saml.
Metz, John Wm.
Merrit, James
Measle Daniel
Measle, Valentine
Mosburgh, Abraham
Myers, Jacob, discharged 3 Aug
Myers, Martin, 28 Jul - 13 Oct
McDamot, [McDumot, McDermot] Richard
Nusz, Michael
Ott, Frederick, sick in Frederick-Town 25 Aug
Patrick, Robert
Peacock, William
Pitt, Thomas
Richards, Zachariah
Reynolds, Horatio
Rohr, Peter, furlough since 23 Sep
Riddlemoser, Abraham, deserted 11 Sep
Row, Frederick, discharged 3 Aug
Randall, Robert
Shultz, David
Stouffer, George
Snavely, John
Smith, John,
Shryoc, John
Smith, William
Stall, Andrew, sick in Baltimore since 20 Sep
Smith, Benjamin
Shaffer, John
Siers, Alexander
Tingstrum, Peter, sick in Frederick-Town since 30 Sep
Tschudy, Martin, enlisted 4 Sep
Vanblarkcum, Evert
Wilkinson, Linor W.
Wissinger, Leonard, discharged 6 Sep
Wilson, John of Alex.
Wincel, John
Wilson, John
Walker, Jonathan
Winters, Ignatius, joined 25 Aug, discharged 28 Sep
Welsh, Henry, joined 28 Aug
Young, John
Yerk/Yirk, James, sick in quarters since 2 Oct
Yowler, George William, Captain's servant, joined 8 Aug

Roll (2) 14 Oct 1814 - 10 Jan 1815:
Joseph Green, capt., resident of Emmitsburgh
Thomas W. Morgan, 1st lt., Fredericktown
George W. Hoffman, 2nd lt., Fredericktown
David Barnett, ens., Hagerstown
George W. Holler, 1st sgt., Fredericktown
Martin Shultz, 2nd sgt., Fredericktown
Alfred Ridgly, 3rd sgt., Fredericktown
Vachel Stinchcomb, 4th sgt., Fredericktown, discharged at Baltimore 6 Dec by surgeon
Levi Davis, 1st cpl., Fredericktown
John Heisly, 2nd cpl., Fredericktown, substitute for Frederick A. Heisley
Benjamin Smith, 3rd cpl., resident of Emmittsburgh
William Lewis, 4th cpl., Fredericktown, discharged at Baltimore 6 Dec
George Shade, principal musician, deserted 5 Nov
Michael Benglbreck, musician
John Stauffer, drummer, Fredericktown, deserted 25 Sep, returned 24 Oct, deserted 8 Dec, returned 24 Dec

Privates:
Ankrum, George, Fredericktown
Aldworth, John, deserted 10 Nov
Andrew, Bernard, substitute for Wm. Gillen,
deserted
Beall, Thomas N., deserted 27 Oct
Brooke, Richard, Fredericktown
Brish, David, deserted 12 Dec
Britten, John, Fredericktown
Beard, John, deserted 8 Dec
Burk, Daniel, deserted 16 Dec
Conner, Thomas,

FREDERICK COUNTY MILITIA IN THE WAR OF 1812

Fredericktown
Crumbecker, David, deserted 14 Dec
Conrad, Joseph, Fredericktown, deserted 21 Dec, returned 2 Jan
Carns, Jacob, Fredericktown, discharged Baltimore 6 Dec by surgeon
Cox, William, deserted 8 Dec
Crilly, Michael, deserted 8 Dec
Cockran, James, enlisted 3 Nov
Dorff, Patrick, Fredericktown, taken prisoner at Bladensburgh 24 Aug
Datroff, Andrew, Fredericktown
Dunavin, William, deserted 8 Dec, returned 2 Jan
Dennis, John, deserted 8 Dec
Elberts, George, Baltimore Town, deserted 21 Dec, returned 30 Dec
Feaga, Frederick, deserted 27 Oct
Fagan, George, Frederick Co., discharged by surgeon
Fischer, William, promoted to quartermaster sgt. 7 Dec
Funk, Henry, deserted 30 Oct
Fletcher, James, Baltimore Town, substitute for Thomas Hays
Gomber, John, Fredericktown
Garey, Sabred, Fredericktown, deserted 8 Dec, returned 24 Dec
Gittings, William, Baltimore Town, substitute for John Boner
Holler, George, deserted 8 Dec
Hull, Henry, deserted 8 Dec
Hoffman, John, Fredericktown
Hoffman, William, Fredericktown
Hauer, Adam, deserted 12 Dec
Haller, Elisha, Fredericktown, deserted 8 Dec, returned 27 Dec
Holler, Jacob, Fredericktown
Hummell, John, deserted 8 Dec
Hoover, George, deserted 8 Dec
Henry, Joseph, Baltimore Town, substitute for James Brickett
Johnson, Thomas, Fredericktown
Kuhn, Peter, deserted 5 Dec
Keller, Frederick, Fredericktown, deserted 14 Dec, returned 2 Jan
Keiting, George S., Fredericktown
Keller, John, deserted 27 Oct
Sutton, Henry, deserted 29 Oct
McConley, Samuel, enlisted 3 Nov
Metz, William John, deserted 12 Dec
Merritt, James, Fredericktown
Measle, Daniel, deserted 4 Dec
Measle, Valentine, enlisted 28 Nov
Mosburg, Abraham, Fredericktown
Myers, Martin, deserted 8 Dec
McDermot, Richard, deserted 16 Dec
Moore, Thomas, Baltimore Town, substitute for Ignatius Jacobs
Nusz, Michael, deserted 2 Dec
Ott, Frederick,
deserted 8 Dec
Peacock, William, deserted 27 Oct
Pitt, Thomas, deserted
Richards, Zachariah, Baltimore Town
Reynolds, Horatio, Fredericktown, deserted 8 Dec, returned 30 Dec
Rohr, Peter, Fredericktown, discharged 6 Dec by surgeon in Baltimore
Randell, Robert, deserted 27 Oct
Shultz, David, deserted 8 Dec
Stauffer, George, deserted 17 Dec, returned 24 Dec
Snavely, John, deserted 4 Dec
Smith, John, deserted 8 Dec
Shryoc, John, Baltimore Town, deserted 27 Dec, returned 30 Dec
Smith, William, deserted 8 Dec
Stall, Andrew, deserted 27 Oct
Shaffer, John, deserted 15 Oct
Seers, Alexander, deserted 29 Oct
Slack, James, Baltimore Town, substitute for Joseph Keepers
Vanblarcum, Evert, deserted 5 Nov
Wilkinson, Liner(?) W., Fredericktown
Wilson, John of Alex., Fredericktown, discharged 6 Dec by surgeon
Wincel, John, deserted 7 ...
Wilson, John, deserted 7 ...
Walker, Jonathan, deserted 20 Nov
Welch, Henry,

APPENDIX D: MUSTER ROLLS OF THE ACTIVE UNITS

deserted 20 Nov
Whitlock, John, Baltimore Town
Young, John, Fredericktown

Yirk, James, Emmettsburgh
Yowler, George, Fredericktown, deserted 8 Dec, returned 2 Jan

William, servant, discharged 8 Dec
John, servant, Fredericktown

This rolls shows the second tour of active duty performed by Getzendanner's company. The company arrived in Annapolis around 26 Jul 1814. Many of the same men had marched with Captain Getzendanner on the previous deployment to Annapolis in the summer of 1813. They were discharged at Annapolis on 21 August 1814 and allowed travel pay for 5 days for the march home, a distance of 75 miles.

Jacob Getzendanner, Capt.
John A. Dean, 1st lt.
John Hildebrand, 2nd lt.
Christian Greenwald, 1st sgt.
Jacob Teshner, 2nd sgt.
George Getzendanner, 3rd sgt.
John Musser, 4th sgt.

James Dean, 1st cpl.
Robert Dean, 2nd cpl.
Frederick Kline, 3rd cpl.
William Albert, 4th cpl.
George Fagler, musician
John Geldz, musician

Privates:
Getzendanner, Solomon
Bready, John
Widrick, John
Hughs, Hugh
Yowler, Michael
Shinn, Joseph
Engle, Frederick
Woodward, Nathaniel
Hefner, Lawrence
Cannon, Jacob

Kline, Henry
...ok(?), ...
Mosburg, John
Kemp, ...k
Cline, ...
Herring, ...
Main, Jacob
Hughs, Edward
Winpigler, Michael
Trout, John
Evans, Elisha
Brain, John
Kline, John

Murry, Mathias
Layman, John
Hill, John
Miller, George
Kursman, Christian
Meland, Edward, 4 Aug - 21 Aug
Friday, Henry, served 22 days
Moore, John, served 15 days
William, Negro, captain's servant

The company of Basil Dorsey was active from 30 July to 27 Sep 1814. They discharged at Baltimore, having served in Annapolis, Bladensburg and Baltimore. [Throughout the muster roll of Dorsey's company are annotations of discharge by General Foreman, indicating that this company was under the command of the 1st Brigade while at Baltimore.]

Basil Dorsey, Capt.
Samuel Wright, Lt.
John Hamilton, Ens.
Elisha Falconer, Ens.
Benjamin Wright, 1st sgt.
Enos Hutton, 2nd sgt.
James Montgomery, 3rd sgt.
Ruben Hogen, 4th sgt.

Richard Sans, 1st cpl., acted 30 days as cpl.
Charles Young, acted 30 days as cpl.
Daniel Simmons, 3rd cpl., discharged by General Foreman 24 Sep
Taylor, Isreal. 4th cpl.
Vore, Wm., drummer

Privates:
Anderson, George
Armstrong, James
Barret, William
Billingsley, Walter
Kirfman, Christian

Clary, Nathaniel
Davison, William
Darby, Perry
Davison, Samuel
Fine, Peter
Forest, Rezin
Glover, Francis

Hornblower, William
Hopper, Benjamin
Harris, Kinsey
Hagar, Francis
Hill, Bennet, missing since 24

FREDERICK COUNTY MILITIA IN THE WAR OF 1812

Aug
Hobbs, Samuel,
  served as cpl. 30
  days
Engle, Peter
Johnson, Thomas
Mark, George
Mount, George
Mulinix, Rezin
Murray, James
Reed, James
Rhyne, John
Sanders, Thomas
Sans, William
Selby, Henry

Simmons, George,
  discharged 20 Sep
Simmons, Isaac,
  discharged by
  Gen. Foreman 20
  Sep
Simmons, Thomas
Sims, Patrick
Stephens, Charles
Snyder, Christian
Taneyhill, Carlton
Unglebee,
  Zachariah
Unglebee, Erasmus
Wagers, Henry

West, Stephen
Whetter, Leonard
Williams, Lilburn,
  discharged by
  Gen. Foreman 24
  Sep
Wilson, William,
  acted as cpl. 30
  days
Yingling, Philip
Yingling, David
Perdum, Mordecai,
  furloughed 9 Sep
  until well

Captain Denton Darby's company served at Annapolis and then went on to meet the British at Bladensburg. Aquilla Teller [Tulley?] was wounded and Henry Zimmerman was taken prisoner. Captain Darby stated that he was placed under Lieutenant Colonel Cramer and at some point he was placed under Major Kizer of the U. S. Army. In Washington, following the Bladensburg disaster, he was attached to the "City Brigade." Darby's company served from 3 August to 8 Nov 1814 when they were discharged in Georgetown, D.C.

Denton Darby, Capt.
Richard Clark, Lt.
Thomas Goggin, sgt.
Ambrose Ingman, sgt.
George Klay, sgt.

Jonathan Browning, cpl., absent
  6 days
Benjamin Brown, cpl.
Frederick Brown, cpl.

Privates:
Atir, Solomon,
  absent 6 days
Atir, Lazurus
Applebee, William,
  absent 6 days
Allison, John,
  absent 30 days
Allnutt, Jesse,
  joined 1 Sep
Brandenburgh,
  Jesse, absent 38
  days
Bear, Michael,
  absent 6 days
Basford, Thomas
Belt, Bennoni,
  deserted 18 Aug
Buress, Proverb,
  absent 12 days
Buress, Nicholas,
  absent 12 days
Ball, John D.,
  absent 4 days
Berry, John,
  joined 1 Sep
Chaney, Elijah,
  deserted 22 Aug
Clark, Levi,
  absent 6 days

Campbell, George,
  absent 17 days
Cary, Joseph,
  joined 30 Aug
Durall, Elisha,
  absent 6 days
Davis, Joseph,
  drowned 16 Aug
Elms, Joseph,
  joined 1 Sep
Fisher, Asa,
  absent 6 days
Fowler, Thomas,
  absent 35 days
Gibbs, John
Goodlin, Thomas,
  deserted 17 Aug
Gaither, George
Harvey, Elisha
Hillery, James,
  deserted
Harding, John,
  deserted
Harding, Philip
Harding, Solomon
Hutchison,
  Benedick,
  deserted
Johnson, William,
  deserted

Klay, John,
  drowned
Lishure, John,
  deserted
Lishure, Samuel
  deserted
Lishure, Joshua,
  deserted
Logan, George,
  deserted 30 Aug
Medary, John,
  absent 6 days
Moran, William,
  absent 8 days
Minor, William,
  joined 25 Aug
Owen, John
O'Neal, William
Rippin, William
Richards, William,
  absent 31 days
Roach, Gustavus
Swan, William,
  deserted 19 Aug
Suit, Nathaniel
Stone, James,
  joined 14 Aug
Smith, Solomon,
  joined 30 Aug
Teller, Aquila,

APPENDIX D: MUSTER ROLLS OF THE ACTIVE UNITS

wounded in action
Taylor, John
Taylor, Isreal, absent 6 days

Urvin, James of James, joined 27 Sep
Urvin, James

White, Walter
Wilson, Andrew, died 5 Sep
Zimmerman, Henry, taken prisoner 24 Aug Henry

Rewards were offered for those deserted from this company while at camp in Bladensburg on or about 20th Aug: William Swan, 26 yrs, 5ft 10-11 inches, dark complexion, labourer. Elijah Chaney, 25 yrs, 5 ft 8 inches, dark complexion, labourer. James Fillery, 25 yrs, 5 ft 10-11 inches, dark complexion, labourer. Thomas Goodlin, 24 yrs, 5 ft 8-9 inches, light complexion, taylor. William Johnson, 33 yrs, 5 ft 8-10 inches, dark complexion, a miller, mason, drunkard. Samuel, John and Joshua Lishures, aged about 22 yrs, sandy complexions, red hair, labourers. Bennoni Belt, 25 yrs, 5 ft 10-11 inches, light complexion, black hair, labourer. "Deliver at camp Hill, Washington City and receive $5.00 each. Denton Darby."

Captain Samuel Duvall's company left Frederick County around 3 Aug 1814, served in Annapolis and then participated in the Battle of Bladensburg; they were discharged in Georgetown, D. C. around 9 November 1814. Some members were from the Woodsboro area.

Samuel Duvall, Capt.
Christopher Musseter, 1st lt.
Frederick Ridgley, 2nd lt.
Henry Schley, 3rd lt.
Henry Glisan, ens.
John Wolf, 1st sgt.
Simpson Hammond, 2nd sgt.
John Groff, 3rd sgt.
Samuel Carmack, 4th sgt.

James Cochran, 5th sgt.
Michael Gilbert, cpl.
Jacob Christ, cpl.
David Gross, cpl.
John Rock, cpl.
Anthony Echart, cpl.
William Boyd, cpl.
Solomon Sticher, musician
Samuel Crager, musician

Privates:
Anderson, Alexander
Alexander, Muhail G.
Buzard, Peter
Burch, Henry
Barnhart, Solomon
Barthalow, Elias
Butler, Thomas
Brily, Coloson
Buffington, John
Boston, George
Barrukman, Christian
Barnhouse, Richard
Burk, Isaac
Carpenter, Solomon
Curry, John
Cain, Thomas
Chew, William
Donn/Dorner, George
Eckman, John

Edmundston, James N.
Fisk, Daniel
Fout, Christian
Fout, Peter
Frishouse, Adam
Frushouse, Jacob
Golden, John
Gusey, Christian
Green, Laurance
Goff, Richard
Hammon, Denton
Hummock, George
Harris, John
Holiger, Phillip
Hughes, Joseph A.
Jones, Nathan
Loon, Michael
Litt, Jacob
Lightner, George
Lucas, John
Lowe, Jacob
Limbaugh, William
Lafaver, John

McIntire, James
Miller, Henry
Miller, Peter
Moser, Henry
Owen, Isaiah
Piper, Michael
Pumphrey, William
Potter, William
Rifle, John
Rainey, John
Rollins, John C.
Revell, James
Strine, Peter
Smith, John
Sheetenhelm, Jacob
Sponsler, William
Sargeant, Jacob
Shaum, John
Sewell, Charles B.
Talhelm, Peter
Vile, William
Vile, Peter
Wilhide, Jacob, Jr.

FREDERICK COUNTY MILITIA IN THE WAR OF 1812

Wilhide, Jacob 2nd
Warner, Daniel
Wickam, Andrew
Yeonits, Christian

Tilghman, John,
  servant, 1 Sep -
  3 Oct
Riley, Charles,
  servant, 10 Sep -
  3 Oct

Solomon, Negro,
  servant, 14 Sep -
  29 Sep
Pinter, Thomas,
  servant, 2 Oct -
  3 Oct

Rewards were offered by Captain Duvall in the local Frederick newspaper for the following who deserted while at camp at Bladensburg, on Sunday, 14th August, 1814, "privates in my company, now in the service of the U. States,": Daniel Misinger, substitute, dark eyes, dark hair, one fore finger off at the first joint, by profession a laborer. On the same day, Philip Bidinger, a drafted man, about 29-30 yrs old, 5 ft 8-9 inches, light complexion, light hair, grey eyes, by profession a laborer. On 16th Aug, Benjamin Butler, 19-20 yrs old, 5 ft, 9-10 inches, darkish complexion, blue eyes, black hair, a laborer, substitute from Creager's Town. On same, John Redenour, drafted man, 21-22 yrs old, 5 ft 8-9 inches, dark complexion, dark eyes, dark hair, by profession a blacksmith. On 17th of same, William Hinton, substitute, aged about 22 yrs, 5 ft 8-9 inches, fair complexion, light eyes, light hair, by profession a house carpenter and joiner. On 18th of same, Amos Harbaugh, a draft, aged 18-19, dark complexion, black eyes, black hair, and by profession a cabinet maker. On same, Henry Lear, substitute, aged 24-25 yrs, light complexion, grey eyes, light hair, by profession a hatter. On same James Jemeson, aged about 22-23 yrs, 5 ft 7-8 inches, further description cannot be given, as he deserted the very night he was taken as a substitute. On 24 Aug, Hezekiah Metcalf, a substitute, aged 45-50 yrs, dark complexion, grey eyes, dark hair, about 5 ft 7-8 inche, by profession a collier, laborer or drunkard. On 25th of the same from Montgomery Court House, William Fields, a substitute, near 6 ft high, one leg very much perished, his age about 24-25 yrs, light complexion, blue eyes, light hair, and snaggled toothed, his profession a collier or laborer. On 26th of the same, Jacob Litt, a draft, aged 20-21 yrs, 5 ft 9-10 inches, dark complexion, black eyes, black hair, by profession a laborer. On 29th of Aug, from Washington City, Peter Cartnail, aged 49-50, near 6 ft high, dark complexion, dark eyes, very hollow, dark hair, by profession a laborer or drunkard. Five dollars for each. signed Samuel Duvall, Capt.

Capt. Daniel Zacharias Troop of Cavalry of the Second Regiment first Cavalry Distirct Maryland Militia. Service 7 Aug - 10 Sep 1814. Zacharias's company formed at Westminster and was discharged at Port Tobacco, Charles County. Zacharias was later succeeded by John Shuee.

Daniel Zacharias, Capt.
John L. Wells, 1st Lieut.
John Shuee, 2nd Lieut.
John C. Cockey, Cornet
Jacob Grove, Qt. M. Sgt.
Adam Swigart, 1st Sgt.

David Stonecipher, 2nd Sgt.
Michael Clapsadle, 3rd Sgt.
George Swigart, 4th Sgt.
Fredrick Hoppy, trumpeter
Jacob Coppensmith, farriar

Privates:
William Hanes, 10
  Aug - 10 Sep 1814
Jacob Lawyer
Fredrick Bachman
William Campbell

Christopher
  Knipple
Adam Sterner
George Zachareias
Christian Garver
Lee Tipton

David Shuee
Robert Crawford
Bazil Hayden
Jacob Grammer
Nicholas Corbin
Peter Nail

APPENDIX D: MUSTER ROLLS OF THE ACTIVE UNITS

Miles Mitten,
 served 10 Aug -
 10 Sep 1814
Jacob Stonecipher

Thomas Mitten,
 served 10 Aug -
 10 Sep 1814
Samuel Long

John Stonecipher
Benjamin Campbell
John Erb
James Edwards

The Troop of Horse of Captain Nicholas Hall formed in Frederick as a "Detachment of Cavalry in the actual service of the United States under the command of Major John Cook in the Second Regiment of Maryland Militia commanded by Lt. Col. Henry Kemp from the 7th August 1814 to the 10th Septr. 1814 When discharged." All were discharged in Charles County. They were allowed "5 days ... for travelling home." According to some of the men, as expressed in their pension and bounty land claims, the unit was engaged in the Battle of Indian Head. Some of the men came from New Market.

Nicholas Hall, Capt.
Thomas Burgee, 1st Liuet.
Barrack Hall, 2nd Lieut.
Micl (Miel?) Burgee, Cornet

Daniel Collins, Qtr. M. Sgt.
Archd. Browning, 2nd Sgt.
John Montgomery, 3rd Sgt.
Henry Houser, 4th Sgt.

Privates:
Benjamin Beall
William Hyatt
Asa Hyatt
John Ellis
Danl. Browning
Edwd. Linton
Benjamin Hagan
Philip McCelfresh,
 served 7 Aug - 21
 Aug 1814
Philip Smith

Ephraim Thornburgh
Joseph Purdy,
 Senr.
Asa Ward
John Griffith
Elisha Fisher
James Kinney
Isaac Davis
George Davis
Samuel Paine
William Lupton
Thomas Eader

William Salmon
John Miller
Benjamin Colehorse
Paul Talbot
Jacob Ijams,
 served 25 Aug -
 10 Sep 1814
William Carney
Joseph Purdy, Jun.
Henry Baker,
 trumpeter

Muster roll of the Infantry company of Capt. George W. Ent (sometimes called the Blues Company) which served in the 3rd Regiment of Maryland Militia under Lieut. Colonel Henry Stemble [Stembel], in the service of the United States, 24 Aug - 30 Sep 1814. This company was drafted at Fredericktown, marched to Baltimore and stationed at Hampstead Hill. [From T.J.C. Williams and Folger McKinsey, *History of Frederick County Maryland*, originally printed in 1910, reprinted Baltimore: Regional Publishing Company, 1979.]

George W. Ent, capt.
Leonard J.M. Littlejohn, 1st lt.
Jacob Nichols, 2nd lt.
John J. McCally, ens.
George Rohr, orderly sgt.
Joshua Dill, 1st sgt.
Michael Peter, 2nd sgt.
John Hurley, 3 rd sgt.
Cyrus Carey, 4th sgt.

Leonard Mitchell, 1st cpl.
Ezra Stoner, 2nd cpl.
John Durst, 3rd cpl., furnished
 substitute, Ezra Dill
Adam Titlow, 4th cpl.
Peter Storm, 5th cpl.
Jacob Knouff, 6th cpl.
George Lowe, drum major
John Keller, fife major

Privates:
Absalom Albaugh
William Baer
Henry Burgess
Stephen Bacon

John Bentz, Jr.
William Bearshank
George Buckey
Oswald Blasford
David Bennett

Thomas Caywood
Henry Crouse
Abraham Crum
Emanuel Carpenter,
 discharged 1 Sep

351

FREDERICK COUNTY MILITIA IN THE WAR OF 1812

William Conner
Vincent Crutcher
Lawrence Doyle
James Dixon
Daniel Durst
Henry Days
Joseph Ebberts
John Ebberts
Daniel Ely
Joseph Evans
Henry Fogler
Charles Ferdon
Peter Folkner
Ezra Gomber
Zeal (Cecilius) Head
James Howe
Frederick Hawman
George Hinkle
George J. Houx
John Jacobs
Corbin Jacobs
Joseph Johnson
Ramer Kolb
Casper Klein (Cline)

Henry Korns
George Keltz
Michael Hoffman
George W. Littlejohn
Michael Lambrecht
George Lambrecht
Otho H.W. Luckett
Peter Mantz
John McDevitt
William Mitten
John Miler
Noble Moling
Israel Mayberry
William Morgan
Lewis Medtart
Robert McCleery
John Mosier
Jacob Nusz
David Newport
John Paine
William Poole
Henry Piney
John Rinner

Mordacai Randall
Christian Stoner
Wesley Stevenson
John Smith
George Showacre
Jacob Showacre
Henry Shotz
Philip Shankel
Ellett Sallers
Jacob Sponseller
Daniel Stover
Ezra Schell
George Shafer
Samuel Thomas
John Taylor
Otho Wilson
John Warthen
Branton Woodward
Ephriam Wiley
George Whipp
John York
Charles Yager
Jacob Ebberts
Jacob Stoner

The rifle company of Captain William Durbin, Jr., (20th Regiment) made its rendezvous at New Windsor on 24 August 1814 and marched off for Baltimore. They were discharged at Camp Diehl, Baltimore, on 27 October.

William Durbin, Jr., Capt.
William Miltin, 1st lt., discharged 1 Sep for inability
Daniel Sulivan, 2nd Lt., promoted to 1st lt. 10 Sep
William Brown, 2nd Lt. & Adjutant, 10 Sep - discharged 12 Oct 1814
Thomas Murray, 1st sgt.
John Yingling, 2nd sgt.

David Sulivan, 3rd sgt.
William Sulivan, 4th sgt.
Robert Smith, 1st cpl.
Jacob Powder, 2nd cpl.
Jacob Casner, 3rd cpl.
Joseph Steel, 4th cpl.
John Michael, fifer
John Sharner, drummer, absent without leave 25 Oct

Privates:
Arthur, John, absent without leave 25 Oct
Adams, William
Bricker, George, absent without leave 25 Oct
Burns, Peter, absent without leave 25 Oct
Burns, George
Beam/Beams, Jacob
Byer, David, never joined service
Burns, John
Bowlin/Bolding, Benjamin
Cox, Jacob, never joined service
Cullison, Joseph, never joined service
Craver, Henry, absent without leave 25 Oct
Davis, Alban, deserted 5 Sep
Erbaugh, Peter, absent without leave 25 Oct
Grimes, James, absent without leave 23 Oct
Gorrell, Samuel
Haines/Hines, Eli, never joined service
Haines, Isaac, never joined service
Harman, John
Harman, Jacob
Haun/Hawn, David, absent leave 25 Oct
Harriss, George, discharged 2 Sep for inability
Hines, John, deserted 25 Sep
Kemp, John, deserted 13 Sep
King, Gilbreth,

APPENDIX D: MUSTER ROLLS OF THE ACTIVE UNITS

joined 15 Oct
Lambert, George, never joined service
Lambert, David, never joined service
Marshall, Henry
Major, Laurence, discharged for inability
Miller, Valentine
Marker, John
Medcalf, Thomas, enlisted 15 Sep
Marker, David, deserted 6 Sep
Ospert/Orpert, John, never joined service
Proby/Praby, John, joined 14 Oct
Peusey, George, never joined service
Peusey, Joel, never joined service
Robinson /Robertson, John, absent without leave 29 Sep
Robinson /Robertson, Joshua
Smeltzer, Jacob, never joined service
Sulivan, Abraham, discharged 3 Sep for inability
Swigert, John, never joined service
Slife, (?) Henry, deserted 30 Sep
Sulivan, Jacob
Segruff/Synuff, Michael, never joined service
Starry, George, absent without leave 25 Oct
Storrap/Slarrap, Jacob
Sense, Peter
Storrap/Slarrap, John
Stoner, John, never joined service
Sharrar/Sharan, Jacob, never joined service
Shepherd, Thomas, never joined service
Tauney/Tourney, John, absent without leave 22 Oct
Turner, Benjamin, absent without leave, 23 Oct
Turner, Jesse
Turner, Solomon
Vaughn, Thomas
Walter/Walton, Christian, absent without leave 25 Oct
Williams, James, never joined service
Warner, George, never joined service
Warner, Abraham, never joined service
Rait, Hammond, never joined service
Fauney, Jacob, bugler, discharged 6 Sep for inability

The company of Henry Steiner served from 25 Aug to 27 Sep 1814. They formed as volunteers at Fredericktown, in Aug 1814. They were discharged at Baltimore Oct 1814. [One member said they fought at the Battle of North Point; stationed on Louderslagers Hill; he said he was in charge of a battery of 6 guns.]

Henry Steiner, capt., sick
Robert G. McPherson, 1st lt.
Lewis Green, 2nd lt.
John Buckey, 1st sgt.
William Hauser, 2nd sgt.
George Dertzback, 3rd sgt.
David Mantz, 4th sgt.

Jacob Kieffer, 1st cpl.
William Steiner, 2nd cpl.
Henry Hauer, 3 cpl. Henry
Marcus Y. Graff, 4th cpl.
Jacob Fouble, musician
John Stouffer, musician

Privates:
Ambrose, Peter
Baer, Michael of John
Barns, Samuel
Blackford, Thomas
Belt, Lloyd
Briant, Samuel
Boyd, David, sick on furlough
Boone, Robert
Burkhart, Daniel
Cossell, William
Dean, Thomas
Dixon, James
Evitt, George
Freburger, Peter
Feagler, Jacob
Goldsborough, Nicholas
Graham, Thomas
Hanshew, Henry
Hauer, George
Harding, John L.
Heffner, Michael
Holler, Henry
Holter, Daniel, furlough
Jamieson, John, sick on furlough
Jenkins, William
Johnson, William
Jolly, Thomas M.
Koontz, John
McClain, George
McFarland, Peter

FREDERICK COUNTY MILITIA IN THE WAR OF 1812

McPherson, William
Murdoch, Richard B.
Miller, John, sick, could not join
Neaff, Abraham
Nixdorff, Henry

Nichols, Adam, sick on furlough
Pyfer, Philip
Potts, Philip T.
Rye, Henry
Schaffner, Jacob
Salmon, Charles

Steiner, John Thomas
Shellman, Jacob
Scott, Thomas
Somervill, James
Schissler, John
Schriver, Jacob

Captain Brengle's company left Fredericktown around 23-25 Aug 1814 and according to one veteran, marched to Clarksburgh on the way to the City of Washington; at Clarksburgh their orders were countermanded to return to Frederick. After their return to Frederick they were ordered to march to Baltimore where they were placed in the service of the United States in the First Regiment on 25 August. They were discharged at Baltimore on 19 Sep 1814.

John Brengle, capt.
Mathias E. Bartgis, 1st lt.
William Kolb, 2nd lt.
Ormond F. Butler, ens.
Alexander Robertson, 1st sgt.
Joseph Adlum, 2nd sgt.
Otho Woltz, 3rd sgt.,
  transferred to the 3rd regiment in Sep
John Brunner, 4th sgt.
John D. Smith, 1st cpl.
John Wilson, 2nd cpl.
Henry Bantz, 3rd cpl.
John Sloan, 4th cpl.

Privates:
Applebee, Hezekiah
Balderson, John
Bartle, Christian
Bantz, John
Bear, David
Brengle, Lawrence
Bevans, Alexander
Bougher, Jacob
Buttler, Tobias
Coleleasure, Abram
Coffman, Henry
Devitt, David B.
Dean, Joshua
Doll, Peter
Drewery/Druery, James
Doll, Michael
Ely, William
Ebbert, Ely
Firestone, Jacob
Gayer/Goyer, Jacob
Goyer/Geyer, Jonas
Gonso, Jacob
Gonso, John
Grave, Reuben
Houck, John
Heisley, John
Hittan/Hilton, Miles, deserted
Hane, David
Hoffman, Andrew
Harrison, Zeph
Hane, David
Holler/Haller, Philip
Kefner/Hefner, Jacob
Kelly, George
Knouf, Greenbury*
Keller, Charles
Kessler, Jacob
Leohr, George, deserted
Lieply/Lickly, Peter
Markey, David
Mattingly, Gabriel J.
Mobly, Bazil, deserted
Mixell/Muell, Jacob, deserted
McVicker, David
Ortner, John
Porter, John
Peters, Charles
Pool, Frederick
Pobst, John
Richtor/Riehl, Jacob
Reckter, John
Rattle, William
Rowe, William
Sholl/Shall, Henry
Springer, Daniel
Shotz, John
Shindler, John
Salmon/Solman, George
Shoup, George
Seize, George
Strickstroke, Jacob
Steahl, Henry
Snowtickle, George
Snyder, Henry, deserted
Wissinger, George
Webster, David
Webster, Samuel
Wissinger, Peter
Young, David
Young, Thomas, deserted
Young, Andrew

* The copy held by the National Archives reads, "William Knaup." However Ensign Ormond F. Butler later submitted a copy of the muster roll to the Federal auditor in support of Greenbury Knouff's claim which shown the name of "Greebery Knouff" in place of "William Knaup."

APPENDIX D: MUSTER ROLLS OF THE ACTIVE UNITS

Matthew Murray's company, "The Middletown Blues," served 25 Aug - 27 Oct 1814. The men were drafted at Middletown, around 25 Aug 1814; they were in Montgomery County when the Battle of Bladensburg took place; from there they marched to Baltimore where they were discharged at Camp Hampstead around 31 Oct 1814.

Matthew Murray, capt.
Francis Richment, 1st lt.
John Nelson, 2nd lt.
Henry Herring, ens.
Charles Miller, 1st sgt.
Jonathan Powell, 2nd sgt.
John Nulton, 3rd sgt.

Leonard Miller, 4th sgt.
Peter Nickem, 1st cpl.
Jacob Custard, 2nd cpl.
Jacob Delawder, 3rd cpl.
Jacob Rowhan, 4th cpl.
William Lane, drummer

Privates:
Alexander, Henry, deserted 23 Oct
Alexander, George
Buzzard, David
Baker, Jacob, sick present
Beckenbaugh, John
Boyer, Jonathan, on furlough from 21 Oct
Bochman, Andrew
Boden, Samuel, never joined service
Bell, Thomas
Delphia, Thomas
Dehaven, William
Dern, Frederick
Dever, Richard
Fox, John
Fish, William
Frederick, John
Frazier, Jeremiah, deserted 24 Oct

Frazier, Fielder, deserted 22 Oct
Boodger, Peter
Gilbert, Reuben
Harlan, Stephen
Herring, John
Hawn, David
Haupt, Jacob
Hile, Adam, absent from 6 Oct
Hickson, Robert
Harquishimer, Jacob
Hicks, George, deserted 27 Aug
Kephart, Simon
Larkins, John
Levy, David
McMulen, Charles
Minnick, George
Muck, (Much) Frederick
Michael, Lewis
Mayberry, Thomas
Mertina, Jacob, absent from 4 Oct

Marlow, Thomas
Muck, Henry
Nussmith, Thomas
Nickem, Joseph
Pape, William
Roads, Jacob
Richards, John
Ridgely, Richard
Shafner, Peter
Smur, Jacob, deserted 21 Oct
Smithy, John
Shank, Peter
Snyder, Abraham
Snyder, George
Unshippen, Peter
Wichter, John
Whitmore, George, absent from 30 Sep
Wiles, James, deserted 27 Aug
Wadsworth, Samuel
Winpigler, John
Henry, servant

The rifle company of Captain Knox of the 1st Battalion of Major Beall Randall served during the period 26 Aug - 27 Oct 1814. Members were from the Taneytown area. The company was discharged at Camp Diehl, Baltimore, around 30 Oct 1814. According to one of the members this unit was encamped at the Rope Walk on Federal Hill. One member served in the capacity of a scout during the Battle of North Point; he said he saw the bombardment of Fort McHenry and witnessed the destruction of the three barges that passed the Fort; after performing the duty as a scout he returned to Baltimore and encamped on Federal Hill until he was mustered out of service. During the Battle of North Point the regiment marched down on the bayside to prevent the soldiers engaged in battle from being flanked. According to Joshua Green, the company was positioned in a corn field in sight of the British Army with orderes to fire on the British if the Americans were driven back. After the battle the command was employed in guarding Baltimore. Some were discharged at Louderslager Hill.

FREDERICK COUNTY MILITIA IN THE WAR OF 1812

William Knox, capt.
John Slick, 1st lt.
George Oyster, 2nd lt.
Henry Hickson, ens.
William Moore, 1st sgt.
John Little, 2nd sgt.
James Ross, 3rd sgt.
Patrick Burk, 4th sgt.
James Drummon, 5th sgt.

Ethelbert Taney, 1st cpl.
Peter Ec..es, 2nd cpl.
John Six, 3rd cpl.
James Rogers, 4th cpl.
Samuel Gault, 5th cpl.
Abraham Linn, 6th cpl.
John Flegal, fifer
Andrew Walker, drummer

Privates:
Angel, George
Albaugh, Adam
Armstrong, William
Bramwell, William
Burk, Michael
Bartlet, Joseph
Brack, Frederick,
 deserted, 26 Sep
Bentley, George
Brown, John
Bowman, George
Clabaugh, Jacob,
 deserted 15 Sep
Crouse, Christian,
 deserted 11 Sep
Calf, Martin,
 deserted 10 Sep
Cochran, John
Clingan, William
Coblents, Jacob,
 discharged by
 doctor 8 Sep
Cornell, Thomas
Dorsey, Michael
Delosure,
 Ignatious
Damoot, John
Davidson, Jesse
Eckes, Nicholas
Eck, Peter
Flegal, David
Fair, Michael,
 discharged by
 doctor 8 Sep
Grace, Michael
Gougher, Jacob
Greason, Nathan
Green, Joshua
Hiteshoe, John,
 deserted 23 Sep
Hiteshoe, Gideon
Hiteshoe, Jacob
Hollinberger,
 Peter
Hawn, Isaac
Hann, Henry
Hann, Jacob
Hesson, John
Hayes, Abraham
Hiner, Harbert
Hann, William
Hollenberger,
 William
Hiteshoe, Abraham
Iser, George,
 deserted 11 Sep
Knouf, Jacob
Koons, Jacob
Martin, David, 17
 Sep - 27 Oct
Naille, Samuel
Newcomer, John,
 deserted 15 Sep
Naile, William
Ott, Michael
Orendorf, John
Pepper, Abraham,
 absent without
 leave 24 Oct
Paxton, John
Rinedoller, John
Rafesnider, John
Richards, John,
 deserted 28 Aug
Sharrah, William
Sharrah, George
Slider, Jacob
Shealy, Andrew
Stiner, John,
 deserted 15 Sep
Smith, Jacob
Stinchecome,
 Nathaniel
Sypher, Henry
Smith, Joseph
Sellers, Jacob,
 deserted 27 Aug
Shurp, Conrad, 17
 Sep - 27 Oct
Vanzant, John
Wickard, Phillip
Wetzel, Daniel
Wetzel, John
Walker, William
Young, John
Zumbren, Jacob
Zumbren, George
Zollinger, George
Hunt, John O.

At least three cavalry companies of the First Cavalry District, 2nd Regiment (Frederick County), were called up as the British approached Washington, D.C. 1st Lieutenant Upton Reid's Troop of Horse served in Washington, D. C. from 26 Aug to 3 Sep 1814.

Upton Reid, brevet 1st lt.
George Troxel, 2nd lt.

Leonard Six, cornet

Privates:
Willson, Edward J.
McWilliams,
 Clement
Delaplane, Daniel
Sheets, Jacob
Elder, Nathaniel

Stulz, Nicholas
Haugh, Daniel
Six, John
Heiner, John
Elder, Jesse
Price, George
Koons, John

Troxel, Peter
Koons, Jacob
Phares(?), William
Spalding, Basil
Henning, John
Spalding, Henry
Hainer, Andrew

APPENDIX D: MUSTER ROLLS OF THE ACTIVE UNITS

Galt, Moses
Nead, Henry
Elder, Henry
Quynn, Patrick
Shoup, Jacob
Shorl, John

Troxel, Jacob
Keepers, Michell
Barrick, Samuel
Hersch(?), Philip
Wolfe, George
Six, George

Koons, William
Boyle, Peter
Gillmeyer, Francis
Koons, Henry

The company of Captain Nicholas Turbutt of the Fredericktown area was called up on 1 Sep 1814. They marched from Frederick Town on 2 Sep and arrived at Camp Hampstead on Sunday the 4th Sept. The were discharged at Camp Hampstead, Baltimore on 27 Oct 1814. Annotations in brackets are from Williams, *History of Frederick County*.

Nicholas Turbutt, capt.
Jacob Crumbaker, 1st lt.
Otho Wooltz, 2nd lt., 5 Sep
Daniel Burkhartt, ens., 8 Sep
Asa Aud, orderly sgt.
Joshua Davis, 1st sgt.
Jacob Teshner, 2nd sgt.
Benjamin Beckett, 3rd sgt.

Philip Rightsel, 4th sgt.
Daniel Shotts, 1st cpl.
Eli Williams, 2nd cpl.
John Fouble, 3rd cpl.
Owing Fling, 4th cpl.
George Zimmerman, fifer
John Degrange, drummer
Reson Hobbs

Privates:
Albough, William [Wm. H. Albaugh]
Applebee, Hezekiah
Armstrong, Richard, 8 Sep, deserted 12 Oct
Adkins, Benjamin, never joined
Bopst, Daniel
Baltzel, John [hatter]
Bready, David
Beard, Jacob
Beall, Ninian
Clineheart, Frederick, on furlough 12 Oct
Copenhaver, John
Cook, Benjamin
Colier, Steven, deserted 3 Oct
Cannon, Jacob
Calton, William, never joined
Crum, John
Crum, Isaac, not yet joined
Canaga, Jacob, not yet joined
Dick, John, discharged by surgeon
Delashmutt, Otho
Davis, James
Englebright, [Englebrecht] William
Egnew, [Agnew] Henry
Fouble, [Fauble] Casper
Febus, [Phebus] Peter
Finck, [Finch] John, joined 8 Sep
Fout, Balser, not yet joined
Farding, Charles, 15 Sep, deserted 24 Sep
Gosson?, Oliver C., absent?
Gates, Robert, deserted 20 Oct
Gilbert, Jacob, not yet joined
Glison, Thomas, absent without leave Sep
Hatten, [Holer] Jacob
Hawkins, James
Hufman, [Hoffman, sr.] George
Hickson, Thomas
Hobbs, Reson [Regin]
Hilkey, George
Hossefross [Hassefross],
John
Holter, William
Holter, George
Hempey, Henry
Haris, [Harris] Reson, 8 Sep
Harts, Peter, 8 Sep, deserted 2 Oct
Jarvis, Zadock
Johnson, Erasmus
Jacobs, Philip
Kline [Klein], Peter
Klink, John
Keller, Peter
Kelly, Edward, deceased in hospital
Keafer, Henry
Kessler, David, 8 Sep
Lakins [Lakin], William
Lakins [Lakin], John, not yet joined
Lohr, Frederick, not yet joined
McClay, William, deserted 17 Oct
Moore, George, deserted 20 Oct
Marlowe, Hanson
Medary, Andrew
Moling, Edward

FREDERICK COUNTY MILITIA IN THE WAR OF 1812

McCormick, George
Macmillan, Thomas
More [Moore], Charles
Miles [Niles], John
Mottern, Peter
Main, John, 8 Sep
Measel, Jacob
Miller, George, not yet joined
Ott, Peter
Ropp, Samuel
Ramburgh, Frederick
Richards, William, 8 Sep
Shell [Schell, Charles, [Jr.]
Sponseller, Frederick
Smith, Henry

Stailey [Staley], Abraham
Stallings, Richard
Spahn, Elias, discharged by surgeon
Sprangle [Sprengle], David
Swigard, Peter
Smith, Thomas, 8 Sep
Stone, Jacob, 8 Sep
Sponseller, John, sick absent without leave
Stailey [Staley], Peter, 8 Sep
Shafer, Simon
Stone, Henry
Taylour [Taylor], William

Tudor, John
Titlow, Daniel
Tabler, William
Troutman, Peter
Tolbort [Talbott], Wilson
Tidy, James, not yet joined
Wherett [Whirett], Bennett
Ward, Edward, enlisted Sep 1814
Wenrick, John
Ways, Basel, 3 Sep
Widerick, Christian
Wilson, Greenbury, deserted 19 Sep
Williamson, James, not joined
Williams, David
Zimmerman, Valentine

Captain Joseph Wood's company served from 3 Aug until 28 Oct 1814. They were at the entrenchments during the Battle of North Point. Made their rendezvous at Campt Diehl.

Roll (1) 3 Aug - 13 Oct 1814:
Joseph Wood, capt.
George Barrick, 1st lt.
Jacob Winebrener, 2nd lt., joined 27 Aug
Jacob Beard, ens.
John Corcoran, 1st sgt.
Ezra Barrick, 2nd sgt.

Charles Elder, 3rd sgt.
Benjamin McHenry, 4th sgt., on furlough 4 Oct
John Champer, 1st cpl.
Jefferson Godman, 2nd cpl.
William Carmack, 3rd cpl.
Frederick Miller, 4th cpl.

Privates:
Algeyer/Allgoyer, Henry, enlisted 11 Oct
Armstrong, James
Barrick, Cornelius
Bauston, Philip
Beaumont, Basil
Byroad, Peter, deserted 29 Sep
Colliflower, Michael
Colliflower, George
Colliflower, Samuel
Condon, Edward
Creager, William, on furlough 18 Sep
Doyle, Lago [Jago, Leg?]
Davis, Thomas,
    deserted 21 Sep
Davis, Richard
Erwin/Ervin, John
Eyelor, Henry
Filler, Solomon
Filler, William
Glisan, Charles
Griffith, Lemuel
Hefner, Daniel
Hartsack, Peter
Hicks, Joseph
Harbaugh, Benjn.
Horn, Jesse
Houk/Houx, John
Hider, William
Huffard, John
Harlan, James
Hoffman, John
Iselnaugel, Michl.
Jacobs, Philip
James, Basil, joined 16 Sep

Johnson/Johnston, Thomas
Jones, Jeremiah
Kerby/Kurbey, John
Klein, Frederick
Keeny, Jacob, deserted 12 Sep
Lightlider, George
Late, George
Long, George
Loch/Lock, Abraham
Lookbaugh, John
Lyda/Lydd, James
McFarlan, Peter, sick absent with leave 12 Oct
McBee, William
McCloud, Thomas
McUlroy, James, joined 10 Sep
Martin, John
Myers, John

APPENDIX D: MUSTER ROLLS OF THE ACTIVE UNITS

Metcalf, William
Meckan/Mechan, John
Nusbaum, Jacob
Rider, George
Ryder/Rider, Frederick
Ross, Frederick
Robertson, George
Robbins, Benjn.
Staup, Adam
Staup, Eli
Staup, Jacob
Saffill, Orlandor, furloughed 27 Sep
Staub, John
Smith, George
Shroyer, William
Smith, John
Shryock, Henry
Stoner, David
Speaker, John, deserted 13 Sep
Seward/Steward, David, deserted 1 Oct
Smith, John, deserted 24 Sep
Smith, Joseph
Spruttsman, Jacob, joined 27 Sep
Shaffer, Daniel, joined 27 Sep
Tuner, [Tener, Teener] Phillip, joined 27 Aug
Tuner, [Tener?] David, joined 27 Aug
Taneyhill, Samuel, joined 9 Oct
Willhide, Henry, joined 27 Aug
Waggoner, John
Watts, John
Savoy, Samuel, captain's servant

Roll (2) 14 Oct - 28 Oct 1814:
Joseph Wood, capt.
George Barrick, 1st lt.
Jacob Winebrunner, 2nd lt.
Jacob Beard, ens.
John Cocoran, 1st sgt.
Ezra Barrick, 2nd sgt.
Charles Elder, 3rd sgt.
Benj. McHenry, 4th sgt., joined 27 Aug, furloughed 4 Oct, returned 16 Oct
Jefferson Godman, 1st cpl.
William Carmack, 2nd cpl.
Frederick Miller, 3rd cpl.
Henry Shryock, 4th cpl.

Privates:
Armstrong, James
Barrick, Cornelius
Baustin/Bauston, Philip
Beaumont, Buscal/Bascal
Colliflouer, Michael
Colliflouer, Gorge
Colliflouer, Samuel
Condon, Edward
Champer, John, deserted 23 Oct
Doyle, Jago
Davis, Richard, absent 27 Oct
Erwin, John
Eyelor, Henry
Filler, Solomon
Filler, William, on furlough 26 Oct
Glisan, Charles, furlough 26 Oct
Griffith, Lamuel
Gilbert, John
Hefner, Daniel
Hartzack, Peter
Hix, Joseph, furlough 26 Oct
Harbaugh, Benjn.
Han/Horn, Jesse
Houx, John, furlough 26 Oct
Hider, William
Hufford/Huffard, John, furlough 26 Oct
Harland, James
Hoffman, John
Iselnaughle, Michl.
Jacobs, Philip
James, Basil
Johnson, Thomas
Jones, Jeremiah, deserted 24 Oct
Kurby, John
Klein, Frederick
Liglider, George
Late, George
Long, George
Lock, Abraham, deserted 24 Oct
Lookbaugh, John
Lyda, James
McBee, William
McCloud, Thomas, sick in hospital
McAlroy, James
Martin, John
Myers, John
Metcalf, William
McCahan, John, lost cartridge box
Nusbaum, Jacob
Rider, George
Rider, Frederick
Robertson, George, absent 28 Oct
Robbins, Benjamin
Staup, Adam
Staup, Eli, deserted 26 Oct
Staup, Jacob
Staup/Staub, John
Smith, George, furlough 26 Oct
Shroyer, William
Smith, John
Stoner, David
Smith, Joseph
Spruttsman, Jacob
Shafer, Daniel
Tener/Teener, Philip
Tener, David
Taneyhill, Samuel
Willhide, Henry
Waggoner, John
Watts, John, deserted 14 Oct, musket not delivered up
Savoy, Samuel, waiter

FREDERICK COUNTY MILITIA IN THE WAR OF 1812

Captain Marker's Mountain Rangers from Middletown was activated a second time on 25 Aug 1814, this time for Baltimore; discharged at Camp Hampstead, 27 Oct 1814.

Daniel Marker, capt.
Otho Thomas, 1st lt.
James Shawen, ens.
Joseph Johnson, 1st sgt.
Christian Tabler, 2nd sgt.,
  furloughed 1 Oct
Edward Butler, 3rd sgt.,
  furloughed
John Woolard, furloughed 25 Sep
Henry Allen, 1st cpl.
John Delashmutt, 2nd cpl.
John Simmons, 3rd cpl
William Brookover, 4th cpl.

Privates:
Arnold, John
Allen, Alexander
Bear, George
Custard, John
Copland, Samuel
Castle, Eli
Conner, Thomas
Delashmutt, Nelson
Davis, Walter
Daily, John
Davis, Elijah
Delashmutt, Denis
Eaton, Joseph
Everhart, William
Forrest, Solomon
Forrest, Owen
Fox, Peter
Gladhill, John,
  deserted 12 Oct
Gibbons, Orwell
Hatten, William

Hanshaw, George
Jenkins, Theodora
Koon, George
Lineweaver, Casper
Martin, Jacob
Mattingly, Thomas
Murphy, James,
  deserted 28 Sep
Nichols, John
Osburn, Joseph
Ortman, Daniel,
  deserted 19 Sep
Ohagan, Imishade
Pickens, Robert
Roberts, William
Smith, Samuel
Stewart, Daniel
Stotlemire, David,
  deserted 20 Oct
Strailman, George,
  deserted 20 Oct

Stephens, James,
  deserted 25 Aug
Thralls, John,
  deserted 25 Sep
Tolbott, Benjamin
Thomas, Archibald
Winpigler, John
Winpigler, George
Wian, Henry
Woodard,
  Nathaniel,
  furloughed 11 Oct
Winfield, Lawrence
Wise, James,
  deserted 29 Aug
Wian, John
Crap, Boler,
  servant, resident
  Baltimore
Thomson, Bithy,
  servant, resident
  of Baltimore

Captain Galt's company (3rd Regiment, 2nd Divisions, 11th Brigade) left Emmittsburg around 26 August 1814, marched to Taneytown and then to Baltimore. Most of the men were from Emmittsburg/Taneytown area. They arrived at Camp Hampstead on 31 August and were placed as reserves in the entrenchments. Henry Green recalled the company being stationed at the Chincapin Hill entrenchments. "It rained a great deal. Mud and water were almost knee deep." Some men said they were discharged as late as 3 November 1814. The muster roll reads, 31 Aug - 27 Oct 1814.

According to Lieutenant Snider, Galt's company was designated 1st company of the 2nd Battalion commanded by Major George M. Eichelberger, 3rd Regt, Infantry commanded by Col. Henry Stemble. He said that the company was mustered into the service of the United States at Camp Hampstead on 31 August 1814. The last number in the entry is the distance from residence to point of rendezvous (Taneytown unless stated otherwise).

John Galt, capt., 3
Nicholas Snider, 1st lt., 0
Jacob Row, 1st lt., 7
Peter Crapster, Ens., 2
Henry Green, 1st sgt, 16
Henry Gueyer, 2nd sgt., 10
John Herbaugh, 3rd sgt, 21

Elias Herbaugh, 4th sgt., 21
Jacob Lane, 1st cpl., 13
James Storm, 2nd cpl., 10
Felix Taney, 3rd cpl, 2 miles from Hampstead
Jacob Trout, 4th cpl., 10 miles from Hampstead

APPENDIX D: MUSTER ROLLS OF THE ACTIVE UNITS

John Durf, drummer, 7
Daniel Baldwin, fifer, 3

Privates:
Atlespurier, Sebastian 3
Armstrong, Oliver, 1, deserted 15 Sep
Bowmaster, John, 5
Bowersock, Daniel, 3
Black, Jacob, 6
Boner, Joseph, 10
Barton, Samuel, 10
Barkdoll, Christian, 15
Baldwin, Isaac, 3
Baker, Henry, 10
Beard, John, 1
Black, Henry, 0 from Hampstead
Baker, Jacob, 10 miles from Hampstead
Colwell, David, 0, sick absent 15 Oct
Cover, Joseph, 12 miles from Hampstead
Cornel, Richard, 5
Crouse, Lewis, 12 miles from Hampstead
Craton, James, 8 miles from Hampstead
Cover, Jacob, 12
Dowd, George, resident of Baltimore
Davis, Joshua, 3
Emerly, James, 5
Flegle, George, 9
Fuss, Conrad, 10
Flaut, Jacob, 23, sick absent 19 Sep
Gooker, Peter, resident of Baltimore Co.
Gump, Isaac, 13
Hammond, James, 5, deserted 21 Oct
Harriet, Henry, 10
Houkman, Henry, 9
Hannah, Elijah, 10
Hovis, Adam, 11

Hynson, John, Sr., resident of Baltimore
Hyson, John, Jr., resident of Baltimore
Herbaugh, Jonathan, 21
Herbaugh, Jacob, 21
Henning, Adam, 10
Hockensmith, David, 7
Heck, Jacob, 3
Hull, Andrew, 4
Iodum, Daniel, 13, deserted 22 Oct
Jones, William, 2
Jones, John, 7
Jordan, William, 13
Kesslering, Lewis, 3
Keefer, Lewis, 7
Knouf, John, 10
Kephart, David, 11
Kelly, John, joined 7 Sep, resident of Baltimore
Khuntz, Simon, 10
Lane, Joseph, 12
Lynn, John, 2
Larew, William, 5 miles from Hampstead
Lare, Samuel, resident of Baltimore Co., 10
McVay, John, 10
Mooney, Daniel, 21
McKissic, James, 20, sick absent 14 Oct
McKinney, John, 5
Manahan, James, 20
Myles, James, Baltimore Co.
Murdock, John B., resident of Baltimore, dead 18 Oct
Newry, John, 20
Ott, George, 7
Odonal, James, 10
Ocker, Henry, 10
Oyler, John, 17
Oyler, George, joined 7 Sep, 18 miles from Hampstead

Oler, John, joined 28 Sep, 7
Perkins, John, 8, deserted 26 Sep
Peterman, Jacob, 10
Reinicker, Paul, 0
Robinson, George, resident of Baltimore
Rife, Abraham, 5
Row, Samuel, 6
Row, Michael, 10
Robinson, Charles, 15
Rader, Michael, 13
Rickets, Benjamin, joined 6 Sep, 20 miles from Hampstead, deserted 15 Sep
Shilling, Michael, resident of Baltimore
Sell, Lewis, 10
Smith, Henry, 10
Shoemaker, John, 0
Sumbrum, David, 3, deserted 15 Sep
Smith, Charles, 20
Strine, William, 5, deserted 15 Sep
Shafer, Jacob, 16
Sumbrum, John, 5
Secrist, Jonas, 4
Stoufer, Henry, 20
Smith, Frederick, 17
Stine, Patrick, 13
Shorts, Jacob, 10
Shoup, Baltzer, joined 6 Sep, 2 miles from Hampstead
Shriner, George, 3 miles from Hampstead
Stults, James, 3 miles from Hampstead
Sheely, John, 3
Tarlton, Elisha, resident of Baltimore
Tresler, Henry, 22
Tronberger, Frederick, 2
Toophorn, George, 10, waiter to Maj. Eickelberger.

FREDERICK COUNTY MILITIA IN THE WAR OF 1812

Uphold, Sebastian, 12
Willyard, Lawrence, joined 3 Oct, 20 miles from Hampstead
Willyard, John, 20, deserted 10 Sep
Whitmore, Frederick,
discharged 5 Sep
Whetsel, William, discharged 5 Sep
Weller, Henry, 15, sick absent 19 Sep
Wyman, John
Wivel, John, 5
Wharton, Ralph, 10
Welch, Jacob, 10
Winter, Jacob, resident of Baltimore Co, rendezvous at Hampstead, 0
Yingling, John, 5, sick absent 15 Sep
Young, John, 10
Young, Andrew, 20
Zacharias, Mathias, 10

The company of Captain Barton Hackney, from the Fredericktown and Middletown area, participated in the Battle of North Point, according to one of its members, P. Charles Hackney. Their entire period of service covered was from 1 Sep 1814 until 29 Oct 1814.

Barton Hackney, capt., furloughed 22 Oct
James Simmons, 1st lt.
Benjamin Lakins, 2nd lt.
Robert Johnson, ens.
Joseph West, 1st sgt.
Josiah Frazier, 2nd sgt.
Henry Filler, 3rd sgt.

Andrew M. Clopper, 4th sgt.
Elisha Howard, 5th sgt.
Ralph Nichols, 1st cpl.
William Stover, 2nd cpl.
George Kephart, 3rd cpl.
Walter Gill, 4th cpl.
Francis Daus, 5th cpl.

Privates:
Alsop, Joseph, deserted 23 Oct
Aler, Jacob
Berry, Samuel, deserted 14 Sep
Ball, Samuel
Bryan, William
Beall, Thomas
Baily, William
Baughman, Adam, joined 17 Sep
Beachtle, George, joined 25 Sep, deserted 23 Oct
Cartnail, Jacob
Cline, Frederick, deserted 14 Sep
Cooley, James, sick in hospital 15 Sep
Dawson, Nicholas, deserted 14 Sep
Downing, Dory
Flanagan, Joseph
Friday, Henry, sick furloughed 4 Oct
Garrott, Middleton
Galwith, John W., joined 30 Sep
Hestand, Daniel,
deserted 23 Oct
Horn, Abraham
Hackney, Charles P.
Hestand, John, joined 6 Sep
Hays, John
Hershabarger, John B., furloughed 20 Oct
Jones, Thomas, discharged by surgeon 4 Oct
Johnson, John H. [K.?]
Jones, James
Jinkens, Simon
Knouft, George
Krouse, John
Kephart, George
Kesler, William
Long, John
Leaply, John
Martin, Thomas
Miller, Christian
Myres, Peter
Marshal, Augustus
Michael, John, joined 10 Sep
May, John, joined 10 Sep
McDavitt, Peter,
deserted 23 Oct
Nickles, Benjamin
Polman, Michael, joined 10 Sep
Polman, John, joined 10 Sep, deserted 21 Oct
Queen, William
Richards, Michael
Reeder, James, sick in hospital 17 Oct
Reed, Benjamin, deserted 24 Oct
Recruit, (?)
Richard, sick in hospital 22 Oct
Richter, Frederick
Relien, Jacob S.
Slagle, Charles
Slagle, Jacob
Shover, Adam
Stover, George
Squire, Thomas
Umbaugh, John
Warthon, Nicholas
Weddle, George
Wilson, Aquilla
Woolf, George, deserted 23 Oct
Wasky, Christian
Way,, joined 10

APPENDIX D: MUSTER ROLLS OF THE ACTIVE UNITS

Sep Jacob
Williard, Elias,
joined 30 Sep

Yacke, Peter,
joined 25 Sep,
deserted 23 Oct

Bill, Negro
servant,
discharged 19 Sep

Company of Captain Upton Norris, later succeeded by Captain John Fonsten. The men were enrolled at New Windsor and Westminster and marched from Westminster to Baltimore where they engaged in the defense of the city. This company served from 2 Sep until 27 Oct 1814. Last number in the entry is the distance from rendezvous (Westminster) to the soldier's residence.

John Fonsten, capt., 15
Jacob Copenhaver, 1st lt., 8
John Lowe, 2nd lt., 15
John Mathias, 1st sgt., 2
Carroll Hammond, 2nd sgt, 16
Abalard Stevenson, 3rd sgt., 5
Lewis Green, 4th sgt., 17
Philip Griffith, 5th sgt., 15

Andrew Groaner, 1st cpl., 15
Jacob Myerly, 2nd cpl., 2
John Powder, 3rd cpl., 3
Abraham Wampler, 4th cpl., 0
William Eckman, 5th cpl., 16
Michael Fogle, drummer, 10
Charles Michael, fifer, 2

Privates:
Andrews, Henry, 7
Aerhart, Valentine, 7
Attic, George, 7
Baldwin, Peter, 4
Bloom, Peter, 10
Baldwin, George, 6
Biggle, Jacob, 8
Bowhorn, George, 16
Bowhorn, William, 16
Beal, David, discharged by certificate 26 Sep
Bittle, Henry, 12
Bond, John, 10
Bever, John, 2
Bond, Benjamin, 8
Bankert, Mathias, 4
Bowers, Adam, 6
Brown, John, 16
Brightwill, Thomas, 16
Brown, Robert, 15
Burgoon, Jacob, 6
Crawmer, Daniel, 15
Clabough, Thomas, 9
Crawmer, Helpher, 15
Crous, William, 2
Cain, Benjamin, deserted 13 Sep 1814

Clary, Daniel, deserted 20 Sep 1814
Cook, Thomas, 13
Crowl, David, 2
Chamberlain, Walter, sick absent 3 Oct 1814
Crumrine, Peter, 12
Crumrine, John, 9
Clary, Samuel, sick absent 16 Sep
Crawford, William, 8
Crawford, Samuel, 7
Cramlet, Andrew, deserted 14 Sep
Chew, William, deserted 6 Sep
Davis, John, deserted 30 Sep
Dunn, Edward, 18
Dorsey, Otho, sick absent 26 Sep
Dayhoof, Christian, deserted 20 Sep
Eves, Elias, 14
Evans, James, 8
Fogle, David, 11
Finch, Adam, 20
Frock, William, 8
Flugle, John, 6
Fetterling, John, 2
Fringer, George, 2

Gilbert, Jacob, 2
Gausnel, Beal, deserted 17 Sep
Hughes, Patrick, 8
Hahn, Abraham, 8
Humbert, George, 10
Horn, Basil, 8
Horn, Benjamin [Hook according to sick/dead list], sick absent 9 Oct
Homes, James, 2
Jones, Samuel, discharged by certificate 11 Oct
Johns, Thomas, deserted 15 Sep
Keeny, Nathaniel, 13
Kingsley, Samuel, enlisted 25 Sep
Kelly, John, 12
Key, William, 18
Kint, Abraham, 8
Kuntz, George, 12
Kelly, Patrick, sick absent 24 Sep
Lowman, John, deserted 14 Sep
Leese, Philip, 7
Louderslagle, Solomon, 2
Lippie, David, 9
Laman, Jacob, deserted 1 Oct

FREDERICK COUNTY MILITIA IN THE WAR OF 1812

Lookinbeel, Samuel, 16
Martin, Anthony, sick absent 29 Sep, died 21 Oct
Messler, John, 12
Mock, Peter, deserted 14 Sep
Manahan, Thomas, deserted 14 Sep
Myerly, Solomon, 3
McInzey, Austin, 3
Myerly, David, deserted 25 Sep
Myerly, Benjamin, deserted 28 Sep
Mobley, Elias, 2
McDaniel, Joseph, 15
Mulnix, John, 16
Myers, John of Peter, 7
Myers, John, 6
McGee, James, sick absent 24 Sep
McOye, Henry, 15
McKley, George, enlisted 27 Sep
McWilliams, James, 6
Neusbaum, John, 15
Ourent, Daniel, 15
Peters, Samuel, 1
Powel, Jacob, 8
Powel, George, 6
Pool, Basil, sick absent 3 Oct
Preston, John, furloughed from 21 Oct for 7 days
Packwood, John, deserted 9 Oct
Rees, Benjamin, 6
Roadpouch, Peter, 7
Rowsen, Jacob, 9
Reichart, Christian, 13
Rutter, Thomas, 11
Stansbury, Isaac, 4
Smith, George, deserted 4 Oct
Stoufer, Jacob, deserted 7 Oct
Shriver, Samuel, 8
Stoufer, David, 8
Selby, Obadiah, 8
Staly, Malachiah, deserted 14 Sep
Spurrier, Greenbury, 16
Shoemaker, Christoph, deserted 14 Oct
Shuey, Daniel, 2
Simpson, Benjamin, sick absent 14 Oct
Shafer, John, 4
Sneck, Henry, 9
Stegner, Jacob, 12
Stegner, George, 12
Sneck, John, 9
Stone, George, 9
Smeethe, [Smith?] Peter, discharged by certificate 8 Oct
Stone, John, deserted 14 Sep
Stuller, Conrad, 8
Shanabrooke, Casper, deserted 1 Oct
Sponsaler, Jacob, sick absent 7 Oct
Seabrookes, Samuel, 16
Shroyer, Frederick, 8
Shriver, John, 10
Shilling, John, deserted 1 Oct
Stone, Jacob, 7
Souder, Conrad, deserted 16 Sep
Stall, Jacob, deserted 15 Sep
Shelton, Thomas, deserted 14 Sep
Shafer, Frederick, deserted 4 Oct
Stuller, Ulerich, deserted 9 Oct
Sheets, Samuel, 6
Taman, Aquilla, 5
Trump, Casper, deserted 24 Sep
Walterson, John, deserted 20 Sep
Walter, Joseph, 12
West, Joshua, deserted 15 Sep
Woods, Michael, 10
Weaver, Philip, 6
Whitmier, Simon, 12
Ways, Thomas, deserted 14 Sep
Walter, Jacob, deserted 21 Sep
Walter, William, 12
Wilson, William, deserted 14 Sep
West, William, deserted 13 Sep
Wine, Jacob, deserted 14 Sep
Welk, George, 10
Wood, Bennet, deserted 28 Sep
Williams, Lilburn, 17
Wampler, Lewis, ...?
Yingling, Henry, deserted 3 Oct
Yorkee(?), John, dist.?
Yingling, John, deserted 20 Sep
Bevins, Henry, enlisted 2 Oct 1814
Boring, Zacharias, deserted 30 Sep
Byers, Michael, 3

Captain Shawen's company was comprised of men from the Fredericktown and Middletown area; they served 5 Sep - 27 Oct 1814.

Daniel Shawen, capt.
Henry Culler, lt.
Lewis Birely, ens.
King English, 1st sgt.
Jno. H.P. Castle, 2nd sgt.
Jacob Grove (Grave), 3rd sgt., deserted 24 Oct
Isaac Sewman, 4th sgt.
Jno. Miller, 1st cpl.
Jacob Derner, 2nd cpl.
Joseph Scott, 3rd cpl.
Henry Flook, 4th cpl., deserted 15 Oct

APPENDIX D: MUSTER ROLLS OF THE ACTIVE UNITS

Albert, William
Allisander,
 (Alexander) Jacob
Burns, Jacob
Beckly, Henry
Buzerd, Samuel
Boyer, Jonathan,
 deserted 1 Oct
Colwell, Charles,
 discharged 11 Oct
Collinger, Phillip
Casy, Daniel
Colbert, Joseph,
 resident of
 Washington Co.,
 deserted 13 Oct
Colens, Mathew,
 resident of
 Washington Co.
Derner, George
Dutrow, Henry
Dickson, Jno.
Delawder, George,
 discharged 10 Oct
Eckman, Jacob
Frey, Michael
Geisendurf,
 William
Grove, Leonard,
 deserted 24 Oct
Gladden, James,
 deserted 13 Oct
Green, Jno.,
 deserted 12 Sep
Gladhill, William,
 deserted 13 Oct
Gilbert, George,
 deserted 3 Oct
Gladden, George
Hunsbury,
 Frederick
Huffman, Jno.
Hart, Ezra
Huffman, Henry
Henning, Tho.
Infield, George
Ifirt, Henry
Johnson, Jacob,
 discharged 19 Oct
Lewis, Jno.
Lefever, George
Masaw, Jno.
Miller, Jno.,
 deceased 9 Oct
 1814
Miller, George,
 sick absent 6 Oct
Martial, Tho.,
 deserted 15 Sep
Neff, George
Natt, Joseph
Padget, Allison
Plummer, William,
 deserted 2 Oct
Prutzman,
 Christian
Plickenstarve
 (Plickenstemer),
 Christian
Piper, Jacob
Parter (Porter),
 Reason, resident
 of Baltimore Co.,
 deserted 22 Sep
Rise, Wm., sick
 absent 21 Oct
Rothrock, Lewis,
 deserted 24 Oct
Rensberg, Ezra
Rensberg, Joseph
Steevens
 (Stevens), Joseph
Stottlemeyer,
 Joseph
Slusser, Andrew
Shink, Phillip
Smey, Daniel
Siling, Andrew
Stemp, George
Snur, Henry
Shink, Peter
Summer, Jacob
Suman, Jno.
Smith, Jacob
Shilling, William,
 deserted 18 Sep
Tarrence, James
Woolf, Jacob
Yentes, William

Some British prisoners and British deserters were marched up from Washington following the Battle of Bladensburg. Thirty-four men of Captain Markey's company (16th Regiment), under the command of 1st Lieutenant William Kolb, engaged in guarding the British prisoners (around 80 privates and two officers according to Marine, *British Invasion of Maryland, 1812-1815*.) at the Barracks at Frederick. This unit served from 13 Oct, or earlier, until 15 Nov 1814 at which time (according to private Bennet Carlen), a troop of cavalry from Baltimore took the prisoners into custody.

William Kolb, 1st lt.
George Shultz, 1st sgt.

Eli Ogle, 2nd sgt.

Privates:
Bivins, Alexander
 (payroll lists
 Benjamin vice
 Alexander)
Carlen, James
Carlen, Bennet
Clopper, Nicholas,
 joined 25 Oct
Creglow, George
Dowdle, William
Eador, Jacob
Febus, Peter,
 joined 3 Nov
Fields, William
Gibbs, George
Getzendanner,
 Solomon
Hopper, John,
 joined 6 Nov
Hoffman, Andrew
Killian, Philip,
 joined 16 Oct
Kinkerly, John
Bopst, John,
 joined 16 Oct
Linton, Zachariah,

FREDERICK COUNTY MILITIA IN THE WAR OF 1812

 joined 2 Nov
Medley, Thomas
Mattingly, Gabriel
McDevitt, Peter,
 joined 2 Nov
McVickers, David
Miller, John
Quynn/Quinn,
 William, joined 6
 Nov
Rowe, Michael
Shultz, Henry
Stall, Henry
Tull, Walter
Warthen, Benjamin
Ways, Basil,
 joined 1 Nov
Wandle, David
Young, David

INDEX

-A-
ABBOTT, Mrs.
John, 142
ABRECHT,
Catherine, 231
ADAMS, J. W.,
126
James F., 315
John, 323
John C., 30, 323,
333
Margaret, 49
William, 30, 352
ADDELSPERGER,
Sebastian, 252
ADDLESPERGER,
Robina, 200
ADER, Sussana,
277
ADKINS,
Benjamin, 30, 357
Charles, 36
Kaby, 36
William, 36
ADLESPERGER,
James, 290
Josiah, 52, 290
ADLUM, John, 4
Joseph, 30, 354
Mary, 30
AERHART,
Valentine, 30, 363
AGNEW, Henry,
30, 357
Jane, 67
Samuel, 30, 325,
334
AHLBACH,
Christian, 30
AKERS, Eliza

Jane, 118
Peter G.
Zemiah B., 92
ALBACH, Adam,
30
Maria, 30
ALBAUGH,
Abraham, 114
Absalom, 351
Absolom, 30
Adam, 30, 356
Adeline, 30
Amanda, 30
Amanda E., 30
Annie M., 30
Daniel, 30
David, 30
Elizabeth, 30
Ellenore, 114
Emma J., 30
Emma Jane, 30
Frances, 30
George, 30
George P., 194
Isaac, 30
Jacob, 30
John P., 319
Louesa, 30
Margaret, 276
Mary Ann, 30
Maurice, 30
Morris, 30
Rebecca, 30
Sally Francis, 30
Samuel, 30
Solomon, 30
Susan, 31
Susanna, 30
William, 155
William H., 30,

31, 96, 357
ALBEN, H. B., 310
ALBERT, William,
31, 337, 347, 365
ALBOUGH,
William, 357
ALBOUGHT,
Barbary, 309
ALCOT, Joel, 31,
335
ALDRIDGE,
Corrilla, 76
Eleanor, 67
ALDRIGE, Aurella,
76
ALDWORTH,
John, 31, 344, 345
ALER, Jacob, 31,
362
ALEXANDER,
Captain, 10, 15
Cornelia, 49
Elizabeth, 32
George, 31, 355
Hellen, 31
Henry, 31, 334,
338, 355
Jacob, 10, 11, 12,
31, 334, 340, 341,
365
Lawson, 221, 235
Maria, 31
Matilda C., 31
Michael G., 31
Muhail G., 31,
349
Rebecca, 31
Rebeckey, 31
Robertson, 31
Sarah, 31

Tilghman, 31
Valentine, 31
Valuntine, 341
ALGEYER, Henry, 358
ALGUIRE, 32
Henry, 32
ALLEN,
Alexander, 32, 360
Henry, 32, 360
James W., 104
ALLGEYER, 32
Henry, 32
ALLGOYER, 32
Henry, 32, 358
ALLISANDER,
Jacob, 32, 365
ALLISON, John, 348
John P., 32
Joseph P., 168
ALLNUTT, Jesse, 32, 348
ALNUT, Thomas, 32
ALRICK,
Catharine, 231
ALSOP, Joseph, 32, 334, 362
ALTOO, Samuel, 36
AMATTHIAS,
John, 328
AMBROS,
Hannah, 280
AMBROSE,
Catherina, 104
Catherine, 32
Christopher, 32
Elizabeth, 79
John, 32

Mary, 32
Matthias, 32
Peter, 32, 323, 333, 353
Sophia, 128
AMICH, George, 32
AMICK, George, 32, 342
ANDERS,
Elizabeth, 33
Henry, 33
John, 33, 279, 338
ANDERSON,
Alexander, 33, 349
Ann, 33
Elizabeth, 33
George, 33, 347
J. M., 33
James, 33
Jerusa, 260
John, 33
Jonathan M., 33
Louisa, 33
Lusindia, 33
Margarett Ann, 33
Mary, 33
Rebecca, 62
Sharloty, 33
ANDES, Mary Ann
Catharine, 77
William, 271
ANDREW,
Bernard, 33, 345
Herbert, 33, 335
ANDREWS,
Abraham, 318
Adam, 33, 335
Elizabeth, 33

Henry, 33, 34, 363
Jacob, 34
ANDRUM, George, 344
ANGEL, David, 34
George, 34, 356
ANGELL, Samuel, 261
ANGLE,
Catharine, 34
David, 34
George, 34
Isaac, 34, 321
John, 34, 321, 322
ANKROM, George, 34
ANKRUM, George, 34, 345
ANMAN, Andrew, 299
ANNON, Robert L., 34, 329
ANSTEE, John, 328
ANTHONEY,
Henry, 339
ANTHONY,
Henry, 34, 338
APPENZELLAR,
Henry, 65
APPLEBEE,
Hezekiah, 34, 354, 357
APPLEBER,
William, 34, 348
APPLER,
Abraham, 325
William, 34
ARANALD,

INDEX

Antony, 321
ARAWALD,
 Antony, 34
ARBAUGH,
 Elizabeth, 34
 Jacob, 34
ARBOUGH, Jacob, 34
ARBUCKLE,
 Mary, 73
ARCHBOLD,
 Elizabeth, 95
ARCHIBALD,
 James, 34
 James K., 34
ARCHIBOLD,
 James, 34
 James K., 34
ARMBERGER,
 Michael, 320
ARMSTRONG,
 Abraham, 83
 James, 35, 322, 336, 347, 358, 359
 Oliver, 35, 361
 Richard, 35, 357
 William, 35, 356
ARNOLD,
 Anthony, 55
 Ezra, 35
 John, 35, 323, 333, 360
 Joshua, 35
 Mahlon, 35
 Margaret, 160
 Martin, 35
 Matilda, 35
 Samuel, 35
 Sarah, 35
 Thomas, 35
ARTHUR, Celestia

E., 35
 Daniel, 35
 Frederick, 35
 John, 35, 352
 Maranda, 35
 Nerva F., 35
 Sarah C., 35
 Susan, 35
ARTZ, Abraham, 35
 Catherine, 36
 Mattie L., 36
ASHAMAN,
 Henry, 318
ASHBAUGH,
 David, 150
ATHO, Samuel, 36
ATIR, Lazarus, 102, 348
 Lazurus, 36
 Solomon, 36, 348
ATKINS, Charles, 36, 337
 Charles of William, 36, 332
 James, 36, 332
 Mary, 36
 Samuel, 36
ATLESPURIER,
 Sebastian, 36, 361
ATLOO, Samuel, 36
ATTERHOLT,
 Emiline, 114
 John, 114
 Susanna, 114
ATTIC, George, 36, 363
ATTLEY,
 Margaret, 128
ATWOOD, Henry,

42
 Priscilla, 37
 William, 37
AUBERT, A. E., 37
 Hannah, 37
 Jacob, 37, 337
 Louisa, 37
AUD, Asa, 37, 357
 Catharine, 37
 William E., 37
AULGUIRE,
 Henry, 32
AUMAN, Andrew, 299
AVES, Ann, 162
AYERS, M. C., 296

-B-

BABB, Charles, 38
BABINGTON,
 Joseph, 120
BACHMAN,
 Fredrick, 38, 350
BACKENBAUGH,
 George, 326
BACON, Stephen, 38, 351
BADER, Gabriel, 38
BAER, Ann E., 39
 Anna Maria, 39
 Catharine, 231
 Charlotte, 38
 David, 38
 Elizabeth W., 38
 Ezra, 39
 George, 38
 Harriet, 39
 Jack, 328
 Jacob, 38, 331

FREDERICK COUNTY MILITIA IN THE WAR OF 1812

Johannes, 39
Mary, 51
Matilda C., 38
Michael, 331, 333
Michael of John,
38, 39, 323, 353
Michael S., 38
Philip, 51
William, 245,
323, 333, 351
William of
Henry, 39, 320
BAGLEY, James,
313
BAIL, Abraham,
39, 321
 Elizabeth, 39
 Ludwick, 39, 321
 Sarah, 39
 William, 39, 321,
322
BAILE, Eliza, 39
 Ludwick, 39
BAILEY, Ann, 49
 Nancy, 49
BAILY, Silas, 320
 William, 39
BAKER, Basil, 39
 Catharine, 257
 Catherine, 309
 Christian, 331
 Hannah, 39
 Henry, 39, 63,
68, 311, 328, 351,
361
 Jacob, 39, 355,
361
 John A., 268
 Magdalena, 303
 Philip, 40
 Sarah, 68

William, 89
BALDERSON,
Drucilla, 40
John, 40, 354
Margaret, 40
BALDERSTON,
John, 40
BALDWIN, Daniel,
361
 George, 40, 363
 Isaac, 40, 361
 Nicholas, 40, 344
 Peter, 363, 40
BALL, Frances E.,
58
 Frances
Elizabeth, 58
 John, 40
 John D., 348
 Owen D., 58
 Samuel, 362
 Samuel B., 40
BALLET,
Jonathen, 22, 317
BALNS, Robert,
244
BALTZEL, John,
357
BALTZELL,
Albert, 41
 Alice, 41
 Charles, 40
 Charlotte, 40
 Cornelia, 41
 Eliza A., 41
 Fanny, 41
 Frederick, 41
 George, 320, 323
 Jacob, 317
 John, 41, 328
 John of Nicholas,

40
 John R., 41
 Philip Thomas,
41
 Ruth, 41
BAND, Elijah, 41,
321
BANKARD, Jacob,
41, 309, 337
 John, 41, 309,
337
 Mary, 41
BANKER, Jacob,
41
 John, 41, 341
BANKERD,
Samuel, 41
BANKERT, Isaac,
86
 Jacob, 109
 Mathias, 41, 363
 Samuel, 41
BANKHART,
Peter, 41
BANTZ, Dr., 25
 Henry, 41, 354
 John, 41, 354
 Uriah S., 213
 William, 331
BARCKMON,
Daniel, 42
BARE, George, 317
BARGEN, George,
319
 Valintine, 319
BARICKMAN,
Christian, 45
 Enock, 45
 Henry, 45
BARING, Jesse,
41, 321

INDEX

BARKDALL, Christian, 361
BARKDOLL, Christian, 42
  Joseph, 97
BARKER, James W., 156
BARKMAN, Catherine, 42
  Daniel, 42, 341
BARNERD, Hezekiah, 42, 336
BARNES, Anne Lavina, 42
  Archibald, 319
  Dorsey, 319
  Ellen, 42
  Henry, 42
  John, 42
  Mary, 42
  Samuel, 42
  Thomas, 319
  Zachariah, 319
BARNETT, David, 42, 345
BARNHART, Solomon, 42, 349
BARNHOUSE, John, 43
  Jonas P., 43
  Joseph, 43
  Margaret Jane, 43
  Randolph, 43
  Richard, 43, 349
  Sarah Jane, 43
  Sidney, 43
BARNOVER, David, 43, 335, 341, 342
  George, 43

BARNS, John, 67
  Samuel, 353
BAROLL, Lewis, 43, 335
BARR, David J., 233
  John, 43
BARRETT, Mary J., 236
  William, 43, 347
BARRICK, Abert, 43
  Ann Eliza, 44
  Charles, 44
  Cornelius, 43, 358, 359
  Edward, 43
  Elizabeth, 44
  Ellen, 44
  Ester, 44
  Esther, 44
  Eugenia, 44
  Ezra, 43, 44, 358, 359
  Frederick, 44
  George, 44, 358, 359
  George Lewis, 44
  George of Peter, 44
  H., 6, 335
  Henry, 44, 327
  Hetty, 45
  Isaiah, 43
  John, 44
  John W., 44
  Joshua, 43
  Lewis, 44
  Mary J., 43
  Nancy Lucretia, 44

  Richard H., 44
  Robert, 43
  Samuel, 44, 45, 323, 333, 357
  Sarah, 44
  Sarah S., 43
  Simon, 43
  Solomon, 318
  Sophia, 43
  William, 45, 318
BARRICKMAN, Catherine, 42
  Christian, 45
  Daniel, 42
  Elizabeth, 45
BARRIKMAN, Christian, 349
BARRUKMAN, Christian, 45
BART, Cornelius, 45
BARTEL, Christian, 45
  John, 68
BARTGIS, Benjamin F., 45
  James, 37, 112
  Margret, 45
  Mathew E., 334
  Mathias E., 45, 354
  Matthias E., 45, 320
BARTHALOW, Elias, 45, 349
  Hester Ann, 45
  John, 46
  Joshua, 46, 321
BARTHELOW, Elias, 46
  Esther, 46

BARTHOLOW,
  Andrew J., 46
  Hester Ann, 46
  J., 322
  Michael, 46, 321
BARTLE,
  Christian, 46, 354
BARTLES, John,
  46
BARTLET, Joseph,
  46, 356
BARTON, Amy, 46
  Elisha, 155
  Samuel, 14, 46,
  83, 361
  Sarah E., 46
  Sarah Elizabeth,
  46
BARTZELL, John,
  46
BASFORD,
  Martha, 77
  Thomas, 46, 348
BASH, Elizabeth,
  139
BASORD, Anna,
  242
BATES, Marlene
  S., 28
BATTER, Richard
  W., 324
BATZIN, Samuel,
  319
BAUCHER, Henry,
  325
BAUER, David E.,
  154
BAUGHMAN,
  Adam, 46, 362
BAUMGARDNER,
  Jacob, 13, 115,
  151, 252
BAUMGARTEN,
  Jacob, 46
BAUMGARTNER,
  John, 325
BAUNGANTOUS,
  Jacob, 46
BAUSMAN,
  Elizabeth, 278
BAUSTIN, Philip,
  359
BAUSTON, Philip,
  46, 358, 359
BAXTER, John,
  319
BAYER, Abraham,
  335
  Abrahma, 46
  Peter, 325
BAYLEY, M., 22
BAYLY, Mountjoy,
  1
BEACHTEL,
  Henry, 52
BEACHTLE,
  George, 46, 362
BEAIL, Abraham,
  85
BEAL, David, 47,
  363
BEALE, Ann
  Marie Elizabeth,
  51
BEALER, George,
  318
BEALL, Benjamin,
  47, 351
  Catharine, 47
  Daniel, 47
  Mordecai, 325
  Ninian, 47, 357
  Thomas, 47, 334,
  362
  Thomas N., 344,
  345
  William, 36
  William D., 5
  Zepheniah, 47
BEALLE, Thomas,
  47
BEAM, Elizabeth,
  47
  Jacob, 47, 352
  William, 47
BEAMS, Anna, 47
  Elizabeth, 47
  Jacob, 47, 352
  William, 47
BEAR, Caroline,
  232
  Catharine, 48
  Catherine, 231
  Charles A., 232
  David, 38, 354
  Frances, 232
  George, 47, 74,
  232, 360
  Henry, 231
  Jane, 232
  John, 232
  Mary, 47
  Michael, 48, 348
  William, 231
BEARD, Abraham,
  48
  Amelia, 48
  Daniel, 48
  Jacob, 48, 271,
  357, 358, 359
  James Elder, 48
  John, 48, 197,
  341, 344, 345, 361

372

INDEX

Joseph, 41
Magdalene, 160
Mary C., 197
Richard, 48, 339
William, 268
BEARSHANK,
William, 48, 351
BEATTY,
Ebenezer, 48
John M., 320
Lewis A., 48
Thomas, 318
BEAUMONT,
Bascal, 359
Basil, 358
Bazil, 48
Buscal, 359
BEAVER, Andrew
J., 49
Eliza, 182
John, 48, 49, 209, 245
BEAVIN, Walter, 324
BECHTELL,
George, 47
Jacob, 47
Samuel, 47
BECKENBAUGH,
Ann R., 49
Catharine, 49
Elizabeth, 49
Henry, 49
John, 49, 355
John T., 49
Mary, 49
Peter, 49
Sarah A., 49
Susan, 49
BECKER, Egbert
T. E., 168

BECKERBAUGH,
Barbara, 256
BECKET, James, 344
BECKETT,
Benjamin, 49, 357
BECKLEY, Ann, 49
Henry, 49
Nancy, 49
BECKLY, Henry, 365
BECKWITH,
Benjamin, 49
Lenox, 49
Rebecca, 49
Susanna, 234
Susannah, 234
BECKWORTH,
Lenore, 340
Lenox, 49
BEECHER, Annie
E., 250
John, 250
BEECKELY,
Henry, 326
BEEKLESS,
Philip, 49
BEILY, William, 362
BELL, Catherine, 280
George, 49
Thomas, 50, 326, 355
Thomas N., 50
BELMEAR,
Captain, 10
BELT, Ann C., 101
Bennoni, 24, 50, 348, 349

Elizabeth, 50
Lloyd, 50, 353
Rufus, 24
BENDER,
Elizabeth, 107
BENGLBRECK,
Michael, 345
BENITT, Lloyd, 50, 321
Robert, 321
BENN, John, 50
BENNET, David, 335
John, 119
Sarah, 119
Susan A., 214
BENNETT, Asaph, 234
Auther, 67
Benjamin W., 132
David, 50, 351
Elizabeth, 50
J. M., 223
James, 50
John, 334
John B., 50, 338
Margaret, 67
Robert, 50, 322
BENNSBURGH,
David, 285
BENTLEY,
Berman H., 240
George, 50, 356
BENTZ, John, 50, 351
BEONER, John, 50, 344
BERGAN,
Frederick, 319
BERIER,

373

FREDERICK COUNTY MILITIA IN THE WAR OF 1812

Abraham, 317
BERKMAN,
 Christian, 45
BERNARD,
 Hezekiah, 50, 270
BERRET, Samuel, 236
BERRY, James, 51, 326
 John, 51, 126, 348
 Maria A., 126
 Mary, 51
 Samuel, 51, 362
BERRYMAN,
 William M., 311
BERTIN,
 Benjamin, 51, 339
BETES, Fanney, 138
BETHEL, Mary Ann, 293
BETT, Rufus, 24, 51
BEVANS,
 Alexander, 51, 354
 Sarah, 213
BEVER, John, 48, 363
BEVINS, Henry, 364
 Susanna, 213
BICKETT, James, 51
BIDDLE, Mary, 51
 Thomas, 51, 280
 Thopmas, 337
BIDINGER, Philip, 24, 51, 350
BIEHL, Isaac, 86
BIERLY, Lewis A.,
278
BIERSHENK,
 Henry, 51, 332
 Rachael, 51
BIERSHING,
 Henry, 51
 Rachael, 51
 William, 212
BIGELOW, Susan, 51
BIGGLE, Jacob, 52, 363
BIGGS, Catharine, 181
 William of Ben, 323
BIGHAM, Mary, 168
 Robert, 52, 317
BILL, 363
BILLINGSLEY,
 Walter, 347
 Walter R., 52
BIRCKHEAD,
 Abraham, 319
BIRCKMAN,
 Christian, 45
BIRELY, Charlotte, 52
 Evalina, 52
 Lewis, 52, 364
 Valentine, 52
BISER, Catherine, 247
 Jacob, 326
 John, 324
BISHOP, Mark, 220
BITTINGER,
 Elizabeth, 200
BITTLE, Ann
Marie Elizabeth, 51
 Catherine, 171
 Daniel Howard, 51
 David Frederick, 51
 Elizabeth, 51
 Frank D., 51
 George, 171
 George Michael, 51
 Henry, 52, 363
 Lydia, 51
 Mary, 51
 Susan, 51
 Thomas, 51, 104, 194, 220
BIVENS,
 Alexander, 52
 Benjamin, 52
 Henry, 52
BIVINS,
 Alexander, 51, 365
BIXLER, Peter, 325
BLACK, Henry, 52, 361
 Isaac, 52, 341
 Jacob, 52, 361
 John, 53
 Joseph, 317
 Mary E., 190
 Philip, 53, 342
 Rebecca, 52
 Sam, 53, 343
 Sarah, 52
 William J., 72
BLACKBURN,
 Catharine, 44
BLACKFORD,

INDEX

Caroline, 53
John, 330
Major, 330
Thomas, 353
Thomas
Thornburg, 53
W. H., 53
William H., 53
BLACKMAN,
Mary, 229
BLAIR, Elizabeth, 280
John, 280
BLANCHFORD,
Harriet, 293
James, 53, 293, 333
BLASFORD,
Oswald, 351
BLAXFORD,
Oswald, 53
BLAZE, William, 53
BLENSINGER,
Mary, 175
BLESSING,
Abraham, 53, 323, 332
Anna M., 54
Elizabeth E., 54
Francis T., 54
George W., 54
Jacob, 54, 326, 333
Margaret, 113
Mary, 54
Mary J., 54
Mary M., 53
Michael, 113, 323
Penelope R., 54
Rebecca, 187

William H., 54
BLEWBAUGH,
John, 341
BLEWBOUGH,
John, 54, 342
BLIZARD, Beal, 341
BLIZZARD, Beal, 54, 342
BLOCHER,
Elizabeth, 101
John, 101
BLOIS, Mordicai, 54
BLOOM, Adam, 54
Catherine, 54
Peter, 54, 363
BLUER, Mary, 147
BLUFFORD,
Henrey, 341
Henry, 54
BOBLETS,
Caroline, 124
Ephraim, 124
BOBLETTS,
Caroline Emilie, 124
Ephraim, 124
BOBST, Daniel, 56
John, 56
Lydia, 56
Mary, 56
BOCHMAN,
Andrew, 54, 355
BODEN, Samuel, 54, 355
BOERSTLER,
Charles G., 54
Christian, 54
George W., 330, 331

Rev., 35
BOGGS, John W., 93
BOHAM,
Elizabeth, 54
Jacob, 54
Peter, 54, 333
BOHER, Henry, 54, 335
BOHN, Adam, 168
BOILEAU, David, 216
BOLDING,
Benjamin, 55, 58, 352
BOLI, Elizabeth, 110
BOLIE, Catharine, 178
BOLTON, Amanda
Catharine, 255
George, 255
BOLY, Catherine, 110
Daniel, 55
BOND, Abigail, 55
Alexander, 55, 338
Benjamin, 55, 363
Caroline F., 55
Charles, 13, 55, 341, 342
Elijah, 55, 334
Emeline, 55
John, 55, 363
Joshua, 55, 321
Juliana, 55
Juliann, 55
Mary J., 55
Peter, 55, 321,

375

FREDERICK COUNTY MILITIA IN THE WAR OF 1812

322
 Sarah E., 55
BONDER, David, 325
BONEBRAKE, Elizabeth, 246
BONER, Jane, 55
 John, 128, 344
 Joseph, 55, 361
BONERS, Elizabeth, 314
BONNER, John Andrew, 191
 Sarah L., 191
 William F., 191
BONSALL, J. Stapleton, 39
BOODGER, Peter, 355
BOOKERLY, William, 327
BOONE, Catherine, 56
 Jerningham, 56
 Leonard J., 323
 Robert, 55, 56, 353
BOONER, John, 50
BOOSE, John, 52
BOOSER, George, 56
BOOSES, George, 24, 56
BOOTH, Robert, 339
BOOTMAN, Jacob, 56, 338
BOOVEY, Jacob, 56, 339
BOPST, Ann M.,

56
 Daniel, 56, 357
 Elizabeth, 56
 John, 56, 365
 John H., 56
 Joshua D., 56
 Lydia, 56
 Marietta, 56
 Mary, 56
 Othaniel A., 56
 Ruanna, 56
 Samuel A., 56
 Sarah, 198
 Sophia, 56
 William, 56
BORDER, David, 56, 335
 Ellen, 56
BOREING, Peter, 57, 341, 342
BORING, Peter, 57, 325, 335
 Zachariah, 57, 335
 Zacharias, 57, 364
BOROUGHS, Isaac, 67, 338
BORTLE, Elizabeth, 68
BOSLEY, George, 319
BOSSARD, Soloman, 69
BOSSERT, Jacob, 202
 Susanna, 202
BOSTAIN, Philip, 57
BOSTON, George, 57, 349

BOSWELL, Catharine, 242
BOTELAR, Elias, 318
BOTELER, Arthur, 323
 Ed., 116
 Edward L., 57
 Edward Sims, 57
 Jane, 116
 Jeff. O., 57
 Lingen, 57
 Prudence, 57
BOTLER, Ann, 140
 Henry, 139, 140
BOTTOMFIELD, Hannah, 257
 Jacob, 257
BOUGHER, Jacob, 57, 354
BOWARD, David, 190
 Sallie, 190
BOWER, Christian, 57
 Hannah, 280
 Henry, 220
BOWERS, Adam, 52, 57, 363
 Elias W., 102
 Elizabeth, 300
 Jacob, 57
 John H., 35
 Joseph, 299, 300
 Mary, 80
BOWERSOCH, Daniel, 58
BOWERSOCK, Daniel, 58, 361
BOWHAN, George,

376

INDEX

58
William, 58
BOWHORN,
  George, 58
  Goerge, 363
  William, 58, 363
BOWLES, David, 58
BOWLIN,
  Benjamin, 58, 352
BOWLUS,
  Magdalene, 235
BOWMAN,
  George, 58, 356
  Jacob, 97
BOWMASTER,
  John, 58, 361
BOYD, Caline, 58
  David, 58, 323, 333, 353
  Edna, 58
  Frances Elizabeth, 58
  Hamilton, 58
  Jane, 272
  John H., 58
  Mary, 58
  Singleton W., 58
  William, 58, 349
BOYER, Anna, 218
  David K., 154
  Gabriel, 70
  George, 70, 324, 332
  John, 59, 153, 324, 332
  Johnathan, 59
  Jonathan, 59, 355, 365
  Josiah E., 154
  Mary Ann, 259

Peter, 196
Thomas, 325
BOYLE, Charles, 59, 338
  D. Scott, 88
  Elizabeth, 59
  James, 327
  John B., 66
  Peter, 59, 357
BRACK, Frederick, 59, 356
BRADFIELD,
  Rachel, 80
BRADSHAW,
  Solomon, 59, 324, 334
BRAIN, John, 59, 347
BRAMWELL,
  John, 61
  William, 59, 356
BRANCKEL, John, 60
BRANDENBERGER, Elisabeth, 59
  Jacob, 59
  Jesse, 59
BRANDENBURG,
  Frank E., 59
  Henry, 177
  Howard Wilson, 59
  Jane, 100
  John M., 179
  Joseph, 100
  O. D., 59
BRANDENBURG H, Allen T., 59
  Jacob, 59
  Jesse, 12, 59, 348
  Matilda, 59

BRANGLE,
  Lawrence, 354
  Lucy, 60
  Mary, 61
BRANNARD,
  George, 59
BRASHEAR, Bett, 327
  Edna, 58
  Richard M., 58
BRASHEARS, Eli, 59
  Ely, 21
BRASHER, Ely, 322
BRAWER, Emal., 319
  Emanuel, 321
  Jacob, 319
BRAWN, John, 221
BRAWNER,
  Elizabeth, 240
  Emanuel, 60
  Ignatius, 323
  William, 60, 321
BRAWNING,
  Achsah, 63
  Archabald, 63
  David, 63
BREADSHAW,
  Solomon, 60
BREADY, Ann Elizabeth, 68
  Calvin, 60
  Curtis, 60
  David, 60, 357
  E. Tobias, 60
  Edward, 60
  Elizabeth, 60
  Eugene, 60

FREDERICK COUNTY MILITIA IN THE WAR OF 1812

George, 60, 68
George A., 60
John, 60, 337, 347
  Luther, 60
  Mary, 60
  Ormond, 60
  Richard, 60
BRECKON, Moses, 254
BRENCKEL,
  Elizabeth, 60
  Johannes, 60
  John, 60
BRENGEL, John, 60
BRENGLE,
  Ann Rebecca, 71, 72
  Anna Maria, 60
  Barbara, 68, 289
  Catharine, 234
  Catherine, 61
  Christian, 68
  Daniel, 60
  Elizabeth, 60
  Eva, 60
  Eva Margaret, 60
  Johannes, 60
  John, 9, 16, 60, 333, 354
  John Nicholas, 60
  John of Christian, 323
  Lawrence, 60
  Lawrence John, 60
  Lawrence of Christian, 61
  Lewis A., 71, 72
  Lorenz, 60
  Margaret, 60
  Maria, 60
  Mariah Barbara, 68
  Mary, 60
  Nicholas, 320
  Nicolas, 322
  Peter, 72, 320, 322
  Rachel, 233
BRIAN, Samuel, 353
BRIANT, Samuel, 61
BRICKER, David, 61, 341, 342
  George, 61, 352
  Henry, 61, 341, 342
BRICKET, James, 153
BRICKNER, W. G., 222
BRIGGS, Asa, 61, 334
  Ignatius, 326
BRIGHLEY, Marcy, 324
BRIGHTWELL, Thomas, 61, 363
BRILEY, Collison, 61
  Sarah, 61
BRILL, Mary Catharine, 255
BRILY, Coloson, 61, 349
  Joseph, 61
BRINGLE, Laurence, 317
BRISBIN, William, 110
BRISCOE, Isabella, 47
BRISH, Ann, 61
  David, 61, 344, 345
BRITTEN, John, 61, 344, 345
BRITTON, John, 61
BROMWELL,
  John, 61
  William, 59
BRONER, John, 62
BROOK, Richard, 328
BROOKE, Mary R., 206
  Richard, 61, 326, 328, 344, 345
BROOKOVER,
  Eleanor, 73
  William, 62, 360
BROONER, John, 61, 335
  John of Jacob, 63
  Maria, 63
BROTHER, Henry, 317
  Valentine, 317
BROTHERTON, Robert, 325
BROW, Emanuel, 321
BROWER, David, 319, 325
BROWMAN, Jacob, 324

378

INDEX

BROWN,
 Alexander H., 172
 Benjamin, 62, 233, 348
 Catharine, 62
 Christian, 62
 Deborah, 62
 Elizabeth, 126
 Ellen, 44
 Emanuel, 62
 Francis, 62, 332
 Frederick, 62, 348
 George, 126
 Jacob, 57
 Jane, 62
 John, 62, 261, 325, 356, 363
 Joseph, 315
 Mary, 36, 62, 105
 Nancy, 74
 Rebecca, 62
 Robert, 62, 363
 Sarah, 62, 96
 Thomas, 62
 William, 63, 216, 352
 William G., 290
 William S., 88, 152, 293
BROWNING,
 Archibald, 63, 351
 Daniel, 351
 David, 63
 Jeremiah, 318
 Jonathan, 63, 348
 Joseph, 318
 Maria, 63
 Rebecca, 63
BROWNLEY, John S., 325
BROY, Elizabeth, 249
BRUAN, William, 63
BRUNDAGE, Thomas, 311
BRUNER, Elias, 22, 317
 George, 324
 John, 63
 Sarah Ann, 226
BRUNNER,
 Caroline, 63
 Edward J., 63
 Elizabeth, 202
 Ellen C., 63
 James, 251
 John, 61, 63, 199, 354
 John of Jacob, 63
 Lewis A., 63
 Margaret, 199
 Maria, 63
 Mary, 63
 Valentine S., 63
BRUSH, Eliza, 132
 Henry C., 132
 Platt, 132
BRYAN, Amey, 63
 James, 63
 Mary R., 215
 William, 362
BRYANT, Henry L., 209
 James, 11, 63, 340, 341
BUCHER, Christena, 291
BUCHLY, Edward B., 134
BUCKAWAY, George A., 292
BUCKEY, Catharine Louisa, 167
 Catherine, 64, 234
 David, 320, 323
 George, 63, 195, 351
 Henry, 64
 John, 64, 323, 333, 353
 Marion, 195
 Matilda, 64
 Michael, 64, 234, 322
 Nicholas, 320
 Rachel, 144
 Rebecca, 144
 Susan, 64
BUCKINGHAM,
 Alfred W., 194
 Basil, 64, 322
 David, 132
 Epheriam, 321
 Ephraim, 64
BUCKMAN, Patience, 274
BUCKY, John, 64
BUFFINGTON, John, 64, 349
 Magdalena, 79
BUMPERS, Priscilla, 80
BUNTZ, Caroline, 63
 William S., 63
BURALL, Ann, 110

FREDERICK COUNTY MILITIA IN THE WAR OF 1812

George, 110
Jane C., 110
BURCH, Henry, 64, 349
BURCKHARTT, John, 320
BURCKHEAD, Daniel of Christopher, 64
BURDETT, Elias, 240
BURESS,
　Nicholas, 64, 348
　Proverb, 64, 348
BURGAN,
　Rebecca, 31
　Rebeckey, 31
BURGEE, Ann, 64
　Mary, 64
　Micl, 351
　Miel, 64, 351
　Thomas, 64, 351
BURGER, Jacob, 190
　William, 40
BURGESS,
　Captain, 10
　Henry, 65, 351
BURGOON,
　Catharine, 65
　F. J., 116
　Jacob, 65, 363
　Norman Aaron, 65
　Sarah, 65
　William, 65
BURK, Daniel, 65, 344, 345
　Elizabeth, 65
　Isaac, 65, 349
　Michael, 65, 333,
356
　Milton, 65
　Patrick, 65, 302, 356
　Thomas, 319
BURKARD, Jacob, 65, 336
BURKE,
　Catharine, 65
　Isaac, 265
　John, 65, 66
　Mary, 65, 66
　Polly, 65
　Thomas C., 66
　William A., 66
BURKET, Jacob, 66, 342
BURKETT,
　Charles, 36
BURKHARD,
　Jacob, 65, 66
BURKHARDT,
　Elizabeth, 264
BURKHART,
　Charles H., 315
　Daniel, 66, 323, 333, 353
　John, 66, 333
　William, 148
BURKHARTT,
　Daniel, 357
BURKITT, Henry, 318
BURNHAM, Mrs., 196
BURNS,
　Andrew, 66
　Ann Rebeca, 67
　David, 67
　George, 66, 352
　George Frederic,
67
　Jacob, 66, 199, 200, 256, 365
　James, 66
　James D., 344
　Jarvis Francis, 67
　John, 66, 67, 352
　John Jeremiah, 67
　Mary, 66, 67
　Mary J. F., 67
　Peter, 16, 67, 352
　Polly, 67
BUROUGHS,
　Isaac, 67, 339
BURR, John, 69
BURRIS, Nicholas R., 67
　Sarah, 67
BURRISS, Nicholas R., 67
　Sarah, 67
BURROUGHS,
　Isaac, 67
BURROWS,
　Nicholas R., 67
　Sarah, 67
BURT, Hiram, 106
BUSSARD, Daniel, 67, 336
　Eleanor, 67
　Henry, 60
　Peter, 69
　Sarah, 69
BUTCHER, Jacob, 322
BUTLER, Agnes, 166
　Amelia, 68
　Ann Elizabeth,

INDEX

68
Anna Margareth, 68
Anna Maria, 68
Benjamin, 24, 67, 350
Betzy, 68
Catharina Barbara, 68
Charles, 68
Christina Mocabee, 68
Edward, 360
Elias, 67
Elizabeth, 68, 69
F. L., 102
George, 68
Harriet, 68
Heneretta T., 94
James, 68, 341
Jane, 68
John Tobias, 68
Maria Anna, 68
Mariah Barbara, 68
Mary A., 68
Ormon F., 68
Ormond, 68, 183
Ormond F., 45, 56, 68, 182, 250, 334, 354
Richard, 68, 69, 331
Richard W., 68
Richardt William, 68
Robert, 68
Sarah, 68
Thomas, 349, 68
Tobias, 317
Tobias H., 68

BUTTLER, Tobias, 354
William, 331
BUXTON, John, 324
BUZARD, Peter, 69, 349
Sarah, 69
BUZERD, Samuel, 69, 365
BUZZARD, Daniel, 322
David, 69, 355
Mary, 69
Samuel, 69
BYARD, John, 299
Josephine, 299
BYER, David, 69, 352
George, 70, 332
BYERLY, George S., 132
Lewis, 70, 110
BYERS, Elizabeth, 70, 232
Martin L., 212
Michael, 70, 364
Mrs. Joseph, 70
Sally, 219
BYROAD, Peter, 70, 358
BYRODD, Peter, 70

-C-
CABLE, Henry, 70
CAFFMAN, Henry, 70, 175
CAFRY, Catherine, 74
CAIL, Joseph, 70,

321
CAIN, Benjamin, 70, 363
Elizabeth, 70
Ephraim, 322
J. W., 91
Jacob, 70, 335
John, 326
John T., 70
John W., 91
Joseph E., 70
Kezia D., 265
Leticia, 70
Levinia, 70
Louisa A., 91
Mary, 42, 70
Mary J., 70
Sarah A., 70
Solomon, 70
Thomas, 70, 336, 349
CAINALL, William, 322
CALE, Joseph, 319
CALF, Martin, 71, 356
CALHOON, Robert L., 71, 334
CALISON, Elizabeth, 300
CALL, Mathew, 71, 333
Mathias, 71, 341
Matthias, 343
CALTON, William, 357
CAMPBELL, Benjamin, 71, 351
E. T., 91
George, 71, 348
James T., 118

FREDERICK COUNTY MILITIA IN THE WAR OF 1812

John, 71, 336
Samuel J., 168
William, 71, 350
CANADAY, John, 71, 321
CANAGA, Jacob, 357
CANDLER,
  Adelade S., 39
  Anne E., 39
  Augusta B., 39
  Daniel H., 39
  Mariah L., 39
  Osker H., 39
  Sarah, 163
  Sarah C., 39
CANNON,
  Christian, 71
  Daniel, 71
  Elizabeth, 71
  Jacob, 71, 347, 357
  Julian M., 71
CANTLEBARY, P. F., 182
CANTNER, Mary, 224
CAOSHING, Joseph, 322
CAPOOTE, Mary, 224
CARBIN, Nicholas, 71, 335
CAREGEIR, Catharine, 192
CAREGUR, Catharine, 192
CAREY, Cyrus, 71, 351
  George, 323
CARLEN, Bennet, 71, 365
  James, 71, 365
CARLETON, Ann Rebecca, 71
  Eliza, 71
  Mary, 71
  Thomas, 71, 331
CARLIN,
  Cornelius, 71, 334, 337
  Elizabeth, 101
  Nicholas, 71
CARLTON, Ann Rebecca, 71, 72
  Edward, 72
  Edward A., 71, 72
  Eliza, 71
  Eliza Jenett, 72
  Mary, 71
  Mary P., 72
  Thomas, 71, 72, 324
  William, 72
CARMACK,
  Caroline, 72
  Elizabeth, 103
  Ephraim, 189, 216
  Francis, 72
  Isabelle, 72
  Lydia, 72
  Mary, 275
  Salome, 72
  Samuel, 31, 33, 72, 112, 114, 257, 301, 349
  Sarah Jane, 72
  William, 72, 358, 359
CARMAN,
  Rebecca, 91
CARMICKLE,
  James, 72
CARNE, Adam, 73, 341
CARNELL,
  Margaret, 316
CARNES,
  Catharine, 102
  Jacob, 73, 344
  John, 73, 331
  Thomas, 73, 339
CARNEY, Patrick, 73, 338, 339
  William, 73, 351
CARNS, Jacob, 73, 346
CARPENTER,
  Emanuel, 73, 351
  John, 73
  Louisa G., 147
  Robert, 147
  Solomon, 73, 349
CARR, James H., 270
  Joseph, 166
  Mary Ann, 166
  Ruth, 256
  Thomas, 73, 336
CARRIEL, Robert A., 58
CARRIER,
  Jonathan, 229
CARROL, William, 341
CARROLL,
  Marcus, 264
CARSON, Mrs., 67
CARTER,
  Catherine, 73
  Joseph, 73, 332

382

INDEX

Mary, 46
William, 73, 325, 335
CARTNAIL,
  Eleanor, 73
  Jacob, 73, 362
  Peter, 24, 322, 350
CARTY, C. C., 214
  James, 73, 341
  John, 73, 341
  Margaret, 73
  Mrs. Joseph W. L., 196
CARTZDAFFNER, Ann, 239
CARTZENDAFNER, Joseph, 218
CARUL, John, 325
CARVEL, William, 73, 341
CARY, Cyrus, 73
  Eliza, 132
  Joseph, 74, 348
  Mary, 73
CASE, Aaron, 311
CASEY, Jason, 74, 338, 339
  Martha, 287
CASH, John S., 271
CASNER, Eleanor, 74
  Jacob, 325, 74, 352
  John, 74, 341, 343
CASS, 74
CASSELL,
  Catherine, 222
  Charles P., 89

Rachel, 222
William, 323
CASSIDY, Charles L., 273
CASSIL, William, 40
CASSNER, Jacob, 74, 335
  John, 74, 335
CASTER, Martha, 228
CASTLE,
  Catharine, 74
  Eli, 74, 360
  Elijah, 338
  Elisha, 74, 339
  Ely, 74
  George V., 74
  James, 318
  John H., 74
  John H. P., 364
  Nancy, 74
  Noah, 74
  Samuel, 324
  Sarah A., 74
  Thomas P., 74
CASTNER,
  Rassellas, 34
CASY, Daniel, 74, 365
CATROW,
  Catharine, 180
  George, 180
CATSDEAFLER, Anna, 239
CAUFMAN, Christian, 80
CAUGH, Balser, 74, 321
  David, 74, 321, 322

Jacob, 74, 321
CAWOOD,
  Thomas, 75
CAYWOOD,
  Catherin, 75
  Elizabeth, 75
  Hannah, 75
  John, 75
  Joseph, 75
  Mahjala, 75
  Martin, 75
  Samuel, 75
  Thomas, 75, 351
  William, 75
CEARLY, Joseph, 75, 338
CEASE, John, 75
CECIL, Henry B., 75
CHAMBERLAIN, Walter, 363
CHAMPER, John, 76, 358, 359
CHANBERLAIN, Walter, 75
CHANEY,
  Aurella, 76
  Charles, 76
  Charles J., 334
  Elijah, 24, 76, 348, 349
  John, 76
  Mary, 76
  Prudence, 57
CHAPMAN, J. F., 168
CHAPPEL, Howard, 62
CHARLES, 76, 330, 331
CHARLTON, Mary

383

FREDERICK COUNTY MILITIA IN THE WAR OF 1812

E., 130
CHENEY, Corrilla, 76
  Elijah, 76
  Ezekiel, 116
CHEW, Ann M., 163
  Charles E., 163
  Mary J., 163
  Samuel, 163
  William, 76, 163, 334, 349, 363
  William H., 163
CHINCOTH, Enoch, 279
CHORIN, James, 318
CHRINHER, Mary Magdalena, 267
CHRISMAN, Alta, 75
  George P., 75
CHRIST, Anna Juliana, 76
  Anna Sophia, 76
  Charlotte Emilia, 76
  Christina, 76
  Elizabeth, 76
  Henrietta Angelica, 76
  Israel, 76
  Jacob, 76, 349
  Jesse B., 76
  John Rudolph, 76
  Maria Elizabeth, 76
  Rebecca Louisa, 76
  T. H., 176

William Henry, 76
CHRISTMAN, Christr., 75
  E. D., 75
  Frank, 75
CHURCHHILL, Israel, 76
CLABAUGH, Elizabeth Norris, 220
  Jacob, 76, 356
  James, 325
  John, 77
  Mary, 77
  Thomas, 77
CLABOUGH, Thomas, 363
CLAIRY, Adin, 78
CLANTICE, Peter, 200
CLANTS, Charles, 77, 336
  Mary Ann Catharine, 77
CLANTZ, Charles, 77
  Mary Ann Catharine, 77
CLAPSADDLE, Michael, 77
  Paul, 77
CLAPSADLE, Michael, 350
CLAREY, John, 324
CLARK, Ann Maria, 77
  Arthur Younzey, 77
  David M., 223

Johan, 77
John, 77, 338, 339
John Henry, 77
Joshia, 338
Josiah, 77, 339
Levi, 77, 348
Margaret, 77
Martha, 77
Martha Ann, 77
Mary, 77
Rhoday, 77
Richard, 77, 322, 336, 348
Thomas S., 78
CLARKE, Hugh, 78, 332
  Joseph B., 92
  Richard, 291
CLARY, Adin, 78
  Daniel, 78, 363
  Nathaniel, 78, 347
  Samuel, 78, 363
  Zachariah, 78
CLAY, Alfred C., 55
  Elizabeth, 65
  Henry, 78, 321
CLAYBAUGH, Elizabeth, 91
  Sarah, 316
  Thomas, 77
CLEARY, Zachariah, 78
CLEMENTS, Hezekiah, 240
  Josias, 319
CLEMSON, James, 78
CLERAMER, Ann,

INDEX

124
CLINARD,
  Frederick, 178,
  230, 297
CLINE, 78, 347
  Alexander, 78
  Casper, 78, 352
  Catherine, 78
  Charles, 78
  Corilla, 78
  Elizabeth, 79
  Frederick, 79,
    362
  Hezekiah, 282
  Nicholas, 78
  Philip, 79, 104,
    194, 220, 280
CLINEFERBURCK
  Cornelius, 79,
    335
CLINEHEART,
  Frederick, 357
CLINGAN,
  Elizabeth, 79
  William, 79, 325,
    356
  Winchester, 45,
    162
CLINK, Andrew,
  79
CLOPPER,
  Andrew, 79
  Andrew M., 362
  Nicholas, 79, 365
COAKER, Walter,
  79, 341, 343
COALE, Catherine,
  233
  Humphrey, 324
  William, 80
COBB, John

Devin, 184
COBBRETZ, Peter,
  327
COBELANCE,
  Fanny, 276
COBLENTS,
  Jacob, 79, 356
COBLENTZ,
  Catharine, 79, 80
  David, 85
  Elizabeth, 79
  Jacob, 79, 80
  John, 79, 80
  Malinda, 79
  Mary M., 85
  Peter, 79, 80
COCHRAN, Allen,
  63
  Cornelius, 135
  Hugh, 63
  James, 80, 344,
    349
  John, 80, 324,
    356
  Rachel, 80
COCKEY, John C.,
  80, 350
  Richard, 328
COCKRAN, James,
  346
COCRAN, John,
  359
COFFIN, Thomas
  W., 260
COFFMAN,
  Andrew, 143
  Christian, 80
  Henry, 354
  Joseph, 143
COLBERT, Joseph,
  80, 365

COLE, Benjamin
  G., 330
  Enser, 80, 343
  Enzer, 341
  Humphrey, 80,
    332
  Major, 330
  Nathan, 238
  William, 80, 339
COLEGATE,
  George, 80, 325,
    328
COLEHORSE,
  Benjamin, 351
COLELASURE,
  Abraham, 80
COLELEASURE,
  Abram, 354
COLEMAN, Jacob,
  318
COLENS, Mathew,
  365
COLGAZIER,
  Abraham, 80
  Mary, 80
COLGLAZIER,
  John, 131
COLIER, Steven,
  357
COLISON,
  Washington, 300
COLLASSON,
  Washington, 299
COLLENS,
  Mathew, 80
COLLIFLOUER,
  Gorge, 359
  Michael, 359
  Samuel, 359
COLLIFLOWER,
  George, 80, 358

385

FREDERICK COUNTY MILITIA IN THE WAR OF 1812

Hannah, 80
Mary, 80
Michael, 80, 358
Samuel, 80, 358
Susannah, 80
COLLINGER,
  Phillip, 81, 365
COLLINS, Daniel,
  81, 136, 351
  Elijah, 81, 334
  James, 81
COLLISON,
  Washington, 299
COLOURS, Mary,
  308
COLWELL,
  Charles, 81, 365
  David, 81, 361
CONDON,
  Edward, 358, 359
  Thomas, 81, 336,
  341, 343
CONLY, James,
  338
CONNEL,
  Benjamin, 90
CONNER, Aquila,
  81, 341
  Catherine, 81
  James, 81, 341
  Jane, 55
  Martha, 81
  Peggy, 81
  Thomas, 81, 344,
  345, 360
  William, 81, 319,
  352
CONRAD, Aolser,
  319
  Crisher, 81
  Elizabeth, 82

Joseph, 81, 82,
  215, 346
CONRADT,
  Joseph, 81, 344
CONROD, Balser,
  94
CONROY,
  Margaret, 306
CONTEE, Jane,
  309
COO, John R., 238
COOK, Benjamin,
  82, 357
  Edward, 331
  George W., 43
  John, 14, 82,
  172, 327, 338, 351
  Joseph, 59
  Orlando, 244
  Thomas, 82, 363
COOKERLY,
  Catherine, 240
  Darcus, 164
  Jacob, 318
  John, 318
  William, 82, 318
COOLEY, James,
  82, 362
  Joseph, 82, 344
COOMES,
  Elizabeth, 82
  John, 82, 321
  William, 82, 341
COONS, Abraham,
  322
COOPER, David,
  317
  Edward H., 292
  John, 82, 341,
  343
  W. C., 156

COOSHING,
  Joseph, 82
COOSIN, Joseph,
  82, 343
COOSIX, Joseph,
  82, 341, 343
COPELIN,
  Elizabeth, 82
  Samuel B., 82
COPENHAVER,
  Barbara, 82
  Jacob, 82, 363
  John, 82, 357
  William, 82, 343
COPENHEAVER,
  William, 341
COPLAND,
  Samuel, 82, 360
COPPENSMITH,
  Jacob, 350
COPPERSMITH,
  Elizabeth, 83
  Jacob, 82, 83
CORBIN, Edward,
  83
  Nicholas, 83, 325,
  350
CORCORAN,
  John, 83, 358
CORD, Stephen,
  83
CORNEL, Richard,
  83, 361
CORNELL,
  Margaret, 316
  Richard, 83
  Smith, 83
  Thomas, 83, 356
CORRELL,
  Christian, 14, 83
  Elizabeth, 83

INDEX

Mary E., 83
COSKERY, Michael, 317
COSNEL, Richard, 84
COSS, Peter, 84, 339
  Susanna, 84
COSSELL, William, 84, 333, 353
COST, Christian, 84, 318
COSTIN, Mortimer D., 69
COUGH, Jacob, 84, 321
  Mary, 84
COURTNEY, Liberty, 187
COVER, Adeline, 84
  Anna Rebecca, 84
  Cyrus, 84
  David, 84
  Erastus, 84
  Eveline, 84
  George Alfred, 84
  Jacob, 84, 361
  Jacob H., 84
  Joseph, 84, 361
  Joseph Hanson, 84
  Levi, 84
  Margaret, 84
  Sophia, 84
  Susanna, 84
  Susannah, 84
  Wesley Alexander, 84
  William, 84

COWAN, Hugh, 192
  James, 178
COWLEY, James, 339
COX, Jacob, 84, 352
  L. L., 40
  William, 84, 344, 346
COY, John, 324
CR..., Nathan, 84, 334
CRABBS, B. Franklin, 134
CRABSTER, Peter, 84
CRAFT, Elizabeth, 179
CRAGER, Eliza, 85
  Elizabeth, 85
  George Washington, 85
  Jeremiah Augustus, 85
  Mary Ann, 85
  Rebecca, 85
  Samuel, 84, 349
  Sarah Anna, 85
CRAIG, Mary, 215
CRAIN, William P., 204
CRALL, Christion, 318
CRAMER, Eve Catharine, 85
  Ezra, 305
  Jacob, 85, 291, 327
  Lt. Colonel, 12
  Magdalena, 85

  Margaret, 85
  Mary M., 85
  Oliver, 259
  William, 43
CRAMLET, Andrew, 85, 363
CRAMPTON, Joshua, 111
CRANDLE, James, 85, 339
CRANE, Henry R., 53
CRANER, Samuel, 324
CRANSLET, Andrew, 85
CRAP, Boler, 85, 360
CRAPSTER, John, 85, 154
  Mary E., 154
  Peter, 84, 324, 360
  William, 154
CRATON, James, 85, 87, 361
CRAVER, Clem., 334
  Clements, 85, 332
  Henry, 85, 352
  Samuel, 324
CRAWELL, Michael, 85, 321
CRAWFORD, Evan, 319, 321, 325
  Evan L., 85, 321
  Eve, 86
  George, 86

FREDERICK COUNTY MILITIA IN THE WAR OF 1812

George W., 86
James, 86
Rebecca, 86
Robert, 86, 350
Samuel, 86, 363
Scena, 86
William, 86, 319, 363
CRAWMER, Basil, 86
  Daniel, 86, 363
  George, 86
  Helpher, 86, 363
  Margaret, 86
CRAYTON, Hugh, 86
  Joshua, 111
CREAGER,
  Amanda Louisa, 37
  Captain, 14
  George, 320, 323
  Jacob, 21, 87
  John of Lawrence, 87
  John W., 276
  Lewis, 327
  Michael, 302
  William, 87, 358
CREAK, George, 87, 333
CREATIN, Lucy Ann, 141
CREEGER, Samuel, 84
CREEK, Robert, 331
CREGLOW, George, 87, 365
CREMER, John, 233
CRESS, Jacob, 317

CRETIN, James, 87
  John T., 87
  Mary A., 87
  Mary C., 286
CREW, Elizabeth, 87
  William, 87, 257, 332
CRIDER, D. L., 309
CRILLY, Michael, 87, 344, 346
CRISE,
  Barbara, 87
  George, 87, 88
CRISHER, Conrad, 88
  Conrod, 343
  Coonrod, 81, 88, 341
CRIST, Christina, 76
  Jacob, 76
  John, 88
CROMBACKER, 88
  Jacob, 89
CROMWELL,
  Nathan, 330, 331
CRONICE, Henry, 88
CRONISE, Henry, 88
CROSBERY,
  James B., 88
CROSBURY,
  James, 341
CROSS, Ann S., 159
  Elizabeth, 32

  Thomas, 88, 339
CROUS, William, 88, 363
CROUSE,
  Christian, 88, 356
  Christopher, 88
  Elizabeth, 88
  Henry, 88, 351
  Ira E., 49, 312
  John, 88, 335
  Joseph, 88, 325, 335
  Lewis, 88, 361
  Margaret, 88
  Salley, 88
  Samuel, 111
  Sarah, 111
  William, 88, 123
CROUT, John, 89, 325, 335
  Rachel, 89
CROW, William J., 86
CROWEL,
  Catharine, 219
CROWL, David, 89, 109, 363
  George, 187
  Jacob, 64
CRUM, Abraham, 89, 212, 351
  Casper, 78
  Edward L., 78
  Elisabetha, 89
  Harriet, 78
  Henry, 326
  Hetty, 45
  Isaac, 78, 357
  John, 318, 357
  Jonathan W., 185
  Mary, 30

INDEX

Nathan, 326
Susan, 135
Susanna, 89
William, 89, 135
CRUMAGE,
Frederick, 89, 341
CRUMBACHER,
Hans, 89
John, 89
CRUMBAKER,
David F., 89
Elias Smitley, 90
Elisabeth, 90
Grofton Porter, 90
Jacob, 16, 89, 90, 357
John, 24, 90
Joseph Monroe, 90
Joshua Randolph, 90
M. W., 24
Oliver Hazzard Perry, 90
Rosanna, 89
Rossanna, 90
Sarah, 90
Zikiah, 90
CRUMBECKER, 90
David, 344, 346
David F., 89
Mary, 89
CRUMPACKER,
Hans, 90
CRUMPTON,
William, 313
CRUMRINE,
Henry, 90, 325, 335

John, 90, 363
Judith, 90
Peter, 90, 363
CRUTCHER,
Barbara, 90
Vincent, 90, 352
CRYNER, Michael, 318
CULISON, Joseph, 90
Mary, 299
Washington, 299
CULLEN, Charles, 116
CULLER, Anna, 90
Henry, 90, 364
CULLERS, Mary, 308
CULLISON,
Joseph, 90, 352
CULLOM, Abigail, 227
CUMMING,
Casper, 325
Robert, 2, 317
CUMMINGS,
Robert, 327
CUNNINGHAM,
James, 90, 333
John, 244
John F., 32
Martha Ann, 77
CUNTZ, Jacob, 318
CURENCE, Elijah, 91, 333
CURFMAN, Adam, 91
Christian, 91
Christopher, 91

Elizabeth, 91
Rebecca, 91
CURNEL, James, 317
CURRENS, Elijah, 325
CURRUN, Elijah, 325
CURRY, James, 24, 91, 336
John, 91, 349
CURSMAN,
Christian, 91, 337
CURTIS, Channcy E., 215
Sarah M., 215
CURTZ, Abraham, 325
CUSTARD, Jacob, 91, 355
John, 91, 360
CUTSAIL, Henry, 322
CUTSHALL,
Samuel, 91
CYRUS, Cary, 331

-D-
DADDISMAN,
Mary, 139
DADDS, Robert, 91, 321
DAGAN, John, 321
DAGEN, John, 91
DAGETT, Joab, 92, 330
DAHOOF,
Andrew, 92
Christian, 92
DAILEY,
Archibald, 92, 335

FREDERICK COUNTY MILITIA IN THE WAR OF 1812

John, 92
DAILY, John, 360
DALAUTER,
Mary, 70
DAMOND, John, 323
DAMOOT, John, 92, 97, 356
DANIEL, 92, 330, 331
DANNER, Zach., 140
DARBY, Denton, 12, 15, 92, 348, 349
  Elizabeth, 92
  Perry, 92, 347
  Zemiah B., 92
DARLING, James, 295
DARNALL, John, 322
DARNELL, Benedick, 92, 336
DARNER, Andrew, 171
  Mary, 91
DARTZABAUGH, George, 45
  Margret, 45
DARTZBAUGHH, Catherine, 97
  George, 97
  Sophia R., 97
DASHON, Margret, 250
DATROFF, Andrew, 92, 346
DAUS, Francis, 92, 362
DAVID, Catharine

C., 206
John N., 206
Joshua, 357
Mathan, 338
DAVIDGE, Rezin, 317
DAVIDSON,
  Catherine, 92, 93
  Ella May, 93
  Jesse, 92, 356
  Samuel, 92, 93
DAVIS, Alban, 93, 352
  Alexander, 93, 325, 335
  Anna, 257
  Catharine, 177
  Eli, 93
  Elijah, 93, 360
  Elizabeth, 93, 94
  Ephraim, 64, 138
  George, 351
  George E., 93
  Isaac, 93, 351
  James, 93, 95, 357
  James Y., 106
  Jane, 94
  Jesse T. H., 146
  John, 93, 94, 338, 339, 363
  Jonathan, 94, 338, 339
  Joseph, 94, 348
  Joshua, 94, 324, 332, 361
  Laura Littlejohn, 193
  Levi, 94, 344, 345
  Luke, 325

Mary Ann, 93
Nathan, 94, 339
Paris, 94, 338
Permilla, 93
Rachel, 93
Richard, 21, 94, 321, 358, 359
Sarah Ann, 94
Thomas, 94, 358
Thomas C., 44
Walter, 94, 360
William, 95
William E., 199
DAVISON, Alice, 183
  Robert, 322
  Samuel, 92, 95, 347
  William, 95, 347
DAWES, James, 95
DAWSON,
  Captain, 16
  Nicholas, 95, 362
  Sam, 338
  Samuel, 6, 9, 12, 95, 325, 334, 338, 339
DAYHOOF, Christian, 95, 363
DAYS, Henry, 95, 352
DE LAWTER, Jacob, 70
  Sarah, 70
DEAN, Catharine, 95
  Elizabeth, 95
  James, 95, 337, 347
  John A., 23, 95,

INDEX

337, 347
  Joshua, 95, 354
  Peter, 95
  Robert, 95, 214, 337, 347
  Thomas, 95, 333, 353
DEAVER,
  Benjamin, 95
DEBERRY,
  Susanna, 138
DEETERING,
  Catharine, 252
DEGRANGE, Ann R., 95
  Catharine M., 95
  Daniel W. F., 95
  David J., 95
  Elizabeth, 95, 96
  George W., 95
  John, 95, 96, 357
  Nathaniel C., 95
DEHAVEN,
  William, 96, 355
DEHOFF, Andrew, 344
DEHOOF,
  Catharine, 65
  John, 96, 341
DELAPLAIN,
  Daniel, 96
DELAPLANE,
  Daniel, 96, 356
DELASHMITT,
  Bazil, 96
  Sampson, 96
  Samson, 339
DELASHMUT,
  Andrew J., 213
DELASHMUTT,
  Denis, 96, 360

  John, 96, 360
  Nelson, 96, 334, 360
  Otho, 96, 357
  Sampson, 96, 334
DELAUDER,
  David, 96
  John, 96
DELAUTEN,
  Frederic, 338
DELAUTER,
  Frederic, 96
DELAWDER,
  George, 96, 365
  Jacob, 96, 355
DELAWTEN,
  Daniel, 337
DELAWTER,
  Alpheus, 96
  Catherine, 96
  Daniel, 96
  David, 96, 337
  Elizabeth, 96
  Ezra, 96
  Jacob, 96
  Jonas, 96
  Lewis, 96
  Mary A., 96
  Rebecca, 96
  Sarah, 96
  Sarah A., 96
DELEPLANE,
  Daniel, 318
DELL, Adam, 97, 321, 322
  David, 97, 321, 322
  Elizabeth, 136
  Harriet, 293
DELOSIER,
  Ignatius, 97

DELOSURE,
  Ignatious, 356
  Ignatius, 97
  Susanna, 97
DELPHA, Thomas, 97, 341
DELPHIA,
  Thomas, 97, 355
DELUSHMUTT,
  Basil, 338
  Sampson, 338
DEMMIL, Henry, 319
DEMOTH, John, 325
DEMRY, John, 97
DEMUTH,
  Catharine, 92, 97
  Johann, 92, 97
  John, 97, 335
  Sophia Theresia, 92, 97
DENNIS, John, 97, 344, 346
DENSMORE,
  Adam, 22, 317
DERN, Frederick, 97, 355
  John Philip, 27
  Susie, 184
DERNE, Frederick, 97
DERNER, George, 97, 365
  Jacob, 97, 364
DERR, Abraham, 325
  Catherine, 97, 237
  Daniel, 97, 306
  John, 235

FREDERICK COUNTY MILITIA IN THE WAR OF 1812

Sophia, 243
Theodore, 88
DERTZABAUGH,
Susan, 182
DERTZBACH,
Catherine, 97
Margaret, 97
Mary, 97
DERTZBACK,
Catherine, 97
George, 97, 333, 353
DERTZBAUGH,
Catharine, 97
Elizabeth, 178
G. W., 142
George, 97, 323
DESHAN,
Margret, 250
DESHER, Jacob, 98
DESHNER, Jacob, 337
DEVELBISS,
Charles, 98, 341
DEVER, Richard, 98, 355
DEVILBISS, Anna Elizabeth, 145
Catharine, 34
Charles, 98, 290
George, 98
DEVITT, Amelia, 98
Ann P., 98
Anna M., 98
David B., 98, 324, 354
Edward J., 98
Elizabeth, 98
Margaret, 98

Philip H., 98
DICK, Christian, 98, 332
John, 357
DICKSON, John, 98, 365
DIEL, Philip, 325
DIELMAN, Mary C., 87
DIFFENBAUGH,
James A., 89
DILL, Ezra, 98, 101, 351
George, 98
Joshua, 98, 351
Lewis H., 162
Louis H., 56
Margaret, 98
Mary, 98
Mary M., 98
DILT, Jacob, 277
DINSMORE,
Margaret, 98
DIONEBURGH,
Jacob, 322
DISCORNEY,
Augustis J., 98, 341
Augustis P., 341
Augustis S., 98
Augustus P., 342
Augustus S., 342
DISON, Richard R., 99
DITTER,
Abraham, 98, 344
DIXON, Benjamin F., 99
Hezekiah, 99, 339
James, 99, 352, 353
James M., 99
Joseph A., 99
Joshua, 126
Sophia, 99, 126
Sophia E., 99
DOAN, Sarah, 242
DOCKERTY,
Daniel, 99
DODGE, Lewis, 33
Lusindia, 33
DODS, Robert, 328
DOFLER,
Elizabeth, 261
George, 261
DOHERTY, Daniel, 99
DOLL, Elizabeth, 126
George, 126
Michael, 99, 354
Miss, 63
Peter, 99, 324, 354
DONGAN, James, 100
DONN, George, 99, 349
DONNELY,
Frank, 268
Mary Jane, 268
DORF, Patrick, 344
DORFF, George, 99, 334
Patrick, 99, 346
DORNER, George, 99, 349
DORSEY,
Abraham, 99, 341
Alter, 320

392

INDEX

Ariana, 273
Basil, 12, 322, 347
Basil of Evan, 99
Caleb, 38
Captain, 16
Eliza Ann, 158
Elizabeth W., 38
Ely C., 324
Henry C., 99
Lloyd, 218
Maria Ann, 173
Mary, 273
Michael, 99, 356
Mr., 76
Nancy, 221
Nancy Ann, 312
Otho, 99, 324, 363
Robert E., 173
Roderick, 60
Rosetta, 173
Samuel T., 324
William H., 173
DOUB, Jacob, 324
John, 324
DOUBLE, Andrew, 162
DOUGAN, James, 100
DOUGHERTY, Andrew, 110
Charles, 99
Daniel, 99
John, 174
DOURY, James, 100
DOW, Charles H., 69
DOWD, George, 100, 361
DOWDEN, Mary, 125
DOWDLE, William, 100, 365
DOWLIN, Emma H., 107
DOWNEY, Jane, 217
John, 100, 333
Lydia, 100
DOWNING, Dory, 100, 362
DOYL, Jago, 100
DOYLE, George, 324
Jago, 358, 359
John, 100
Lago, 358
Lawrence, 100, 352
Leg, 358
Margaret, 100
Sarah, 100
DRAPER, William, 100
DREW, Solomon, 215
DREWERY, James, 354
DRILL, Andrew, 150
Elizabeth, 150
DRISKOL, Cecila, 297
DRONENBURG, Jane, 100
John T., 100
Lucay A., 100
DRONENBURGH, Jacob, 100, 336
Joseph M., 100
Mary M., 100
DRUERY, James, 100, 354
DRUMMON, James, 100, 356
DUBEL, John, 199
DUCKNESS, Maria, 84
DUDERAR, George, 100, 341, 343
DUFFEY, James, 100, 341
DUFFIELD, John, 100
DUGAN, James, 100
James P., 69
John, 325
DUGEN, Isabela, 269
DULL, Mary, 279
DUNAGAN, Thomas, 69
DUNAVIN, William, 101, 344, 346
DUNCAN, Martha, 117
DUNGAN, Jane R., 117
Jane Rebecca, 107
Maria, 107
Martha, 117
William, 117
DUNGEN, Martha, 117
DUNN, Edward, 101, 363
DUNNING, Dora,

101, 341
DUPLAINT,
  Dominic, 101
  Dominick, 341
DUPLIANT,
  Dominic, 343
DURBIN,
  Catharine, 101
  Dan, 325
  Elizabeth, 101
  Polly, 278
  Thomas W., 323
  William, 16, 26, 101, 352
DURF, John, 140, 361
DURST, Daniel, 101, 352
  Elizabeth, 101
  John, 98, 101, 351
DUTRO,
  Catherine, 145
  Catherine A., 145
  George, 145
  John, 145
  Lewis, 145
DUTROW,
  Elizabeth, 70
  Henry, 101, 365
DUTTERO,
  Catherine, 145
  George, 145
  Margt., 70
DUTTEROW,
  David, 13, 101
DUTTROW,
  Catherine, 145
  George, 145
DUVAL, Gabriel, 292

DUVALL, Ann C., 101
  Ann E., 101
  Captain, 350
  Daniel, 101, 336
  Daniel B., 101
  Elisha, 101, 348
  John, 102
  Joseph, 306
  Julia, 101
  Lloyd, 101
  Lloyd T., 101
  Samuel, 12, 15, 102, 349, 350
  Susan V., 101
  Thomas, 102, 172
  William T., 150, 172
DYER, Edward H., 280

-E-
EADER, Alice, 102
  Amelia M., 102
  Ann, 102
  Ann E., 102
  Anna C., 102
  Augustus L., 102
  Catharine, 102
  Catherine, 102
  David, 102, 320, 322
  Henrietta E., 102
  Laura, 102
  Lazarus, 102
  Lazurus, 36
  Margaret, 102
  Mary Ann, 176
  Mary C., 102
  Mary Hellen, 102
  Sarah Catherine, 102
  Solomon, 36
  Susan, 102
  Thomas, 102, 351
  William, 102, 230, 336
  William M., 103
EADOR, Jacob, 103, 365
EAGENBROAD, Daniel, 318
EAREHART, George, 343
EAREHEART, George, 103
EARHART,
  George, 341
  J. William, 252
  Jacob, 325
  William, 312
EARNEST, Joseph H., 269
EARNST, Abraham, 103, 336
EASTER, Ann, 33
EASTERDAY,
  Abraham, 103
  Elizabeth, 131
  John, 326
EASTERLINE, George, 341
EATON, Joseph, 103, 360
EBB, Jeremiah, 103, 339
EBBARTS, Mary, 270
EBBERT, Elyu, 354
  John, 103
  Joseph, 103, 333

INDEX

EBBERTS, 103
 Elizabeth, 103
 George, 104
 Jacob, 103, 352
 John, 103, 352
 Joseph, 103, 352
 Joseph M., 39,
 108, 251
 Michael, 103
 Susanna, 103
EBERT, 103
 Ann Rebecca,
 103
 Eli, 104
 Elizabeth, 103
 John, 103, 149
EBERTS, Cathrine,
 103
 George, 104, 344
 Jacob, 103
 Michael, 280
EBLEN, Isaac, 234
EBY, Samuel, 104,
 336
ECARD, Henry, 79
 John, 79
ECCARD,
 Catherina, 104
 Peter, 104, 337
 Sarah Maria, 104
ECHAR,
 Christopher, 104,
 322
ECHART,
 Anthony, 104, 349
ECHISS, Samuel,
 325
ECK, Ellen, 312
 Peter, 104, 356
ECKAR,
 Christopher, 321

David, 104, 322
ECKART, Peter,
 104
ECKER,
 Christopher, 104
 Solomon, 220
 William, 220
ECKERT, Peter,
 104
 Salley, 88
 Sarah, 65
ECKES, Nicholas,
 104, 356
 Peter, 356
ECKHART,
 Anthony, 104, 274
 Betsy, 104
 Catharine, 104
 Susan, 104
ECKIS, Peter, 105,
 335
 Samuel, 105, 335
ECKMAN, Jacob,
 105, 365
 John, 105, 349
 Polly, 155
 William, 105, 363
EDELIN, Ignatius,
 244
EDMONDSON,
 Robert, 105
EDMUNDSTON,
 James N., 105, 349
EDWARDS,
 James, 105, 351
EGNEW, Henry,
 357
 Samuel, 30
EICHELBERGER,
 George M., 19,
 105, 331, 360

Jane, 105
 Martin, 209
 Peter, 233
 William A., 105
EICKELBERGER,
 Major, 361
EICLEBERGER,
 George M., 328
EIKER, David, 190
ELBERTS, George,
 105, 346
ELDER, Catharine,
 105, 141
 Charles, 105,
 332, 358, 359
 Eleanor, 193
 Francis, 105
 Guy, 193
 Henry, 105, 357
 James A., 299
 Jesse, 106, 356
 Judith, 193
 Lucy, 141
 Mary, 146
 Nathaniel, 106,
 317, 356
ELEMA, Joseph,
 106
ELINE, Jacob, 325
ELKINS, Mary,
 106
 William, 106
ELLER, Elias, 106
 Elizabeth, 106
 Jacob of Jacob,
 106
 John T., 106
 Martha, 106
ELLIOTT, James
 M., 34
ELLIS, Anna

FREDERICK COUNTY MILITIA IN THE WAR OF 1812

Maria, 106
Daniel, 288
John, 91, 106, 351
William, 324
ELMES, Joseph, 106
ELMS, Asseneth, 106
  Cena, 106
  Cenett, 106
  Joseph, 106, 348
  Sena, 106
ELY, Daniel, 107, 324, 352
  David, 114
  Ezra, 61, 107
  Glovenia, 107
  Julia, 114
  Martha, 107
  Sarah, 107, 232, 280
  William, 107, 354
EMERLY, James, 107, 361
ENGEL, Susanna, 180
ENGELBRECHT, Jacob, 108
  Margaretta, 251
  Michael, 108
ENGELBRIGHT, William, 108
ENGELL, Peter, 107
ENGLAND, Andrew, 107, 341, 343
  Harriet, 107, 128
  Nathan, 107
  Samuel, 335
ENGLAR, Elizabeth, 47
ENGLE, Andrew, 325
  Catharine, 62
  David, 107, 321
  Frederick, 107, 337, 347
  George, 180
  Jacob, 265
  John, 107, 321, 324
  Mary Ann, 293
  Peter, 107, 318, 348
  Susan, 265
  Susanna, 180
  Susannah, 265
ENGLEBRECHT, Louisa F., 108
  Luther M., 108
  Mary A., 108
  Michael, 108, 344
  Rebecca, 108
  Susanna, 108
  William, 108, 357
ENGLEBRIGHT, William, 357
ENGLEMAN, John, 108, 341, 343
ENGLER, Philip, 108, 343
  Phillip, 341
ENGLISH, James J., 288
  John, 108, 321
  Jonathan D., 128
  King, 108, 364
ENSBERGER, Robina, 200
ENSEY, Dennis, 319
ENSOR, Luke C., 220
ENT, George W., 10, 16, 53, 103, 108, 212, 351
  John, 108, 332
  Margaret, 108
  Mary M., 53
EPLEY, John, 264
ERB, John, 109, 351
ERBAUGH, Peter, 109, 352
ERHARD, George, 109
  James, 109
  Julia A., 109
  Margaret, 109
ERHART, George, 109, 333
ERNEST, Solomon, 271
ERTER, George, 320, 322
ERVIN, Jane, 62
  John, 109, 358
  William T., 116
ERWIN, John, 358, 359
ESEBERGER, Henry, 318
ESTER, Sophia, 99
ESTERLINE, George, 109, 343
  Rachel, 252
ESTHER, Elizabeth, 225
EVANS, Catherine,

INDEX

78
  Corilla, 78
  Currilla, 78
  David, 109, 321
  Elisha, 109, 347
  James, 109, 363
  John F., 182
  Joseph, 109, 352
  Lydia, 100
  Robert, 78
EVERETT,
  Samuel, 109, 339
EVERHART,
  William, 109, 360
EVERLY, David, 109
  Elizabeth, 109
EVERS, Mary, 204
EVES, Elias, 109, 363
EVITT, Catherine, 140
  George, 109, 353
  George W., 323, 333
  Woodward, 109
EWING, Samuel, 90
  William, 319
EYELOR,
  Elizabeth, 109
  Henry, 109, 358, 359
EYLER, Aaron, 110
  Andrew Jackson, 110
  Catharine, 110
  Cecilia Ann Elizabeth, 110
  Charlotte Rebecca, 110
  Edwin Frederick, 110
  Elias, 110
  Elizabeth, 109, 110
  Henry, 109, 110, 336
  John, 110
  John C., 110
  John Cyrus, 110
  Joseph, 110
  Joseph Elizabeth, 110
  Laura Jane, 110
  Lewis Francis, 110
  Martha Adeline, 110
  Mary Amanda, 110
  Rebecca, 110
  Sarah, 110, 143
EYLOR, Henry, 110, 333
  John, 332

-F-
FAGAN, Anna Maria, 106
  Catherine, 110
  Elizabeth, 111
  George, 110, 215, 344, 346
FAGLER, George, 51, 111, 347
FAIR, Elizabeth, 111
  Mary, 111
  Michael, 111, 337, 356
  Peter, 325
  Rebecca, 111
  Samuel, 111
  Sarah, 111
  Susan, 111
  Valentine, 111
  Volusia, 111
FALCONAR,
  Ralph J., 106
FALCONER,
  Elisha, 111, 347
  Maria, 63
FALKNER, Maria, 63
FALKS, Cunrade, 318
FARDING,
  Charles, 357
FARNER, Jacob, 325
FARQUHAR,
  William P., 9, 13, 111
FARRELL,
  William, 44
FARRIS, William, 136
FARST, Michael, 111, 341, 343
FAUBEL, Caspar, 111
  David, 111
  Elizabeth, 112
  George, 111
  Jacob, 111, 112, 146
  John, 111, 112
  Joseph Degrange, 111
  Margaret, 111
  Rufus E., 112

FREDERICK COUNTY MILITIA IN THE WAR OF 1812

FAUBLE, 111
A. Degrange, 112
Ann, 112
Casper, 112, 357
Catherine, 112
Elizabeth, 112
George, 112, 332
Jacob, 112, 333
John, 72, 112, 226
Margaret, 112
Marion, 112
Mattie E., 112
FAUBOE, Jacob, 112
FAUNEY, Jacob, 112, 353
FAVORITE,
Elizabeth, 85
Maria, 152
FAWCETT, C. W., 37
FAWLAN, James, 319
FEAGA, Catharine, 200
Frederick, 113, 344, 346
FEAGLER, Jacob, 113, 353
John, 320
FEASHAKE,
Adolphus, 301
FEASTER, Jacob, 115
FEBUS, Peter, 113, 357, 365
FECHTIG, Charles Christian, 330
FECTAR, Andrew, 113, 321

FEISTER, Jacob, 115
FELDY, Elizabeth, 115
FELTY, Elizabeth, 115
Jacob F., 113, 332
FENFROCK,
William, 225
FERDON, Charles, 352
FERGUSON,
Hugh, 165
Mrs. A. L., 315
William, 324
FERNANDERS,
Adam, 113, 343
FERNANDES,
Thomas, 113, 339
FERNANDY,
Thomas, 113, 338
FERNANDZ,
Thomas, 338
FERNDON,
Charles, 113
FERNUNDY,
Thomas, 338
FERREE,
Elisabeth, 253
Mary, 253
FERRELL,
Abraham, 113
Eliza, 113
James R., 113
John, 113
Margaret, 113
Richard, 113
Sarah Virginia, 113
Susan, 113

FESSLER, John, 113
FESTER, Daniel, 113, 341
FETTERLING,
John, 113, 363
Rachel, 89
FICK, Daniel, 113, 333
FICKEL, Daniel, 113
FICKLE, Daniel, 338
FIEGA, Christena, 251
FIEGLER, Henry L., 97
Margaret, 97
FIELDS, William, 24, 113, 350, 365
FILLER, Daniel H., 114
Elizabeth, 113, 114
Henry, 113, 336, 362
John, 113, 338, 339
Mary J., 114
Solomon, 113, 114, 263, 358, 359
Solomon A., 114
William, 114, 358, 359
FILLERY, James, 24, 349
FINCH, Adam, 114, 363
Eliza, 114
Elizabeth, 114, 130

398

INDEX

John, 114, 226, 357
Rosetta, 114
Susanna, 114
FINCK, John, 357
FINE, John, 114, 332
Peter, 114, 322, 336, 347
FINK, Elizabeth, 122
John, 318
Mary, 47
Solamon, 318
FINLEY, Philip, 81
FINNEY,
Charlotte, 38, 39
Christian K., 39
James, 38, 39
Mary F., 39
FIPS, Nathaniel, 114, 333
FIRESTONE, Jacob, 114, 328, 354
FIRSTER, Jacob, 115
FIRZZLE, Nimrod, 325
FISCHER, Adam, 114, 324, 331, 332, 334
Amelia, 68
John, 326
William, 114, 346
FISH, Daniel, 349
Helen, 115
Hellen, 115
William, 115, 355
FISHBACK, Rhoda, 44

FISHBURN, David, 319, 322
FISHER, Adam, 114, 330
Asa, 115, 348
Catherine, 73
Elisha, 114, 351
Isaac R., 236
John, 38, 97, 328
Mary, 66, 67, 89, 114
Thomas, 317
William, 114, 330, 344
FISK, Barton, 322
Daniel, 115
FISTER, Anna, 90
Jacob, 115
FITTING, F. M., 192
FITZHUGH, Daniel, 330, 331
FITZPATRICK, John, 115, 335
FLANAGAN, Joseph, 115, 362
FLANT, Jacob, 115
FLAUT, Captain, 323
Christian, 317
George, 323
Jacob, 115
FLAUTT, George, 6, 8, 115, 332
Margaret, 115
FLEAGAL, John of Charles, 116
Susan, 116
FLEAGLE, John, 116, 137
John of Charles,

116
S. Franklin, 116
Susan, 116
FLEGAL, David, 115, 356
John, 356
John of Charles, 116
Susan, 116
FLEGLE, George, 115, 361
Jacob, 325
John, 116, 232
FLEMING, Arthur, 22, 317
Captain, 22
Charles F., 288
Eleanor, 163
John, 318
Joseph, 163
Mary, 76
Samuel, 75, 320, 322
FLEMMING, Mary, 76
FLENNER, Catharine, 115
Elizabeth, 115, 116
Philip, 116
Phillip, 24, 115
Rachael, 116
FLETCHER, Jacob, 317
James, 116, 346
Joseph, 116
FLICK, Adam, 115
FLICKINGER, John, 325
FLIFER, Devid, 318

Samuel, 318
FLING, Jane, 116
  Owen, 116
  Owing, 357
FLINN, Jane, 116
  Owen, 116
FLINTIN, Betsey, 254
FLOOK, Henry, 115, 364
  Margaret, 246
  Peter, 318
FLOYD, Hezekiah, 51
  Lydia, 51
FLUGEL, John of Charles, 116
  Susan, 116
FLUGLE, John, 116, 363
FLYNN, Jane, 116
  Owen, 116
FOGLE, Abraham, 117, 325, 335
  David, 117, 363
  Elizabeth, 117
  John M., 270, 271
  Mary Ann, 271
  Mathias, 271
  Matthias, 270
  Michael, 363
  Solomon, 271
  Susannah, 270
FOGLER, Henry, 117, 352
  Margaret, 117
  Martha, 107, 117
  Mary, 280
FOLKNER, Peter, 117, 352

FOLTZ, M. A., 182
FONCE, George W., 268
FONSTEN, John, 10, 20, 26, 122, 363
  Lt., 21
FOOT, George D., 172
FORCE, Joseph, 117, 338
FORD, Ann M., 117
  Clemm S., 117
  Edward, 117
  F. M., 37
  Ignatius, 117
  Jerome, 117
  John L., 117
  Joseph, 117, 324, 332, 338
  July A., 117
  Mary, 205
  Peter, 117
  Robert, 41
  Stephen, 117
FORE, Mordica, 322
FOREMAN, Danial, 341
  Daniel, 117, 343
  David, 117, 341, 343
  General, 12, 348
  Jacob, 117, 324, 335, 341, 343
  Valentine, 117
FOREST, Jeremiah, 338
  Nelson, 117, 321
  Rezin, 117, 347

FORGASON, John, 318
FORMWALT, Emanuel, 146
  Solomon, 137
FORNEY, Catharine, 261
  John, 323
FORRESST, Solomon, 118
FORREST, Absalom, 117
  Ann R., 118
  Daniel, 118
  Elizabeth, 118
  Hanson, 118
  Henrietta, 118
  Jeremiah, 117, 339
  Julia, 117
  Mahlon, 118
  Maria, 118
  Mary S., 118
  Owen, 360
  Solomon, 360
  Susan, 118
  W. Catharine, 118
  Wastiann, 117
FORSYTH, Nancy, 255
  William, 255
FORTNER, Maria, 63
FOSTER, James, 118, 341, 343
FOUBLE, 118
  Casper, 357
  George, 324
  Jacob, 323, 353
  John, 357

INDEX

Sarah, 283
FOUCH, Mary, 197
FOUND, Moses, 255
FOUT, Balser, 357
  Baltzer, 134
  Christian, 13, 118, 349
  David, 283
  Elizabeth, 98
  Jacob, 22, 317
  John H., 305
  Lewis, 22, 317
  Nancy, 118
  Peter, 98, 118, 320, 323, 349
  Rebecca, 134
FOUTS, Henry H., 254
FOWBLE, Jacob, 112
FOWLER,
  Bartholomew Thomas, 118
  Charlotte, 239
  Eliza Jane, 118
  Elizabeth, 234
  Ellen, 214
  John, 118, 339
  Mary, 114
  Matilda, 136
  Thomas, 348
FOX, C. F.
  Aldolphus, 47
  Catherine, 118
  Ernst A. C., 79
  George, 118
  Henry, 318
  Henry S., 190
  Jacob, 140

  John, 118, 355
  Peter, 118, 360
  Samuel, 119
FRAILEY,
  Solomon, 216
FRALEY,
  Elizabeth, 111
  Henry, 111
FRAME, Jacob, 119, 344
FRANCISCO,
  Hiram, 104
FRANK, George K., 305
FRANKFOLTHER,
  John, 119
  Mary, 119
FRANKFORTER,
  John, 119, 341, 343
  Mary, 119
FRANKFORTHER,
  Amos, 119
  Catherine, 119
  Daniel, 119
  David, 119
  Elizabeth, 119
  George, 119
  Jacob, 119
  John, 119
  Martha, 119
  Mary, 119
  Rebecca, 119
FRANKFUTHER,
  John, 119
  Mary, 119
FRANKLIN,
  Francis, 119, 321, 325, 341, 343
  Frencis, 335
  John, 119, 321

  Joshua, 324
  Thomas, 119, 322
FRANS, Peter, 22, 317
FRANTZ, Susan, 250
  Susanna, 250
FRAZER, Eveline, 120
  Josiah, 120
FRAZIER,
  Catharine, 119, 120
  Cornelius, 119
  David, 120
  Eveline, 120
  Fielder, 119, 355
  George W., 120
  James L., 120
  Jeremiah, 119, 120, 139, 211, 355
  Josephine, 120
  Josiah, 106, 120, 362
  Margaret, 139
  Mary, 33
  Sarah Ann, 119
  Sarah W., 120
  Susan A., 120
  William, 139
FREBURGER,
  Peter, 120, 353
FREDERICK,
  James F., 94
  John, 120, 355
  Mary I., 120
FREESE, George, 194
FREESONG,
  Peter, 48
FREEZE, David, 323

FREISE, George, 318
FRENCH, Amelia, 68
　Elizabeth, 116
　George, 68
　John, 116
FRESHOUR,
　Adam, 317
　Jacob, 120
FREY, Magdalena, 201
　Mary, 256
　Michael, 120, 365
FRIAR, Elizabeth, 170
FRIDAY, Henry, 120, 121, 347, 362
　Mary, 121
FRINGER, George, 20, 25, 121, 363
　Rachel, 121
FRISHOUSE,
　Adam, 121, 349
FRITCHEY, John G., 86
FRITCHIE, Ann Rebecca, 103
　Barbara, 142
　Mrs., 149
FRITRCHIE, John, 324
FRIZEL, Jacob, 121, 321
FRIZELL, Nimrod, 121, 334
FRIZIL, Mearad, 121, 321
FRIZILL, Jacob, 121
FRIZZELL, Jacob, 121, 322
FROCK, Catherine, 121
　Jacob William, 121
　Lydia, 146
　Michael, 121
　William, 121, 363
FROLICH,
　Elizabeth, 111
　Henry, 111
FROOCK, John, 83
FROSCHAUER,
　Adam, 121
　Fredrich, 121
　Jacob, 121
　Johannes, 121
　Margaretha, 121
　Sophia, 121
FROST, Major, 182
　Robert, 121, 332
FRUSAR, Adam, 121
FRUSHOUR,
　Adam, 121, 334
　Catherine, 120
　Jacob, 120, 121
　Jaocb, 332
FRUSHOUSE,
　Jacob, 121, 349
FRY, Joseph, 324
FRYMAN,
　Margaret, 216
FUBBS, Nathaniel, 323
FULLER, Ann Rebeca, 67
　Francis, 323
FULTON, Captain, 14
　Robert, 21, 121, 318
FULTONE,
　George, 319
FUNK, Henry, 122, 344, 346
FUNSON, John, 122, 325
FUNSTON, John, 122
FURGISON,
　William, 122, 334
FURGUS, James, 180
FURGUSON,
　Rebecca, 86
FURNEY, David, 325
FURRY, Abraham, 70
FUSS, Conrad, 122, 361
　Elizabeth, 65

-G-

GADEN, George, 55
GADULTICK,
　George, 332
GADULTIG,
　George, 122, 332
GAITHER, George, 122, 348
　H. H., 314
　Lott, 336, 122
　Ruth, 208
　Samuel, 208
　Sarah, 208
GALLASPY,
　James, 122

INDEX

GALLIGHER, Michael P., 220
GALT, Captain, 14
  John, 10, 18, 123, 319, 360
  Moses, 122, 357
  Sarah, 123
GALTON, Ignatius, 122
GALWITH, Elizabeth, 122
  John W., 122, 362
GAMBRILL, Anne E., 105
  Charles A., 105
GAMMER, Jacob, 123
  Mary, 123
GANER, Peter, 326
GANZAU, Jacob, 129
  Margaret, 129
GARBER, Jacob, 192
GARDINER, Elizabeth, 266
  James, 266
GARDNER, Elizabeth, 230
GAREY, Sabred, 123, 344, 346
GARHEART, Henry, 317
GARLING, David, 194
GARLYLE, David, 123
GARLYTLE, David, 322

GARMSHAUSEN, John, 125
GARNHEART, Henry, 317
GARRETT, Erasmus, 123
GARROTT, Middleton, 123, 362
GARVER, Christian, 123, 323, 350
  Jacob, 192
  Mary, 123
  Michael, 325
  Samuel, 324
GASAWAY, Thomas, 7, 336
GASSAWAY, Thomas, 123, 336
GASTON, John, 22, 317
GASWAY, Thomas, 322
GATES, Robert, 123, 357
GATH, Samuel, 111
GATTAN, B. F., 223
GAUER, Peter, 326
GAUFMAN, Georg, 321
  George, 123
GAULT, John, 123
  Joseph, 123, 344
  Samuel, 123, 356
  Sarah, 123
GAUSNEL, Beal, 123, 363

GAVER, George, 123, 323, 337, 338, 339
  Henry, 124, 338
  Hiram, 84
  John, 3, 124, 337
  Malinda, 124
  Martin, 124
  Mary, 124
  Mrs. Joseph, 235
  Peter, 124, 326, 334
GAWULTIG, George, 324
GAYER, Jacob, 354
GEARBO, Ignatious, 124, 341
GEAREY, Christopher, 124, 336
GEARY, Christian, 7, 335
GEASE, George, 318
GEDULDIG, George, 122
GEDULIG, Catharina, 122
  George, 122
  Jacob, 122
  Wilhelm, 122
GEISBERT, Catharine M., 263
GEISBURT, Jonathan, 263
GEISENDARF, William, 320
GEISENDURF, William, 124, 365
GEISINGER,

403

Catharine, 124
David, 124
Elizabeth, 192
GELDZ, John, 124, 347
GELTZ, John, 124, 337
GEORGE, Mrs. Thomas S., 273
GEPHARD, John, 318
GERCY, Jacob, 124
GERNAND, Adam, 124
  Anna Catharina, 124
  Anna Catharine, 124, 125
  Anna Elizabetha, 124
  Caroline Emilie, 124
  Elizabeth, 124
  Harriet S., 124
  John Adam, 124
  Joseph, 124
  Joseph Alfred, 124
  Mary Melinda, 124
  Sarah Ann Elizabeth, 124
  William, 124
GESLIN, Levin, 324
GETROST, Susan, 236
GETTIER, George, 125
  Henry, 125
  Jacob, 125
  Lewis P., 125
  Margaret, 125
  Margurite, 125
GETZ, Henry, 125, 337
GETZENDANNER Adam, 125, 337
  Adam H., 126
  Alexander, 126
  Anna, 125
  Anna Elizabeth, 125
  Anna Maria, 126
  Balthasar, 125
  Catharine, 126
  Catherine, 126
  Cathrine Maria, 126
  Christian, 323
  Edward T., 278
  Elizabeth, 125, 126
  George, 125, 347
  Harriet, 126
  Harriett, 305
  Henry, 126
  Isaac Jacob, 126
  Jacob, 7, 11, 51, 337, 347
  Jacob of Adam, 125
  John, 23, 300
  John J., 305
  John Joseph, 126
  Joseph, 126
  Maria A., 126
  Mary, 51, 125
  Mary Ann, 126
  Solomon, 126, 337, 347, 365
  Solomon J., 126
  Sophia, 126
  Susan, 126
  Susannah, 126
GETZENDONER, Christian, 320
GEYER, D. S., 126
  Dorcas, 126
  Jacob, 126
  Jonas, 126, 354
GHOLSIN, Ambrose, 126
GHOSLIN, Ambrose, 332
GIBBENY, John, 328
GIBBONS, Mathew, 127, 341
  Orwell, 127, 360
GIBBS, George, 127, 365
  John, 127, 348
GIBSON, Catharine, 268
  David B., 315
  Thomas, 127, 317, 319
  William, 325
GIES, John, 311
GIGER, Adam, 104
GILBERT, Barnhart, 318
  Benjamin, 150
  George, 365
  Jacob, 127, 357, 363
  John, 127, 359
  John B., 189
  Michael, 127, 349
  Reuben, 127, 355
  Thomas, 324

INDEX

GILKINSON,
Burris, 174
James, 174
GILL, James, 127, 338, 340
Walter, 127, 362
GILLAN,
Elizabeth, 83
GILLASPEY,
James, 122
GILLASPIE,
James, 127
GILLASPY, 127
James, 127
Johannes, 127
John, 127, 187, 338
Margaret, 186
Mathew, 339
Matthew, 127
Thomas C., 187
GILLELAND,
Elizabeth, 83
GILLEN, William, 14, 33, 127, 336, 344, 345
GILLENWATER, James, 187
GILLESPIE, Maria, 248
Mary, 127, 186, 248
Mathew, 127, 186
Mathias, 127, 186
Matthew, 127
GILLILAN,
Elizabeth, 83
GILLMEYER,
Francis, 127, 357
GILSON, Samuel W., 119

GIRD, William F., 127, 344
GIRTY, Samuel, 127, 324, 335
GISBERT,
Catharine M., 263
GISENDERFER,
William, 322
GIST, Charles, 127
John, 128
Joshua C., 128
Margaret, 128
Mary A., 128
Thomas, 128
Thomas B., 49, 89, 152
GITTINGER,
James, 56
GITTINGS, Jane, 68
William, 128, 346
GITZENDANNER,
Captain, 10
Jacob of Adam, 320
GLADDEN,
George, 365
James, 365
GLADHILL, James S., 128
John, 128, 360
Sophia, 128
Thomas, 128, 333
William, 128, 333, 365
GLADVILL, John, 128
GLASCOW, Ann B., 46
GLASE, Jacob W., 236

Maggie, 236
GLAUT, Jacob, 361
GLESON,
Margaret, 291
GLISAN, Charles, 128, 358, 359
Elisea, 195
Henry, 349
John, 70, 128
Margaret, 291
Mary, 195
GLISON, John, 128
Thomas, 357
GLISSAN, John, 128
GLOVER, Francis, 128, 347
GODDARD, John, 326
GODMAN,
Jefferson, 129, 358, 359
GOFF, Richard, 129, 349
GOGGIN, Thomas, 129, 348
GOLDEN, John, 129, 349
GOLDSBOROUGH
Charles H., 129
Charles W., 129
Edward Y., 129
Nicholas, 353
Nicholas W., 129
Sarah, 129
William, 129
GOLT, John, 317
GOMBER, Ann C., 270

FREDERICK COUNTY MILITIA IN THE WAR OF 1812

Ezra, 352
Ezra M., 129
John, 129, 344, 346
GONSE, Ann Sophia, 129
Catharen Matilda, 129
Charles Jacob, 129
Charlotte Keller, 129
Mary Elizabeth, 129
William Henry, 129
GONSO, Jacob, 129, 354
John, 129, 354
Margaret, 129
Mary, 129
Matilda, 129
GONZE, Jacob, 129
Margaret, 129
GONZO, Jacob, 129
John, 129
Margaret, 129
GOOD, Adam, 317
GOODING, Lambert T., 342, 343
Lampert T., 129
GOODLAND, Elizabeth, 130
Thomas, 130, 335
GOODLIN, Elizabeth, 130
Thomas, 24, 130, 348, 349

GOODMAN, Elizabeth, 305
John, 171
Rachel, 178
William, 171
GOODWIN, John E., 91
GOOKER, Peter, 130, 361
GORDEN, William, 130
GORDON, Rebecca Ann, 193
Sarah, 100
William, 130
GORRELL, Samuel, 130, 352
GOSLIN, Ambrose, 324
Mary, 212
GOSNELL, Margaret, 86
Richard, 84
GOSS, Sallie, 69
GOSSON, Oliver C., 357
GOTSCH, Julius, 269
GOUGHER, Jacob, 130, 356
GOYER, Jacob, 354
Jonas, 354
GRABELL, Ann, 229
GRABLE, Nancy, 308
GRACE, Charles P., 130, 334
Michael, 130, 356
William, 130, 339

GRADY, Caroline M., 187
GRAFF, E. Beaty, 311
George, 130, 323, 333
Joseph, 130
Marcus Y., 130, 132, 353
Mary E., 130
Sabastian, 328
GRAHAM, Caroline Worthington G., 131
Elizabeth C., 196
Ephraim, 130
John, 317
Thomas, 353
Thomas Johnson, 131
Walter, 196
GRAHAME, Ann, 131
Caroline Worthington G., 131
John Colin, 131
Thomas Johnson, 131
GRAMMAR, Jacob, 123
Mary, 123
GRAMMER, Godig, 22, 317
Jacob, 123, 131, 350
Mary, 123
GRAU, Jacob, 323
GRAVE, Jacob, 364

INDEX

Reuben, 354
GRAY, George, 322
  Walter, 131, 340
  William, 169, 332
GRAYSON, Jane, 105
GREASON, Jane, 105
  Nathan, 131, 356
GREEN, Benedick, 125
  Benedict, 131
  Benjamin, 132
  Eliza, 132
  Elizabeth, 82, 131, 290
  Emma V., 134
  Francis, 131
  George, 131, 336
  George W., 106
  Henry, 18, 131, 325, 360
  John, 121, 132, 322, 365
  John T., 131
  Joseph, 8, 13, 132, 325, 334, 344, 345
  Joshua, 20, 132, 355, 356
  Laurance, 349
  Lawrance, 216
  Lawrence, 132
  Lewis, 20, 25, 132, 137, 138, 323, 353, 363
  Mary, 132
  P. J., 132
  Samuel, 132, 324, 334
  Susanna, 131

GREENAMIRE, William, 132
GREENHALS, John, 132, 322
GREENHOLTZ, Jacob, 132, 321
  John, 132, 321
GREENTREE, Ezra, 93
GREENWALD, Catherine, 133
  Christian, 132, 133, 337, 347
  Emanuel, 133
  Livinia, 133
  Mary Magdalena, 133
  Susan, 133
GREENWALT, Catherine, 133
  Christian, 132, 133
  David, 133
  Mary, 133
  Mary Magdalena, 133
  Wilson, 133
GREENWELL, Elizabeth, 155
GREENWOOD, Jeremiah, 220
  John, 133, 321, 322
  Ludwick, 319
GREGG, John, 106
GREGORY, David R., 75
  John, 75
GREIDER, George T., 176
GREY, Zachariah, 133, 335
GRIAR, John, 195
  Sarah, 195
GRIBBEL, Polly, 65
GRIFFAN, William, 342
GRIFFIN, Thomas, 133
  William, 133, 342
GRIFFITH, Caleb, 133
  John, 133, 351
  Lemuel, 133, 358, 359
  Philemon, 2
  Philip, 133, 363
GRIMES, Elizabeth, 106
  Ephraim, 130
  George, 133, 341, 343
  Jacob, 133, 336
  James, 133, 352
  Nicholas, 133
  Rebecca, 133
  Sarah, 222
GRINEL, Cornelus, 318
GROANER, Andrew, 134, 363
GROCE, Henry, 326
GROF, Samuel, 319
GROFF, John, 134, 349
GROSHON, Abraham, 134
  Catherine, 134
  Elias, 134

FREDERICK COUNTY MILITIA IN THE WAR OF 1812

Mary Ann, 134
GROSS, David,
134, 349
  Jacob, 134
  John, 134, 336
  Mary A., 134
  William, 134,
339, 340
GROVE, Ann M.,
135
  Ann M. R., 135
  Annie, 135
  Barbara, 135
  Barbary, 135
  Catharine, 135
  Catherine, 135
  Charles B., 135
  Christianna S.,
135
  David, 135
  Edward, 135
  Elias, 135
  Ellen, 135
  Greenberry F.,
135
  Hannah, 37
  Harriett, 135
  Jacob, 77, 123,
318, 320, 327, 350,
364
  John, 134, 135
  Leonard, 135,
365
  Leonard S., 134,
135
  Lydia, 135
  Maria, 135
  Mariah, 135
  Mary, 135
  Rebecca, 134,
135, 140

  Reuben, 16, 37,
135
  Susan, 135
GROVENS,
George, 318
GUEYER, Henry,
360
GUISEBERT,
Catharine M., 263
GUMP, Anna
Maria, 135
  Benjamin, 6, 135,
325, 334, 335
  Elias, 135
  Elizabeth, 135
  Elizabeth
Juliana, 135
  Ester, 135
  Isaac, 135, 361
  John, 135
  Jonathan, 135
  William, 135
GUNDY, Abraham,
319
GUNTHER, Helen
L., 193
GUSEY, Christian,
135, 349
GUSS, Elizabeth,
217
  William, 217
GUYER, Samuel,
322
GUYMON,
Prestley, 270
GWINN, John, 319

-H-

HAAS, Christian,
319
HABBS, Warner,

158, 321
HACKNEY,
Barton, 20, 136,
362
  Charles P., 136,
362
  Elizabeth, 136
  P. Charles, 362
HAFER,
Catherine, 135
  Samuel, 135
HAGAN, Adam,
64, 138
  Benjamin, 136,
351
  Francis, 136
  Matilda, 136
  Richard, 136
HAGAR, Francis,
347
HAGER, William,
319
HAGLEN, Isaac,
136, 337
HAGON, Francis,
136
  Matilda, 136
HAHN, Abraham,
26, 136, 363
  Bazil, 21, 24, 136
  Benjamin, 136
  Catharina, 137
  Daniel, 137
  Elizabeth, 136,
137
  Henry, 137, 338
  Israel, 137
  Jacob, 137
  Joseph, 137
  Lydia, 137
  Mary A., 136

INDEX

Michael, 137
Polly, 226
Samuel, 137
HAILEY, John, 137
HAINER, Andrew, 137, 356
HAINES, Albert L., 138
  Charles, 138
  Daniel, 137, 319, 321
  David, 138, 319, 324
  Eli, 137, 156, 352
  Elizabeth, 137, 138
  Francis, 138
  Henry, 137, 319, 321
  Isaac, 138, 352
  Israel, 138
  Jacob, 324
  Jesse, 138
  John, 138, 321, 322
  Mary, 138
  Phebe, 137
  Phebea, 137
  Samuel of Jo, 323
  Sarah, 39
  Susanna, 138
HALDERMAN, Nathaniel, 168
HALL, Amey, 63
  Barrack, 351
  Barrock, 138
  Barruck, 138
  Henry, 324
  Isaac, 138, 340
  James, 145
  John S., 3, 319, 320
  Joshua, 138, 334, 338, 339
  Nehemiah, 259
  Nicholas, 14, 138, 351
  Nickolas, 320
  Richard, 138
  Thomas B., 138, 329
  William, 327
  William H., 176
HALLEN, George William, 139
HALLER, Ann, 139
  Ann Luesa, 139
  Carlene, 242
  Christiana, 211
  Elisha, 138, 344, 346
  Elizabeth, 139
  Fanney, 138
  George, 139, 344
  George W., 344
  George William, 139
  Henry, 139
  Henry H., 139
  Hillary, 306
  Jacob, 51, 139, 246, 344
  Jacob B., 139
  Joseph, 211
  Juliann C., 139
  Margaret, 139
  Mary, 139
  Mary A., 147
  Mary Magdalene, 281
  Nicholas, 139
  Philip, 139, 354
  Samuel, 56, 195
  Samuel M., 139
  Sarah M., 139
  Tobias, 139, 140, 323
  Tobias W., 139
  Wilhelmina, 139
  William, 140, 338
HAMBLETON, Catherine, 140
  John, 140
  Louisa, 140
HAMILTON, Catherine, 140
  John, 140, 347
  William, 140, 344
HAMLER, Sarah, 258
HAMM, W. N., 314
HAMMER, Jacob, 323
HAMMON, Denton, 140, 349
  James, 140
  Mary Ann, 140
  Ormond, 322
  Sarah Ann, 140
  Sharlot R., 140
HAMMOND, Carroll, 140, 363
  David C., 51
  Denton, 140
  Edin, 322
  Eliza. M., 140
  Francis Simpson, 141
  Hannah, 140

Hezekiah, 140
James, 140, 361
Ormond W., 95
Simpson, 140, 349
Thomas, 141
Washington, 258
William, 141, 329
HAMN, Erhart, 325
HAMOND,
Denton, 140
Hezekiah, 140
Rebecca, 140
Simpson, 12, 141
HAMPTON,
Rachel, 268
HAN, Jesse, 359
HANDSCHUH,
Frederick, 103
HANE, Anna, 108
Daniel, 141
David, 141, 306, 354
Jacob, 108
Maria, 141
HANEMAN, F., 96
HANES, Daniel, 329
William, 141, 350
HANEY, Charles, 147
Charles W., 147
Margaret, 147
HANICKER, Peter, 141, 335
HANIFER, John, 141, 332
HANIPIN, John, 332
HANN, Adam, 141, 342, 343
Bethilda, 141
Bridget, 141
Henry, 141, 356
Jacob, 141, 356
Lucy, 141
Mary Magdalene, 141
Monica, 141
Sarah, 316
William, 142, 342, 343, 356
HANNAH, Elijah, 142, 361
HANSCHUH, Rev., 142
HANSHAW, Catharine Susan, 142
George, 142, 360
Henry, 142
HANSHEW, Allen, 142
Charles A., 142
Daniel, 142
Daniel S., 142
Emily, 142
Emily E., 142
Frederick, 142
Fritchie, 142
George, 142
Harriet C., 142
Henry, 353
John, 103, 142
John Frederick William, 142
Julia A., 142
Mary, 142
HANSON, A. B., 143
Alexander B., 142
John, 143
Susan H., 143
Susan W., 143
HAPE, George, 318
HAPLER,
Elizabeth, 45
HARBAUGH,
Adaline, 143
Alexander, 143, 323
Amos, 24, 350
Ann, 143
Anna B., 143
Anna Margaretha, 124
Anna Maria, 84
Benjamin, 143, 358, 359
Catharine, 110
Christian, 143
David, 110
Elias, 143
Elixander, 332
Ephraim, 143
Felix V., 143
Frederick Alexander, 143
George, 143
George C., 143
Henry, 143
Hiram, 143
Jacob, 143
Jonathan, 97
Laura Jane, 110
Margaret, 115
Maria E., 143
Maria Elizabeth, 143
Mary, 143

INDEX

Milton, 110
Rebecca, 110
Rosanna, 143
Sarah, 143
Simon W., 110
Stansbury, 143
Susan, 143
Washington, 143
Winfield, 143
HARBOLD, Mary A., 134
HARBOLT, Mary A., 134
HARCUSHIMER, John, 287
HARDER, Henry, 144
HARDING, Annie V., 144
  Basil, 144, 195
  Eleanor, 144
  Eleanora, 144
  Hannah, 144
  James, 232
  James M., 177
  Jane, 144
  John, 24, 144, 243
  John L., 353
  John Lackland, 144
  Julia Ann, 144
  Lucinda C., 144
  Margaret, 144
  Martha, 145
  Philip, 12, 144, 145, 348
  Rebecca, 144
  Rutha H., 171
  Sarah, 165
  Solomon, 144, 348
HARDISTA, William, 318
HARDMAN, George, 145
  Michael, 81
HARDT, John C., 203
HARDY, Catharina, 145
  Catherine, 145
  Ezra, 145
  George, 145
  Jeannine M., 145
  Johan Caspar, 145
  John, 145
  John Caspar, 145
  Joseph, 145, 344
  Susanna, 145
HARGESHEIMER, Joseph, 145, 341
HARIS, Reson, 357
HARKRIDER, Mary, 199
HARLAN, James, 145, 358
  James W., 145
  Joshua, 145
  Mary, 145
  Mary M., 145
  Stephen, 355
HARLAND, James, 145, 359
HARLEN, James W., 145
  John M., 145
  Nancy, 145
HARLIN, James, 308
  James W., 308
HARMAN, Christian, 7, 335
  David, 145, 332
  Elizabeth, 200
  George, 84, 132, 323
  Jacob, 145, 146, 323, 333, 352
  John, 146, 352
  Lewis, 116
  Margaret, 145, 146, 234
  Mary, 146, 220
HARMON, Jacob, 145, 146
  Margaret, 145
  Mary, 146
HARNE, Overton, 146
HARNS, Halban, 146, 321
HARPER, Abram, 147
  Francis T., 257
  Harrison, 43
  Priscilla, 147
  Richard, 129
HARQUISHIMER, Jacob, 355
HARRIET, Henry, 146, 361
HARRIN, Elizabeth, 153
  Jacob, 153, 340
HARRINGTON, George, 135
  Margaret, 135
HARRIS, C. A., 296
  Catherine, 147, 230

FREDERICK COUNTY MILITIA IN THE WAR OF 1812

Daniel, 146, 324, 332
George, 146
Jacob, 319
John, 146, 349
Joseph of Mord, 323
Kinsey, 147, 347
Lydia, 146
Mary, 146, 147
Michael, 147, 342, 343
Mrs. E. H., 315
Nancy, 146
Regin, 147
Reson, 357
Rezin, 34
Thomas, 317
Thomas H., 53
Zepheniah, 147
HARRISON,
Edward, 147
Kinsey, 147
Margaret, 147
Mary, 147
Mary A., 147
P. L., 147
Rebecca, 249
Samuel, 249
William, 249
Zeph, 354
Zephaniah, 147
Zepheniah, 147
HARRISS, George, 352
HARRY, 148, 337
HARSHMAN, Christian, 281
HART, Amanda, 148
Elizabeth, 148
Ezra, 148, 365
Jerusha, 148
Liddia, 148
Margaret, 148
Mary, 148
Michael, 148, 337, 338
Nicholas, 292
Oliver, 148
Peter S., 148
Sara, 148
Sarah, 148
Susanna, 148
Theophilus, 148
HARTLEY, James, 324
HARTS, Peter, 357
HARTSACK, Peter, 358
HARTSOCK, Ann, 215, 216
Anna, 215
John, 259, 324
Sarah, 246
Susanna, 215, 216
HARTZ, Margaret, 306
HARTZACK, Peter, 148, 359
HARVEY, Elisha, 148, 348
George, 148
HARVY, Seth, 322
HASLET, Jacob, 150
Major, 25
HASPELHORN, Henry, 124
Mary, 124
HASSEFROSS,
John, 148, 357
HATCH, Samuel, 148, 325, 334
HATTEN, Jacob, 139, 357
William, 148, 360
HAUBERT, Eve, 86
HAUCK, John, 289
HAUER, Adam, 148, 346
Ann C., 149
Catharine, 60, 149
Catherine, 148, 149
Daniel, 148, 149, 320, 322
Daniel J., 149
Elizabeth, 149
Elizabeth Margaret, 148
Georg, 148
George, 148, 149, 353
Henry, 149, 331, 353
John H., 149, 333
John Henry, 149
Lucretia L., 149
Margaret, 148
Margaret Ann, 149
Mary L., 149
Nicholas D., 142, 149
Susan, 149
William, 149
HAUERT, Catharina, 149

INDEX

Henrich, 149
Nicolaus, 149
HAUFFMAN,
John, 320
HAUGH, Daniel,
149, 356
HAUGHN, Adam,
342
Jonathan, 149,
342
HAUKER, John,
149, 333
HAUMAN,
Frederick, 150
HAUN, Adam, 141
David, 149, 352
HAUPT, Elizabeth,
162
Jacob, 162, 355
HAUSE, Levin,
106, 107
HAUSER, 103
Isaac, 259
Michael, 64, 149
Susan, 64
Susanna, 149
Wilhelm, 149
William, 149,
323, 333, 353
HAVENER,
Augustus D., 249
John, 317
HAVER, George of
Peter, 323
Peter, 323
HAWK, Daniel,
258
Hannah E., 258
Henry, 325
Mary J., 258
Peter, 325

HAWKINGBURG,
Scott, 136
HAWKINS, James,
150, 357
HAWKINSBURG,
Alice, 136
HAWMAN, F., 100
Frederick, 112,
139, 150, 177, 185,
216, 246, 250, 280,
352
Margaret, 277
HAWN, Anna M.,
137
David, 149, 150,
352, 355
Henry, 137
Isaac, 150, 356
Mary, 150
HAY, Mary, 281
Susannah, 80
HAYDEN, Basil,
77, 150, 162
Bazil, 350
Catherine, 161
Elizabeth, 161
Joseph, 161
HAYES, Abraham,
150, 356
Abraham W., 150
Deborah, 150
Henrietta, 150
Joseph, 150
HAYNES, Daniel,
150, 322
George, 319
HAYS, Abigail, 163
Abraham, 163
Abraham W., 150
D. S., 241
Eleanor, 163

James L., 32
John, 150, 362
John O., 163
Leonard, 163
Sarah, 163
Thomas, 150, 344
William S., 163
HAZLET, Jacob,
150
John, 155
Mary, 155
HAZLETT, Jacob,
150
HEAD, Catherine,
151
Ceceliour, 318
Cecilius, 151,
289, 352
James, 325
John, 151
William
Beckwith, 317
Zeal, 151, 352
HEASTON, Elsa,
259
HEATER, William,
151, 335
HEATH, Richard
K., 334
Richard Key, 9
HECK, Jacob, 13,
115, 151, 361
HECKMAN,
George, 53
HEDGES, Joseph,
327
HEFFNER,
Charlotte, 151
Daniel, 151
George W., 151,
152

Harriet, 151
Jacob, 151, 332, 337
John, 151
John of Frederick, 151, 324
Julia Ann, 151
Lavina, 151
Lawrence, 151, 337
Lewis H., 151
Margaret, 151, 152
Mary, 151, 207
Mary S., 151
Michael, 151, 152, 207, 333, 353
Michael of Frederick, 323
Susannah, 181
HEFNER, Daniel, 151, 358, 359
Jacob, 354
Lawrence, 151, 347
HEGES, Isaac, 324
HEICHEW, George, 325
HEIGHE, James, 273
Mary, 273
HEIGHTER, John, 181
HEIM, Andrew, 152
Jacob B., 152
William, 152
HEINER, Jacob, 293
John, 152, 356
HEINES,

Elizabeth, 160
Jamnes, 160
HEISELY, Frederick Augustus, 152
HEISLEY, Frederick A., 320, 344
Frederick Augustus, 152
John, 152, 354
John D., 344
HEISLY, John, 345
HEITCHEW, Elizabeth, 88
HELBYDLE, Jacob, 321
HELDERBRAND, George, 155
HELFENSTEIN, Rev., 31
HELM, Samuel, 342
HELMES, Samuel, 152
HELMS, Samuel, 343
HELTABIDLE, Antony, 152
Elizabeth, 152
Maria, 152
Sabina, 152
HELTBRIDLE, Anthony, 321
HELTBYDLE, Antony, 152, 321
Elizabeth, 152
George, 321
Maria, 152
HELTIBIDDLE, David, 152

HEMP, John, 324
HEMPEY, Henry, 152, 357
HEMPY, Catharine, 152
Henry, 152
Kitty, 152
HENLEY, Moses B., 166
HENLY, Margaret, 125
HENNING, Adam, 153, 361
Catherine, 153
John, 153, 356
Thomas, 365
HENNYMAN, Gabriel, 325
HENRICKS, George, 222
HENRY, 355
David, 317
Joseph, 153, 346
HENSELL, Daniel, 34
HEPPER, Mary, 201
HERBAUGH, Elias, 143, 360
Henry, 323
Jacob, 361
John, 360
Jonathan, 153, 361
HERBERT, Perry, 153, 326, 334
HERFERT, Abraham, 323
HERGESHEIMER, David, 223
HERMAN, John,

INDEX

153, 337
HERRING, 153, 347
  Elizabeth, 153, 284
  George, 326
  Henry, 115, 118, 153, 211, 216, 217, 355
  Jacob, 153, 334
  John, 355
  John of A., 153
HERSCH, Philip, 153, 357
HERSH, Coonrade, 317
HERSHABARGER, John B., 153, 362
HERSHMAN, Christian, 324
HESS, Charles, 153
  Daniel, 316
  Martha A., 316
HESSER, Amy, 181
  George, 181
HESSON, Abraham, 325
  John, 153, 356
  Joseph, 280
  Margaret, 221
  Mary, 154
  Peter, 154, 342, 343
HESSONG, Catherine, 221
  Margaret, 221
  Margret, 221
HESTAND, Daniel, 154, 362

John, 154, 362
HETHYDLE, Jacob, 154
HIATTS, Jase, 167
  Joseph, 167
HIBBERT, Daniel, 311, 312
HICHEW, 154
  David, 154
  George, 157, 335
HICKEY, Catharine H., 296
  James D., 296
  James F., 296
  Mary J., 296
HICKMAN, Catharine, 37
  Isaac, 154
HICKS, George, 355
  Joseph, 154, 358
HICKSON, Heinrich, 154
  Henry, 356
  Henry H., 154
  Maria, 154
  Mary E., 154
  Robert, 355
  Thomas, 154, 317, 357
  Thomas V., 155
  William C., 154
HIDE, Adam, 155, 334
  Valentine, 326
HIDER, William, 155, 358, 359
HIGGINS, Rev. James, 33
HIGH, Frederick, 155, 322

Polly, 155
HILARD, Johnson, 155, 343
HILBERT, Henry, 250
HILDEBRAND, Georg, 155
  George, 344
  John, 155, 347
  Joseph, 155
  Magdalena, 155
  Margaret, 155
HILDEBRANT, John, 155
  Margaret, 155
HILDEBREAND, John, 337
HILDERBRAND, George, 155
HILE, Adam, 355
HILHIDE, John, 303
HILKEY, George, 155, 357
  Sarah, 155
  Siloma, 155
  Soloma, 155
HILL, Anna E., 191
  Anna Maria, 126
  Bennet, 155, 347
  Charlotte, 190, 191
  John, 155, 347
  Littelton, 212
  Rachel, 212
  Richard, 190
  Squire S., 212
  William F., 212
HILLEARY, Doctor, 331

John, 323
Priscilla, 37
William, 156, 331
HILLERY,
 Augustus, 155
 Edward, 155
 Elizabeth, 155
 James, 155, 348
 Lpouisa, 155
 Osborn, 155
 Perry, 308
 William, 155, 327, 330
HILTABIDEL,
 George, 156
HILTABIDLE,
 George, 156
 Martha, 156
 Mary A., 156
 Serena E., 156
HILTABYDEL,
 George, 321
HILTABYDLE,
 George, 156
HILTEBRIDLE,
 Mary, 199
HILTON, Henry, 108
 Miles, 156, 354
 Polly, 176
HIMELICK, John, 45
HINER, Harbert, 156, 356
HINES, Christian, 156
 Eli, 137, 156, 352
 Jacob, 156
 John, 156, 333, 352
 Michael, 156, 342, 343
 Peter, 156
 Sarah, 228
HINKE, William J., 27
HINKLE,
 Catherine, 157
 George, 156, 157, 352
HINKLIE, George, 22, 317
HINKS, Samuel, 223
 Susan, 223
HINSILL, Fredrick, 330
HINTON, William, 24, 350
HITCHEW, David, 157, 338
HITE, Abraham H., 153
HITECHEW,
 Gideon, 157
 Julian, 157
HITER, Abraham, 157
HITESHEW,
 Abraham, 157
 Amanda, 157
 Anna Maria, 157
 Catharine, 159
 Catherine, 54, 157
 David, 157, 167
 Emeline, 157
 George, 157, 158
 Gideon, 88, 157
 Hannah, 54
 Jacob, 88, 157
 John, 157, 333
 Mary, 157
 Mary Ann, 157
 Philip L., 157
 Regina, 157
 Rejoiner, 157
HITESHOE,
 Abraham, 157, 356
 Catherine, 157
 Gideon, 157, 356
 Jacob, 158, 356
 John, 158, 356
HITSELBERGER,
 Mary, 248
 Mary Fitzhugh, 27
HITTAN, Miles, 354
HIX, Joseph, 154, 359
 Leticia, 70
HOBART, John H., 173
HOBB, Warner, 327
HOBBS, Brice, 158
 Eliza Ann, 158
 Elizabeth, 158
 Louis J., 225
 Mary, 243
 Mary J. C., 225
 Regin, 357
 Reson, 158, 357
 Rezin, 158
 Samuel, 158, 348
 Warner, 158
 William, 324
 William C., 324
HOCH, Catherine, 190
 R. H., 190
HOCK, Catharine,

INDEX

190
  Catherine, 191
  Raleigh, 190
HOCKENSMITH,
  Catharine, 158
  David, 158, 361
HOCKERSMITH,
  David, 158, 325
  Henry, 237
HOCKINSMITH,
  David, 158, 335
  George, 158
  John, 158
HOCKMAN,
  Elizabeth, 314
HOEK, John, 358
HOERSHMAN,
  Philip, 318
HOFF, Peter, 22, 317
HOFFMAN,
  Andrew, 158, 354
  Ann, 159
  Casper, 158
  Catharine, 159
  Charlotte, 159
  Ezra, 159
  George, 158, 357
  George W., 158, 344, 345
  Henry, 158
  Jacob, 158
  John, 158, 159, 338, 344, 346, 358, 359
  Mary, 159
  Michael, 159, 352
  Sally, 159
  Samuel, 86
  William, 159, 344, 346

HOGEN, Ruben, 159, 347
HOHN, Daniel, 137, 336
HOHNE, Ann S., 159
  Westol, 159
HOLBROOK,
  Thomas, 159, 343
HOLBRUNER,
  Adam, 268
HOLBRUNNER,
  John, 44
  Thomas M., 269
HOLBURNER,
  Adam, 268
HOLDCRAFT,
  Jacob Mehrling, 27
HOLDER, 160
  Anna Margreth, 160
  Anna Margretha, 160
  Anna Maria, 160
  Daniel, 160
  Georg, 160
  George, 160
  Johann Georg, 160
HOLEDGER,
  Phillip, 159
HOLER, Jacob, 139, 357
HOLIDA, George, 31
HOLIGER, Phillip, 159, 349
HOLLAR, George William, 139
HOLLEN, George William, 139

HOLLENBERGER,
  Anna, 262
  Elizabeth, 159
  Magdalena, 160
  Peter, 160
  William, 159, 356
HOLLENBERRY,
  Anna, 262
HOLLER, 159
  Ann, 139
  Daniel, 323
  George, 139, 346
  George W., 345
  George William, 139
  Henry, 353
  Jacob, 139, 346
  John, 326
  Mary, 139
  Philip, 354
  Tobias, 140, 333
HOLLINBERGER,
  Peter, 160
HOLLINGER,
  Phillip, 159
HOLLINGERGER,
  Peter, 356
HOLLINGSWORT
H, Francis, 160
HOLMES, Jacob, 293
HOLSTEIN, M., 173
  Rachel, 173
HOLTER, 160
  Anna Maria, 160
  Catharine, 160
  Daniel, 160, 333, 353
  Elizabeth, 160
  George, 160, 357

George B., 160
Jacob, 160
Johann Georg, 160
John, 160
Magdalene, 160
Margaret, 160
Mary, 160
Peter, 160
Samuel L., 160
Sarah, 160
Susan, 160
William, 48, 160, 357
HOLTZ, Jacob, 317
John, 161
Margaret, 73
Mary, 308
Nicholas, 317
HOLTZAPPLE, Abraham, 326
Daniel, 324
HOLTZMAN, Catherine, 161
John, 161, 334
HOLTZOPPLE, Abraham, 161
HOLVER, David, 161, 321
HOMES, James, 161, 363
HONE, John Westol, 341
Westol, 161
HONNIWATT, John, 317
HOOD, Colonel, 11
Lt. Colonel, 10
HOOFFMAN, John, 332

HOOK, Benjamin, 161, 363
James, 319, 338, 339
John, 161
William James, 161
HOOKER, Johnsey, 161, 343
Jonsey, 342
HOOPER, Barton, 161
Esther, 46
Hester Ann, 45
John, 161, 321
Urilla, 46
HOOPES, John, 241
HOOPS, Daniel, 96
Mary A., 96
HOOVER, Daniel, 161, 189, 323, 332
George, 161, 344, 346
Henry, 161, 337
Jacob, 161, 324, 332
HOPKINS, Resin, 324
HOPPE, Catharine, 161, 162
Frederick, 161
HOPPER, Benjamin, 162, 322, 336, 347
John, 365
William A., 226
HOPPY, Fredrick, 350
HORINE, Catharine, 74

Rebecca, 269
HORKINSON, Norris, 162, 334
HORN, Abraham, 162, 362
Basil, 162, 363
Benjamin, 161, 363
Jesse, 162, 358, 359
HORNBEY, William, 162, 333
HORNBLOWER, Ann, 162
William, 162, 347
HORNER, George W., 44
HORNICKER, Peter, 325
HORNS, Polly, 67
HOSKINS, George, 108, 147
HOSLER, Anna Juliana, 76
George, 76
HOSSEFROSS, John, 357
HOTTER, Catharine, 47
HOUCK, Ann, 162
Catharine, 195
Charles, 162
Eleanor, 162
Ellenora, 162
Ezra, 245
George, 162
Jacob, 195, 320, 323
John, 162, 354
Mary Ann, 183
Philip, 119

INDEX

Polly, 227
William, 88
HOUCKMAN,
Henry, 162, 361
HOUCKS,
Elizabeth, 163
HOUNG, John, 324
HOUPT, Elizabeth, 162
  Henry, 324
  Jacob, 162
HOUSE, Caleb, 318
  George, 318
  John, 318, 326
  Nathan, 81
  Richard, 318
  Steven, 318
HOUSER, Henry, 162, 351
  Jacob, 317
HOUSMAN, Frederick, 280
HOUSTON, Agnes, 166
  James F., 166
HOUTZER, Sarah E., 215
HOUX, Catherine, 111
  Elizabeth, 163
  George J., 162, 352
  George Jacob, 111
  John, 163, 358, 359
HOVIS, Adam, 163, 361
HOWARD, Adam, 163, 344
  Betsy, 212
  Cornelius, 272
  Dorcus, 212
  Edward, 173
  Eleanor, 163
  Elenor, 163
  Elisha, 163, 362
  Elizabeth, 212
  Elizabeth R., 217
  Joseph, 163, 212, 332
  Richard, 163
  Sarah R., 217
  Thomas, 163, 320, 323, 332
HOWE, James, 163, 352
HOWELL, Jerim, 89
HOWER, Henry, 324
HOWSER, Sarah, 67
HUBBARD, William B., 163
HUBER, A. J., 66
  Abraham H., 123
HUEY, William, 163, 340
HUFFARD, Elizabeth, 163
  John, 163, 358, 359
HUFFER, Hannah, 75
HUFFMAN, Henry, 365
  John, 163, 318, 332, 365
  Mrs. G. E., 104
HUFFORD, Elizabeth, 163
  John, 359
HUFMAN, George, 357
HUGESS, Hiram Harry, 164
HUGHES, Amanda, 165
  Amanda Cecelia, 164
  Andrew, 326
  Daniel, 164
  Daniel Boyle, 163
  Edward, 165, 226
  Eleanor, 164
  Elizabeth, 165
  Elizabeth H., 164
  George R., 44
  Hiram, 165
  Hugh, 164, 165, 324, 332
  James, 164
  Joseph, 317
  Joseph A., 164, 349
  Levi, 164
  Mary, 112
  Otho, 24, 164
  Otho Williams, 164
  Patrick, 135, 164, 333, 363
  Richard, 164, 165, 323, 333
  Samuel, 165
  Sarah M., 274
  Sophia, 165, 226
  William D., 168
HUGHS, Edward, 165, 347

FREDERICK COUNTY MILITIA IN THE WAR OF 1812

Hugh, 165, 337, 347
John, 141
Richard, 164
HUHN, Joseph L., 320
HULL, Andrew, 165, 361
  Christianna, 165
  Henry, 165, 344, 346
  John, 165, 340
  Rebecca, 289
HULSTINE, Elizabeth, 271
HUMBERT, George, 165, 363
  Jacob, 325
HUMEL, Catharine, 200
HUMMEL, John, 165
HUMMELL, John, 332, 344, 346
HUMMOCK, George, 165, 349
HUNDLEY, Matthew C., 269
HUNSBURY, Frederick, 365
HUNT, A. H., 108
  John O., 165, 356
HUNTER, Dorcas, 126
HUPPY, 165
HURLEY, Clemtinea S., 143
  James, 314
  James J., 51
  John, 165, 340, 351
  Maria, 314
  Moses B., 166
  Sarah, 165
  Thomas A., 165
  Urilla, 166
HURLY, John, 338
HUSH, Hannah M., 166
  Mary Ann, 166
  Samuel, 166, 342, 343
  Samuel C., 166
  William, 166, 340
HUSTON, Agnes, 166
  James F., 9, 14, 166, 328, 344
  John, 328
HUTCHINGS, Elisabeth, 111
HUTCHINSON, Benedick, 167
HUTCHISON, A., 223
  Benedick, 166, 348
  Benedict, 166
HUTTON, Enos, 167, 320, 347
  Rebeccah, 167
HYATT, Asa, 167, 351
  Eli, 93
  Elizabeth, 93
  Jase, 167
  Joseph, 167
  Margaret, 167
  Mary Ann, 167
  William, 167, 351
HYCHEW, David, 167
HYDER, Margaret, 184
HYMES, Mary, 242
HYNES, John, 156
HYNSON, John, 87, 167, 361
HYSON, John, 361

-I-

ICENOGAL, David, 168
ICKES, Mathias, 56
IDEN, B. C., 84
IFIRT, Henry, 365
IJAMS, Ellen A., 218
  Jacob, 351
  Jemima, 218
  Plummer, 218
  Ruth, 218
INFIELD, George, 167, 365
INGMAN, Ambrose, 167, 348
  Catharine Louisa, 167
INGRM, Nancy, 253
INGRMAN, Ambrose, 64
  Catherine, 64
INLOES, Abraham, 167, 340
INLOWS, Abraham, 338
IODUM, Daniel, 167, 361
IRELAND,

INDEX

Benjamin, 22, 317
IRVIN, John, 168
IRVINE, Amanda M., 168
  John, 167, 335
  Mary, 168
IRVING, David, 168, 324, 332
IRWIN, John, 325
ISANOGLE, Michael, 168
ISBELL, Henry, 168
ISELNAUGEL, Michael, 168, 358
ISELNAUGHLE, Michael, 359
ISEMINGER, Henry, 168
ISENBARG, John, 319
ISER, Christianna, 165
  George, 168, 356
ISERMINGER, Henry, 168
ISINTIARG, Peter, 319
ISNOGLE, David, 168
IZOR, Enoch, 168, 342

-J-
JACK, 331
JACKSON, A., 118
  Archabald, 168
  Archable, 332
  Archibald, 342
  Charles, 163
  Elias, 223

Jacob, 326
Nancy, 118
JACOB, 331
JACOBS, Ann E., 169
  Corbin, 168, 352
  Francis, 169
  Helen, 169
  Henry, 169
  Ignatius, 168, 214, 301, 345
  Jacob, 169
  Jane, 169
  Jane A., 169
  John, 169, 352
  Margaret J., 180
  Martha Jane, 168
  Mary Ann, 168
  Parmelia, 288
  Philip, 169, 288, 324, 332, 357, 358, 359
  Susan V., 169
  Thomas, 169
  William, 169
JAMES, Amos, 169, 336, 338
  Basil, 358, 359
  Bazil, 169
  Brickett, 346
  Charles Wesley, 169
  Daniel, 178
  Harriet, 169
  Isaac, 169, 342
  Jacob H., 169
  John, 169, 325, 327, 335
  Joseph, 320, 322
  Margaret, 178
  Sydney Ann, 178

Tudor, 338
JAMIESON, John, 169, 353
JAMISON, James, 169, 345
  John, 169
  Lt. Colonel, 3
JARVIS, Zadock, 169, 357
JAY, William, 169, 332
JEKES, George, 222
JEMESON, James, 24, 350
JEMISON, James, 170
  Robert J., 316
JENKINS, Elizabeth, 170
  Felix, 170, 340
  Feliz, 338
  Hannah, 170
  Job, 170
  Mandy J., 125
  Simon, 326
  Theodora, 170, 360
  Thomas, 46
  William, 170, 323, 333, 353
JENKINSON, William, 170
JENNINGS, Ann, 131
JESSE, Samuel, 106
JIMMISON, Francis, 317
JINKENS, Simon, 362

FREDERICK COUNTY MILITIA IN THE WAR OF 1812

JINKINS, Simon, 170, 334
JOFFMAN, Andrew, 365
JOHN, 170, 331, 347
JOHNE, William, 182
JOHNS, Thomas, 170, 335, 363
JOHNSON, Ann Margaret, 170
  Anna Elizabetha, 124
  Baker, 131
  Caroline, 172
  Caroline Worthington G., 131
  Catharine, 172
  Catherine, 171
  Charles W., 171
  Crerciller, 172
  Delila, 172
  Delina, 172
  Erasmus, 170, 357
  Jacob, 170, 171, 337, 365
  James, 327
  John, 170, 171
  John H., 362
  John K., 167, 185, 362
  John Knite, 171
  John T., 172
  John V., 171
  Joseph, 171, 324, 332, 336, 352, 360
  Magdalane, 170
  Malinda, 172
  Maria Ann, 173
  Mary, 185
  Nathaniel, 172
  Polly, 185
  Rebecca, 171
  Richard, 171
  Robert, 172, 362
  Rutha H., 171
  Samuel, 328
  Samuel B., 171
  Sarah E., 172
  Thomas, 172, 173, 322, 335, 336, 340, 345, 346, 348, 358, 359
  Thomas B., 324
  Thomas Brashear, 156
  William, 24, 173, 185, 319, 348, 349, 353
  William G., 86
  William T., 172
  Worthington R., 112
JOHNSTON, Thomas, 172, 173, 358
JOLLY, Rachel, 173
  Thomas M., 173, 353
JONED, Richard, 174
JONERS, David, 335
JONES, Abigail, 243
  Amos, 169, 338, 339
  Auberry, 58
  Benjamin, 331
  Charles M., 174
  David, 173, 325
  Frances, 174
  George, 173, 338
  Jacob, 129
  James, 173, 362
  Jeremiah, 173, 358, 359
  John, 129, 174, 325, 326, 338, 340, 361
  John W., 174, 334
  Joseph, 327
  Margaret, 129
  Mary, 58
  Morris, 264
  Nathan, 174, 349
  Richard, 174, 326, 334
  Samuel, 363
  Thomas, 174, 362
  William, 174, 361
  Zachariah, 174
JORDAN, William, 174, 361
JOY, Benedict, 42
  Helen, 115
  Hellen, 115
JUDY, Martin, 174, 340
JULIAN, Isaac W., 90
JUNKIN, 174

-K-

KAIN, Mary, 265
KALKLOESCHER, Abraham, 174
KANDALE, John,

INDEX

125
KANE, Jacob, 174
KANODE, Anna
  A., 175
  Catharine M.,
  175
  David, 175
  Jacob C., 175
  John T., 175
KANTNER, Adam,
  177
  Elizabeth, 30
  George, 30, 213
KARN, Adam, 189
KARNES,
  Catharine, 102
KARNS, Hannah,
  257
  Peter, 257
KAUFFMAN,
  Henry, 175
KAUFMAN, John,
  322
KAUGLE, Daniel,
  216
KEAFAUVER,
  Catharine, 289
  George, 162
  John, 289
KEAFER, Henry,
  357
  Jacob, 323
KEAGLER, Susan,
  104
KEATING, George
  S., 175
KEEFAR, Philip,
  318
KEEFER, 175
  Ann R., 178
  Charlotte, 178

Ellen S., 178
Harriet V., 178
Harry K., 183
Henry, 175
Jacob, 178, 319
Lewis, 175, 361
Mary, 106
Mary C., 178
Matilda, 262
Peter, 324
KEEFFER, Jacob,
  178
KEEGER, James,
  123
KEEMAN,
  Catharine, 190
KEENAN,
  Catharine, 190
  Catherine, 190
  Katharine, 190
  Patrick, 190
KEENY, Jacob,
  175, 358
  Nathaniel, 363
KEEPERS, Joseph,
  175, 266, 345, 346
  Micah, 175
  Micha, 175
  Michell, 175, 357
  Susan, 175
KEETING, George
  S., 345
KEFNER, Jacob,
  354
KEIL, Philip, 215
KEIPERS, Joseph,
  266
KEITING, George,
  346
  George S., 175
KELLAR, David,

326
KELLENBERGER,
  Peter, 325
KELLER,
  Catherine, 126, 227
  Charles, 175, 354
  Conrad, 175
  Edward, 176
  Elizabeth, 162
  Frederick, 175,
  176, 238, 336, 345,
  346
  George, 325
  Henry T., 169,
  176
  Jacob, 176, 322,
  336
  John, 175, 176,
  345, 346, 351
  John H., 31
  Louisa, 261
  Margaret, 129
  Maria, 175, 176
  Mary, 175
  Mary Ann, 176
  Peter, 176, 357
  Ruben, 176
  Rubin, 176
  Rudy, 169
KELLEY, John,
  319
  Joshua, 176
  Maria O., 222
  Savilla, 102
  Solomon, 176
  William, 176
KELLY, Edward,
  357
  Elizabeth, 103
  George, 176, 354
  Henry, 107, 306

James, 183
John, 177, 361, 363
Jonathan, 91
Joshua, 176, 342, 343
Patrick, 363
Solomon, 176
William, 342
KELSELRING,
Lewis, 178
KELTEN, John, 325
KELTZ, George, 177, 352
KEMP, 347
Catharine, 126
Christian, 320, 323
Conrad, 177, 319, 321
David, 320, 322
Elizabeth, 125
Frederick, 177
George, 264
Henry, 14, 82, 329, 351
John, 177, 332, 352
Joseph, 265
Mary M., 264
Sophia, 264
Theadore, 264
Walter B., 223
KENEDY, William, 177, 342, 343
KENNEDY, John W., 206
Sarah Ann, 274
KENTNER, Adam, 177, 338, 340

KENUFF, Deborah M., 183
Jacob, 183
Mary Ann, 183
KENWIP, Conrad, 177, 321
KEPELRING,
Barbara, 311
KEPHART,
Catharine, 177
David, 177, 361
George, 177, 182, 362
Margaret, 177
Ormand, 177
Simon, 355
KEPLER,
Araminta, 178
David, 178
KEPLINGER,
Catharine, 178
John, 178, 322, 336
Joseph, 259
KEPPART, David, 317
KERBY, John, 358
KERNEY, Michael, 41
KESLER, William, 178, 362
KESSELRING,
Lewis, 178
KESSLER,
Andrew, 135
Araminta, 178
David, 178, 357
Elizabeth, 70
Jacob, 178, 265, 354
Rachel, 178

Rebecca A., 178
KESSLERING,
Lewis, 178, 361
KETTLE, William, 178
KETZENTURNER,
Jacob, 317
KEY, John Ross, 184
William, 363
KEYSER, Samuel, 264
KHUNTZ, Simeon, 178
Simon, 361
KIDD, William, 280
KIEFER,
Charlotte, 38
Christian, 38
George, 319
KIEFFER, Jacob, 178, 333, 353
KIENS, Joseph, 258
KILB, Ramer, 352
KILLIAN, Philip, 178, 365
KILLION,
Elizabeth, 178
Philip, 178
KIMMEL, Alfred, 178
Anthony, 178
Anthony Zaarr, 179
Edmund Clemson, 178
Hampden, 178
Marion Louise, 179

INDEX

Sydney Ann, 178
KIMMELL,
Anthony, 179
KIMPEY, Peter, 323
KINE, Abraham, 325
KINEY, Margaret, 167
KING, Francis, 326
  Gilbreth, 179, 352
  Gilbrith, 179
  James J., 94
KINGADE, Joseph, 179
KINGSLEY, Samuel, 363
KINKADE, Joseph, 179, 333, 343
KINKEAD, Joseph, 342
KINKERLY, John, 365
KINKLEY, John, 179
KINNA, Amanda, 179
  Cassiah, 179
  Cassira, 179
  Catharine, 179
  Catherine, 179
  David, 179
  Deborah, 179
  Elizabeth, 179
  James, 167, 179
  James H., 179
  Mary, 179
  Polly, 179
  Sallie, 179
  Sampson, 179
  Samuel, 171
  Sarah, 179
  Thomas, 179
  William, 179
KINNEY, James, 351
  John T., 152
  John W., 179
KINNY, William, 179, 336
KINT, Abraham, 363
KIPLER, Andrew, 185
KIPLINGER, Catharine, 149
KIPP, Henry W., 241
KIRFMAN, Christian, 180, 347
  Christopher, 91
KIRKPATRICK, Margarett Ann, 33
KIRKWOOD, Mary J., 110
  Robert, 83
  Thomas, 110
KISER, Margaret M., 316
  William, 316
KITTING, John, 180, 335
KITTLE, William, 178
KIZER, Daniel, 151
  Major, 12
KLAY, George, 180, 348
  John, 180, 348
KLEIN, Casper, 78, 352
  Edward D., 180
  Frederick, 180, 358, 359
  Henry, 180
  Peter, 180, 357
  Ruanna Mathilda, 180
KLEINHART, Mary, 98
KLEINHOFF, Sarah, 123
KLINE, Charles, 180, 337
  Edward D., 180
  Elisabeth, 180
  Elizabeth, 39, 181
  Frederick, 37, 79, 180, 337, 347
  George, 180, 338
  Henry, 180, 347
  John, 180, 347
  Malinda, 181
  Peter, 180, 192, 357
  Philip, 79, 131, 181, 337
  Ruanna Mathilda, 180
  Stephen J., 231
  Stephen Jacob, 288
  Susanna, 180
  Thomas, 181
KLINEHOFF, Sarah, 123
KLINK, Henry, 325
  John, 181, 337, 357
KLISE, Levi, 181

Susannah, 181
William, 181
KNAFF, Amy, 181
  Catharine, 181
  Ellen Rebecca, 181
  John, 181, 335
  Mary, 181
  Sarah Ann Rebecca, 181
KNAUF,
  Greenbery, 182
  Greenbury, 182
  Susan, 182
  William, 354
KNAUFF, Amy, 181
  Asbury, 255
  Catharine, 181
  Charles E., 183
  Deborah M., 183
  Diana, 183
  Eliza W., 181
  Ellen Rebecca, 181
  George U., 183
  Greenbury, 181
  Howard, 183
  Jacob, 181, 183
  Jennie, 183
  John, 181
  Lewis H., 183
  Mary, 181
  Mary A. E., 183
  Mary Ann, 183
  Sarah Ann Rebecca, 181
  Susan, 183
  Virginia, 183
KNAUP, William, 182

KNIGH, Peter, 322
KNIGHT, Conley M., 69
  Peter, 181, 321
KNIPPLE,
  Christopher, 350
  Jacob, 280
KNOT, Caleb, 181
KNOTT, Caleb, 181, 345
  Francis, 181
  Ruth, 181
KNOUF, Eliza, 182
  Greenbury, 181, 182, 354
  Jacob, 182, 356
  John, 183, 361
  Osee J., 183
  Susan, 182
KNOUFE, George, 182
  Mary M., 182
KNOUFF,
  Catherine, 120, 181
  Deborah M., 183
  Eliza W., 181
  George, 181, 182
  Greenbery, 182
  Greenbury, 183
  Jacob, 181, 183, 351
  John, 181
  Mary Ann, 183
  Mary M., 182
  Susan, 182
KNOUFT, George, 182, 362
  Mary M., 182
KNOUX, Jacob, 225
KNOWER, John, 183
KNOX, Barbara, 183
  Captain, 355
  James, 183
  Jane, 183
  John, 183
  John Robison, 183
  William, 19, 183, 328, 356
KNUFF, Deborah M., 183
  Eliza W., 181
  Jacob, 181, 183
  Mary Ann, 183
KOCH, George, 84
  John, 183, 336
  Maria, 84
  Susannah, 84
KOFFMAN, David, 228
  Nancy, 228
KOHLHOSS, Eliza J., 169
  George B., 169
  Rebeccah, 169
KOLB, 183
  Ann Catharine, 211
  David, 146
  David William, 184
  Eve Maria Ann, 184
  George, 146
  John F., 183, 332
  John W., 157
  John William, 184
  Margaret, 146

INDEX

Ramer, 183
Stanley
Denmead, 184
William, 15, 183, 184, 354, 365
Wilson, 146
Wilson W., 146
KOLP, Jacob, 184
KOOGLE, George, 171
Jacob, 324
John, 241
KOON, George, 184, 360
Henry, 184
Jacob, 184
John, 184
William, 184
KOONS,
Catharine, 184
George, 184
Henry, 184, 357
Jacob, 184, 356
John, 184, 356
Joseph, 184
Margaret, 184
Mary, 184
Peter, 184
Susannah, 184
Susie, 184
William, 357
KOONTZ,
Catharine, 246
George, 184, 324
Godfrey, 257
Henry, 184
Jacob, 184
John, 184, 185, 324, 332, 353
Margaret, 185
William A., 184

KOONTZE, Jacob, 184
KORNS, Henry, 185, 352
KRAEMER,
Catharine C., 175
John, 175
Maria, 175
KRAMER, Peter, 85
KRAMMER, Maria C., 196
KREGLOE,
Catherine, 97
KREIS, Maria, 30
Peter, 200
KREISE, Sophia, 267
KREMER, Maria, 175
KRIEGER, Anna Maria, 84
Lawrence, 84
Samuel, 84
KRISE, H. J., 263
KRISHER, Mary Magdalena, 267
KRMER, Anna Maria, 143
KROFT, Margurite, 125
KROUS, John, 283
KROUSE, John, 88, 185, 362
Sarah, 111
William, 88
KRUG, Elizabeth, 103
John Andrew, 103
KRUMRINE,

Henry, 90
KUEHL, Hilda, 117
KUHN, Catherine Elizabeth, 272
Henry, 3
Joseph, 322
Peter, 185, 325, 345, 346
Zebulon, 272
KULP, Jacob, 184
KUNTZ, George, 363
KURBEY, John, 185, 358
KURBY, John, 359
KURFMAN,
Christ, 91
KURSMAN,
Christian, 91, 185, 347
KURTZ, Abraham, 325
Esther, 44
Rev., 31

-L-

LABAN, Paul, 338
LAFAVER, John, 185, 349
LAKIN, Abraham, 319
Daniel, 319
Elizabeth R., 185
George P., 185
John, 185, 357
Susan, 185
Susan A., 185
Susanna, 185
William, 185, 357
William H., 185

LAKING, Daniel
T., 246
LAKINS,
Benjamin, 185, 362
John, 357
Susan, 185
William, 185, 357
LAMAN, Isaac, 188
Jacob, 186, 363
LAMAR, Mary, 185
Polly, 185
Richard, 185
Richard J., 288
LAMBERT,
Catherine, 148
David, 186, 353
Frederick, 231
George, 186, 353
LAMBETH, John, 318
LAMBRECHT,
George, 186, 352
Michael, 186, 352
Rachel, 186
LAMBRIGHT,
Ammamary, 186
Ann M., 186
Charles O. L., 186
John, 107, 250
Mary, 186
Michael, 186, 225
LAMPBRIGHT,
George, 186
Rachel, 186
LANDERMAN,
Joseph, 186, 337
LANDES, Jacob, 186
Margaret, 186

LANDIS, Jacob, 186, 321
LANDISS, Jacob, 325
LANE, Jacob, 360
Joseph, 186, 361
William, 186, 343, 355
LANG, Samuel, 186, 335
LANTZ, Henry, 135
John, 110
Margaret, 135
Maria, 135
LAPE, Samuel, 186, 337
LAPOLE, 186
George, 188, 338, 340
LARE, Samuel, 186, 361
LAREW, William, 186, 361
LARKIN, John, 186
Margaret, 186, 187
LARKINS, Jacob, 180
John, 355
LARN, William, 187, 343
LAROVETT,
Michael, 187
Philip, 187
LASHORN, Mary, 300
LATE, Catherine, 187
George, 187, 263,

358, 359
George
Washington, 85
Irane, 187
Isaac, 187
Jacob, 187
Margaret, 302
Mary Ann, 85
Rebecca, 85
LATHGIVER,
Maria, 263
LAUGHLIN,
William, 303
LAURENCE,
Elizabeth, 50
LAVARETT,
Philip, 187, 335
LAVORETT,
Michael, 335
LAWLESS, 187
Phillip, 193
LAWRENCE,
Adam, 177
Daniel, 33
James, 187, 345
LAWYER, Jacob, 350
LAYMAN, John, 187, 324, 332, 347
Rebecca, 187
LEAB, Elizabeth, 306
Jacob, 126, 306
LEACH, Benjamin, 187
LEAKIN, Sheppard
C., 42
LEAKINS, John
T., 114
LEAMING,
Reuben, 180

INDEX

LEAMON, Hugh, 322
LEAPLEY,
  Elizabeth, 187
  John, 187
LEAPLY, John, 362
LEAR, Henry, 24, 188, 350
LEARY, Mary Ann, 166
LEASE, Charles, 258
  Elizabeth, 258
  Franklin M., 280
  George, 95
LEASER, Peter, 188, 334
LEATHER, John of George, 320, 323
  John of John, 320, 322
LEATHERMAN,
  Charles T., 198
  George, 179
  Hannah, 259
LECALLEET, John, 188, 321
LECALLERT, George, 321
LECALLUT, George, 188
LEE, Garrett, 188, 324, 332
  Henry P., 212
  William, 107
LEECH, Benjamin, 187
LEEMAN, Isaac, 188
LEESE, Philip, 188, 363
LEEZER, Peter, 188
LEFEVER, Elias, 318
  George, 188, 365
  John, 188
  Mary, 188
  William, 204
LEFTWICH,
  Alexander T., 53
LEGG, William, 188, 340
LEGLIDER, Mary, 121
LEHR, Catherine, 151
LEICSTER, Mary, 311
LEINBACH, Anna Rosina, 76, 201
  Christian, 76, 201
  Christina, 76
  Elizabeth, 201
  Frederick, 201
  Sarah, 201
LEISTER, David, 325
  Jacob, 90
LEIZER, Peter, 188
LEMAR, Richard, 188, 341
LEOHR, George, 188, 354
LEONARD, Ann R., 90
  Harriet, 233
  Richard, 188, 326, 334
LEOPOLD,
  George, 188
LEOPOLE, George, 188
  Henry, 189
LEPPO, Peter, 325
  Petter, 189
LESCALLAT,
  Richard, 189, 321
LESCALLECH,
  George, 189
  Richard, 189, 321
LESCALLECT,
  George, 322
LESCALLEECH,
  John, 189, 321
LESCOLADE,
  George, 325
LEVI, Elizabeth, 136
LEVY, David, 103, 355
  David T., 189
  Elizabeth, 189
  John Leonard, 150
  Jonathan, 22, 327
  Louisa, 149
LEWEN, Paul, 189, 338
LEWIS, Columbia E., 189
  John, 189, 365
  Louis, 154
  Rebecca, 63
  William, 189, 344, 345
  William D., 189
LEYERS, Thomas, 325

FREDERICK COUNTY MILITIA IN THE WAR OF 1812

LEZEN, Peter, 188
LICHLIGHTER, Conrad, 192
LICHLITER, Conrad, 192
LICKLY, Peter, 354
LIDAY, Jacob, 189, 335
  Sarah, 189
LIDDY, John, 190, 197
LIDIE, Jacob, 189
  Sarah, 189
LIEPLY, Peter, 190, 192, 354
LIGHLIDER, George, 358
LIGHTEWAY, John, 221
  William, 221
LIGHTLIDER, George, 190
LIGHTNER, Elizabeth, 190
  George, 190, 349
  George M., 190
LIGHTWAY, John, 221
  William, 221
LIGLIDER, George, 359
LILLY, Joseph, 192
LIMBAUGH, John, 191
  William, 349
LIMEBAUGH, Susan, 191
LINDSAY, Elish, 321
  Elisha, 190
  Thomas, 59
LINDSEY, Elisha, 325
  Juliana, 55
  William, 325
LINEBAUGH, Betsy, 190
  Catharine, 191
  Fanny, 191
  Fanny E., 190
  Jennie, 190
  Susan, 191
  William, 190
LINEWEAVER, Casper, 191, 360
LINGANFELTER, Michael, 325
LINGENFELTER, Michael, 191, 335
LINK, Adam, 114
  Elizabeth, 113
  Joseph, 325
  Lewis, 114
LINN, Abraham, 191, 356
  Kitty, 246
LINTON, Ann, 61
  Deward, 351
  Zachariah, 191, 365
LIPPA, Ann, 191
  David, 191
LIPPIE, Ann, 191
  David, 191, 363
LIPPS, Jay, 180
LIPPY, Ann, 191
  David, 191
  George, 83
  Joseph, 252
  Nancy, 191
LIPSLEY, Peter, 192
LISHURE, John, 24, 192, 348
  Joshua, 24, 192, 348
  Samuel, 24, 192, 348
LISHURES, John, 349
  Joshua, 349
  Samuel, 349
LITCHLIGHTER, Conrad, 192
LITER, John, 58
LITLE, John, 323
LITT, Catharine, 192
  Jacob, 24, 192, 349, 350
LITTLE, Barbara, 87
  David, 192, 342
  John, 192, 332, 356
  Joseph, 317
  P. J., 125
  Peter, 192
LITTLEJOHN, Elizabeth, 192
  George, 192
  George W., 352
  Leonard, 193
  Leonard J. M., 192, 331, 351
  Leonard James, 193
  Rebecca, 192
LIVERS, Elizabeth, 59
  Judith, 193
  Mary A., 87

430

INDEX

Thomas, 193, 317, 334
LIZEN, Peter, 188
LIZER, George, 281
  Margaret, 281
LLOYD, Catherine, 147
  Elizabeth, 193
  John D., 190
  William A., 193, 324
  William Ambrose, 193
LOARA, Mary, 283
LOBEN, Paul, 193
LOCH, Abraham, 358
LOCHER, Adam, 193, 342
LOCK, Abraham, 193, 358, 359
LOCKARD, William, 49
  William of John, 49
LOCKE, Ellen Ridgely, 42
  George, 193
  Nathaniel, 42
  Rebecca Ann, 193
LOCKER, Adam, 193
LOERHER, Adam, 342
LOGAN, Donna, 313
  George, 193, 348
  John, 193, 335
  Mary, 285

LOHR, Frederick, 357
LOLLIS, Phillip, 193
LOMAN, Edward, 193, 340
LOMAX, Lawson, 193
LOMDON, Nancy, 237
LONG, Elisabeth, 194
  George, 194, 358, 359
  George J., 255
  James, 114
  John, 194, 333, 362
  Peter, 194
  Samuel, 351
  Samuel of Jacob, 325
  Stoffel, 326
LONGMAN, Eve, 194
  Henry, 194
  Jacob, 194
  Joseph, 194
  Martha A. M., 194
  Matilda, 194
  Susanna, 194
LONGMON, Jacob, 337
LONGSTRETH, Thomas, 313
LOOKBAUGH, John, 194, 358, 359
LOOKENINBEEL, Samuel, 194

LOOKINBEAL, Samuel, 295
LOOKINBEEL, Samuel, 364
LOON, Michael, 194, 349
LORAN, Mary, 283
LORENTZ, Adam, 177
  Henry, 257
  Jacob, 153, 323
  John, 40
  Joseph, 221
LOUD, Baltzer, 333
LOUDERSLAGLE, Solomon, 195, 363
LOUDON, John, 148
LOVE, David, 195
LOVEN, Paul, 340
LOW, Andrew, 96, 195
  Jacob, 195, 336
  John, 195
  Marion, 195
LOWE, Alexander, 195
  George, 195, 351
  Jacob, 195, 324, 332, 349
  John, 195, 363
  Mary, 195
  Samuel A., 195
  William, 93
LOWEN, Paul, 193, 195
LOWERY, Frederick, 195, 338, 340
  John, 195, 338,

340
 Joseph, 91, 195, 338, 339
 Mary, 91
LOWMAN, John, 195, 334, 363
 John B., 43
LOWRYE, Henry, 9, 15
LOY, Charlotte, 260
 Frederick, 189, 325
LOYD, William A., 193, 332
LUCAS,
 Christiana, 196
 Henry, 196, 342, 343
 Jesse, 319
 John, 196, 349
 Samuel C., 136
LUCKABAUGH, Elizabeth, 109
LUCKABUGH, Peter, 110
LUCKENBACH, Elizabeth, 109
LUCKENBEEL, John, 196
LUCKET, Elizabeth, 196
 Thomas Husey, 196
LUCKETT, Otho H. W., 352
 Otho Holland William, 196
 Valentine Peyton, 196
 William, 318

LUDWICK, Mary, 150
LUGEN, Moses, 341
LUGENBEEL, D. W. C., 196
 John, 196
 Maria C., 196
 Moses, 196, 341, 342
 Pinkney, 196
LUKINGBEAL, Mary, 197
 Samuel, 197
LUPTON, William, 351
LUTAN, George, 318, 319
LUTES, John, 197, 342
LUTTON, Henry, 197, 345
LUTZ, John, 325
 Mary Ann, 106
LYDA, James, 197, 358, 359
LYDAY, John, 197, 336
LYDD, James, 358
LYDENBERG, Marianna, 36
LYDEY, John, 197
 John C., 197
 Mary C., 197
 Mary M., 197
LYDIE, John, 190, 197
LYETH, Benjamin S., 285
 Sarah R., 285
LYMBAUGH,

Catharine, 191
LYNCH, John, 197
 John A., 246
 Michael, 252
LYNN, John, 197, 361
 Joseph, 197, 325, 335
LYON, Isaac, 324
LYTLE, Peter, 192

-M-

MCAFEE, Archibald, 323
MCALROY, 202
 James, 206, 359
MCARTER, Arthur T., 240
MCATEE, Leonard, 202
MCBARE, Charles, 202
MCBEAR, Charles, 342
MCBEE, William, 202, 358, 359
MCBRIDE, Anthony, 300
MCCAFFREY, William H., 72
MCCAHAN, 202
 John, 207, 359
MCCALISS, John, 140
MCCALISTER, John, 317
MCCALLEY, Elizabeth, 202
 John J., 331
 John James, 202
MCCALLY, John

INDEX

J., 351
MCCANN,
  Eleanor, 162
  John, 203, 321
MCCARLIN,
  Thomas, 22, 317
MCCARTY, 150
  Anthony, 203
  Joseph, 203
MCCAY, Samuel, 203, 338
MCCELFRESH, Philip, 351
MCCLAIN, George, 203, 324, 353
  James, 203, 342
MCCLALLEN, John, 75
MCCLASKEY, William, 203, 340
MCCLAY, William, 357
MCCLEAN,
  Charles, 203
  Julia A., 203
MCCLEERY, Robert, 203, 331, 352
MCCLOUD, Thomas, 203, 358, 359
MCCLY, William, 46
MCCOLEN, Samuel, 203, 340
MCCOLLUM, William, 146
MCCONLEY, Samuel, 203, 345, 346
MCCORMICK,
  Elizabeth, 103
  George, 203, 358
MCCOY, Joseph, 74
  Samuel, 203, 335, 338, 339
MCCRAY, James, 203, 338
  William, 203, 338, 340
M'CREA, Ann Mary, 79
  Catharine Elizabeth, 79
  James William Thomson, 79, 80
MCCREA, Joseph, 317
M'CREA, Margaret Jane, 79
MCCREA, William, 317
MCCULIN, James, 341
  William, 341
MCCULLEY, Elizabeth, 203
MCCULLY, John J., 324
MCCUMSAY, William, 204, 321
MCCUMSTY, Mary, 311
  William, 311
MCDADE, David, 56
MCDAMOT, Richard, 345
MCDANIEL, Ann, 241
  Cammilla, 268
  David, 204, 324
  Elizabeth, 187
  George, 204, 338
  Harriet, 268
  Jacob, 204, 336
  John, 204, 323, 333
  Joseph, 204, 364
  Mary, 204
  Sherman, 204
MCDAVITT, Peter, 204, 362
  William, 204, 334
MCDERMOT, Richard, 204, 345, 346
MCDEVITT, John, 204, 352
  Peter, 204, 366
MCDONALD,
  George, 238
  Pat, 40
MCDOWELL,
  James, 240
  Mrs. Ray, 152
  Reuben R., 209
MCDUMOT, Richard, 345
MCELFRESH,
  Caleb, 322
  Henry, 327
MCELROY, Gilbert, 91
MCFARLAN, Peter, 204, 358
MCFARLAND, M. C., 156
  Peter, 204, 353
MACFERSON, Nathan, 322
MCGARY, John,

433

MCGEE, George
W., 325
  James, 204, 364
  Joseph, 91
MCGILL, Patrick,
  317, 318
MCGINIS,
  Thomas, 204, 335
MCGINLEY, John
  W., 250
  Theresa, 179
MCGINNISS,
  Henry, 204, 334
MCGRATH,
  Thomas K., 33
MCGRAW, John,
  204
MCGREGOR,
  Joseph W., 311
MCGUFFIN,
  Elizabeth, 79
MCHENRY,
  Benjamin, 205,
  334, 358, 359
  Solomon, 260
MACHHOLD,
  Sevilla, 315
MCHUGH, H., 116
MCINSEY,
  Augustine, 205
  Austin, 205
  Mary, 205
MCINTIRE,
  James, 205, 349
  Sarah, 295
MCINZEY, Austin,
  364
MCINZIE,
  Augustine, 205
  Austin, 205
  Mary, 205
MCKARNS,
  Thomas, 303
MACKELFRESH,
  David, 321
  Philip, 327
MCKENZIE, Ada
  K., 56
MACKETT, James,
  322
MCKEY, Lydia H.,
  46
MACKEY, William,
  197, 335
MCKINNEY, John,
  205, 361
  Solomon, 260
MCKINSEY,
  Augustine, 205
  Austin, 205
  Folger, 5, 22, 351
  Mary, 205
MCKINSTREY,
  Joseph, 205, 341,
  342
MCKINZIE,
  Augustine, 205
  Austin, 205
  James S., 32
  Mary, 205
MCKISSIC, James,
  205, 361
MCKLEY, George,
  205, 364
MCKNITT,
  William, 205, 341,
  342
MCKULLEN,
  Samuel, 324
MACKY, William,
  325
MCLAIN, Charles,
  203
  Charles A., 203
  Fanny B., 203
  George E., 203
  Julianna, 203
  Margarett E., 203
MCLAUGHLIN,
  Ann C., 218
MCLEANE,
  Charles, 203
  Julia A., 203
MCMAHAN,
  Jerry, 205, 334
MACMILLAN,
  Thomas, 358
MCMILLAN,
  Thomas, 205
MCMULEN,
  Charles, 355
MCMULIN, James,
  205
  William, 205
MCMULLEN,
  Margaret, 108
  Rebecca, 108
  Samuel, 205, 295,
  338
  Susanah, 295
  William, 295
MCMULLIN,
  Charles P., 149
  Elizabeth, 149
  John, 205, 334
  Samuel, 205, 338
  Thomas, 205
MCNEAL, John,
  74
MCNEIL, John, 74
MCOYE, Henry,
  205, 364

INDEX

MCPHERSON,
Catharine C., 206
Harriet, 206
Henry, 206
Howard, 206
John, 2, 22, 205, 317
Maria, 205
Robert, 333
Robert G., 323, 353
Robert Grier, 205
Sarah Ann, 206
W. S., 216
William, 206, 213, 335, 354
William Smith, 206
MCSHERRY,
Bernard, 317
Henry F., 285
MCULROY, 202
James, 206, 358
MCVAY, Jane, 206
John, 206, 207, 361
MCVEY, Jane, 206
MCVICKER,
David, 207, 354
MCVICKERS,
David, 207, 366
MCVIKER, David, 207
MCWAY, John, 207
MCWILLIAMS,
Amy, 46
Clement, 207, 356
James, 207, 364
MADARY,

Andrew, 197
MADERY, Mary M., 100
MAETZGER, Jacob, 318
MAGEE, Captain, 15
George W., 9, 197, 321, 342
George Washington, 13, 341
MAGERS,
Laurence, 197, 322
Lawrance, 321
William, 197, 336
MAGRUDER,
Louise E., 120
Rezin, 198, 340
MAGRUTER,
Margaret, 281
MAGUIRE,
Bridget, 141
MAHANEY, Polly, 231
MAHONEY, Mrs.
John J., 87
MAHUE, James, 198, 334
MAIN, Catharine, 172, 307
D. M., 198
Daniel, 172
Frederick, 324
George, 172, 323
Jacob, 347
John, 198, 358
John Jacob, 198
Ruth, 172
Ruthe, 172
William F., 198

MAJOR, Laurence, 198, 353
MAKIN, Samuel, 199
MALAHAN,
William, 319
MALLONER,
John, 319
MANAHAN,
James, 198, 361
Thomas, 198, 364
MANKERT, Adam, 324
MANLY, Jesse L., 94
MANN, John, 198, 338
MANNAHAM,
Thomas, 319
MANSFIELD,
John, 198
MANTZ, Ann P., 98
Casper, 324
Catharine, 60
Charlotte, 52
David, 198, 333, 353
David of Peter, 323
Eleanor, 144
Elizabeth, 198
Ezra, 4, 5, 322, 326
Francis, 52, 144
Harriet, 39
Mary, 60, 245
Mrs., 149
Peter, 60, 149, 198, 212, 352
MANZER,

Elizabeth, 137
MARANT,
  Abraham, 75
MARAT, Catherine
  A., 36
MARFOOT,
  Charles, 198, 321
  John, 198, 321
MARGRATT, H., 33
MARGUART,
  George, 139
MARINE, William
  M., 24
MARK, Elizabeth, 255
  George, 199, 348
MARKALL, John, 199, 330, 331
MARKEL, Jacob, 210
MARKELL, Ezra, 199
  George, 142
  Jacob, 149, 199, 215, 324, 331
  John, 199, 217, 320, 323
  Lewis, 63
  Louis, 217
  Mary, 63, 199
  Rebecca, 199
  Samuel, 199
  Sophia, 199
MARKEN, Samuel, 199
  Wesley, 199
MARKER,
  Captain, 7
  Daniel, 10, 19, 199, 200, 337, 360

  David, 199, 353
  John, 199, 200, 337, 353
  Mary, 199
  Rachel, 200
MARKEY, Captain, 15, 365
  Catharine, 200
  David, 200, 320, 354
MARKILL, John, 330
MARKIN,
  Margaret, 199
  Samuel, 199, 337
MARKLE, John, 326, 328
MARKS, Elizabeth, 255
MARLIN, Thomas, 200
MARLOW,
  Hanson, 200
  Henry Frazier, 200
  John S., 323
  Louisa, 200
  Mary W., 43
  Thomas, 355
MARLOWE,
  Hanson, 357
MARLOY, John, 22, 317
MARQUERT,
  George, 200
MARQUEST,
  George, 61
MARS, Robert, 322
MARS.., Robert, 200
MARSH, David,

324
  Joel, 323
  Mason R., 99
MARSHAL,
  Augustus, 362
MARSHALL,
  Augustus, 200
  Eleanor, 144
  Eleanora, 144
  Henry, 200, 353
  John L., 144
  Marian, 144
  Robert, 200, 321
MARSTELLER,
  Eliza, 154
MARTHOLOW,
  Michael, 322
MARTIAL,
  Thomas, 200, 365
MARTIN, Abram
  B., 69
  Anthony, 200, 364
  B. F., 238
  Catherine, 226
  Charles, 71, 72
  David, 200, 259, 356
  Eliza, 71
  Eliza Jenett, 72
  Ezra, 200
  George, 323
  Hannah, 259
  Jacob, 201, 318, 360
  Jeremiah, 181
  Jesse, 317
  John, 201, 336, 358, 359
  Mary, 181
  Peter, 201, 326,

INDEX

334
 Rev., 36
 Robina, 200
 Sarah C., 316
 Thomas, 362
 William N., 146
MARTZ,
 Catherine, 201
 Catherine E., 315
 Daniel, 324
 Ezra, 328
 George, 201, 315
 Margaret, 148
 Mary Ann, 315
MARY, 331
MASAW, John, 210, 365
MASON,
 Elizabeth, 83
 Lernira, 223
 Luther J., 220
 Mrs. Charles L., 120
MASSEY, Cora Schaeffer, 314
 Robert, 287
MATHEW, Captain, 334
MATHIAS, Griff, 201, 336
 Griffith, 201
 Jacob, 162, 201
 John, 201, 363
 Susan, 201
MATHIAS L.,
 Joseph L., 49
MATILDA, 331
MATTEN, William, 285
MATTERN,
 Elizabeth, 71
 Peter, 201
MATTHEWS,
 James, 325
 Jonas, 325
 Lewis, 201, 325
 Louis, 201
 Philip, 201
 Sarah, 201
MATTHIAS,
 Daniel, 272
 David, 119
 Jacob, 328
 Joseph, 325
MATTHUS, Louis, 201
MATTINGLEY, Gabriel J., 201
MATTINGLY,
 Gabriel, 366
 Gabriel J., 201, 354
 Thomas, 202, 360
MATZENBAUGH,
 Barbary, 202
 Daniel, 95, 202
 John, 202
 Samuel, 202
MAUDY, Mary, 304
MAUS, Catharine, 315
MAXWELL,
 Frances, 174
 Nancy Lucretia, 44
 Thomas, 44
MAY, Benjamin, 202, 337
 Charles, 202, 338, 340
 Henrietta, 202
 James A., 43
 John, 202, 362
 Magdalena, 202
 Sarah Jane, 43
MAYBERRY,
 Israel, 202, 352
 Sophia, 212
 Thomas, 355
MAYERS,
 Lawrence, 202
MAYHUE, James, 326
MAYN, John Jacob, 198
 Sarah, 198
MAYNARD, H. G., 243
 Nathan of Thomas, 243
MAZER, Leonard, 216
 Nancy, 216
MEALEY, Isiah, 307
MEALS, William B., 250
MEARLE, Nicholas, 207, 337
MEARSH, Joel, 320
MEARTY, John, 318
MEASEL, Jacob, 358
MEASELL, Jacob, 207
 Mary, 207
MEASLE, Daniel, 207, 345, 346
 Jacob, 207
 Mary, 207

FREDERICK COUNTY MILITIA IN THE WAR OF 1812

Valentine, 207, 345, 346
MEAZLE, Valentine, 207
MECHAN, 202
John, 207, 359
MECKAN, John, 359
MEDARY, Andrew, 357
John, 207, 348
MEDCALF, Thomas, 207, 353
MEDDART, Jacob, 317
MEDLEY, Thomas, 208, 366
MEDTART, Godfrey, 223
Jacob, 223
Lewis, 208, 275, 352
Susanna, 223
MEGUOHAN, James, 319
MEIXEL, Betsy, 212
Elizabeth, 212
Jacob, 212
MEIXSEL, Elizabeth, 212
MEIXSELL, Mrs., 58
MELAND, Edward, 208, 347
MENCHEY, Mary, 61
MENTOR, 331
MERCER, Cornelius, 208
Elizabeth, 54
Sarah, 208
MERCHANT, John O., 37
MERCIER, Cornelius, 208
Richard, 208
Sarah, 208
MERITT, James, 340
MERRIT, James, 345
MERRITT, James, 208, 346
MERSER, Araminta, 178
MERTINA, Jacob, 208, 355
MESSERSMITH, Henry, 257
Philip C., 257
MESSINGS, John, 208
MESSLER, John, 208, 364
MESSTER, John, 319
METCALF, Hezekiah, 24, 208, 350
John, 323
Martha, 210
Mordecai, 208
Thomas, 208
William, 209, 359
METZ, George, 209, 340
John William, 209, 345
Mary, 186
William John, 209
METZGAR, Mattie E., 112
METZGER, George, 72, 142
MEYER, Catharine, 315
MEYERS, Calvin, 315
MICHAEL, Andrew, 209, 338, 340
Ann, 139
Charles, 363
Charles W., 25, 209
Elizabeth, 92
Henry, 115, 209
John, 209, 352, 362
Lewis, 209, 324, 334, 355
Maria C., 209
Sabra S., 217
William, 322
MICHAELS, William, 320
MICKLE, Conrad, 209, 337
MICKLEY, Daniel, 247
MILER, John, 352
MILES, George S., 72
John, 358
William, 209, 340
MILLEN, Charles, 209
Christian, 209
Jacob, 209, 335
MILLER, Amanda M., 81

INDEX

Ann Catharine, 211
Barbara, 82
Caroline C., 36
Catharine, 152, 158
Catherine, 32, 210
Charles, 210, 355
Charles M., 223
Charlotte, 40
Christian, 362
Christiana, 211
David, 32, 210
Eliza, 223
Elizabeth, 210, 238, 261
Eve Maria Ann, 184
Frederick, 210, 336, 358, 359
General, 333
George, 210, 324, 332, 336, 347, 358, 365
George A., 35, 89
George D., 281
George W., 210
Gottlob, 199
Henry, 210, 349
Hiram, 210
Isaac, 295
Jacob, 210, 323, 325, 333, 338
Jacob F., 199
Jacob L., 210
Jacob T. C., 139
Jeremiah, 182
John, 9, 22, 210, 211, 229, 317, 318, 324, 334, 338, 339,
342, 343, 351, 354, 364, 365, 366
John I., 210
John W., 182, 211, 264
Julia M., 223
Kitty, 152
Leonard, 118, 211, 217, 334, 355
Lewis E., 210
Mahlon, 179
Manerva A., 210
Martha, 36
Martin, 211, 334, 338, 340
Mary, 210, 256
Mattie L., 36
Peter, 211, 349
Philip, 211, 338
Polly, 210
Rebecca, 199
Samuel, 40, 171
Sarah, 210
Solomon, 295, 324
Thomas E., 210
Thomas J., 210
Valentine, 211, 353
Washington, 210
William C., 6, 8
William E., 70
William H., 210
MILLS, Ezra, 211, 334
Izrael, 326
Malinda, 172
MILTIN, John, 211
William, 211, 352
MILTON, John, 211, 321

MINICK, Catherine, 311
MINNICK, George, 211, 355
MINOR, William, 211, 348
MISINGER, Daniel, 24, 350
MISSELL, 211
Valentine, 207
MISSINGER, Daniel, 212
MITCHELL, Heneretta, 296
Leonard, 212, 351
MITTEN, Mary, 212
Miles, 325, 351
Thomas, 351
William, 212
MITTER, John, 212, 321
MIXEL, Jacob, 212
MIXELL, Betsy, 212
Elizabeth, 212
Jacob, 212, 354
Mary, 58
MOBBERLEY, Rachael, 117
MOBBERLY, Amanuel, 198
Eli, 212
Elizabeth, 198
Ely, 212
Isaac, 338
Lewis, 198
Margaret, 198
Martha, 107
Mary E., 198

FREDERICK COUNTY MILITIA IN THE WAR OF 1812

Peter, 198
Sophia, 212
MOBLEY, Basil, 212
Eli, 212
Elias, 212, 364
Ely, 212
Isaac, 213, 340
John, 213, 334
Martha, 107
Rachel, 212
Rebecca, 117
Sophia, 212
MOBLY, Basil, 212
Bazil, 354
Rachael, 107
MOCK, Peter, 213, 364
MODOCK,
  Augustus, 217
  Eliza, 217
  Horris B., 217
  July A., 217
  Lorra, 217
  Lydia H., 217
  Richard B., 217
  Richard H., 217
  Sarah R., 217
  Susan L., 217
MOLAND, Edward, 337
MOLING, Edward, 213, 357
  Noble, 213, 352
  Sarah, 213
  Susanna, 213
  William, 213
MONDAY,
  Daddeus, 213
  Dadies, 213
  Dahdeua, 213
  Dodies, 341
MONSON, Rebeca P., 213
MONTGOMERY,
  Caroline E., 213
  James, 213, 214, 347
  John, 213, 214, 351
  Mary, 214
  Thomas H., 130
MOONEY, Daniel, 214, 361
  William, 252
MOONY, Daniel, 214
MOOR, Charles, 149
MOORE, Ann M., 242
  Charles, 210, 214, 324, 332, 358
  Daniel M., 329
  Edward N., 242
  Fanny E., 190
  George, 357
  James, 214, 277, 328
  John, 214, 347
  L. Tilden, 28
  Thomas, 214, 346
  William, 214, 356
MOORING, John, 325
MORAN, William, 214, 348
MORE, Charles, 358
  James, 214
  Mary A., 214
  William, 214, 327
MORGAN, Ellen W., 214
  George, 214
  Margaret, 98
  Mary, 199, 214
  Mary A., 214
  Thomas, 214, 324
  Thomas W., 149, 214, 245, 332, 344, 345
  Thomas William, 139
  Virginia D., 214
  William, 215, 352
MORIARITY,
  John, 338
MORIARTY, John, 215
MORNINGSTAR,
  Jess, 159
  Mary, 123
  Michael, 318
  Philip, 323
MORRISON,
  James, 215, 323, 338, 340
  W. H., 229
MORSE, Charles, 322
MORSELL, Rachel, 93
  William, 93
MORT, George, 215, 335
  John, 215
  Mary, 215
  William, 215, 336
MORYATTA,
  John, 215, 340
MOSBURG,
  Abraham, 215, 346

440

INDEX

John, 215, 337, 347
MOSBURGH, Abraham, 215, 334, 345
Daniel, 215, 334
MOSBURY, Abraham, 215
John, 215
MOSE, Henry, 349
MOSER, Angelina, 216
Ann, 215
Anna, 215
Anna C., 216
Anna Margaret, 216
Benjamin, 324
Daniel, 216
E. Leonard, 216
Frederick Arnold, 216
Henry, 215, 216
John, 216, 334
Leonard, 216
Leonard Ephraim, 216
Leonidas, 216
Lydia Anna, 216
Lyvina, 216
Nancy, 216
Sarah Elizabeth, 216
MOSIER, John, 216, 352
MOSLER, John, 216
MOSSBURGH, Daniel, 215, 338
MOSSER, Ann, 215
Anna, 215
Henry, 215
MOSSITIER, Christopher, 216
MOSSMAN, Mary, 32
Robert, 32
MOTTER, George, 326
Joshua, 291
Lewis, 328
Lewis M., 87
Rebecca, 248
MOTTERN, Catherine, 133
Peter, 358
MOUNT, George, 216, 348
MOWERY, Henry, 216, 338, 340
MOXBURY, John, 215, 216
MOXLEY, Ezekiel, 265
MOZER, Leonard, 216, 280
Nancy, 216
MUCH, Frederick, 355
MUCK, Frederick, 216, 355
Henry, 216, 217, 355
Margaret, 216
MUCKELFRESH, David, 217
MUEL, Jacob, 354
MULDORE, David, 318
MULINIX, Rezin, 217, 348
MULLENDORE, David, 47, 326
MULLINIX, E. E., 214
MULNIX, John, 217, 364
MUMFORD, Thomas, 324
MURDOCH, Richard B., 217, 354
Sallie B., 217
MURDOCK, George W., 217, 323, 333
John B., 217, 361
Richard B., 217
Sarah R., 217
MURFEY, John, 217, 342
MURPHY, Hezekiah, 217
James, 217, 360
Jane, 217
Sabra S., 217
Thomas, 217, 334, 335, 338, 340
MURRAY, Anna, 218
Basil, 218
Bazil, 218, 341
Captain, 24
James, 100, 218, 348
John, 319
Joshua, 218, 339
Lucay A., 100
Margaret Amelia, 220
Mary, 218
Mathew, 10

FREDERICK COUNTY MILITIA IN THE WAR OF 1812

Matthew, 16,
218, 355
 Rachel, 278
 Thomas, 218, 352
MURRY, Abigail,
55
 Charles, 319
 Frederick, 318
 James, 218, 321,
322
 John, 218, 321
 Joshua, 218, 338
 Mathias, 218, 347
 Samuel, 218, 322
 Solomon, 218,
321
 Stephen, 322
MUSGRAVE,
 Henrietta, 150
MUSSER, John,
218, 337, 347
MUSSETER,
 Christopher, 218,
349
 Ruth, 218
MUSSETTER,
 Ann, 218
 Elizabeth, 218
MUSZ, Michael,
218, 334
MYERHEFFER,
 John, 333
MYERHEIFER,
 John, 218
MYERLY,
 Benjamin, 219, 364
 Catharine, 219
 David, 219, 364
 Jacob, 219, 363
 Sally, 219
 Solomon, 219,
364
MYERS, Abraham,
116
 Adam, 324
 Benjamin, 319
 Catharine, 315
 Elizabeth, 189
 George W., 219
 Henry, 22
 Isael, 324
 Israel, 324
 Jacob, 219, 345
 Jerry, 219, 339,
340
 John, 219, 319,
358, 359, 364
 John of Peter,
219, 364
 Margaret, 27, 155
 Martin, 219, 345,
346
 Mary, 146
 Mary Susan, 261
 Michael, 219
 Peter, 219, 325
MYLES, James,
219, 361
MYRES, Peter,
219, 362
MYTINGER,
 George, 332

-N-

NAFE, George, 221
 Margaret, 221
NAIL, Mary, 220
 Peter, 220, 350
NAILE, Elizabeth,
220
 Samuel, 220
 William, 220, 356
NAILLE,
 Elizabeth, 220
 Mary, 220
 Peter, 220
 Samuel, 220, 356
NAILOR, John,
220
NASE, Adam, 168
NASH, Archabald,
321
 Archibald, 220
NATT, Joseph,
220, 365
NEAD, Henry,
220, 357
NEAFF, Abraham,
220, 354
NEAL, Abner, 295
 Samuel, 220
NED, 330
NEFF, Abraham,
220, 324
 Andrew, 220, 337
 Daniel Jacob, 220
 Dorothe, 220
 Elizabeth, 221
 George, 221, 365
 George
Washington, 221
 Jacob, 221, 338
 John, 171
 Magdalena, 221
 Magdelana, 221
 Margaret, 221
 Margaret Amelia,
220
 Susanna, 221
NEHART, Jacob,
223
NEIL, Ellen, 220
 Rebecca, 220

INDEX

Samuel, 220
Sophia, 220
NEILL, John W., 72
  Mary P., 72
NEIR, Harriet, 68
  John, 68
NELSON, Amos, 322
  Arthur, 221, 327, 330, 331
  David, 168
  Doctor, 330
  John, 38, 221, 323, 333, 355
  Nathan, 243
NESMITH, James H., 222
  John H., 221
  Nancy, 221
  Thomas J., 221
NETH, Harriet, 206
  Louis, 206
NETZ, William, 346
NEUSBAUM, John, 222, 364
NEVINS, Thomas, 333
NEWCOMER, John, 222, 356
  Mary, 222
  Susan, 116
  William, 222
NEWINS, Thomas, 222
NEWPORT, David, 222, 352
  Margarett, 306
  Mary, 222

NEWRY, John, 222, 361
NEWTON, Elizabeth, 202
  Mahlon A., 202
NICADEMUS, Andrew, 222, 321, 322
  Henry, 222, 321, 322
NICHEM, Amy, 223
  Joseph, 223
NICHODEMUS, John, 256
NICHOLAS, Peter, 321
  Ralph, 326
  Sarah, 61
  Susanna, 97
NICHOLLS, Daniel, 93
  Jacob, 222, 334
  Raphael, 222, 334
  Sarah, 222
NICHOLS, Adam, 222, 354
  Benjamin, 222
  Jacob, 222, 351
  John, 222, 223, 360
  Maria O., 222
  Peter, 323
  Ralph, 223, 362
  Rebecca, 223
  Sarah, 222
  Sophia, 186
  Thomas F., 136
NICHOLSON, Susanna, 97
NICKEM, Joseph, 355
  Peter, 223, 355
NICKLES, Benjamin, 223, 362
NICKUM, Amy, 223
  Joseph, 223
NICODEMUS, Andrew, 222
  Catherine, 222
  Henry, 222
  Rachel, 222
NICODUMUS, Henry, 223
NICOL, Jacob, 222
  Johann, 222
  Philippina, 222
NIHART, Jacob, 223
NILES, John, 223, 358
NISWANGER, Christian, 326
NIXDORFF, Barbara, 223
  Eliza, 223
  Elizabeth, 223
  Georg, 223
  George A., 223
  Henrich, 223
  Henry, 142, 223, 275, 334, 354
  Henry M., 223
  Julia M., 223
  Lewis M., 223
  Magdalena, 223
  Mary E., 223
  Samuel, 223
  Susan, 223
  Susanna, 223
  Tobias, 223

NIXENDORFF,
Henry, 323
NOBLE, John, 224
  Joseph, 342
  Mrs. John W.,
242
NOEL, Blazon,
224, 335
NOGGLE, Joseph,
224, 343
NOLAND,
Thomas, 326
NOLEN, Barnabas,
224
NOLIN, Barnabas,
224
NOLING, Hannah
E., 136
NOOVER, George,
335
NORRIS, Captain,
25
  Eleanor, 235
  Elizabeth, 112
  Hannah, 144
  Henry, 224, 341
  Isac, 323
  Margaret, 185
  Upton, 20, 24,
363
NOURSE,
Asseneth, 106
  Cena, 106
  Cenett, 106
  Sena, 106
NOUSE, Asseneth,
106
  Cena, 106
  Cenett, 106
  Sena, 106
NULTON, John,

224, 355
NURSER, Ann, 93
  Ann Margaret,
224
  Elizabeth C., 224
  Henry, 93
  Jesse, 224
  Louisa, 224
  Mary Ann, 224
NUSBAUM,
Henry, 224
  Jacob, 224, 359
  Sarah, 224
NUSBOM, Henry,
224, 321
NUSSBAUM,
Jacob, 224
  Johannes, 224
  Margaretha, 224
NUSSEAR, Jesse,
224
  Mary A., 224
NUSSER, John,
224
NUSSMITH, 224
  Nancy, 221
  Thomas, 355
  Thomas J., 221
NUSZ, Elizabeth,
225
  Jacob, 224, 352
  Mary, 224
  Michael, 218,
225, 345, 346

-O-
O'BRIAN, Mashac,
225
  Meshack, 225
O'BRIEN, Edward,
342, 343

OBRIEN, Edward,
225
O'BRYAN, Mashac,
225
  Meshack, 225
OCKER, Henry,
225, 256, 361
  Mary Magdalene,
141
  Sarah, 52
OCKS, Jacob, 225,
340
ODONAL, James,
225, 361
ODONALD, John,
225, 335
OFFICER, James,
89
OGB., John W.,
114
  Mary, 184
OGBUM,
Benjamin, 325
OGLE, Alexander,
317
  Benjamin, 181,
325
  Catharine, 181
  Eleanor, 193
  Eli, 225, 365
  John, 325
  Joseph, 318
  Mary J. C., 225
  Samuel, 6, 9,
325, 334
  Samuel V., 225
  Theo A., 57
  Thomas, 320
OHAGAN,
Imishade, 360
OHLER, Elizabeth,

INDEX

225
 John Thomas, 316
 Joseph, 225
 Peter, 225
OILER, George, 225
OLER, Elizabeth, 225
 John, 225, 361
 Joseph, 225, 339
 Peter, 225, 335
O'NEAL, William, 225, 348
ORDNER, Sophia, 165
ORENDORF, John, 356
ORNDERF, Jacob, 226
 Joseph, 226
ORNDORF, Aloysius F., 288
ORNDORFF, A. F., 87
 Aloysius F., 226
ORNDURFF, Jacob, 339
ORPERT, John, 226, 353
ORPIT, John, 226, 322
 Thomas, 226, 321
ORPRIT, Thomas, 321
ORR, John, 319
ORTMAN, Daniel, 360
ORTNER, John, 226, 354
 May, 143
 Sophia, 226
OSBURN, Joseph, 360
OSPERT, John, 226, 353
OTT, An. Marg., 226
 Anna Elisabeth, 226
 Barnhardt, 226
 Catherine, 226
 Frederick, 226, 345, 346
 Friedrich, 226
 George, 226, 361
 Lydia, 72
 Mary, 226
 Michael, 226, 356
 Peter, 47, 56, 99, 125, 126, 178, 226, 230, 297, 358
 Polly, 226
 Rebecca, 133
 Sarah Ann, 226
OTWILL, Ann Eliza, 44
OURENT, Daniel, 226, 364
OVELMAN, Joseph, 65
OVERLY, Catherine, 255
OWEN, Abigail, 227
 Isaiah, 226, 349
 John, 226, 227, 348
 William Otway, 53
OWINGS, Samuel, 234
OWSLEY, Joshua B., 140
OYLER, George, 227, 361
 Henry, 323
 John, 227, 323, 361
OYSTER, George, 227, 325, 356
 Polly, 227

-P-
PACK, Thomas, 51
PACKWOOD, John, 227, 364
PADGET, Allison, 227, 365
 Richard, 326
PADGETT, Elizabeth, 276
 John, 227, 334
 Mary, 223
 Rebecca, 223
 Solomon, 227
PAIN, Catherine, 227
 James, 227, 319, 335
 John, 227
PAINE, James, 227
 John, 227, 352
 Samuel, 351
PALMER, Matthew, 227, 340
PANABAKER, Samuel, 324
PAPE, William, 227, 355
PARK, William, 227

445

PARKE, George M., 89
PARKER, Samuel, 227, 337
PARKS, William, 227, 342, 343
PARR, Henry, 227, 335
PARRISH, Benjamin, 80
PARROTT, Dale K., 160
 Irma Holter, 160
PARSONS, William B., 305
PARTER, Reason, 232, 365
PATRICK, Robert, 227, 345
PATTERSON, Robert, 172
 William, 91
PAUL, Michael, 227
PAUS, Anna Rosina, 201
 Christian, 201
 Magdalena, 201
PAXTON, John, 228, 356
 John William, 228
PEACOCK, Jacob, 228, 334
 Sarah, 228
 William, 228, 345, 346
PEARCE, Catharine Russell, 124
 Lemuel, 228, 321
 William, 228, 321, 325
PEARL, Susanna, 216
 Thomas, 216
PEARSON, Isaac E., 35, 88
PECOR, Charlotta, 93
PEDDICORD, Caleb J., 216
PEERS, Clemmen, 333
PEERY, Jasper M., 153
PENN, Elizabeth, 94
PENNINGTON, Catherine C., 253
 John P., 118
 Lee R., 253
PENNYBAKER, Elizabeth, 95
 Samuel, 228, 335
 Susannah, 228
PEPPER, Abraham, 228, 356
PEPPLE, Abraham, 228
 Caroline, 228
 Jacob, 325
 Maria, 228
PERDUM, Mordecai, 228, 348
PERKINS, John, 228, 361
PERRIOG, J. J., 107
PERRY, Debbie, 179
 Elizabeth, 179
 Johnathan, 179
 Martin, 179
PETER, John, 339
 Michael, 351
PETERMAN, Georg Washington Golden, 229
 Jacob, 229, 361
 Jacob S., 228, 229
 John, 229, 335
 Lizze Amanda, 229
 Martha, 228, 229
 Marthew, 229
 Maryan, 229
 Simson Thomas, 229
 William Alja, 229
 William E., 229
PETERS, Ann, 229
 Anna, 229
 Anna Cecilia, 229
 Charles, 229, 354
 Elizabeth, 229
 John, 229, 339
 Mary Margaret, 229
 Michael, 229
 Polly, 229
 Samuel, 229, 364
 Sarah, 229
PETTER, Leppo, 335
PETTIBON, David, 189
PEUSEY, George, 229, 353
 Joel, 229, 353
PEWSEY, George, 229

INDEX

Joel, 229
PFEISTER, Jacob, 115
PHARES, William, 356
  Williams, 230
PHEBUS, Ann R., 230
  Benjamin, 230
  Catherine A., 230
  Elizabeth, 230
  Peter, 230, 357
PHELPS, Adoram, 46
  Charles, 230, 340
PHFER, John, 323
PHILIP, 331
PHILIPS, J. R., 53
PHILLIP, Eli, 318
PHILLIPS,
  Catherine, 69, 230
  Deborah M., 183
  Elie, 230
  John, 234
  Mary Ann, 167
  Sarah Ann, 119
PHILPOT, John H. 147
  Shepherd B., 147
PHILPS, George, 320
PHLEGER, Edward, 160
PHRATER, James, 342
PICKEL, Mary, 71
PICKENS, Robert, 360
PICKET, Ezekiel, 253
PICKETT, Charles, 324
  Juliann, 60
PICKING, Leonard, 124
PICKINS, Catharine, 119
PIGEON, Amos, 322
PIGMAN, Bene T., 320
PINEY, Henry, 352
PINNEY, M. P., 202
PINTER, Thomas, 230, 350
PIPER, Jacob, 230, 365
  Michael, 230, 349
PIPPENGER, William, 190
PITT, Thomas, 230, 345, 346
PLESTER, Stephen, 230, 332
PLICKENSTARVE, Christian, 230, 365
PLICKENSTEMER Christian, 230, 365
PLUMMER,
  Deborah, 303
  Louisa, 140
  Nelson, 140
  Rebeccah, 167
  William, 230, 365
  William of Jacob, 322
PLUNK, Susannah, 228
POAST, W. P., 41
POBST, Daniel, 56
  John, 56, 230, 354
  Lydia, 56, 230
  Mary, 56
POFFENBERGER, Isaac, 51
  Mary, 51
POLAND,
  Absolem, 169
  Harriet, 169
POLE, Thomas, 230, 319, 321
  William, 319
POLING, Virginia S., 90
POLLACK,
  Christian, 140
  David, 140
POLMAN, John, 230, 362
  Michael, 230, 362
POMEROY, L. C., 269
POOL, Basil, 230, 364
  Cornelius, 103, 230, 336
  Frederick, 354
  George, 102
  Henry M., 231, 342
  John, 231
POOLE, Benjamin, 261
  Catharine, 231
  Catherine, 231
  Cornelius, 230
  Frederick, 180, 231
  Hanson, 231
  Henry, 231
  Henry M., 231,

FREDERICK COUNTY MILITIA IN THE WAR OF 1812

335
  Jacob, 231, 334
  John, 231
  Joseph, 319
  Lucretia L., 231
  Martha H., 231
  Mary, 231
  Polly, 231
  Sally, 241
  Sarah Elizabeth, 180
  William, 231, 352
POPE, William, 333
PORTER,
  Catharine, 231
  Catherine, 232
  Clinkton, 174
  James, 231
  John, 354
  John A., 231, 232
  John W., 85
  Mary A., 218
  Mary Ann, 231
  Reason, 232, 365
POSEY, F. J., 52
POTTER, William, 232, 349
POTTORFF,
  Thomas J., 69
POTTS, Elizabeth, 164, 232
  Elizabeth H., 164
  Philip, 232
  Philip T., 354
  Philip Thomas, 232
  Richard, 164, 232
  S., 239
POUDER,
  Elizabeth, 232
POWDER,
  Andrew, 48
  Elizabeth, 232
  Jacob, 26, 232, 245, 352
  John, 363
  Mary, 48
POWEL, Elizabeth, 232
  George, 232, 364
  Jacob, 232, 364
  Margaret, 268
  Nathan, 232, 321
POWELL,
  Catherine, 240
  Elizabeth, 232
  Ellen, 166
  Henry, 166
  Jacob, 232
  Jonathan, 232, 355
  Sam, 338
  Samuel, 232, 339
POWERS, Thomas, 232, 340
PRABY, John, 232, 353
PRATHER, James, 232, 343
PRATZMAN,
  Christian, 233
PRAUGH, Abner, 232, 321
  John, 232, 321
PRENDORF, John, 226
PRENGELL, John, 60
PRESTON, John, 232, 364
PRETSMAN,
  George, 233
PRETZMAN,
  Elisabeth, 233
  George, 233
  Jacob, 233
PRICE, Catherine, 233
  Elizabeth, 313
  George, 233, 356
PRIESTMAN,
  George, 233, 336
PRIMROSE,
  Samuel F., 166
PRISTMAN,
  Elisabeth, 233
  Jacob, 233
PROBY, John, 232, 353
PROPHET, H. S., 121
PROTZMAN,
  Barbara, 282
  Elisabeth, 233
  Jacob, 233
PROUD, John G., 206
  Robert M., 206
PROUTZ, Rodrick, 107
PRUDENCE,
  Sarah, 229
PRUGH, George, 319
  Henery, 319
PRUTZMAN,
  Christian, 233, 365
  Elisabeth, 233
  Jacob, 233
PRYAR, John, 233
PRYOR, John, 339

INDEX

PUL, Conrad, 230
  Cornelius, 230
  Eleonora, 230
  Magdalena, 230
  Susanna, 230
  Wilhelm, 230
PUMPHREY,
  Annie, 306
  William, 349
  William of
    Samuel, 233
PUMPHRY, Annie
  M., 306
PURDY, Henry,
  233, 335
  Joseph, 351
PURKEY, J., 86
PURSELL, Sarah,
  238
PYFER, John, 233,
  334
  Philip, 233, 234,
    323, 334, 354
  Philip Henry,
    233
  Rachel, 233
  Warner, 234
PYFFER, Ann C.,
  233
  Margaret M., 233
  Rachael, 233
PYLE, John, 234,
  339
PYOTT, James,
  234
  Samuel, 234
  Susannah, 234

-Q-
QUANTRILL,
  Thomas, 5

QUEEN, Elizabeth,
  234
  William, 234, 362
QUINN, Allen, 317
  Mary, 142
  William, 366
QUYNN, Patrick,
  234, 357
  William, 234, 366

-R-
RADER, Calvin
  M., 268
  Michael, 234, 361
RAFESNIDER,
  John, 234, 356
RAGAN, Colonel,
  13, 21
  John, 9, 234, 330
RAINEY, John,
  234, 349
RAIT, Eleanor, 235
  Hammond, 234,
    235, 353
RAITT, Harmand,
  317
RAMBURGH,
  Frederick, 358
RAMER, John,
  235, 337
  Susannah, 235
  William Perry,
    235
RAMSBERG,
  Joseph, 307
  Susan, 185
RAMSBURG, Ann
  Catharine, 235
  Ann Eliza, 235
  Ann Rebekah,
    235

Anna Maria, 160
Benjamin, 156
Charlotte, 235
Edward, 235
Elizabeth, 56
Frederick, 235
Frederick J., 235
Jane B., 236
Joseph, 74, 235
Josephus, 235
Levi, 235
Lewis, 235, 236,
  332
Lydia, 235
Magdalen, 235
Magdalene, 235
Mary, 142
Mary A., 236
R. M., 142
Susan B., 235,
  236
Urias, 235
William E., 236
RAMSBURGER,
  Anna Elizabeth,
    145
  Catherine, 145
  Jacob, 145
RAMSBURGH,
  Dennis, 61, 235
RAMSEY, John,
  317
RAMSOUR,
  Henry, 236
RAMSOWER,
  Elizabeth, 158
  Henry, 236
RAMSPARKE,
  Stephen, 47
RAMSPEY, Lewis,
  324

449

RANDALL, Beall, 19, 355
  Mordacai, 236, 352
  Robert, 345
RANDELL, Robert, 236, 346
RANDLE, Nicholas, 236, 321, 322
RANDOLPH, John, 126
RANKIN, Samuel, 153
RAPE, Ann, 191
  Nancy, 191
RAPP, Barbara, 236
  Barbara Ann, 236
  Jacob, 236
  Jesse, 168
  John, 287
  Philipp, 236
  Samuel, 236
  Susanna, 236
RATLIFF, Thomas, 322
RATLIFFE, Urilla, 166
RATTLE, William, 237, 354
RATTLER, William, 237
RAVEN, William, 267
RAWLIN, Sarah, 222
RAWLINGS, Elizabeth, 213
RAWLINS, Wilson, 237, 339, 340
RAY, Elizabeth, 237
  John, 237, 342
RAZOR, Jacob, 237
REA, William B., 168
READ, Stephen H., 69
REAM, George, 237
REAMOUS, Mary, 39
REAMS, John, 237
REAMY, Martha, 28
REASE, Jacob, 225
REASER, Jacob, 237
REAVER, Mary, 226
  Washington, 226
RECK, Rebecca, 52
RECKTER, John, 354
RECRUIT Richard, 237, 362
RECTOR, John, 240
REDEMOUR, John, 350
REDENOUR, John, 24, 237
REED, Benjamin, 237, 362
  Elizabeth, 238
  George, 6, 237, 325, 335
  Jacob, 324
  James, 237, 348
  John, 238, 334
  Joseph, 174
  Mary, 238
  Nancy, 237
  Philip, 238, 335, 339, 340
  Phillip, 229
  Sallie, 69
  Sarah, 238
  Susan, 237
REEDER, James, 238, 362
REEDY, Jacob, 318
REES, Benjamin, 238, 364
REESE, Catherine, 237
  Catherine E., 315
  Elizabeth, 101
  George A., 123
  Jacob, 47, 72, 123, 237
  John, 235, 315
REEVES, Finley, 165
  Finly, 164
REICH, Philip, 213
REICHART, Christian, 238, 364
  Hannah, 80
REID, James, 237, 238, 332
  Susan, 237
  Upton, 14, 356
  Upton Scott, 238
REIDENOUR, Sarah, 69
REIFSNEIDER, Joshua L., 173
REILLY, Wilson,

INDEX

159
REINDOLLAR,
Amelia, 272
James, 272
William, 111
REINECKER,
John, 324
REINHART,
Catharine, 115
REINICKER, Paul, 238, 361
REITZEL, Philip, 238
REITZELL, Maria, 238
Philip, 238
RELIEN, Jacob S., 238, 362
RELKEY, Susanna, 121
REMLEY, William, 304
REMSBERG,
Charlotte, 278
Joseph, 235
Lewis, 278
Magdalene, 235
REMSBURG,
Christian, 40
Ezra, 238
George W., 40
RENNER,
Barbara, 79
Daniel, 317, 318
John, 324
Peggy, 253
Solomon, 325, 79
RENSBERG, Ezra, 365
Joseph, 365
RENSBERT,

Joseph, 238
REPP, Jacob, 156
RESLINGS,
Thomas, 323
REVELL, James, 239, 349
REYNALDS,
Samuel, 320
REYNOLD,
Christina, 290
REYNOLDS,
Horatio, 239, 345, 346
John, 10, 331
Margaret, 111
Samuel, 323
RHENICHER,
Peter, 342
RHIEL, Catherine, 242
Jacob, 242
John H., 242
RHINECHER,
Peter, 239
RHINEHART,
John F., 119
Sarah Ann, 119
RHODERICK, 239
G. C., 47
Lewis, 245
Mahlon, 40, 47
Margaret, 246
RHODES, Anna, 239
John, 183
Samuel, 239
RHODRUC, Lewis, 245, 246
Margaret A., 246
RHYNE, John, 239, 348

RICE, Benjamin, 319
Perry, 45, 72
Philip, 239
Rebecca, 30
RICHARDS, Ann, 239
Charlotte, 239
George, 173
Jacob, 326
John, 239, 326, 334, 355, 356
Michael, 239, 362
Rebecca, 239
William, 239, 348, 358
Zachariah, 240, 345, 346
RICHARDSON,
Elijah, 240, 321
Elizabeth, 240
Joseph, 240
Susannah, 240
William, 265
Zachariah, 240
RICHART,
Washington C., 234
RICHMEND,
Daniel, 240
Francis, 240
Sussan, 240
RICHMENT,
Catherine, 240
Francis, 240, 355
RICHMOND,
Catherine, 240
Francis, 240
George, 240
RICHTER,
Catharina, 240

FREDERICK COUNTY MILITIA IN THE WAR OF 1812

Catherine, 240
Frederick, 240, 362
Henrich, 240
Johannes, 240
John, 240
RICHTOR, Jacob, 354
RICKETS, Alina, 240
Bazel, 240
Benjamin, 361
RICKETTS, B. M., 241
Benjamin, 241
Hezekiah, 241
John T., 241
Sally, 241
Sarah, 241
RIDDLEMOSER, Abraham, 241, 345
RIDER, Ann, 241
Frederick, 241, 359
George, 241, 359
RIDGELEY, Bethany, 185
RIDGELY, Alfred, 241, 344
Charles, 41
Henry, 241, 339, 340
Joshua, 241, 341
Matilda C., 38
Rebecca, 49
Richard, 38, 355
Ruth, 41
Sarah H., 285
William A., 306
RIDGLEY, Ana, 242
Asa, 241
Daniel, 242
Elias, 242
Elizabeth, 242
Ezra Eligah, 242
Frederick, 241, 349
John Lawrence, 242
Joshua, 241
Margaret, 241
Mary, 242
Mary Ann Martha, 242
Rebecca, 242
Richard, 242
Sarah, 242
Westall, 242
William, 242
RIDGLY, Alfred, 241, 345
RIDINGEN, Peter, 335
RIDINGER, Catharine, 242
Peter, 242
Stephen, 110
RIEHL, Anna, 242
Catharine, 242
Elisabeth, 242
George, 242
Jacob, 242, 354
Johannes, 242
Sophia, 242
RIFE, Abraham, 243, 361
Daniel, 243, 342, 343
Elizabeth, 243
RIFFLE, John, 243, 337
Sophia, 243
RIFLE, John, 243, 349
RIGDON, Columbia E., 189
RIGGLE, Adam, 243, 343
RIGGS, Asha, 243, 340
Henry, 21, 243, 322
Mary, 243
Osha, 243, 339
RIGHTSEL, Philip, 357
RIGISON, James C., 243
RIGLE, Adam, 342
RIGNEY, John, 5, 326, 328
RILEY, Charles, 243, 350
Daniel, 243, 321
RIMEL, John J., 190
Martha, 190
RIMPEY, Peter, 333
RINCHART, Daniel, 323
RINE, Catherine, 93
John, 239
RINEDOLLAR, George, 325
RINEDOLLER, John, 243, 356
RINEHART, John, 243
RINEHEART, Daniel, 243, 343

452

INDEX

John, 243, 342
RINER, Abigail, 243, 244
 Catey, 244
 Catharine, 244
 Catherine, 243
 George, 243, 244, 336
 Mary, 243
 William, 244, 332
RINGER,
 Catharine, 256
 Elisabeth, 233
 John, 233
 Susanna, 89
RINHART, Daniel, 333
RINNER, John, 244, 352
RIPPEN, Thomas, 244
 William, 244
RIPPIN, Henry, 244
 John T., 244
 Josephine, 244
 Margaret, 244
 Thomas, 244
 William, 244, 348
RIPPON, Thomas, 244
RISE, William, 244, 365
RISER, Jacob, 318
RITCHIE, Abner, 317
 John, 5, 317, 320, 328
 Thomas, 244
ROACH, Dennis, 244

Gustavus, 244, 348
ROADPOUCH, Elizabeth, 244
 Peter, 244, 364
ROADS, Ann, 239
 Elizabeth, 261
 Jacob, 355
 Samuel, 239
ROBBINS,
 Benjamin, 359
ROBERT, 330
ROBERTS,
 Benjamin, 244, 332
 Ephraim, 33
 Grace, 306
 P., 33
 William, 245, 360
ROBERTSON,
 Alexander, 245, 354
 George, 245, 359
 John, 245, 353
 Joshua, 245, 353
 Mary, 48, 245
 Susan, 245
 Walter, 38
 William, 245, 342
ROBINETT,
 Richard, 245
ROBINS,
 Benjamin, 245
ROBINSON,
 Charles, 245, 361
 George, 245, 361
 John, 245, 353
 Joshua, 245, 353
 Susan, 245
ROBISON, James C., 342
 William, 342

ROBISSON, John Wesly, 67
ROBSON, John Wesly, 67
ROCK, John, 245, 349
ROCKNEY,
 Elisabeth, 194
ROCKWELL,
 Tolbert, 245, 343
RODERICK,
 Lewis, 235, 245, 246
 Margaret, 246
 Mary Ann Magdaline, 246
RODGERS,
 Andrew, 293
 James, 65, 182
RODHRICK,
 Lewis, 245
RODRICK, J. S. L., 245, 246
 Jacob Randolph, 246
 Lewis, 245, 246
 Margaret, 246
RODROCK, Lewis, 245
ROGERS, James, 246, 356
 Mary, 299
ROHR, Catharine, 246
 George, 246, 351
 Peter, 246, 345, 346
ROHRBACK, Ellen C., 63
 Martin N., 63
ROHRER,

453

Magdalena, 202
Samuel, 152
ROLLINS, John C., 246, 349
ROOL, Frederick, 80
ROOP, Daniel, 246
 Elizabeth, 237, 246
 Jacob, 246, 247, 321
 Jesse, 246
 Joel, 246
 Joseph, 246
 Kitty, 246
 Samuel, 246
 Sarah, 246, 247
 Upton, 220
ROOPE, Jacob, 325
ROOSS, Jacob, 246
ROOT, Basil, 200
 Harriet, 107
ROPP, Samuel, 247, 341, 358
ROSE, Elizabeth, 275
 Walter, 287
ROSS, Alexander, 309
 Frederick, 247, 359
 James, 247, 356
 Lewis W., 209
 William, 131
ROTHERY, George, 120
ROTHROCK, 247
 Lewis, 245, 365
ROTRUCK, Lewis, 245, 246

ROUGH, Philip, 323
ROUSER, Abraham, 317
ROUTSON, John, 247, 335
ROUTSONG, Catherine, 247
 John, 247, 342, 343
ROUTZAHN, Benjamin, 51
 Edward, 198
 Elizabeth, 51
 Joseph, 213
ROUTZAN, Benjamin, 48
ROUTZAWN, Daniel, 326
 Jacob, 324
ROUTZONG, Benjamin, 48
ROW, Frederick, 247, 345
 Jacob, 19, 360
 John, 247, 332, 339
 Mary, 297
 Michael, 247, 341, 361
 Samuel, 247, 361
 Sarah, 107
ROWE, Ezra, 306
 George, 247
 Michael, 232, 247, 320, 323, 366
 William, 247, 323, 354
ROWHAM, Jacob, 247
ROWHAN, Jacob,

355
ROWLAND, Percival, 57
ROWSEN, Jacob, 247, 364
RUBERT, Jacob, 247, 335
RUCKER, Eleanor, 287
RUDISIL, Anna Mary, 272
 Thomas, 272
RUDY, Catherine, 36
 Christianus, 247
 Christopher, 247, 339
 Dieterich, 247
 Suss., 247
RUMLER, George, 325
RUMM, Isaac, 47
RUMSPARK, Henry, 326
RUNNER, Christena, 290
RUPERT, William M., 237
RUPIRT, George, 323
RUSH, William, 248, 340
RUSSELL, Donna Valley, 27
 Elizabeth, 69
 John, 69
RUTH, Caroline Mary Ann, 275
RUTTER, Joseph, 333
 Thomas, 248, 364

INDEX

RYAN, Catherine, 92
  James, 248, 336
  John, 202
RYDER, Frederick, 359
RYE, Anne, 248
  Henry, 248, 354

-S-
SACKER, John, 248, 342, 343
SAFFELL, Deborah, 248
  Mary Rebecca, 248
  Orlander, 248
  Orlando, 248
  Samuel, 248
SAFFILL, Orlandor, 359
SAFILL, Orlander, 248
SALLERS, Ellett, 248, 352
SALMON, Catherine, 248
  Charles, 248, 354
  George, 182, 248, 354
  Sarah, 94
  William, 351
SALTKILD, Elizabeth, 33
SAM, 330
SAMDEAL, Peter, 248
SAMPSELL, Anna Mary, 249
  Catherine, 249
  Devalt, 248, 249

Elizabeth, 249
Hiram, 249
Isaac, 249
Jacob, 249
John, 249
Maria, 248
Mary, 248, 249
Peter, 248, 249
Serena, 249
SAMSEAL, Devalt, 248
  Maria, 248
  Mary, 248
  Peter, 341
SAMSELL, Devalt, 248
  Maria, 248
  Mary, 248
  Peter, 248
SANDERS, Henrietta, 249
  Thomas, 249, 348
SANDERSON, Raymond, 320
SANDES, Abraham, 319
SANDS, Ann, 249
  George, 249
  Rebecca, 249
  Rebecca D., 249
  Richard, 249
SANS, Ann, 249
  Rebecca, 249
  Richard, 249, 347
  William, 249, 348
SANSENY, John, 249, 321
SANTMAN, Catharine, 172
  Emanuel, 172
  Jacob, 172

SARGEANT, Jacob, 249, 349
SARGENT, Jacob, 249, 319, 336
  James, 333
SATHGIVER, Maria, 263
SAUNDERS, Henrietta, 249
  Thomas, 249
SAVOY, Samuel, 249, 359
SAYLER, Solomon A., 159
SAYLOR, Em, 250
  John Frederick, 21, 249, 250
  Susan, 250
  Susanna, 250
SCAGGS, Leonard, 304
  Mahala, 304
  Richard, 326
  Richard D., 250
SCARFF, Mary, 160
SCHAEFER, John G., 225
SCHAEFFER, David F., 24
SCHAFFNER, George, 250, 334
  Jacob, 250, 354
SCHARF, J. Thomas, 24, 28
SCHEATENHELM Catharine, 104
SCHEIB, Catharine C., 175
SCHELL, Charles, 250, 358

FREDERICK COUNTY MILITIA IN THE WAR OF 1812

Ezra, 250, 334, 352
Jesse, 250, 324, 331
Margret, 250
Mary, 250
SCHEPLEY, Frederick, 251, 338
SCHINDLER, Hannah, 259
John, 259
Louisa, 259
SCHISLER, Ann M., 251
Catherine, 251
Catherine S., 251
Hiram, 251
John, 323
Margaretta R. M., 251
SCHISSLER, Adam, 320
Catherine, 251
John, 146, 251, 334, 354
Margaretta R. M., 251
SCHIVALLER, John, 251
SCHLAGLE, Helene, 314
SCHLEICHK, Isaac, 251, 336
SCHLEY, Charles, 251
Clarence, 251
Fairfax, 251
Frederick A., 331
Harriet, 251
Henry, 251, 349
Louesa, 251

Sarah M., 251
Sarah Maria, 251
William, 251
SCHLIFE, Henry, 267
SCHLIM, Elizabeth Magdalena, 143
SCHLYOCK, Jacob, 22, 317
SCHNEIDER, Elisabeth, 242
SCHNYDER, John, 251
SCHOLL, Christena, 251
Dennis, 45
Henry, 251
SCHOOL, Catharina, 251
Christian, 251
Henrich, 251
SCHOOLER, Joan J., 249
SCHR?DTER, Susanna, 154
SCHRINER, Jacob, 318
SCHRIVER, Jacob, 251, 354
SCHROYER, Frederick, 252
Mary M., 197
Rachel, 252
SCHRYOCK, John, 318
SCHU, Barbara, 236
SCHUANTIEGEL, George, 252
SCHUCKERS, Emanuel, 81

SCHULTZ, David, 252, 332
SCHUR, Barbara, 236
SCLIGH, Isaac, 322
SCNYDER, John, 334
SCOTT, Catharen Matilda, 129
Elizabeth, 68
J. McPherson, 212
James, 323
Joseph, 252, 364
Major General, 26
Maria C., 209
Thomas, 252, 323, 354
SEABOLD, Catharine, 252
Peter, 252
SEABROOKES, Samuel, 252, 364
SEAMAN, Amanda M., 168
George W., 168
SEAPLEY, Mary M., 182
SEAPOLD, Catharine, 252
Peter, 252
SEAPOLT, Anastasia, 252
Andrew, 252
Isabel, 252
Joseph, 252
William, 252
SEARLY, Joseph, 75, 252, 337

456

INDEX

SEARS, John, 264
SEBOLD,
  Catharine, 252
  Peter, 252
SECRIST,
  Catherine, 153
  Jonas, 252
SEDWICK,
  Caroline E., 213
  Caroline Elizabeth, 213
  Elizabeth, 213
  John, 213
  Rebecca Prisciller, 213
  Sophia Jane, 213
SEERLY, Joseph, 252, 339, 340
SEERS, Alexander, 252, 346
SEFER, Joseph, 253
SEGRUFF, Michael, 253, 353
SEIFERT, Eliza, 228
SEIS, George, 253
  Peggy, 253
SEIZE, George, 253, 354
  Peggy, 253
SELBY, Elisabeth, 253
  Henry, 253, 348
  Larkin, 253
  Obadiah, 253, 364
  Susan Boteler, 253
  Susannah Boteler, 253

SELL, Daniel, 323
  Lewis, 253, 361
  Margaret, 146
SELLERS, Henry A., 173
  Jacob, 253, 356
SELLMAN, Beale, 323
  William, 21, 253
SELMAN, Beal, 333
SEMAN, Hugh, 320
SENIOR, Jacob, 253
SENSE, Peter, 253, 353
SENSENEY, John, 253, 321
SENSENY, Isaac, 253, 322
  Mary, 84
SENTMAN, Peter, 319
SENTZ, Susan, 305
SERGEANT, John, 336
SERGENT,
  George, 24, 253
  James, 24, 254
  John, 253
SERGIANT, James, 323
SEVERN, Edwin F., 59
SEVERS, Evalina, 52
  Henry, 52
SEVRIST, Jonas, 361

SEWARD, David, 359
SEWELL, Charles B., 254, 349
SEWMAN, Isaac, 254, 364
SGSS, Anna Maria, 143
  Godfrey, 143
  Rosanna, 143
SHAAFF, Casper, 317
SHABAKER,
  George, 262
  George W., 262
  Jacob, 262
  Matilda, 262
SHADE, George, 254, 323, 330, 344, 345
  W. G., 7
SHAEFFER,
  Betsey, 254
  George, 254
  Jacob, 325
SHAFER, Betsey, 254
  Catherine, 157, 314
  Conrad, 321, 323
  Daniel, 254, 359
  E. Elizabeth, 254
  Elizabeth, 275
  Frederick, 254, 335, 364
  George, 254, 352
  Heneretta A., 254
  Isaac, 229
  Jacob, 254, 361
  John, 22, 67,

254, 327, 364
  Simon, 358
  Washington L., 254
SHAFF, Ather, 318
SHAFFER,
  Conrad, 317
  Daniel, 21, 254, 359
  George, 254, 317, 340
  Jacob, 254
  John, 254, 345, 346
  Margaret, 88
SHAFFNER,
  Caspar, 331
  Harriet, 255
  Jacob, 255, 336
SHAFNER, Peter, 255, 355
SHALL, Henry, 354
SHAMER, John, 255
SHAMHART,
  Amanda Catharine, 255
  Catherine, 255
  David, 255
  Henry, 255
  John, 255
  Mary Catharine, 255
  Rachel, 255
  Rezin, 255
  William Henry, 255
SHAMHARTT,
  Amanda Katharine, 255
  Elisabeth Anne, 255
  Emily Caroline, 255
  Ephraim, 255
  Fovina, 255
  George, 255
  Henry, 255
  Jane, 255
  John, 255
  Katharine, 255
  Martha, 255
  Mary, 255
  Pheby, 255
  Reason, 255
  Tompson Luther, 255
  William Henry, 255
SHANABROOKE,
  Casper, 255, 364
SHANEN, Mary, 218
SHANER,
  Elizabeth, 255
  Julean A., 255
  Luvina M., 255
  Mary J., 255
  Melcher, 255, 340
  Melki, 255
SHANEYBROOK,
  Jacob, 255, 325, 335
SHANK, Barbara, 256
  John, 256, 318
  Mary, 69, 256
  Peter, 69, 256, 326, 355
  Philip, 256
  Susan, 256
SHANKEL, Philip, 256, 352
SHANNABROOKE
  Casper, 256
SHANNON, Ann, 249
SHANTZ, Bessie, 191
  George, 191
SHAPE, Catherine, 274
  George B., 261
  Louesa, 261
SHARAN, Jacob, 256, 353
SHARER, George, 256
  J., 256
  Mary, 256
  Ruth, 256
SHARNER, John, 255, 256, 352
SHARPE, Caroline Rebecca, 272
  George W., 272
SHARRAH,
  George, 256, 356
  Mary, 256
  William, 256, 356
SHARRAR,
  George, 256
  Jacob, 256, 353
  Mary, 256
SHARRER,
  George, 256
  Mary, 256
SHARTZ,
  Catharine, 256
  Daniel, 256
SHAUEN, Mary, 218

INDEX

SHAUM, John, 256, 349
SHAW, Evalina L., 154
  George M., 308
  Hugh, 328
SHAWBAKER, George, 262
  Jacob, 256, 262
  Matilda, 262
SHAWEN, Andrew J., 257
  Catharine, 257
  Cornelius, 257
  Daniel, 10, 20, 256, 257, 364
  Edward M., 257
  Isabella, 257
  James, 257, 360
  Joseph, 257
  Lucretia M., 257
  Mary, 218, 257
  Oscar S., 257
  Samuel, 257
  Samuel T., 257
SHAWHAM, James, 320
SHAWN, Catharine, 257
  James, 257
  John, 257, 332
SHEALY, Andrew, 257, 356
  Hannah, 257
SHEATS, Henry, 299
SHEELEY, Andrew, 257
  Baltzer, 257
  Christian, 323
  Hannah, 257

SHEELY, Andrew, 257
  John, 257, 361
SHEET, Jacob, 356
SHEETENHELM, Elizabeth, 258
  Jacob, 258, 349
  Mary, 258
  Reuben, 258
SHEETINGHELLUM, Jacob, 258
  Mary, 258
SHEETS, Ann M., 258
  Eliza, 299
  Henry, 299
  Jacob, 258
  Samuel, 258, 364
SHEICY, Henry, 258, 321
SHELL, Charles, 358
SHELLEY, James T., 234
SHELLMAN, Catherine, 148
  Jacob, 149, 258, 354
  John, 149
  Sarah, 258
  William, 149, 321, 323
SHELTON, Thomas, 258, 364
SHENK, Christian, 118
SHEPHERD, Nancy, 258
  Thomas, 258, 353
SHEPPERD, Joseph, 67

SHERLEY, John, 296
SHERMAN, Conrad, 314
  Helene, 314
  Jacob, 317
  Susan, 314
SHERRADEN, Anner, 242
  Henry, 242
SHETINGHELLERN, Jacob, 258
  Mary, 258
SHEU, Jacob, 342
SHIELDS, Henry, 278
SHILLING, David, 259
  Hannah, 259
  Jacob, 312
  Jesse, 259
  John, 259, 364
  Michael, 259, 361
  William, 259, 365
SHINAFIELD, John W., 159
SHINDLER, Hannah, 259
  John, 259, 354
SHINEFIELD, William, 247
SHINK, Peter, 365
  Phillip, 365
SHINN, Joseph, 259, 347
SHIPLEY, Ann, 93
  Daniel, 324
  Denton, 259
  Elias, 259, 335
  Frederick, 196
  George L., 311

FREDERICK COUNTY MILITIA IN THE WAR OF 1812

Isaac, 259
Magdelana, 221
Mary Ann, 259
Ruth, 208
Samuel, 104, 259, 337
SHIPLY, Samuel, 335
SHIPP, William M., 241
SHIRLEY, Henrietta, 296
SHISLER, Adam, 323
SHIVERS, Clara, 260
  Cornelius, 259, 260
  Micha, 260
  Susanna, 260
  Washington, 260
SHLIFE, Henry, 267
  John, 267
  Mary Magdalena, 267
SHOACRE, George, 37
SHOCK, John, 342
SHOCKNEY, Jerusa, 260
  John, 260, 333, 343
SHOE, Charlotte, 260
  Jacob, 260
  John, 260, 321
  Philip, 260
SHOEMAKER, Christopher, 260
  Christoph, 260, 364
  Elizabeth, 261
  Henrietta, 262
  Jacob, 318
  John, 260, 262, 361
  Nicholas, 260, 261, 336
SHOLL, Christian, 261, 337
  Henry, 261, 354
  John, 261
SHOMEL, John, 318
SHOOK, Adam, 261, 342
  Barbara, 135
  Granison, 135
  Lydia, 56
  Mary, 56
SHOPE, Alice Ellen, 261
  Augustus K., 261
  Elizabeth, 261
  Ernest R., 261
  George Brengle, 261
  Horace A., 261
  Louisa, 261
  Marie Louise, 261
  Milton W., 261
  Sophia, 226
SHORB, Catharine, 261
  Conrad, 261
  John, 261, 323, 333
  John A., 261
  Joseph, 323
SHORL, John, 261
SHORTS, Jacob, 261, 361
SHOTO, John, 261
SHOTS, Elizabeth, 261
  Henry, 261
  John, 261
SHOTTS, Daniel, 357
  H., 261
  Mary Susan, 261
SHOTZ, Henry, 261, 352
  John, 354
SHOUP, Baltzer, 262, 361
  Elizabeth, 261
  George, 22, 317, 354
  George Brengle, 261
  Jacob, 262, 357
  Louisa, 261
  Sophia, 226
SHOVALTER, Catherine, 249
SHOVER, Adam, 262, 362
SHOWACRE, George, 180, 262, 352
  Jacob, 262, 352
  Matilda, 262
SHOWBAKER, George, 262
  George W., 262
  Mariah Barbara, 68
  Matilda, 262
SHOWER, Daniel, 257

460

INDEX

Melcher, 339
SHOWERS, Jacob, 157
SHOWN, John, 257, 324
  Margaret, 290
SHOWY, Henry, 323
SHRADER, Eliza, 299
  Jacal, 299
  John, 262
SHRAWYER, Frederick, 252
  Rachel, 252
SHRAYER, Henry, 318
SHRINER, Anna, 262
  George, 262, 361
SHRIVER, 262
  Abraham, 252
  Andrew, 61
  Benjamin, 262, 321, 322
  Catharine, 242
  Catherine, 61
  David, 3
  Isaac, 252, 262, 329
  J. Thomas, 117
  Jacob, 117, 251
  John, 262, 364
  Samuel, 262, 364
  T., 263
  Thomas, 262
  Walter, 263
SHRODER, Sanford, 67
SHROTES, John, 263, 339

SHROYER, Frederick, 252, 263, 364
  Matthias, 317
  Rachel, 252
  Susannah, 184
  William, 263, 359
SHRYOC, John, 263, 345
SHRYOCK, Captain, 15
  Catharine M., 263
  Catherine, 263
  Christina, 263
  George, 9
  George W., 263
  Henry, 21, 94, 263, 359
  Henry V., 263
  James W., 263
  John J., 263
  Mary E., 263
  Mary H., 263
  Rebecca, 263
  Rebecca C., 263
  Sarah A., 263
  Sarah A. D., 263
  Valentine, 263
SHUCKE, Lydia, 230
SHUE, Jacob, 263
SHUEE, David, 350
  John, 350
SHUEY, Daniel, 263, 364
SHULTZ, Carline A., 264
  Caroline A., 264
  David, 263, 324, 345, 346
  George, 263, 365
  Henry, 162, 225, 264, 366
  Lewis H., 264
  Martin, 264, 344, 345
  Sophia, 264
SHUNK, Benjamin, 288
SHURP, Catharine, 261
  Conrad, 261, 356
SHUTT, William H., 90
SHYROC, John, 346
SIAS, Micademus, 321
  Nicademis, 264
SICKAFOOSE, Henry, 284
SIDES, Mary Ann, 93
SIDNEY, Edward, 264
SIER, John, 264
SIERS, Alexander, 252, 264, 345
SIESS, Rosanna, 143
SIFERT, Sarah, 189
SIGAFOOS, Henry, 284
SIGAFOOSE, Henry, 284
SIGENFOOS, Henry, 284
SIGLER, Peter, 264, 339

SILAS, 335
SILING, Andrew, 365
J. Andrew, 264
SILVERSON, Mrs. Charles, 286
SILVERTHORN, William, 264, 340
SIM, Henry, 323
SIMM, Zachariah, 319
SIMMONDS, John, 325
SIMMONS, Annie C., 236
  Charles S., 265
  Daniel, 264, 347
  George, 265, 348
  Isaac, 265, 348
  James, 265, 362
  John, 236, 265, 360
  John H., 322
  Kezia D., 265
  Mary, 265
  Mary R., 265
  Peter, 145
  Samuel S., 230
  Serena, 265
  Sophia, 265
  Stella Barnes, 285
  Susan, 265
  Susannah, 265
  Thomas, 265, 348
  Zachariah, 265
SIMMS, John, 265
SIMON, Catherine, 118
SIMPSON, B. J. F., 260
  Benjamin, 265, 364
  Jackson, 206
  Sarah, 206
  Sophia, 265
  Walter, 322
SIMS, John, 265
  Patrick, 265, 348
SINN, Edward, 106
  Henry, 320
  Jacob, 72
SINSTACK, Wilhelmina, 139
SISLER, Elizabeth, 310
SITES, Mary Ann, 140
SIUTZER, John, 334
SIX, Catherine, 266
  George, 265, 357
  John, 266, 356
  Leonard, 266, 356
  Sarah A., 266
SIZE, John, 323
  Nathan, 333
SKILES, Margaret, 186
SKINNER, Alfred, 240
SLACK, James, 266, 346
SLACKS, Elizabeth, 266
SLADE, George, 333
SLAGLE, Charles, 266, 362
  Jacob, 266, 334, 362
  Ruth, 181
SLANGENHOUPT Jacob, 325
  John, 325
SLARRAP, Jacob, 266, 353
  John, 266, 353
SLATER, James B., 267, 341, 342
SLATES, Conrad, 144
  Daniel, 178
  John, 339
SLAUGENHEPT, John, 335
SLAUGHENHEPT, John, 267
SLEGLE, Lydia, 146
SLICE, Michael, 267, 336
SLICK, Frances, 267
  Francis, 342
  John, 267, 356
  Philip, 325
SLIDER, Jacob, 267, 356
  Sophia, 267
SLIFE, Henry, 267, 353
  John, 267, 342, 343
  Mary Magdalena, 267
  Mary McElener, 267
SLIFER, Devid, 318

INDEX

Samuel, 318
SLITE, John, 343
SLOAN, John, 267, 354
SLOTHOUN, Francis, 267, 335
SLOTHOUR, Francis, 267
SLOTTSHOUR, Francis, 325
SLUSSER, Andrew, 267, 365
SMALL, Jacob, 5, 331
  Maria, 291
  Sarah S., 43
  William, 291
SMALLWOOD, George N., 187
SMART, Robert M., 62
SMEETHE, Peter, 267, 364
SMELLSER, George, 292
SMELTZER, Henry, 326
  Jacob, 267, 353
SMEY, Daniel, 267, 365
SMITH, Adam, 170
  Alina, 240
  Ann C., 270
  Anne, 248
  Annie M., 268
  Baltzer, 22, 317
  Barbara, 90
  Benjamin, 33, 267, 345
  Captain, 335
  Caroline, 72
  Caspar, 267
  Catharine, 268
  Catherine, 248, 251
  Charles, 248, 267, 361
  Charles D., 248
  Christian B., 267
  Daniel, 248
  Daniel W., 269
  Elijah, 268, 339, 340
  Elizabeth, 269, 271, 279
  Ellen, 56
  Ephraim, 270
  Ester, 135
  Felix, 268, 325, 335
  Frederick, 268, 336, 361
  Gaspar, 267, 268
  George, 223, 268, 321, 322, 359, 364
  George Gibson, 268
  George M., 268, 342
  George N., 342
  George W., 268
  Harriet, 255
  Harriet E., 268
  Hellen S., 268
  Henry, 260, 268, 344, 358, 361
  Herbert, 325
  Isaac, 269, 332
  Isabela, 269
  Jacob, 128, 230, 235, 246, 269, 307, 356, 365
  Jacob S., 269
  James, 260, 269, 339
  James David, 216
  James H., 270
  Jane, 215
  Jeremiah, 260
  John, 169, 179, 254, 269, 283, 320, 322, 336, 341, 342, 345, 346, 349, 352, 359
  John A., 207
  John D., 323, 354
  John Dinsmore, 270
  John of John, 269
  John of M., 269
  Jonas H., 269
  Joseph, 270, 336, 356, 359
  Joseph M., 270
  Joseph S., 1
  Joshua, 325
  Larr Klise, 181
  Lewis, 318
  Loretta C., 268
  Martha L., 43
  Mary, 268, 270
  Mary Ann, 271
  Mary E., 83, 223
  Mary Jane, 268
  Mary Magdalena, 133
  Micha, 260
  Michael, 270
  Middleton, 327
  Nancy, 303
  Peter, 364

Philip, 6, 7, 270, 335, 336, 351
Rachel, 268
Randolph, 270
Rebecca, 248, 269
Robert, 260, 270, 332, 352
Samuel, 148, 271, 323, 336, 360
Samuel Price, 271
Sarah C., 269
Sarah Catherine, 102
Solomon, 21, 271, 336, 348
Susan, 237, 245, 269, 270
Susannah, 270
Theresa, 268
Thomas, 271, 339, 340, 358
Thomas A., 213
William, 135, 181, 186, 215, 271, 272, 324, 325, 326, 332, 334, 339, 340, 345, 346
William T., 86
SMITHY, John, 272, 355
SMITLEY, Eve, 90
George, 90
Rosanna, 89
Rossanna, 90
SMOOK, Dennis, 64
Matilda, 64
Peter, 318
SMUR, Jacob, 272, 355

SNACK, John, 272
SNAVELY, John, 272, 346
SNECK, Henry, 272, 364
John, 272, 364
SNEEMAN, David William, 341
William, 272
SNERR, Charles, 272, 338
SNIDER, Amelia, 272
Angeline, 272
Anna Mary, 272
Caroline Rebecca, 272
Catharine, 149
Catherine Elizabeth, 272
Elizabeth, 117
Ellen M., 273
Ellen Margaret, 272
Jacob, 272, 342
Jeremiah, 272
John N., 31
Joseph, 272, 343
Margaretta, 272, 273
Nicholas, 18, 19, 123, 272, 289, 300, 360
Samuel Thomson, 273
Susanna Hickson, 30
SNOOK, Henry, 273, 336
Lydia, 235
Simon, 235

SNOUFFER, J. J., 301
Jacob, 325
SNOUFFLER, Catharine, 161
SNOWDAGLE, George, 273, 334
SNOWTICKEL, George, 252, 273
SNOWTICKLE, George, 354
SNUR, Henry, 273, 365
SNYDER, Abraham, 273, 355
Ann E., 273
Ann Mary, 273
Catharine, 149
Catherine, 278
Christian, 273, 322, 348
Elizabeth, 273
George, 273, 355
Henry, 219, 273, 320, 322, 354
Jacob, 273, 340
John, 273, 338, 340
Margaret, 273
Nicholas, 84
Sarah, 224
Susan, 31
SOHWEN, 273
John, 257, 332
SOLLERS, Ariana, 273
John, 273
Mary, 273
Sabritt, 273
Sobret, 328
Thomas, 273

INDEX

SOLMAN, George, 354
SOLOMON, 273, 350
SOMERS, John, 273, 334
SOMERVILL, James, 273, 354
SOMMERS,
  Elizabeth, 284
  Jacob, 284
SOUDER, Conrad, 274, 364
SOUTHGATE,
  Samuel, 324
  Susannah, 240
SOWERS,
  Elizabeth, 274
  Jacob, 274
  John, 325
SPAHN, Elias, 358
SPALDING, Basil, 274, 356
  Catharine, 105
  Edward, 288
  Henry, 274, 356
  Sarah M., 274
SPARKS,
  Catharine, 257
SPAULDING,
  Susannah, 126
SPEACHT, Sophia, 306
SPEAKER, John, 274, 359
  Magdelena, 274
SPEALMAN,
  Andrew, 274, 322
SPEELMAN,
  Andrew, 274, 325, 342, 343

SPIELMAN, J. R., 191
SPONSALER,
  Elizabeth, 274
  Jacob, 274, 364
  William, 274
SPONSELER,
  Anna, 274
  Arthur, 274
  Catherine, 274
  David, 274
  George, 274
  Jacob, 274
  Patience, 274
  William, 274
SPONSELLAR,
  Adam, 301
  Elizabeth, 288
SPONSELLER,
  Catherine, 274
  Frederick, 274, 358
  Jacob, 274, 352
  John, 358
  William, 274, 336
SPONSLER,
  David, 342, 343
  Elizabeth, 274
  Jacob, 275
  Jess, 274
  William, 275, 349
SPOON, Jacob, 118
SPOONER, H. K., 207
  Joseph, 318
SPRANGLE,
  David, 358
SPRENGLE,
  Caroline Mary Ann, 275

David, 275, 358
SPRIGG, Otho, 327
SPRINGER,
  Daniel, 182, 275, 354
  Elizabeth, 275
SPRUTTSMAN,
  Jacob, 359
SPRUTTZMAN,
  Jacob, 275
SPRUTZMAN,
  Elizabeth, 233
  Jacob, 233
SPURGIN, Joseph E., 268
SPURRIER, Green, 275
  Greenbury, 275, 364
  Lancelot, 275
SQUIRE, Henry, 44
  Josephine, 44
  Thomas, 275, 362
SRIVER,
  Benjamin, 319
STAGE, Andrew, 319
STAHL, Henry, 275
STAHR, Mary, 236
STAILEY,
  Abraham, 358
  Peter, 358
STALEY,
  Abraham, 275, 358
  Abraham T., 276
  Ann Elizabeth, 276
  Anne S., 276

FREDERICK COUNTY MILITIA IN THE WAR OF 1812

Catherine, 275
Cornelius, 276
Elizabeth, 275
Frederick of
Jacob, 324
  George, 56
  Jacob, 22
  Jacob of Joseph, 317
  John, 22, 317
  Joseph, 22, 317
  Malinda, 79
  Margaret, 276
  Moses, 275
  Peter, 276, 358
  Sarah, 276
STALL, Andrew, 276, 345, 346
  Henry, 276, 366
  Jacob, 276, 364
STALLING, Ann, 102
STALLINGS, Catherine, 230
  Charles T., 276
  Deliah R., 276
  Delila, 172
  Mary A. M., 276
  Otho, 276
  Richard, 276, 358
  William H., 276
STALY, Ann E., 275
  Henry, 275, 319
  John A., 275
  Josiah Oliver, 275
  Lewis, 275
  Lewis Edward, 275
  Malachiah, 276, 364
  Moses, 275, 276, 337
  Phebe A., 275
STAM, Nathan, 276, 321
STAMP, Elizabeth, 276
  George, 276, 334
STANSBURY, Isaac, 276, 364
  William, 295
STANTON, John, 277
STARBUCK, George, 131
STARLING, Rachel, 80
STARNER, Henry, 325
  Jonathan, 276
STARR, Jesse W., 112
STARRY, George, 276, 353
STATES, John, 276, 339
STAUB, Jacob, 276
  John, 359
STAUF, Catharine, 125
STAUFFER, Christina, 277
  Daniel, 277
  Georg, 277
  George, 277, 346
  John, 277, 344, 345
STAUP, Adam, 277, 359
  Andrew J., 277
  Ann E., 277
  Catherine, 277
  David, 134
  Edward T., 277
  Eli, 277, 359
  Francis J., 277
  Jacob, 276, 277, 359
  James E., 134
  Jerome, 277
  John, 277, 359
  Lucinda, 277
  Margaret, 277
  Mary Ann, 134
STAUTON, John, 277
STEAHL, Henry, 275, 277, 354
STEEL, Andrew, 77
  Buzaleel, 77
  Daniel, 277, 336
  George H., 149
  John R., 190
  John T., 277
  Joseph, 277, 336, 352
  Sussana, 277
STEELE, David, 52
  Rachael, 51
STEERS, John, 277, 340
STEEVENS, Joseph, 365
STEGNER, George, 277, 364
  Jacob, 278, 364
STEINBERGER, Caroline, 53
STEINER, Anna,

466

INDEX

125
  Barbara, 278
  Charlotte, 235, 278
  Christian, 276
  Elizabeth, 278
  Frederick B., 278
  George, 278
  Henry, 4, 5, 6, 8, 18, 23, 64, 278, 323, 333, 353
  Jacob, 149, 278
  John J., 323
  John T., 334
  John Thomas, 278, 354
  Mrs., 149
  Rachel, 278
  Rachel Rebecca, 278
  S., 235
  Stephen, 5, 8, 9, 13, 21, 278, 320, 328, 330
  William, 278, 353
STEM, Elizabeth, 137, 159
STEMBEL,
  Frederick, 327
  Henry, 10, 327, 351
  John, 327
STEMBLE, Henry, 278, 331, 351, 360
STEMMELL, Daniel, 323
STEMP, George, 278, 365
STENLEY, Virginia, 25, 273
STEPHENS,
  Catherine, 278
  Charles, 278, 348
  David, 9
  James, 278, 360
STERM, Lend., 300
STERNER, Adam, 350
  Jonathan, 276, 342
  Judith, 90
STEVENS,
  Jemima, 293
  Joseph, 278, 365
  Polly, 278
  Reason, 278, 321
  Renzin, 278
  Rezen, 258
  Susan, 175
  Thomas, 33
STEVENSON,
  Abalard, 363
  Abelard, 278
  David, 279, 341, 342
  Joshua, 3, 328
  Levi L., 279
  Richard, 319
  Wesley, 279, 352
STEWARD, David, 279, 359
  Margaret, 294
  William, 294
STEWART,
  Benjamin, 177
  Daniel, 279, 360
  Elizabeth, 264
  Jordan, 326
  Polly, 229
  William, 279, 336
  William H., 38
  William R., 264
STICHER, George, 279, 336
  Peter, 279, 337
  Solomon, 279, 349
STICK, William, 301
STICKEL, Mary, 279
  Solomon, 279
STICKER,
  Elizabeth, 302
  Ely, 223
  Solomon, 279
STICKLE, Maria, 63
STILLY, Peter, 317
STIMMEL, Daniel, 320
  Elizabeth, 279
  Henrietta J., 279
  Henry, 317
  John, 279
  John B., 21, 72, 103, 279
  Magdalena, 85
  Margaret, 84
  Peter, 85
  Susanna, 103
STIMMELL,
  Catharine, 184
  John B., 94
STINCHACOMB, Vachel, 279, 344
STINCHCOMB,
  Elizabeth, 279
  Nathaniel, 279
  Vachel, 345
STINCHECOME, Elizabeth, 279

Nathaniel, 279, 356
STINCHECUMB, Vachel, 323
STINCHICUM, Elizabeth, 280
Nathaniel, 280
STINE, Patrick, 280, 361
STINER, John, 280, 356
STITELY, Jacob, 55
STOCKS, Joshua, 43
William, 43
STOKER, Bolzear, 111
STOKERS, George, 280
Hannah, 280
STOKES, George, 104, 216, 274
Henry, 280
STONE, George, 280, 364
George R., 311
Hannah, 280
Henry, 358
Jacob, 52, 280, 358, 364
James, 280, 348
John, 280, 364
Rachel, 311
Rebecca, 239
STONEBRACKER, Mary A., 136
STONEBUNN, John, 90
STONECIPHER, David, 350
Jacob, 351
John, 351
STONECYPHER, John, 34
STONER, 280
Abraham, 282
Catherine, 280
Christian, 280, 352
Daniel, 140
David, 280, 359
Elenor, 282
Ezra, 280, 351
Hannah, 140
Jacob, 281, 352
John, 115, 281, 353
Mary, 117, 280
Stephen, 317
STONESIFER, Ephraim A., 277
STORM, Catharine, 65
Jacob, 281
James, 281, 360
John Peter, 281
Julianna, 281
Mary Magdalene, 281
P. L., 281
Peter, 281, 351
STORRAP, Jacob, 281, 353
John, 281, 353
STOTELMYER, Catherine, 42
David, 11, 281, 340, 341
Jacob John, 341
John K., 281, 340
John of D., 282
Joseph, 281, 341
William Jacob, 341
STOTLEMIRE, David, 281, 360
STOTLEMYER, Barbara, 282
David, 281
Jacob, 282
STOTTLEMEYER, Joseph, 281, 365
STOTTLEMIER, Catharine, 42
STOTTLEMYER, Barbara, 281, 282
Daniel, 281, 282
David, 281, 334
George, 281, 333
George of George, 323
Jacob, 281, 282
Jacon, 281
John, 281, 282, 334
John K., 324
John of D., 282
Johns, 281
Joseph, 281, 282, 324
Margaret, 281
Mary, 281
Susan, 281
STOTTSHOUR, Francis, 325
STOUB, Adam, 282
STOUFER, David, 282, 364
Henry, 282, 319, 361

Jacob, 282, 364
STOUFFER,
David, 282
  Elenor, 282
  George, 333
  Jacob, 282
  John, 282, 344, 353
  John of Joseph, 282
STOULEMYER, Joseph, 281
STOUP, Adam, 282
STOVER,
Catharine Susan, 142
  Christian, 55
  Daniel, 282, 352
  George, 282, 362
  John, 142
  Margaret, 142
  Mrs., 149
  William, 282, 362
STOYKES, George, 280
  Hannah, 280
  Susan, 280
STRAIGLE, Maria, 238
STRAILMAN, George, 118, 282, 360
STRAITMAN, George, 231
STRASBERGER, George, 114
STRAUSE, Henry, 329
STRETCHER, John E., 212

STRICKSTOCK, Adam, 282
  Catharina, 282
  Ottilia, 282
STRICKSTROCK, Jacob, 282
STRICKSTROKE, Jacob, 354
STRICKSTRUCK, Jacob, 282
STRINE, Peter, 282, 349
  William, 283, 323, 361
STRIXTRUCK, Catherine, 282
STROBRIDGE, William, 40
STROHM, Katherine Mary, 300
STRONG, Catharine, 207
STUDAY, Henry, 283, 321
  Jacob, 283
STUDY, Jacob, 321
STULL, Ann Elizabeth, 276
  Benjamin, 283, 321
  Catherine, 266
  John, 318
  Susan, 256
STULLER, Conrad, 137, 283, 364
  Ulerich, 283, 364
STULTS, James, 283, 361
STULTZ, James, 283

Nicholas, 356
STUMP, George, 326
  John, 70
STUP, Annie, 135
  Franklin, 135
STYERS, Cornelius, 283
SUIT, Nathaniel, 283, 348
SUITZER, John, 283
SULIVAN, Abraham, 283, 353
  Daniel, 352
  David, 283, 352
  Jacob, 283, 353
  Sarah, 283
  William, 283, 352
SULLIVAN, Abraham, 283
  Daniel, 283
  Mary, 283
  Sarah, 283
  William, 245
SULTZER, John, 326
SUMAN, Isaac, 139, 283
  John, 284, 365
  Juliann C., 139
SUMBRUM, David, 284, 361
  John, 284, 361
SUMBRUN, Elizabeth, 243
SUMMER, Catherine, 284
  Elizabeth, 284
  Jacob, 284, 365
SUMMERS, Jacob,

323
 William, 284
SUMMONS,
 James, 318
SUTLZ, Nicholas, 284
SUTTON, Henry, 284, 346
 William W., 130
SWAENY, William, 323
SWAINE,
 Elizabeth, 193
 General, 193
SWALES, Eleanor, 74
SWAN, William, 24, 284, 348, 349
SWARTZ, Daniel, 284
SWEANEY, William, 135
SWEARENGAN,
 Elizabeth, 284
 Van, 284, 341
SWEARINGEN,
 Jo, 318
 Joseph, 326
SWEENEY,
 William, 165, 333
SWIGARD,
 Christian, 319
 John, 319
 Peter, 358
SWIGART, Adam, 350
 George, 350
SWIGERT, John, 284, 353
SWITZER, James L., 201

Ulrick, 323
SWOPE, Barney, 323
 Elizabeth, 221
 Henry, 317
 Samuel, 66
SYBERT, David, 284, 340
SYCAFOOSE,
 Henry, 284, 339, 340
SYER, Nichodemus, 284, 343
 Nichodimus, 342
 Nickodemus, 284
SYMS, John, 284
SYNUFF, Michael, 253, 285, 353
SYPHER,
 Catherine, 285
 Henry, 285, 356

-T-
TABLER,
 Benjamin L., 285
 Christian, 360
 Christian of William, 285
 Sarah R., 285
 William, 285, 358
TACWELL,
 Robert, 285, 334
TALBOT,
 Benjamin, 136
 Paul, 351
 Polly, 310
TALBOTT, 285
 David, 285
 Wilson, 285, 358
TALHELM, Mary, 285

Peter, 285, 349
TALL, Walter, 285, 319
TALLHAMMER,
 Mathias, 285
TALLHELM, 285
 Mary, 285
 Peter, 285, 336
TAMAN, Aquilla, 285, 364
TANEY, David, 260
 Ethelbert, 286, 356
 Felix, 360
 Felix B., 14, 83, 286
 Mary C., 286
TANEYHILL,
 Carlton, 286, 348
 Samuel, 286, 359
TANNEHILL,
 Carlton, 286
TANNER, Jacob, 286, 317, 335
 James, 286, 336
TANZEY, Arthur, 320
TAPMAN,
 Obediah, 286
TARLTON, Elisha, 286, 361
TARNER, Jacob, 325
TARRENCE,
 James, 290, 365
TARREYHILL, 286
TARWELL,
 Robert, 285, 334
TASWELL, Robert, 285

INDEX

TATE, T. T., 250
TAUNEY, John, 286, 353
TAWNEY, David, 323
  Henry, 323
TAWNSEND, Thomas, 319
TAXWELL, Robert, 334
TAYLOR, Charles P., 98
  Frederick, 286
  Hesse, 286
  Hezekiah, 286, 342, 343
  Isreal, 286, 347, 349
  James, 229
  Jesse, 336
  Jessy, 322
  John, 287, 349, 352
  M. H., 229
  Phoebe, 286
  William, 287, 358
  William B., 171
TAYLOUR, William, 358
TEAGARDEN, Ezekiel L., 107
TEENER, Philip, 359
  Phillip, 359
TELLER, Aquila, 12, 287
  Aquilla, 348
TEMPLE, Catharine, 257
TEMPLIN, Richard, 326

TENER, David, 287, 359
  Philip, 287, 359
  Phillip, 359
TESHNER, Jacob, 287, 347, 357
THOMAS, Archibald, 287, 360
  Benjamin, 287, 336, 338, 339
  Christian, 172
  David, 155, 287
  Elijah, 287, 321, 325
  Elizabeth Causlet, 50
  George, 324
  Henry, 324
  Jacob, 326
  James, 103
  John, 330
  John E., 253
  John Hanson, 329
  Martha, 287
  Otho, 287, 360
  Philip D., 311
  Richard, 323
  Richard P., 320
  Samuel, 287, 352
  William, 287, 319, 324, 333, 338
THOMPSON, Elizabeth, 94, 288
  George, 287
  Henry K., 288
  James, 94
  John, 288
  Levy, 322
  Parmelia, 288
  Richard, 288

  Thomas, 288
  William B., 87, 288, 324, 332
THOMSON, Bithy, 288, 360
  Elizabeth, 288
  Hugh, 14, 19, 272, 288
  Jane, 272
  John, 288
  Margaretta, 272
  Samuel, 317
  William, 25
THORNBURGH, Ephraim, 351
THRALLS, John, 289, 360
THRASHER, Benjamin, 319
  Eli, 319
  Elias, 318
  Thomas, 319
THUMB, Susan, 250
THURSTON, Emma, 190
  John, 190
TICE, Henry K., 51
TIDY, James, 358
TIER, John, 289, 336
TIFFANY, Angeline, 272
TILGHMAN, Frisby, 329
  John, 289, 350
TINGSTRUM, Peter, 289, 345
TIPTON, Lee, 350
TITLOW, Adam,

FREDERICK COUNTY MILITIA IN THE WAR OF 1812

289, 351
Daniel, 289, 358
Elizabeth, 289
George, 289, 323, 334
Lewis S., 147
Mary Catherine, 289
Ophelia C. Y., 289
Rebecca, 289
Sophia S., 289
TODD, Benjamin, 60
Lucy, 60
TODHUNTER, Isaac N., 305
Jury, 305
TOHAY, John, 289, 339, 340
TOLBORT, Wilson, 358
TOLBOTT, Benjamin, 289, 360
TOLL, Walter, 289, 341
TOM, 289, 330
TOMBS, John, 323
TOMKINS, Lewis H., 168
TOONEY, Abraham, 84
TOOPHORN, George, 289, 361
TOOSANG, Francis T., 342
TOOSONG, Francis T., 289
TOPPER, Ann J., 176
TORRANCE,
Benjamin S., 309
TORRENCE, James, 290
TOURNEY, John, 286, 290, 353
TOWNSEN, Samuel, 290, 322
Thomas, 290
TOWNSON, Samuel, 321
Thomas, 321
TRACEY, Basil, 290, 341, 342
TRACY, John S., 322
William L., 305
TRAIL, Abigail, 163
TRAVERS, Mary Ann, 126
TRESLER, Henry, 290, 361
TREXLER, Peter, 290, 335
TRIC, Thomas, 290, 335
TRICKER, Eleanor, 164
TRIMMER, Daniel, 134, 250
TRITT, Peter, 326
Susanna, 84
TROMBO, George, 290
TRONBERGER, Frederick, 290
TRONBRGER, Frederick, 361
TROUT, Elizabeth, 313
Jacob, 360
John, 290, 347
Margaret, 290, 313
TROUTMAN, Christena, 290
Christina, 290
Peter, 290, 358
TROXALL, George of Jacob, 325
John, 325
TROXEL, Catherine, 134
Elizabeth, 290
Felix J., 291
George, 290, 356
Jacob, 290, 317, 357
Magdalene, 291
Peter, 291, 356
Peter of Peter, 328
TROXELL, Elizabeth, 290
Jacob, 290, 335
TRUCKS, John, 317
TRUMBO, 291
George, 342, 343
TRUMP, Casper, 291, 364
Christena, 291
Sebastiana, 252
TRUNDLE, Hezekiah, 326
TRUNNEL, Henrietta, 249
TSCHUDY, Martin, 291, 332, 345
TUBBS, Nathaniel, 323

472

INDEX

TUCKER, William, 318
TUDOR, James, 291
 John, 95, 291, 358
TULL, Walter, 366
TULLEY, Aquilla, 291
 Margaret, 291
TUNER, David, 359
 Phillip, 359
TUPPLE, Robert, 325
TURBOTT, Nicholas, 320
TURBUTT, Maria, 291
 Nicholas, 10, 16, 291, 357
TURFIEL, Lewis, 291, 343
TURNER, Allen C., 59
 Benjamin, 291, 353
 Daniel, 339
 Elias, 153
 Elizabeth, 47
 Jacob, 325
 Jesse, 291, 353
 Joshua, 21, 59, 291, 292
 Matilda, 59
 Solomon, 292, 353
TURTON, Fielder, 326
TURVILL, Lewis, 291

TWIG, Thomas, 292, 339
TWIGG, Thomas, 292
TWINER, Daniel, 293, 339
TYLER, Maria, 205
 William, 326
 William Bradley, 206

-U-
UHLER, David, 293, 343
ULER, David, 342
ULRICH, George, 135
 Lydia, 135
UMBAUGH, John, 293, 362
UMBERGER, Michael, 24, 293
 Nancy, 293
UNDERDARZK, Henry, 299
UNGEEFEHN, John, 319
UNGLEBEE, Erasmus, 348
 Mary Ann, 293
 Zachariah, 293, 348
UNGLESBEE, Erasmus, 293
UNGLESBY, Mary Ann, 293
 Zachariah, 293
UNSHIPPEN, Peter, 355
UPDEGRAFF, David, 293

UPHOLD, Sebastian, 293, 362
UPRAFT, Thomas, 293
URVIN, James, 293, 349
 James of James, 293, 349
UTZ, Jacob, 123
 Mary, 123

-V-
VALENTINE, John J., 263
 Mary E., 263
VAN MARTER, William, 76
VAN SWEARINGEN, Cyrus J., 153
VANBLARCUM, Evert, 293, 346
VANBLARKCUM, Evert, 345
VANBLARKEUM, Evert, 293
VANFERSON, Jemima, 293
 Nathan, 293
VANHORN, Mary, 41
VANORSDEL, Hezekiah, 95
VANPHERSON, Nathan, 7, 336
 Nathaniel, 293, 336
VANZANT, John, 293, 356
VARLEE, Henry, 294, 334

FREDERICK COUNTY MILITIA IN THE WAR OF 1812

VARNUM, James M., 244
VAUGHAN, Emeline, 55
VAUGHN,
  Catharine, 148
  Elizabeth, 33
  James, 148
  Thomas, 294, 353
VERNON,
  Charlotte L., 294
  George W. F., 294
  Nathaniel, 294
VERTINBECKER, Magdalane, 170
VICKERS, Solomon, 319
VILE, Peter, 294, 349
  William, 294, 349
VORE, William, 294, 320, 347

-W-
WACHTEL, John, 3
WACKTER, George, 326
WADAMS, Frederick, 207
WADKINS, John, 294
WADSWORTH, Samuel, 294, 355
WAGERS, Henry, 294, 348
  Upton, 327
WAGGONER, John, 294, 359
WAGNER,
  Catherine, 285
  George, 310
WALKER, Amy, 223
  Andrew, 294, 356
  Catharine, 48
  Edward, 322
  George B., 12, 294, 326, 334
  James, 33
  James S., 260
  John W., 294
  Jonathan, 294, 345, 346
  Margaret, 294
  Mary Jane, 294
  Rebecca, 192
  Samuel L., 294
  Stephen, 294, 339
  Thomas L., 53
  W. W., 195
  William, 192, 317, 321, 356
  William W., 195, 260
WALLACE, Joseph, 294, 339
WALLER, Betzy, 69
  Elizabeth, 69
WALLING, Jacob, 257
  James, 140
WALTER,
  Christian, 295, 353
  Jacob, 295, 325, 342, 343, 364
  Joseph, 295, 364
  Mary, 258
  Mary J. F., 67
  Susanah, 295
  William, 295, 364
WALTERS,
  Christiana, 196
  Mary, 258
WALTERSON, John, 295, 364
WALTON, Christian, 295, 353
WAMPLER,
  Abraham, 306, 363
  Abram, 295
  David, 325
  Elizabeth, 306
  George E., 47
  George Edw., 295
  George Edward, 132
  Jacob, 319
  John, 3, 328
  Lewis, 252, 295, 364
  Susanah, 295
WANDLE, David, 295, 366
WANTS, Frederick, 232
WANTZ, Elizabeth, 232
WARCK, Andrew, 295, 339
  Sarah, 295
WARD, Asa, 351
  Captain, 14
  Edward, 295, 358
  Henrietta E., 102
  John F., 67
WARDECK, John, 22, 317
WARE, William, 296

INDEX

WARFIELD,
  Achsah, 63
  Andrew, 91
  Henry R., 328
  John, 296, 321
  Jon, 320
  Prewsley, 326
WARMAN, Noah, 296, 321
WARNER,
  Abraham, 296, 353
  Daniel, 296, 350
  David B., 151
  Eliza W., 181
  George, 296, 324, 353
  Henry, 296, 339, 340
  William, 296, 340
WARNON, Noah, 296, 322
WARTHAN,
  Henrietta, 296
WARTHEN,
  Benjamin, 296
  Heneretta, 296
  Henrietta, 296
  John, 296, 352
  Nicholas, 296
WARTHEY,
  Benjamin, 366
WARTHING,
  Francis, 319
WARTHON,
  Nicholas, 362
WASKEY,
  Christian, 297
  Sarah, 155
WASKY, Christian, 362
WASSKEY, Eli, 96

WATER, Jacob, 333
WATERS, Ann, 64
  Anne, 64
  Benjamin, 323
  Horatio, 72, 288
  Joal, 327
  Joel, 327
  Sarah Ann Elizabeth, 124
WATKINS,
  Gassaway, 7, 335
  John, 149, 297
  Leonard, 327
  Margaret, 149
  Thomas, 32
WATSON,
  Catharine, 75
  James C., 91
  John, 83
  Samuel, 294
WATT, 331
  Mary, 297
  Mary Ann, 231
  Robert, 297, 324, 332
WATTERS, Joab, 320
WATTS, Jane, 169
  John, 297, 359
  Maria R., 36
WAY, 362
  David, 320
  Jacob, 297
WAYS, Basel, 358
  Basil, 297, 366
  Basil J., 297
  Cecila, 297
  Thomas, 297, 364
WEAGLY,
  Catherine E., 67

WEAKLEY, Otho, 120
WEAKLY, Mary, 238
WEANT, Samuel, 180
WEAR, Bernard T., 33
  Louisa, 33
WEAVER, Captain, 14, 16
  Catharine, 95
  Jacob, 297
  Lewis, 9, 14, 297, 344
  Margaret, 102
  Mary, 143
  Michael, 297, 323, 334
  Philip, 297, 339, 364
WEBB, Henry, 322
  John, 298, 335
WEBER, Mary, 143
WEBSTER, David, 298, 354
  Samuel, 298, 354
WECKLEY, William, 252
WEDDEL,
  Rebecca, 171
WEDDLE, George, 298, 362
  John, 298, 325, 339, 340
  Rebecca, 171
WEDELLE, John, 298
WEDRICK,
  George, 317

475

FREDERICK COUNTY MILITIA IN THE WAR OF 1812

WEEBER,
Nathaniel, 325
WEEKLEY,
William, 290, 298,
343
WEEKLY, William,
342
WEEKS, John, 33
  Sharloty, 33
WEIMER,
  Deborah, 150
WEIRS, Thomas,
  22, 317
WEIST, John, 298
WELCH, Henry,
  298, 346
  Jacob, 298, 362
  William, 339
WELK, George,
  298, 364
WELLCOS, Jacob,
  216
WELLER, Anna
  Catharina, 124
  Anna Catharine,
  124
  Anna
  Margaretha, 124
  Elizabeth
  Juliana, 135
  Henry, 298, 362
  John Jacob, 124
WELLMORE,
  Lucretia C., 38
WELLS, John L.,
  350
  Richard, 329
WELSH, Adam,
  317
  Henry, 345
  William, 298

WELTY, Joseph,
  299
WENRICK, John,
  298, 358
WENTZEL,
  Benjamin, 64
WENTZELL,
  Grace A., 64
WERBLE,
  Catharine, 162
  Frederick, 162
WERING, George
  T., 66
WEST, Abiham,
  298
  Abraham, 298,
  321, 322, 342, 343
  Eugene, 298
  Isaac, 298
  John, 332
  Jonathan, 319
  Joseph, 298, 362
  Joshua, 298, 321,
  364
  Levin, 298, 326
  Mary Elizabeth,
  298
  Nathaniel, 298,
  342, 343
  Shadrick, 319
  Stephen, 298,
  324, 348
  Thomas, 319, 323
  William, 298, 364
WESTBROOK, N.
  B., 116
WESTERMAN,
  Henry, 111
WESTOVER,
  Mary, 148
  Oliver, 148

  Sara, 148
WETSEL, John
  H., 299
WETTZEL,
  William, 333
WETZEL, Annie,
  300
  Betty Ann, 299
  Daniel, 299, 300,
  356
  Eliza, 299, 300
  Elizabeth, 300
  Jacob, 299
  John, 299, 300,
  356
  Josiah, 299, 300
  Margaret, 299,
  300
  Samuel, 299
WETZELL,
  William, 323
WHARTON,
  Ralph, 300, 362
  Ralphael, 300
WHAT, Maria R.,
  118
WHEELER,
  Edward, 300, 321
WHERETT,
  Bennett, 358
WHERRITT,
  Bennett, 300
WHETSEL,
  William, 300, 362
WHETTER,
  Leonard, 300, 348
WHETTLE, John,
  300, 334
WHIFFERY,
  Andrew, 300
WHIFFEY,

476

INDEX

Andrew, 300
WHILHOUP,
  John, 326
WHIP, Charlotte,
  258
  Shellman, 258
WHIPP, George,
  300, 324, 352
  Mary, 300
WHIRETT,
  Bennett, 358
WHITACRE,
  James, 32
  Jonas, 32
WHITAKER,
  Elender, 69
WHITE, Albert A.,
  118
  Joseph, 300, 322,
  336
  Margaret Jane,
  43
  Martha, 81
  Thomas, 300,
  339, 340
  Walter, 12, 301,
  349
WHITEMAN,
  Henry, 266
WHITLOCK, John,
  301, 347
WHITMIER,
  Simon, 301, 364
WHITMORE,
  Frederick, 301, 362
  George, 324, 355
  George of
  George, 323
  James, 301
  Matilda, 194
WHITTAKER,

James K., 69
WHITTER,
  Leonard, 301
WIAN, Henry, 360
  John, 360
WIAND, Henry,
  301
  John, 301
WICHTER, John,
  355
WICKAM, Andrew,
  301, 302, 350
WICKARD, Adam,
  302
  Philip, 302
  Phillip, 302, 356
WICKART, Adam,
  342
WICKHAM,
  Andrew, 301, 302,
  336
  Elizabeth, 302
  Jacob, 302, 336
  John, 302
WIDERICK,
  Christian, 358
  Elizabeth, 302
  John, 302
WIDRICK,
  Christian, 302
  John, 302, 337,
  347
WIESINGER,
  Catharina, 307
  Maria Susanna,
  307
  Peter, 307
WIEST, John, 298,
  332
WIGLE, Frederick,
  302, 334

WILCALIDEL,
  Jacob G., 302, 321
WILCOTT, James,
  43
WILDER, D. S.,
  310
WILES, Henry G.,
  116
  James, 355
WILEY, Ephriam,
  302, 352
WILHERS, Ann
  Luesa, 139
WILHIDE,
  Catharine, 302
  Catherine Ann,
  303
  Daniel, 302
  Elizabeth, 303
  Henry, 303
  Jacob, 302, 349,
  350
  Margaret, 302,
  303
  Mary A., 303
  Niles, 302
  Reuben, 302
  Susan, 303
WILHITE, Jacob,
  302
  Margaret, 302
WILKINSON,
  Joseph, 322
  Liner W., 303,
  346
  Linor W., 345
WILL, John P., 89
WILLARD, Elias,
  303
  Elizabeth, 280
  Magdalena, 303

WILLERY, Jacob, 110
WILLEY, John, 324
WILLGERD, John, 318
WILLHIDE,
Captain, 7, 335
George, 302, 303
Henry, 93, 303, 359
Jacob, 303, 336
Mary E., 47
Susan, 93
WILLHITE,
George, 302, 303, 336
WILLIAM, 303, 345, 347
Elizabeth Magdalena, 143
Peter, 143
WILLIAMS, David, 303, 358
Deborah, 303
Eli, 303, 357
H. J., 270
Hilleary, 322
James, 303, 353
John, 3, 121, 303, 336, 340
John B., 303, 322
Levi, 215
Lilben, 303
Lilburn, 303, 348, 364
Livinia, 133
Nancy, 303
Otho H., 249, 329
Peter, 133

R. W., 37
Rachel, 121, 255
Sarah, 62
T. J. C., 5, 22, 27, 351
Temperance, 303
WILLIAMSON,
Dorsie, 319
James, 358
Rebecca, 51
WILLIAR, Anna Maria, 135
Maria Elizabeth, 143
WILLIARD,
Charlotte Rebecca, 110
Elias, 303, 363
Henry, 303
John Adam, 110
Magdalena, 303
Samuel, 303
WILLIS, Henry, 85, 303, 325
WILLS, William, 322
WILLSON, Edward J., 303, 356
WILLYARD,
Andrew, 323
Elias, 323
Eline, 318
Jacob, 318
John, 304, 318, 362
Lawrence, 304, 362
Peter, 318
Philip, 318
WILSON, Andrew, 12, 304, 349

Aquilla, 304, 362
Elizabeth, 87
Greenbury, 358
John, 304, 324, 332, 345, 346, 354
John A., 282
John of Alexander, 304, 345, 346
Joshua, 233
Nancy, 146, 258
Otho, 304, 324, 332, 352
Thomas, 325
William, 304, 348, 364
WILT, Jacob, 277
WINBIGLER,
Elizabeth, 305
Henry, 304
John, 304
John J., 304
Mary, 304
Michael, 305
Richard, 304
WINCEL, John, 304, 345, 346
WINCHESTER,
Richard, 318
WINDER, Lev. [General], 10, 23
WINDPIGLER,
George, 304, 332
Harriett, 305
Jacob, 326
John, 305
Mahala, 304
WINDSOR, Elenor, 315
John H., 315
WINE, Christean,

INDEX

318
  Jacob, 305, 364
WINEBRENER,
  Christian, 305
  Eve, 305
  Jacob, 305, 358
  John, 305
  Peter, 305
  Philip, 305
WINEBRENNER,
  Jacob, 305
  John, 134
  Peter, 305
WINEBRUNNER,
  Jacob, 305, 359
WINFIELD,
  Lawrence, 305, 360
WINGAFAIR,
  John, 321
WINGIFAIR, John, 305
WINK, George, 305
  Susan, 305
WINKLER,
  Harriet, 306
WINKLEY,
  Harriet, 306
WINPEAGLER,
  Catherine, 307
WINPEGLER,
  Harriet, 126
  John, 126
WINPIGLER,
  Elizabeth, 165, 305
  George, 304, 305, 332, 360
  Harriett, 305
  John, 305, 355, 360
  Manuel, 306
  Michael, 305, 347
  Richard, 181
WINRAT, John, 306, 322
WINRATT, John, 306, 321
WINTER, Jacob, 306, 362
  John, 306
  Susanna, 108
WINTERS, David, 36
  Elizabeth, 306
  Frederick, 306, 321
  Ignatious, 306
  Ignatius, 345
  Jacob, 333
  John, 306, 319, 325, 335, 341, 342
  Margaret, 306
WIRTENBAKER,
  William, 310
WIRTZ, Elizabeth, 153
WISE, Betsy, 190
  James, 306, 360
  Jon., 186
  Joshua D., 116
  Samuel, 306
  Sarah E., 116
  William W., 280
WISINGER,
  Catherine, 307
  Leonard, 307
WISMAN, George, 318
  Jacob, 318
  John, 323
  Peter, 318
  Voluntine, 318
WISONG, George R., 129
WISSINGER,
  Catharine, 307
  Elizabeth, 306
  George, 306, 326, 354
  Harriet, 306
  Leonard, 307, 345
  Peter, 307, 354
  Solomon, 307
  Sophia, 306
WISSMAN,
  Canrode, 318
WITHEROW,
  William, 325
WITMAR, David, 142
  Henry, 142
WITMER, 307
  James, 301
WITTEN, William, 283
WITTER, David, 119
  Mary, 119
WITTINGTON,
  Mrs., 230
WIVEL, John, 307, 362
WODKINS, John, 294
WOLD, George, 317
WOLF, Catharine, 307
  George W., 250
  Jacob, 307
  John, 308, 349
  Mary, 308

FREDERICK COUNTY MILITIA IN THE WAR OF 1812

WOLFART, Lydia
Anna, 216
WOLFE, 307
  Abraham, 323
  Catharine, 307
  George, 308, 357
  Jacob, 307
  John, 308
  Mary, 308
WOLGAMOTT,
  Joseph, 308, 340
WOLLE, Nath. S., 176
WOLTZ,
  Hezekiiah, 324
  Margaret, 108
  Maria, 141
  Mary, 108
  Otho, 308, 324, 334, 354
  Peter, 108
WOOD, Aaron, 308
  Bennet, 308, 364
  Charles, 308
  David, 333
  Henry, 327
  Joel, 308, 325, 335
  John, 138
  Joseph, 9, 20, 308, 336, 358, 359
  Mary, 145
  Nancy, 293, 308
  Thomas, 323
WOODARD,
  Nathaniel, 308, 360
WOODS, Mary, 308
  Michael, 308, 364
WOODWARD,
  Ann Margaret, 170
  Anthony, 22, 317
  Branton, 308, 352
  John J., 30
  Lewis, 309
  Marg., 309
  Mary, 308
  Nathaniel, 308, 309, 337, 347
  Susannah, 309
WOOLARD, John, 309, 360
WOOLF, George, 362
  Jacob, 307, 309, 365
WOOLFE, George, 309
WOOLFORD,
  Nancy, 216
WOOLTZ,
  Hezekiah, 309, 331
  Otho, 309, 332, 357
WOOLVERTON,
  John, 34
WOONDER, John, 309, 342, 343
WOOTEN, W. J., 176
WOOTTEN,
  William T., 112
WOOTTON, John, 291
  Richard, 309
WORTHAN,
  Elizabeth, 59
  Joseph, 59
WORTHEN,
  Martin, 319
WORTHINGTON,
  Elizabeth, 206
  Jane, 309
  Thomas C., 320, 324
  Thomas Contee, 5, 22, 309, 331
  William, 309
WRIGHT, 310
  Ann Rebecca, 310
  Benjamin, 309, 310, 347
  Henry, 310
  James, 310, 332
  Jesse, 94, 320
  John, 310, 335
  John A., 310
  John H., 310
  John of David, 310, 335
  John R., 306
  Lewis, 310
  Polly, 310
  Reuben, 310
  Samuel, 310, 347
  Sarah, 310
WYANT,
  Elizabeth, 225
WYERS, Jacob, 321
WYMAN, John, 310, 362
WYSONG, Isaac, 324

-Y-

YACKE, Peter, 310, 363
YAGER, Caroline, 310
  Charles, 310, 352

INDEX

YANDES, George, 310, 321
YANDIS, George, 321
YANDISS, Jacob, 323
 William, 323
YANTIS, Christian, 310, 332
 Daniel, 324
 Elizabeth, 310
 George, 310
 Henry, 318
 Jacob, 333
 William, 310
YANTIZ, Christian, 310
 Elizabeth, 310
 Susannah, 310
YARDLY, William, 322
YATES, Catharine, 311
 Catherine, 311
 Charles, 311, 339
 Georgetta, 311
YEATS, Robert A., 126
YEISER, Barbara, 311
 Daniel, 90, 311, 335
 Danuel, 325
YENTES, Christian, 310
 Elizabeth, 310
 William, 310, 365
YEONITIS, Christian, 311
YEONITS, Christian, 350

YERK, James, 311, 345
 James S., 311
 Margaret M., 311
 Margarett Ann, 311
YINGLING,
 Banjamin, 328
 Benjamin, 306
 David, 311, 323, 341, 342, 348
 David G., 311
 Elizabeth, 244
 Ellen, 312
 Henry, 311, 312, 364
 Jacob, 325
 Jeremiah, 89
 John, 312, 352, 362, 364
 John of Jacob, 325
 Philip, 312, 348
 Rachel, 311
 Sophia, 54
 Sophia L., 54
YIRK, 312
 James, 311, 345, 347
YOAKLEY, Peter, 268
YOKEY, John, 295
YONILS, Christian, 312, 335
YONITZ, Christopher, 324
YORK, John, 312, 352
YORKEE, John, 312, 364
YOST, Elizabeth,

190
YOUNG, Allen M., 281
 Andrew, 312, 317, 354, 362
 Ann, 312
 Casper, 318
 Catharine, 289
 Charles, 312, 347
 Conrad, 36, 312, 339, 340
 Conrad of Jacob, 318
 Conrod, 312
 Daniel, 233, 313
 Davault, 312
 David, 312, 313, 354, 366
 Devault, 334
 Dewalt, 312
 Dewault, 326
 Edward, 183
 Elizabeth, 289, 313
 George, 313, 318, 321, 322
 Harriett, 135
 Henry, 240, 274
 Henry James, 27
 Jacob, 313, 325, 335
 John, 313, 324, 332, 345, 347, 356, 362
 Joseph E., 312
 Joshua, 97
 Louisa, 200
 Magdelena, 274
 Margaret, 312
 Mary, 97
 Nancy, 312

Nancy Ann, 312
Oliver, 135
Sophia, 289
Sue, 183
Susanna, 180
Thomas, 71, 313, 354
William, 229, 313, 339
YOUNGMAN, William H., 313, 324, 332
YOUNKIN, Amos, 314
  Eli, 314
  Elizabeth, 313, 314
  Ephraim P., 314
  Isaac, 314
  John, 313
  Lydia, 314
  Margaret, 313, 314
  Rudolph, 314
  Susanna, 314
  William, 314
YOUNTZ, John, 314
YOUTSEY, George, 326
YOUTZ, John, 314
YOUTZEY, Hannah, 39
YOUWLER, Elizabeth, 314
  George, 314
YOWLER, Catherine, 314
  George, 334, 345, 347
  Michael, 314, 337, 347

-Z-
ZACHAREIAS, George, 350
ZACHARIAS, Appolonia, 314
  Daniel, 14, 31, 314, 350
  Helen, 314
  John Daniel, 314
  Mathias, 314, 362
  Susan, 314
ZACHARY, John, 339
ZACKARY, John, 314
ZEALER, Adam, 314, 324, 332
  George, 320
  Margaret, 145
ZEGLER, Margaret, 145
ZEHRING, Lewis, 70
ZEILERT, Frederick, 314
ZEISO, George, 314
ZELER, Ann Luesa, 139
ZEPP, Elizabeth, 229
  George, 272
ZIEGLER, Henry, 97
ZIEHLER, Elizabeth, 60
  Henry, 60
ZIELER, Anna S., 129

John D., 129
ZILHART, Frederick, 314
ZIMBRAN, George, 325
ZIMMERMAN, Barbara, 315
  Barbary, 202
  Catherine, 258
  George, 315, 318, 357
  George Valentin, 315
  Henry, 12, 315, 349
  J. F., 110
  Jacob, 235
  Johannes, 315
  Joseph, 202
  Joshua J., 99
  Mary, 268
  Mary Ann, 315
  Michael, 318
  Nicholas, 317
  Samuel, 133
  Solomon J., 258
  Susan, 35, 133
  Valentine, 315, 358
ZOLLINGER, Anne Elizabeth, 315
  Benton George, 315
  Catharine, 315
  Catherine Meyers, 315
  Eleonora Francisca, 315
  George, 315, 356
  John H., 315

INDEX

Lewis Augustus, 315
Margaret Sivilla, 315
Mary Catharine, 315
Sevilla, 315
Susanna Angelica, 315
ZUMBREN, George, 316, 356
Jacob, 316, 356
Margaret, 316
Sarah, 316
ZUMBRUM, Jacob, 182, 316
Julian, 157
Margaret, 316
Sarah, 316
ZUMBRUN, George, 316
Henry, 316, 336
Jacob, 111, 316
Margaret, 316
Sarah, 316

Other Heritage Books by Sallie A. Mallick:
Sketches of Citizens of Baltimore City and Baltimore County, Maryland

Other Heritage Books by F. Edward Wright:
Abstracts of Bucks County, Pennsylvania Wills, 1685-1785
Abstracts of Cumberland County, Pennsylvania Wills, 1750-1785
Abstracts of Cumberland County, Pennsylvania Wills, 1785-1825
Abstracts of Philadelphia County Wills, 1726-1747
Abstracts of Philadelphia County Wills, 1748-1763
Abstracts of Philadelphia County Wills, 1763-1784
Abstracts of Philadelphia County Wills, 1777-1790
Abstracts of Philadelphia County Wills, 1790-1802
Abstracts of Philadelphia County Wills, 1802-1809
Abstracts of Philadelphia County Wills, 1810-1815
Abstracts of Philadelphia County Wills, 1815-1819
Abstracts of Philadelphia County Wills, 1820-1825
Abstracts of Philadelphia County, Pennsylvania Wills, 1682-1726
Abstracts of South Central Pennsylvania Newspapers, Volume 1, 1785-1790
Abstracts of South Central Pennsylvania Newspapers, Volume 3, 1796-1800
Abstracts of the Newspapers of Georgetown and the Federal City, 1789-99
Abstracts of York County, Pennsylvania Wills, 1749-1819
Bucks County, Pennsylvania Church Records of the 17th and 18th Centuries Volume 2: Quaker Records: Falls and Middletown Monthly Meetings
Anna Miller Watring and F. Edward Wright
Caroline County, Maryland Marriages, Births and Deaths, 1850-1880
Citizens of the Eastern Shore of Maryland, 1659-1750
Cumberland County, Pennsylvania Church Records of the 18th Century
Delaware Newspaper Abstracts, Volume 1: 1786-1795
Early Charles County, Maryland Settlers, 1658-1745
Marlene Strawser Bates and F. Edward Wright
Early Church Records of Alexandria City and Fairfax County, Virginia
F. Edward Wright and Wesley E. Pippenger
Early Church Records of New Castle County, Delaware, Volume 1, 1701-1800
Frederick County Militia in the War of 1812
Sallie A. Mallick and F. Edward Wright
Inhabitants of Baltimore County, 1692-1763
Land Records of Sussex County, Delaware, 1769-1782
Land Records of Sussex County, Delaware, 1782-1789
Elaine Hastings Mason and F. Edward Wright
Marriage Licenses of Washington, District of Columbia, 1811-1830
Marriages and Deaths from the Newspapers of Allegany and Washington Counties, Maryland, 1820-1830

Marriages and Deaths from The York Recorder, *1821-1830*
Marriages and Deaths in the Newspapers of Frederick and Montgomery Counties, Maryland, 1820-1830
Marriages and Deaths in the Newspapers of Lancaster County, Pennsylvania, 1821-1830
Marriages and Deaths in the Newspapers of Lancaster County, Pennsylvania, 1831-1840
Marriages and Deaths of Cumberland County, [Pennsylvania], 1821-1830
Maryland Calendar of Wills Volume 9: 1744-1749
Maryland Calendar of Wills Volume 10: 1748-1753
Maryland Calendar of Wills Volume 11: 1753-1760
Maryland Calendar of Wills Volume 12: 1759-1764
Maryland Calendar of Wills Volume 13: 1764-1767
Maryland Calendar of Wills Volume 14: 1767-1772
Maryland Calendar of Wills Volume 15: 1772-1774
Maryland Calendar of Wills Volume 16: 1774-1777
Maryland Eastern Shore Newspaper Abstracts, Volume 1: 1790-1805
Maryland Eastern Shore Newspaper Abstracts, Volume 2: 1806-1812
Maryland Eastern Shore Newspaper Abstracts, Volume 3: 1813-1818
Maryland Eastern Shore Newspaper Abstracts, Volume 4: 1819-1824
Maryland Eastern Shore Newspaper Abstracts, Volume 5: Northern Counties, 1825-1829
F. Edward Wright and Irma Harper
Maryland Eastern Shore Newspaper Abstracts, Volume 6: Southern Counties, 1825-1829
Maryland Eastern Shore Newspaper Abstracts, Volume 7: Northern Counties, 1830-1834
Irma Harper and F. Edward Wright
Maryland Eastern Shore Newspaper Abstracts, Volume 8: Southern Counties, 1830-1834
Maryland Militia in the Revolutionary War
S. Eugene Clements and F. Edward Wright
Newspaper Abstracts of Allegany and Washington Counties, Maryland, 1811-1815
Newspaper Abstracts of Cecil and Harford Counties, Maryland, 1822-1830
Newspaper Abstracts of Frederick County, Maryland, 1816-1819
Newspaper Abstracts of Frederick County, Maryland, 1811-1815
Sketches of Maryland Eastern Shoremen
Tax List of Chester County, Pennsylvania 1768
Tax List of York County, Pennsylvania 1779
Washington County Church Records of the 18th Century, 1768-1800
Western Maryland Newspaper Abstracts, Volume 1: 1786-1798
Western Maryland Newspaper Abstracts, Volume 2: 1799-1805
Western Maryland Newspaper Abstracts, Volume 3: 1806-1810
Wills of Chester County, Pennsylvania, 1766-1778